THE MENNONITE HYMNAL

FAITH AND LIFE PRESS, NEWTON, KANSAS
HERALD PRESS, SCOTTDALE, PENNSYLVANIA

THE MENNONITE HYMNAL

Copyright © 1969 by Herald Press, Scottdale, Pa. 15683 and
Faith and Life Press, Newton, Kansas 67114.
Library of Congress Catalog Card Number: 69-18131

Third Printing, 1970

Printed in the United States

All rights reserved. No part of this book may be copied or reproduced in any form except for brief quotations for use in magazine or newspaper reviews without written permission from the publishers.

Acknowledgments

The publishers wish to acknowledge with grateful appreciation the cooperation and support of individuals, trusts, and publishers who have granted permission for the use of copyrighted songs.

We have earnestly and carefully endeavored to ascertain the copyright status of each song. If any songs have been included without proper permission or credit, the publishers will upon notification gladly make necessary corrections. For a detailed listing of acknowledgments for both the Hymns and Worship Resources sections, see pages 608-611.

Preface

Music has a significant place in the life of the Christian church, especially the church at worship. The stream of church music, springing from its Judaic origins almost two thousand years ago, has been a constant and vital force in the life and faith of the church. Indeed one cannot imagine Christianity without the "psalms and hymns and spiritual songs" already an important part of worship in the Apostolic Church.

Moreover, this stream of music is as something alive, discarding the unusable, adaptive to new circumstances, creative in meeting needs as they may exist. Church music has not been contained in rigid, unyielding forms or patterns, but in different ways has supplied musical expression for the church in its developing life and worship. Hymnology, too, as a significant part of the musical heritage of the church, has not been locked in the closed canon of an ancient and unchanging tradition, but has been alive and growing, dynamically ministering to a living and growing Christendom.

Church music has also been important in the Anabaptist-Mennonite family of the church, ever since its birth in the Reformation. And here, too, church music by and large has been living rather than static, as may be attested by the many hymnals used or published at various times and places during the past four centuries.

Thus it was to be expected when two of the Mennonite brotherhoods, the (Old) Mennonite Church and the General Conference Mennonite Church, independently decided the hymnbook each was using, the *Church Hymnal* (1927) and *The Mennonite Hymnary* (1940) respectively, needed to be brought up to date. The delegates at the 1953 triennial session of the General Conference Mennonite Church discussed the need for revising *The Mennonite Hymnary* and a committee was appointed by the Conference's Board of Education and Publication to work on a revision. Similarly in 1957 the Music Committee of the Mennonite Church began work on revision of the *Church Hymnal*.

For several years each of the two music committees carefully examined its own and other hymnals, trying to determine to what extent its hymnal should be revised and developing a list of hymns it would like to include in a revision. The two committees were conscious of each other's work, shared the minutes of their meetings, and occasionally met jointly to compare notes and discuss the results of their work. Two convictions seemed to emerge from this period of independent work and informal sharing: each group believed a major revision of its hymnbook was necessary and each believed the attempt should be made to publish one rather than two hymnbooks.

Upon approval of a joint hymnal project by the two conferences, a joint hymnal committee was appointed in 1961 from the membership of the two music committees: Lester Hostetler, J. Harold Moyer, and George Wiebe of the General Conference; and Chester K. Lehman, Mary Oyer, and Walter E. Yoder of the (Old) Mennonite Church. Vernon H. Neufeld, who had convened the earlier exploratory sessions, was asked to continue as chairman of the Committee. Edward Stoltzfus joined the group in 1964 upon the death of Walter E. Yoder. The publishers were represented at meetings of the Committee by Ellrose Zook of Herald Press and Willard Claassen of Faith and Life Press.

PREFACE

The Joint Hymnal Committee subsequently became the principal working group in carrying the responsibility for producing one hymnal for the two brotherhoods. The Committee considered and synthesized the work of the separate music committees, using the results to develop a basic list of hymns for the collection. The Committee, through its members and specially appointed subcommittees, gave careful attention to the hymn texts and the available tunes, making appropriate selections and editing and arranging where it believed this necessary. The Introduction to *The Mennonite Hymnal* provides greater detail of the Committee's work with the texts and tunes.

Included in *The Mennonite Hymnal* is also a section entitled "Additional Worship Resources" to provide for greater congregational participation in Christian worship. Along with the singing of hymns this section will provide worshipers with opportunities for additional worship experiences.

There were many who in various ways contributed to the publication of the hymnal, but it is not possible to name them all. The following committees, however, and the members who served at various times are recognized for their participation and assistance in the project:

Joint Hymnal Committee

Vernon H. Neufeld, Chairman
J. Harold Moyer, Vice-chairman
Mary Oyer, Executive Secretary
Lester Hostetler, Coeditor
Walter E. Yoder, Coeditor
Chester K. Lehman
Edward Stoltzfus
George Wiebe (Walter Thiessen, alternate)
Willard Claassen, Publisher's Representative
Ellrose Zook, Publisher's Representative

General Conference Music Committee

Marvin Dirks
John Gaeddert
Walter H. Hohmann
Lester Hostetler
William Klassen
 (Chairman, 1965-   )
Russell Lantz
J. Harold Moyer
Vernon H. Neufeld
 (Chairman, 1960-65)
George Wiebe

(Old) Mennonite Music Committee

John Duerksen
Chester K. Lehman
Earl M. Maust
Mary Oyer
Roy D. Roth
J. Mark Stauffer
Edward Stoltzfus
 (Chairman, 1964-   )
Dwight Weldy
Walter E. Yoder
 (Chairman until 1964)

Text Committee

Marvin Dirks
Paul Erb
Walter Klaassen
William Klassen

Chester K. Lehman, Chairman
John Ruth
Edward Stoltzfus

Tune Committee

J. Harold Moyer, Chairman
Mary Oyer
Orlando Schmidt

J. Mark Stauffer
Dwight Weldy
George Wiebe

Worship Aids Section Committee

William Klassen
John H. Mosemann, Chairman

Orlando Schmidt
Howard Zehr

PREFACE

In addition to the committee members, Arlene Hartzler served as consultant for the hymns for children and J. P. Classen provided valuable information on the chorales. Special recognition is given to Erik Routley, British hymnologist, who served generously as resource consultant.

Those who worked on the hymnal project sincerely believe that *The Mennonite Hymnal* will increase and deepen an appreciation among the churches for the rich hymnody of the Christian church; that through singing the hymns of the church members in the congregations will find themselves drawn together, with Christians everywhere, in oneness in Christ; and above all that through the singing of these hymns all will render their prayer and praise to God the Father and His Son Jesus Christ.

"Let the word of Christ dwell in you richly, as you teach and admonish one another in all wisdom, and as you sing psalms and hymns and spiritual songs with thankfulness in your hearts to God" (Colossians 3:16).

Vernon H. Neufeld
Chairman
Joint Hymnal Committee

Introduction

The Mennonite Hymnal is the successor to two Mennonite hymnbooks, the *Church Hymnal*, 1927, of the (Old) Mennonite Church and *The Mennonite Hymnary*, 1940, of the General Conference Mennonite Church. The committees responsible for its compilation began their work with these books. From these each congregation has developed a collection of its own familiar hymns which express its own situation and around which it builds valuable associations. The committees tried to select those hymns and tunes which are indispensable to the present life of Mennonite congregations. To these they added a large number of works from a wide variety of sources with the conviction that each congregation's experience would be invigorated by new expressions from Christians of other places and times.

They examined the texts for their theological appropriateness, clarity of expression, quality and durability, as well as for their present pertinence. Tunes were judged for their suitability for the text, quality and interest, ease of singing, and congregational usefulness—bearing in mind that most congregations would sing in four parts and frequently without accompaniment.

The *Church Hymnal*, 1927, and *The Mennonite Hymnary*, 1940, hold many hymns in common. However, details of text often differ, from one or two words to several stanzas. Means for reconciling these differences had to be found. The committees agreed to start with the author's original wording and to use it whenever possible. John Wesley, in his Preface to *A Collection of Hymns for the . . . People Called Methodists*, 1779, articulated a grievance of many hymn writers:

> Many gentlemen have done my brother and me . . . the honour to reprint many of our hymns. Now they are perfectly welcome so to do, provided they print them just as they are. But I desire they would not attempt to mend them; for they are really not able. None of them is able to mend either the sense or the verse. Therefore I must beg of them one of these two favours: either to let them stand just as they are, to take them for better for worse; or to add the true reading in the margin, or at the bottom of the page; that we may no longer be accountable either for the nonsense or for the doggerel of other men.

However, Wesley himself changed Watts' first stanza of Psalm 100:

> Sing to the Lord with joyful Voice;
> Let ev'ry Land his Name adore;
> The British Isles shall send the Noise
> Across the Ocean to the Shore.

to our present hymn, "Before Jehovah's Awful Throne" (48); and the committees for this hymnal found other changes desirable. Watts' "Alas and Did My Savior Bleed" has one line, "When God, the mighty Maker died," which is altered almost universally—as it is in this hymnal (170). John Cennick's "Lo! He Comes, with Clouds Descending" of 1752 (192) was rewritten by two other eighteenth-century authors.

The Text Committee tried to maintain the integrity of the author's statement. Alterations made for theological, linguistic, or traditional reasons are indicated immediately after the author's name, as follows:

INTRODUCTION

† a slight change—generally one word
‡ alteration extends to several words or one line
"and Others" indicates extensive alterations; if possible the "Others" are identified.

Examination of the original texts, which often consist of many stanzas, yielded previously unused stanzas and even new hymns. The Text Committee discovered, for example, that the last four stanzas of the nine for "Praise to God, Immortal Praise" had a particular contribution to make; out of this poem came two hymns (524 and 525). The Committee selected five from thirteen stanzas for "There's a Wideness in God's Mercy" (78); several of these are new to Mennonite hymnals. The Committee members tried to include more complete sections and continuous versions of metrical Psalms and moved rather frequently beyond a four-stanza norm in order to enlarge the content of the hymn chosen.

The Tune Committee examined the original form of the music in most cases. Frequently the tune appeared originally as a single-line melody only, or as the tenor voice in a four-part version. Here it seemed appropriate to follow the standard procedure in hymnal editing—that of adjusting the musical arrangement to the needs of the text and the possibilities for congregational use. Music for *The Mennonite Hymnal* has been arranged for four-part singing, with the melody in the soprano voice. Only rarely is unison required, although any congregation may choose to sing many of the tunes in unison.

The *Church Hymnal* and *The Mennonite Hymnary* frequently differ in the choice of tunes used with texts they hold in common. The Joint Hymnal Committee was responsible for decisions on combinations of texts with tunes for *The Mennonite Hymnal*. For these judgments they considered common usage in Christendom, effectiveness for four-part singing, and vitality of expression for the twentieth century. *Stephanos* was chosen over *Bullinger* for "Art Thou Weary" (230), for example, because it seemed to be the more direct, congregational vehicle. *Warrington* was judged better for the structure of the Psalm setting, "Give to Our God Immortal Praise" (34), than *Lasst uns erfreuen*, which was used in a more suitable combination (51); furthermore, *Warrington* seemed the more appropriate companion to a Watts' Psalm because it is an English Psalm tune. For "Christ for the World We Sing" *Kirby Bedon* was replaced by *Malvern* and a new, dynamic setting, *Milton Abbas* (424 and 425). Occasionally a tune used by both groups seemed too worn to perpetuate further. The combination of "O Happy Day" with *Rockingham New* (398) from Joseph Funk's *Harmonia Sacra* replaces the more familiar setting. Only rarely did the attempt to reconcile differences between hymnals result in the use of a text twice to accommodate the version from each book.

Rhythm is more varied here than in previous Mennonite hymnals. Time signatures are used when the meter is regular and the song leader can be assured of one basic pattern. Signatures are omitted if measures differ in length or character. In some of these cases the result is simpler for the congregation, if not for the song leader. The music seems to flow more naturally in *Dundee*, for example (258), if the note lengths are varied rather than uniform. In other cases the character of the melody depends largely upon rhyth-

INTRODUCTION

mic interest. The rhythms of some of the Reformation tunes have been restored for variety and vitality (91, 118, 284). Fermatas (⌒) have been used sparingly—only where they seem helpful to group participation or where, as in certain Gospel Songs, they function as an integral part of the style.

Dynamics are not indicated unless permission for the use of the music called for their inclusion.

Amens are not always used; rather, they appear with hymns of prayer and praise. The congregation is free to use or omit them as they wish.

Some of the more difficult numbers are placed in the Choral Section near the end of the book. However, even these can be congregational.

Dates of composition for text and music are indicated immediately after the author's and composer's name. The specific date is in most cases that of the first appearance in print, unless the actual date of writing is certain. The latter, however, is not so designated.

The Mennonite Hymnal will be published in both round- and shape-note editions. The first Mennonite singing-school book, *Genuine Church Music*, by Joseph Funk, 1832, used the American system of four shape-notes (mi, fa, sol, la) to facilitate reading. These expanded to seven shapes in his 1851 edition. Since that time most (Old) Mennonite hymnals have been available in shape-note editions—usually with the Jesse B. Aiken shapes, which are used in the shape-note edition of *The Mennonite Hymnal*.

The Mennonite Hymnal is a testimony to the richness of the Christian tradition of singing and to Mennonites' indebtedness to the church of all times and places. It draws on various cultural backgrounds of Mennonites. Their most distinctive book, the *Ausbund* of 1564, which is still in use, is represented by brief portions of three texts joined with tunes that the sixteenth-century Anabaptists might have known (40, 344, 384). Mennonites who have remained close to their German background still sing Lutheran chorales; chorale texts and tunes are well represented. Those who spoke English in the early nineteenth century absorbed the American tradition of Watts' texts—along with authors such as Wesley and Newton—and replaced their Germanic past with American tunes and folk hymns from the singing-school tradition. These strands—German and American—join in this book to enrich the resources of each. The Mennonites' use of the more recent Gospel Songs is perpetuated in this book with a collection in a separate section.

To the major emphases of previous books this hymnal adds a variety of materials. The number of Greek and Latin texts in translation has been enlarged. These were chosen on the basis of their timelessness and durability through centuries of use. Six non-Western hymns (55, 209, and 362, for example) express, at least in token, the committees' interest in being a part of the worldwide church. A search for works in contemporary idiom yielded only a few which seemed usable and singable for Mennonite congregations (Text examples: 295 and 457; Tunes: 172, 207, 228, and 353).

The Mennonite Hymnal offers a more varied group of tunes than previous books. Latin chants (92, for example), Welsh tunes (62, 253, 459), French Calvinist Psalm tunes (70 and 121), French church melodies from the seventeenth and eighteenth centuries (44 and 456), and French Psalm tunes from

INTRODUCTION

the past few decades (617 and 618) are included. Folk tunes from various countries—England (71), Denmark (218), Sweden (335)—supplement the larger number of American folk hymns (112, 147, 273, and 322, to mention a few).

The Mennonite Hymnal, thus, is a collection of widely varied hymns and tunes. It represents a number of approaches to taste and to the function of hymns in worship. All of the persons who have had a part in its preparation hope that each congregation can draw from the whole of over six hundred hymns a collection of its own which will be appropriate to its character and size, its musical experience, and its spiritual needs.

> Mary Oyer
> Executive Secretary
> Joint Hymnal Committee

Contents

THE HYMNS

GOD, 1-88

Adoration and Praise ...	1-41
Majesty and Holiness...	42-48
Creator of Heaven and Earth	49-62
His Love and Mercy	63-78
His Providence and Care	79-85
His Laws and Judgment.	86-88

JESUS CHRIST, 89-204

Praise and Glory	89-110
Advent	111-121
Birth	122-138
Epiphany	139-143
Life and Ministry	144-153
Triumphal Entry	154-156
Passion	157-173
Resurrection	174-183
Ascension	184-191
Second Coming	192-197
Reign and Kingdom.....	198-204

THE HOLY SPIRIT 205-217

THE HOLY SCRIPTURES, 218-224

LIFE IN CHRIST, 225-371

Call of Christ	225-232
Repentance and Forgiveness	233-248
Faith and Assurance....	249-264
Love and Gratitude	265-270
Joy and Peace	271-278
Purity and Holiness	279-283
Hope and Aspiration....	284-295
Prayer	296-302
Communion with Christ .	303-310
Pilgrimage and Guidance	311-320
Conflict and Victory	321-332
Courage and Comfort ...	333-342
Obedience and Consecration	343-358
Stewardship	359-365
Life Eternal...........	366-371

THE CHURCH, 372-418

Its Foundation and Nature	372-380
Fellowship of Believers..	381-387
The Ministry: Pastors and Teachers	388-389
The Lord's House	390-393
Communion of Saints ...	394-397
Sacraments	
Baptism	398-399
The Lord's Supper..	400-409
Foot Washing	410-411
Marriage	412
Consecration of Children and Parents	413-415
Burial of the Dead	416-418

MISSION OF THE CHURCH, 419-459

Evangelism and Missions	419-429
Service and Witness	430-441
Education	442-445
Christian Citizenship ...	446-448
Peace and Nonresistance	449-456
Social Justice	457-459

HOME AND FAMILY, 460-476

The Christian Home	460-463
Hymns for Children	464-476

TIMES AND SEASONS, 477-526

Morning	477-486
Evening	487-496
The Lord's Day	497-501
Close of Worship	502-507
Old and New Year	508-511
Spring-Summer-Autumn-Winter	512-517
Harvest and Thanksgiving	518-526

GOSPEL SONGS 527-594

CHORAL HYMNS........595-619

MUSICAL AIDS TO WORSHIP 620-653

CONTENTS

ADDITIONAL WORSHIP RESOURCES

Section I. Scripture Readings 654-719
Section II. Affirmations of Faith 720-723
Section III. Congregational Responses 724-733
Section IV. Prayers 734-752

ACKNOWLEDGMENTS

	Page
Hymns	608
Additional Worship Resources	611

INDEXES

Index of Authors, Translators, and Sources	611
Index of Composers, Arrangers, and Sources	614
Metrical Index of Tunes	617
Alphabetical Index of Tunes	620
Index of Scriptural Allusions	623
Topical Index	625
Index of First Lines	634
Index of German First Lines	640

HOLY GOD, WE PRAISE THY NAME 1

GROSSER GOTT, WIR LOBEN DICH 7.8.7.8.7.7.

Late 4th century
Te Deum laudamus
Tr. Clarence Augustus Walworth†, 1853

Katholisches Gesangbuch, Vienna, 1776

1. Ho-ly God, we praise Thy name; Lord of all, we bow be-fore Thee;
   All on earth Thy scep-ter claim, All in heav'n a-bove a-dore Thee.
   In-fi-nite Thy vast do-main, Ev-er-last-ing is Thy reign.

2. Hark, the loud ce-les-tial hymn, An-gel choirs a-bove are rais-ing,
   Cher-u-bim and ser-a-phim, In un-ceas-ing cho-rus prais-ing,
   Fill the heav'ns with sweet ac-cord: Ho-ly, ho-ly, ho-ly Lord.

3. Lo! the ap-os-tol-ic train Join Thy sa-cred name to hal-low;
   Proph-ets swell the glad re-frain, And the white-robed mar-tyrs fol-low;
   And, from morn till set of sun, Through the church the song goes on.

4. Ho-ly Fa-ther, Ho-ly Son, Ho-ly Spir-it, three we name Thee;
   Though in es-sence on-ly one, Un-di-vid-ed God we claim Thee,
   And a-dor-ing bend the knee, While we own the mys-ter-y. A-men.

Tr. Ignaz Franz, 1771

1. Grosser Gott, wir loben dich!
    Herr, wir preisen deine Stärke!
   Vor dir neigt die Erde sich
    und bewundert deine Werke.
   Wie du warst vor aller Zeit,
    so bleibst du in Ewigkeit.

2. Alles, was dich preisen kann,
    Cherubim und Seraphinen,
   stimmen dir ein Loblied an,
    alle Engel, die dir dienen,
   rufen dir stets ohne Ruh:
    Heilig, heilig, heilig zu.

3. Auf dem ganzen Erdenkreis
    loben Grosse und auch Kleine
   dich, Gott Vater; dir zum Preis
    singt die heilige Gemeine,
   sie verehrt auf seinem Thron
    deinen eingebornen Sohn.

4. Stehe denn, o Herr, uns bei,
    die wir dich in Demut bitten,
   die dein Blut dort machte frei,
    als du für uns hast gelitten.
   Nimm uns nach vollbrachtem Lauf
    zu dir in den Himmel auf.

GOD: ADORATION AND PRAISE

2 ALL PEOPLE THAT ON EARTH DO DWELL
OLD HUNDREDTH L.M.

William Kethe, 1561
Version of the *Scottish Psalter*, 1650

Pseaumes octante trois..., Geneva, 1551

1 All peo-ple that on earth do dwell, Sing to the Lord with cheer-ful voice.
2 Know that the Lord is God in-deed, With-out our aid He did us make:
3 O en-ter then His gates with praise, Ap-proach with joy His courts un-to:
4 For why? the Lord our God is good, His mer-cy is for-ev-er sure:

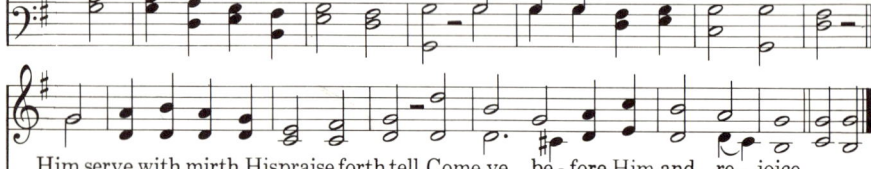

Him serve with mirth, His praise forth tell, Come ye be-fore Him and re-joice.
We are His flock, He doth us feed, And for His sheep He doth us take.
Praise, laud, and bless His name al-ways, For it is seem-ly so to do.
His truth at all times firm-ly stood, And shall from age to age en-dure. A-men.

3 ALL PEOPLE THAT ON EARTH DO DWELL
OLD HUNDREDTH L.M.

William Kethe, 1561
Version of the *Scottish Psalter*, 1650

MELODY IN TENOR

Pseaumes octante trois..., Geneva, 1551
Setting by Claude Goudimel, 1565

1 All peo-ple that on earth do dwell, Sing to the Lord with cheer-ful voice.
2 Know that the Lord is God in-deed, With-out our aid He did us make:
3 O en-ter then His gates with praise, Ap-proach with joy His courts un-to:
4 For why? the Lord our God is good, His mer-cy is for-ev-er sure:

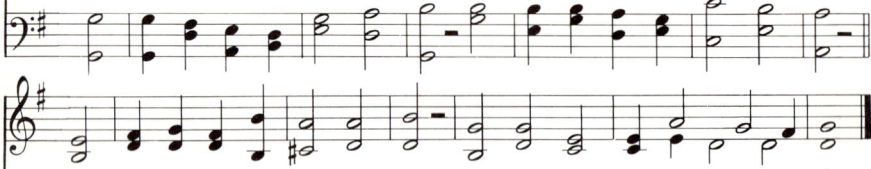

Him serve with mirth, His praise forth tell, Come ye be-fore Him and re-joice.
We are His flock, He doth us feed, And for His sheep He doth us take.
Praise, laud, and bless His name al-ways, For it is seem-ly so to do.
His truth at all times firm-ly stood, And shall from age to age en-dure.

For other settings of the tune see 638 and 639.

GOD: ADORATION AND PRAISE

GOD: ADORATION AND PRAISE

7 GOD HIMSELF IS WITH US

WUNDERBARER KÖNIG 6.6.8.6.6.8.3.3.6.6.

Gerhard Tersteegen, 1729
Gott ist gegenwärtig
Tr. *Hymnal 1940*

A und Ω, Glaub-und Liebesübung
Bremen, 1680

1. God Himself is with us; Let us all adore Him, And with awe appear before Him. God is here within us; Soul, in silence fear Him, Humbly, fervently draw near Him. Now His own Who have known God, in worship lowly, Yield their spirits wholly.

2. Come, abide within me; Let my soul, like Mary, Be Thine earthly sanctuary. Come, indwelling Spirit, With transfigured splendor; Love and honor will I render. Where I go Here below, Let me bow before Thee, Know Thee, and adore Thee.

3. Gladly we surrender Earth's deceitful treasures, Pride of life, and sinful pleasures: Gladly, Lord, we offer Thine to be forever, Soul and life and each endeavor. Thou alone Shalt be known Lord of all our being, Life's true way decreeing. Amen.

GOD: ADORATION AND PRAISE

9 PRAISE TO THE LORD, THE ALMIGHTY

LOBE DEN HERREN 14.14.4.7.8.

Joachim Neander, 1680
Lobe den Herren, den mächtigen König der Ehren
Tr. Catherine Winkworth, 1863

Gesangbuch, Stralsund, 1665

1. Praise to the Lord! the Al-might-y, the King of cre-a-tion!
O my soul, praise Him, for He is thy health and sal-va-tion!
All ye who hear, Now to His tem-ple draw near,
Join me in glad a-do-ra-tion!

2. Praise to the Lord! who o'er all things so won-drous-ly reign-eth,
Shel-ters thee un-der His wings, yea, so gen-tly sus-tain-eth;
Hast thou not seen How thy de-sires have been
Grant-ed in what He or-dain-eth?

3. Praise to the Lord! who doth pros-per thy work and de-fend thee;
Sure-ly His good-ness and mer-cy here dai-ly at-tend thee;
Pon-der a-new What the Al-might-y can do,
If with His love He be-friend thee!

4. Praise to the Lord! O let all that is in me a-dore Him!
All that hath life and breath, come now with prais-es be-fore Him!
Let the A-men Sound from His peo-ple a-gain,
Glad-ly for aye we a-dore Him! A-men.

GOD: ADORATION AND PRAISE

1 Lobe den Herren, den mächtigen König der Ehren!
  Meine geliebete Seele, das ist **mein** Begehren.
        Kommet zu Hauf!
        Psalter und Harfe, wacht auf!
     Lasset den Lobgesang hören!

2 Lobe den Herren, der alles so herrlich regieret,
  der dich auf Flügeln des Adelers sicher geführet,
        der dich erhält,
        wie es dir selber gefällt.
  Hast du nicht dieses verspüret?

O THAT I HAD A THOUSAND VOICES 10

O DASS ICH TAUSEND ZUNGEN 9.8.9.8.8.8.

Johann Mentzer, 1704
O dass ich tausend Zungen hätte
Tr. Catherine Winkworth, 1863, and Others

Johann Balthasar König, 1738

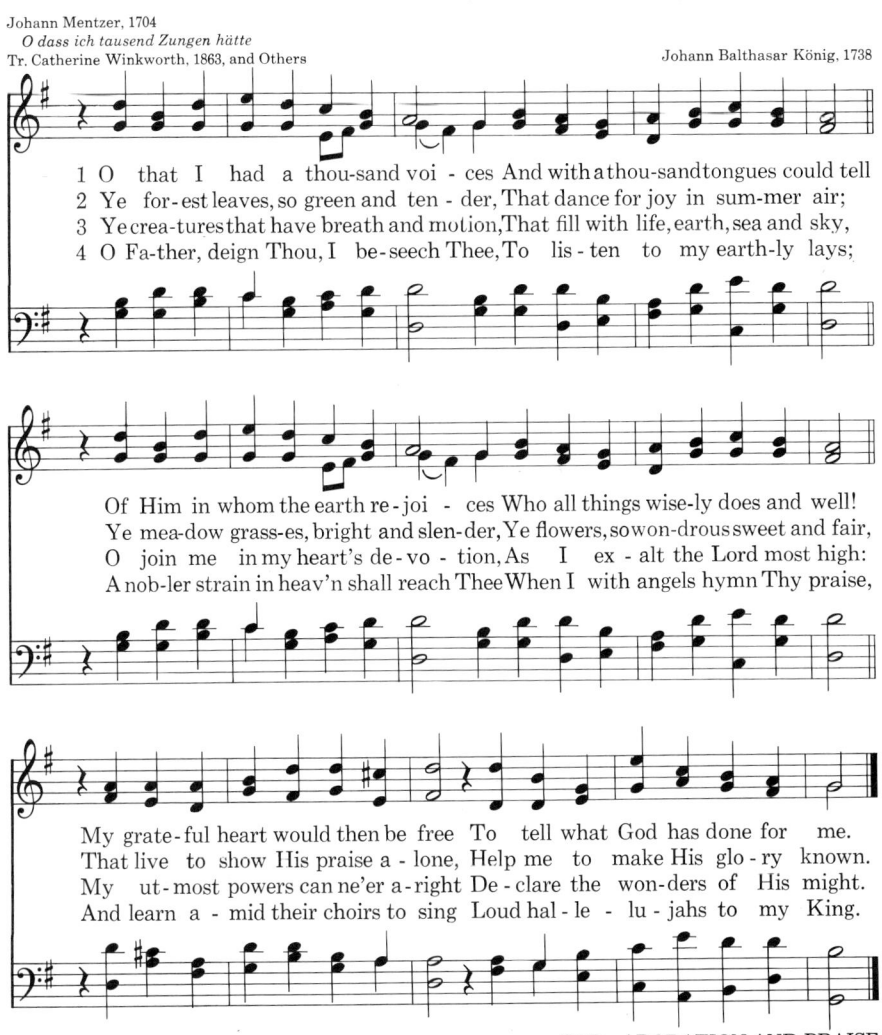

1 O that I had a thou-sand voi - ces And with a thou-sand tongues could tell
2 Ye for-est leaves, so green and ten - der, That dance for joy in sum-mer air;
3 Ye crea-tures that have breath and motion, That fill with life, earth, sea and sky,
4 O Fa-ther, deign Thou, I be-seech Thee, To lis - ten to my earth-ly lays;

Of Him in whom the earth re-joi - ces Who all things wise-ly does and well!
Ye mea-dow grass-es, bright and slen - der, Ye flowers, so won-drous sweet and fair,
O join me in my heart's de-vo - tion, As I ex - alt the Lord most high:
A nob-ler strain in heav'n shall reach Thee When I with angels hymn Thy praise,

My grate-ful heart would then be free To tell what God has done for me.
That live to show His praise a - lone, Help me to make His glo-ry known.
My ut-most powers can ne'er a-right De - clare the won-ders of His might.
And learn a - mid their choirs to sing Loud hal - le - lu - jahs to my King.

GOD: ADORATION AND PRAISE

O COME, LOUD ANTHEMS LET US SING 14

SALISBURY L.M. with Refrain

Based on Psalm 95
Tate and Brady's *New Version
of the Psalms*†, 1696
Refrain added

"Haydn" in Lowell Mason's
*Boston Handel and Haydn Society
Collection* . . . , 1822

1. O come, loud anthems let us sing, Loud thanks to our Almighty King; For we our voices high should raise, When our salvation's Rock we praise.
2. Into His presence let us haste, To thank Him for His favors past; To Him address, in joyful songs, The praise that to His name belongs.
3. The depths of earth are in His hand, Her secret wealth at His command; The strength of hills that reach the skies, Subjected to His empire lies.
4. O let us to His courts repair, And bow with adoration there; Down on our knees, devoutly all, Before the Lord, our Maker, fall.

REFRAIN

Great is the Lord! what tongue can frame An equal honor to His name. Amen.

GOD: ADORATION AND PRAISE

17 MY SOUL, AWAKE AND RENDER
WACH AUF, MEIN HERZ 7.7.7.7.

Paul Gerhardt, 1648
Wach auf, mein Herz, und singe
Tr. Johann Christian Jacobi, 1720, and Others

N. Selnecker's
Christliche Psalmen . . . , 1587

1. My soul, awake and render To God, thy great defender, Thy prayer and thy thanksgiving For all the joys of living.
2. O Lord, be Thou my treasure, Fulfill in me Thy pleasure, And let Thy Spirit guide me Lest evil should betide me.
3. Thy love be my salvation, My heart Thy habitation, Thy Word my food and gladness Till heaven dispels all sadness.

18 MY GOD, HOW ENDLESS IS THY LOVE
WARD L.M.

"Scotch Tune"

Isaac Watts, 1709

Arranged by Lowell Mason, 1860

1. My God, how endless is Thy love! Thy gifts are ev'ry evening new;
2. Thou spread'st the curtains of the night, Great Guardian of my sleeping hours;
3. I yield my pow'rs to Thy command; To Thee I consecrate my days;

GOD: ADORATION AND PRAISE

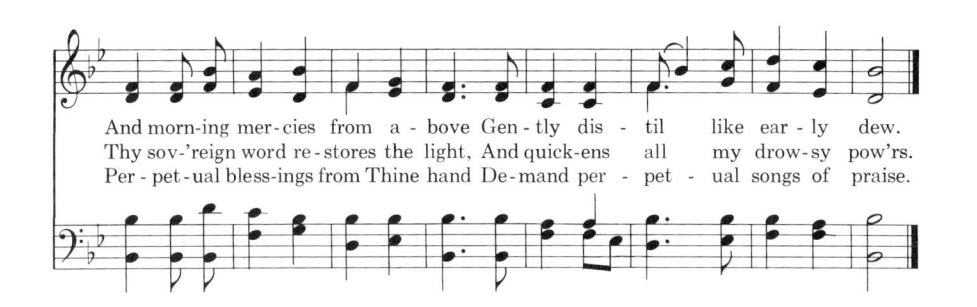

And morn-ing mer-cies from a-bove Gen-tly dis - til like ear - ly dew.
Thy sov-'reign word re-stores the light, And quick-ens all my drow-sy pow'rs.
Per - pet-u-al bless-ings from Thine hand De-mand per - pet - u-al songs of praise.

ERE THE BLUE HEAVENS 19

GERMANY L.M.

Isaac Watts, 1707
W. Gardiner's *Sacred Melodies*, 1815

1 Ere the blue heav'ns were stretched a-broad, From ev - er-last-ing was the Word; With God He was; the Word was God, And must di - vine - ly be a-dored.
2 By His own power were all things made; By Him sup-port - ed, all things stand; He is the whole cre - a - tion's head, And an - gels fly at His com - mand.
3 Mor - tals with joy be-held His face, Th' e - ter - nal Fa - ther's on - ly Son; How full of truth! how full of grace! When through His eyes the God-head shone.
4 Arch - an - gels leave their high a - bode To learn new mys - t'ries here, and tell The loves of our de - scend - ing God, The glo - ries of Em - man - u - el.

GOD: ADORATION AND PRAISE

20 PRAISE THOU THE LORD, O MY SOUL

LOBE DEN HERREN, O MEINE SEELE 10.8.10.8.8.8.8.8.

Based on Psalm 146
Johann Daniel Herrnschmidt, 1714
Lobe den Herren, o meine Seele
Tr. Lester Hostetler, 1938

New-vermehrte Christliche Seelenharf
Ansbach, 1664

1. Praise thou the Lord, O my soul, sing prais-es! Him let me bless in life and death. All through my days His great love a-maz-es, Him let me praise with ev-ery breath, Who life and light hath giv'n to me. Bless, O my soul, e-ter-nal-ly. Hal-le-lu-jah! Hal-le-lu-jah!

2. Praise, all ye peo-ple, His name all-glo-rious, Him who in heav'n and earth doth reign. All that hath life and breath, sound the cho-rus, Sing ye His praise with glad re-frain. Ye chil-dren of our ho-ly God, Fa-ther and Son, and Spir-it, laud. Hal-le-lu-jah! Hal-le-lu-jah! A-men.

GOD: ADORATION AND PRAISE

22 LET ALL THE WORLD
LUCKINGTON 10.4.6.6.6.6.10.4.

George Herbert, 1633 — Basil Harwood, 1908

1 Let all the world in ev-ery corn-er sing "My God and King!"
2 Let all the world in ev-ery corn-er sing "My God and King!"
The heavens are not too high; His praise may thith-er fly:
The church with psalms must shout, No door can keep them out:
The earth is not too low; His prais-es there may grow,
But, a-bove all, the heart Must bear the long-est part.
Let all the world in ev-ery corn-er sing "My God and King!"
Let all the world in ev-ery corn-er sing "My God and King!"

GOD: ADORATION AND PRAISE

24 HOLY LORD, HOLY LORD

FAHRE FORT 6.7.8.7.8.9.6.

Christian Gregor, 1778
Heiliger, Heiliger, Heiliger, Herr Zebaoth
Tr. F. W. Foster, C. G. Clemens, J. Swertner‡, 1789

J. A. Freylinghausen's *Neues
Geistreiches Gesangbuch,*
1704

1. Ho - ly Lord, ho - ly Lord, Ho - ly and al - might - y Lord,
Thou, who, as the great Cre - a - tor, Art by all Thy works a - dored;
Source of u - ni - ver - sal na - ture, And to man re - deemed by Je - sus' blood, Lord, our God! Lord, our God!

2. Thanks and praise, thanks and praise, Thanks and praise be ev - er Thine,
That Thy Word to us is giv - en, Teach - ing us with pow'r di - vine,
That the Lord of earth and heav - en, Ev - er - last - ing life for us to gain, Once was slain, once was slain.

3. Lord, our God, Lord, our God, May Thy pre - cious sav - ing Word,
Till our race is here com - plet - ed, Light un - to our path af - ford;
And, when in Thy pres - ence seat - ed, We to Thee will ren - der for Thy grace Cease - less praise, cease - less praise. A - men.

GOD: ADORATION AND PRAISE

I'LL PRAISE MY MAKER 25

NASHVILLE 8.8.8.8.8.8.

Based on Psalm 146
Isaac Watts, 1719

Lowell Mason, 1832

1. I'll praise my Mak-er with my breath, And when my voice is lost in death, Praise shall em-ploy my no-bler powers; My days of praise shall ne'er be past, While life, and thought, and be-ing last, Or im-mor-tal-i-ty en-dures.

2. Hap-py the man whose hopes re-ly On Is-rael's God; He made the sky And earth and seas, with all their train: His truth for-ev-er stands se-cure; He saves th'op-pressed, He feeds the poor, And none shall find His prom-ise vain.

3. The Lord hath eyes to give the blind; The Lord sup-ports the sink-ing mind; He sends the la-b'ring con-science peace; He helps the stran-ger in dis-tress, The wid-ow and the fa-ther-less, And grants the pris-'ner sweet re-lease.

4. I'll praise Him while He lends me breath, And when my voice is lost in death, Praise shall em-ploy my no-bler powers; My days of praise shall ne'er be past, While life, and thought, and be-ing last, Or im-mor-tal-i-ty en-dures. A-men.

GOD: ADORATION AND PRAISE

26 LORD, WHO CAN BE WITH THEE COMPARED

HERR, DIR IST NIEMAND 9.9.8.9.9.8.9.8.9.8.

Johann A. Cramer, 1763
Herr, Dir ist niemand zu vergleichen
Tr. Harriett R. Spaeth, 1913

Justin Heinrich Knecht, 1793

1. Lord, who can be with Thee com-par-ed? Or who Thy great-ness hath de-clar-ed? What ar-dent thought dis-cerned a-right? Fur-ther than our poor reck-'ning stretch-es, Be-yond the ken of mor-tal eye, Or bound-less depths of star-ry reach-es, There hast Thou set Thy throne on high.

2. Ex-alt, my soul, ex-alt the glo-ry Of my Cre-a-tor, all the liv-ing, Thy daz-zling vest-ment is the light! Praise, hon-or, maj-es-ty re-ceiv-ing, Thou Source and Life of all the liv-ing, Sing thy tri-um-phant songs be-fore Him, Re-peat them, all His saints, a-dore Him Who holds us by His might-y hand! Re-joice in Him, ye hosts of heav-en, To Him a-lone your voic-es raise; Wor-thy is He, to whom be giv-en Hon-or and wor-ship, thanks and praise. A-men.

GOD: ADORATION AND PRAISE

PRAISE THE LORD, YE HEAVENS 27
FABEN 8.7.8.7.D.

Based on Psalm 148
Foundling Hospital Collection, c. 1796, St. 1 and 2
Edward Osler, 1836, St. 3

John H. Wilcox, 1849

1. Praise the Lord: ye heav'ns, a-dore Him; Praise Him, an-gels in the height;
Sun and moon, re-joice be-fore Him, Praise Him, all ye stars of light.
Praise the Lord, for He hath spo-ken; Worlds His might-y voice o-beyed;
Laws which nev-er shall be bro-ken For their guid-ance He hath made.

2. Praise the Lord, for He is glo-rious; Nev-er shall His prom-ise fail:
God hath made His saints vic-to-rious; Sin and death shall not pre-vail.
Praise the God of our sal-va-tion; Hosts on high, His power pro-claim;
Heav'n and earth and all cre-a-tion, Laud and mag-ni-fy His name.

3. Wor-ship, hon-or, glo-ry, bless-ing, Lord, we of-fer un-to Thee;
Young and old, Thy praise ex-press-ing, In glad hom-age bend the knee.
All the saints in heav'n a-dore Thee; We would bow be-fore Thy throne:
As Thine an-gels serve be-fore Thee, So on earth Thy will be done. A-men.

GOD: ADORATION AND PRAISE

28 O GOD, WE PRAISE THEE
TALLIS' ORDINAL C.M.

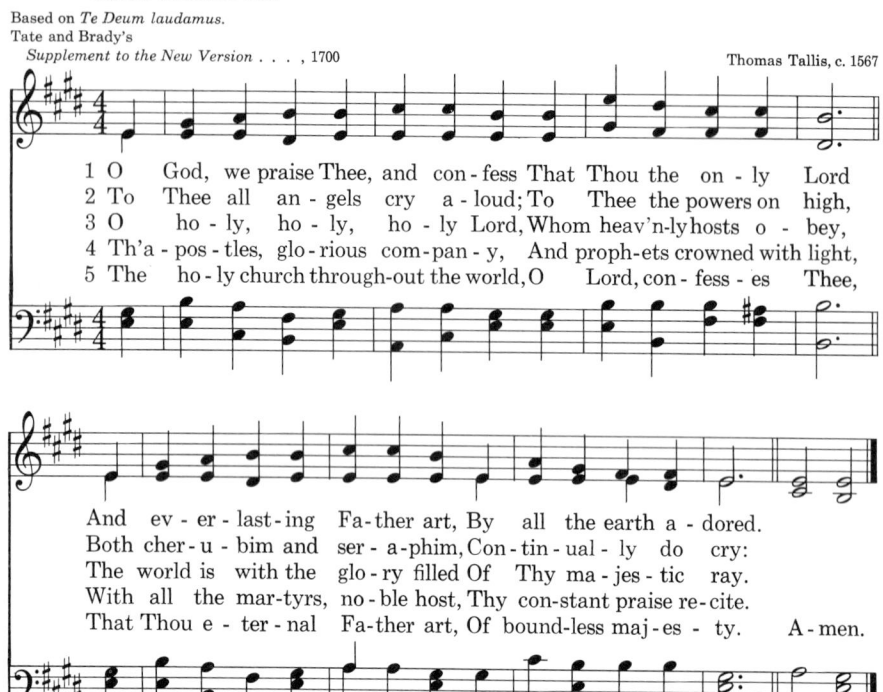

Based on *Te Deum laudamus*.
Tate and Brady's
Supplement to the New Version . . . , 1700

Thomas Tallis, c. 1567

1. O God, we praise Thee, and confess That Thou the only Lord
And everlasting Father art, By all the earth adored.
2. To Thee all angels cry aloud; To Thee the powers on high,
Both cherubim and seraphim, Continually do cry:
3. O holy, holy, holy Lord, Whom heav'nly hosts obey,
The world is with the glory filled Of Thy majestic ray.
4. Th'apostles, glorious company, And prophets crowned with light,
With all the martyrs, noble host, Thy constant praise recite.
5. The holy church throughout the world, O Lord, confesses Thee,
That Thou eternal Father art, Of boundless majesty. A-men.

29 SONGS OF PRAISE THE ANGELS SANG
MONKLAND 7.7.7.7.

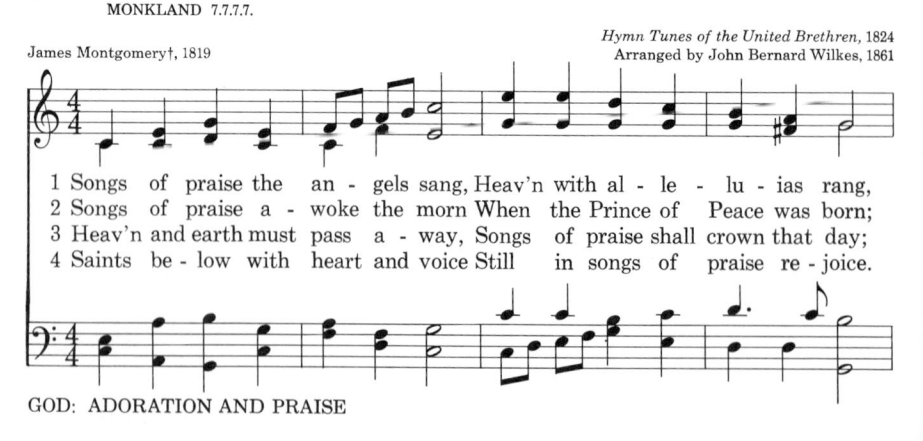

James Montgomery†, 1819

Hymn Tunes of the United Brethren, 1824
Arranged by John Bernard Wilkes, 1861

1. Songs of praise the angels sang, Heav'n with alleluias rang,
2. Songs of praise awoke the morn When the Prince of Peace was born;
3. Heav'n and earth must pass away, Songs of praise shall crown that day;
4. Saints below with heart and voice Still in songs of praise rejoice.

GOD: ADORATION AND PRAISE

When cre-a-tion was be-gun, When God spake and it was done.
Songs of praise a-rose when He Cap-tive led cap-tiv-i-ty.
God will make new heav'ns and earth, Songs of praise shall hail their birth.
Learn-ing here, by faith and love, Songs of praise to sing a-bove. A-men.

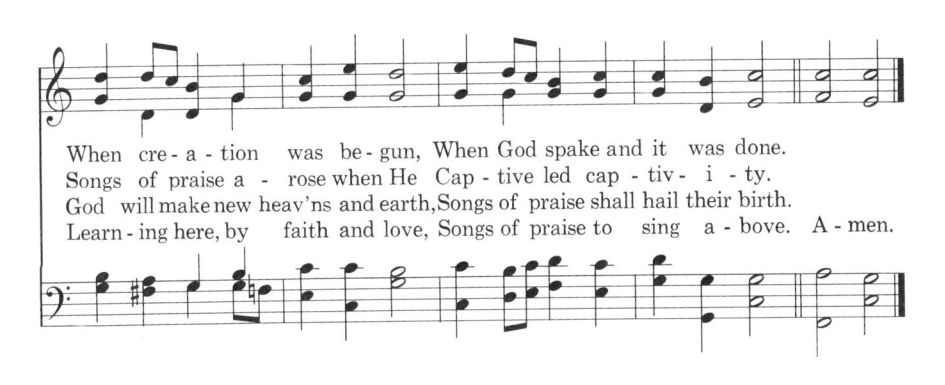

ANGELS HOLY, HIGH AND LOWLY 30
WINDERMERE 8.7.8.8.7.

Based on *Benedicite*
John Stuart Blackie, 1845

Frederick Charles Maker, 1891

1 An-gels ho-ly, High and low-ly, Sing the prais-es of the Lord! Earth and sky, all liv-ing na-ture, Man, the stamp of thy Cre-a-tor, Praise ye, praise ye, God the Lord!

2 Bond and free man, Land and sea man, Earth, with peo-ples wide-ly stored, Wan-d'rer lone o'er prai-ries am-ple, Full-voiced choir, in cost-ly tem-ple, Praise ye, praise ye, God the Lord!

3 Praise Him ev-er, Boun-teous Giv-er; Praise Him, Fa-ther, Friend, and Lord! Each glad soul its free course wing-ing, Each glad voice its free song sing-ing, Praise the great and might-y Lord! A-men.

GOD: ADORATION AND PRAISE

31 NOW THANK WE ALL OUR GOD

NUN DANKET ALLE GOTT 6.7.6.7.6.6.6.6.

Martin Rinckart, 1636
Nun danket alle Gott
Tr. Catherine Winkworth, 1858

Johann Crüger, 1647

1. Now thank we all our God With heart and hands and voices,
Who won-drous things hath done, In whom His world rejoices;
Who, from our moth-ers' arms Hath blessed us on our way
With count-less gifts of love, And still is ours to-day.

2. O may this boun-teous God Through all our life be near us,
With ev-er joy-ful hearts And bless-ed peace to cheer us;
And keep us in His grace, And guide us when per-plexed,
And free us from all ills In this world and the next.

3. All praise and thanks to God, The Fa-ther, now be giv-en,
The Son, and Him who reigns With Them in high-est heav-en,
The one e-ter-nal God, Whom earth and heav'n a-dore;
For thus it was, is now, And shall be ev-er-more. A-men.

GOD: ADORATION AND PRAISE

1 Nun danket alle Gott
mit Herzen, Mund und Händen,
der grosse Dinge tut
an uns und allen Enden;
der uns an Leib und Seel
von früher Kindheit an
unzählig viel zu gut
bis hieher hat getan.

2 Der ewig reiche Gott
woll uns in unserm Leben
ein immer fröhlich Herz
und edlen Frieden geben,
und uns in seiner Gnad
erhalten fort und fort
und uns aus aller Not
erlösen hier und dort.

3 Lob, Ehr und Preis sei Gott,
dem Vater und dem Sohne
und dem, der beiden gleich
im höchsten Himmelsthrone,
dem dreimal einen Gott,
wie er ursprünglich war
und ist und bleiben wird
jetzund und immerdar!

ALL PRAISE TO HIM WHO REIGNS ABOVE 32

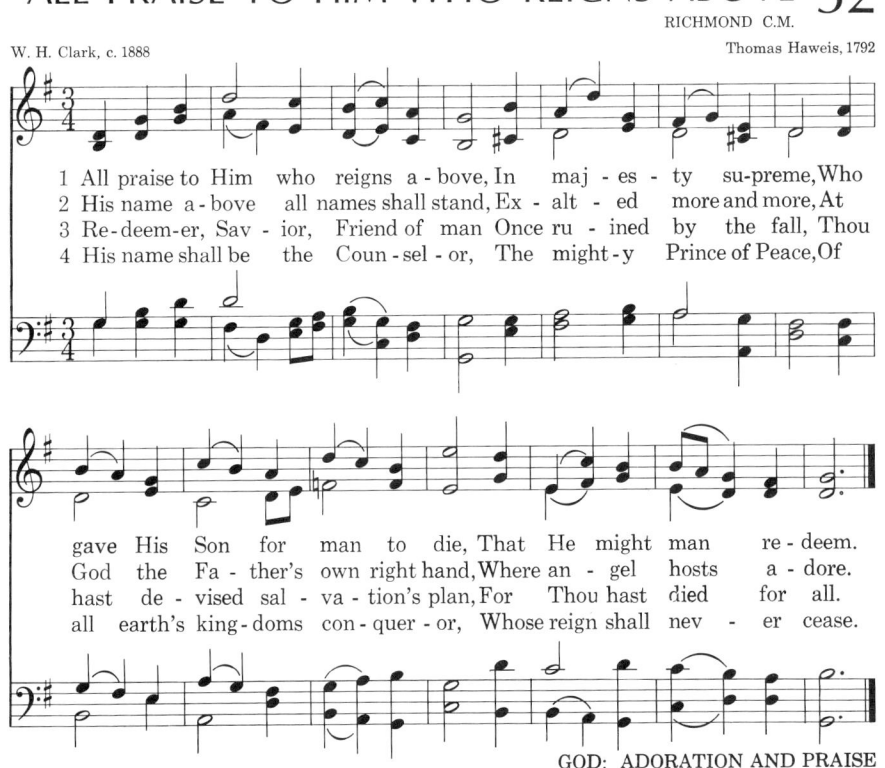

RICHMOND C.M.

W. H. Clark, c. 1888
Thomas Haweis, 1792

1 All praise to Him who reigns a-bove, In maj-es-ty su-preme, Who gave His Son for man to die, That He might man re-deem.
2 His name a-bove all names shall stand, Ex-alt-ed more and more, At God the Fa-ther's own right hand, Where an-gel hosts a-dore.
3 Re-deem-er, Sav-ior, Friend of man Once ru-ined by the fall, Thou hast de-vised sal-va-tion's plan, For Thou hast died for all.
4 His name shall be the Coun-sel-or, The might-y Prince of Peace, Of all earth's king-doms con-quer-or, Whose reign shall nev-er cease.

GOD: ADORATION AND PRAISE

33 I WILL EVER SING THY PRAISES

WOMIT SOLL ICH 8.7.8.7.8.8.7.7.

Ludwig Andreas Gotter, 1697
Womit soll ich dich wohl loben
Tr. Rudolph A. John, 1912

Justin Heinrich Knecht, 1797

1. I will ever sing Thy praises, Might-y God and gra-cious King;
Glad my heart its trib-ute rais-es, And to Thee my psalms I'll sing;
Thou art King of all cre-a-tion, Ev-ery land and ev-ery na-tion;
"Thou-sand, thou-sand thanks to Thee, Might-y God," my song shall be! A-men.

2. All the peo-ple shall pro-claim Thee, Sing Thy praise from shore to shore;
Ev-ery hu-man heart shall name Thee God and King for ev-er-more;
On Thy throne in heav-en vault-ed, In Thy maj-es-ty ex-alt-ed,

3. When at last my feet have found Thee, When at last I am Thine own;
When the ran-somed hosts sur-round Thee, On Thy great e-ter-nal throne;
When in yon-der land of glo-ry, An-gels tell re-demp-tion's sto-ry,

GOD: ADORATION AND PRAISE

GIVE TO OUR GOD IMMORTAL PRAISE 34

WARRINGTON L.M.

Based on Psalm 136
Isaac Watts, 1719

Ralph Harrison, 1784

1. Give to our God immortal praise; Mercy and truth are all His ways: Wonders of grace to God belong; Repeat His mercies in your song.

2. Give to the Lord of lords renown; The King of kings with glory crown; His mercies ever shall endure, When lords and kings are known no more.

3. He built the earth, He spread the sky, And fixed the starry lights on high: Wonders of grace to God belong; Repeat His mercies in your song.

4. He fills the sun with morning light; He bids the moon direct the night: His mercies ever shall endure, When suns and moons shall shine no more. A-men.

5. He sent His Son with power to save
From guilt, and darkness, and the grave:
Wonders of grace to God belong;
Repeat His mercies in your song.

6. Through this vain world He guides our feet,
And leads us to His heav'nly seat:
His mercies ever shall endure,
When this vain world shall be no more.

GOD: ADORATION AND PRAISE

35 GREAT GOD, INDULGE MY HUMBLE CLAIM
HAGERSTOWN L.M.

Based on Psalm 63
Isaac Watts, 1719

John David Brunk, 1902

1. Great God, indulge my humble claim, Thou art my hope, my joy, my rest; The glories that compose Thy name Stand all engaged to make me blest.
2. Thou great and good, Thou just and wise; Thou art my Father and my God; And I am Thine by sacred ties, Thy son, Thy servant, bought with blood.
3. With early feet I love t'appear Among Thy saints, and seek Thy face; Oft have I seen Thy glory there, And felt the pow'r of sov-'reign grace.
4. I'll lift my hands, I'll raise my voice, While I have breath to pray or praise; This work shall make my heart rejoice, And spend the remnant of my days. A-men.

36 FROM ALL THAT DWELL BELOW
DEUS TUORUM MILITUM L.M.

Based on Psalm 117
Isaac Watts, 1719

Grenoble Antiphoner, 1753

1. From all that dwell below the skies Let the Creator's praise arise;
2. Eternal are Thy mercies, Lord; Eternal truth attends Thy Word;

GOD: ADORATION AND PRAISE

Let the Re-deem-er's name be sung Through ev-ery land, by ev-ery tongue.
Thy praise shall sound from shore to shore Till suns shall rise and set no more. A-men.

ETERNAL FATHER, WHEN TO THEE 37

WAREHAM L.M.

Hervey Doddridge Ganse, c. 1870　　　　　　　　　　　　　　　William Knapp, 1738

1 E - ter - nal Fa - ther, when to Thee, Be - yond all worlds, by faith I soar, Be - fore Thy bound - less maj - es - ty I stand in si - lence, and a - dore.

2 But, Sav - ior, Thou art by my side; Thy voice I hear, Thy face I see: Thou art my Friend, my dai - ly Guide; God o - ver all, yet God with me.

3 And Thou, great Spir - it, in my heart Dost make Thy tem - ple day by day; The Ho - ly Ghost of God Thou art, Yet dwell - est in this house of clay.

4 Blest Trin - i - ty, in whom a - lone All things cre - a - ted move or rest, High in the heav'ns Thou hast Thy throne; Thou hast Thy throne with - in my breast. A - men.

GOD: ADORATION AND PRAISE

38 ALL GLORY BE TO GOD ON HIGH
ALLEIN GOTT IN DER HÖH 8.7.8.7.8.8.7.

Based on *Gloria in Excelsis*
Nicolaus Decius, 1522
Allein Gott in der Höh
Tr. Catherine Winkworth†, 1863

Nicolaus Decius, 1522

1 All glo-ry be to God on high, Who hath our race be-friend-ed!
2 We praise, we wor-ship Thee, we trust, And give Thee thanks for ev - er,
3 O Je-sus Christ, our God and Lord, Son of Thy heav'n-ly Fa - ther,
4 O Ho-ly Spir-it, pre-cious Gift, Thou Com-fort-er un-fail - ing,

To us no harm shall now come nigh, The strife at last is end - ed;
O Fa-ther, that Thy rule is just And wise, and chang-es nev - er:
O Thou who hast our peace re-stored And the lost sheep dost gath - er,
O'er Sa-tan's snares our souls up-lift, And let Thy power a-vail - ing

God show-eth His good-will toward men, And peace shall dwell
Thy bound-less power o'er all things reigns, Done is what-e'er
Thou Lamb of God, to Thee on high From out our depths
A-vert our woes and calm our dread, For us the Sav-

on earth a-gain; O thank Him for His good - ness.
Thy will or-dains; Well for us that Thou rul - est!
we sin-ners cry, Have mer-cy on us, Je - sus!
ior's blood was shed; We trust in Thee to save us! A - men.

GOD: ADORATION AND PRAISE

1 Allein Gott in der Höh sei Ehr
   und Dank für seine Gnade,
darum, dass nun und nimmermehr
   uns rühren kann ein Schade.
Ein Wohlgefalln Gott an uns hat;
nun ist gross Fried ohn Unterlass.
   All Fehd hat nun ein Ende.

2 Wir beten an und loben dich,
   wir bringen Ehr und danken,
dass du, Gott Vater, ewiglich
   regierst ohn alles Wanken.
Ganz unbegrenzt ist deine Macht;
allzeit geschieht, was du bedacht.
   Wohl uns solch eines Herren!

3 O Jesu Christe, Gottes Sohn,
   für uns ein Mensch geboren,
gesandt von deines Vaters Thron
   zu retten, was verloren;
Lamm Gottes, heilger Herr und Gott,
nimm an die Bitt von unsrer Not:
   Erbarm dich unser aller!

4 O heilger Geist, du höchstes Gut,
   mit deinem Heil uns tröste;
vor Satans Macht nimm uns in Hut,
   die Jesus Christ erlöste
durch Marter gross und bittern Tod.
Wend ab all unser Leid und Not!
   Auf dich wir uns verlassen.

HIGH IN THE HEAVENS, ETERNAL GOD 39

TRURO L.M.

Based on Psalm 36
Isaac Watts, 1719

Thomas Williams' *Psalmodia Evangelica*, 1789

1 High in the heav'ns, Eternal God, Thy goodness in full glory shines; Thy truth shall break through ev-ery cloud That veils and darkens Thy designs.
2 Forever firm Thy justice stands, As mountains their foundations keep; Wise are the wonders of Thy hands; Thy judgments are a mighty deep.
3 My God, how excellent Thy grace, Whence all our hope and comfort springs! The sons of Adam in distress Fly to the shadow of Thy wings.
4 Life, like a fountain, rich and free, Springs from the presence of my Lord; And in Thy light our souls shall see The glories promised in Thy Word. A-men.

GOD: ADORATION AND PRAISE

40 I SING WITH EXULTATION

NUN WEND IHR HÖREN SAGEN 7.5.7.5.7.6.7.6.

Felix Manz, c. 1526
Mit Lust so will ich singen
Tr. Marion Wenger, 1966

"Bentzenauer Ton," Nürnberg, 1540

1. I sing with exultation, All my heart delights
In God, who brings salvation, Frees from death's dread might.
I praise Thee, Christ of heaven, Who ever shall endure,
Who takes away my sorrow, Keeps me safe and secure.

2. Whom God sent as example, Light my feet to guide.
Before my end He bade me In His realm abide.
That I might love and cherish His righteousness divine;
That I with Him forever Bliss eternal might find.

3. Sing praise to Christ our Savior, Who in grace inclined
To us reveals His nature, Patient, loving, kind.
His love divine outpouring He shows to everyone,
Unfeigned and like His Father's, As no other has done.

4. Christ bids us, none compelling, To His glorious throne.
He only who is willing Christ as Lord to own,
He is assured of heaven Who will right faith pursue,
With heart made pure do penance, Seal'd with baptism true.

GOD: ADORATION AND PRAISE

THROUGH ALL THE CHANGING SCENES 41

IRISH C.M.

Based on Psalm 34
Tate and Brady's *New Version*
of the Psalms, 1696 and 1698

A Collection of Hymns and
Sacred Poems, Dublin, 1749

1. Through all the changing scenes of life, In trouble and in joy, The praises of my God shall still My heart and tongue employ.
2. O magnify the Lord with me, With me exalt His name; When in distress to Him I called, He to my rescue came.
3. The hosts of God encamp around The dwellings of the just; Deliv'rance He affords to all Who on His succor trust.
4. O make but trial of His love; Experience will decide How blest are they, and only they, Who in His truth confide. A-men.

5. Fear Him, ye saints, and you will then
   Have nothing else to fear;
   Make you His service your delight;
   Your wants shall be His care.

6. For God preserves the souls of those
   Who on His truth depend;
   To them and their posterity
   His blessings shall descend.

GOD: ADORATION AND PRAISE

42 O GOD, THE ROCK OF AGES

GREENLAND 7.6.7.6.D.

Edward Henry Bickersteth, 1880

Johann Michael Haydn, 1806

1. O God, the Rock of Ages, Who evermore hast been,
What time the tempest rages, Our dwelling place serene;
Before Thy first creations, O Lord, the same as now,
To endless generations The everlasting Thou!

2. Our years are like the shadows On sunny hills that lie,
Or grasses in the meadows That blossom but to die:
A sleep, a dream, a story By strangers quickly told,
An un-remaining glory Of things that soon are old.

3. O Thou, who canst not slumber, Whose light grows never pale,
Teach us aright to number Our years before they fail.
On us Thy mercy lighten, On us Thy goodness rest,
And let Thy Spirit brighten The hearts Thyself hast blessed.

4. Lord, crown our faith's endeavor With beauty and with grace,
Till, clothed in light forever, We see Thee face to face:
A joy no language measures; A fountain brimming o'er;
An endless flow of pleasures; An ocean without shore. Amen.

GOD: MAJESTY AND HOLINESS

IMMORTAL, INVISIBLE, GOD 43

ST. DENIO 11.11.11.11.

Walter Chalmers Smith†, 1867
Welsh Hymn Melody, 1839

1. Im-mor-tal, in-vis-i-ble, God on-ly wise,
In light in-ac-ces-si-ble hid from our eyes,
Most bless-ed, most glo-rious, the An-cient of Days,
Al-might-y, vic-to-rious, Thy great name we praise.

2. Un-rest-ing, un-hast-ing, and si-lent as light,
Nor want-ing, nor wast-ing, Thou rul-est in might;
Thy jus-tice like moun-tains high soar-ing a-bove
Thy clouds which are foun-tains of good-ness and love.

3. To all, life Thou giv-est to both great and small;
In all life Thou liv-est, the true life of all;
We blos-som and flour-ish as leaves on the tree,
And with-er and per-ish, but naught chang-eth Thee.

4. Great Fa-ther of glo-ry, pure Fa-ther of light,
Thine an-gels a-dore Thee, all veil-ing their sight;
All praise we would ren-der; O help us to see
'Tis on-ly the splen-dor of light hid-eth Thee. A-men.

GOD: MAJESTY AND HOLINESS

44 O SPLENDOR OF GOD'S GLORY
SOLEMNIS HAEC FESTIVITAS L.M.

Ambrose of Milan, d. 397
Splendor paternae gloriae
Tr. Louis F. Benson, 1910

Paris Gradual, 1689

1. O Splendor of God's glory bright, From light eternal bringing light, Thou Light of light, light's living Spring, True Day, all days illumining:

2. Come, very Sun of heaven's love, In lasting radiance from above, And pour the Holy Spirit's ray On all we think or do today.

3. Confirm our will to do the right, And keep our hearts from envy's blight; Let faith her eager fires renew And hate the false, and love the true.

4. Dawn's glory gilds the earth and skies, Let Him, our perfect Morn, arise, The Word in God the Father One, The Father imaged in the Son.

GOD: MAJESTY AND HOLINESS

O SPLENDOR OF GOD'S GLORY 45

SPLENDOR PATERNAE L.M.

Ambrose of Milan, d. 397
Splendor paternae gloriae
Tr. Louis F. Benson, 1910

Sarum Plainsong

1. O Splendor of God's glory bright, From light eternal bringing light, Thou Light of light, light's living Spring, True Day, all days illumining:
2. Come, very Sun of heaven's love, In lasting radiance from above, And pour the Holy Spirit's ray On all we think or do today.
3. Confirm our will to do the right, And keep our hearts from envy's blight; Let faith her eager fires renew, And hate the false, and love the true.
4. Dawn's glory gilds the earth and skies, Let Him, our perfect Morn, arise, The Word in God the Father One, The Father imaged in the Son. A-men.

GOD: MAJESTY AND HOLINESS

46 GREAT GOD, HOW INFINITE ART THOU
WINDSOR C.M.

Isaac Watts†, 1707 *W. Damon's Booke of Musicke, 1591*

1, 5 Great God, how in-fi-nite art Thou! How poor and weak are we! Let the whole race of crea-tures bow, And pay their praise to Thee.
2 Thy throne e-ter-nal a-ges stood, Ere seas or stars were made: Thou art the ev-er-liv-ing God, Were all the na-tions dead.
3 E-ter-ni-ty, with all its years, Stands pres-ent in Thy view; To Thee there's noth-ing old ap-pears; Great God, there's noth-ing new.
4 Our lives through var-ious scenes are drawn, And vexed with tri-fling cares, While Thine e-ter-nal thought moves on Thine un-dis-turbed af-fairs. A-men.

47 O LORD, OUR LORD, IN ALL THE EARTH
DUNFERMLINE C.M.

Based on Psalm 8
Psalter, 1912 *Scottish Psalter, 1615*

1 O Lord, our Lord, in all the earth How ex-cel-lent Thy name!
2 When I re-gard the won-drous heav'ns, Thy hand-i-work on high,
3 O what is man, in Thy re-gard To hold so large a place!
4 On man Thy wis-dom hath be-stowed A power well nigh di-vine;
5 Thy might-y works and won-drous grace Thy glo-ry, Lord, pro-claim.

GOD: MAJESTY AND HOLINESS

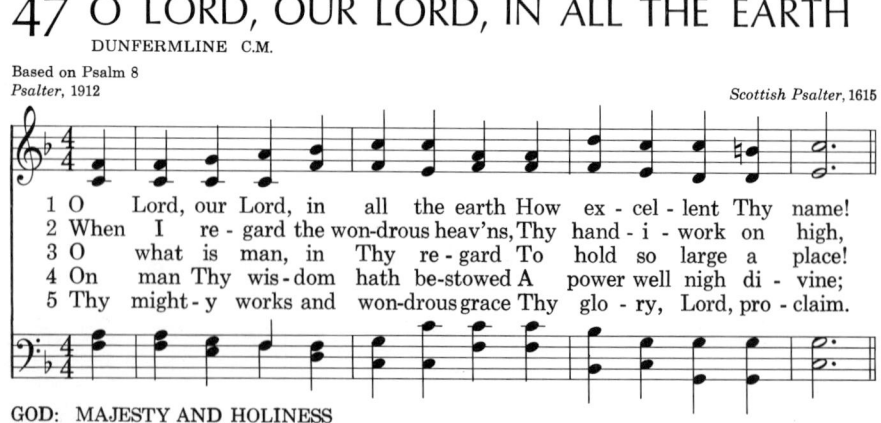

Thy glo-ry Thou hast spread a-far In all the star-ry frame.
The moon and stars or-dained by Thee, O what is man! I cry.
And what the son of man, that Thou Dost vis-it him in grace!
With hon-or Thou hast crowned his head With glo-ry like to Thine.
O Lord, our Lord, in all the earth How ex-cel-lent Thy name! A-men.

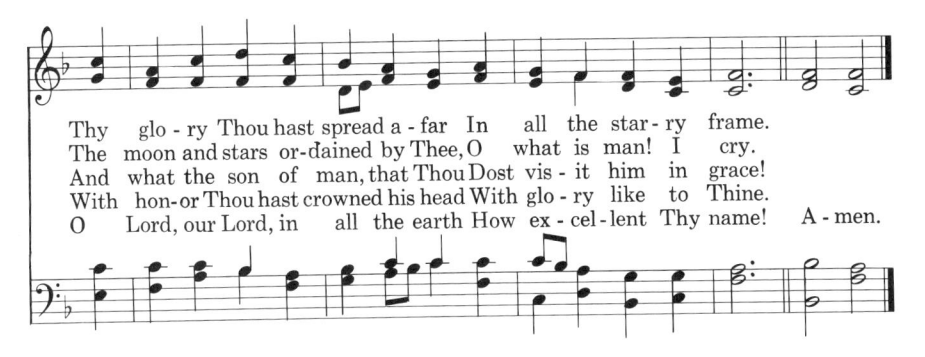

BEFORE JEHOVAH'S AWEFUL THRONE 48
WATTS L.M.

Based on Psalm 100
Isaac Watts, 1719
Altered by John Wesley, 1736

John D. Brunk, 1910

1. Be-fore Je-ho-vah's awe-ful throne, Ye na-tions, bow with sa-cred joy: Know that the Lord is God a-lone: He can cre-ate, and He de-stroy.
2. His sov-'reign power with-out our aid, Made us of clay, and formed us men; And when like wan-d'ring sheep we strayed, He brought us to His fold a-gain.
3. We are His peo-ple, we His care, Our souls, and all our mor-tal frame; What last-ing hon-ors shall we rear, Al-might-y Mak-er, to Thy name?
4. We'll crowd Thy gates with thank-ful songs, High as the heav'ns our voic-es raise; And earth, with her ten thou-sand tongues, Shall fill Thy courts with sound-ing praise.
5. Wide as the world is Thy com-mand, Vast as e-ter-ni-ty Thy love; Firm as a rock Thy truth must stand, When roll-ing years shall cease to move. A-men.

GOD: MAJESTY AND HOLINESS

49 THIS IS MY FATHER'S WORLD
TERRA BEATA S.M.D.

Maltbie D. Babcock, 1901
Franklin L. Sheppard, 1915

1 This is my Father's world, And to my list'ning ears, All
nature sings, and round me rings The music of the spheres.
This is my Father's world: I rest me in the thought Of
rocks and trees, of skies and seas; His hand the wonders wrought.

2 This is my Father's world, The birds their carols raise, The
morning light, the lily white, Declare their Maker's praise.
This is my Father's world: He shines in all that's fair; In the
rustling grass I hear Him pass, He speaks to me ev'rywhere.

3 This is my Father's world, O let me ne'er forget That
though the wrong seems oft so strong, God is the Ruler yet.
This is my Father's world: The battle is not done, Jesus, who died shall be satisfied, And heav'n and earth be one. A-men.

GOD: CREATOR OF HEAVEN AND EARTH

I SING THE MIGHTY POWER OF GOD 50

ELLACOMBE C.M.D.

Isaac Watts‡, 1715

Adapted from *Gesangbuch . . . ,* Württemberg, 1784

1 I sing the might-y power of God, That made the moun-tains rise;
That spread the flow-ing seas a-broad, And built the loft-y skies.
I sing the wis-dom that or-dained The sun to rule the day;
The moon shines full at His com-mand, And all the stars o-bey.

2 I sing the good-ness of the Lord, That filled the earth with food;
He formed the crea-tures with His word, And then pro-nounced them good.
Lord, how Thy won-ders are dis-played, Wher-e'er I turn my eye:
If I sur-vey the ground I tread, Or gaze up-on the sky!

3 There's not a plant or flower be-low, But makes Thy glo-ries known;
And clouds a-rise, and tem-pests blow, By or-der from Thy throne;
While all that bor-rows life from Thee Is ev-er in Thy care,
And ev-ery-where that man can be, Thou, God, art pres-ent there. A-men.

GOD: CREATOR OF HEAVEN AND EARTH

51 ALL CREATURES OF OUR GOD AND KING
LASST UNS ERFREUEN L.M. with Alleluias

Francis of Assisi, d. 1226
Laudato sia Dio mio Signore
Tr. William Henry Draper, 1931

Kirchengesangbuch, Köln, 1623
Harmonized and arranged
by Ralph Vaughan Williams, 1906
Arrangement altered

1 All creatures of our God and King, Lift up your voice and with us sing
2 Thou rush-ing wind that art so strong, Ye clouds that sail in heav'n a-long,
3 Thou flow-ing wa-ter, pure and clear, Make mu-sic for thy Lord to hear,
4 And all ye men of ten-der heart, For-giv-ing oth-ers, take your part,
5 Let all things their Cre-a-tor bless, And wor-ship Him in hum-ble-ness,

Al-le-lu-ia, Al-le-lu-ia! Thou burn-ing sun with gold-en beam,
O praise Him, Al-le-lu-ia! Thou ris-ing morn in praise re-joice,
Al-le-lu-ia! Al-le-lu-ia! Thou fire so mas-ter-ful and bright,
O sing ye, Al-le-lu-ia! Ye who long pain and sor-row bear,
O praise Him, Al-le-lu-ia! Praise, praise the Fa-ther, praise the Son,

Thou sil-ver moon with soft-er gleam, O praise Him, O praise Him,
Ye lights of eve-ning, find a voice, O praise Him, O praise Him,
That giv-est man both warmth and light, O praise Him, O praise Him,
Praise God and on Him cast your care, O praise Him, O praise Him,
And praise the Spir-it, three in one, O praise Him, O praise Him,

Al-le-lu-ia, al-le-lu-ia, al-le-lu-ia!
Al-le-lu-ia, al-le-lu-ia, al-le-lu-ia!
Al-le-lu-ia, al-le-lu-ia, al-le-lu-ia!
Al-le-lu-ia, al-le-lu-ia, al-le-lu-ia!
Al-le-lu-ia, al-le-lu-ia, al-le-lu-ia! A-men.

GOD: CREATOR OF HEAVEN AND EARTH

ALL CREATURES OF OUR GOD AND KING 52

LASST UNS ERFREUEN L.M. with Alleluias

Francis of Assisi, d. 1226
Laudato sia Dio mio Signore
Tr. William Henry Draper, 1931

Kirchengesangbuch, Köln, 1623
Original form of melody
Harmony by J. Harold Moyer, 1965

1. All creatures of our God and King, Alleluia! Lift up your voice and with us sing Alleluia! Thou burning sun with golden beam, O praise Him! Thou silver moon with softer gleam, O praise Him! Alleluia, alleluia, alleluia!

2. Thou rushing wind that art so strong, Alleluia! Ye clouds that sail in heav'n along, Alleluia! Thou rising morn, in praise rejoice, O praise Him! Ye lights of evening, find a voice, O praise Him! Alleluia, alleluia, alleluia!

3. Thou flowing water, pure and clear, Alleluia! Make music for thy Lord to hear, Alleluia! Thou fire so masterful and bright, O praise Him! That givest man both warmth and light, O praise Him! Alleluia, alleluia, alleluia!

4. And all ye men of tender heart, Alleluia! Forgiving others, take your part, Alleluia! Ye who long pain and sorrow bear, O praise Him! Praise God and on Him cast your care, O praise Him! Alleluia, alleluia, alleluia!

5. Let all things their Creator bless, Alleluia! And worship Him in humbleness, Alleluia! Praise, praise the Father, praise the Son, O praise Him! And praise the Spirit, three in one, O praise Him! Alleluia, alleluia, alleluia! A-men.

GOD: CREATOR OF HEAVEN AND EARTH

53 COME, O MY SOUL, IN SACRED LAYS
PARK STREET L.M.

Author Unknown
Sometimes attributed to
Thomas Blacklock, d. 1791

Frederick M. A. Venua, c. 1810

1 Come, O my soul, in sacred lays, At-tempt thy great Cre-a-tor's praise: But O what tongue can speak His fame? What mor-tal verse can reach the theme? What mor-tal verse can reach the theme?

2 En-throned a-mid the ra-diant spheres, He glo-ry like a gar-ment wears; To form a robe of light di-vine, Ten thou-sand suns a-round Him shine, Ten thou-sand suns a-round Him shine.

3 In all our Mak-er's grand de-signs, Al-might-y power with wis-dom shines; His works, through all this won-drous frame, De-clare the glo-ry of His name, De-clare the glo-ry of His name.

4 Raised on de-vo-tion's loft-y wing, Do thou, my soul, His glo-ries sing; And let His praise em-ploy thy tongue, Till lis-t'ning worlds shall join the song, Till lis-t'ning worlds shall join the song.

54 GOD OF THE EARTH, THE SKY, THE SEA
SHELTERING WING L.M.

Samuel Longfellow, 1864

Joseph Barnby, 1872

1 God of the earth, the sky, the sea, Mak-er of all a-bove, be-low,
2 Thy love is in the sunshine's glow, Thy life is in the quick-ening air;
3 We feel Thy calm at eve-ning's hour, Thy grand-eur in the march of night;
4 But high-er far, and far more clear, Thee in man's spir-it we be-hold:

GOD: CREATOR OF HEAVEN AND EARTH

Cre - a - tion lives and moves in Thee, Thy pres-ent life through all doth flow.
When lightnings flash and stormwinds blow, There is Thy power; Thy law is there.
And when the morn-ing breaks with power, We hear Thy word, "Let there be light!"
Thine im-age and Thy-self are there, Th'in-dwell-ing God, pro-claimed of old.

GOD, THE LORD OMNIPOTENT 55

TOASIA 7.8.7.9.

Taiwan
Tr. Boris and Clare Anderson, 1961

Toasia
Pepuhoan

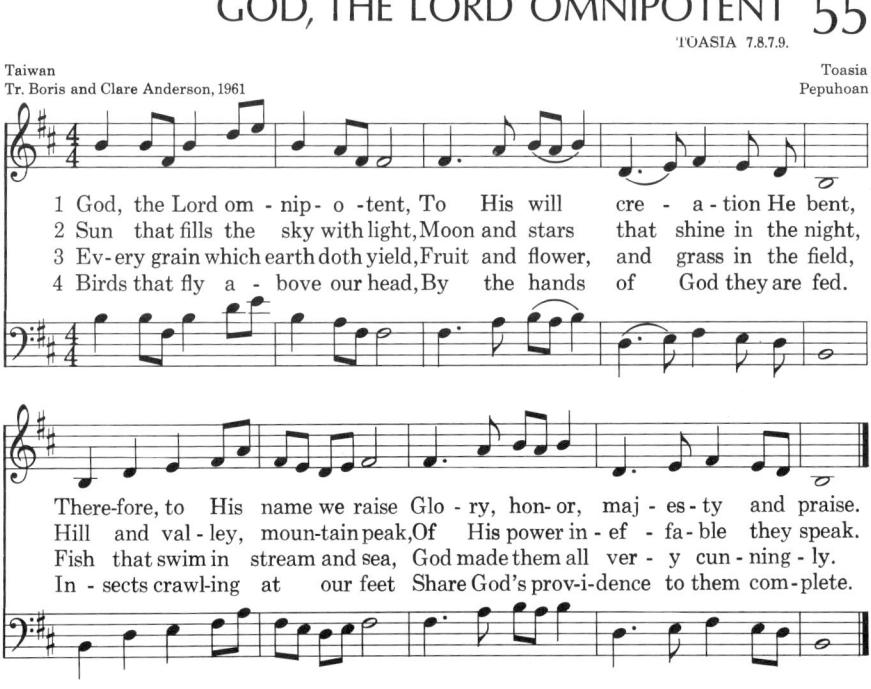

1 God, the Lord om - nip - o -tent, To His will cre - a - tion He bent,
2 Sun that fills the sky with light, Moon and stars that shine in the night,
3 Ev-ery grain which earth doth yield, Fruit and flower, and grass in the field,
4 Birds that fly a - bove our head, By the hands of God they are fed.

There-fore, to His name we raise Glo - ry, hon - or, maj - es - ty and praise.
Hill and val - ley, moun-tain peak, Of His power in - ef - fa - ble they speak.
Fish that swim in stream and sea, God made them all ver - y cun - ning - ly.
In - sects crawl-ing at our feet Share God's prov-i-dence to them com-plete.

5 People too in every land
Live out of His bountiful hand.
He alone their needs provides,
His the will that all their way decides.

6 God is God, and only He,
Idols are merely vanity.
He alone to men can be
Life that springs to all eternity.

GOD: CREATOR OF HEAVEN AND EARTH

56 THE SPACIOUS FIRMAMENT ON HIGH

CREATION L.M.D.

Joseph Addison†, 1712 — Arranged from Franz Joseph Haydn, 1798

1. The spa-cious fir-ma-ment on high, With all the blue e-the-real sky, And span-gled heav'ns a shin-ing frame, Their great O-rig-i-nal pro-claim. Th'un-wea-ried sun, from day to day, Does his Cre-a-tor's power dis-play, And pub-lish-es, to

2. Soon as the eve-ning shades pre-vail, The moon takes up the won-drous tale; And night-ly to the lis-t'ning earth, Re-peats the sto-ry of her birth; Whilst all the stars that round her burn, And all the plan-ets in their turn, Con-firm the ti-dings

3. What though, in sol-emn si-lence, all Move round the dark ter-res-trial ball? What though no re-al voice, nor sound, A-midst their ra-diant orbs be found? In rea-son's ear they all re-joice, And ut-ter forth a glo-rious voice; For-ev-er sing-ing

GOD: CREATOR OF HEAVEN AND EARTH

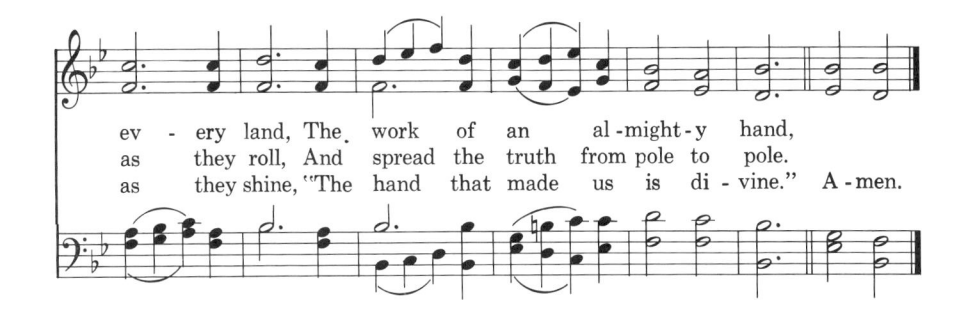

ev - ery land, The work of an al-might-y hand,
as they roll, And spread the truth from pole to pole.
as they shine, "The hand that made us is di-vine." A-men.

LORD OF ALL BEING, THRONED AFAR 57

LOUVAN L.M.

Oliver Wendell Holmes, 1848   Virgil C. Taylor, 1846

1. Lord of all be-ing, throned a-far, Thy glo-ry flames from sun and star; Cen-ter and soul of ev-ery sphere, Yet to each lov-ing heart how near!
2. Sun of our life, Thy wak-ening ray Sheds on our path the glow of day; Star of our hope, Thy sof-tened light Cheers the long watch-es of the night.
3. Our mid-night is Thy smile with-drawn; Our noon-tide is Thy gra-cious dawn; Our rain-bow arch, Thy mer-cy's sign; All, save the clouds of sin, are Thine.
4. Grant us Thy truth to make us free, And kin-dling hearts that burn for Thee; Till all Thy liv-ing al-tars claim One ho-ly light, one heav'n-ly flame. A-men.

GOD: CREATOR OF HEAVEN AND EARTH

58 FOR THE BEAUTY OF THE EARTH
DIX 7.7.7.7.7.7.

Folliott Sandford Pierpoint‡, 1864

Arranged from Conrad Kocher
by William Henry Monk, 1861

1 For the beau-ty of the earth, For the beau-ty of the skies,
2 For the beau-ty of each hour Of the day and of the night,
3 For the joy of hu-man love, Broth-er, sis-ter, par-ent, child,
4 For Thy church, that ev-er-more Lift-eth ho-ly hands a-bove,

For the love which from our birth O-ver and a-round us lies:
Hill and vale, and tree and flower, Sun and moon, and stars of light:
Friends on earth, and friends a-bove; For all gen-tle thoughts and mild:
Of-fering up on ev-ery shore Her pure sac-ri-fice of love:

Lord of all, to Thee we raise This our hymn of grate-ful praise. A-men.

59 HEAVEN AND EARTH, THE SEA AND AIR
GOTT SEI DANK 7.7.7.7.

Joachim Neander, 1680
Himmel, Erde, Luft und Meer
Tr. Catherine Winkworth, 1858
and Frances Elizabeth Cox, 1841

J. A. Freylinghausen's *Neues
Geistreiches Gesangbuch*, 1704

1 Heav'n and earth, the sea and air, All their Mak-er's praise de-clare;
2 See the sun, with glo-rious ray, Pierce the clouds at ope-ning day;
3 See how He hath ev-ery-where Made this earth so rich and fair;
4 Lord, great won-ders work-est Thou! To Thy sway all crea-tures bow;

GOD: CREATOR OF HEAVEN AND EARTH

Wake, my soul, a-wake and sing; Now thy grate-ful prais-es bring.
Moon and stars, in splen-dor bright. Praise their God through si-lent night.
Hill and vale and fruit-ful land, All things liv-ing show His hand.
Write Thou deep-ly in my heart What I am, and what Thou art. A-men.

GOD, WHO MADEST EARTH AND HEAVEN 60
GOTT DES HIMMELS 8.7.8.7.7.7.

Heinrich Albert, 1642
Gott des Himmels und der Erde
Tr. Richard Massie, 1857, and Catherine Winkworth, 1855

Heinrich Albert, 1642

1 God, who mad-est earth and heav-en, Fa-ther, Son, and Ho-ly Ghost,
2 Help me, that I may this morn-ing In the Spir-it al-so rise;
3 Lead me, and di-rect my do-ings By Thy ho-ly Word and will;

Who the day and night hast giv-en, Sun, and moon, and star-ry host;
And my soul with grace a-dorn-ing, Lord, pre-pare it in such wise,
Or-der all my ways and go-ings, Keep me, Lord, this day, from ill;

Whose strong hand the world sus-tains, And what-ev-er it con-tains;
That I may, with-out dis-may, Look for Thy great judg-ment day.
No-where else, ex-cept with Thee, Can I safe-ly guard-ed be. A-men.

GOD: CREATOR OF HEAVEN AND EARTH

61 PRAISE THE LORD, HIS GLORIES SHOW

GWALCHMAI 7.7.7.7. with Alleluias

Based on Psalm 150
Henry Francis Lyte, 1834

Joseph David Jones, 1868

1 Praise the Lord, His glories show, Alleluia!
  Saints within His courts below, Alleluia!
  Angels round His throne above, Alleluia!
  All that see and share His love. Alleluia!

2 Earth to heav'n, and heav'n to earth, Alleluia!
  Tell His wonders, sing His worth, Alleluia!
  Age to age and shore to shore, Alleluia!
  Praise Him, praise Him evermore! Alleluia!

3 Praise the Lord, His mercies trace, Alleluia!
  Praise His providence and grace, Alleluia!
  All that He for man hath done, Alleluia!
  All He sends us through His Son. Alleluia! A-men.

GOD: CREATOR OF HEAVEN AND EARTH

LET THE WHOLE CREATION CRY 62

LLANFAIR 7.7.7.7. with Alleluias

Based on Psalm 148
Stopford A. Brooke†, 1881

Robert Williams, 1817

1. Let the whole cre - a - tion cry Al - le - lu - ia!
2. Praise Him, all ye hosts a - bove, Al - le - lu - ia!
3. War - riors fight-ing for the Lord, Al - le - lu - ia!
4. Men and wom - en, young and old, Al - le - lu - ia!

Glo - ry to the Lord on high! Al - le - lu - ia!
Ev - er bright and fair in love! Al - le - lu - ia!
Pro - phets burn - ing with His word, Al - le - lu - ia!
Raise the an - them man - i - fold; Al - le - lu - ia!

Heav'n and earth, a - wake and sing, Al - le - lu - ia!
Sun and moon, up - lift your voice, Al - le - lu - ia!
Those to whom the arts be - long, Al - le - lu - ia!
And let chil - dren's hap - py hearts, Al - le - lu - ia!

"God is God and there - fore King," Al - le - lu - ia!
Night and stars in God re - joice, Al - le - lu - ia!
Join the rush - ing of the song, Al - le - lu - ia!
In this wor - ship bear their parts: Al - le - lu - ia!

GOD: CREATOR OF HEAVEN AND EARTH

63 MY SHEPHERD WILL SUPPLY MY NEED

RESIGNATION C.M.D.

Based on Psalm 23
Isaac Watts, 1719

Folk Hymn.
F. Lewis' *Beauties of Harmony*, c. 1828
Version from Joseph Funk's *Genuine Church Music*, 1832
Harmony by J. Harold Moyer, 1965

1 My Shepherd will supply my need; Jehovah is His name: In pastures fresh He makes me feed, Beside the living stream. He brings my wand'ring spirit back, When I forsake His ways; And leads me,

2 When I walk through the shades of death Thy presence is my stay; One word of Thy supporting breath Drives all my fears away. Thy hand, in sight of all my foes, Doth still my table spread; My cup with

3 The sure provisions of my God Attend me all my days; O may Thy house be my abode, And all my work be praise. There would I find a settled rest, While others go and come; No more a

GOD: HIS LOVE AND MERCY

for His mer - cy's sake, In paths of truth and grace.
bless - ings o - ver - flows, Thine oil a - noints my head.
stran - ger, nor a guest, But like a child at home.

O LOVE OF GOD, HOW STRONG 64
ALFRETON L.M.

Horatius Bonar, 1864
William Beastall, c. 1818

1. O love of God, how strong and true! E - ter - nal and yet ev - er new, Un - com - pre - hend - ed and un - bought, Be - yond all knowl - edge and all thought.

2. O wide - em - brac - ing, won - drous love, We read thee in the sky a - bove, We read thee in the earth be - low, In seas that swell and streams that flow.

3. We read thee best in Him who came, To bear for us the cross of shame; Sent by the Fa - ther from on high, Our life to live, our death to die.

4. We read thy power to bless and save, E'en in the dark - ness of the grave; Still more in res - ur - rec - tion light, We read the full - ness of thy might.

5. O love of God, our shield and stay, Through all the per - ils of our way; E - ter - nal love, in thee we rest, For - ev - er safe, for - ev - er blest!

GOD: HIS LOVE AND MERCY

65 THE KING OF LOVE MY SHEPHERD IS

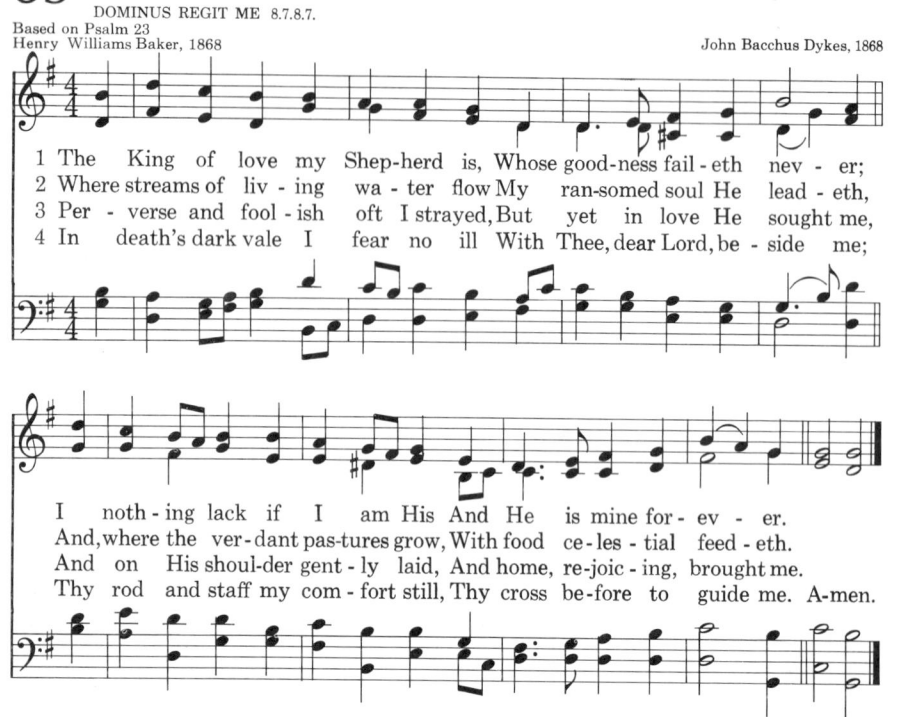

DOMINUS REGIT ME 8.7.8.7.
Based on Psalm 23
Henry Williams Baker, 1868

John Bacchus Dykes, 1868

1. The King of love my Shepherd is, Whose goodness faileth never;
I nothing lack if I am His And He is mine forever.

2. Where streams of living water flow My ransomed soul He leadeth,
And, where the verdant pastures grow, With food celestial feedeth.

3. Perverse and foolish oft I strayed, But yet in love He sought me,
And on His shoulder gently laid, And home, rejoicing, brought me.

4. In death's dark vale I fear no ill With Thee, dear Lord, beside me;
Thy rod and staff my comfort still, Thy cross before to guide me. A-men.

5. Thou spread'st a table in my sight,
Thy unction grace bestoweth,
And O what transport of delight
From Thy pure chalice floweth.

6. And so through all the length of days
Thy goodness faileth never;
Good Shepherd, may I sing Thy praise
Within Thy house forever.

66 THE LORD MY SHEPHERD IS

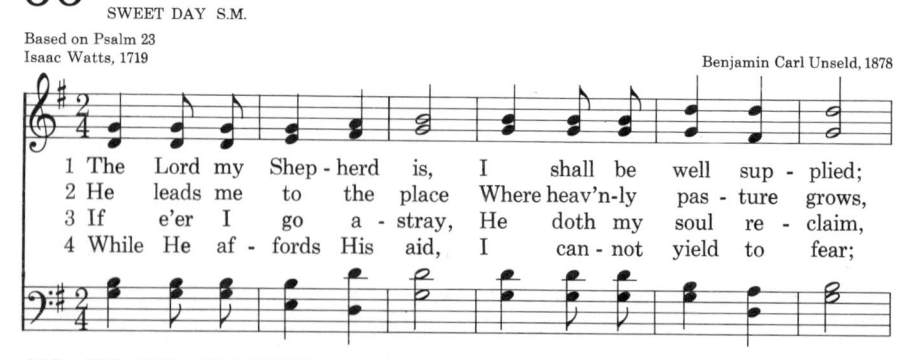

SWEET DAY S.M.
Based on Psalm 23
Isaac Watts, 1719

Benjamin Carl Unseld, 1878

1. The Lord my Shepherd is, I shall be well supplied;
2. He leads me to the place Where heav'nly pasture grows,
3. If e'er I go astray, He doth my soul reclaim,
4. While He affords His aid, I cannot yield to fear;

GOD: HIS LOVE AND MERCY

Since He is mine and I am His, What can I want beside?
Where living waters gently pass, And full salvation flows.
And guides me in His own right way, For His most holy name.
Tho' I should walk thro' death's dark shade, My Shepherd's with me there. A-men.

5 In spite of all my foes
    Thou dost my table spread,
    My cup with blessings overflows,
    And joy exalts my head.

6 The bounties of Thy love
    Shall crown my following days;
    Nor from Thy house will I remove
    Nor cease to speak Thy praise.

THE LORD'S MY SHEPHERD 67

CRIMOND C.M.

Based on Psalm 23
Scottish Psalter, 1650

Jessie Seymour Irvine, 1872

1 The Lord's my Shepherd, I'll not want. He makes me down to lie
2 My soul He doth restore again; And me to walk doth make
3 Yea, though I walk in death's dark vale, Yet will I fear none ill:
4 My table Thou hast furnished In presence of my foes;
5 Goodness and mercy all my life Shall surely follow me:

In pastures green; He leadeth me The quiet waters by.
Within the paths of righteousness, Ev'n for His own name's sake.
For Thou art with me; and Thy rod And staff me comfort still.
My head Thou dost with oil anoint, And my cup overflows.
And in God's house for-ev-er-more My dwelling place shall be. A-men.

GOD: HIS LOVE AND MERCY

68 WHAT MERCY AND DIVINE COMPASSION

MIR IST ERBARMUNG 9.8.9.8.8.8.

Philipp Friedrich Hiller, 1767
Mir ist Erbarmung widerfahren
Tr. Frieda Kaufman, 1938

J. G. Schicht's
Allgemeines Choral-Buch . . . , 1819

1. What mer-cy and di-vine com-pas-sion Has God in Christ re-vealed to me! My haugh-ty spir-it would not ask it, Yet He be-stowed it, full and free. In God my heart doth now re-joice: I praise His grace with heart doth now re-joice:

2. E-ter-nal wrath should be my por-tion: The Lamb of God, for sin-ners slain, Re-moved the curse and con-dem-na-tion, His blood a-toned for ev-ery stain. God's love in Christ on Cal-v'ry's tree From guilt and shame has

3. Great God, ac-cept my ad-o-ra-tion; Help me Thy mer-cy to con-fess, In Je-sus Christ is my sal-va-tion; He is my hope in life and death; His blood, His right-eous-ness a-lone I claim be-fore Thy

4. Thy boun-teous grace is my as-sur-ance, The blood of Christ my on-ly plea, Thy heart of love my con-so-la-tion Un-til Thy glo-rious face I see; My theme, through nev-er-end-ing days, Shall be Thy great re-

GOD: HIS LOVE AND MERCY

grate - ful voice. I praise His grace with grate - ful voice.
set me free. From guilt and shame has set me free.
judg - ment throne. I claim be - fore Thy judg - ment throne.
deem - ing grace. Shall be Thy great re - deem - ing grace.

AWAKE, MY SOUL, AWAKE MY TONGUE 69
DUKE STREET L.M.

Anne Steele, 1760

H. Boyd's *Psalm and Hymn Tunes*, 1793
Attributed to John Hatton, d. 1793

1 A - wake, my soul, a - wake my tongue, My God de -
2 Di - vine - ly free His mer - cy flows, For - gives my
3 His mer - cy, with un - chang - ing rays, For - ev - er
4 While all His works His praise pro - claim, And men and

mands the grate - ful song; Let all my in - most powers re -
sins, al - lays my woes, And bids ap - proach-ing death re -
shines, while time de - cays: And chil-dren's chil - dren shall re -
an - gels bless His name, O let my heart, my life, my

cord The won-drous mer - cy of the Lord.
move, And crowns me with in - dul - gent love.
cord The truth and good - ness of the Lord.
tongue At - tend, and join the bliss - ful song! A - men.

GOD: HIS LOVE AND MERCY

70 LET US, WITH A GLADSOME MIND
GENEVA 136 7.7.7.7.

Based on Psalm 136
John Milton‡, 1623

Les cent cinquante pseaumes..., Geneva, 1562
Harmony adapted from Claude Goudimel, 1565

1. Let us, with a gladsome mind, Praise the Lord, for He is kind:
2. Let us blaze His name abroad, For of gods He is the God:
3. He with all-commanding might Filled the new-made world with light:

Refrain (Omit after Stanza 5.)

For His mercies aye endure, Ever faithful, ever sure.

4. All things living He doth feed,
His full hand supplies their need:
Refrain

5. Let us, with a gladsome mind,
Praise the Lord, for He is kind.

71 GOD IS LOVE, HIS MERCY BRIGHTENS
SUSSEX 8.7.8.7.

John Bowring, 1825

From an English Traditional Melody
Ralph Vaughan Williams, 1906

1. God is love, His mercy brightens All the path in which we rove:
2. Chance and change are busy ever; Man decays, and ages move;
3. E'en the hour that darkest seemeth Will His changeless goodness prove;
4. He with earthly cares entwineth Hope and comfort from above;

GOD: HIS LOVE AND MERCY

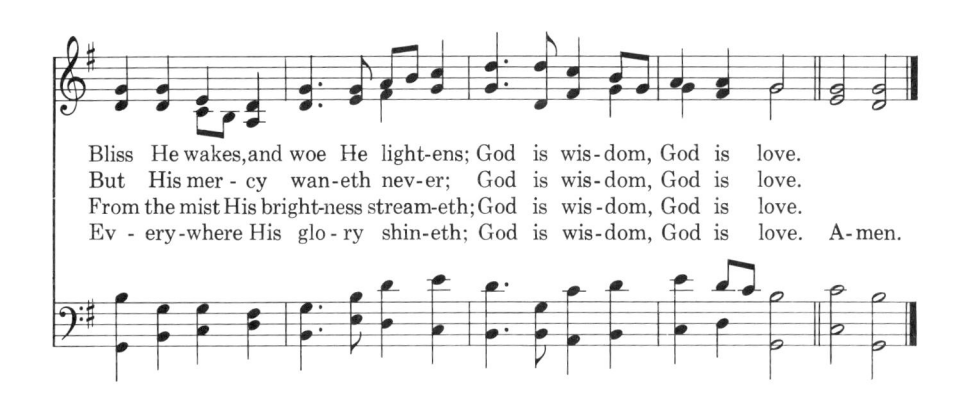

Bliss He wakes, and woe He light-ens; God is wis-dom, God is love.
But His mer-cy wan-eth nev-er; God is wis-dom, God is love.
From the mist His bright-ness stream-eth; God is wis-dom, God is love.
Ev-ery-where His glo-ry shin-eth; God is wis-dom, God is love. A-men.

BLESS, O MY SOUL, THE LIVING GOD 72

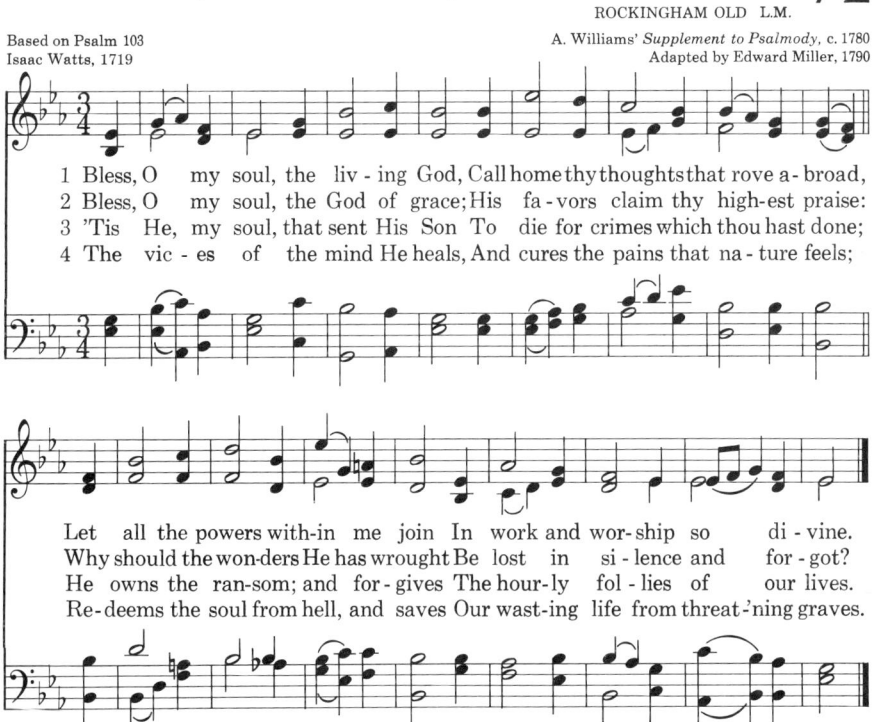

ROCKINGHAM OLD L.M.

Based on Psalm 103
Isaac Watts, 1719

A. Williams' *Supplement to Psalmody*, c. 1780
Adapted by Edward Miller, 1790

1. Bless, O my soul, the liv-ing God, Call home thy thoughts that rove a-broad,
   Let all the powers with-in me join In work and wor-ship so di-vine.
2. Bless, O my soul, the God of grace; His fa-vors claim thy high-est praise:
   Why should the won-ders He has wrought Be lost in si-lence and for-got?
3. 'Tis He, my soul, that sent His Son To die for crimes which thou hast done;
   He owns the ran-som; and for-gives The hour-ly fol-lies of our lives.
4. The vic-es of the mind He heals, And cures the pains that na-ture feels;
   Re-deems the soul from hell, and saves Our wast-ing life from threat'ning graves.

5. Our youth decayed His power repairs;
   His mercy crowns our growing years:
   He satisfies our mouth with good,
   And fills our hopes with heav'nly food.

6. He sees th' oppressor and th' oppressed,
   And often gives the sufferers rest:
   But will His justice more display
   In the last great rewarding day.

GOD: HIS LOVE AND MERCY

73 BE STILL, MY SOUL
FINLANDIA 10.10.10.10.10.10.

Catharina A. D. von Schlegel, 1752
Stille, mein Wille
Tr. Jane Laurie Borthwick, 1855

From Jean Sibelius, 1899
Arranged for *The Hymnal*, 1933 (Presbyterian)

1 Be still, my soul! the Lord is on thy side; Bear pa-tient-ly the cross of grief or pain; Leave to thy God to or-der and pro-vide, In ev-ery change He faith-ful will re-main. Be still, my soul! thy best, thy heav'n-ly Friend Through thorn-y ways leads to a joy-ful end.

2 Be still, my soul! thy God doth un-der-take To guide the fu-ture as He has the past. Thy hope, thy con-fi-dence, let noth-ing shake; All now mys-te-rious shall be bright at last. Be still, my soul! the waves and winds still know His voice who ruled them while He dwelt be-low.

3 Be still, my soul! the hour is has-t'ning on When we shall be for-ev-er with the Lord, When dis-ap-point-ment, grief, and fear are gone, Sor-row for-got, love's pur-est joys re-stored. Be still, my soul! when change and tears are past, All safe and bless-ed we shall meet at last. A-men.

GOD: HIS LOVE AND MERCY

WHEN ALL THY MERCIES, O MY GOD 74

GENEVA C.M.

Joseph Addison, 1712

John Cole, 1805
Version from Joseph Funk's *Harmonia Sacra.*

1 When all Thy mercies, O my God, My rising soul surveys, Transported with the view, I'm lost In wonder, love and praise.

2 Ten thousand thousand precious gifts My daily thanks employ; Nor is the least a cheerful heart, That tastes those gifts with joy.

3 Through every period of my life Thy goodness I'll pursue; And after death, in distant worlds, The glorious theme renew.

4 Through all eternity, to Thee
A joyful song I'll raise;
But O eternity's too short
To utter all Thy praise!

Soprano and Tenor parts have been exchanged.

GOD: HIS LOVE AND MERCY

75 LOVE DIVINE, ALL LOVES EXCELLING
BEECHER 8.7.8.7.D.

Charles Wesley, 1747 — John Zundel, 1870

1. Love divine, all loves excelling, Joy of heav'n, to earth come down;
Fix in us Thy humble dwelling, All Thy faithful mercies crown.
Jesus, Thou art all compassion, Pure, unbounded love Thou art;
Visit us with Thy salvation, Enter every trembling heart.

2. Breathe, O breathe Thy loving Spirit Into every troubled breast;
Let us all in Thee inherit, Let us find the promised rest;
Take away the love of sinning; Alpha and Omega be;
End of faith, as its beginning, Set our hearts at liberty.

3. Come, Almighty to deliver, Let us all Thy grace receive;
Suddenly return, and never, Nevermore Thy temples leave.
Thee we would be always blessing, Serve Thee as Thy hosts above,
Pray, and praise Thee without ceasing, Glory in Thy perfect love.

4. Finish, then, Thy new creation; Pure and spotless let us be;
Let us see Thy great salvation Perfectly restored in Thee;
Changed from glory into glory, Till in heav'n we take our place,
Till we cast our crowns before Thee, Lost in wonder, love, and praise. A-men.

GOD: HIS LOVE AND MERCY

LOVE DIVINE, ALL LOVES EXCELLING 76

BLAENWERN 8.7.8.7.D.

Charles Wesley‡, 1747
William Penfro Rowlands, 1915

1. Love di-vine, all loves ex-cell-ing, Joy of heav'n, to earth come down,
Fix in us Thy hum-ble dwell-ing, All Thy faith-ful mer-cies crown:
Je - sus, Thou art all com-pas-sion, Pure, un - bound-ed love Thou art;
Vis - it us with Thy sal - va-tion, En - ter ev - ery trem-bling heart.

2. Breathe, O breathe Thy lov - ing Spir - it In - to ev - ery trou - bled breast;
Let us all in Thee in - her - it, Let us find the prom-ised rest;
Take a - way the love of sin-ning, Al - pha and O - me - ga be;
End of faith, as its be - gin-ning, Set our hearts at lib - er - ty.

3. Come, Al - might-y to de - liv - er, Let us all Thy grace re - ceive;
Sud - den - ly re - turn, and nev - er, Nev - er - more Thy tem - ples leave.
Thee we would be al - ways bless-ing, Serve Thee as Thy hosts a - bove,
Pray, and praise Thee with-out ceas-ing, Glo - ry in Thy per-fect love.

4. Fin - ish, then, Thy new cre - a - tion: Pure and spot-less let us be;
Let us see Thy great sal - va-tion, Per - fect - ly re - stored in Thee,
Changed from glo - ry in - to glo - ry, Till in heav'n, we take our place,
Till we cast our crowns be-fore Thee, Lost in won - der, love, and praise. A-men.

GOD: HIS LOVE AND MERCY

77 WHAT GOD HATH DONE IS DONE ARIGHT
WAS GOTT TUT, DAS IST WOHLGETAN 8.7.8.7.4.4.7.7.

Benjamin Schmolck, 1720
Was Gott tut, das ist wohlgetan
Tr. Frances Elizabeth Cox, 1864

Severus Gastorius, 1681

1. What God hath done is done a-right, So think all true be-liev-ers;
They feel His love, they own His might, Though fond hopes prove de-ceiv-ers:
Mid seem-ing ill God loves them still, And, e'en by sor-row's leav-en,
Would raise their hearts to heav-en.

2. What God hath done is done a-right, In gifts with-held or sent us;
And what suf-fic-eth in His sight, Should al-ways well con-tent us:
'Tis for our sakes He gives or takes; Then, hum-bly bowed be-fore Him,
In si-lence we a-dore Him.

3. What God hath done is done a-right, May He sub-mis-sive make us!
His gra-cious prom-ise He doth plight, That He will ne'er for-sake us:
Our Sav-ior knows Our wants and woes, And all we need pro-vid-eth:
Praise God, what-e'er be-tid-eth! A-men.

GOD: HIS LOVE AND MERCY

1 Was Gott tut, das ist wohlgetan,
    so denken Gottes Kinder.
  Er sieht sie oft gar strenge an
    und liebt sie doch nicht minder;
  er zieht ihr Herz nur himmelwärts,
    wenn er sie lässt auf Erden
  ein Ziel der Plagen werden.

2 Was Gott tut, das ist wohlgetan.
    Gibt er, so kann man nehmen;
  Nimmt er, wir sind nicht übler dran,
    wenn wir uns nur bequemen.
  Die Linke schmerzt, die Rechte herzt,
    und beide Hände müssen
  wir doch in Demut küssen.

3 Was Gott tut, das ist wohlgetan.
    Er weist uns oft den Segen,
  und eh er noch gedeihen kann,
    muss sich die Hoffnung legen.
  Weil er allein der Schatz will sein,
    so macht er andre Güter
  durch den Verlust uns bitter.

THERE'S A WIDENESS IN GOD'S MERCY 78

WELLESLEY 8.7.8.7.

Frederick William Faber, 1862

Lizzie Shove Tourjée, 1878

1 There's a wide-ness in God's mer-cy, Like the wide-ness of the sea: There's a kind-ness in His jus-tice, Which is more than lib-er-ty.
2 There is wel-come for the sin-ner, And more grac-es for the good; There is mer-cy with the Sav-ior; There is heal-ing in His blood.
3 There is grace e-nough for thou-sands Of new worlds as great as this; There is room for fresh cre-a-tions In that up-per home of bliss.
4 For the love of God is broad-er Than the mea-sures of man's mind; And the heart of the E-ter-nal Is most won-der-ful-ly kind.
5 But we make His love too nar-row By false lim-its of our own; And we mag-ni-fy His strict-ness With a zeal He will not own. A-men.

GOD: HIS LOVE AND MERCY

79 LORD, THOU HAST SEARCHED AND SEEN
BERA L.M.

Based on Psalm 139
Isaac Watts, 1719

John Edgar Gould, 1849

1. Lord, Thou hast searched and seen me through: Thine eye commands, with piercing view, My rising and my resting hours, My heart and flesh with all their powers.
2. My thoughts, before they are my own, Are to my God distinctly known; He knows the words I mean to speak, Ere from my opening lips they break.
3. Within Thy circling power I stand; On every side I find Thy hand: Awake, asleep, at home, abroad, I am surrounded still with God.
4. O may these thoughts possess my breast, Where'er I rove, where'er I rest; Nor let my weaker passions dare Consent to sin, for God is there. A-men.

80 GOD MOVES IN A MYSTERIOUS WAY
DUNFERMLINE C.M.

William Cowper, 1773

Scottish Psalter, 1615

1. God moves in a mysterious way, His wonders to perform;
2. Ye fearful saints, fresh courage take; The clouds ye so much dread
3. Judge not the Lord by feeble sense, But trust Him for His grace;
4. His purposes will ripen fast, Unfolding every hour;
5. Blind unbelief is sure to err, And scan His work in vain;

GOD: HIS PROVIDENCE AND CARE

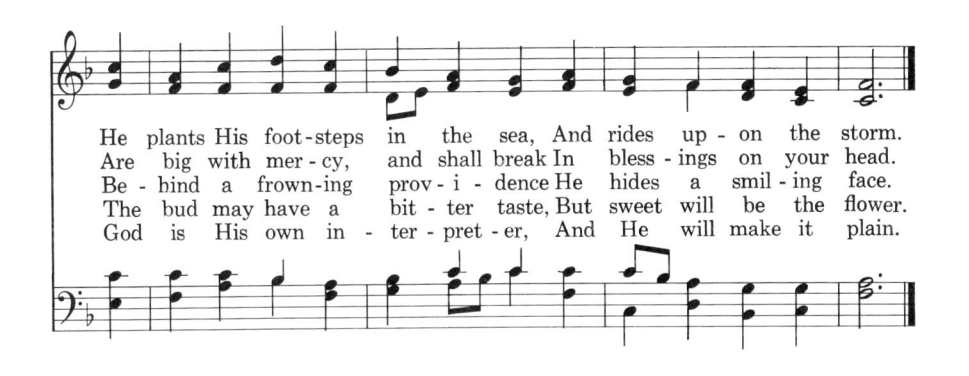

He plants His foot-steps in the sea, And rides up-on the storm.
Are big with mer-cy, and shall break In bless-ings on your head.
Be-hind a frown-ing prov-i-dence He hides a smil-ing face.
The bud may have a bit-ter taste, But sweet will be the flower.
God is His own in-ter-pret-er, And He will make it plain.

HAST THOU NOT KNOWN 81
ST. MAGNUS C.M.

Based on Isaiah 40: 28-31
Isaac Watts, 1707
Altered in *Scottish Paraphrases*, 1781

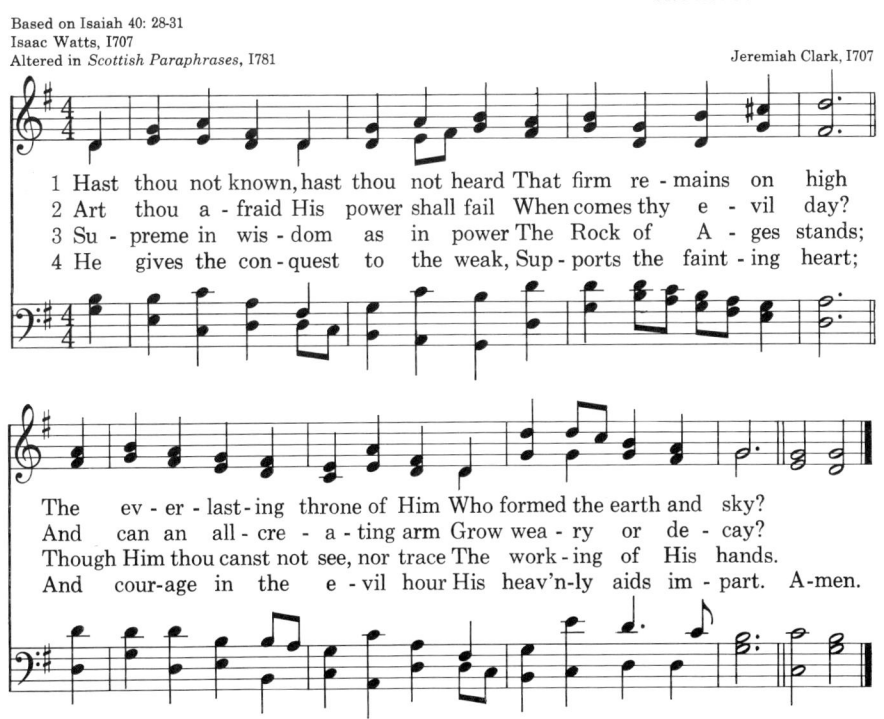

Jeremiah Clark, 1707

1. Hast thou not known, hast thou not heard That firm re-mains on high
2. Art thou a-fraid His power shall fail When comes thy e-vil day?
3. Su-preme in wis-dom as in power The Rock of A-ges stands;
4. He gives the con-quest to the weak, Sup-ports the faint-ing heart;

The ev-er-last-ing throne of Him Who formed the earth and sky?
And can an all-cre-a-ting arm Grow wea-ry or de-cay?
Though Him thou canst not see, nor trace The work-ing of His hands.
And cour-age in the e-vil hour His heav'n-ly aids im-part. A-men.

5 Mere human power shall fast decay,
   And youthful vigor cease;
But they who wait upon the Lord
   In strength shall still increase.

6 They with unwearied feet shall tread
   The path of life divine,
With growing ardor onward move,
   With growing brightness shine.

GOD: HIS PROVIDENCE AND CARE

82 PRAISE WAITS FOR THEE IN ZION

ABRIDGE C.M.

Based on Psalm 65
Scottish Psalter, 1650
Altered by Nichol Grieve, 1940

Isaac Smith, c. 1780

1. Praise waits for Thee in Zi-on, Lord; To Thee our vows paid shall be; O Thou that hear-er art of prayer, All flesh shall come to Thee.
2. Our sins have proved too strong for us And led us far a-stray. Our man-i-fold in-iq-ui-ties We pray Thee purge a-way.
3. Blessed is the man whom Thou didst choose And mak'st ap-proach to Thee, That he with-in Thy tem-ple courts May still a dwell-er be.
4. We sure-ly shall be sat-is-fied With Thy a-bun-dant grace, And with the good-ness of Thy house, Ev'n of Thy ho-ly place. A-men.

83 O GOD OF BETHEL

SALZBURG C.M.

Based on Genesis 28: 19-21
Philip Doddridge, d. 1751 and John Logan, d. 1788
Altered in *Scottish Paraphrases*, 1781

Johann Michael Haydn, 1806

1. O God of Beth-el, by whose hand Thy peo-ple still are fed;
2. Our vows, our prayers, we now pre-sent Be-fore Thy throne of grace;
3. Through each per-plex-ing path of life Our wan-d'ring foot-steps guide;
4. O spread Thy cov-'ring wings a-round, Till all our wan-d'rings cease,
5. Such bless-ings from Thy gra-cious hand Our hum-ble prayers im-plore;

GOD: HIS PROVIDENCE AND CARE

Who through this wea - ry pil-grim-age Hast all our fa - thers led:
God of our fa - thers, be the God Of their suc - ceed-ing race.
Give us each day our dai - ly bread, And rai - ment fit pro - vide.
And at our Fa - ther's loved a - bode Our souls ar - rive in peace.
And Thou shalt be our cho-sen God, And por - tion ev - er - more. A-men.

O GOD, OUR HELP IN AGES PAST 84

ST. ANNE C.M.

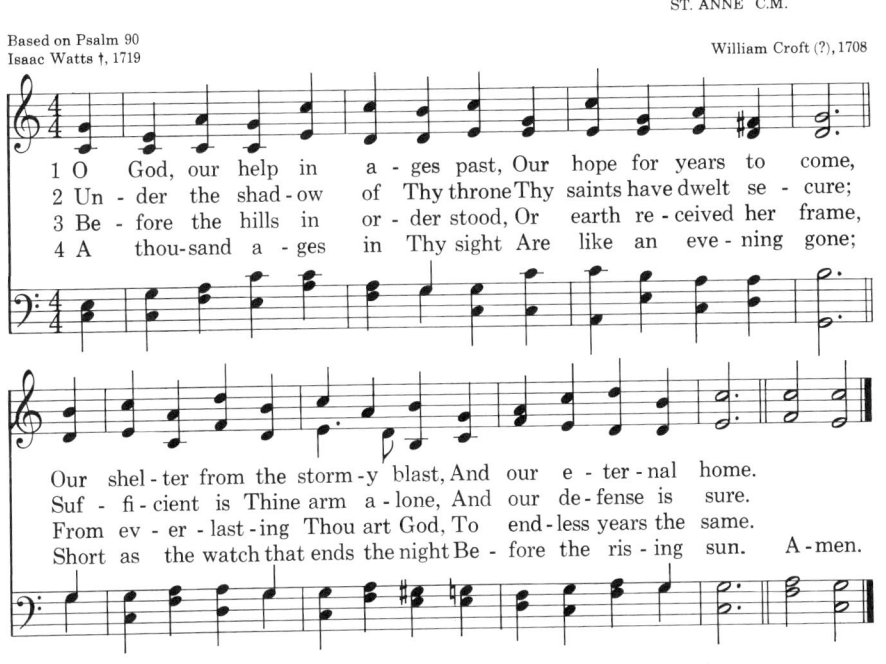

Based on Psalm 90
Isaac Watts †, 1719

William Croft (?), 1708

1. O God, our help in a - ges past, Our hope for years to come,
2. Un - der the shad - ow of Thy throne Thy saints have dwelt se - cure;
3. Be - fore the hills in or - der stood, Or earth re - ceived her frame,
4. A thou-sand a - ges in Thy sight Are like an eve - ning gone;

Our shel - ter from the storm - y blast, And our e - ter - nal home.
Suf - fi - cient is Thine arm a - lone, And our de - fense is sure.
From ev - er - last - ing Thou art God, To end - less years the same.
Short as the watch that ends the night Be - fore the ris - ing sun. A - men.

5. Time, like an ever-rolling stream,
   Bears all its sons away;
   They fly forgotten, as a dream
   Dies at the opening day.

6. O God, our help in ages past,
   Our hope for years to come,
   Be Thou our guard while troubles last,
   And our eternal home.

GOD: HIS PROVIDENCE AND CARE

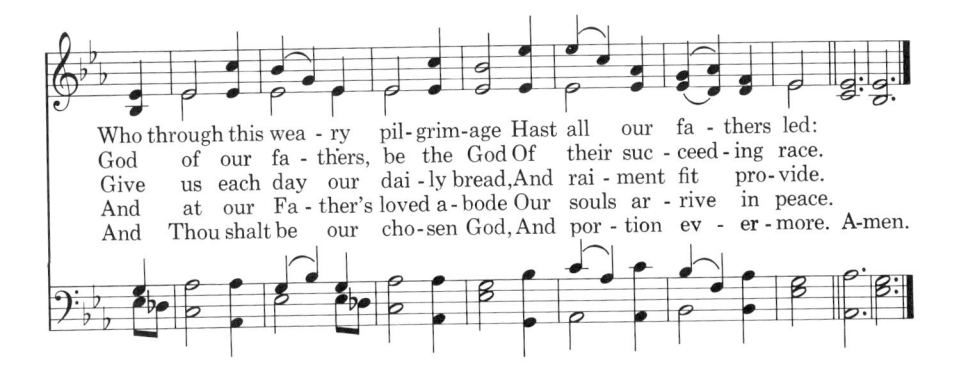

85 GOD IS MY LIGHT

GOTT IST GETREU 4.6.6.4.6.6.9.9.4.

Johann Heinrich Karl Hengstenberg, 1825
Gott ist mein Licht
Tr. Ernst William Hengstenberg, c. 1835

Johann Rudolph Ahle, c. 1661

1 God is my light! My soul, do not de-spair In hours of thy dis-tress! The sun with-draws, And earth is dark and drear: My light will nev-er cease. On days of joy with splen-dor beam-ing, Through nights of grief its rays are gleam-ing; God is my light!

2 God is my trust! My soul, be not a-fraid, Thy help-er will a-bide; "I'll not for-sake thee!" He has kind-ly said, He's ev-er at thy side; In fee-ble age will yet stand by thee, No re-al good will He de-ny thee: God is my trust!

3 The king-dom His! Thro'-out the earth He reigns With wis-dom, grace, and might; The stars go on, And time its course main-tains Be-neath His watch-ful sight; In si-lence on-ward still pro-ceed-ing, The u-ni-verse o-beys His lead-ing, The king-dom His! A-men.

GOD: HIS PROVIDENCE AND CARE

GOD THE OMNIPOTENT 86

RUSSIAN HYMN 11.10.11.9.

Henry Fothergill Chorley‡, 1842, St. 1 and 2
John Ellerton‡, 1870, St. 3 and 4

Alexis Lvov, 1833

1. God the om - nip - o - tent! King, who or - dain - est
Thun - der Thy clar - ion, the light - ning Thy sword,
Show forth Thy pit - y on high where Thou reign - est:
Give to us peace in our time, O Lord.

2. God the all - mer - ci - ful! Earth hath for - sak - en
Thy ways all ho - ly, and slight - ed Thy Word;
Bid not Thy wrath in its ter - rors a - wak - en:
Give to us peace in our time, O Lord.

3. God the all - right - eous one! Man hath de - fied Thee;
Yet to e - ter - ni - ty stand - eth Thy Word;
False - hood and wrong shall not tar - ry be - side Thee:
Give to us peace in our time, O Lord.

4. God the all - prov - i - dent! Earth by Thy chas - t'ning
Yet shall to free - dom and truth be re - stored;
Through the thick dark - ness Thy king - dom is has - t'ning:
Thou wilt give peace in Thy time, O Lord. A - men.

GOD: HIS LAWS AND JUDGMENT

87 THAT DAY OF WRATH
WINDHAM L.M.

Thomas of Celano, 13th century
Dies irae, dies illa
Tr. Walter Scott‡, 1805

Daniel Read, 1785

1. That day of wrath, that dreadful day, When heav'n and earth shall pass away! What power shall be the sinner's stay? How shall he meet that dreadful day?
2. When, shriv'ling like a parched scroll, The flaming heav'ns together roll, And louder yet, and yet more dread, Swells the high trump that wakes the dead?
3. O on that day, that wrathful day, When man to judgment wakes from clay, Be Thou, O Christ, the sinner's stay, Tho' heav'n and earth shall pass away. A-men.

88 O DAY OF GOD, DRAW NIGH
BELLWOODS S.M.

Robert B. Y. Scott‡, 1937

James Hopkirk, 1938

1. O day of God, draw nigh In beauty and in power; Come with Thy timeless judgment now To match our present hour.
2. Bring to our troubled minds, Uncertain and afraid, The quiet of a steadfast faith, Calm of a call obeyed.
3. Bring justice to our land, That all may dwell secure, And finely build for days to come Foundations that endure.
4. Bring to our world of strife Thy sovereign word of peace, That war may haunt the earth no more And desolation cease.
5. O day of God, draw nigh, As at creation's birth, Let there be light again, and set Thy judgments in the earth. A-men.

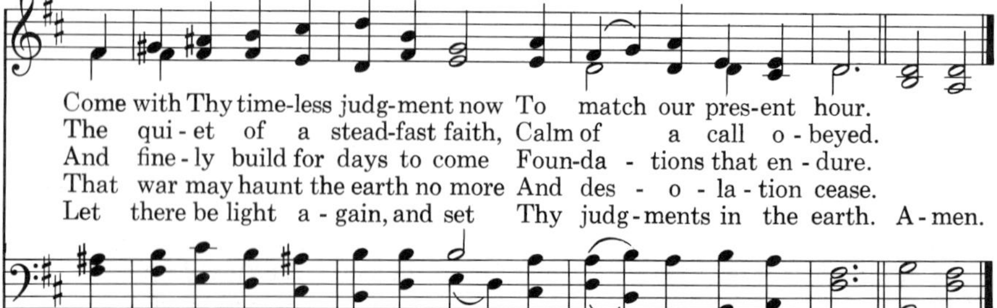

GOD: HIS LAWS AND JUDGMENT

Nikolaus Ludwig von Zinzendorf, 1742
So lange Jesus bleibt der Herr
Tr. Esther Bergen, 1959

Chor
Gemeinden Russlands, ...

1. The Lord is King, O praise His name, O'er all the earth His grace proclaim! From age to age, from day to day, His wonders grow more gloriously.

2. O see the mighty hand of God, His love and mercy changeth not! His blood and righteousness avail; His grace and pardon never fail!

3. This shall the song forever be Of saints before the crystal sea: O Christ, that on the cross hath bled, Hast safely through life's valley led.

4. O star that lights the pilgrim's way! Our Lord of lords, our hope and stay! The head to whom we homage bring, The rock to which our faith may cling! A-men.

1. So lange Jesus bleibt der Herr,
   wird's alle Tage herrlicher.
   So war's, so ist's, so wird es sein
   bei seiner gläubigen Gemein.

2. Es bleibt bei dem bekannten Wort
   von Zeit zu Zeit, von Ort zu Ort:
   Christi Blut und Gerechtigkeit
   bleibt der Gemeine Schmuck und Kleid.

3. Das Psalmlied am krystallnen Meer,
   das Losungswort vom kleinen Heer
   ist: "Eines hat uns durchgebracht,
   Lamm Gottes, dass du warst geschlacht."

4. Du bist und bleibest unser Herr,
   der Leitstern deiner Wanderer,
   der Deinen teures Oberhaupt,
   dem keiner Feinde Macht sie raubt.

JESUS CHRIST: PRAISE AND GLORY

IN THEE IS GLADNESS

IN DIR IST FREUDE 5.5.7.D.5.5.5.5.9.D.

Johann Lindemann, c. 1595
In Dir ist Freude
Tr. Catherine Winkworth, 1858 and 1863

Adapted from Giovanni Giacomo Gastoldi, 1591

1. In Thee is gladness Amid all sadness, Jesus, sunshine of my heart!
By Thee are given The gifts of heaven, Thou the true Redeemer art!
Our souls Thou wakest, Our bonds Thou breakest, Who trusts Thee surely
Hath built securely, He stands forever: Hallelujah!
Our hearts are pining To see Thy shining, Dying or living

2. If He is ours We fear no powers, Nor of earth, nor sin, nor death;
He sees and blesses In worst distresses, He can change them with a breath!
Wherefore the story Tell of His glory With heart and voices;
All heav'n rejoices In Him forever: Hallelujah!
We shout for gladness. Triumph o'er sadness, Love Thee and praise Thee,

JESUS CHRIST: PRAISE AND GLORY

To Thee are cleaving, Naught can us sever: Hallelujah!
And still shall raise Thee Glad hymns forever: Hallelujah!

LORD JESUS CHRIST, BE PRESENT NOW 91
HERR JESU CHRIST, DICH ZU UNS WEND L.M.

Pensum sacrum, Altenberg, 1648, St. 1-3
Cantionale sacrum, Gotha, 1651, St. 4
Herr Jesu Christ, dich zu uns wend
Tr. Catherine Winkworth‡, 1863

Cantionale Germanicum, Gochsheim, 1628

1. Lord Jesus Christ, be present now, Our hearts in true devotion bow, Thy Spirit send with grace divine, And let Thy truth within us shine.
2. Unseal our lips to sing Thy praise, Our souls to Thee in worship raise, Make strong our faith, increase our light That we may know Thy name aright,
3. Till we with saints in glad accord Sing "Holy, holy, holy is the Lord!" And in the light of heav'n above Shall see Thy face and know Thy love.
4. All glory to the Father, Son, And Holy Spirit, three in one! To Thee, O blessed Trinity, Be praise throughout eternity! Amen.

JESUS CHRIST: PRAISE AND GLORY

92 OF THE FATHER'S LOVE BEGOTTEN
DIVINUM MYSTERIUM 8.7.8.7.8.7.7.

Aurelius Clemens Prudentius, d. 413
Cordus natus ex Parentis
Tr. John Mason Neale and Henry W. Baker, 1861

13th-century Plainsong
Harmony by Winfred Douglas, 1940

1 Of the Father's love be-got-ten, Ere the worlds be-gan to be,
2 O ye heights of heav'n, a-dore Him; An-gel hosts, His prais-es sing;
3 Thee let old men, Thee let young men, Thee let boys in cho-rus sing;
4 Christ, to Thee with God the Fa-ther, And, O Ho-ly Ghost, to Thee,

He is Al-pha and O-me-ga, He the source, the end-ing He,
Powers, do-min-ions, bow be-fore Him, And ex-tol our God and King;
Ma-trons, vir-gins, lit-tle maid-ens, With glad voic-es an-swer-ing:
Hymn and chant and high thanks-giv-ing, And un-wear-ied prais-es be:

Of the things that are, that have been, And that
Let no tongue on earth be si - lent, Ev - ery
Let their guile-less songs re - ech - o, And the
Hon - or, glo - ry, and do - min - ion, And e -

JESUS CHRIST: PRAISE AND GLORY

fu - ture years shall see, Ev - er-more and ev - er - more!
voice in con-cert ring, Ev - er-more and ev - er - more!
heart its mu - sic bring, Ev - er-more and ev - er - more!
ter - nal vic - to - ry, Ev - er-more and ev - er - more! A - men.

COME, LET US TUNE OUR LOFTIEST SONG 93

MOZART L.M.

Robert Athow West, 1849 — Arranged from a *Kyrie*, published in Mainz, 1821

1 Come, let us tune our loft - iest song, And raise to Christ our joy - ful strain; Wor - ship and thanks to Him be - long, Who reigns, and shall for - ev - er reign.

2 His sov -'reign power our bod - ies made; Our souls are His im - mor - tal breath; And when His crea - tures sinned, He bled, To save us from e - ter - nal death.

3 Burn ev - ery breast with Je - sus' love; Bound ev - ery heart with rap - turous joy; And saints on earth, with saints a - bove, Your voic - es in His praise em - ploy.

4 Ex - tol the Lamb with loft - iest song; As - cend for Him our cheer - ful strain; Wor - ship and thanks to Him be - long, Who reigns, and shall for - ev - er reign.

JESUS CHRIST: PRAISE AND GLORY

94 AT THE NAME OF JESUS
KING'S WESTON 6.5.6.5.D.

Caroline Maria Noel, 1875

Ralph Vaughan Williams, 1925
Arranged for *The Hymnbook*, 1955, (Presbyterian)

1. At the name of Jesus Every knee shall bow,
Every tongue confess Him King of glory now;
'Tis the Father's pleasure We should call Him Lord,
Who from the beginning Was the mighty Word.

2. At His voice creation Sprang at once to sight,
All the angel faces, All the hosts of light,
Thrones and dominations, Stars upon their way,
All the heav'nly orders, In their great array.

3. Humbled for a season, To receive a name
From the lips of sinners Unto whom He came,
Faithfully He bore it Spotless to the last,
Brought it back victorious, When from death He passed;

4. In your hearts enthrone Him; There let Him subdue
All that is not holy, All that is not true:
Crown Him as your Captain In temptation's hour;
Let His will enfold you In its light and power.

5. Brothers, this Lord Jesus Shall return again,
With His Father's glory, With His angel train;
For all wreaths of empire Meet upon His brow,
And our hearts confess Him King of glory now. A-men.

JESUS CHRIST: PRAISE AND GLORY

ALL HAIL THE POWER OF JESUS' NAME 95

CORONATION C.M.

Edward Perronet, 1779 and 1780
Altered by John Rippon

Oliver Holden, 1792

1 All hail the power of Jesus' name! Let angels prostrate fall;
2 Ye chosen seed of Israel's race, Ye ransomed of the fall,
3 Let every kindred, every tribe, On this terrestrial ball,
4 O that with yonder sacred throng We at His feet may fall!

Bring forth the royal diadem,
Hail Him who saves you by His grace,
To Him all majesty ascribe,
We'll join the everlasting song,

And crown Him Lord of all; Bring forth the royal
And crown Him Lord of all; Hail Him who saves you
And crown Him Lord of all; To Him all majes-
And crown Him Lord of all; We'll join the ever-

diadem, And crown Him Lord of all!
by His grace, And crown Him Lord of all!
ty ascribe, And crown Him Lord of all!
lasting song, And crown Him Lord of all! A-men.

Another setting of this hymn may be found at No. 601

JESUS CHRIST: PRAISE AND GLORY

96 JESUS, THOU MIGHTY LORD
DOANE 6.4.6.4.D.

Fanny Crosby, c. 1883 — William Howard Doane, 1883

1. Jesus, Thou mighty Lord, Great is Thy name; Still through eternal years, Thou art the same; Changeless Thy holy Word, True evermore; Thy name we glorify, Thy name adore.
2. Jesus, Thou mighty Lord, Jesus, our King, Praise for Thy wondrous love Gladly we sing. Love in Thy diadem Shines evermore; Thy name we glorify, Thy name adore.
3. Sought by Thy mercy, Lord, Saved by Thy power, Led by Thy gracious hand, Kept every hour. Thine shall the honor be, Thine evermore; Thy name we glorify, Thy name adore. A-men.

97 FAIREST LORD JESUS
CRUSADERS' HYMN 5.6.8.5.5.8.

Gesangbuch, Münster, 1677, St. 1 and 3
Heinrich August Hoffmann von Fallersleben, 1842, St. 2
Schönster Herr Jesu!
Tr. R. S. Willis' *Church-Chorals*... †, 1850

H. A. Hoffmann von Fallersleben's, *Schlesische Volkslieder*, 1842
Harmony by Richard Storrs Willis, 1850

1. Fairest Lord Jesus, Ruler of all nature, O Thou of God and man the Son;
2. Fair are the meadows, Fairer still the woodlands, Robed in the blooming garb of spring;
3. Fair is the sunshine, Fairer still the moonlight, And all the twinkling, starry host;

JESUS CHRIST: PRAISE AND GLORY

Thee will I cher-ish, Thee will I hon-or, Thou, my soul's glo-ry, joy and crown.
Je-sus is fair-er, Je-sus is pur-er, Who makes the woe-ful heart to sing.
Je-sus shines bright-er, Je-sus shines pur-er Than all the an-gels heav'n can boast.

JESUS, THOU JOY OF LOVING HEARTS 98

SHELTERING WING L.M.

Bernard of Clairvaux? c. 1150
Jesu dulcis memoria
Tr. Ray Palmer, 1858

Joseph Barnby, 1872

1. Je-sus, Thou joy of lov-ing hearts! Thou fount of life! Thou light of men! From the best bliss that earth im-parts, We turn un-filled to Thee a-gain.
2. Thy truth un-changed hath ev-er stood; Thou sav-est those that on Thee call; To them that seek Thee, Thou art good, To them that find Thee, all in all.
3. We taste Thee, O Thou liv-ing bread, And long to feast up-on Thee still; We drink of Thee, the foun-tain head, And thirst our souls from Thee to fill!
4. Our rest-less spir-its yearn for Thee, Wher-e'er our change-ful lot is cast; Glad, when Thy gra-cious smile we see, Blest, when our faith can hold Thee fast.
5. O Je-sus, ev-er with us stay; Make all our mo-ments calm and bright; Chase the dark night of sin a-way, Shed o'er the world Thy ho-ly light! A-men.

JESUS CHRIST: PRAISE AND GLORY

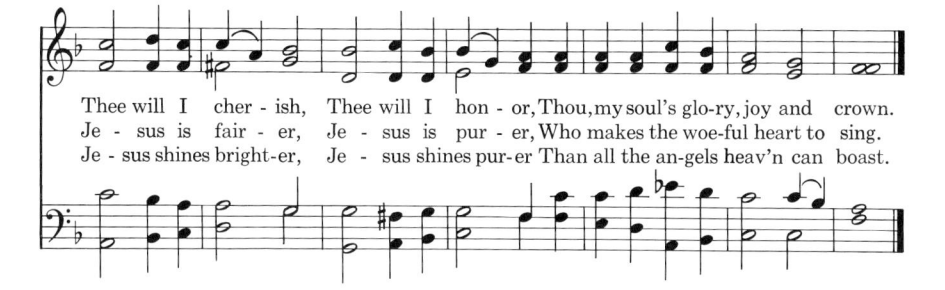

99 O COULD I SPEAK

ARIEL 8.8.6.8.8.6.

Samuel Medley†, 1789

From Wolfgang Amadeus Mozart, 1791
Arranged by Lowell Mason, 1836

1. O could I speak the matchless worth, O could I sound the glories forth, Which in my Savior shine! I'd soar and touch the heav'nly strings, And vie with Gabriel while he sings In tones almost divine, In tones almost divine.

2. I'd sing the precious blood He spilt, My ransom from the dreadful guilt, Of sin, and wrath divine; I'd sing His glorious righteousness, In which all-perfect heav'nly dress My soul shall ever shine, My soul shall ever shine.

3. I'd sing the characters He bears, And all the forms of love He wears, Exalted on His throne; In loftiest songs of sweetest praise, I would to everlasting days Make all His glories known, Make all His glories known.

4. Well, the delightful day will come When my dear Lord will bring me home, And I shall see His face; Then with my Savior, Brother, Friend A blest eternity I'll spend, Triumphant in His grace, Triumphant in His grace.

JESUS CHRIST: PRAISE AND GLORY

YE SERVANTS OF GOD 100
HANOVER 10.10.11.11.

Charles Wesley†, 1744
William Croft(?), 1708

1 Ye servants of God, your Master proclaim,
2 God ruleth on high, almighty to save;
3 "Salvation to God, who sits on the throne!"
4 Then let us adore, and give Him His right,

And publish abroad His wonderful name;
And still He is nigh, His presence we have.
Let all cry aloud, and honor the Son:
All glory and power and wisdom and might,

The name all-victorious, of Jesus extol;
The great congregation His triumphs shall sing,
The praises of Jesus the angels proclaim,
All honor and blessing, with angels above,

His kingdom is glorious, And rules over all.
Ascribing salvation to Jesus, our King.
Fall down on their faces, and worship the Lamb.
And thanks never ceasing for infinite love. A-men.

JESUS CHRIST: PRAISE AND GLORY

101 GLORY TO GOD ON HIGH
ITALIAN HYMN 6.6.4.6.6.6.4.

James Allen, 1761, and Others
Felice de Giardini, 1769

1. Glory to God on high! Let heav'n and earth reply,
"Praise ye His name!" His love and grace adore, Who all our
sorrows bore; Sing loud for evermore, "Worthy the Lamb!"

2. While they around the throne Cheerfully join in one,
Praising His name. Ye who have felt His blood Sealing your
peace with God, Sound His dear name abroad, "Worthy the Lamb!"

3. Join, all ye ransomed race, Our Lord and God to bless:
Praise ye His name! In Him we will rejoice, And make a
joyful noise, Shouting with heart and voice, "Worthy the Lamb!"

4. Soon must we change our place, Yet will we never cease
Praising His name: To Him our songs we bring; Hail Him our
gracious King; And through all ages sing, "Worthy the Lamb!" Amen.

102 HOW SWEET THE NAME OF JESUS
ST. PETER C.M.

John Newton, 1779
Alexander Robert Reinagle, c. 1836

1. How sweet the name of Jesus sounds In a believer's ear!
2. It makes the wounded spirit whole, And calms the troubled breast;
3. Dear name! the rock on which I build, My shield and hiding place;
4. Weak is the effort of my heart, And cold my warmest thought;
5. Till then I would Thy love proclaim With every fleeting breath;

JESUS CHRIST: PRAISE AND GLORY

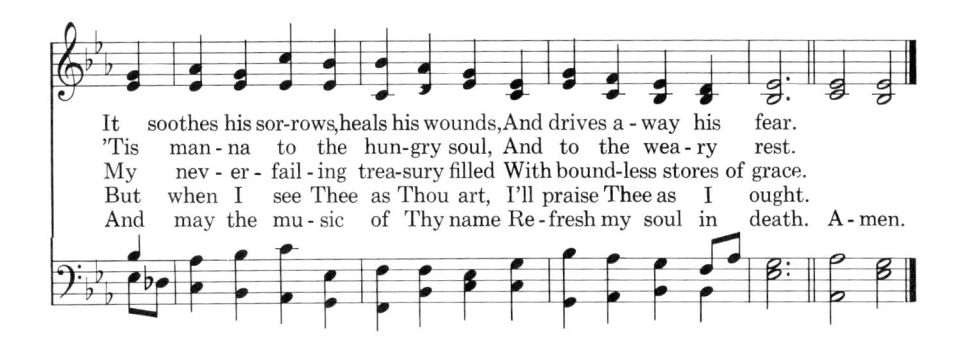

It soothes his sorrows, heals his wounds, And drives away his fear.
'Tis manna to the hungry soul, And to the weary rest.
My never-failing treasury filled With boundless stores of grace.
But when I see Thee as Thou art, I'll praise Thee as I ought.
And may the music of Thy name Refresh my soul in death. A-men.

HOW BEAUTEOUS WERE THE MARKS 103
MARYTON L.M.

Arthur Cleveland Coxe†, 1840
Henry Percy Smith, 1874

1. How beauteous were the marks divine That in Thy meekness used to shine; That lit Thy lonely pathway, trod In wondrous love, O Son of God!
2. O who like Thee so humbly bore The scorn, the scoffs of men before? So meek, forgiving, Godlike, high, So glorious in humility!
3. And all Thy life's unchanging years, A man of sorrows and of tears, The cross, where all our sins were laid, Upon Thy bending shoulders weighed.
4. And death, that sets the pris'ner free, Was pang and scoff and scorn to Thee; Yet love through all Thy torture glowed, And mercy with Thy lifeblood flowed.
5. O in Thy light be mine to go, Illuming all this way of woe; And give me ever on the road To trace Thy footsteps, Son of God! A-men.

JESUS CHRIST: PRAISE AND GLORY

104 O FOR A THOUSAND TONGUES
AZMON C.M.

Charles Wesley, 1739

Carl Gotthelf Gläser, d. 1829
Arranged by Lowell Mason, 1839

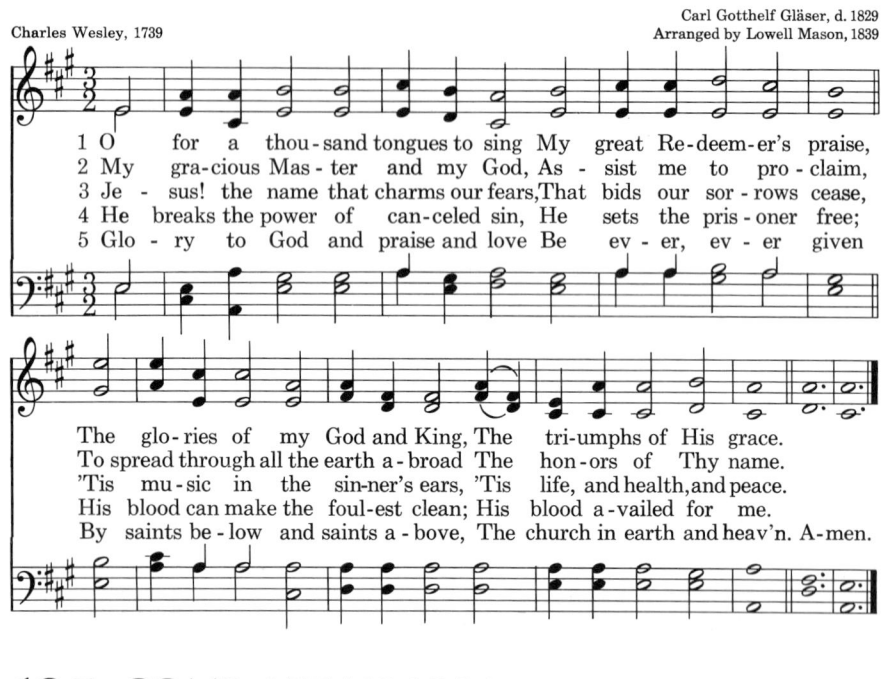

1. O for a thou-sand tongues to sing My great Re-deem-er's praise, The glo-ries of my God and King, The tri-umphs of His grace.
2. My gra-cious Mas-ter and my God, As-sist me to pro-claim, To spread through all the earth a-broad The hon-ors of Thy name.
3. Je-sus! the name that charms our fears, That bids our sor-rows cease, 'Tis mu-sic in the sin-ner's ears, 'Tis life, and health, and peace.
4. He breaks the power of can-celed sin, He sets the pris-oner free; His blood can make the foul-est clean; His blood a-vailed for me.
5. Glo-ry to God and praise and love Be ev-er, ev-er given By saints be-low and saints a-bove, The church in earth and heav'n. A-men.

105 COME, LET US JOIN
NEWBOLD C.M.

Isaac Watts, 1707

George Kingsley, 1847

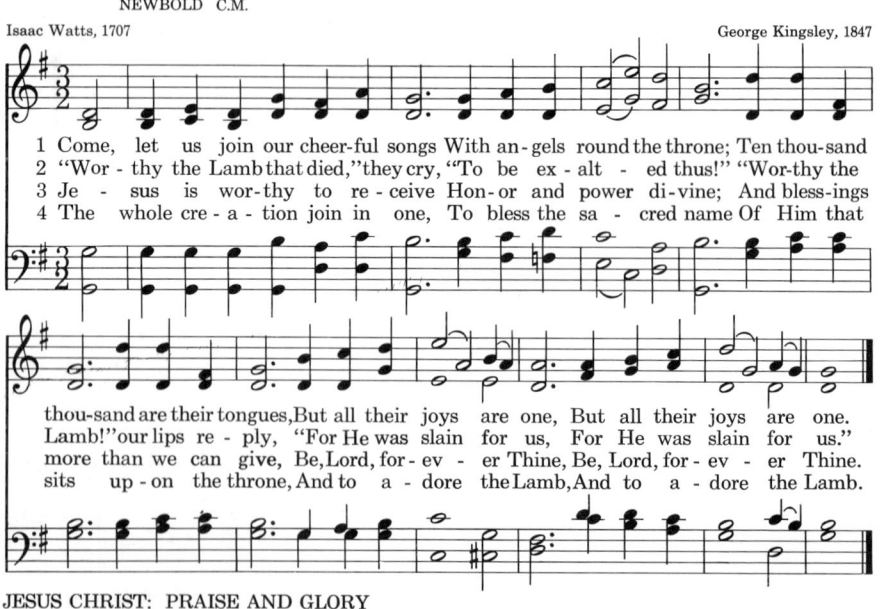

1. Come, let us join our cheer-ful songs With an-gels round the throne; Ten thou-sand thou-sand are their tongues, But all their joys are one, But all their joys are one.
2. "Wor-thy the Lamb that died," they cry, "To be ex-alt-ed thus!" "Wor-thy the Lamb!" our lips re-ply, "For He was slain for us, For He was slain for us."
3. Je-sus is wor-thy to re-ceive Hon-or and power di-vine; And bless-ings more than we can give, Be, Lord, for-ev-er Thine, Be, Lord, for-ev-er Thine.
4. The whole cre-a-tion join in one, To bless the sa-cred name Of Him that sits up-on the throne, And to a-dore the Lamb, And to a-dore the Lamb.

JESUS CHRIST: PRAISE AND GLORY

O POWER OF LOVE 106

ST. PETERSBURG 9.8.9.8.9.9.

Gerhard Tersteegen, 1757
Ich bete an die Macht der Liebe
Tr. Herman Brückner‡, d. 1942

Dimitri S. Bortniansky, 1825

1. O power of love, all else tran-scend-ing In Je-sus pres-ent ev-er-more, I wor-ship Thee, in hom-age bend-ing, Thy name to hon-or and a-dore: Yea, let my soul, in deep de-vo-tion, Bathe in love's might-y bound-less o-cean.

2. Thou art my rest, no earth-ly treas-ure Can sat-is-fy my yearn-ing heart, And naught can give to me the pleas-ure I find in Thee, my cho-sen part, Thy love, so ten-der, so pos-sess-ing, Is joy to me, and ev-ery bless-ing.

3. To Thee my heart and life be giv-en, Thou art in truth my high-est good; For me Thy sa-cred side was riv-en, For me was shed Thy pre-cious blood. O Thou who art the world's sal-va-tion, Be Thine my love and ad-o-ra-tion. A-men.

JESUS CHRIST: PRAISE AND GLORY

107 WHEN MORNING GILDS THE SKIES
LAUDES DOMINI 6.6.6.6.6.6.

Katholisches Gesangbuch, Würzburg, 1828
Beim frühen Morgenlicht
Tr. Edward Caswall†, 1854

Joseph Barnby, 1868

1. When morn-ing gilds the skies, My heart a-wak-ing cries: May Je-sus Christ be praised! A-like at work or prayer To Je-sus I re-pair: May Je-sus Christ be praised!
2. Does sad-ness fill my mind, A sol-ace here I find: May Je-sus Christ be praised! Or fades my earth-ly bliss, My com-fort still is this: May Je-sus Christ be praised!
3. The night be-comes as day, When from the heart we say: May Je-sus Christ be praised! In heav'n's e-ter-nal bliss, The love-liest strain is this: May Je-sus Christ be praised!
4. Be this, while life is mine, My can-ti-cle di-vine, May Je-sus Christ be praised! Be this th'e-ter-nal song, Through all the a-ges on: May Je-sus Christ be praised! A-men.

108 JESUS, THE VERY THOUGHT OF THEE
ST. AGNES C.M.

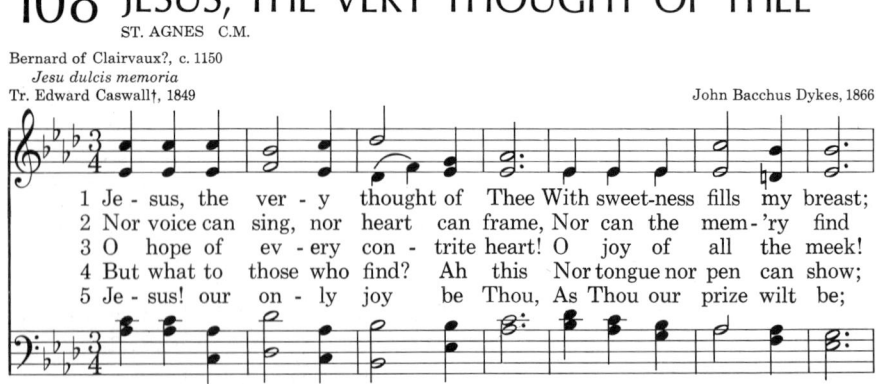

Bernard of Clairvaux?, c. 1150
Jesu dulcis memoria
Tr. Edward Caswall†, 1849

John Bacchus Dykes, 1866

1. Je-sus, the ver-y thought of Thee With sweet-ness fills my breast;
2. Nor voice can sing, nor heart can frame, Nor can the mem-'ry find
3. O hope of ev-ery con-trite heart! O joy of all the meek!
4. But what to those who find? Ah this Nor tongue nor pen can show;
5. Je-sus! our on-ly joy be Thou, As Thou our prize wilt be;

JESUS CHRIST: PRAISE AND GLORY

But sweet-er far Thy face to see, And in Thy pres-ence rest.
A sweet-er sound than Thy blest name, O Sav-ior of man-kind!
To those who fall, how kind Thou art! How good to those who seek!
The love of Je - sus, what it is, None but His loved ones know.
Je - sus! be Thou our glo - ry now, And through e-ter - ni - ty. A-men.

BEHOLD THE GLORIES OF THE LAMB 109

ST. MARTIN'S C.M.

Isaac Watts†, c. 1696
William Tans'ur, c. 1755

1. Be - hold the glo - ries of the Lamb, A - mid the Fa-ther's throne,
   Pre - pare new hon - ors for His name, And songs be - fore un-known.
2. Let eld - ers wor - ship at His feet, The church a - dore a - round,
   With vi - als full of o - dors sweet, And harps of sweet - er sound.
3. Those are the prayers of all the saints, And these the hymns they raise.
   Je - sus is kind to our com-plaints, He loves to hear our praise.
4. Now, to the Lamb that once was slain, Be end - less bless - ings paid;
   Sal - va - tion, glo - ry, joy, re - main For - ev - er on Thy head.
5. Thou hast re - deemed our souls with blood, Hast set the pris - 'ners free,
   Hast made us kings and priests to God, And we shall reign with Thee.

JESUS CHRIST: PRAISE AND GLORY

110 AWAKE, MY SOUL, IN JOYFUL LAYS

LOVING KINDNESS L.M. with Refrain

Samuel Medley, 1782

Folk Hymn
Joshua Leavitt's *Christian Lyre*, 1831

1. A-wake, my soul, in joy-ful lays, And sing thy great Re-deem-er's praise; He just-ly claims a song from me, His lov-ing-kind-ness, O how free! Lov-ing-kind-ness, lov-ing-kind-ness, His lov-ing-kind-ness, O how free!

2. He saw me ru-ined in the fall, Yet loved me not-with-stand-ing all; He saved me from my lost es-tate, His lov-ing-kind-ness, O how great! Lov-ing-kind-ness, lov-ing-kind-ness, His lov-ing-kind-ness, O how great!

3. Though nu-m'rous hosts of might-y foes, Though earth and hell my way op-pose, He safe-ly leads my soul a-long, His lov-ing-kind-ness, O how strong! Lov-ing-kind-ness, lov-ing-kind-ness, His lov-ing-kind-ness, O how strong!

4. When trou-ble, like a gloom-y cloud, Has gath-ered thick, and thun-dered loud, He near my soul has al-ways stood, His lov-ing-kind-ness, O how good! Lov-ing-kind-ness, lov-ing-kind-ness, His lov-ing-kind-ness, O how good!

JESUS CHRIST: PRAISE AND GLORY

O COME, O COME, EMMANUEL   111

VENI EMMANUEL L.M. with Refrain

Anonymous
Veni, veni Emmanuel
Tr. John Mason Neale, 1851,
and Compilers of *Hymns Ancient and Modern*, 1861

Fifteenth Century Trope Melody
The Hymnal Noted, Part II, 1854

1. O come, O come, Emmanuel, And ransom captive Israel, That mourns in lonely exile here, Until the Son of God appear.
2. O come, Thou Rod of Jesse, free Thine own from Satan's tyranny; From depths of hell Thy people save, And give them victory o'er the grave.
3. O come, Thou Day-spring, come and cheer Our spirits by Thine advent here; Disperse the gloomy clouds of night, And death's dark shadows put to flight.
4. O come, Thou Key of David, come, And open wide our heav'nly home; Make safe the way that leads on high, And close the path to misery.
5. O come, O come, Thou Lord of might, Who to Thy tribes, on Sinai's height, In ancient times didst give the law In cloud and majesty and awe.

Rejoice! Rejoice! Emmanuel Shall come to thee, O Israel! Amen.

JESUS CHRIST: ADVENT

112 HARK, THE GLAD SOUND
COMMUNION C.M.D.

Philip Doddridge, 1755

Folk Hymn
"Robison" in J. Wyeth's *Repository of Sacred Music, Part Second*, 1813
Harmony by J. Harold Moyer, 1965

1. Hark, the glad sound! the Savior comes! The Savior promised long!
Let every heart prepare a throne, And every voice a song.
On Him the Spirit largely poured, Exerts its sacred fire;
Wisdom and might and zeal and love, His holy breast inspire.

2. He comes the prisoners to release, In Satan's bondage held;
The gates of brass before Him burst, The iron fetters yield.
He comes the broken heart to bind, The bleeding soul to cure,
And with the treasures of His grace T'enrich the humble poor.

3. His silver trumpets publish loud The jub'lee of the Lord;
Our debts are all remitted now, Our heritage restored.
Our glad hosannas, Prince of Peace, Thy welcome shall proclaim;
And heav'n's eternal arches ring With Thy beloved name.

JESUS CHRIST: ADVENT

HAIL TO THE LORD'S ANOINTED 113

CRÜGER 7.6.7.6.D.

James Montgomery†, 1821

Johann Crüger, 1640
Adapted by William Henry Monk, 1861

1. Hail to the Lord's a-noint-ed, Great Da-vid's great-er Son! Hail to the time ap-point-ed, His reign on earth be-gun! He comes to break op-pres-sion, To set the cap-tive free, To take a-way trans-gres-sion, And rule in eq-ui-ty.

2. He comes with suc-cor speed-y To those who suf-fer wrong; To help the poor and need-y, And bid the weak be strong; To give them songs for sigh-ing, Their dark-ness turn to light, Whose souls, con-demned and dy-ing, Were pre-cious in His sight.

3. He shall come down like show-ers Up-on the fruit-ful earth; And love, joy, hope like flow-ers, Spring in His path to birth. Be-fore Him, on the moun-tains Shall peace, the her-ald, go; And right-eous-ness, in foun-tains, From hill to val-ley flow.

4. O'er ev-ery foe vic-to-rious, He on His throne shall rest, From age to age more glo-rious, All bless-ing and all blest. The tide of time shall nev-er His cov-e-nant re-move; His name shall stand for-ev-er; That name to us is Love. A-men.

JESUS CHRIST: ADVENT

114 VEILED IN DARKNESS JUDAH LAY
EBELING 7.7.7.7.7.7.

Douglas LeTell Rights, 1915 — Johann Georg Ebeling, 1666

1. Veiled in darkness Judah lay, Waiting for the promised day, While across the shadowy night Streamed a flood of glorious light, Heav'nly voices chanting then, "Peace on earth, good-will to men."

2. Still the earth in darkness lies. Up from death's dark vale arise Voices of a world in grief, Prayers of men who seek relief; Now our darkness pierce again, "Peace on earth, good-will to men."

3. Light of light, we humbly pray, Shine upon Thy world today; Break the gloom of our dark night, Fill our souls with love and light, Send Thy blessed word again, "Peace on earth, good-will to men." Amen.

JESUS CHRIST: ADVENT

COME, THOU LONG-EXPECTED JESUS 115

HYFRYDOL 8.7.8.7.D.

Charles Wesley†, 1745

Rowland Hugh Prichard, c. 1830
Harmonized by Ralph Vaughan Williams, 1951

1 Come, Thou long-ex-pect-ed Je-sus! Born to set Thy peo-ple free,
2 Born Thy peo-ple to de-liv-er, Born a child, and yet a King,

From our fears and sins re-lease us, Let us find our rest in Thee.
Born to reign in us for-ev-er, Now Thy gra-cious king-dom bring,

Is-rael's strength and con-so-la-tion, Hope of all the earth Thou art;
By Thy own e-ter-nal Spir-it, Rule in all our hearts a-lone;

Dear De-sire of ev-ery na-tion, Joy of ev-ery long-ing heart.
By Thy all suf-fi-cient mer-it, Raise us to Thy glo-rious throne. A-men.

JESUS CHRIST: ADVENT

116 O SAVIOR, REND THE HEAVENS WIDE
O HEILAND, REISS DIE HIMMEL AUF L.M.

Friedrich von Spee, 1623
O Heiland, reiss die Himmel auf
Tr. Martin L. Seltz, 1965

Gesangbuch, Augsburg, 1666
Harmony by Esther Wiebe, 1964

1. O Savior, rend the heavens wide;
Come down, come down with mighty stride.
Unbar the gates, the doors break down;
Unbar the way to heaven's crown.

2. O Father, dew from heaven send;
As gentle dew, O Son, descend.
Drop down, you clouds, and torrents bring;
To Jacob's line rain down a King.

3. O earth, in flow'ring bud be seen;
Clothe hill and dale in garb of green.
O earth, bring forth this Blossom rare;
O Savior, rise from meadow fair.

4. Here dreadful doom upon us lies;
Death looms so grim before our eyes.
O come, lead us with mighty hand
From exile to our fatherland.

5. There will we all our praises bring
Ever to Thee, our Savior King;
There will we laud Thee and adore
For ever and for evermore. A-men.

JESUS CHRIST: ADVENT

LET ALL MORTAL FLESH KEEP SILENCE 117

PICARDY 8.7.8.7.8.7.

Liturgy of St. James
Σιγησάτω πᾶσα σὰρξ βροτεία
Tr. Gerard Moultrie, 1864

French Carol Melody

In Unison

1. Let all mortal flesh keep silence, And with fear and trembling stand; Ponder nothing earthly minded, For with blessing in His hand, Christ our God to earth descendeth, Our full homage to demand.

2. King of kings, yet born of Mary, As of old on earth He stood, Lord of lords, in human vesture, In the body and the blood, He will give to all the faithful His own self for heav'nly food.

3. Rank on rank the host of heaven Spreads its vanguard on the way, As the Light of light descendeth From the realms of endless day, That the powers of hell may vanish As the darkness clears away.

4. At His feet the six-winged seraph; Cherubim with sleepless eye, Veil their faces to the presence, As with ceaseless voice they cry, Alleluia, Alleluia, Alleluia, Lord most high.

JESUS CHRIST: ADVENT

118 WAKE, AWAKE, FOR NIGHT IS FLYING

WACHET AUF, RUFT UNS DIE STIMME 8.9.8.8.9.8.6.6.4.8.8.

Philipp Nicolai, 1599
Wachet auf, ruft uns die Stimme
Tr. Catherine Winkworth, 1858

Philipp Nicolai, 1599

1. Wake, awake, for night is flying, The watch-men on the heights are crying; Awake, Jerusalem, at last! Midnight hears the welcome voices, And at the thrilling cry rejoices: Come forth, ye virgins, night is past!

2. Zion hears the watch-men singing, And all her heart with joy is springing, She wakes, she rises from her gloom; For her Lord comes down all-glorious, The strong in grace, in truth victorious, Her Star is risen, her Light is come!

JESUS CHRIST: ADVENT

The Bride-groom comes, a-wake, Your lamps with gladness take;
Ah come, Thou bless-ed Lord, O Je-sus, Son of God,
Al-le-lu-ia! And for His mar-riage feast pre-pare,
Al-le-lu-ia! We fol-low till the halls we see
For ye must go to meet Him there.
Where Thou hast bid us sup with Thee. A-men.

3 Now let all the heav'ns adore Thee,
And men and angels sing before Thee,
  With harp and cymbal's clearest tone;
Of one pearl each shining portal,
Where we are with the choir immortal
  Of angels round Thy dazzling throne;
    Nor eye hath seen, nor ear
    Hath yet attain'd to hear
      What there is ours,
But we rejoice, and sing to Thee
Our hymns of joy eternally.

JESUS CHRIST: ADVENT

119 O HOW SHALL I RECEIVE THEE
VALET WILL ICH DIR GEBEN 7.6.7.6.D.

Paul Gerhardt, 1653
Wie soll ich dich empfangen
Tr. Arthur Tozer Russell, 1851, and Others

Melchior Teschner, 1613

1. O how shall I receive Thee, How meet Thee on Thy way, Blest hope of every nation, My soul's delight and stay? O Jesus, Jesus, give me Now by Thy own pure light To know whate'er is pleasing And welcome in Thy sight.

2. Thy Zion palms is strewing, And branches fresh and fair; My soul, to praise awaking, Her anthem shall prepare. Unending thanks and praises From my glad heart shall spring; And to Thy name the service Of all my powers I bring.

3. Love caused Thy incarnation; Love brought Thee down to me. Thy thirst for my salvation Procured my liberty. O love beyond all telling, That led Thee to embrace, In love all love excelling, Our lost and troubled race.

4. Thou comest, Lord, with gladness, In mercy and good will, To bring an end to sadness And bid our fears be still. We welcome Thee, our Savior; Come gather us to Thee, That in Thy light eternal Our joyous home may be.

JESUS CHRIST: ADVENT

LIFT UP YOUR HEADS, YE MIGHTY GATES 120
MACHT HOCH DIE TÜR 8.8.8.8.8.8.8.6.6.

Based on Psalm 24
Georg Weissel, 1642
Macht hoch die Tür, die Tor macht weit
Tr. Catherine Winkworth, 1863

J. A. Freylinghausen's *Neues
Geistreiches Gesangbuch*, 1704

1 Lift up your heads, ye mighty gates, Behold the King of glory waits;
2 The Lord is just, a Helper tried, Mercy is ever at His side,
3 O blest the land, the city blest, Where Christ the Ruler is confessed!
4 Redeemer, come! I open wide My heart to Thee; here, Lord, abide!

The King of kings is drawing near, The Savior of the world is here;
His kingly crown is holiness, His scepter, pity in distress,
O happy hearts and happy homes To whom this King in triumph comes!
Let me Thy inner presence feel, Thy grace and love in me reveal,

Life and salvation doth He bring, Wherefore rejoice and gladly sing:
The end of all our woes He brings; Wherefore the earth is glad and sings:
The cloudless Sun of joy He is, Who bringeth pure delight and bliss:
Thy Holy Spirit guide us on Until our glorious goal is won!

We praise Thee, Father, now! Creator, wise art Thou!
We praise Thee, Savior, now, Mighty in deed art Thou!
O Comforter divine, What boundless grace is Thine!
Eternal praise and fame We offer to Thy name. A-men.

JESUS CHRIST: ADVENT

121 COMFORT, COMFORT YE MY PEOPLE
GENEVA 42 8.7.8.7.7.7.8.8.

Based on Isaiah 40
Johann Olearius
Tröstet, tröstet meine Lieben
Tr. Catherine Winkworth†, 1863

Pseaumes octante trois . . ., Geneva, 1551
Harmony adapted from Claude Goudimel, 1565

1. Com-fort, com-fort ye My peo-ple, Speak ye peace, thus saith our God;
Com-fort those who sit in dark-ness, Mourn-ing 'neath their sor-rows' load.
Speak ye to Je-ru-sa-lem Of the peace that waits for them;
Tell her that her sins I cov-er, And her war-fare now is o-ver.

2. Yea, her sins our God will par-don, Blot-ting out each dark mis-deed;
All that well de-served His an-ger He no more will see or heed.
She hath suf-fered man-y a day, Now her griefs have passed a-way;
God will change her pin-ing sad-ness In-to ev-er-spring-ing glad-ness.

3. Hark, the voice of one that cri-eth In the des-ert far and near,
Bid-ding all men to re-pent-ance Since the king-dom now is here.
O that warn-ing cry o-bey! Now pre-pare for God a way;
Let the val-leys rise to meet Him And the hills bow down to greet Him.

4. Make ye straight what long was crook-ed, Make the rough-er plac-es plain;
Let your hearts be true and hum-ble, As be-fits His ho-ly reign.
For the glo-ry of the Lord Now o'er earth is shed a-broad,
And all flesh shall see the to-ken That His Word is nev-er bro-ken. A-men.

JESUS CHRIST: ADVENT

JOY TO THE WORLD 122

ANTIOCH C.M.

Based on Psalm 98
Isaac Watts, 1719

"From Handel"
Lowell Mason, 1836

1. Joy to the world! the Lord is come; Let earth re-ceive her King; Let ev-ery heart pre-pare Him room, And heav'n and na-ture sing, And heav'n and na-ture sing, And heav'n, and heav'n and na-ture sing.

2. Joy to the earth; the Sav-ior reigns; Let men their songs em-ploy; While fields and floods, rocks, hills, and plains, Re-peat the sound-ing joy, Re-peat the sound-ing joy, Re-peat, re-peat the sound-ing joy.

3. No more let sins and sor-rows grow, Nor thorns in-fest the ground, He comes to make His bless-ings flow Far as the curse is found, Far as the curse is found, Far as, far as the curse is found.

4. He rules the world with truth and grace, And makes the na-tions prove The glo-ries of His right-eous-ness, And won-ders of His love, And won-ders of His love, And won-ders, won-ders of His love.

JESUS CHRIST: BIRTH

123 CHRISTIANS, AWAKE
YORKSHIRE 10.10.10.10.10.10.

John Byrom, c. 1749
John Wainwright, c. 1749

1. Christians, awake! salute the happy morn Whereon the Savior of the world was born; Rise to adore the mystery of love, Which hosts of angels chanted from above; With them the joyful tidings first begun Of God incarnate and the Virgin's Son.

2. Then to the watchful shepherds it was told, Who heard th'angelic herald's voice, "Behold, I bring good tidings of a Savior's birth To you and all the nations upon earth; This day hath God fulfilled His promised word, This day is born a Savior, Christ the Lord."

3. He spake; and straightway the celestial choir In hymns of joy, unknown before, conspire; The praises of redeeming love they sang, And heav'n's whole orb with alleluias rang; God's highest glory was their anthem still, Peace upon earth, and unto men good will.

4. Then may we hope, th'angelic hosts among, To sing, redeemed, a glad triumphal song; He that was born upon this joyful day Around us all His glory shall display; Saved by His love, forever we shall sing Eternal praise to heav'n's almighty King.

JESUS CHRIST: BIRTH

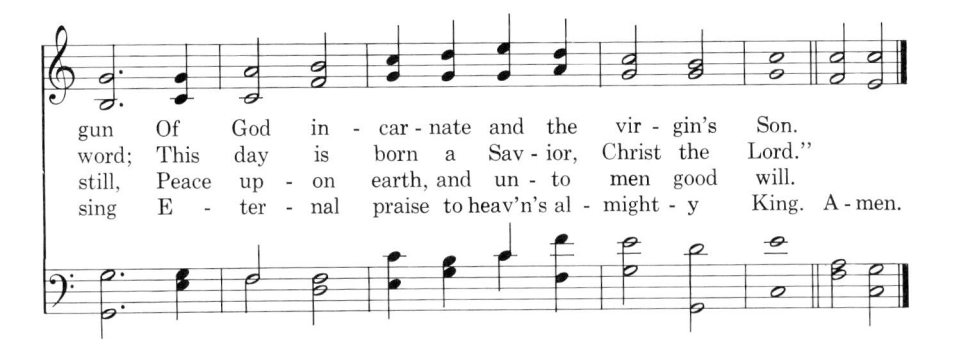

gun Of God in-car-nate and the vir-gin's Son.
word; This day is born a Sav-ior, Christ the Lord."
still, Peace up-on earth, and un-to men good will.
sing E-ter-nal praise to heav'n's al-might-y King. A-men.

ALL MY HEART THIS NIGHT REJOICES 124
WARUM SOLLT ICH MICH DENN GRÄMEN 8.3.3.6.D.

Paul Gerhardt, 1653
Fröhlich soll mein Herze springen
Tr. Catherine Winkworth, 1855

Johann Georg Ebeling, 1666

1 All my heart this night re-joic-es. As I hear, Far and near, Sweet-est an-gel voic-es. "Christ is born," their choirs are sing-ing, Till the air Ev-ery-where Now with joy is ring-ing.

2 Come then, let us has-ten yon-der; Here let all, Great and small, Kneel in awe and won-der! Love Him who with love is yearn-ing! Hail the star That from far Bright with hope is burn-ing!

JESUS CHRIST: BIRTH

125 TO US A CHILD OF HOPE IS BORN

ZERAH C.M.

Based on Isaiah 9: 6-7
John Morison in
Scottish Paraphrases, 1781

Lowell Mason, 1837

1. To us a Child of hope is born, To us a Son is giv'n; Him shall the tribes of earth obey, Him all the hosts of heaven, Him shall the tribes of earth obey, Him all the hosts of heaven.

2. His name shall be the Prince of Peace, For evermore adored, The Wonderful, the Counselor, The great and mighty Lord, The Wonderful, the Counselor, The great and mighty Lord.

3. His power, increasing, still shall spread; His reign no end shall know; Justice shall guard His throne above, And peace abound below, Justice shall guard His throne above, And peace abound below.

JESUS CHRIST: BIRTH

IT CAME UPON THE MIDNIGHT CLEAR 126

CAROL C.M.D.

Edmund Hamilton Sears†, 1849

Richard Storrs Willis, 1850

1 It came up-on the mid-night clear, That glo-rious song of old,
2 Still through the clo-ven skies they come, With peace-ful wings un-furled,
3 And ye, be-neath life's crush-ing load, Whose forms are bend-ing low,
4 For lo, the days are has-t'ning on, By proph-et bards fore-told,

From an-gels bend-ing near the earth To touch their harps of gold:
And still their heav'n-ly mu-sic floats O'er all the wea-ry world:
Who toil a-long the climb-ing way With pain-ful steps and slow:
When with the ev-er-cir-cling years Comes round the age of gold;

"Peace on the earth, good will to men, From heav'n's all-gra-cious King."
A-bove its sad and low-ly plains They bend on hov-'ring wing,
Look now! for glad and gold-en hours Come swift-ly on the wing:
When peace shall o-ver all the earth Its an-cient splen-dors fling,

The world in sol-emn still-ness lay, To hear the an-gels sing.
And ev-er o'er its Ba-bel-sounds The bless-ed an-gels sing.
O rest be-side the wea-ry road, And hear the an-gels sing.
And the whole world give back the song Which now the an-gels sing.

JESUS CHRIST: BIRTH

127 ANGELS WE HAVE HEARD ON HIGH

GLORIA 7.7.7.7. with Refrain

Traditional French Carol
Altered by Earl Marlatt, b. 1892

French Carol

1. Angels we have heard on high, Singing sweetly through the night,
And the mountains in reply Echoing their brave delight.

2. Shepherds, why this jubilee? Why these songs of happy cheer?
What great brightness did you see? What glad tidings did you hear?

3. Come to Bethlehem and see Him whose birth the angels sing;
Come, adore on bended knee Christ, the Lord, the newborn King.

4. See Him in a manger laid Whom the angels praise above;
Mary, Joseph, lend your aid, While we raise our hearts in love.

Refrain

Gloria in excelsis Deo,
Gloria in excelsis Deo.

JESUS CHRIST: BIRTH

ANGELS FROM THE REALMS OF GLORY 128

REGENT SQUARE 8.7.8.7.8.7.

James Montgomery, 1816 — Henry Smart, 1867

1. Angels, from the realms of glory, Wing your flight o'er all the earth, Ye who sang creation's story, Now proclaim Messiah's birth; Come and worship, Come and worship, Worship Christ the newborn King.

2. Shepherds, in the field abiding, Watching o'er your flocks by night, God with man is now residing, Yonder shines the infant-light; Come and worship, Come and worship, Worship Christ the newborn King.

3. Sages, leave your contemplations, Brighter visions beam afar; Seek the great desire of nations; Ye have seen His natal star; Come and worship, Come and worship, Worship Christ the newborn King.

4. Saints, before the altar bending, Watching long in hope and fear, Suddenly the Lord descending, In His temple shall appear; Come and worship, Come and worship, Worship Christ the newborn King.

5. Sinners, wrung with true repentance, Doom'd for guilt to endless pains, Justice now revokes the sentence, Mercy calls you, break your chains; Come and worship, Come and worship, Worship Christ the newborn King.

JESUS CHRIST: BIRTH

129 WHAT CHILD IS THIS

GREENSLEEVES 8.7.8.7. with Refrain

William Chatterton Dix, c. 1865

English Traditional Melody

1. What child is this, who, laid to rest, On Mary's lap is sleeping?
Whom angels greet with anthems sweet, While shepherds watch are keeping?

2. Why lies He in such mean estate Where ox and ass are feeding?
Good Christian, fear: for sinners here The silent Word is pleading.

3. So bring Him incense, gold, and myrrh, Come, peasant, king, to own Him,
The King of kings salvation brings, Let loving hearts enthrone Him.

Refrain
This, this is Christ the King, Whom shepherds guard and angels sing:
Haste, haste to bring Him laud, The babe, the son of Mary.

JESUS CHRIST: BIRTH

SILENT NIGHT, HOLY NIGHT 130

SILENT NIGHT Irregular

Joseph Mohr, 1818
Stille Nacht, Heilige Nacht
Tr. John Freeman Young, 1863

Franz Gruber, 1818

1. Si - lent night, ho - ly night, All is calm, all is bright
Round yon vir - gin moth-er and child. Ho - ly in-fant so ten-der and mild,
Sleep in heav-en-ly peace, Sleep in heav-en-ly peace.

2. Si - lent night, ho - ly night, Shep-herds quake at the sight,
Glo - ries stream from heav-en a - far, Heaven-ly hosts sing al - le - lu - ia;
Christ, the Sav - ior is born! Christ, the Sav - ior is born!

3. Si - lent night, ho - ly night, Son of God, love's pure light
Ra - diant beams from Thy ho-ly face, With the dawn of re - deem - ing grace,
Je - sus, Lord, at Thy birth, Je - sus, Lord, at Thy birth.

1 Stille Nacht, heilige Nacht!
Alles schläft, einsam wacht
nur das traute, hochheilige Paar,
das im Stalle zu Bethlehem war
bei dem himmlischen Kind,
bei dem himmlischen Kind.

2 Stille Nacht, heilige Nacht!
Hirten erst kund gemacht;
durch der Engel Hallelujah
tönt es laut von fern und nah:
Christ, der Retter, ist da!
Christ, der Retter, ist da!

3 Stille Nacht, heilige Nacht!
Gottes Sohn, o wie lacht
Lieb aus deinem holdseligen Mund,
da uns schlägt die rettende Stund,
Christ, in deiner Geburt!
Christ, in deiner Geburt!

JESUS CHRIST: BIRTH

131 LO, HOW A ROSE E'ER BLOOMING

ES IST EIN ROS' 7.6.7.6.6.7.6.

Köln, 1599, St. 1 and 2; Berlin, 1844, St. 3
Es ist ein Ros' entsprungen
Tr. Theodore Baker, 1894, St. 1 and 2
and Harriet R. Spaeth, 1875, St. 3

Alte Catholische Geistliche Kirkengeseng,
Köln, 1599
Harmony by Michael Praetorius, 1609

1. Lo, how a rose e'er bloom-ing From ten-der stem hath sprung, Of Jes-se's lin-eage com-ing, As men of old have sung. It came, a flow-'ret bright, A-mid the cold of win-ter, When half-spent was the night.

2. I-sai-ah 'twas fore-told it, The rose I have in mind, With Ma-ry we be-hold it. The Vir-gin moth-er kind. To show God's love a-right She bore to them a Sav-ior, When half-spent was the night.

3. This flower, whose fra-grance ten-der With sweet-ness fills the air, Dis-pels with glo-rious splen-dor The dark-ness ev-ery-where. True Man, yet ver-y God, From sin and death He saves us And light-ens ev-ery load.

JESUS CHRIST: BIRTH

O COME, ALL YE FAITHFUL 132
ADESTE FIDELES Irregular

Anonymous, 18th c.
Adeste fideles laeti triumphantes
Tr. Frederick Oakeley, 1842, and Others, St. 1, 3, 4
and William Mercer‡, 1854, St. 2

John Francis Wade? c. 1740-43

1. O come, all ye faith-ful, Joy-ful and tri-um-phant, O come ye, O come ye to Beth-le-hem; Come and be-hold Him, Born the King of an-gels;
2. True God of true God, Light of light e-ter-nal, Our low-ly na-ture He hath not ab-horred; Son of the Fa-ther, Be-got-ten, not cre-a-ted;
3. Sing, choirs of an-gels, Sing in ex-ul-ta-tion, Sing, all ye cit-i-zens of heav'n a-bove; Glo-ry to God... In... the... high-est;
4. Yea, Lord, we greet Thee, Born this hap-py morn-ing, Je-sus, to Thee be... glo-ry giv'n; Word of the Fa-ther, Now in flesh ap-pear-ing:

REFRAIN

O come, let us a-dore Him, O come, let us a-dore Him,
O come, let us a-dore Him, Christ the Lord.

JESUS CHRIST: BIRTH

133 O LITTLE TOWN OF BETHLEHEM
ST. LOUIS 8.6.8.6.7.6.8.6.

Phillips Brooks, 1868   Lewis Henry Redner, 1868

1. O little town of Bethlehem, How still we see thee lie! Above thy deep and dreamless sleep The silent stars go by; Yet in thy dark streets shineth The everlasting Light; The hopes and fears of all the years Are met in thee tonight.

2. For Christ is born of Mary, And gathered all above, While mortals sleep, the angels keep Their watch of wond'ring love. O morning stars, together Proclaim the holy birth! And praises sing to God the King, And peace to men on earth.

3. How silently, how silently, The wondrous gift is giv'n! So God imparts to human hearts The blessings of His heav'n. No ear may hear His coming, But in this world of sin, Where meek souls will receive Him still, The dear Christ enters in.

4. O holy Child of Bethlehem! Descend to us, we pray; Cast out our sin, and enter in; Be born in us today. We hear the Christmas angels The great glad tidings tell; O come to us, abide with us, Our Lord Emmanuel. A-men.

JESUS CHRIST: BIRTH

FROM HEAVEN ABOVE TO EARTH 134
VOM HIMMEL HOCH L.M.

Martin Luther, 1535
Vom Himmel hoch, da komm' ich her
Tr. Catherine Winkworth†, 1855

V. Schumann's *Geistliche Lieder*, 1539

1. From heav'n above to earth I come
To bear good news to ev'ry home;
Glad tidings of great joy I bring,
Whereof I now will say and sing:

2. To you this night is born a child
Of Mary, chosen mother mild;
This little child, of lowly birth,
Shall be the joy of all your earth.

3. Now let us all with gladsome cheer
Follow the shepherds and draw near
To see this wondrous gift of God,
Who hath His only Son bestowed.

4. Welcome to earth, Thou noble Guest,
Through whom e'en wicked men are blest!
Thou com'st to share our misery;
What can we render, Lord, to Thee?

5. My heart for very joy doth leap,
My lips no more can silence keep;
I, too, must raise with joyful tongue
That sweetest ancient cradle-song:

6. Glory to God in highest heaven,
Who unto us His Son hath given!
While angels sing with joyful mirth
A glad new year to all the earth.

JESUS CHRIST: BIRTH

135 HARK! THE HERALD ANGELS SING

MENDELSSOHN 7.7.7.7.D. with Refrain

Charles Wesley, 1739, and Others
Arranged from Felix Mendelssohn, 1840

1. Hark! the herald angels sing, "Glory to the newborn King;
Peace on earth, and mercy mild, God and sinners reconciled!"
Joyful all ye nations, rise, Join the triumph of the skies;
With th'angelic host proclaim "Christ is born in Bethlehem."

2. Christ, by highest heav'n adored; Christ, the everlasting Lord;
Late in time behold Him come, Offspring of the virgin's womb:
Veil'd in flesh the Godhead see; Hail th'incarnate Deity,
Pleas'd as man with man to dwell; Jesus, our Emmanuel!

3. Hail, the heav'n-born Prince of Peace! Hail, the Sun of Righteousness!
Light and life to all He brings, Ris'n with healing in His wings.
Mild He lays His glory by, Born that man no more may die,
Born to raise the sons of earth, Born to give them second birth.

JESUS CHRIST: BIRTH

Hark! the her-ald an-gels sing, "Glo-ry to the new-born King." A-men.

LET ALL TOGETHER PRAISE OUR GOD 136
LOBT GOTT, IHR CHRISTEN C.M.

Nicolaus Herman, c. 1554
Lobt Gott, ihr Christen alle gleich
Tr. Arthur Tozer Russell†, 1851

Nicolaus Herman, 1554
Harmony by Johann Sebastian Bach, c. 1735-1740

1. Let all to-geth-er praise our God Up-on His loft-y throne; For He un-clos-es heav'n to-day And gives to us His Son, And gives to us His Son.
2. He lays a-side His maj-es-ty And seems as noth-ing worth, And takes on Him a serv-ant's form, Who made the heav'n and earth, Who made the heav'n and earth.
3. Be-hold the won-der-ful ex-change Our Lord with us doth make! Lo, He as-sumes our flesh and blood, And we of heav'n par-take, And we of heav'n par-take.
4. The glo-rious gates of par-a-dise The an-gel guards no more; This day a-gain those gates un-fold. With praise our God a-dore, With praise our God a-dore! A-men.

JESUS CHRIST: BIRTH

137 THE FIRST NOEL THE ANGEL DID SAY

THE FIRST NOEL Irregular

Traditional Carol

English Carol, published 1833

1. The first Noel the angel did say
Was to certain poor shepherds in fields as they lay;
In fields where they lay keeping their sheep,
On a cold winter's night that was so deep.

2. They looked up and saw a star
Shining in the east, beyond them far,
And to the earth it gave great light,
And so it continued both day and night.

3. And by the light of that same star,
Three wise men came from country far;
To seek for a king was their intent
And to follow the star wherever it went.

4. This star drew nigh to the north-west,
O'er Bethlehem it took its rest,
And there it did both stop and stay,
Right over the place where Jesus lay.

5. Then entered in those wise men three,
Full reverently upon their knee,
And offered there, in His presence,
Their gold, and myrrh, and frankincense.

JESUS CHRIST: BIRTH

Noel, Noel, Noel, Noel, Born is the King of Is - ra - el.

WHILE SHEPHERDS WATCHED 138
CHRISTMAS C.M.

Nahum Tate, 1703
George Frideric Handel, 1728

1. While shep-herds watched their flocks by night, All seat-ed on the ground, The an-gel of the Lord came down, And glo-ry shone a-round, And glo-ry shone a-round.
2. "Fear not!" said he; for might-y dread Had seized their trou-bled mind; "Glad ti-dings of great joy I bring, To you and all man-kind, To you and all man-kind.
3. "To you, in Da-vid's town, this day Is born, of Da-vid's line, The Sav-ior, who is Christ the Lord, And this shall be the sign: And this shall be the sign:
4. "The heav'n-ly babe you there shall find To hu-man view dis-played, All mean-ly wrapped in swath-ing bands, And in a man-ger laid, And in a man-ger laid."
5. Thus spake the ser-aph; and forth-with Ap-peared a shin-ing throng Of an-gels prais-ing God, and thus Ad-dressed their joy-ful song: Ad-dressed their joy-ful song:
6. "All glo-ry be to God on high, And to the earth be peace: Good will hence-forth from heav'n to men Be-gin and nev-er cease! Be-gin and nev-er cease!"

JESUS CHRIST: BIRTH

139 WORSHIP THE LORD

WAS LEBET, WAS SCHWEBET 12.10.12.10.

John Samuel Bewley Monsell†, 1863

Manuscript Chorale Book, Üttingen, 1754

1. Worship the Lord in the beauty of holiness,
Bow down before Him, His glory proclaim;
Gold of obedience and incense of lowliness
Bring and adore Him; the Lord is His name!

2. Low at His feet lay thy burden of carefulness,
High on His heart He will bear it for thee,
Comfort thy sorrows, and answer thy prayerfulness
Guiding thy steps as may best for thee be.

3. Fear not to enter His courts in the slenderness
Of the poor wealth thou wouldst reckon as thine;
Truth in its beauty, and love in its tenderness,
These are the offerings to lay on His shrine.

4. These, though we bring them in trembling and fearfulness,
He will accept for the name that is dear;
Mornings of joy give for evenings of tearfulness,
Trust for our trembling, and hope for our fear.

5. Worship the Lord in the beauty of holiness,
Bow down before Him, His glory proclaim;
Gold of obedience and incense of lowliness
Bring and adore Him; the Lord is His name!

JESUS CHRIST: EPIPHANY

FROM THE EASTERN MOUNTAINS 140

PRINCETHORPE 6.5.6.5.D.

Godfrey Thring†, 1873
William Pitts, 1871

1. From the eastern mountains Pressing on they come, Wise men in their wisdom, To His humble home; Stirred by deep devotion, Hasting from afar, Ever journeying onward, Guided by a star.

2. There their Lord and Savior Meek and lowly lay, Wondrous light that led them Onward on their way, Ever now to lighten Nations from afar, As they journey homeward By that guiding star.

3. Thou who in a manger Once hast lowly lain, Who dost now in glory O'er all kingdoms reign, Throw Thy radiance o'er them, Guide them on their way: Ne'er have seen the brightness Of Thy guiding star,

4. Gather in the outcasts, All who've gone astray, Throw Thy radiance o'er them, Guide them on their way: Those who've never known Thee, Those who've wandered far, Guide them by the brightness Of Thy guiding star.

5. Onward through the darkness Of the lonely night, Shining still before them With Thy kindly light, Guide them, Jew and Gentile, Homeward from afar, Young and old together, By Thy guiding star. A-men.

JESUS CHRIST: EPIPHANY

141 HOW BRIGHT APPEARS THE MORNING STAR

WIE SCHÖN LEUCHTET DER MORGENSTERN 8.8.7.8.8.7.4.12.8.

Philipp Nicolai, 1599
Wie schön leuchtet der Morgenstern
William Mercer, 1859

Philipp Nicolai, 1599

1. How bright appears the morning star, With mercy beaming from afar! The host of heav'n rejoices! O righteous branch! O Jesse's rod! Thou Son of man, and Son of God! We too will lift our voices. Jesus! Jesus! Holy, holy! yet most lowly!

2. Rejoice, ye heav'ns, thou earth, reply! With praise, ye sinners, fill the sky! For this His incarnation! Incarnate God, put forth Thy power, Ride on, ride on, great Conqueror, Till all know Thy salvation. Amen, amen! Alleluia, alleluia!

JESUS CHRIST: EPIPHANY

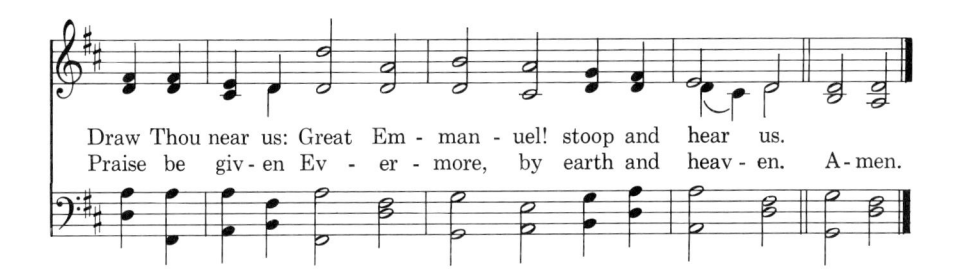

Draw Thou near us: Great Emmanuel! stoop and hear us.
Praise be given Evermore, by earth and heaven. A-men.

AS WITH GLADNESS MEN OF OLD 142
DIX 7.7.7.7.7.7.

William C. Dix, c. 1858

From Conrad Kocher, 1838
Adapted by William Henry Monk, 1861

1. As with gladness men of old Did the guiding star behold;
As with joy they hailed its light, Leading onward, beaming bright;
So, most gracious Lord, may we Evermore be led to Thee.

2. As with joyful steps they sped To that lowly manger-bed,
There to bend the knee before Him whom heav'n and earth adore;
So may we with willing feet Ever seek Thy mercy seat.

3. As they offered gifts most rare, At that manger rude and bare,
So may we with holy joy, Pure and free from sin's alloy,
All our costliest treasures bring, Christ, to Thee, our heav'nly King.

4. Holy Jesus, every day Keep us in the narrow way;
And, when earthly things are past, Bring our ransomed souls at last
Where they need no star to guide, Where no clouds Thy glory hide. A-men.

JESUS CHRIST: EPIPHANY

143 BRIGHTEST AND BEST
MORNING STAR 11.10.11.10.

Reginald Heber, 1811 — James Prockter Harding, 1892

1. Bright-est and best of the sons of the morn-ing,
   Dawn on our dark-ness, and lend us Thine aid;
   Star of the east, the ho-ri-zon a-dorn-ing,
   Guide where our in-fant Re-deem-er is laid.

2. Cold on His cra-dle the dew-drops are shin-ing,
   Low lies His head with the beasts of the stall;
   An-gels a-dore Him in slum-ber re-clin-ing,
   Mak-er, and Mon-arch, and Sav-ior of all.

3. Say, shall we yield Him, in cost-ly de-vo-tion,
   O-dors of E-dom and of-f'rings di-vine,
   Gems of the moun-tain and pearls of the o-cean,
   Myrrh from the for-est, or gold from the mine?

4. Vain-ly we of-fer each am-ple ob-la-tion,
   Vain-ly with gifts would His fa-vor se-cure;
   Rich-er by far is the heart's ad-o-ra-tion,
   Dear-er to God are the prayers of the poor.

5. Bright-est and best of the sons of the morn-ing,
   Dawn on our dark-ness, and lend us Thine aid;
   Star of the east, the ho-ri-zon a-dorn-ing,
   Guide where our in-fant Re-deem-er is laid. A-men.

JESUS CHRIST: EPIPHANY

FORTY DAYS AND FORTY NIGHTS 144
AUS DER TIEFE 7.7.7.7.

George Hunt Smyttan, 1856
Altered by Francis Pott and Others, 1861

Gesangbuch, Nürnberg, 1676

1 For-ty days and for-ty nights Thou wast fast-ing in the wild;
2 Shall not we Thy watch-ings share, And from earth-ly joys ab-stain,
3 And if Sa-tan, vex-ing sore, Flesh or spir-it should as-sail,
4 Keep, O keep us, Sav-ior dear, Ev-er con-stant by Thy side;

For-ty days and for-ty nights Tempt-ed, and yet un-de-filed.
Fast-ing with un-ceas-ing prayer, Glad with Thee to suf-fer pain?
Thou, his van-quish-er be-fore, Grant we may not faint nor fail.
That with Thee we may ap-pear At the e-ter-nal Eas-ter-tide. A-men.

O MASTER OF THE LOVING HEART 145
ABRIDGE C.M.

Calvin W. Laufer, 1927

Isaac Smith, c. 1780

1 O Mas-ter of the lov-ing heart, The Friend of all in need,
2 Thy days were full of kind-ly acts, Thy speech was true and plain;
3 Thy face was warm with sym-pa-thy, Thy hand God's strength re-vealed;
4 O grant us hearts like Thine, dear Lord, So joy-ous, true, and free,

We pray that we may be like Thee, In thought and word and deed.
And no one ev-er sought Thee, Lord, Who came to Thee in vain.
Who saw Thy face, or felt Thy touch, Were com-fort-ed and healed.
That all Thy chil-dren ev-ery-where Be drawn by us to Thee. A-men.

JESUS CHRIST: LIFE AND MINISTRY

146 YE FAIR GREEN HILLS OF GALILEE
STELLA 8.8.8.8.8.8.

Eustace R. Conder, 1887

Easy Tunes for Catholic Schools, 1852

1. Ye fair green hills of Galilee, That girdle quiet Nazareth, What glorious vision did ye see, When He who conquered sin and death Your flow-'ry slopes and summits trod, And grew in grace with man and God?

2. "We saw no glory crown His head As childhood ripened into youth; No angels on His errands sped; He wrought no sign; but meekness, truth, And love to man, and love to God."

3. Jesus! my Savior, Master, King, Who didst for me the burden bear, While saints in heav'n Thy glory sing, Let me on earth Thy likeness wear; Mine be the path Thy feet have trod, Duty, and love to man and God. A-men.

JESUS CHRIST: LIFE AND MINISTRY

MY DEAR REDEEMER AND MY LORD 147

SOCIAL BAND L.M.D.

Isaac Watts, 1707-1709

Folk Hymn
J. Ingalls' *Christian Harmony,* 1805
Harmony by J. Harold Moyer, 1965

1. My dear Redeemer and my Lord, I read my duty in Thy Word;
But in Thy life the law appears Drawn out in living characters.
Such was Thy truth, and such Thy zeal, Such deference to Thy Father's will,
Such love, and meekness so divine, I would transcribe and make them mine.

2. Cold mountains and the midnight air Witnessed the fervor of Thy prayer;
The desert Thy temptations knew, Thy conflict and Thy vict'ry too.
Be Thou my pattern; make me bear More of Thy gracious image here;
Then God the Judge shall own my name Among the fol-l'wers of the Lamb.

JESUS CHRIST: LIFE AND MINISTRY

148 FIERCE RAGED THE TEMPEST
ST. AËLRED 8.8.8.3.

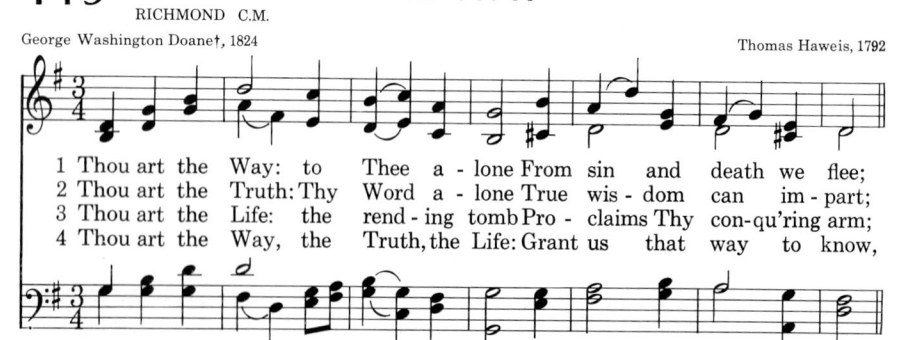

Godfrey Thring, 1861

John Bacchus Dykes, 1862

1. Fierce raged the tempest o'er the deep,
Watch did Thine anxious servants keep;
But Thou wast wrapped in guileless sleep, Calm and still.

2. "Save, Lord, we perish!" was their cry,
"O save us in our agony!"
Thy word above the storm rose high, "Peace! be still."

3. The wild winds hushed; the angry deep
Sank, like a little child, to sleep;
The sullen billows ceased to leap, At Thy will.

4. So, when our life is clouded o'er,
And storm-winds drift us from the shore,
Say, lest we sink to rise no more, "Peace! be still."

149 THOU ART THE WAY
RICHMOND C.M.

George Washington Doane†, 1824

Thomas Haweis, 1792

1. Thou art the Way: to Thee alone From sin and death we flee;

2. Thou art the Truth: Thy Word alone True wisdom can impart;

3. Thou art the Life: the rending tomb Proclaims Thy conqu'ring arm;

4. Thou art the Way, the Truth, the Life: Grant us that way to know,

JESUS CHRIST: LIFE AND MINISTRY

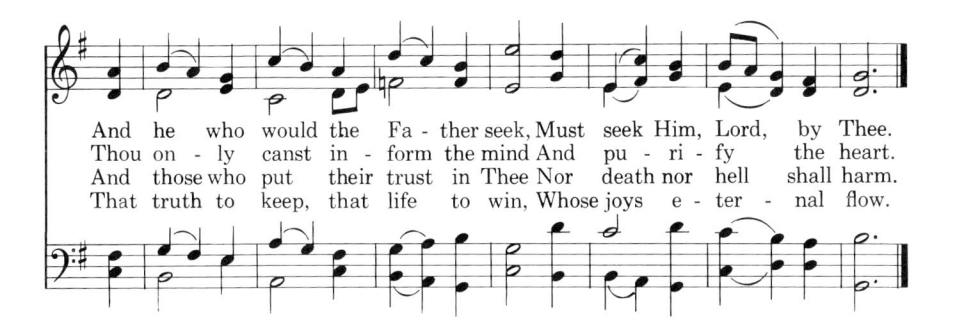

And he who would the Father seek, Must seek Him, Lord, by Thee.
Thou on-ly canst in-form the mind And pu-ri-fy the heart.
And those who put their trust in Thee Nor death nor hell shall harm.
That truth to keep, that life to win, Whose joys e-ter-nal flow.

IMMORTAL LOVE, FOREVER FULL 150

SERENITY C.M.

John Greenleaf Whittier, 1866

William V. Wallace, 1856

1. Im-mor-tal love, for-ev-er full, For-ev-er flow-ing free, For-ev-er shared, for-ev-er whole, A nev-er-ebb-ing sea!
2. Our out-ward lips con-fess the name All oth-er names a-bove; Love on-ly know-eth whence it came, And com-pre-hend-eth love.
3. We may not climb the heav'n-ly steeps To bring the Lord Christ down, In vain we search the low-est deeps, For Him no depths can drown.
4. The heal-ing of His seam-less dress Is by our beds of pain; We touch Him in life's throng and press, And we are whole a-gain.
5. O Lord and Mas-ter of us all, What-e'er our name or sign, We own Thy sway, we hear Thy call, We test our lives by Thine. A-men.

JESUS CHRIST: LIFE AND MINISTRY

151 THOU TO WHOM THE SICK AND DYING
JESUS, JESUS, NICHTS ALS JESUS 8.7.8.7.7.7.

Godfrey Thring, 1870 — Bonner's *Vollkommenes* . . . *Choral-Buch*, 1715

1. Thou to whom the sick and dying Ever came, nor came in vain, Still with healing words replying To the wearied cry of pain, Hear us, Jesus, as we meet Suppliants at Thy mercy seat.

2. Still the weary, sick, and dying Need a brother's, sister's care; On Thy higher help relying May we now their burden share, Bringing all our off'rings meet, Suppliants at Thy mercy seat.

3. May each child of Thine be willing, Willing both in hand and heart, All the law of love fulfilling, Ever comfort to impart; Ever bringing off'rings meet, Suppliant to Thy mercy seat.

4. So may sickness, sin, and sadness, To Thy healing power yield, Till the sick and sad, in gladness, Rescued, ransom'd, cleansed and healed, One in Thee together meet, Pardon'd at Thy judgment seat. A-men.

JESUS CHRIST: LIFE AND MINISTRY

THINE ARM, O LORD, IN DAYS OF OLD 152

ST. MATTHEW C.M.D.

Edward Hayes Plumptre, 1864
William Croft? 1708

1 Thine arm, O Lord, in days of old, Was strong to heal and save;
   It triumphed o'er disease and death, O'er darkness and the grave.
   To Thee they went: the blind, the dumb, The palsied, and the lame,
   The leper and his tainted life, The sick with fevered frame:

2 And lo! Thy touch brought life and health, Gave speech, and strength, and sight;
   And youth renewed and frenzy calmed Owned Thee, the Lord of light.
   And now, O Lord, be near to bless, Almighty as of yore,
   In crowded street, by restless couch, As by Gennesaret's shore.

3 Be Thou our great Deliv'rer still, Thou Lord of life and death,
   Restore and quicken, soothe and bless, With Thine almighty breath;
   To hands that work and eyes that see Give wisdom's heav'nly lore,
   That whole and sick, and weak and strong, May praise Thee evermore. A-men.

JESUS CHRIST: LIFE AND MINISTRY

153 NOT ALWAYS ON THE MOUNT
LOB SEI DEM ALLMÄCHTIGEN L.M.

Frederick L. Hosmer, 1882 — Johann Crüger, 1640

1. Not always on the mount may we
Rapt in the heav'nly vision be:
The shores of thought and feeling know
The Spirit's tidal ebb and flow.

2. "Lord, it is good, abiding here,"
We cry, the heav'nly presence near;
The vision vanishes, our eyes
Are lifted into vacant skies.

3. Yet, hath one such exalted hour
Upon the soul redeeming power,
And in its strength through after days
We travel our appointed ways.

4. Till all the lowly vale grows bright,
Transfigured in remembered light,
And in untiring souls we bear
The freshness of the upper air.

5. The mount for vision: but below
The paths of daily duty go,
And nobler life therein shall own
The pattern on the mountain shown.

JESUS CHRIST: LIFE AND MINISTRY

ALL GLORY, LAUD, AND HONOR 154

VALET WILL ICH DIR GEBEN 7.6.7.6. with Refrain

Theodulph of Orleans, c. 820
Gloria laus et honor
Tr. John Mason Neale†, 1851

Melchior Teschner, 1613

REFRAIN (Sing after each stanza)

All glory, laud, and honor To Thee, Redeemer, King,
To whom the lips of children Made sweet hosannas ring.

1 Thou art the King of Israel, Thou David's royal Son,
Who in the Lord's name comest, The King and blessed one.

2 The company of angels Are praising Thee on high,
And mortal men, and all things Created, make reply.

3 The people of the Hebrews With palms before Thee went;
Our praise and prayer and anthems Before Thee we present.

4 To Thee, before Thy passion, They sang their hymns of praise;
To Thee, now high exalted, Our melody we raise.

5 Thou didst accept their praises; Accept the prayers we bring,
Who in all good delightest, Thou good and gracious King.

JESUS CHRIST: TRIUMPHAL ENTRY

155 HOSANNA, LOUD HOSANNA
ELLACOMBE C.M.D.

Jennette Threlfall, d. 1880

Adapted from *Gesangbuch* . . . ,
Württemberg, 1784

1. Ho-sanna, loud hosanna The little children sang;
Through pillared court and temple The lovely anthem rang;
To Jesus, who had blessed them Close folded to His breast,
The children sang their praises, The simplest and the best.

2. From Olivet they followed 'Mid an exultant crowd,
The victor palm-branch waving, And chanting clear and loud;
The Lord of men and angels Rode on in lowly state,
Nor scorned that little children Should on His bidding wait.

3. "Hosanna in the highest!" That ancient song we sing,
For Christ is our Redeemer, The Lord of heav'n our King.
O may we ever praise Him With heart and life and voice,
And in His blissful presence Eternally rejoice! A-men.

JESUS CHRIST: TRIUMPHAL ENTRY

RIDE ON, RIDE ON IN MAJESTY 156
WINCHESTER NEW L.M.

From *Musicalisch Hand-buch*, published
by George Rebelein's Widow, 1690
Arranged by William Henry Havergal, 1847

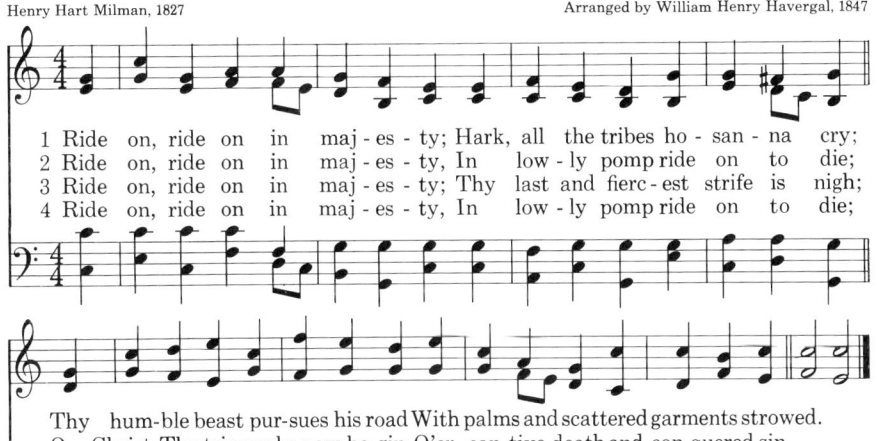

Henry Hart Milman, 1827

1. Ride on, ride on in maj-es-ty; Hark, all the tribes ho-san-na cry;
Thy hum-ble beast pur-sues his road With palms and scattered garments strowed.
2. Ride on, ride on in maj-es-ty, In low-ly pomp ride on to die;
O Christ, Thy tri-umphs now be-gin O'er cap-tive death and con-quered sin.
3. Ride on, ride on in maj-es-ty; Thy last and fierc-est strife is nigh;
The Fa-ther, on His sap-phire throne, Ex-pects His own a-noint-ed Son.
4. Ride on, ride on in maj-es-ty, In low-ly pomp ride on to die;
Bow Thy meek head to mor-tal pain, Then take, O God, Thy power, and reign. A-men.

JESUS CHRIST: TRIUMPHAL ENTRY

O THOU, WHO THROUGH THIS HOLY 157
WETHERBY C.M.

John Mason Neale, 1842

Samuel Sebastian Wesley, 1872

1. O Thou, who through this ho-ly week, Didst suf-fer for us all;
The sick to heal, the lost to seek, To raise up them that fall:
2. We can-not un-der-stand the woe Thy love was pleased to bear:
O Lamb of God, we on-ly know That all our hopes are there.
3. Thy feet the path of suf-f'ring trod, Thy hand the vic-t'ry won:
What shall we ren-der to our God For all that He hath done? A-men.

JESUS CHRIST: PASSION

158 AH, HOLY JESUS
HERZLIEBSTER JESU 11.11.11.5.

Johann Heermann, c. 1630
Herzliebster Jesu
Tr. Robert Bridges, 1899
St. 3 omitted with permission

Johann Crüger, 1640

1. Ah, holy Jesus, how hast Thou offended,
That man to judge Thee hath in hate pretended?
By foes derided, by Thine own rejected,
O most afflicted.

2. Who was the guilty? Who brought this upon Thee?
Alas, my treason, Jesus, hath undone Thee.
'Twas I, Lord Jesus, I it was denied Thee:
I crucified Thee.

3. For me, kind Jesus, was Thy incarnation,
Thy mortal sorrow, and Thy life's oblation:
Thy death of anguish and Thy bitter passion,
For my salvation.

4. Therefore, kind Jesus, since I cannot pay Thee,
I do adore Thee, and will ever pray Thee,
Think on Thy pity and Thy love unswerving,
Not my deserving. A-men.

JESUS CHRIST: PASSION

O SACRED HEAD, NOW WOUNDED 159

HERZLICH TUT MICH VERLANGEN 7.6.7.6.D.

Based on *Salve caput cruentatum*
Paul Gerhardt, 1656
O Haupt voll Blut und Wunden
Tr. James Waddell Alexander†, 1830

Hans Leo Hassler, 1601
Harmony by Johann Sebastian Bach, 1729

1. O sacred Head, now wounded, With grief and shame weighed down! Now scornfully surrounded With thorns, Thy only crown: O sacred Head, what glory, What bliss till now was Thine! Yet, though despised and gory, I joy to call Thee mine.

2. O noblest brow and dearest, In other days the world All feared when Thou appearedst; What shame on Thee is hurled! How art Thou pale with anguish, With sore abuse and scorn; How does that visage languish, Which once was bright as morn!

3. What Thou, my Lord, hast suffered Was all for sinners' gain: Mine, mine was the transgression, But Thine the deadly pain. Lo, here I fall, my Savior! 'Tis I deserve Thy place; Look on me with Thy favor, Vouchsafe to me Thy grace.

4. What language shall I borrow To thank Thee, dearest Friend, For this Thy dying sorrow, Thy pity without end? O make me Thine forever; And should I fainting be, Lord, let me never, never, Outlive my love to Thee.

5. Be near when I am dying, O show Thy cross to me; And for my succor flying, Come, Lord, and set me free; These eyes, new faith receiving, From Jesus shall not move; For he who dies believing, Dies safely, through Thy love. A-men.

JESUS CHRIST: PASSION

160 GO TO DARK GETHSEMANE
REDHEAD NO. 76 (AJALON) 7.7.7.7.7.7.

James Montgomery, 1820 — Richard Redhead, 1853

1. Go to dark Geth-sem-a-ne, Ye that feel the tempt-er's power,
Your Re-deem-er's con-flict see; Watch with Him one bit-ter hour:
Turn not from His griefs a-way; Learn of Je-sus Christ to pray.

2. Fol-low to the judg-ment hall; View the Lord of life ar-raigned.
O the worm-wood and the gall! O the pangs His soul sus-tained!
Shun not suf-f'ring, shame, or loss; Learn of Him to bear the cross.

3. Cal-v'ry's mourn-ful moun-tain climb; There, a-dor-ing at His feet,
Mark that mir-a-cle of time, God's own sac-ri-fice com-plete:
"It is fin-ished!" hear the cry; Learn of Je-sus Christ to die.

4. Ear-ly has-ten to the tomb Where they laid His breath-less clay:
All is sol-i-tude and gloom; Who hath tak-en Him a-way?
Christ is ris'n! He meets our eyes. Sav-ior, teach us so to rise. A-men.

161 'TIS MIDNIGHT, AND ON OLIVE'S BROW
OLIVE'S BROW L.M.

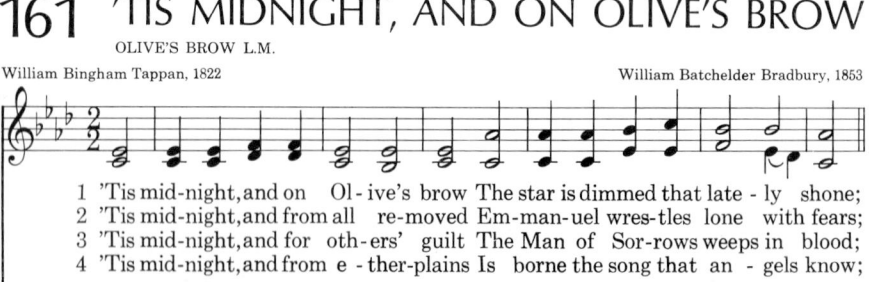

William Bingham Tappan, 1822 — William Batchelder Bradbury, 1853

1. 'Tis mid-night, and on Ol-ive's brow The star is dimmed that late-ly shone;
2. 'Tis mid-night, and from all re-moved Em-man-uel wres-tles lone with fears;
3. 'Tis mid-night, and for oth-ers' guilt The Man of Sor-rows weeps in blood;
4. 'Tis mid-night, and from e-ther-plains Is borne the song that an-gels know;

JESUS CHRIST: PASSION

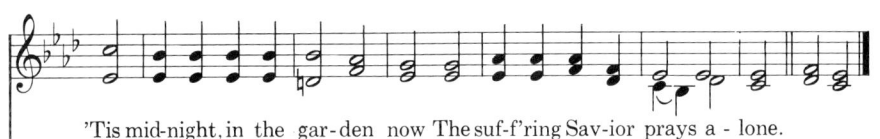

'Tis mid-night, in the gar-den now The suf-f'ring Sav-ior prays a-lone.
E'en the dis-ci-ple whom He loved Heeds not his Mas-ter's grief and tears.
Yet He who hath in an-guish knelt Is not for-sak-en by His God.
Un-heard by mor-tals are the strains That sweet-ly soothe the Sav-ior's woe. A-men.

THRONED UPON THE AWFUL TREE 162

SPANISH HYMN 7.7.7.7.7.7.

John Ellerton, 1875   Arranged by Benjamin Carr, 1824

1 Throned up-on the aw-ful tree, King of grief, I watch with Thee:
2 Si - lent thro' those three dread hours, Wres-tling with the e - vil powers,
3 Hark that cry that peals a-loud Up-ward thro' the whelm-ing cloud!
4 Lord, should fear and an-guish roll Dark-ly o'er my sin-ful soul,

Dark-ness veils Thine an-guished face, None its lines of woe can trace,
Left a-lone with hu-man sin, Gloom a-round Thee and with-in,
Thou, the Fa-ther's on-ly Son, Thou, His own a-noint-ed one,
Thou, who once was thus be-reft That Thine own might ne'er be left,

None can tell what pangs un-known Hold Thee si-lent and a-lone.
Till th'ap-point-ed time is nigh, Till the Lamb of God may die.
Thou dost ask Him, can it be? "Why hast Thou for-sak-en Me?"
Teach me by that bit-ter cry In the gloom to know Thee nigh. A-men.

JESUS CHRIST: PASSION

163 WHAT WONDROUS LOVE IS THIS
WONDROUS LOVE Irregular

Folk text
J. Mercer's *Cluster of Spiritual Songs*, 1836

Folk Hymn
"Christopher" in W. Hauser's *Hesperian Harp*, 1848
Harmony by Alice Parker, 1966

1. What won-drous love is this, O my soul, O my soul! What won-drous love is this, O my soul! What won-drous love is this that caused the Lord of bliss To bear the dread-ful curse for my soul, for my soul, To bear the dread-ful curse for my soul?

2. When I was sink-ing down, sink-ing down, sink-ing down, When I was sink-ing down, sink-ing down, When I was sink-ing down be-neath God's right-eous frown, Christ laid a-side His crown for my soul, for my soul, Christ laid a-side His crown for my soul.

3. To God and to the Lamb I will sing, I will sing, To God and to the Lamb I will sing, To God and to the Lamb who is the great I am, While mil-lions join the theme, I will sing, I will sing, While mil-lions join the theme, I will sing.

4. And when from death I'm free I'll sing on, I'll sing on, And when from death I'm free, I'll sing on, And when from death I'm free, I'll sing and joy-ful be, And through e-ter-ni-ty I'll sing on, I'll sing on, And through e-ter-ni-ty I'll sing on.

JESUS CHRIST: PASSION

WERE YOU THERE 164

WERE YOU THERE Irregular

Negro Spiritual

Traditional Negro Melody

1. Were you there when they cru-ci-fied my Lord?
2. Were you there when they nailed Him to the tree?
3. Were you there when they laid Him in the tomb?
4. Were you there when He rose up from the dead?

Were you there when they cru-ci-fied my Lord?
Were you there when they nailed Him to the tree?
Were you there when they laid Him in the tomb?
Were you there when He rose up from the dead?

O!

Sometimes it causes me to trem-ble, trem-ble, trem-ble.

Were you there when they cru-ci-fied my Lord?
Were you there when they nailed Him to the tree?
Were you there when they laid Him in the tomb?
Were you there when He rose up from the dead?

JESUS CHRIST: PASSION

165 WHEN I SURVEY
ROCKINGHAM OLD L.M.

Isaac Watts†, 1707
A. Williams' *Supplement to Psalmody* . . . , c. 1780
Adapted by Edward Miller, 1790

1. When I survey the wondrous cross, On which the Prince of glory died, My richest gain I count but loss, And pour contempt on all my pride.
2. Forbid it, Lord, that I should boast, Save in the death of Christ my God; All the vain things that charm me most, I sacrifice them to His blood.
3. See, from His head, His hands, His feet, Sorrow and love flow mingled down; Did e'er such love and sorrow meet, Or thorns compose so rich a crown?
4. Were the whole realm of nature mine, That were a present far too small; Love so amazing, so divine, Demands my soul, my life, my all.

166 CROSS OF JESUS, CROSS OF SORROW
CROSS OF JESUS 8.7.8.7.

William John Sparrow Simpson†, 1887
John Stainer, 1887

1. Cross of Jesus, cross of sorrow, Where the blood of Christ was shed,
2. Here the King of all the ages, Thron'd in light ere worlds could be,
3. O mysterious condescending! O abandonment sublime!
4. Evermore for human failure By His passion we can plead;

JESUS CHRIST: PASSION

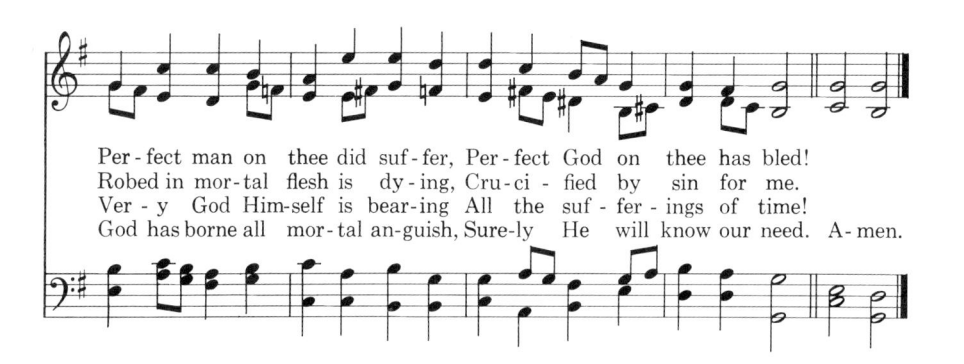

Per - fect man on thee did suf - fer, Per - fect God on thee has bled!
Robed in mor - tal flesh is dy - ing, Cru - ci - fied by sin for me.
Ver - y God Him-self is bear-ing All the suf - fer - ings of time!
God has borne all mor - tal an-guish, Sure-ly He will know our need. A-men.

WHEN I SURVEY 167
HAMBURG L.M.

Isaac Watts, 1707
Lowell Mason, 1824

1 When I sur - vey the won - drous cross, On which the Prince of glo - ry died, My rich - est gain I count but loss, And pour con-tempt on all my pride.
2 For - bid it, Lord, that I should boast, Save in the death of Christ my God; All the vain things that charm me most, I sac - ri - fice them to His blood.
3 See, from His head, His hands, His feet, Sor - row and love flow min - gled down; Did e'er such love and sor - row meet, Or thorns com-pose so rich a crown?
4 Were the whole realm of na - ture mine, That were a pres - ent far too small; Love so a - maz - ing, so di - vine, De-mands my soul, my life, my all. A - men.

JESUS CHRIST: PASSION

168 CHRIST, THE LIFE OF ALL THE LIVING
ALLE MENSCHEN MÜSSEN STERBEN 8.7.8.7.7.7.7.7.

Ernst Christoph Homburg, 1659
Jesu, meines Lebens Leben
Tr. Catherine Winkworth†, 1863

Christoph Anton, c. 1642

1 Christ, the life of all the liv-ing, Christ, the death of death our foe,
  Who Thyself for us once giv-ing To the dark-est depths of woe,
  Pa-tient-ly didst yield Thy breath But to save my soul from death;
  Thousand, thousand thanks shall be, Bless-ed Je-sus, brought to Thee.

2 Thou, ah Thou, hast tak-en on Thee Bit-ter strokes, a cru-el rod;
  Pain and scorn were heaped up-on Thee, O Thou sin-less Son of God;
  On-ly thus for me to win Res-cue from the bonds of sin;
  Thousand, thousand thanks shall be, Bless-ed Je-sus, brought to Thee.

3 Then for all that wrought our par-don, For Thy sor-rows deep and sore,
  For Thine an-guish in the gar-den, I will thank Thee ev-er-more;
  Thank Thee with my lat-est breath For Thy sad and cru-el death,
  For that last and bit-ter cry, And shall praise Thee, Lord, on high. A-men.

JESUS CHRIST: PASSION

IN THE CROSS OF CHRIST I GLORY 169

RATHBUN 8.7.8.7.

John Bowring, 1825 — Ithamar Conkey, 1849

1. In the cross of Christ I glory, Tow-'ring o'er the wrecks of time;
All the light of sa-cred sto-ry, Gath-ers round its head sub-lime.

2. When the woes of life o'er-take me; Hopes de-ceive and fears an-noy,
Nev-er shall the cross for-sake me; Lo! it glows with peace and joy.

3. When the sun of bliss is beam-ing Light and love up-on my way,
From the cross the ra-diance stream-ing, Adds more lus-ter to the day.

4. Bane and bless-ing, pain and plea-sure, By the cross are sanc-ti-fied;
Peace is there that knows no mea-sure, Joys that through all time a-bide.

ALAS! AND DID MY SAVIOR BLEED 170

MARTYRDOM C.M.

Isaac Watts†, 1707 — Hugh Wilson, late 18th century
Adapted by Robert Archibald Smith, 1825

1. A-las! and did my Sav-ior bleed? And did my Sov-ereign die?
Would He de-vote that sa-cred head, For sin-ners such as I?

2. Was it for crimes that I have done He groaned up-on the tree?
A-maz-ing pit-y! grace un-known! And love be-yond de-gree!

3. Well might the sun in dark-ness hide, And shut his glo-ries in,
When Christ, the might-y Mak-er, died For man, the crea-ture's sin.

4. But drops of grief can ne'er re-pay The debt of love I owe;
Here, Lord, I give my-self a-way, 'Tis all that I can do.

JESUS CHRIST: PASSION

171 BENEATH THE CROSS OF JESUS

ST. CHRISTOPHER 7.6.8.6.8.6.8.6.

Elizabeth C. Clephane, 1872
Frederick Charles Maker, 1881

1. Beneath the cross of Jesus I fain would take my stand,
The shadow of a mighty rock Within a weary land;
A home within the wilderness, A rest upon the way,
From the burning of the noontide heat, And the burden of the day.

2. Upon that cross of Jesus My eye at times can see
The very dying form of One Who suffered there for me;
And from my smitten heart with tears Two wonders I confess,
The wonders of His glorious love And my unworthiness.

3. I take, O cross, thy shadow For my abiding place;
I ask no other sunshine than The sunshine of His face,
Content to let the world go by, To know no gain nor loss,
My sinful self my only shame, My glory all the cross.

JESUS CHRIST: PASSION

MY SONG IS LOVE UNKNOWN 172

LOVE UNKNOWN 6.6.6.6.4.4.4.4.

Samuel Crossman, 1664
John Ireland, 1925

1. My song is love un-known, My Sav-ior's love to me, Love to the love-less shown, That they might love - ly be. O who am I, That for my sake My Lord should take Frail flesh, and die?

2. He came from His blest throne, Sal - va - tion to be - stow; But men made strange, and none The longed-for Christ would know. But O, my friend, My friend in - deed, Who at my need His life did spend!

3. Some-times they strew His way, And His sweet prais - es sing; Re - sound-ing all the day Ho - san - nas to their king. Then "Cru - ci - fy!" Is all their breath, And for His death They thirst and cry.

4. Here might I stay and sing, No sto - ry so di - vine; Nev - er was love, dear King, Nev - er was grief like Thine. This is my friend, In whose sweet praise I all my days Could glad - ly spend.

JESUS CHRIST: PASSION

173 O LAMB OF GOD ALL HOLY

O LAMM GOTTES 7.7.7.7.7.7.7.8.

Based on *Agnus Dei*
Nicolaus Decius, 1522 or 1523
O Lamm Gottes unschuldig
Tr. Arthur Tozer Russell, 1851

Nicolaus Decius, 1542

1. O Lamb of God all holy! Who on the cross didst suffer, And patient still and lowly, Thyself to scorn didst offer; Our sins by Thee were taken, Or hope had us forsaken: Have mercy on us, O Jesus!

2. O Lamb of God all holy! Who on the cross didst suffer, And patient still and lowly, Thyself to scorn didst offer; Our sins by Thee were taken, Or hope had us forsaken: Have mercy on us, O Jesus!

3. O Lamb of God all holy! Who on the cross didst suffer, And patient still and lowly, Thyself to scorn didst offer; Our sins by Thee were taken, Or hope had us forsaken: Thy peace be with us, O Jesus! Amen.

JESUS CHRIST: PASSION

THE DAY OF RESURRECTION 174

LANCASHIRE 7.6.7.6.D.

John of Damascus, d. c. 750
Ἀναστάσεως ἡμέρα
Tr. John Mason Neale‡, 1862

Henry Thomas Smart, 1835

1. The day of res-ur-rec-tion! Earth, tell it out a-broad; The pass-o-ver of glad-ness, The pass-o-ver of God. From death to life e-ter-nal, From this world to the sky, Our Christ hath brought us o-ver With hymns of vic-to-ry.

2. Our hearts be pure from e-vil, That we may see a-right The Lord in rays e-ter-nal Of res-ur-rec-tion light; And, lis-t'ning to His ac-cents, May hear, so calm and plain, His own "All hail!" and hear-ing, May raise the vic-tor strain.

3. Now let the heav'ns be joy-ful, Let earth her song be-gin; Let the round world keep tri-umph, And all that is there-in; In-vis-i-ble and vis-i-ble, Their notes let all things blend, For Christ the Lord hath ris-en, Our joy that hath no end.

JESUS CHRIST: RESURRECTION

175 LIFT YOUR GLAD VOICES
RESURRECTION Irregular

Henry Waret, 1817 — John Edgar Gould, c. 1879

1. Lift your glad voic-es in tri-umph on high, For Jesus hath ris-en, and man shall not die; Vain were the ter-rors that gath-ered a-round Him, And short the do-min-ion of death and the grave.
2. He burst from the fet-ters of dark-ness that bound Him, Re-splend-ent in glo-ry, to live and to save: Loud was the cho-rus of an-gels on high, The Sav-ior hath ris-en, and man shall not die.
3. Glo-ry to God, in full an-thems of joy; The be-ing He gave us death can-not de-stroy: Sad were the life we may part with to-mor-row, If tears were our birth-right, and death were our end.
4. But Je-sus hath cheered the dark val-ley of sor-row, And bade us, im-mor-tal, to heav-en as-cend: Lift then your voic-es in tri-umph on high, For Je-sus hath ris-en, and man shall not die.

176 THE LORD IS RISEN INDEED
BENJAMIN S.M.

Thomas Kelly, 1802 — Arranged from Franz Joseph Haydn, 1798

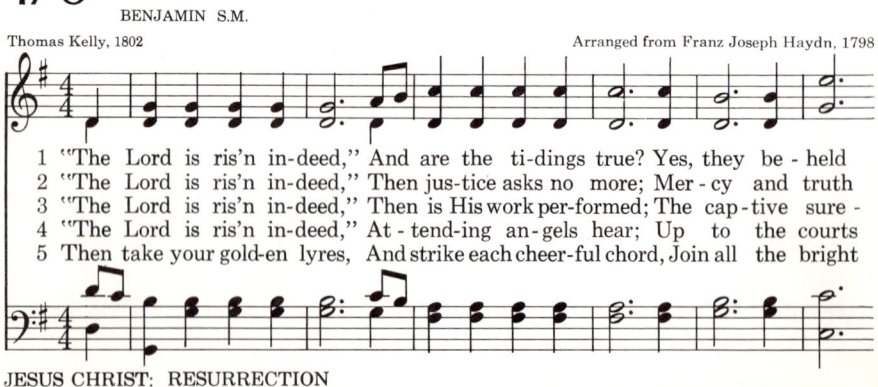

1. "The Lord is ris'n in-deed," And are the ti-dings true? Yes, they be-held
2. "The Lord is ris'n in-deed," Then jus-tice asks no more; Mer-cy and truth
3. "The Lord is ris'n in-deed," Then is His work per-formed; The cap-tive sure-
4. "The Lord is ris'n in-deed," At-tend-ing an-gels hear; Up to the courts
5. Then take your gold-en lyres, And strike each cheer-ful chord, Join all the bright

JESUS CHRIST: RESURRECTION

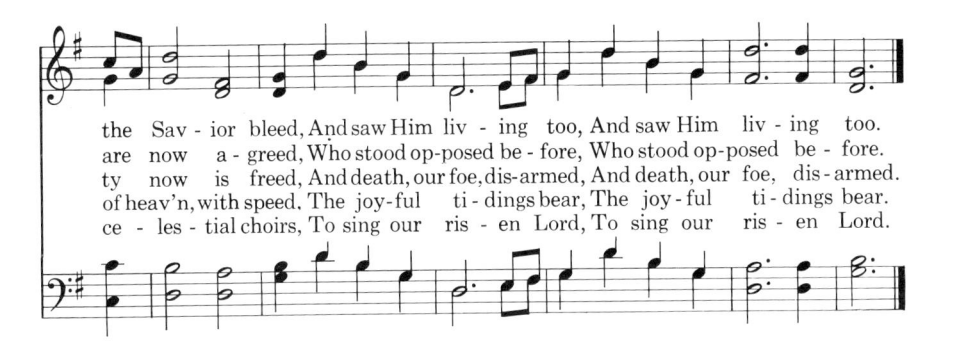

the Sav - ior bleed, And saw Him liv - ing too, And saw Him liv - ing too.
are now a - greed, Who stood op-posed be - fore, Who stood op-posed be - fore.
ty now is freed, And death, our foe, dis-armed, And death, our foe, dis-armed.
of heav'n, with speed. The joy-ful ti - dings bear, The joy-ful ti - dings bear.
ce - les - tial choirs, To sing our ris - en Lord, To sing our ris - en Lord.

CHRIST THE LORD IS RISEN AGAIN 177
STRAF MICH NICHT IN DEINEM ZORN 7.7.7.7. with Refrain

Michael Weisse, 1531
Christus ist erstanden
Tr. Catherine Winkworth, 1858

Hundert . . . geistliche Arien, Dresden, 1694

1 Christ the Lord is risen a - gain! Christ hath bro - ken ev - ery chain!
2 He who gave for us His life, Who for us en - dured the strife,
3 He who bore all pain and loss Com - fort - less up - on the cross,
4 He who slum-ber'd in the grave, Is ex - alt - ed now to save;

Hark, the an - gels shout for joy, Sing - ing ev - er - more on high,
Is our Pas - chal Lamb to - day! We too sing for joy, and say:
Lives in glo - ry now on high, Pleads for us and hears our cry:
Now through Chris-ten-dom it rings That the Lamb is King of kings!

REFRAIN
Christ the Lord, Christ the Lord, Christ the Lord is ris - en! Al - le - lu - ia!

5 Now He bids us tell abroad,
How the lost may be restored,
How the penitent forgiven,
How we too may enter heav'n.
(REFRAIN)

6 Thou our Paschal Lamb indeed,
Christ, today Thy people feed;
Take our sins and guilt away,
That we all may sing for aye,
(REFRAIN)

JESUS CHRIST: RESURRECTION

178 COME, YE FAITHFUL, RAISE THE STRAIN

AVE VIRGO VIRGINUM (GAUDEAMUS PARITER) 7.6.7.6.D.

John of Damascus, d. c. 750
Ἀΐσωμεν πάντες λαοί
Tr. John Mason Neale, 1859

Johann Horn, 1544

1. Come, ye faithful, raise the strain Of triumphant gladness;
   God hath brought His Israel Into joy from sadness;
   Loosed from Pharaoh's bitter yoke Jacob's sons and daughters;
   Led them with unmoistened foot Through the Red Sea waters.

2. 'Tis the spring of souls today; Christ hath burst His prison,
   And from three days' sleep in death As a sun hath risen;
   All the winter of our sins, Long and dark, is flying
   From His light, to whom we give Laud and praise undying.

3. Now the queen of seasons, bright With the day of splendor,
   With the royal feast of feasts, Comes its joy to render;
   Comes to glad Jerusalem, Who with true affection
   Welcomes in unwearied strains Jesus' resurrection.

4. Neither might the gates of death, Nor the tomb's dark portal,
   Nor the watchers, nor the seal Hold Thee as a mortal:
   But today amidst the Twelve Thou didst stand, bestowing
   That Thy peace which evermore Passeth human knowing.

JESUS CHRIST: RESURRECTION

CHRIST THE LORD IS RISEN TODAY 179

EASTER HYMN 7.7.7.7. with Alleluias

Charles Wesley, 1739
Lyra Davidica, 1708

1. "Christ the Lord is ris'n to-day," Sons of men and an-gels say, Raise your joys and tri-umphs high, Sing ye heav'ns, and earth re-ply. Alleluia!
2. Lives a-gain our glo-rious King, Where, O death, is now thy sting? Dy-ing once He all doth save, Where thy vic-to-ry, O grave? Alleluia!
3. Love's re-deem-ing work is done, Fought the fight, the bat-tle won, Death in vain for-bids His rise: Christ has o-pened par-a-dise! Alleluia!
4. Soar we now, where Christ has led? Fol-l'wing our ex-alt-ed Head, Made like Him, like Him we rise, Ours the cross, the grave, the skies! Alleluia!

JESUS CHRIST: RESURRECTION

180 THINE IS THE GLORY

JUDAS MACCABEUS 10.11.11.11. with Refrain

Edmond Bundry, 1884
A toi la gloire, ô Ressuscité
Tr. R. Birch Hoyle‡, 1923

Arranged from George Frideric Handel, 1746

1. Thine is the glo-ry, Ris-en, con-quering Son; End-less is the vic-tory Thou o'er death hast won. An-gels in bright rai-ment Rolled the stone a-way, Kept the fold-ed grave-clothes Where Thy bod-y lay.
2. Lo! Je-sus meets us. Ris-en from the tomb, Lov-ing-ly He greets us, Scat-ters fear and gloom; Let the church with glad-ness Hymns of tri-umph sing, For our Lord now liv-eth; Death hath lost its sting.
3. No more we doubt Thee, Glo-rious Prince of life! Life is nought with-out Thee; Aid us in our strife; Make us more than con-querors, Through Thy death-less love; Bring us safe through Jor-dan To Thy home a-bove.

REFRAIN

Thine is the glo-ry, Ris-en, con-quering Son;

JESUS CHRIST: RESURRECTION

End - less is the vic - t'ry Thou o'er death hast won. A - men.

JOY DAWNED AGAIN ON EASTER DAY 181
PUER NOBIS NASCITUR L.M.

Anonymous 4th or 5th century
Aurora lucis rutilat. Pt. III. *Claro Paschali gaudio*
Tr. *The Hymnary,* 1872

Piae Cantiones, 1582

1 Joy dawned a - gain on Eas - ter day, The sun shone out with fair - er ray, When, to their long - ing eyes re - stored, Th' a - pos - tles saw their ris - en Lord.
2 His ris - en flesh with ra - diance glow'd; His wound-ed hands and side He showed: Those scars their si - lent wit - ness gave That Christ was ris - en from the grave.
3 O Je - sus, King of gen - tle - ness, Do Thou our in - most hearts pos - sess; And we to Thee will ev - er raise The trib - ute of our grate - ful praise.
4 Je - sus, who art the Lord of all, In this our Eas - ter fes - ti - val, From ev - ery weap - on death can wield Thine own re - deemed, Thy peo - ple, shield.
5 All praise, O ris - en Lord, we give To Thee, who, dead, a - gain dost live; To God the Fa - ther e - qual praise, And God the Ho - ly Ghost, we raise. A - men.

JESUS CHRIST: RESURRECTION

182 JESUS CHRIST, MY SURE DEFENSE
JESUS, MEINE ZUVERSICHT 7.8.7.8.7.7.

C. Runge's *Praxis pietatis melica*, 1653
Jesus, meine Zuversicht
Tr. Catherine Winkworth, 1863

C. Runge's *Praxis pietatis melica*, 1653

1. Jesus Christ, my sure defense And my Savior, ever liveth; Knowing this, my confidence Rests upon the hope it giveth, Though the night of death be fraught Still with many an anxious thought.

2. Jesus, my Redeemer, lives! I, too, unto life must waken; He will have me where He is. Shall my courage then be shaken? Shall I fear? Or could the Head Rise and leave His members dead?

3. Nay, too closely am I bound Unto Him by hope forever; Faith's strong hand the rock hath found, Grasped it, and will leave it never; Not the ban of death can part From its Lord the trusting heart.

4. Savior, draw away our heart Now from pleasures base and hollow, Let us there with Thee have part, Here on earth Thy footsteps follow. Fix our hearts beyond the skies, Whither we ourselves would rise. A-men.

JESUS CHRIST: RESURRECTION

ALLELUIA! THE STRIFE IS O'ER 183

VICTORY 8.8.8. with Alleluias

Anonymous, Köln, 1695
Finita jam sunt praelia
Tr. Francis Pott, 1861

Giovanni Pierluigi da Palestrina, 1591
Adapted by William Henry Monk, 1861

Alleluia! Alleluia! Alleluia!

1. The strife is o'er, the battle done;
   The victory of life is won;
   The song of triumph has begun. Alleluia!
2. The powers of death have done their worst,
   But Christ their legions hath dispersed;
   Let shout of holy joy outburst. Alleluia!
3. The three sad days have quickly sped;
   He rises glorious from the dead;
   All glory to our risen Head! Alleluia!
4. Lord, by the stripes which wounded Thee,
   From death's dread sting Thy servants free,
   That we may live and sing to Thee, Alleluia! A-men.

JESUS CHRIST: RESURRECTION

184 REJOICE, THE LORD IS KING

ARTHUR'S SEAT 6.6.6.6. with Refrain

Charles Wesley, 1746

From John Goss, d. 1880
Arranged in *Hymns and Songs of Praise*, 1874

1. Rejoice, the Lord is King: Your Lord and King adore; Mortals, give thanks and sing, And triumph evermore:
2. Jesus, the Savior, reigns, The God of truth and love; When He had purged our stains, He took His seat above:
3. His kingdom cannot fail, He rules o'er earth and heav'n; The keys of death and hell Are to our Jesus giv'n:
4. He sits at God's right hand Till all His foes submit, And bow to His command, And fall beneath His feet:

Refrain: Lift up your heart, lift up your voice; Rejoice, again I say, rejoice. A-men.

JESUS CHRIST: ASCENSION

HAIL THE DAY THAT SEES HIM RISE 185

LLANFAIR 7.7.7.7. with Alleluias

Charles Wesley‡, 1739
Robert Williams, 1817

1. Hail the day that sees Him rise, Alleluia!
Glorious to His native skies; Alleluia!
Christ, awhile to mortals giv'n, Alleluia!
Enters now the highest heav'n. Alleluia!

2. There the glorious triumph waits; Alleluia!
Lift your heads, eternal gates, Alleluia!
Wide unfold the radiant scene, Alleluia!
Take the King of glory in! Alleluia!

3. See, He lifts His hands above! Alleluia!
See, He shows the prints of love! Alleluia!
Hark! His gracious lips bestow, Alleluia!
Blessings on His church below. Alleluia!

4. Lord, beyond our mortal sight, Alleluia!
Raise our hearts to reach Thy height, Alleluia!
There Thy face unclouded see, Alleluia!
Find our heav'n of heav'ns in Thee! Alleluia! A-men.

JESUS CHRIST: ASCENSION

186 LOOK, YE SAINTS
CORONAE 8.7.8.7.4.7.

Thomas Kelly, 1809
William Henry Monk, 1871

1. Look, ye saints, the sight is glorious: See the "Man of Sorrows" now; From the fight returned victorious, Every knee to Him shall bow; Crown Him! Crown Him! Crowns become the Victor's brow.
2. Crown the Savior, angels, crown Him; Rich the trophies Jesus brings; In the seat of pow'r enthrone Him, While the vault of heaven rings: Crown Him! Crown Him! Crown the Savior "King of kings."
3. Sinners in derision crowned Him, Mocking thus the Savior's claim; Saints and angels crowd around Him, Own His title, praise His name: Crown Him! Crown Him! Spread abroad the Victor's fame.
4. Hark, those bursts of acclamation! Hark, those loud triumphant chords! Jesus takes the highest station; O what joy the sight affords: Crown Him! Crown Him! "King of kings, and Lord of lords." A-men.

187 MAJESTIC SWEETNESS SITS ENTHRONED
ORTONVILLE C.M.

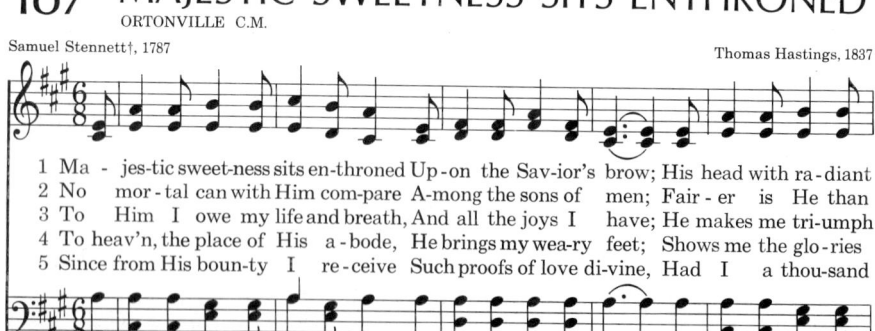

Samuel Stennett†, 1787
Thomas Hastings, 1837

1. Majestic sweetness sits enthroned Upon the Savior's brow; His head with radiant
2. No mortal can with Him compare Among the sons of men; Fairer is He than
3. To Him I owe my life and breath, And all the joys I have; He makes me triumph
4. To heav'n, the place of His abode, He brings my weary feet; Shows me the glories
5. Since from His bounty I receive Such proofs of love divine, Had I a thousand

JESUS CHRIST: ASCENSION

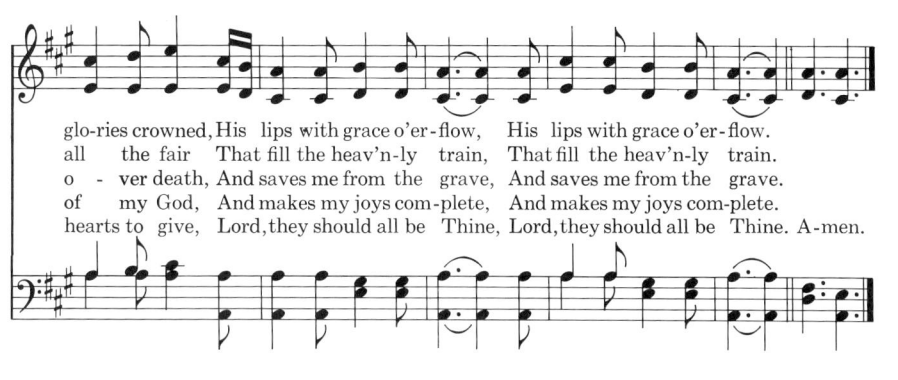

glo-ries crowned, His lips with grace o'er-flow, His lips with grace o'er-flow.
all the fair That fill the heav'n-ly train, That fill the heav'n-ly train.
o - ver death, And saves me from the grave, And saves me from the grave.
of my God, And makes my joys com-plete, And makes my joys com-plete.
hearts to give, Lord, they should all be Thine, Lord, they should all be Thine. A-men.

RISE, GLORIOUS CONQUEROR 188

DORT 6.6.4.6.6.6.4.

Matthew Bridges, 1848   Lowell Mason, 1832

1 Rise, glo-rious Con-qu'ror, rise In - to Thy na - tive skies;
2 Vic - tor o'er death and hell, Che - ru - bic le - gions swell
3 En - ter, in - car - nate God! No feet but Thine have trod
4 Li - on of Ju - dah, hail! And let Thy name pre - vail

As - sume Thy right; And where in many a fold The clouds are
The ra - diant train: Prais - es all heav'n in - spire; Each an - gel
The ser - pent down: Blow the full trum - pets, blow, Wid - er yon
From age to age: Lord of the roll - ing years, Claim for Thine

back-ward rolled, Pass through those gates of gold, And reign in light.
sweeps his lyre, And claps his wings of fire, Thou Lamb once slain!
por - tals throw, Sav - ior, tri - um-phant, go, And take Thy crown!
own the spheres, For Thou hast bought with tears Thy her - it - age. A - men.

JESUS CHRIST: ASCENSION

189 THE HEAD THAT ONCE WAS CROWNED
ST. MAGNUS C.M.

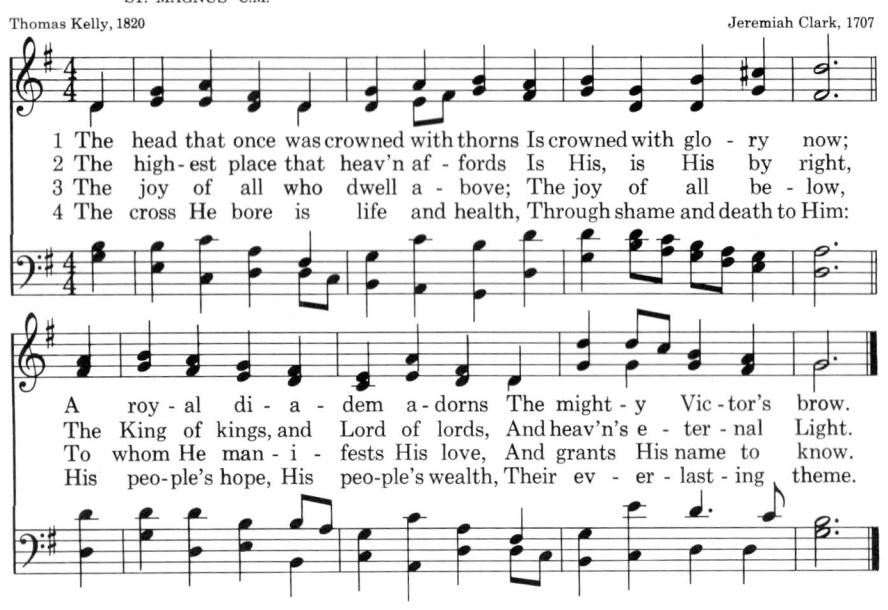

Thomas Kelly, 1820 — Jeremiah Clark, 1707

1. The head that once was crowned with thorns Is crowned with glory now;
   A royal diadem adorns The mighty Victor's brow.
2. The highest place that heav'n affords Is His, is His by right,
   The King of kings, and Lord of lords, And heav'n's eternal Light.
3. The joy of all who dwell above; The joy of all below,
   To whom He manifests His love, And grants His name to know.
4. The cross He bore is life and health, Through shame and death to Him:
   His people's hope, His people's wealth, Their everlasting theme.

190 SING WE TRIUMPHANT HYMNS
DEO GRACIAS L.M.

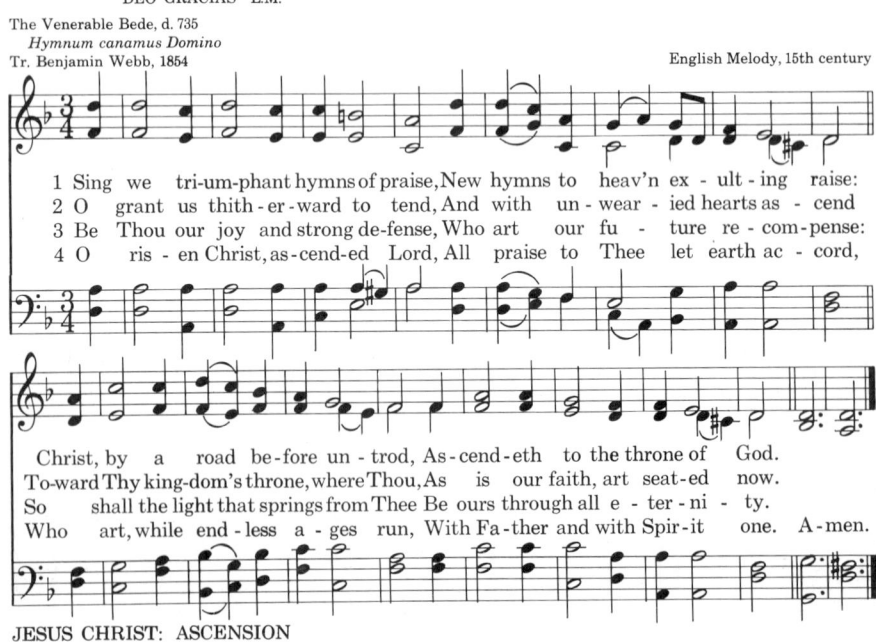

The Venerable Bede, d. 735
Hymnum canamus Domino
Tr. Benjamin Webb, 1854 — English Melody, 15th century

1. Sing we triumphant hymns of praise, New hymns to heav'n exulting raise;
   Christ, by a road before untrod, Ascendeth to the throne of God.
2. O grant us thitherward to tend, And with unwearied hearts ascend
   Toward Thy kingdom's throne, where Thou, As is our faith, art seated now.
3. Be Thou our joy and strong defense, Who art our future recompense;
   So shall the light that springs from Thee Be ours through all eternity.
4. O risen Christ, ascended Lord, All praise to Thee let earth accord,
   Who art, while endless ages run, With Father and with Spirit one. Amen.

JESUS CHRIST: ASCENSION

CROWN HIM WITH MANY CROWNS 191
DIADEMATA S.M.D.

Matthew Bridges, 1851   George Job Elvey, 1868

1. Crown Him with man-y crowns, The Lamb up-on His throne;
Hark! how the heav'n-ly an-them drowns All mu-sic but its own:
A-wake, my soul, and sing Of Him who died for thee,
And hail Him as thy match-less King Through all e-ter-ni-ty.

2. Crown Him the Lord of love: Be-hold His hands and side,
Rich wounds, yet vis-i-ble a-bove, In beau-ty glo-ri-fied:
No an-gel in the sky Can ful-ly bear that sight,
But down-ward bends his burn-ing eye At mys-ter-ies so bright.

3. Crown Him the Lord of peace; Whose pow'r a scep-ter sways
From pole to pole, that wars may cease, Ab-sorbed in prayer and praise:
His reign shall know no end; And round His pierc-ed feet
Fair flow'rs of par-a-dise ex-tend Their fra-grance ev-er sweet.

4. Crown Him the Lord of years, The Po-ten-tate of time;
Cre-a-tor of the roll-ing spheres, In-ef-fa-bly sub-lime:
All hail, Re-deem-er, hail! For Thou hast died for me:
Thy praise shall nev-er, nev-er fail Through-out e-ter-ni-ty. A-men.

JESUS CHRIST: ASCENSION

192 LO! HE COMES
ST. THOMAS (HOLYWOOD) 8.7.8.7.8.7.

John Cennick, 1752
and Charles Wesley, 1758
Alt. by Martin Madan, 1760

John Francis Wade, c. 1743

1. Lo! He comes, with clouds descending Once for our salvation slain; Thousand, thousand saints attending Swell the triumph of His train; Alleluia! Alleluia! God appears on earth to reign.
2. Every eye shall now behold Him Robed in dreadful majesty; Those who set at naught and sold Him, Pierced, and nailed Him to the tree, Deeply wailing, Deeply wailing, Shall the true Messiah see.
3. Every island, sea and mountain, Heav'n and earth shall flee away; All who hate Him must, confounded, Hear the trump proclaim the day: Come to judgment! Come to judgment! Come to judgment! Come away!
4. Now redemption, long expected, See in solemn pomp appear; All His saints, by man rejected, Now shall meet Him in the air: Alleluia! Alleluia! See the day of God appear.
5. Yea, amen! let all adore Thee, High on Thine eternal throne; Savior, take the pow'r and glory, Claim the kingdom for Thine own: Alleluia! Alleluia! Thou shalt reign, and Thou alone.

JESUS CHRIST: SECOND COMING

CHRIST IS COMING! LET CREATION 193
UNSER HERRSCHER 8.7.8.7.8.7.

John Ross MacDuff†, 1853
Joachim Neander, 1680

1. Christ is coming! let creation From her groans and trav-ail cease; Let the glorious proc-la-ma-tion Hope re-store and faith in-crease: Christ is com-ing! Christ is com-ing! Come, Thou blessed Prince of Peace.

2. Earth can now but tell the story Of Thy bitter cross and pain; She shall yet be-hold Thy glory, When Thou com-est back to reign: Christ is com-ing! Christ is com-ing! Let each heart re-peat the strain.

3. Long Thine ex-iles have been pining, Far from rest, and home, and Thee: But, in heav'n-ly ves-tures shining, Soon they shall Thy glo-ry see! Christ is com-ing! Christ is com-ing! Haste the joy-ous ju-bi-lee.

4. With that bless-ed hope be-fore us, Let no harp re-main un-strung; Let the might-y ad-vent cho-rus On-ward roll from tongue to tongue: "Christ is com-ing! Christ is com-ing! Come, Lord Je-sus, quick-ly come!" A-men.

JESUS CHRIST: SECOND COMING

194 REJOICE, ALL YE BELIEVERS
GREENLAND 7.6.7.6.D.

Laurentius Laurenti, 1700
Ermuntert euch, ihr Frommen
Tr. Sarah Borthwick Findlater†, 1854

Johann Michael Haydn, 1806

1. Rejoice, all ye believers! And let your lights appear;
The evening is advancing, A darker night is near.
The Bridegroom is arising, And soon He will draw nigh;
Up! pray, and watch, and wrestle! At midnight comes the cry.

2. See that your lamps are burning; Replenish them with oil;
And wait for your salvation, The end of earthly toil.
The watchers on the mountain Proclaim the Bridegroom near,
Go meet Him as He cometh, With Alleluias clear.

3. Ye saints, who here in patience Your cross and suff'rings bore,
Shall live and reign forever, When sorrow is no more:
Around the throne of glory The Lamb ye shall behold,
In triumph cast before Him Your diadems of gold.

4. Our hope and expectation, O Jesus, now appear;
Arise, Thou Sun so longed for, O'er this benighted sphere.
With hearts and hands uplifted, We plead, O Lord, to see
The day of earth's redemption That brings us home to Thee. A-men.

JESUS CHRIST: SECOND COMING

THE BRIDEGROOM SOON WILL CALL US 195
FREUT EUCH, IHR LIEBEN 7.6.7.6.D.

Johann Walther, 1552
Der Bräutgam wir bald rufen
Tr. Matthias Loy, 1880

Leonhart Schröter, 1587

1. The Bridegroom soon will call us, Come, all ye wedding guests!
May not His voice appall us, While slumber binds our breasts;
May all our lamps be burning, And oil be found in store,
That we, with Him returning, May open find the door.

2. There shall we see delighted Our dear Redeemer's face,
Who leads our souls benighted To glory by His grace;
The patriarchs shall meet us, The prophets' holy band,
Apostles, martyrs, greet us In that celestial land.

3. They will not blush to own us As brothers, sisters dear,
Love ever will be shown us When we with them appear;
We all shall come before Him, Who for us Man became,
As Lord and God adore Him, And ever bless His name.

4. In yonder home shall never Be silent music's voice;
With hearts and lips forever We shall in God rejoice;
The angels shall adore Him, All saints shall sing His praise,
And bring with joy before Him Their sweetest heav'nly lays.

5. In mansions fair and spacious Will God the feast prepare,
And ever kind and gracious, Bid us its riches share;
There bliss that knows no measure From springs of love shall flow,
And never changing pleasure His bounty will bestow.

JESUS CHRIST: SECOND COMING

196 THE KING SHALL COME
ST. MICHEL'S C.M.D.

Based on a Greek text
John Brownlie, 1907

W. Gawler's *Hymns and Psalms*, 1785 to 1788

1. The King shall come when morning dawns, And light triumphant breaks;
When beauty gilds the eastern hills, And life to joy awakes.
But crowned with glory like the sun, That lights that morning sky.

2. O brighter than the rising morn, When He, victorious, rose,
And left the lonesome place of death, Despite the rage of foes;
O brighter than that glorious morn, Shall this fair morning be,
When Christ, our King, in beauty comes, And we His face shall see.

3. The King shall come when morning dawns, And earth's dark night is past;
O haste the rising of that morn, That day that aye shall last.
The King shall come when morning dawns, And light and beauty brings;
Hail! Christ the Lord; Thy people pray Come quickly, King of kings. A-men.

JESUS CHRIST: SECOND COMING

JESUS CAME, THE HEAVENS ADORING 197

BENEDIC ANIMA 8.7.8.7.8.7.

Godfrey Thring, 1864
John Goss, 1869

1. Je-sus came, the heav'ns a-dor-ing, Came with peace from realms on high; Je-sus came for man's re-demp-tion, Low-ly came on earth to die; Al-le-lu-ia! Al-le-lu-ia! Came in deep hu-mil-i-ty.

2. Je-sus comes a-gain in mer-cy, When our hearts are bowed with care; Je-sus comes a-gain in an-swer To an ear-nest, heart-felt prayer; Al-le-lu-ia! Al-le-lu-ia! Comes to save us from de-spair.

3. Je-sus comes to hearts re-joic-ing, Bring-ing news of sins for-given; Je-sus comes in sounds of glad-ness, Lead-ing souls re-deemed to heav'n; Al-le-lu-ia! Al-le-lu-ia! Now the gate of death is riv'n.

4. Je-sus comes in joy and sor-row, Shares a-like our hopes and fears; Je-sus comes, what-e'er be-falls us, Glads our hearts, and dries our tears; Al-le-lu-ia! Al-le-lu-ia! Cheer-ing e'en our fail-ing years.

5. Je-sus comes on clouds tri-um-phant, When the heav'ns shall pass a-way; Je-sus comes a-gain in glo-ry; Let us then our hom-age pay, Al-le-lu-ia! ev-er sing-ing Till the dawn of end-less day.

JESUS CHRIST: SECOND COMING

198 CHRIST IS THE WORLD'S TRUE LIGHT

O GOTT, DU FROMMER GOTT 6.7.6.7.6.6.6.6.

George Wallace Briggs, 1931

A. Fritsch's *Himmels-Lust*, 1679
Harmony by Johann Sebastian Bach, c. 1740

1. Christ is the world's true light, Its captain of salvation,
The day-star clear and bright Of every man and nation;
New life, new hope awakes, Wher-e'er men own His sway:
Freedom her bondage breaks, And night is turned to day.

2. In Christ all races meet, Their ancient feuds forgetting,
The whole round world complete, From sunrise to its setting:
When Christ is throned as Lord, Men shall forsake their fear,
To plowshare beat the sword, To pruning hook the spear.

3. One Lord, in one great name Unite us all who own Thee;
Cast out our pride and shame That hinder to enthrone Thee;
The world has waited long, Has travailed long in pain;
To heal its ancient wrong, Come, Prince of Peace, and reign. A-men.

JESUS CHRIST: REIGN AND KINGDOM

WAKE THE SONG OF JUBILEE 199

AMBOY 7.7.7.7.D.

Leonard Bacon, 1823
Lowell Mason, 1845

1. Wake the song of ju-bi-lee, Let it ech-o o'er the sea! Now is come the prom-ised hour, Je-sus reigns with sov-'reign power. All ye na-tions, join and sing, Christ of lords and kings is King. Let it sound from shore to shore Je-sus reigns for-ev-er-more.

2. Now the des-ert lands re-joice, And the is-lands join their voice, Yea, the whole cre-a-tion sings, "Je-sus is the King of kings." See the ran-som'd mil-lions stand, Palms of con-quest in their hands, This be-fore the throne their strain, Hell is van-quished, death is slain.

3. Bless-ing, hon-or, glo-ry, might, Are the con-q'ror's na-tive right; Thrones and powers be-fore Him fall, Lamb of God and Lord of all. Time has near-ly reached its sum; All things with the bride say, "Come," Je-sus, whom all worlds a-dore, Come, and reign for-ev-er-more. A-men.

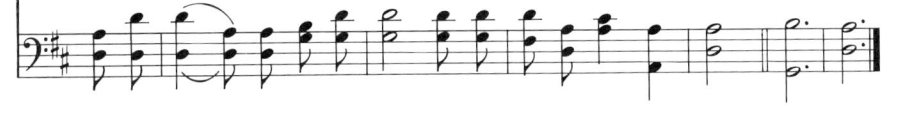

JESUS CHRIST: REIGN AND KINGDOM

200 SEEK YE FIRST THE KINGDOM
KINGDOM OF GOD 6.5.6.5.D.

Norman Elliott, b. 1893

English Melody from *Y Llawlyfr Moliant*, 1890

1. "Seek ye first the king-dom, 'Tis your Fa-ther's will";
   So the voice of Je-sus Bids us fol-low still.
   Sav-ior, we would hear Thee, Fol-low, find, and see;
   And, in life's ad-ven-ture, Thy dis-ci-ples be.

2. As for hid-den trea-sure, Or for match-less pearl,
   When at last dis-cov-ered, Men will sell their all;
   So, when breaks the vi-sion Of that king-dom fair,
   Ours shall be its rich-es And its beau-ty rare.

3. As the si-lent leav-en Works its se-cret way,
   Or as grows the seed grain Through the night and day;
   Lord, so be the in-crease, Peace-a-ble but sure,
   Of Thy Word with-in us And Thy king-dom's power.

4. As the ten-der seed-ling Grows up tall and strong,
   And the birds of heav-en To its branch-es throng;
   So shall all God's chil-dren From the east and west
   Gath-er to His king-dom, In its shad-ow rest.

5. Hum-blest shall be great-est, Poor in spir-it reign;
   Home shall come the child-like Born through Thee a-gain;
   Ea-ger hearts ar-rive there On the pil-grim's road.
   Hail! The king-dom glo-rious Of the liv-ing God!

JESUS CHRIST: REIGN AND KINGDOM

HARK! TEN THOUSAND HARPS 201

HARWELL 8.7.8.7.7.7. with Refrain

Thomas Kelly, 1806
Lowell Mason, 1840

1. Hark! ten thousand harps and voices Sound the note of praise above;
2. King of glory! reign forever, Thine an everlasting crown;
3. Savior! hasten Thine appearing; Bring, O bring the glorious day,

Jesus reigns, and heav'n rejoices; Jesus reigns, the God of love.
Nothing, from Thy love, shall sever Those whom Thou hast made Thine own;
When, the awful summons hearing, Heav'n and earth shall pass away;

See, He sits on yonder throne; Jesus rules the world alone.
Happy objects of Thy grace Destined to behold Thy face.
Then, with golden harps we'll sing, "Glory, glory to our King!"

Alleluia, Alleluia, Alleluia! Amen.

JESUS CHRIST: REIGN AND KINGDOM

202 O WHEREFORE DO THE NATIONS RAGE
UXBRIDGE L.M.

Based on Psalm 2
Psalter, 1912

Lowell Mason, 1830

1. O where-fore do the na-tions rage, And kings and rul-ers strive in vain, A-gainst the Lord of earth and heav'n To o-ver-throw Mes-si-ah's reign?
2. Their strength is weak-ness in the sight Of Him who sits en-throned a-bove; He speaks, and judg-ments fall on them Who tempt His wrath and scorn His love.
3. By God's de-cree His Son re-ceives The na-tions for His her-it-age; The con-qu'ring Christ su-preme shall reign As King of kings, from age to age.

203 JESUS SHALL REIGN
DUKE STREET L.M.

Based on Psalm 72
Isaac Watts, 1719

H. Boyd's *Psalm and Hymn Tunes*, 1793
Attributed to John Hatton, d. 1793

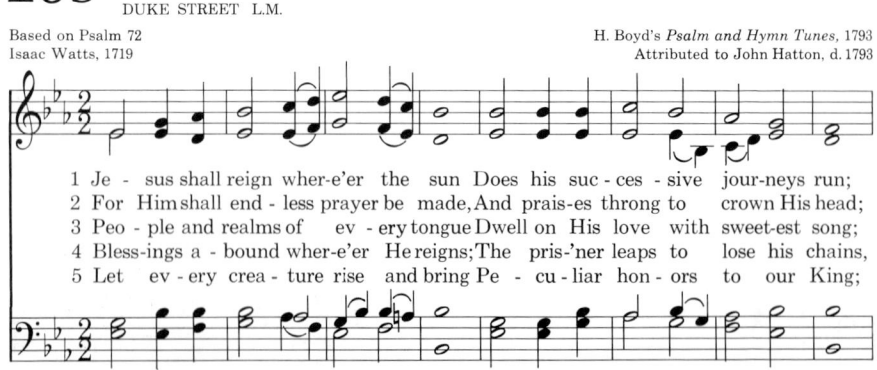

1. Je-sus shall reign wher-e'er the sun Does his suc-ces-sive jour-neys run;
2. For Him shall end-less prayer be made, And prais-es throng to crown His head;
3. Peo-ple and realms of ev-ery tongue Dwell on His love with sweet-est song;
4. Bless-ings a-bound wher-e'er He reigns; The pris-'ner leaps to lose his chains,
5. Let ev-ery crea-ture rise and bring Pe-cu-liar hon-ors to our King;

JESUS CHRIST: REIGN AND KINGDOM

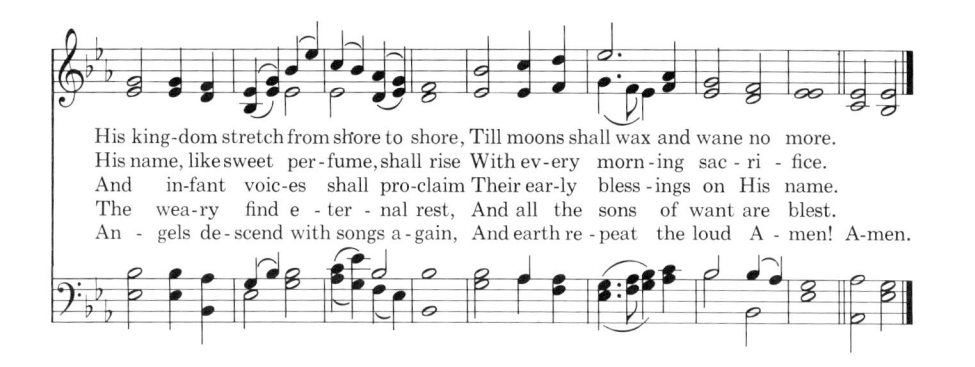

His kingdom stretch from shore to shore, Till moons shall wax and wane no more.
His name, like sweet perfume, shall rise With every morning sacrifice.
And infant voices shall proclaim Their early blessings on His name.
The weary find eternal rest, And all the sons of want are blest.
Angels descend with songs again, And earth repeat the loud Amen! Amen.

THE LORD IS KING 204

CREATION L.M.

Josiah Conder, 1824

Arranged from Franz Joseph Haydn, 1798

1. The Lord is King! lift up your voice, O earth; and all ye heav'ns, rejoice: From world to world the joy shall ring, "The Lord omnipotent is King!"
2. The Lord is King! who then shall dare Resist His will, distrust His care, Or murmur at His wise decrees, Or doubt His royal promises?
3. The Lord is King! Child of the dust, The Judge of all the earth is just; Holy and true are all His ways; Let every creature speak His praise.
4. One Lord, one empire, all secures; He reigns, and life and death are yours: Through earth and heav'n one song shall ring, "The Lord omnipotent is King!"

JESUS CHRIST: REIGN AND KINGDOM

205 O SPIRIT OF LIFE

O HEILIGER GEIST 10.8.8.8.10.

Johann Niedling, 1651
O Heiliger Geist
Tr. John Caspar Mattes, 1913

Geistliche Kirchengesang, Köln, 1623

1. O Spirit of Life, O Spirit of God, In every need Thou bringest aid, Thou camest forth from God's great throne, From God, the Father and the Son; O Spirit of Life, O Spirit of God.
2. O Spirit of Life, O Spirit of God, Make us to love Thy sacred Word; The holy flame of love impart, That charity may warm each heart; O Spirit of Life, O Spirit of God.
3. O Spirit of Life, O Spirit of God, Increase our faith in our dear Lord; Unless Thy grace the power should give, None can believe in Christ and live; O Spirit of Life, O Spirit of God.
4. O Spirit of Life, O Spirit of God, Enlighten us by Thy blest Word; Teach us to know the Father's love, And His dear Son, who reigns above: O Spirit of Life, O Spirit of God. Amen.

206 GRACIOUS SPIRIT! LOVE DIVINE

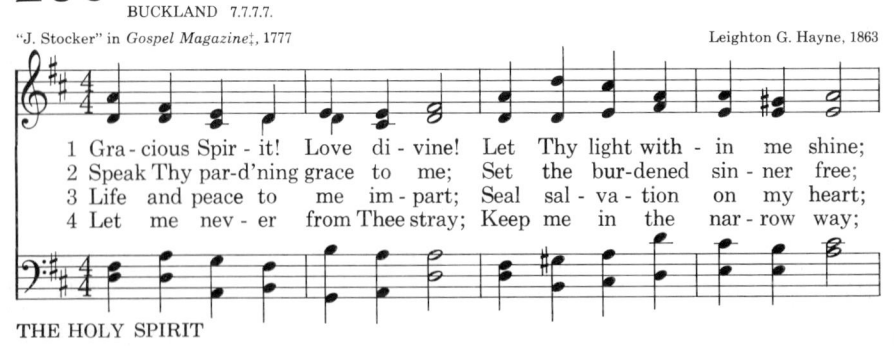

BUCKLAND 7.7.7.7.

"J. Stocker" in *Gospel Magazine*, 1777

Leighton G. Hayne, 1863

1. Gracious Spirit! Love divine! Let Thy light within me shine;
2. Speak Thy pard'ning grace to me; Set the burdened sinner free;
3. Life and peace to me impart; Seal salvation on my heart;
4. Let me never from Thee stray; Keep me in the narrow way;

THE HOLY SPIRIT

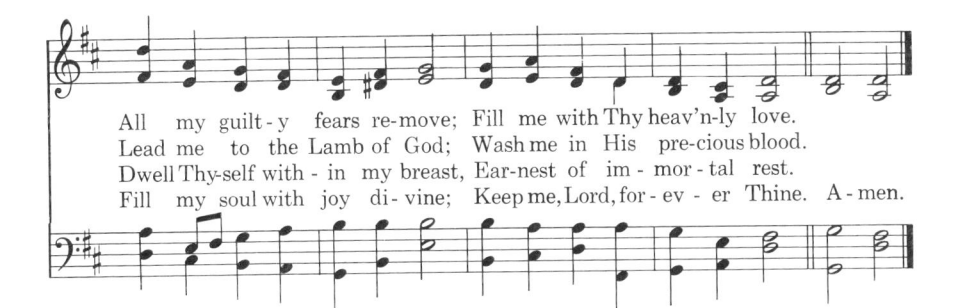

All my guilt-y fears re-move; Fill me with Thy heav'n-ly love.
Lead me to the Lamb of God; Wash me in His pre-cious blood.
Dwell Thy-self with-in my breast, Ear-nest of im-mor-tal rest.
Fill my soul with joy di-vine; Keep me, Lord, for-ev-er Thine. A-men.

HOLY SPIRIT, TRUTH DIVINE 207

WEST END 7.7.7.7.

Samuel Longfellow, 1864
Alice Parker, 1966

1 Ho-ly Spir-it, truth di-vine, Dawn up-on this
2 Ho-ly Spir-it, love di-vine, Glow with-in this
3 Ho-ly Spir-it, power di-vine, Fill and nerve this
4 Ho-ly Spir-it, peace di-vine, Still this rest-less
5 Ho-ly Spir-it, right di-vine, King with-in my

soul of mine; Word of God, and in-ward light,
heart of mine; Kin-dle ev-ery high de-sire;
will of mine; By Thee may I strong-ly live;
heart of mine; Speak to calm this toss-ing sea,
con-science reign; Be my law, and I shall be

Wake my spir-it, clear my sight.
Per-ish self in Thy pure fire.
Brave-ly bear, and no-bly strive.
Stayed in Thy tran-quil-li-ty.
Firm-ly bound, for-ev-er free. A-men.

THE HOLY SPIRIT

208 O HOLY SPIRIT, ENTER IN

WIE SCHÖN LEUCHTET DER MORGENSTERN 8.8.7.8.8.8.7.4.12.8.

Michael Schirmer, 1640
O heilger Geist, kehr bei uns ein
Tr. Catherine Winkworth, 1863

Philipp Nicolai, 1599

1. O Holy Spirit, enter in, Among these hearts Thy work begin, Thy temple deign to make us; Sun of the soul, Thou Light divine, Around and in us brightly shine, To strength and gladness wake us. Where Thou shinest, life from heaven There is given;
2. Left to ourselves, we shall but stray; O lead us on the narrow way, With wisest counsel guide us; And give us steadfastness, that we May henceforth truly follow Thee, What-ever woes betide us: Heal Thou gently hearts now broken, Give some token
3. O mighty rock, O source of life, Let Thy dear word 'mid doubt and strife Be so within us burning, That we be faithful unto death, In Thy pure love and holy faith, From Thee true wisdom learning! Lord, Thy graces on us shower; By Thy power
4. Grant that our days, while life shall last, In purest holiness be passed; Our minds so rule and strengthen That they may rise o'er things of earth, The hopes and joys that here have birth; And if our course Thou lengthen, Keep Thou pure, Lord, from offenses Heart and senses;

THE HOLY SPIRIT

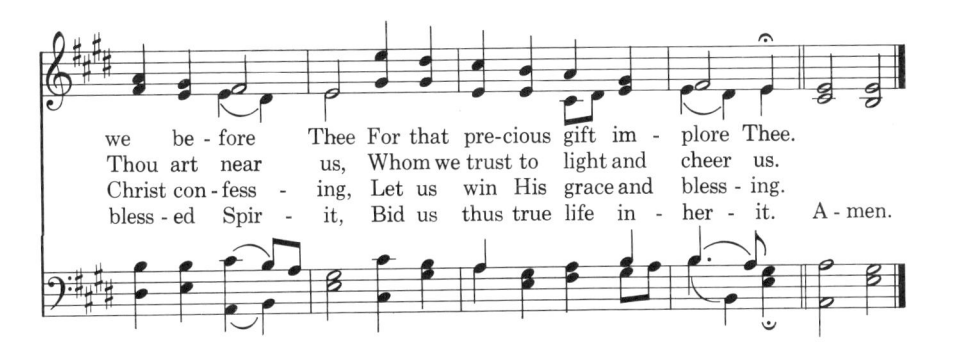

we be-fore Thee For that pre-cious gift im-plore Thee.
Thou art near us, Whom we trust to light and cheer us.
Christ con-fess-ing, Let us win His grace and bless-ing.
bless-ed Spir-it, Bid us thus true life in-her-it. A-men.

MAY THE HOLY SPIRIT'S SWORD 209

JU MENG LING 7.9.7.10.4.10.

Tzu-ch'en Chao, b. 1887
Tr. Frank W. Price, b. 1895

Twelfth-century Chinese Melody

1 May the Ho-ly Spir-it's sword My soul with long-ing pierce, pierce my shield.
2 May the Ho-ly Spir-it pray With strong and word-less sighs, sighs for me.
3 May the Ho-ly Spir-it shine In ra-diant truth and make, make me free.

May He take my ev-ery-thing That I on earth may noth-ing se-cret hoard,
May He com-fort bring and lift The press-ing load and care of life a-way.
May He cast all doubt a-way, His joy and peace and rest be ful-ly mine.

I yield, I yield, To Christ, my Sav-ior, Je-sus Christ, my Lord.
To Thee, to Thee, I come, my Mas-ter. Lo, I come to-day.
On me, on me, Be shed Thy love, O Lord, Thy love di-vine.

THE HOLY SPIRIT

210 COME DOWN, O LOVE DIVINE

DOWN AMPNEY 6.6.11.6.6.11.

Bianco da Siena, d. 1434
Discendi, Amor santo
Tr. Richard Frederick Littledale, 1867

Ralph Vaughan Williams, 1906

1. Come down, O Love divine, Seek Thou this soul of mine,
And visit it with Thine own ardor glowing;
O Comforter, draw near, Within my heart appear,
And kindle it, Thy holy flame bestowing.

2. O let it freely burn, Till earthly passions turn
To dust and ashes in its heat consuming;
And let Thy glorious light Shine ever on my sight,
And clothe me round, the while my path illuming.

3. Let holy charity Mine outward vesture be,
And lowliness become my inner clothing;
True lowliness of heart Which takes the humbler part,
And o'er its own shortcomings weeps with loathing.

4. And so the yearning strong, With which the soul will long,
Shall far outpass the power of human telling;
For none can guess its grace, Till he become the place
Wherein the Holy Spirit makes His dwelling.

THE HOLY SPIRIT

COME, O CREATOR SPIRIT, COME 211
VENI CREATOR SPIRITUS L.M.

Ninth century
Veni Creator Spiritus
Tr. Robert Bridges, 1899
Sts. 3 and 5 omitted with permission

Fourth Century Plainsong

1 Come, O Creator Spirit, come, And make within our hearts Thy home; To us Thy grace celestial give, Who of Thy breathing move and live.
2 O Comforter, that name is Thine, Of God most high the gift divine; The well of life, the fire of love, Our souls' anointing from above.
3 Our senses with Thy light inflame, Our hearts to heav'nly love reclaim; Our bodies' poor infirmity With strength perpetual fortify.
4 May we by Thee the Father learn, And know the Son, and Thee discern, Who art of both; and so adore In perfect faith for evermore. Amen.

THE HOLY SPIRIT

212 COME, O COME, THOU QUICKENING SPIRIT
KOMM, O KOMM 8.7.8.7.7.7.

Heinrich Held, d. 1659
Komm, o komm, du Geist des Lebens
Tr. Edward Traill Horn III, b. 1909

Neu-vermehrtes Gesangbuch, Meiningen, 1693

1. Come, O come, Thou quick-ening Spir-it, God be-fore the dawn of time!
Fire our hearts with ho-ly ar-dor, Bless-ed Com-fort-er sub-lime!
Let Thy ra-diance fill our night, Turn-ing dark-ness in-to light.

2. On-ly that which Thou de-sir-est Be our ob-ject; with Thy hand
Lead our ev-ery thought and ac-tion That they be but Thy com-mand.
All our sin-ful-ness e-rase With the in-crease of Thy grace.

3. Bless-ed Spir-it, who re-new-est All that dwell up-on the earth,
When the e-vil one as-sails us Help us prove our heav'n-ly birth;
Arm us with Thy might-y sword In the le-gions of the Lord.

4. Help us keep the faith for-ev-er; Let not Sa-tan, death or shame
Draw us from Thee, or de-prive us Of the hon-or of Thy name.
When the foe would lure us hence, Be Thou, God, our sure de-fense. A-men.

213 SPIRIT OF HOLINESS, DESCEND
NAOMI C.M.

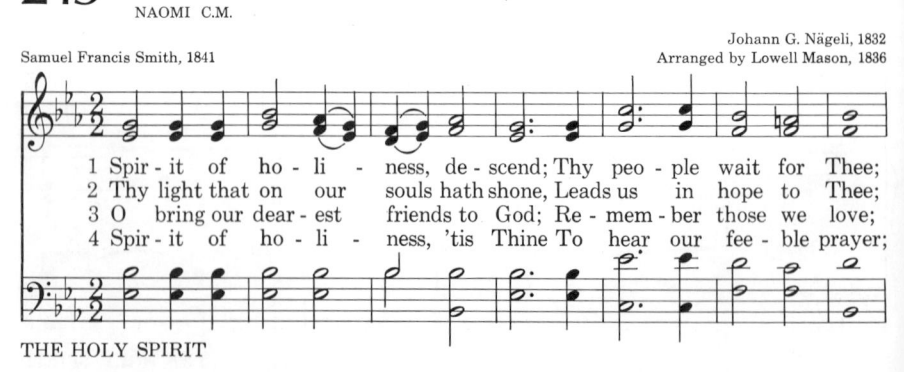

Samuel Francis Smith, 1841

Johann G. Nägeli, 1832
Arranged by Lowell Mason, 1836

1. Spir-it of ho-li-ness, de-scend; Thy peo-ple wait for Thee;
2. Thy light that on our souls hath shone, Leads us in hope to Thee;
3. O bring our dear-est friends to God; Re-mem-ber those we love;
4. Spir-it of ho-li-ness, 'tis Thine To hear our fee-ble prayer;

THE HOLY SPIRIT

Thine ear in kind com - pas - sion lend; Let us Thy mer - cy see.
Let us not feel its rays a - lone, A - lone Thy peo - ple be.
Fit them on earth for Thine a - bode, Fit them for joys a - bove.
Come, for we wait Thy power di - vine, Let us Thy mer - cy share. A-men.

COME, HOLY SPIRIT, COME 214

MORNINGTON S.M.

Joseph Hart, 1759　　　　　　　　　　　　　　　　　　　　Garret Wellesley, c. 1760

1 Come, Ho - ly Spir - it, come! Let Thy bright
2 Re - vive our droop - ing faith, Our doubts and
3 Con - vince us of our sin; Then lead to
4 If Thou, ce - les - tial dove, Thine in - flu -
5 Dwell, there - fore, in our hearts; Our minds from

beams a - rise; Dis - pel all dark - ness from our
fears re - move, And kin - dle in our breasts the
Je - sus' blood, And to our won - d'ring view re -
ence with - draw, What eas - y vic - tims soon we
bond - age free; Then shall we know, and praise, and

minds, And o - pen all our eyes.
flame Of nev - er - dy - ing love.
veal The se - cret love of God.
fall To con - science, wrath, and law!
love, The Fa - ther, Son, and Thee. A - men.

THE HOLY SPIRIT

215 COME, GRACIOUS SPIRIT
BACA L.M.

Simon Browne, 1720, and Others — William Batchelder Bradbury, c. 1858

1. Come, gracious Spirit, heav'nly dove, With light and comfort from above; Be Thou our guardian, Thou our guide, O'er every thought and step preside, O'er every thought and step preside.
2. The light of truth to us display, And make us know and choose Thy way; Plant holy fear in every heart, That we from God may ne'er depart, That we from God may ne'er depart.
3. Lead us to holiness, the road Which we must take to dwell with God; Lead us to Christ, the living way, Nor let us from His pastures stray, Nor let us from His pastures stray.
4. Lead us to God, our final rest, To be with Him forever blest; Lead us to heav'n, its bliss to share, Fullness of joy forever there, Fullness of joy forever there.

216 BREATHE ON ME, BREATH OF GOD
TRENTHAM S.M.

Edwin Hatch†, 1878 — Robert Jackson, 1888

1. Breathe on me, Breath of God, Fill me with life anew, That I may
2. Breathe on me, Breath of God, Until my heart is pure; Until with
3. Breathe on me, Breath of God, Till I am wholly Thine; Until this
4. Breathe on me, Breath of God, So shall I never die, But live with

THE HOLY SPIRIT

love what Thou dost love, And do what Thou wouldst do.
Thee I will one will, To do and to en - dure.
earth - ly part of me Glows with Thy fire di - vine.
Thee the per - fect life Of Thine e - ter - ni - ty. A - men.

SPIRIT OF GOD 217
MORECAMBE 10.10.10.10.

George Croly, 1854   Frederick Cook Atkinson, 1870

1 Spir - it of God! de - scend up - on my heart; Wean it from
2 I ask no dream, no proph - et ec - sta - sies; No sud - den
3 Hast Thou not bid us love Thee, God and King? All, all Thine
4 Teach me to feel that Thou art al - ways nigh; Teach me the
5 Teach me to love Thee as Thine an - gels love, One ho - ly

earth; through all its puls - es move; Stoop to my weak - ness,
rend - ing of the veil of clay; No an - gel vis - it -
own, soul, heart, and strength, and mind; I see Thy cross, there
strug - gles of the soul to bear; To check the ris - ing
pas - sion fill - ing all my frame; The bap - tism of the

might - y as Thou art, And make me love Thee as I ought to love.
ant, no op - 'ning skies; But take the dim - ness of my soul a - way.
teach my heart to cling: O let me seek Thee, and O let me find!
doubt, the reb - el sigh; Teach me the pa - tience of un - an - swered prayer.
heav'n-de-scend-ed dove, My heart an al - tar, and Thy love the flame. A - men.

THE HOLY SPIRIT

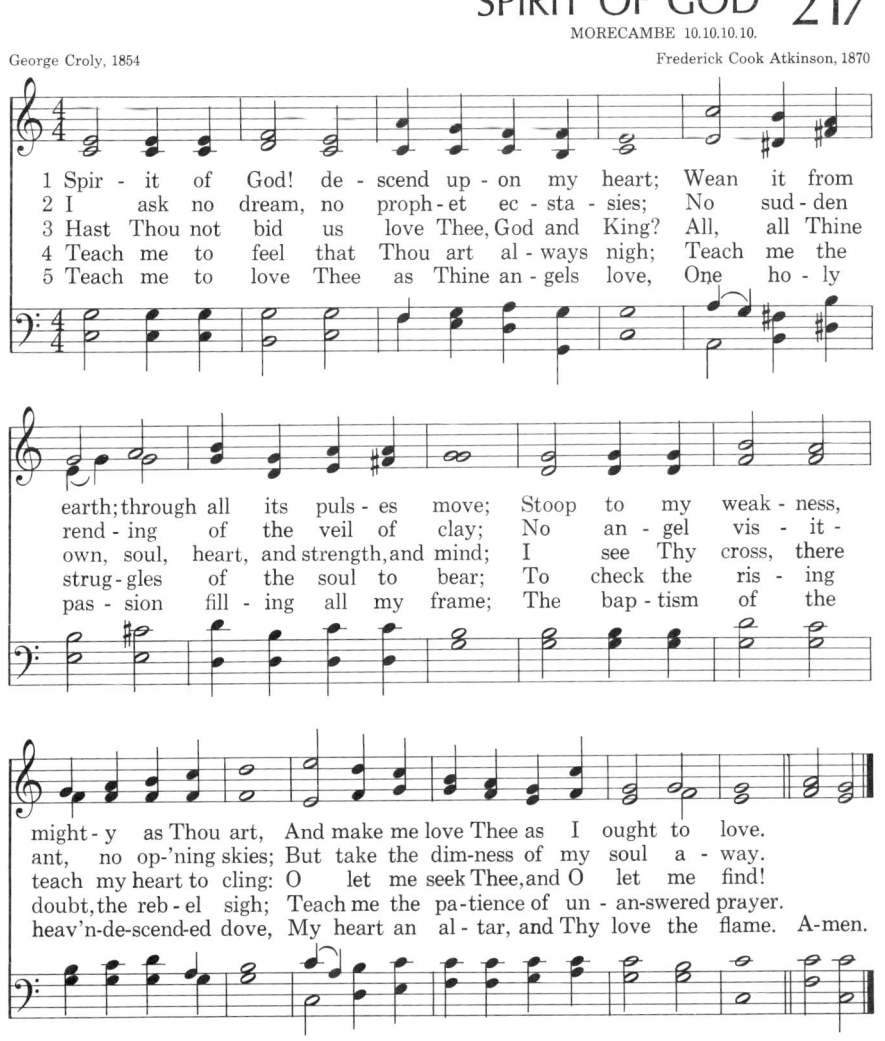

218 THY WORD, O LORD, LIKE GENTLE DEWS
RELEASE C.M.D.

Carl Bernhard Garve, 1825
Dein Wort, O Herr, ist milder Thau
Tr. Catherine Winkworth, 1855, and Others

Danish Melody
Version from *Service Book and Hymnal*, 1958

1. Thy Word, O Lord, like gentle dews, Falls soft on hearts that pine;
Lord, to Thy garden ne'er refuse This heav'nly balm of Thine.
Watered by Thee, let every tree Then blossom to Thy praise,
By grace of Thine bear fruit divine Through all the coming days.

2. Thy Word is like a flaming sword, A wedge that cleaveth stone;
Keen as a fire, so burns Thy Word, And pierceth flesh and bone.
Let it go forth o'er all the earth To cleanse our hearts within,
To show Thy power in Satan's hour, And break the might of sin.

3. Thy Word, a wondrous guiding star, On pilgrim hearts doth rise,
Leads those to God who dwell afar, And makes the simple wise.
Let not its light e'er sink in night, But in each spirit shine,
That none may miss heav'n's final bliss, Led by Thy light divine. A-men.

THE HOLY SCRIPTURES

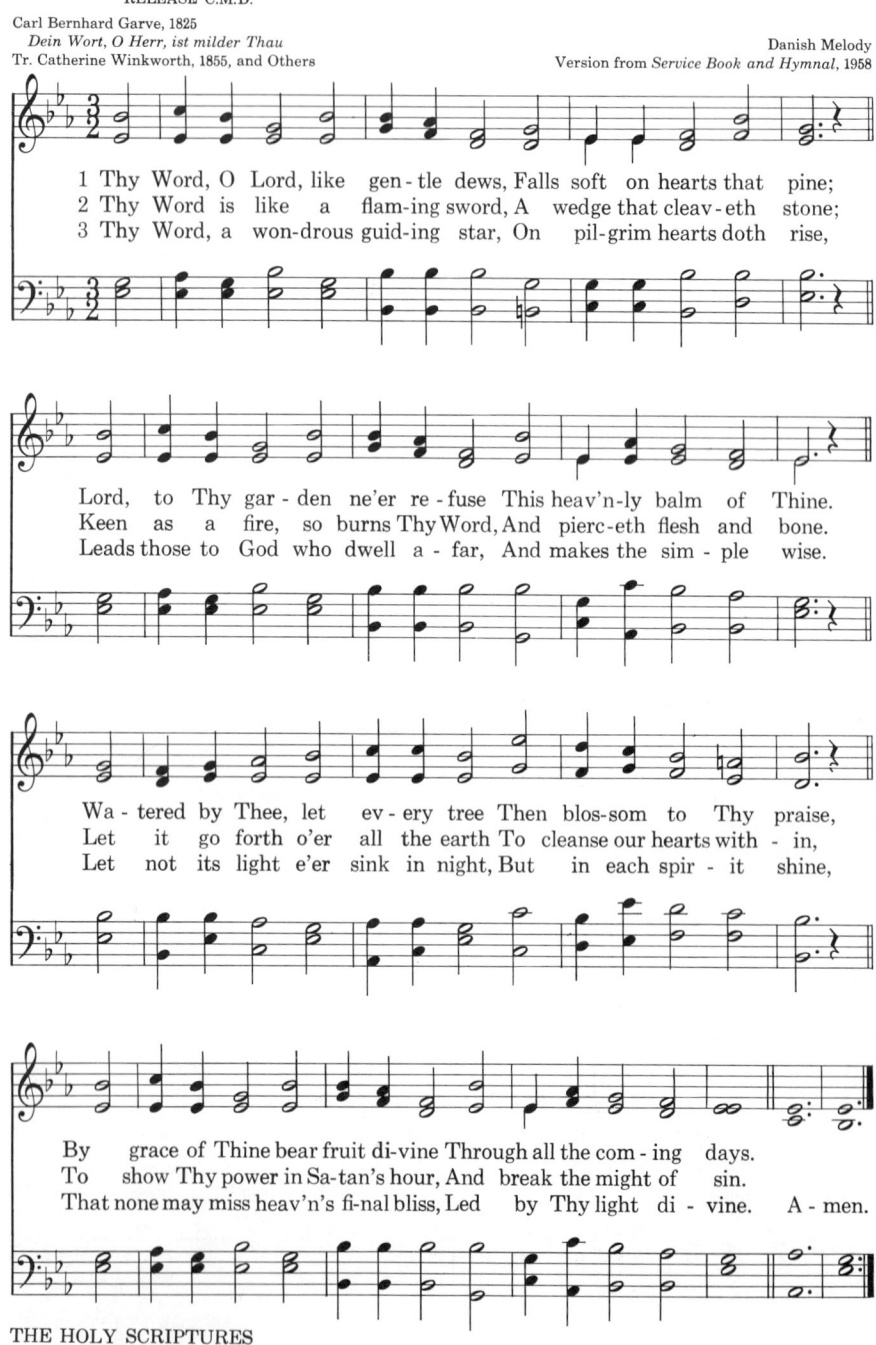

O WORD OF GOD INCARNATE 219

MUNICH 7.6.7.6.D.

William Walsham How, 1867

Neu-vermehrtes Gesangbuch, Meiningen, 1693
Harmony by Felix Mendelssohn, 1847

1. O Word of God incarnate, O wisdom from on high,
O truth unchanged, unchanging, O light of our dark sky:
We praise Thee for the radiance That from the hallowed page,
A lantern to our foot-steps, Shines on from age to age.

2. The church from her dear Master, Received the gift divine,
And still that light she lifteth O'er all the earth to shine.
It is the golden casket, Where gems of truth are stored;
It is the heav'n-drawn picture Of Christ, the living Word.

3. It floateth like a banner Before God's host unfurled;
It shineth like a beacon Above the darkling world.
It is the chart and compass That o'er life's surging sea,
'Mid mists and rocks and quick-sands, Still guides, O Christ, to Thee.

4. O make Thy church, dear Savior, A lamp of purest gold,
To bear before the nations Thy true light, as of old.
O teach Thy wand'ring pilgrims By this their path to trace,
Till, clouds and darkness ended, They see Thee face to face. A-men.

THE HOLY SCRIPTURES

220 THE HEAVENS DECLARE THY GLORY
UXBRIDGE L.M.

Based on Psalm 19
Isaac Watts†, 1719

Lowell Mason, 1830

1. The heav'ns declare Thy glory, Lord, In ev-ery star Thy wisdom shines: But when our eyes behold Thy Word, We read Thy name in fairer lines.
2. Sun, moon and stars convey Thy praise Round the whole earth, and never stand: So when Thy truth began its race, It touched and glanced on ev-ery land.
3. Nor shall Thy spreading gospel rest Till through the world Thy truth has run; Till Christ has all the nations blest That see the light, or feel the sun.
4. Great Sun of righteousness, arise, Bless the dark world with heav'nly light; Thy gospel makes the simple wise; Thy laws are pure, Thy judgments right.
5. Thy noblest wonders here we view In souls renew'd and sins forgiven: Lord, cleanse my sins, my soul renew, And make Thy Word my guide to heav'n. A-men.

221 LORD, THY WORD ABIDETH
RAVENSHAW 6.6.6.6.

Henry W. Baker†, 1861

M. Weisse's *Gesengbuchlein*, 1531
Adapted by William Henry Monk, 1861

1. Lord, Thy Word abideth, And our footsteps guideth;
2. When our foes are near us, Then Thy Word doth cheer us,
3. When the storms are o'er us, And dark clouds before us,
4. Word of mercy, giving Help unto the living;
5. O that we discerning Its most holy learning,

THE HOLY SCRIPTURES

Who its truth be - liev - eth Light and joy re - ceiv - eth.
Word of con - so - la - tion, Mes - sage of sal - va - tion.
Then its light di - rect - eth, And our way pro - tect - eth.
Word of life, sup - ply - ing Com - fort to the dy - ing!
Lord, may love and fear Thee, Ev - er - more be near Thee. A - men.

BREAK THOU THE BREAD OF LIFE 222
BREAD OF LIFE 6.4.6.4.D.

Mary Artemisia Lathbury†, 1877, Sts. 1 and 2
Alexander Groves, 1913, St. 3

William F. Sherwin, 1877

1 Break Thou the bread of life, Dear Lord, to me, As Thou didst break the loaves Be - side the sea; Be - yond the sa - cred page I seek Thee, Lord; My spir - it longs for Thee, O liv - ing Word!
2 Bless Thou the truth, re - vealed This day to me, As Thou didst bless the bread By Gal - i - lee; Then shall all bond - age cease, All fet - ters fall; And I shall find in Thee My All - in - All!
3 Spir - it and life are they, Words Thou dost speak; I has - ten to o - bey, But I am weak; Thou art my on - ly help, Thou art my life; Heed - ing Thy ho - ly Word I win the strife.

THE HOLY SCRIPTURES

223 LAMP OF OUR FEET
NUN DANKET ALL' C.M.

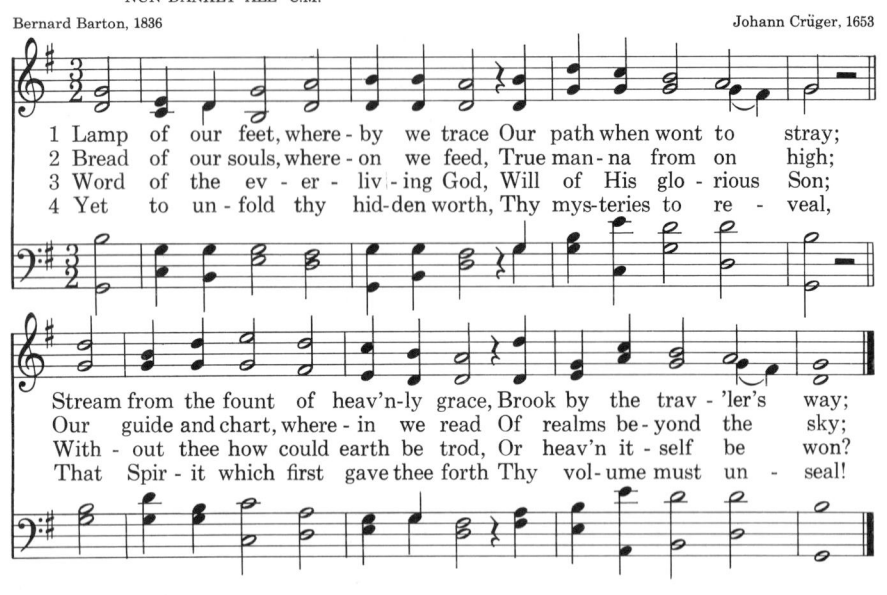

Bernard Barton, 1836 — Johann Crüger, 1653

1. Lamp of our feet, whereby we trace Our path when wont to stray;
   Stream from the fount of heav'nly grace, Brook by the trav'ler's way;
2. Bread of our souls, whereon we feed, True manna from on high;
   Our guide and chart, wherein we read Of realms beyond the sky;
3. Word of the ever-living God, Will of His glorious Son;
   Without thee how could earth be trod, Or heav'n itself be won?
4. Yet to unfold thy hidden worth, Thy mysteries to reveal,
   That Spirit which first gave thee forth Thy volume must unseal!

224 SPREAD, STILL SPREAD, THOU MIGHTY WORD
GOTT SEI DANK 7.7.7.7.

Jonathan Friedrich Bahnmaier, 1827
Walte, walte, nah und fern
Paraphrase by Percy Dearmer, 1931

J. A. Freylinghausen's *Neues Geistreiches Gesangbuch*, 1704

1. Spread, still spread, thou mighty Word, Show the kingdom of the Lord,
   Spread to every soul on earth, Tell them their immortal worth.
2. Tell them how the Father's will Made the world, and makes it still,
   How the Christ proclaimed His love, Taught the wisdom from above.
3. Mighty Word of many hues, Heav'nward pointing, tell the news,
   Word, by Thy divine impact, Teach men how to will and act.
4. Word of life, so clean and strong, Word for which the nations long,
   Spread, till from its tangled night All the earth stirs up to light. A-men.

THE HOLY SCRIPTURES

COME TO THE SAVIOR NOW 225
INVITATION (MAKER) 6.6.6.6.D.

John M. Wigner, 1871
Frederick Charles Maker, 1881

1. Come to the Savior now, He gently calleth thee;
In true repentance bow, Before Him bend the knee:
He waiteth to bestow Salvation, peace, and love,
True joy on earth below, A home in heav'n above.

2. Come to the Savior now, Ye who have wandered far,
Renew your solemn vow, For His by right you are;
Come, like poor wand'ring sheep Returning to His fold;
His arm will safely keep, His love will ne'er grow cold.

3. Come to the Savior, all, What-e'er your burdens be;
Hear now His loving call, "Cast all your care on Me."
Come, and for ev'ry grief In Jesus you will find
A sure and safe relief, A loving Friend, and kind.

LIFE IN CHRIST: CALL OF CHRIST

226 COME UNTO ME, YE WEARY

MEIRIONYDD 7.6.7.6.D.

William Chatterton Dix, 1867
William Lloyd, 1840

1. "Come unto Me, ye weary, And I will give you rest,"
O blessed voice of Jesus, Which comes to hearts oppressed!
It tells of benediction, Of pardon, grace, and peace,
Of joy that hath no ending, Of love which cannot cease.

2. "Come unto Me, ye fainting, And I will give you life,"
O peaceful voice of Jesus, Which comes to end our strife!
The foe is stern and eager, The fight is fierce and long;
But Thou hast made us mighty, And stronger than the strong.

3. "And whosoever cometh, I will not cast him out,"
O patient love of Jesus, Which drives away our doubt!
Which calls us, very sinners, Unworthy though we be
Of love so free and boundless, To come, dear Lord, to Thee!

LIFE IN CHRIST: CALL OF CHRIST

O JESUS, THOU ART STANDING 227

ST. HILDA 7.6.7.6.D.

William Walsham How, 1867

Justin Heinrich Knecht, 1793
and Edward Husband, 1871

1. O Jesus, Thou art standing Outside the fast-closed door,
In lowly patience waiting To pass the threshold o'er:
Shame on us, Christian brothers, His name and sign who bear,
O shame, thrice shame upon us, To keep Him standing there!

2. O Jesus, Thou art knocking; And lo, that hand is scarred,
And thorns Thy brow encircle, And tears Thy face have marred:
O love that passeth knowledge, So patiently to wait!
O sin that hath no equal, So fast to bar the gate!

3. O Jesus, Thou art pleading In accents meek and low,
"I died for you, My children, And will ye treat Me so?"
O Lord, with shame and sorrow We open now the door;
Dear Savior, enter, enter, And leave us nevermore! A-men.

LIFE IN CHRIST: CALL OF CHRIST

228 I SOUGHT THE LORD
FAITH 10.10.10.6.

The Pilgrim Hymnal, 1904
J. Harold Moyer, 1965

1 I sought the Lord, and af-ter-ward I knew He moved my
2 Thou didst reach forth Thy hand and mine en-fold, I walked and
3 I find, I walk, I love, but, O the whole Of love is

soul to seek Him, seek-ing me; It was not I that
sank not on the storm-vexed sea; 'Twas not so much that
but my an-swer, Lord, to Thee! For Thou wert long be-

found, O Sav-ior true, No, I was found of Thee.
I on Thee took hold As Thou, dear Lord, on me.
fore-hand with my soul; Al-ways Thou lov-edst me. A-men.

229 JESUS CALLS US
GALILEE 8.7.8.7.

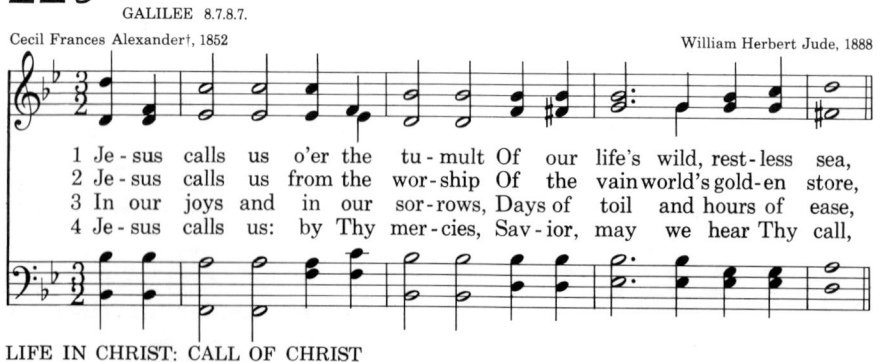

Cecil Frances Alexander, 1852
William Herbert Jude, 1888

1 Je-sus calls us o'er the tu-mult Of our life's wild, rest-less sea,
2 Je-sus calls us from the wor-ship Of the vain world's gold-en store,
3 In our joys and in our sor-rows, Days of toil and hours of ease,
4 Je-sus calls us: by Thy mer-cies, Sav-ior, may we hear Thy call,

LIFE IN CHRIST: CALL OF CHRIST

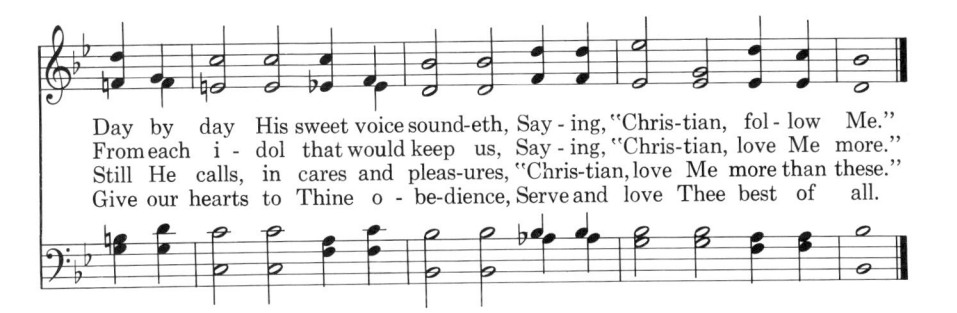

Day by day His sweet voice sound-eth, Say-ing, "Chris-tian, fol-low Me."
From each i-dol that would keep us, Say-ing, "Chris-tian, love Me more."
Still He calls, in cares and pleas-ures, "Chris-tian, love Me more than these."
Give our hearts to Thine o-be-dience, Serve and love Thee best of all.

ART THOU WEARY, ART THOU LANGUID 230

STEPHANOS 8.5.8.3.

John Mason Neale, 1862
Henry Williams Baker, 1868

1. Art thou wea-ry, art thou lan-guid,
   Art thou sore dis-tressed?
   "Come to Me," saith One, "and com-ing, Be at rest."

2. Hath He marks to lead me to Him,
   If He be my Guide?
   "In His feet and hands are wound-prints, And His side."

3. Is there di-a-dem, as Mon-arch,
   That His brow a-dorns?
   "Yea, a crown, in ver-y sure-ty, But of thorns."

4. If I find Him, if I fol-low,
   What His por-tion here?
   "Many a sor-row, many a la-bor, Many a tear."

5. If I still hold closely to Him,
   What hath He at last?
   "Sorrow vanquished, labor ended, Jordan passed."

6. If I ask Him to receive me,
   Will He say me nay?
   "Not till earth and not till heaven Pass away."

LIFE IN CHRIST: CALL OF CHRIST

231 I HEARD THE VOICE OF JESUS
KINGSFOLD C.M.D.

Horatius Bonar, 1846

Melody by Lucy Broadwood
Arranged and harmonized by
Ralph Vaughan Williams, 1906

1. I heard the voice of Jesus say, "Come unto Me and rest;
Lay down, thou weary one, lay down Thy head upon My breast."
I came to Jesus as I was, Weary and worn and sad;
I found in Him a resting place, And He has made me glad.

2. I heard the voice of Jesus say, "Behold, I freely give
The living water; thirsty one, Stoop down and drink and live."
I came to Jesus, and I drank Of that life-giving stream;
My thirst was quench'd, my soul revived, And now I live in Him.

3. I heard the voice of Jesus say, "I am this dark world's light;
Look unto Me, thy morn shall rise, And all thy day be bright."
I looked to Jesus, and I found In Him my star, my sun;
And in that light of life I'll walk, Till trav-'ling days are done. A-men.

LIFE IN CHRIST: CALL OF CHRIST

I HEARD THE VOICE OF JESUS 232

BONAR C.M.D.

Horatius Bonar, 1846
John David Brunk, 1911

1. I heard the voice of Jesus say, "Come unto Me and rest; Lay down, thou weary one, lay down Thy head upon My breast." I came to Jesus as I was, Weary and worn and sad; I found in Him a resting place, And He has made me glad.

2. I heard the voice of Jesus say, "Behold, I freely give The living water; thirsty one, Stoop down and drink and live." I came to Jesus, and I drank Of that life-giving stream; My thirst was quench'd, my soul revived, And now I live in Him.

3. I heard the voice of Jesus say, "I am this dark world's light; Look unto Me, thy morn shall rise, And all thy day be bright." I looked to Jesus, and I found In Him my star, my sun; And in that light of life I'll walk, Till trav'ling days are done.

LIFE IN CHRIST: CALL OF CHRIST

233 DEPTH OF MERCY
BUCKLAND 7.7.7.7.

Charles Wesley, 1740 — Leighton George Hayne, 1863

1. Depth of mer-cy! can there be Mer-cy still re-served for me?
   Can my God His wrath for-bear; Me the chief of sin-ners, spare?
2. I have long with-stood His grace, Long pro-voked Him to His face;
   Would not heark-en to His calls, Grieved Him by a thou-sand falls.
3. I my Mas-ter have de-nied, I a-fresh have cru-ci-fied,
   Oft pro-faned His hal-low'd name, Put Him to an o-pen shame.
4. Now in-cline me to re-pent; Let me now my fall la-ment;
   Now my foul re-volt de-plore, Weep, be-lieve, and sin no more.

234 OUT OF THE DEPTHS I CRY TO THEE
AUS TIEFER NOT 8.7.8.7.8.8.7.

Based on Psalm 130
Martin Luther, 1523
Aus tiefer Not schrei ich zu dir
Tr. Edward Traill Horn III, b. 1909 — *Kirchenampt*, Strassburg, 1525

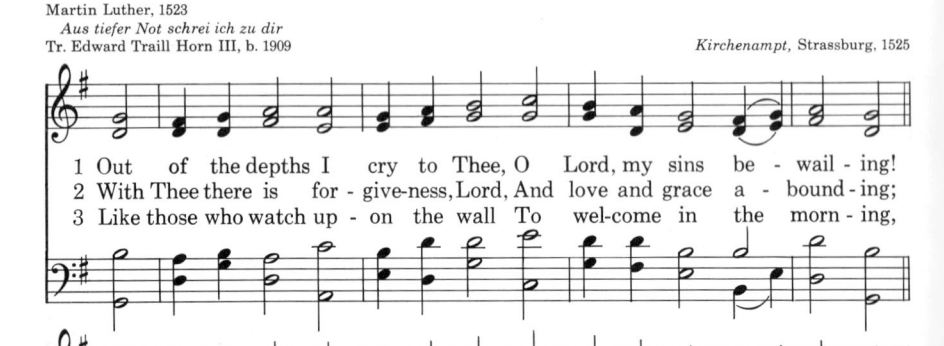

1. Out of the depths I cry to Thee, O Lord, my sins be-wail-ing!
   Bow down Thy gra-cious ear to me, Make Thou my prayer a-vail-ing.
2. With Thee there is for-give-ness, Lord, And love and grace a-bound-ing;
   The no-blest thought and deed and word Were else but emp-ty sound-ing.
3. Like those who watch up-on the wall To wel-come in the morn-ing,
   My soul doth wait Thy qui-et call, Her-self with hope a-dorn-ing.

LIFE IN CHRIST: REPENTANCE AND FORGIVENESS

Mark not my mis-deeds in Thy book, But on my sins in
All guilt-y in Thy sight ap-pear; All to Thy pres-ence
So may all Is-rael look for Thee, And in Thy day find

mer-cy look, Or who can stand be-fore Thee?
come in fear, And find Thy lov-ing-kind-ness.
mer-cy free, And plen-te-ous re-demp-tion. A-men.

JUST AS I AM, WITHOUT ONE PLEA 235
WOODWORTH L.M.

Charlotte Elliott, c. 1834

William Batchelder Bradbury, 1849

1. Just as I am, with-out one plea, But that Thy blood was shed for me,
2. Just as I am, and wait-ing not To rid my soul of one dark blot,
3. Just as I am, though tossed a-bout With many a con-flict, many a doubt,
4. Just as I am, poor, wretch-ed, blind; Sight, rich-es, heal-ing of the mind,
5. Just as I am, Thou wilt re-ceive, Wilt wel-come, par-don, cleanse, re-lieve;
6. Just as I am, Thy love un-known Hath bro-ken ev-ery bar-rier down;

And that Thou bid'st me come to Thee, O Lamb of God, I come, I come!
To Thee whose blood can cleanse each spot, O Lamb of God, I come, I come!
Fight-ings and fears with-in, with-out, O Lamb of God, I come, I come!
Yea, all I need in Thee to find, O Lamb of God, I come, I come!
Be-cause Thy prom-ise I be-lieve, O Lamb of God, I come, I come!
Now, to be Thine, yea, Thine a-lone, O Lamb of God, I come, I come!

LIFE IN CHRIST: REPENTANCE AND FORGIVENESS

236 JESUS, LOVER OF MY SOUL
MARTYN 7.7.7.7.D.

Charles Wesley, 1740 — Simeon Butler Marsh, 1834

1. Jesus, lover of my soul, Let me to Thy bosom fly,
While the nearer waters roll, While the tempest still is high;
Hide me, O my Savior, hide, Till the storm of life is past;
Safe into the haven guide, O receive my soul at last.

2. Other refuge have I none; Hangs my helpless soul on Thee;
Leave, ah, leave me not alone, Still support and comfort me.
All my trust on Thee is stayed, All my help from Thee I bring;
Cover my defenceless head With the shadow of Thy wing.

3. Thou, O Christ, art all I want, More than all in Thee I find;
Raise the fallen, cheer the faint, Heal the sick, and lead the blind.
Just and holy is Thy name, I am all unrighteousness;
False and full of sin I am, Thou art full of truth and grace.

4. Plenteous grace with Thee is found, Grace to cover all my sin;
Let the healing streams abound, Make and keep me pure within.
Thou of life the fountain art, Freely let me take of Thee;
Spring Thou up within my heart, Rise to all eternity. A-men.

LIFE IN CHRIST: REPENTANCE AND FORGIVENESS

JESUS, LOVER OF MY SOUL 237

ABERYSTWYTH 7.7.7.7.D.

Charles Wesley, 1740

Joseph Parry, 1879

1. Jesus, lover of my soul, Let me to Thy bosom fly,
While the nearer waters roll, While the tempest still is high;
Hide me, O my Savior, hide, Till the storm of life is past;
Safe into the haven guide, O receive my soul at last.

2. Other refuge have I none; Hangs my helpless soul on Thee;
Leave, ah, leave me not alone, Still support and comfort me.
All my trust on Thee is stayed, All my help from Thee I bring;
Cover my defenceless head With the shadow of Thy wing.

3. Thou, O Christ, art all I want, More than all in Thee I find:
Raise the fallen, cheer the faint, Heal the sick, and lead the blind,
Just and holy is Thy name, I am all unrighteousness;
False and full of sin I am, Thou art full of truth and grace.

4. Plenteous grace with Thee is found, Grace to cover all my sin;
Let the healing streams abound, Make and keep me pure within.
Thou of life the fountain art, Freely let me take of Thee;
Spring Thou up within my heart, Rise to all eternity. A-men.

LIFE IN CHRIST: REPENTANCE AND FORGIVENESS

238 GOD, BE MERCIFUL TO ME
REDHEAD NO. 76 (AJALON) 7.7.7.7.7.7.

Based on Psalm 51
Psalter, 1912, Sts. 1-4
The Hymnbook, 1955, St. 5

Richard Redhead, 1853

1. God, be mer-ci-ful to me, On Thy grace I rest my plea;
Plen-teous in com-pas-sion Thou, Blot out my trans-gres-sions now;
Wash me, make me pure with-in, Cleanse, O cleanse me from my sin.

2. My trans-gres-sions I con-fess, Grief and guilt my soul op-press;
I have sinned a-gainst Thy grace And pro-voked Thee to Thy face;
I con-fess Thy judg-ment just, Speech-less, I Thy mer-cy trust.

3. I am e-vil, born in sin; Thou de-sir-est truth with-in.
Thou a-lone my Sav-ior art, Teach Thy wis-dom to my heart;
Make me pure, Thy grace be-stow, Wash me whit-er than the snow.

4. Bro-ken, hum-bled to the dust By Thy wrath and judg-ment just,
Let my con-trite heart re-joice And in glad-ness hear Thy voice;
From my sins O hide Thy face, Blot them out in bound-less grace.

5. Gra-cious God, my heart re-new, Make my spir-it right and true;
Cast me not a-way from Thee, Let Thy Spir-it dwell in me;
Thy sal-va-tion's joy im-part, Stead-fast make my will-ing heart. A-men.

239 APPROACH, MY SOUL, THE MERCY SEAT
BYEFIELD C.M.

John Newton, 1779

Thomas Hastings, c. 1840

1. Ap-proach, my soul, the mer-cy seat, Where Je-sus an-swers prayer;
2. Thy prom-ise is my on-ly plea, With this I ven-ture nigh;
3. Bowed down be-neath a load of sin, By Sa-tan sore-ly pressed,
4. O won-drous love! to bleed and die, To bear the cross and shame,

LIFE IN CHRIST: REPENTANCE AND FORGIVENESS

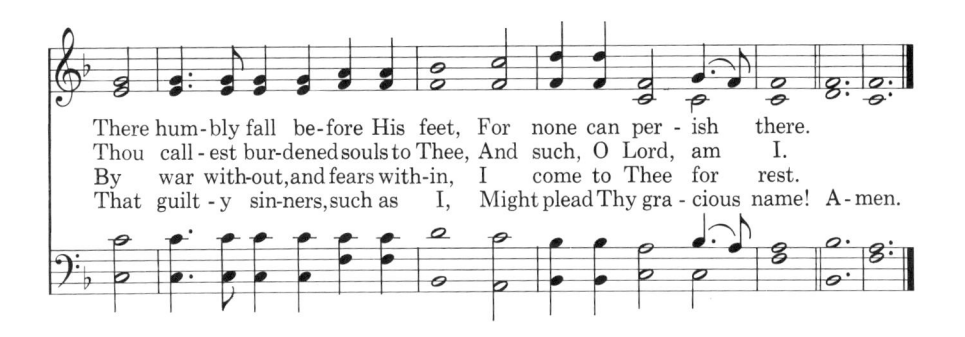

There humbly fall before His feet, For none can perish there.
Thou callest burdened souls to Thee, And such, O Lord, am I.
By war without, and fears within, I come to Thee for rest.
That guilty sinners, such as I, Might plead Thy gracious name! A-men.

LORD, THY MERCY NOW ENTREATING 240

RINGE RECHT 8.7.8.7.

Mary Ann Sidebotham, 1881

J. Thommen's *Erbaulicher Musicalischer Christen-Schatz*, 1745

1. Lord, Thy mercy now entreating, Low before Thy throne we fall; Our misdeeds to Thee confessing, On Thy name we humbly call.
2. Sinful thoughts and words unloving Rise against us one by one; Acts unworthy, deeds unthinking, Good that we have left undone.
3. Hearts that far from Thee were straying, While in prayer we bowed the knee; Lips that, while Thy praises sounding, Lifted not the soul to Thee.
4. Precious moments idly wasted, Precious hours in folly spent; Christian vow and fight unheeded; Scarce a thought to wisdom lent.
5. Lord, Thy mercy still entreating, We with shame our sins would own; From henceforth, the time redeeming, May we live to Thee alone. A-men.

LIFE IN CHRIST: REPENTANCE AND FORGIVENESS

241 LORD, FROM THE DEPTHS TO THEE
CHESHIRE C.M.

Based on Psalm 130
Scottish Psalter†, 1650

Thomas Est's *Psalms*, 1592

1. Lord, from the depths to Thee I cried: My voice, Lord, do Thou hear: Un-to my sup-pli-ca-tion's voice Give an at-ten-tive ear.
2. Lord, who shall stand, if Thou, O Lord, Shouldst mark in-iq-ui-ty? But yet with Thee for-give-ness is, That feared Thou may-est be.
3. I wait for God, my soul doth wait; My hope is in His Word. More than they that for morn-ing watch, My soul waits for the Lord;
4. I say, more than they that do watch The morn-ing light to see, Let Is-ra-el hope ev-er found with Him: And from all his in-iq-ui-ties He Is-rael shall re-deem. A-men.
4. Re-demp-tion al-so plen-te-ous Is in the Lord, For with Him mer-cies be.

242 AMAZING GRACE! HOW SWEET
SOLON (AMAZING GRACE) C.M.

John Newton, 1779

Folk Hymn
Joseph Funk's *Genuine Church Music*, 1832 (*Harmonia Sacra*)

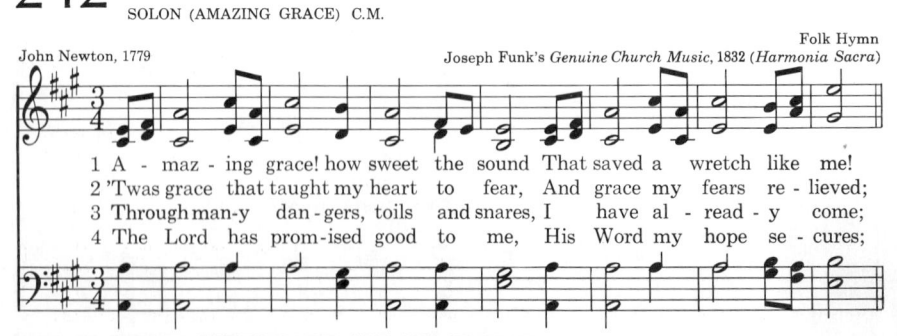

1. A-maz-ing grace! how sweet the sound That saved a wretch like me!
2. 'Twas grace that taught my heart to fear, And grace my fears re-lieved;
3. Through man-y dan-gers, toils and snares, I have al-read-y come;
4. The Lord has prom-ised good to me, His Word my hope se-cures;

LIFE IN CHRIST: REPENTANCE AND FORGIVENESS

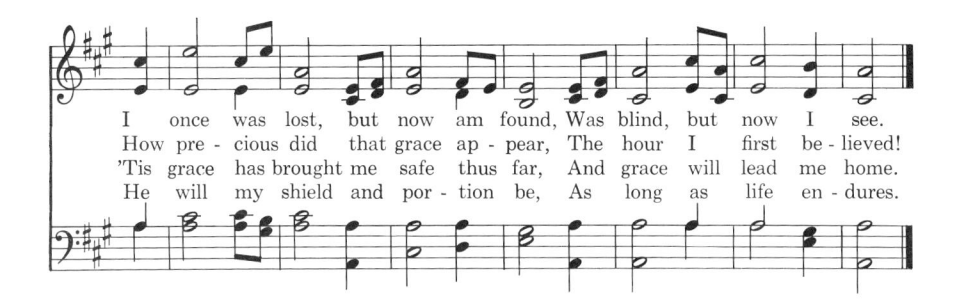

I once was lost, but now am found, Was blind, but now I see.
How precious did that grace appear, The hour I first believed!
'Tis grace has brought me safe thus far, And grace will lead me home.
He will my shield and portion be, As long as life endures.

FAR, FAR AWAY 243

RESTORATION (I WILL ARISE) Irregular

P. P. Bliss' *Gospel Songs*, 1874

Folk Hymn
W. Walker's *Southern Harmony*, 1835

1. Far, far away from my loving Father, I had been wand'ring, wayward, wild, Fearing only lest His anger Overtake His sinful child.
2. Fain had I fed on the husks around me, Till to myself I came, and said, "Plenty have my Father's servants, Perish I for want of bread."
3. "I will arise, though faint and weary, Home to my Father I will go; Woe is me that e'er I wandered, Ah, that I such need should know."
4. "Father," I'll say, "I have sinned before Thee, No more may I be called Thy son: Make me only as Thy servant, Pity me, a wretch undone!"
5. Then I arose and came to my Father, Mercy amazing! Love unknown! He beheld me, ran, embraced me, Pardoned, welcomed, called me "son!"

REFRAIN: I will arise and go to Jesus, He will embrace me in His arms; In the arms of my dear Savior, O there are ten thousand charms.

LIFE IN CHRIST: REPENTANCE AND FORGIVENESS

244 ARISE, MY SOUL, ARISE
LENOX 6.6.6.6.8.8.

Charles Wesley, 1742
Lewis Edson, 1782

1. A-rise, my soul, a-rise, Shake off thy guilt-y fears,
   The bleed-ing sac-ri-fice In my be-half ap-pears;
   Be-fore the throne my sure-ty stands, Be-fore the throne
   my sure-ty stands, My name is writ-ten on His hands.

2. He ev-er lives a-bove For me to in-ter-cede,
   His all-re-deem-ing love, His pre-cious blood to plead;
   His blood a-toned for all our race, His blood a-toned
   for all our race, And sprin-kles now the throne of grace.

3. Five bleed-ing wounds He bears, Re-ceived on Cal-va-ry;
   They pour ef-fec-tual prayers, They strong-ly speak for me;
   For-give him, O for-give, they cry, For-give him, O
   for-give, they cry, Nor let that ran-somed sin-ner die!

4. My God is rec-on-ciled, His pard-'ning voice I hear,
   He owns me for His child, I can no long-er fear;
   With con-fi-dence I now draw nigh, With con-fi-dence
   I now draw nigh, And Fa-ther, Ab-ba Fa-ther, cry!

LIFE IN CHRIST: REPENTANCE AND FORGIVENESS

O BLESS THE LORD, MY SOUL 245

ST. THOMAS S.M.

Based on Psalm 103
Isaac Watts, 1719

Aaron Williams, 1762

1 O bless the Lord, my soul! Let all with-in me join,
2 O bless the Lord, my soul! Nor let His mer-cies lie
3 'Tis He for-gives thy sins; 'Tis He re-lieves thy pain;
4 He crowns thy life with love, When ran-somed from the grave;
5 He fills the poor with good; He gives the suf-f'rers rest;

And aid my tongue to bless His name Whose fa-vors are di - vine.
For - got - ten in un-thank-ful-ness, And with-out prais-es die.
'Tis He that heals thy sick-ness-es, And makes thee young a - gain.
He, that re-deemed my soul from hell Hath sov - ereign power to save.
The Lord hath judg-ments for the proud, And just - ice for th' op-pressed. A-men.

LORD JESUS, THINK ON ME 246

SOUTHWELL S.M.

Synesius of Cyrene, c. 410
Μνώεο Χριστὲ
Tr. Allen W. Chatfield†, 1876

W. Damon's *Psalms*, 1579

1 Lord Je - sus, think on me, And purge a - way my sin;
2 Lord Je - sus, think on me, With care and woe op - pressed;
3 Lord Je - sus, think on me, Nor let me go a - stray;
4 Lord Je - sus, think on me, When flows the tem - pest high:
5 Lord Je - sus, think on me, That, when the flood is past,

From earth-born pas-sions set me free, And make me pure with - in.
Let me Thy lov - ing serv - ant be, And taste Thy prom-ised rest.
Through dark-ness and per - plex - i - ty Point Thou the heav'n-ly way.
When on doth rush the en - e - my, O Sav - ior, be Thou nigh.
I may th' e - ter - nal bright-ness see, And share Thy joy at last. A-men.

LIFE IN CHRIST: REPENTANCE AND FORGIVENESS

247 LORD CHRIST, WHEN FIRST THOU CAM'ST

MIT FREUDEN ZART 8.7.8.7.8.8.7.

Walter Russell Bowie, 1928

Adapted from *Geneva 138, Pseaulmes* . . . , Lyon, 1547
Bohemian Brethren's *Kirchengeseng* . . . , 1566

1. Lord Christ, when first Thou cam'st to men, Upon a cross they bound Thee,
And mocked Thy saving kingship then By thorns with which they crowned Thee;
And still our wrongs may weave Thee now New thorns to pierce that steady brow,
And robe of sorrow round Thee.

2. O aweful love, which found no room In life where sin denied Thee,
And, doomed to death, must bring to doom The power which crucified Thee;
Till not a stone was left on stone, And all a nation's pride o'erthrown,
Went down to dust beside Thee!

3. New advent of the love of Christ, Shall we again refuse Thee,
Till in the night of hate and war We perish as we lose Thee?
From old unfaith our souls release To seek the kingdom of Thy peace,
By which alone we choose Thee.

4. O wounded hands of Jesus, build In us Thy new creation;
Our pride is dust; our vaunt is stilled; We wait Thy revelation.
O love that triumphs over loss, We bring our hearts before Thy cross,
To finish Thy salvation. A-men.

LIFE IN CHRIST: REPENTANCE AND FORGIVENESS

I LAY MY SINS ON JESUS 248
ST. HILDA 7.6.7.6.D.

Horatius Bonar, 1843

Justin Heinrich Knecht, 1793
and Edward Husband, 1871

1. I lay my sins on Jesus, The spotless Lamb of God;
   He bears them all, and frees us From the accursed load.
   I bring my guilt to Jesus, To wash my crimson stains
   White in His blood most precious, Till not a spot remains.

2. I lay my wants on Jesus, All fullness dwells in Him;
   He heals all my diseases, He doth my soul redeem.
   I lay my griefs on Jesus, My burdens and my cares;
   He from them all releases, He all my sorrows shares.

3. I rest my soul on Jesus, This weary soul of mine;
   His right hand me embraces, I on His breast recline.
   I love the name of Jesus: Immanuel, Christ, the Lord;
   Like fragrance on the breezes His name abroad is poured.

4. I long to be, like Jesus, Meek, loving, lowly, mild;
   I long to be, like Jesus, The Father's holy child.
   I long to be with Jesus, Amid the heav'nly throng,
   To sing with saints His praises, To learn the angels' song.

LIFE IN CHRIST: REPENTANCE AND FORGIVENESS

249 FAITH IS A LIVING POWER
SESSIONS L.M.

Petrus Herbert, 1566
Der Glaub' ist ein' lebendig' Kraft
Tr. Composite

Luther Orlando Emerson, 1847

1. Faith is a living power from heav'n Which grasps the promise God has giv'n; Securely fixed on Christ alone, A trust that cannot be o'erthrown.
2. Faith finds in Christ whate'er we need To save and strengthen, guide and feed; Strong in His grace it joys to share His cross, in hope His crown to wear.
3. Faith to the conscience whispers peace; And bids the mourner's sighing cease; By faith the children's right we claim, And call upon our Father's name.
4. Such faith in us, O God, implant, And to our prayers Thy favor grant, In Jesus Christ, Thy saving Son, Who is our fount of health alone. A-men.

250 WE WALK BY FAITH
LOBT GOTT C.M.

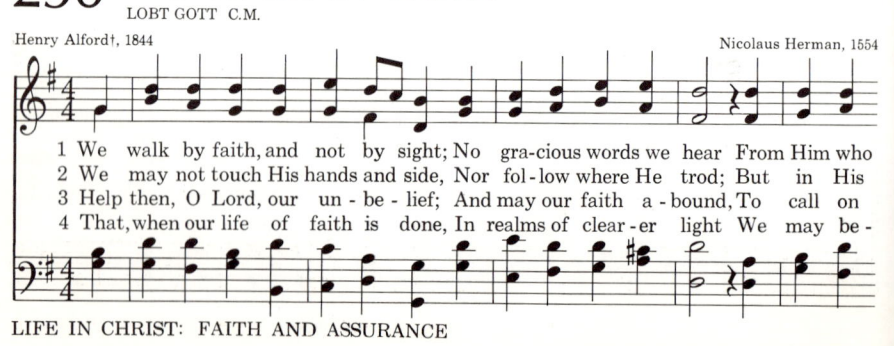

Henry Alford†, 1844

Nicolaus Herman, 1554

1. We walk by faith, and not by sight; No gracious words we hear From Him who
2. We may not touch His hands and side, Nor follow where He trod; But in His
3. Help then, O Lord, our unbelief; And may our faith abound, To call on
4. That, when our life of faith is done, In realms of clearer light We may be-

LIFE IN CHRIST: FAITH AND ASSURANCE

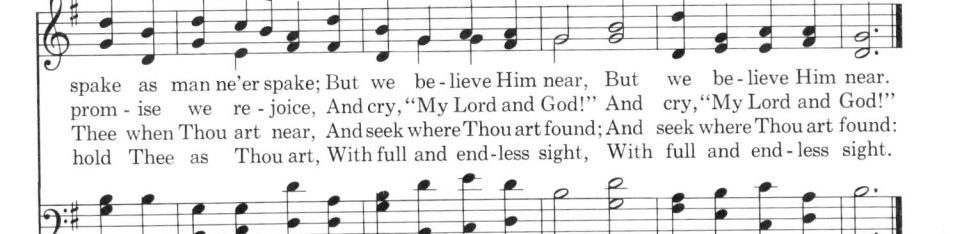

spake as man ne'er spake; But we be-lieve Him near, But we be-lieve Him near.
prom - ise we re - joice, And cry, "My Lord and God!" And cry, "My Lord and God!"
Thee when Thou art near, And seek where Thou art found; And seek where Thou art found:
hold Thee as Thou art, With full and end-less sight, With full and end-less sight.

MY FAITH LOOKS UP TO THEE 251

OLIVET 6.6.4.6.6.6.4.

Ray Palmer, 1830

Lowell Mason, 1832

1 My faith looks up to Thee, Thou Lamb of Cal - va - ry,
2 May Thy rich grace im-part Strength to my faint - ing heart,
3 While life's dark maze I tread, And griefs a - round me spread,
4 When ends life's tran - sient dream, When death's cold, sul - len stream

Sav - ior di - vine: Now hear me while I pray, Take all my
My zeal in - spire; As Thou hast died for me, O may my
Be Thou my guide; Bid dark-ness turn to day, Wipe sor - row's
Shall o'er me roll, Blest Sav - ior, then, in love, Fear and dis -

guilt a - way, O let me from this day Be whol - ly Thine.
love to Thee, Pure, warm, and change-less be, A liv - ing fire.
tears a - way, Nor let me ev - er stray From Thee a - side.
trust re-move; O bear me safe a-bove, A ran-somed soul. A-men.

LIFE IN CHRIST: FAITH AND ASSURANCE

252 IN HEAVENLY LOVE ABIDING

NYLAND 7.6.7.6.D.

Anna Laetita Waring, 1850

Finnish Folk Melody
Harmonized by David Evans, 1927

1. In heav'n-ly love a-bid-ing, No change my heart shall fear,
And safe is such con-fid-ing, For noth-ing chan-ges here.
The storm may roar with-out me, My heart may low be laid;
But God is round a-bout me, And can I be dis-mayed?

2. Wher-ev-er He may guide me, No want shall turn me back;
My Shep-herd is be-side me, And noth-ing can I lack.
His wis-dom ev-er wak-eth, His sight is nev-er dim;
He knows the way He tak-eth, And I will walk with Him.

3. Green pas-tures are be-fore me, Which yet I have not seen;
Bright skies will soon be o'er me, Where the dark clouds have been.
My hope I can-not meas-ure, The path to life is free;
My Sav-ior has my treas-ure, And He will walk with me.

LIFE IN CHRIST: FAITH AND ASSURANCE

SOMETIMES A LIGHT SURPRISES 253

RHYDDID 7.6.7.6.D.

William Cowpert, 1779

J. Parry's *Peroriaeth Hyfryd*, 1837

1. Some-times a light sur-pris-es The Chris-tian while he sings;
It is the Lord who ris-es With heal-ing in His wings;
When com-forts are de-clin-ing, He grants the soul a-gain A
sea-son of clear shin-ing, To cheer it af-ter rain.

2. In ho-ly con-tem-pla-tion We sweet-ly then pur-sue
The theme of God's sal-va-tion, And find it ev-er new;
Set free from pres-ent sor-row, We cheer-ful-ly can say, Let
the un-known to-mor-row Bring with it what it may.

3. It can bring with it noth-ing But He will bear us through;
Who gives the lil-ies cloth-ing Will clothe His peo-ple, too:
Be-neath the spread-ing heav-ens No crea-ture but is fed, And
He who feeds the ra-vens Will give His chil-dren bread.

4. Though vine nor fig tree nei-ther Their wont-ed fruit should bear,
Though all the fields should with-er, Nor flocks nor herds be there;
Yet God, the same a-bid-ing, His praise shall tune my voice; For
while in Him con-fid-ing I can-not but re-joice.

LIFE IN CHRIST: FAITH AND ASSURANCE

254 ROCK OF AGES! CLEFT FOR ME
TOPLADY 7.7.7.7.7.7.

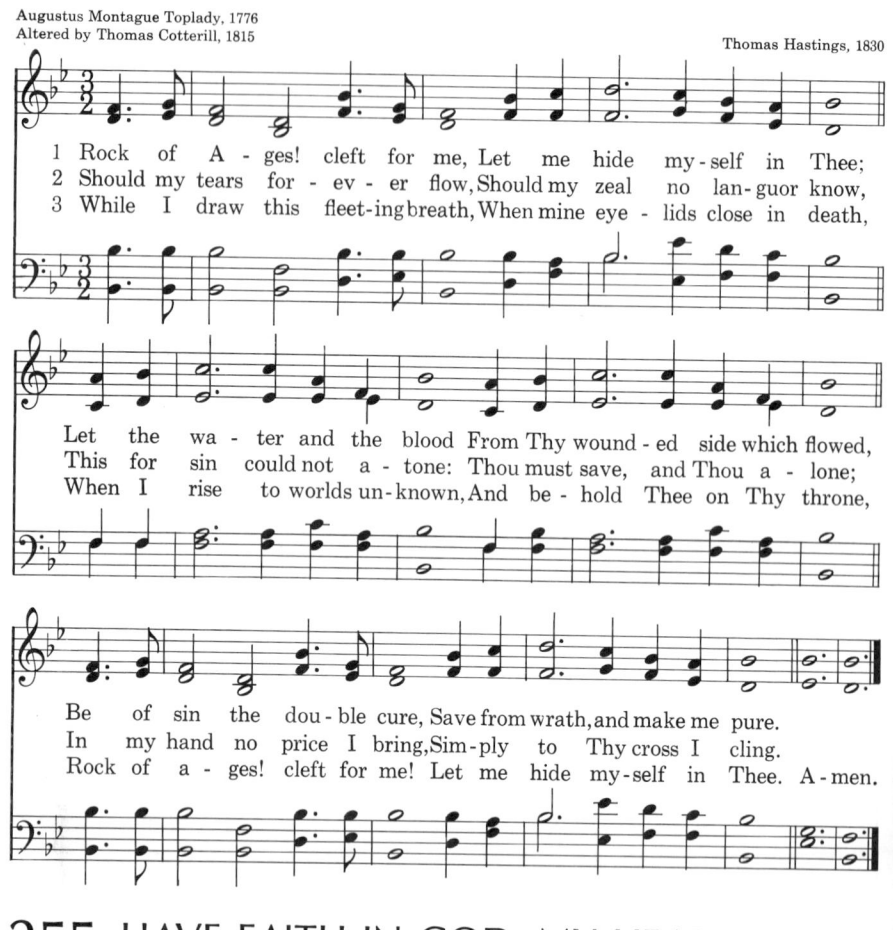

Augustus Montague Toplady, 1776
Altered by Thomas Cotterill, 1815

Thomas Hastings, 1830

1 Rock of Ages! cleft for me, Let me hide my-self in Thee;
2 Should my tears for-ev-er flow, Should my zeal no lan-guor know,
3 While I draw this fleet-ing breath, When mine eye-lids close in death,

Let the wa-ter and the blood From Thy wound-ed side which flowed,
This for sin could not a-tone: Thou must save, and Thou a-lone;
When I rise to worlds un-known, And be-hold Thee on Thy throne,

Be of sin the dou-ble cure, Save from wrath, and make me pure.
In my hand no price I bring, Sim-ply to Thy cross I cling.
Rock of a-ges! cleft for me! Let me hide my-self in Thee. A-men.

255 HAVE FAITH IN GOD, MY HEART
SOUTHWELL S.M.

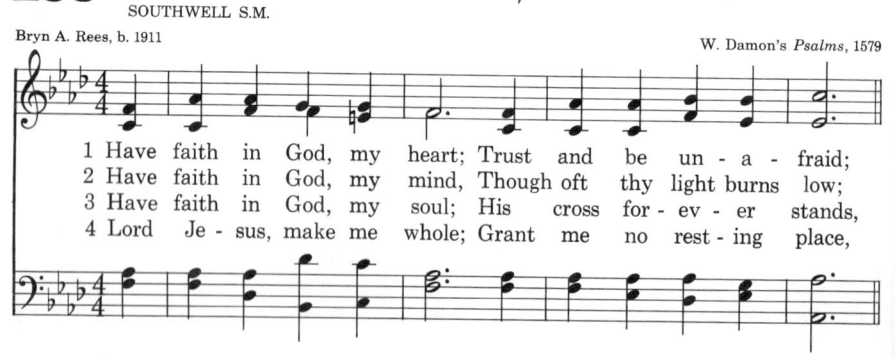

Bryn A. Rees, b. 1911

W. Damon's *Psalms*, 1579

1 Have faith in God, my heart; Trust and be un-a-fraid;
2 Have faith in God, my mind, Though oft thy light burns low;
3 Have faith in God, my soul; His cross for-ev-er stands,
4 Lord Je-sus, make me whole; Grant me no rest-ing place,

LIFE IN CHRIST: FAITH AND ASSURANCE

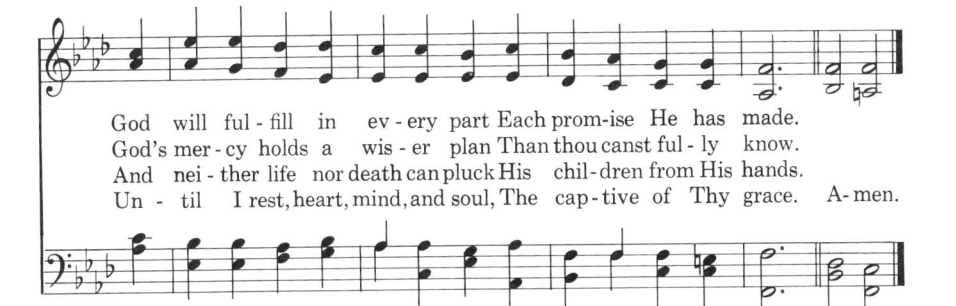

God will ful-fill in ev-ery part Each prom-ise He has made.
God's mer-cy holds a wis-er plan Than thou canst ful-ly know.
And nei-ther life nor death can pluck His chil-dren from His hands.
Un-til I rest, heart, mind, and soul, The cap-tive of Thy grace. A-men.

FATHER, I STRETCH MY HANDS TO THEE 256
CONSOLATION (MORNING SONG) C.M.

Charles Wesley, 1741

Folk Hymn
J. Wyeth's *Repository of Sacred Music,*
Part Second, 1813

1. Fa-ther, I stretch my hands to Thee, No oth-er help I know; If Thou with-draw Thy-self from me, Ah, whith-er shall I go?
2. What did Thy on-ly Son en-dure, Be-fore I drew my breath! What pain, what la-bor to se-cure My soul from end-less death!
3. O Je-sus, could I this be-lieve, I now should feel Thy power; Now my poor soul Thou wouldst re-trieve, Nor let me wait one hour.
4. Au-thor of faith, to Thee I lift My wea-ry, long-ing eyes; O let me now re-ceive that gift, My soul with-out it dies. A-men.

LIFE IN CHRIST: FAITH AND ASSURANCE

257 UNTO THE HILLS AROUND
SANDON 10.4.10.4.10.10.

Based on Psalm 121
John Campbell, 1866

Charles Purday, 1860

1. Un-to the hills a-round do I lift up My long-ing eyes:
O whence for me shall my sal-va-tion come, From whence a-rise?
From God the Lord doth come my cer-tain aid,
From God the Lord who heav'n and earth hath made.

2. He will not suf-fer that thy foot be moved: Safe shalt thou be.
No care-less slum-ber shall His eye-lids close, Who keep-eth thee.
Be-hold, He sleep-eth not, He slum-b'reth ne'er,
Who keep-eth Is-rael in His ho-ly care.

3. Je-ho-vah is Him-self thy keep-er true, Thy change-less shade;
Je-ho-vah thy de-fense on thy right hand Him-self hath made.
And thee no sun by day shall ev-er smite;
No moon shall harm thee in the si-lent night.

4. From ev-ery e-vil shall He keep thy soul, From ev-ery sin:
Je-ho-vah shall pre-serve thy go-ing out, Thy com-ing in.
A-bove thee watch-ing, He whom we a-dore
Shall keep thee hence-forth, yea, for-ev-er-more. A-men.

LIFE IN CHRIST: FAITH AND ASSURANCE

I TO THE HILLS WILL LIFT MINE EYES 258
DUNDEE C.M.

Based on Psalm 121
Scottish Psalter, 1650

Scottish Psalter, 1615

1. I to the hills will lift mine eyes, from whence doth come mine aid?
   My safety cometh from the Lord, who heav'n and earth hath made.
2. Thy foot He'll not let slide, nor will He slumber that thee keeps.
   Behold, He that keeps Israel, He slumbers not, nor sleeps.
3. The Lord thee keeps, the Lord thy shade on thy right hand doth stay:
   The moon by night thee shall not smite, nor yet the sun by day.
4. The Lord shall keep thy soul; He shall preserve thee from all ill.
   Henceforth thy going out and in God keep forever will. A-men.

O FOR A FAITH THAT WILL NOT SHRINK 259
EVAN C.M.

William Hiley Bathurst, 1831

William H. Havergal, d. 1870
Arranged by Lowell Mason, 1850

1. O for a faith that will not shrink Though pressed by many a foe,
   That will not tremble on the brink Of poverty or woe.
2. That will not murmur nor complain Beneath the chastening rod,
   But in the hour of grief or pain Can lean upon its God.
3. A faith that shines more bright and clear When tempests rage without,
   That, when in danger, knows no fear, In darkness feels no doubt.
4. A faith that keeps the narrow way Till life's last spark is fled,
   And with a pure and heav'nly ray Lights up the dying bed.
5. Lord, give me such a faith as this, And then, what-e'er may come,
   I'll taste e'en here the hallowed bliss Of an eternal home. A-men.

LIFE IN CHRIST: FAITH AND ASSURANCE

260 HOW FIRM A FOUNDATION
BELLEVUE (FOUNDATION) 11.11.11.11.

"K"† in John Rippon's *Selection of Hymns*, 1787

Folk Hymn
Joseph Funk's *Genuine Church Music*, 1832 (*Harmonia Sacra*)

1. How firm a foundation, ye saints of the Lord,
Is laid for your faith in His excellent Word!
What more can He say than to you He hath said,
To you who for refuge to Jesus have fled?

2. "Fear not, I am with thee, O be not dismayed;
For I am thy God, and will still give thee aid;
I'll strengthen thee, help thee, and cause thee to stand,
Upheld by My righteous, omnipotent hand.

3. "When through the deep waters I call thee to go,
The rivers of sorrow shall not overflow;
For I will be with thee, thy troubles to bless,
And sanctify to thee thy deepest distress.

4. "When through fiery trials thy pathway shall lie,
My grace, all-sufficient, shall be thy supply;
The flame shall not hurt thee; I only design
Thy dross to consume, and thy gold to refine.

5. "The soul that on Jesus hath leaned for repose,
I will not, I will not desert to his foes;
That soul, though all hell should endeavor to shake,
I'll never, no never, no never forsake!"

LIFE IN CHRIST: FAITH AND ASSURANCE

HOW FIRM A FOUNDATION 261

ADESTE FIDELES 11.11.11.11.

"K"† in John Rippon's *Selection of Hymns*, 1787   John Francis Wade? c. 1740-43

1 How firm a foun - da - tion, ye saints of the Lord, Is
2 "Fear not, I am with thee, O be not dis - mayed; For
3 "When through the deep wa - ters I call thee to go, The
4 "The soul that on Je - sus hath leaned for re - pose, I

laid for your faith in His ex - cel - lent Word! What more can He
I am thy God, and will still give thee aid; I'll strength-en thee,
riv - ers of sor - row shall not o - ver-flow; For I will be
will not, I will not de - sert to his foes; That soul, though all

say than to you He hath said, Who un - to the Sav - ior for
help thee, and cause thee to stand, Up - held by My righ-teous, om -
with thee, thy trou-bles to bless, And sanc - ti - fy to thee thy
hell should en - deav - or to shake, I'll nev - er, no nev - er, no

ref - uge have fled? Who un - to the Sav - ior for ref - uge have fled?
nip - o - tent hand, Up - held by My righ-teous, om - nip - o - tent hand.
deep-est dis - tress, And sanc - ti - fy to thee thy deep-est dis - tress.
nev - er for - sake, I'll nev - er, no nev - er, no nev - er for - sake!"

LIFE IN CHRIST: FAITH AND ASSURANCE

262 FAITH OF OUR FATHERS
ST. CATHERINE L.M. with Refrain

Frederick W. Faber, 1849

Henri Frederick Hemy, 1864
Adapted by James G. Walton, 1874

1 Faith of our fa-thers, liv-ing still In spite of dun-geon, fire, and sword;
2 Our fa-thers, chained in pris-ons dark, Were still in heart and con-science free:
3 Faith of our fa-thers, we will love Both friend and foe in all our strife;

O how our hearts beat high with joy When-e'er we hear that glo-rious word.
How sweet would be their chil-dren's fate, If they, like them, could die for thee.
And preach thee, too, as love knows how, By kind-ly words and vir-tuous life:

Faith of our fa-thers, ho-ly faith. We will be true to thee till death!
Faith of our fa-thers, ho-ly faith. We will be true to thee till death!
Faith of our fa-thers, ho-ly faith. We will be true to thee till death!

263 O HOLY SAVIOR, FRIEND UNSEEN
INTEGER VITAE 8.8.8.6.

Charlotte Elliott, 1836

Friedrich F. Flemming, 1811

1 O ho-ly Sav-ior, friend un-seen, The faint, the weak on Thee may
2 Blest with com-mu-nion so di-vine, Take what Thou wilt, shall I re-
3 Though faith and hope a-while be tried, I ask not, need not aught be-
4 Blest is my lot, what-e'er be-fall; What can dis-turb me, who ap-

LIFE IN CHRIST: FAITH AND ASSURANCE

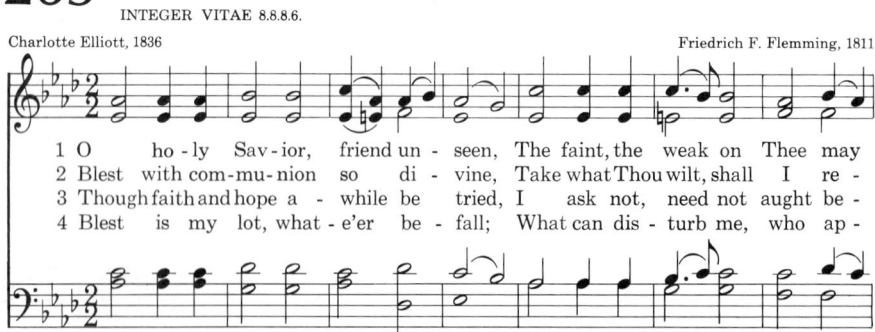

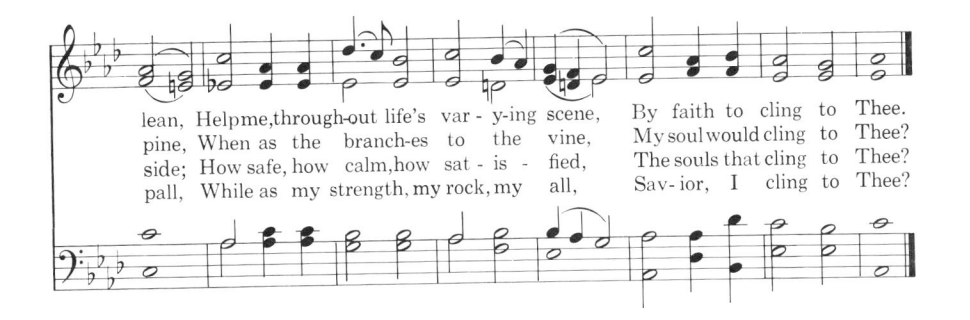

lean, Help me, through-out life's var-y-ing scene, By faith to cling to Thee.
pine, When as the branch-es to the vine, My soul would cling to Thee?
side; How safe, how calm, how sat-is-fied, The souls that cling to Thee?
pall, While as my strength, my rock, my all, Sav-ior, I cling to Thee?

WHEN IN THE HOUR OF UTMOST NEED 264
WENN WIR IN HÖCHSTEN NÖTEN SEIN L.M.

Paul Eber, 1566
Wenn wir in höchsten Nöten sein
Tr. Catherine Winkworth, 1858

Adapted from *Les commandemens de Dieu*
La forme des prieres . . . , Strasbourg, 1545
In German, Wittenberg, 1567

1 When in the hour of ut-most need We know not
2 Then this our com-fort is a-lone, That we may
3 That so with all our hearts we may Once more our

where to look for aid, When days and nights of anx-ious
meet be-fore Thy throne, And cry, O faith-ful God, to
glad thanks-giv-ings pay, And walk o-be-dient to Thy

thought Nor help nor coun-sel yet have brought,
Thee For res-cue from our mis-er-y:
Word, And now and ev-er praise the Lord. A-men.

LIFE IN CHRIST: FAITH AND ASSURANCE

265 MY JESUS, I LOVE THEE

GORDON 11.11.11.11.

William Ralph Featherston, c. 1862

Adoniram J. Gordon, 1876

1. My Jesus, I love Thee, I know Thou art mine,
For Thee all the follies of sin I resign;
My gracious Redeemer, my Savior art Thou;
If ever I loved Thee, my Jesus, 'tis now.

2. I love Thee, because Thou hast first loved me,
And purchased my pardon on Calvary's tree;
I love Thee for wearing the thorns on Thy brow;
If ever I loved Thee, my Jesus, 'tis now.

3. I will love Thee in life, I will love Thee in death,
And praise Thee as long as Thou lendest me breath;
And say when the death-dew lies cold on my brow,
If ever I loved Thee, my Jesus, 'tis now.

4. In mansions of glory and endless delight,
I'll ever adore Thee in heaven so bright;
I'll sing with the glittering crown on my brow,
If ever I loved Thee, my Jesus, 'tis now.

LIFE IN CHRIST: LOVE AND GRATITUDE

JESUS, THY BOUNDLESS LOVE TO ME 266
STELLA 8.8.8.8.8.8.

Paul Gerhardt, 1653
O Jesu Christ, mein schönstes Licht
Tr. John Wesley, 1739

Easy Tunes for Catholic Schools, 1852

1. Jesus, Thy boundless love to me No thought can reach, no tongue declare; O knit my thankful heart to Thee, And reign without a rival there. Thine wholly, Thine alone I am: Be Thou alone my constant flame.

2. O Love, how cheering is Thy ray! All pain before Thy presence flies; Care, anguish, sorrow melt away Where'er Thy healing beams arise: O Jesus, nothing may I see, Nothing hear, feel, or think but Thee!

3. O draw me, Savior, after Thee; So shall I run and never tire: With gracious words still comfort me; Be Thou my hope, my sole desire. Free me from every weight; nor fear Nor sin can come, if Thou art here.

4. In suffering be Thy love my peace, In weakness be Thy love my power; And when the storms of life shall cease, Jesus, in that important hour, In death as life be Thou my guide, And save me, who for me hast died! A-men.

LIFE IN CHRIST: LOVE AND GRATITUDE

267 MY GOD, I THANK THEE
WENTWORTH 8.4.8.4.8.8.4.

Adelaide Anne Procter, 1858
Frederick Charles Maker, 1876

1. My God, I thank Thee, who hast made The earth so bright,
So full of splen-dor and of joy, Beau-ty and light,
So man-y glo-rious things are here, No-ble and right.

2. I thank Thee, too, that Thou hast made Joy to a-bound,
So man-y gen-tle thoughts and deeds Cir-cling us round;
That in the dark-est spot of earth Some love is found.

3. I thank Thee more that all our joy Is touched with pain;
That shad-ows fall on bright-est hours, That thorns re-main,
So that earth's bliss may be our guide, And not our chain.

4. I thank Thee, Lord, that Thou hast kept The best in store;
We have e-nough, yet not too much To long for more,
A yearn-ing for a deep-er peace Not known be-fore. A-men.

268 THE SAVIOR DIED, BUT ROSE AGAIN
WINCHESTER OLD C.M.

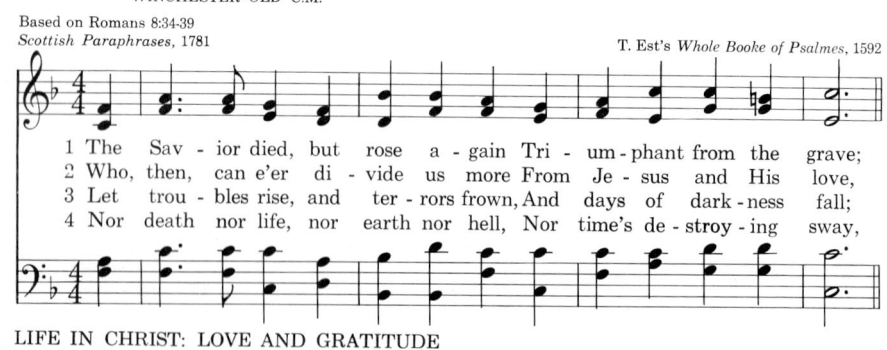

Based on Romans 8:34-39
Scottish Paraphrases, 1781
T. Est's *Whole Booke of Psalmes*, 1592

1. The Sav-ior died, but rose a-gain Tri-um-phant from the grave;
2. Who, then, can e'er di-vide us more From Je-sus and His love,
3. Let trou-bles rise, and ter-rors frown, And days of dark-ness fall;
4. Nor death nor life, nor earth nor hell, Nor time's de-stroy-ing sway,

LIFE IN CHRIST: LOVE AND GRATITUDE

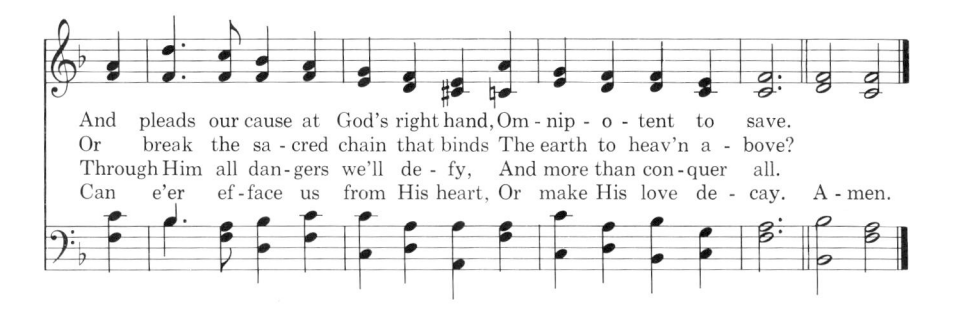

And pleads our cause at God's right hand, Om-nip-o-tent to save.
Or break the sa-cred chain that binds The earth to heav'n a-bove?
Through Him all dan-gers we'll de-fy, And more than con-quer all.
Can e'er ef-face us from His heart, Or make His love de-cay. A-men.

O LOVE THAT WILT NOT LET ME GO 269

ST. MARGARET 8.8.8.8.6.

George Matheson, 1882
Albert Lister Peace, 1884

1. O Love that wilt not let me go, I rest my wea-ry soul in Thee; I give Thee back the life I owe, That in Thine o-cean depths its flow May rich-er, full-er be.

2. O Light that fol-low'st all my way, I yield my flick'ring torch to Thee; My heart re-stores its bor-rowed ray, That in Thy sun-shine's blaze its day May bright-er, fair-er be.

3. O Joy that seek-est me through pain, I can-not close my heart to Thee; I trace the rain-bow through the rain, And feel the prom-ise is not vain That morn shall tear-less be.

4. O Cross that lift-est up my head, I dare not ask to fly from Thee; I lay in dust life's glo-ry dead, And from the ground there blos-soms red Life that shall end-less be. A-men.

LIFE IN CHRIST: LOVE AND GRATITUDE

270 GRACIOUS SPIRIT, HOLY GHOST
CAPETOWN 7.7.7.5.

Christopher Wordsworth, 1862 — Friedrich Filitz, 1847

1. Gra-cious Spir-it, Ho-ly Ghost, Taught by Thee, we cov-et most
Of Thy gifts at Pen-te-cost, Ho-ly, heav'n-ly love.

2. Faith, that moun-tains could re-move, Tongues of earth or heav'n a-bove,
Knowl-edge, all things, emp-ty prove, With-out heav'n-ly love.

3. Love is kind, and suf-fers long, Love is meek, and thinks no wrong,
Love than death it-self more strong; There-fore give us love.

4. Proph-e-cy will fade a-way, Melt-ing in the light of day;
Love will ev-er with us stay; There-fore give us love.

5. Faith and hope and love we see, Join-ing hand in hand, a-gree;
But the great-est of the three, And the best, is love. A-men.

LIFE IN CHRIST: LOVE AND GRATITUDE

271 PEACE, PERFECT PEACE
PAX TECUM 10.10.

Edward Henry Bickersteth, 1875 — George Thomas Caldbeck, 1877

1. Peace, per-fect peace, in this dark world of sin?
The blood of Je-sus whis-pers peace with-in.

2. Peace, per-fect peace, by throng-ing du-ties pressed?
To do the will of Je-sus, this is rest.

3. Peace, per-fect peace, with loved ones far a-way?
In Je-sus' keep-ing we are safe and they.

4. Peace, per-fect peace, our fu-ture all un-known?
Je-sus we know, and He is on the throne.

5. Peace, per-fect peace, death shad-'wing us and ours?
Je-sus has van-quished death and all its powers.

LIFE IN CHRIST: JOY AND PEACE

O HOW HAPPY ARE THEY 272

NEW CONCORD 6.6.9.6.6.9.

Charles Wesley†, 1749

Folk Hymn
Joseph Funk's *Genuine Church Music*, 1832 (*Harmonia Sacra*)
Harmony by J. Harold Moyer, 1965

1. O how happy are they Who the Savior obey,
And have laid up their treasures above,
O what tongue can express The sweet comfort and peace
Of a soul in its earliest love.

2. O that comfort was mine, When the favor divine
I first found in the blood of the Lamb;
When my heart it believed, What a joy it received,
What a heaven in Jesus His name!

3. 'Twas a heaven below My Redeemer to know,
And the angels could do nothing more,
Than to fall at His feet, And the story repeat,
And the lover of sinners adore.

4. Jesus all the day long Was my joy and my song;
O that all His salvation may see!
"He hath loved me," I cried, "He hath suffered and died,
To redeem such a rebel as me!"

LIFE IN CHRIST: JOY AND PEACE

273 O THOU, IN WHOSE PRESENCE

ZION'S PILGRIM 11.8.11.8.D.

Joseph Swain, 1791

Folk Hymn
J. Leavitt's *Christian Lyre*, 1831
Harmony by J. Harold Moyer, 1965

1. O Thou, in whose presence my soul takes delight, On whom in affliction I call, My comfort by day, and my song in the night, My hope, my salvation, my all. Where dost Thou, dear Shepherd, resort with Thy sheep? To feed in the pastures of love? Say, why in the

2. O why should I wander an alien from Thee, Or cry in the desert for bread? Thy foes will rejoice when my sorrows they see, And smile at the tears I have shed. He looks, and ten thousands of angels rejoice, And myriads wait for His word; He speaks, and e-

LIFE IN CHRIST: JOY AND PEACE

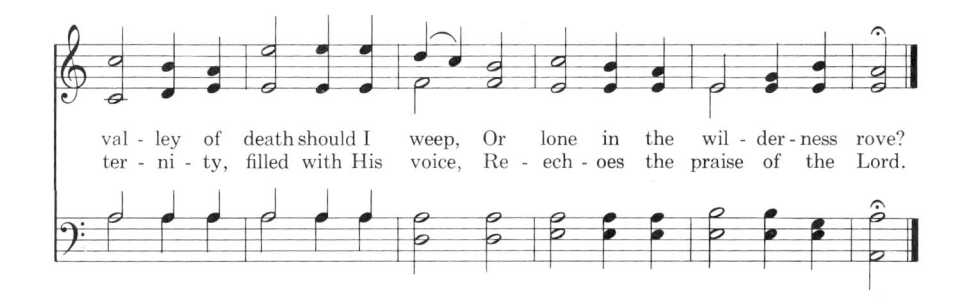

val - ley of death should I weep, Or lone in the wil - der - ness rove?
ter - ni - ty, filled with His voice, Re - ech - oes the praise of the Lord.

DEAR LORD AND FATHER OF MANKIND 274

REST (WHITTIER) 8.6.8.8.6.

John Greenleaf Whittier, 1872
Frederick Charles Maker, 1887

1 Dear Lord and Fa - ther of man-kind, For - give our fool - ish ways;
2 In sim - ple trust like theirs who heard, Be - side the Syr - ian sea,
3 O Sab - bath rest by Gal - i - lee, O calm of hills a - bove,
4 Drop Thy still dews of qui - et - ness, Till all our striv-ings cease;
5 Breathe through the heats of our de - sire Thy cool - ness and Thy balm;

Re - clothe us in our right - ful mind, In pur - er lives Thy
The gra - cious call - ing of the Lord, Let us, like them, with -
Where Je - sus knelt to share with Thee The si - lence of e -
Take from our souls the strain and stress, And let our or - dered
Let sense be dumb, let flesh re - tire; Speak through the earth - quake,

serv - ice find, In deep - er rev - erence, praise.
out a word Rise up and fol - low Thee.
ter - ni - ty, In - ter - pret - ed by love!
lives con - fess The beau - ty of Thy peace.
wind, and fire, O still, small voice of calm! A - men.

LIFE IN CHRIST: JOY AND PEACE

275 ETERNAL SOURCE OF JOYS DIVINE
EDEN (ST. NICHOLAS) C.M.

Anne Steele, 1760
William Henry Havergal, 1853

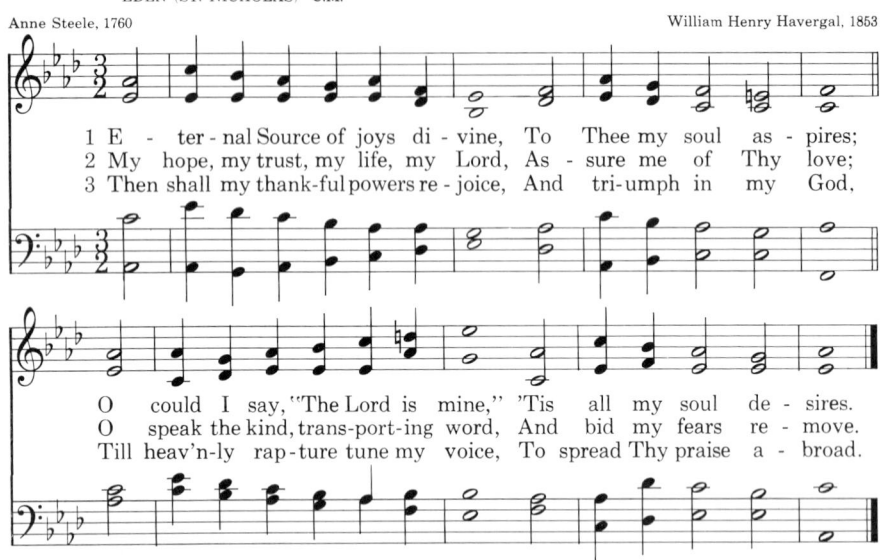

1 E-ternal Source of joys di-vine, To Thee my soul as-pires;
2 My hope, my trust, my life, my Lord, As-sure me of Thy love;
3 Then shall my thankful powers re-joice, And tri-umph in my God,

O could I say, "The Lord is mine," 'Tis all my soul de-sires.
O speak the kind, trans-port-ing word, And bid my fears re-move.
Till heav'n-ly rap-ture tune my voice, To spread Thy praise a-broad.

276 PRINCE OF PEACE, CONTROL MY WILL
ALETTA 7.7.7.7.

Mary Ann Serrett Barber, 1838
William Batchelder Bradbury, 1857

1 Prince of Peace, con-trol my will; Bid this strug-gling heart be still;
2 Thou hast bought me with Thy blood, O-pened wide the gate to God:
3 May Thy will, not mine, be done; May Thy will and mine be one;
4 Sav-ior, at Thy feet I fall, Thou my life, my God, my all!

Bid my fears and doubt-ings cease, Hush my spir-it in-to peace.
Peace I ask, but peace must be, Lord, in be-ing one with Thee.
Chase these doubt-ings from my heart, Now Thy per-fect peace im-part.
Let Thy hap-py serv-ant be One for-ev-er-more with Thee. A-men.

LIFE IN CHRIST: JOY AND PEACE

REJOICE, YE PURE IN HEART 277

MARION S.M. with Refrain

Edward Hayes Plumptre, 1865 — Arthur Henry Messiter, 1883

1 Rejoice, ye pure in heart, Rejoice, give thanks and sing;
  Your festal banner wave on high, The cross of Christ your King.

2 Bright youth and snow-crowned age, Strong men and maidens meek,
  Raise high your free exulting song, God's won-drous praises speak.

3 With all the angel choirs, With all the saints on earth,
  Pour out the strains of joy and bliss, True rapture, noblest mirth.

4 Yes on, through life's long path, Still chanting as ye go,
  From youth to age, by night and day, In gladness and in woe.

Refrain: Rejoice, rejoice, Rejoice, give thanks and sing. A-men.

5 At last the march shall end,
  The wearied ones shall rest,
  The pilgrims find their Father's house,
  Jerusalem the blest.

6 Praise Him who reigns on high,
  The Lord whom we adore,
  The Father, Son, and Holy Ghost,
  One God for evermore.

LIFE IN CHRIST: JOY AND PEACE

278 THAT MAN HATH PERFECT BLESSEDNESS
DUNFERMLINE C.M.

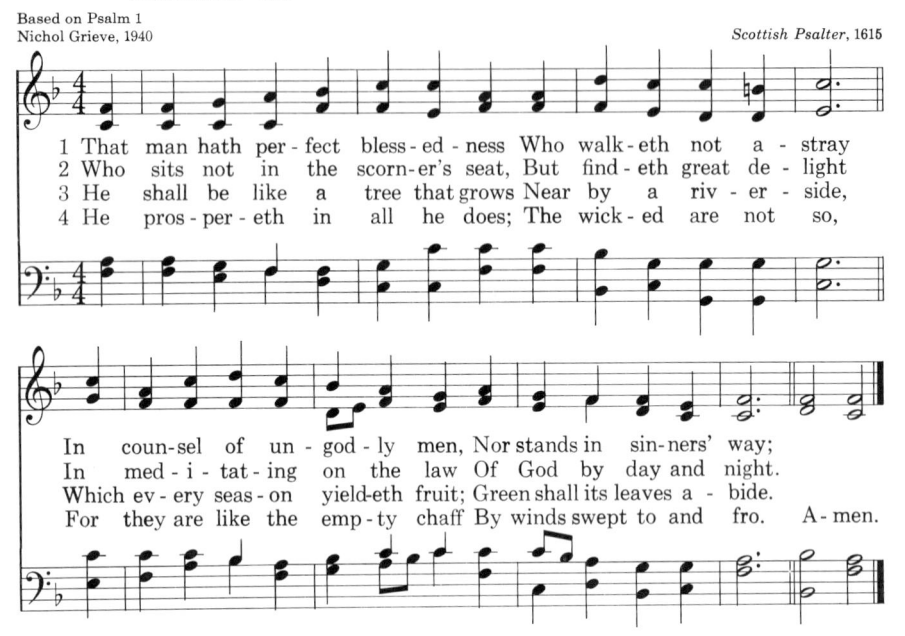

Based on Psalm 1
Nichol Grieve, 1940

Scottish Psalter, 1615

1. That man hath per-fect bless-ed-ness Who walk-eth not a-stray
   In coun-sel of un-god-ly men, Nor stands in sin-ners' way;
2. Who sits not in the scorn-er's seat, But find-eth great de-light
   In med-i-tat-ing on the law Of God by day and night.
3. He shall be like a tree that grows Near by a riv-er-side,
   Which ev-ery sea-son yield-eth fruit; Green shall its leaves a-bide.
4. He pros-per-eth in all he does; The wick-ed are not so,
   For they are like the emp-ty chaff By winds swept to and fro. A-men.

5 For evil-doers shall not stand
  When judgment draweth near;
  Nor in assemblies of the just
  Shall godless men appear.

6 The Lord takes knowledge of the way
  In which the righteous go:
  The course which men of sin pursue
  Ends in their overthrow.

LIFE IN CHRIST: JOY AND PEACE

279 BLEST ARE THE PURE IN HEART
FRANCONIA S.M.

John Keble and Others, 1819 and 1836

J. B. König's *Harmonischer Liederschatz*, 1738
Adapted by William Henry Havergal, 1847

1. Blest are the pure in heart, For they shall see our God;
2. The Lord, who left the heav'ns Our life and peace to bring,
3. Still to the low-ly soul He doth Him-self im-part,
4. Lord, we Thy pres-ence seek; May ours this bless-ing be:

LIFE IN CHRIST: PURITY AND HOLINESS

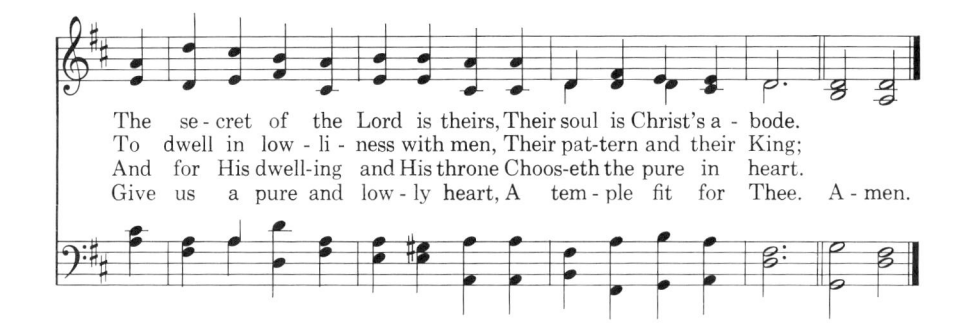

The se-cret of the Lord is theirs, Their soul is Christ's a - bode.
To dwell in low-li-ness with men, Their pat-tern and their King;
And for His dwell-ing and His throne Choos-eth the pure in heart.
Give us a pure and low-ly heart, A tem-ple fit for Thee. A-men.

PURER IN HEART, O GOD 280

PURER IN HEART 6.4.6.4.6.6.6.4.4.

Fannie Estelle Davison, 1877
James Henry Fillmore, 1877

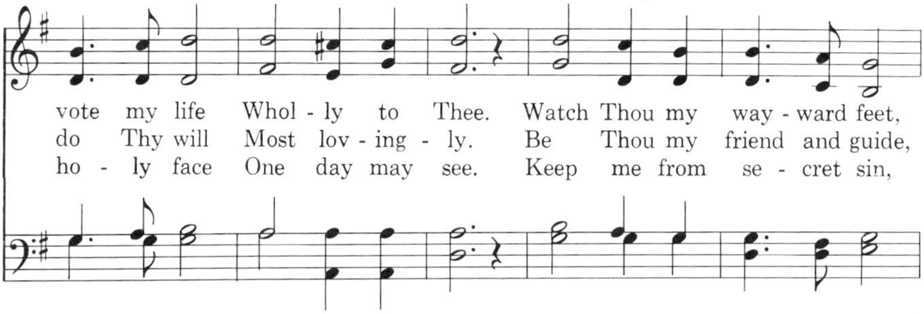

1 Pur-er in heart, O God, Help me to be; May I de-vote my life Whol-ly to Thee. Watch Thou my way-ward feet, Guide me with coun-sel sweet; Pur-er in heart, Help me to be.
2 Pur-er in heart, O God, Help me to be; Teach me to do Thy will Most lov-ing-ly. Be Thou my friend and guide, Let me with Thee a-bide; Pur-er in heart, Help me to be.
3 Pur-er in heart, O God, Help me to be; That I Thy ho-ly face One day may see. Keep me from se-cret sin, Reign Thou my soul with-in; Pur-er in heart, Help me to be. A-men.

LIFE IN CHRIST: PURITY AND HOLINESS

281 KEEP THYSELF PURE
PENTECOST L.M.

Adelaide M. Plumtre, 1908
William Boyd, 1864

1. Keep thyself pure! Christ's soldier, hear, Through life's loud strife, the call rings clear. Thy captain speaks: His word obey; So shall thy strength be as thy day.
2. Keep thyself pure! Thrice blessed he Whose heart from taint of sin is free; His feet shall stand where saints have trod, He with rapt eyes shall see his God.
3. Keep thyself pure! For He who died, Himself for thy sake sanctified; Then hear Him speaking from the skies, And victor o'er temptation rise.
4. O Holy Spirit, keep us pure, Grant us Thy strength when sins allure; Our bodies are Thy temple, Lord; Be Thou in thought and act adored. A-men.

282 WALK IN THE LIGHT
DEDHAM C.M.

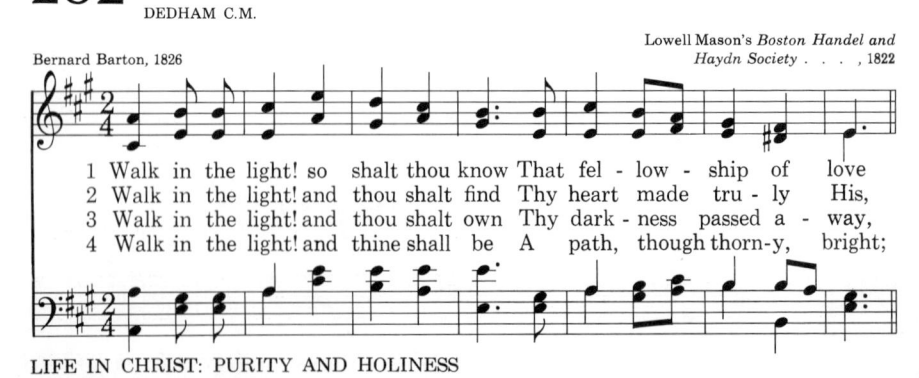

Bernard Barton, 1826
Lowell Mason's *Boston Handel and Haydn Society* . . . , 1822

1. Walk in the light! so shalt thou know That fellowship of love
2. Walk in the light! and thou shalt find Thy heart made truly His,
3. Walk in the light! and thou shalt own Thy darkness passed away,
4. Walk in the light! and thine shall be A path, though thorny, bright;

LIFE IN CHRIST: PURITY AND HOLINESS

His Spir-it on-ly can be-stow Who reigns in light a-bove.
Who dwells in cloud-less light en-shrined, In whom no dark-ness is.
Be-cause that light hath on thee shone In which is per-fect day.
For God, by grace, shall dwell in thee, And God Him-self is light.

O FOR A HEART TO PRAISE 283
KILMARNOCK C.M.

Charles Wesley†, 1742
Neil Dougall, 1831

1. O for a heart to praise my God, A heart from sin set free! A heart that's sprin-kled with the blood So free-ly shed for me.
2. A heart re-signed, sub-mis-sive, meek, My dear Re-deem-er's throne; Where on-ly Christ is heard to speak, Where Je-sus reigns a-lone.
3. A heart in ev-ery thought re-newed, And full of love di-vine; Per-fect, and right, and pure, and good, A cop-y, Lord, of Thine.
4. An hum-ble, low-ly, con-trite heart, Be-liev-ing, true, and clean, Which nei-ther life nor death can part From Him that dwells with-in.
5. Thy na-ture, gra-cious Lord, im-part, Come quick-ly from a-bove, Write Thy new name up-on my heart, Thy new, best name of Love. A-men.

LIFE IN CHRIST: PURITY AND HOLINESS

284 AS THE HART WITH EAGER YEARNING

GENEVA 42 8.7.8.7.7.7.8.8.

Based on Psalm 42
Christine Turner Curtis‡, 1939

Pseaumes octante trois . . . , Geneva, 1551
Harmony adapted from Claude Goudimel, 1565

1. As the hart with eager yearning Seeks the cooling watercourse, So my soul with ardor burning Longs for God, its heav'nly source. When shall I behold His face? When shall I receive His grace? When shall I, His praises

2. Day and night in grievous anguish Bitter tears have been my meat, While my longing soul doth languish To partake His manna sweet. O, my soul, be not dismayed: Trust in God, who is our aid; Hope and joy His love pro-

LIFE IN CHRIST: HOPE AND ASPIRATION

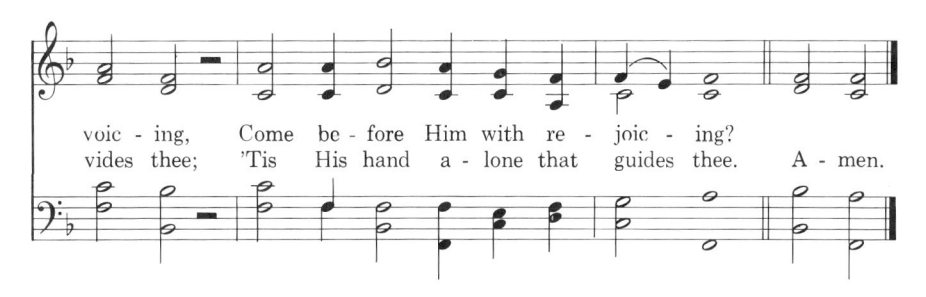

voic - ing, Come be-fore Him with re - joic - ing?
vides thee; 'Tis His hand a - lone that guides thee. A - men.

AS PANTS THE HART 285
MARTYRDOM C.M.

Based on Psalm 42
Tate and Brady's *New Version*
of the Psalms, 1696 and 1698

Hugh Wilson, late 18th century
Adapted by Robert Archibald Smith, 1825

1 As pants the hart for cool - ing streams When
2 For Thee, my God, the liv - ing God, My
3 Why rest - less, why cast down, my soul? Trust
4 God of my strength, how long shall I Like
5 Why rest - less, why cast down, my soul? Hope

heat - ed in the chase, So longs my soul, O
thirst - y soul doth pine; O when shall I be -
God, who will em - ploy His aid for thee, and
one for - got - ten mourn, For - lorn, for - sak - en,
still, and thou shalt sing The praise of Him who

God, for Thee, And Thy re - fresh - ing grace.
hold Thy face, Thou Maj - es - ty di - vine?
change these sighs To thank - ful hymns of joy.
and ex - posed To my op - pres - sor's scorn?
is thy God, Thy health's e - ter - nal spring. A - men.

LIFE IN CHRIST: HOPE AND ASPIRATION

286 CHRIST, OF ALL MY HOPES
SONG XIII 7.7.7.7.

Ralph Wardlaw, 1817

Orlando Gibbons, 1623

1. Christ, of all my hopes the ground, Christ, the spring of all my joy, Still in Thee may I be found, Still for Thee my powers employ!
2. Let Thy love my heart inflame; Keep Thy fear before my sight; Be Thy praise my highest aim; Be Thy smile my chief delight!
3. When new triumphs of Thy name Swell the rap-tured songs above, May I feel the kindred flame, Full of zeal, and full of love!
4. Fountain of o'erflowing grace, Freely from Thy fullness give; Till I close my earthly race, May I prove it "Christ to live!" A-men.

287 O LOVE THAT CASTS OUT FEAR
ST. DENYS 6.6.6.6.

Horatius Bonar, 1861

Frank S. Spinney, 1876

1. O love that casts out fear, O love that casts out sin,
2. True sunlight of the soul, Surround me as I go;
3. Great love of God, come in, Well-spring of heav'nly peace;
4. Love of the living God, Of Father, and of Son,

LIFE IN CHRIST: HOPE AND ASPIRATION

Tar - ry no more with - out, But come and dwell with - in.
So shall my way be safe, My feet no stray - ing know.
Thou liv - ing wa - ter, come, Spring up, and nev - er cease.
Love of the Ho - ly Ghost, Fill Thou each need - y one. A - men.

O CHRIST, OUR HOPE 288

ST. STEPHEN (NEWINGTON) C.M.

Anonymous, 7th or 8th century
Jesu nostra redemptio
Tr. John Chandler, 1837
Doxology added

William Jones, 1789

1. O Christ, our hope, our hearts' de - sire, Re -
2. How vast the mer - cy and the love Which
3. O may Thy might - y love pre - vail Our
4. O Christ, be Thou our pres - ent joy, Our
5. All praise to Thee, as - cend - ed Lord; All

demp - tion's on - ly spring; Cre - a - tor of the
laid our sins on Thee, And led Thee to a
sin - ful souls to spare, O may we come be -
fu - ture great re - ward; Our on - ly glo - ry
glo - ry ev - er be To Fa - ther, Son, and

world art Thou, Its Sav - ior and its King.
cru - el death To set Thy peo - ple free.
fore Thy throne And find ac - cept - ance there!
may it be To glo - ry in the Lord!
Ho - ly Ghost Through all e - ter - ni - ty! A - men.

LIFE IN CHRIST: HOPE AND ASPIRATION

289 NEARER, MY GOD, TO THEE
BETHANY 6.4.6.4.6.6.6.4.

Sarah Adams†, 1841 — Lowell Mason, 1856

1. Near - er, my God, to Thee, Near - er to Thee. E'en though it be a cross
That rais-eth me; Still all my song shall be, Near - er, my God, to Thee,
Near - er, my God, to Thee, Near - er to Thee!

2. Though like the wan - der - er, The sun gone down, Dark-ness be o - ver me,
My rest a stone; Yet in my dreams I'd be Near - er, my God, to Thee,
Near - er, my God, to Thee, Near - er to Thee!

3. There let the way ap - pear Steps un - to heav'n; All that Thou send - est me
In mer - cy giv'n; An - gels to beck - on me Near - er, my God, to Thee,
Near - er, my God, to Thee, Near - er to Thee!

4. Then, with my wak-ing thoughts Bright with Thy praise, Out of my ston - y griefs,
Beth - el I'll raise; So by my woes to be Near - er, my God, to Thee,
Near - er, my God, to Thee, Near - er to Thee!

5. Or if on joy - ful wing, Cleav - ing the sky, Sun, moon, and stars for - got,
Up - ward I fly, Still all my song shall be, Near - er, my God, to Thee,
Near - er, my God, to Thee, Near - er to Thee!

290 ABOVE THE TREMBLING ELEMENTS
DUNDEE C.M.

Anna L. Price, 1890 — *Scottish Psalter*, 1615

1. A - bove the trem - bling el - e - ments, A - bove life's rest - less sea,
2. Great calm-ness there, sweet pa - tience, too, Up - on Thy face I see;
3. I am not wea - ry of Thy work, From earth I would not flee;
4. That I may bless my ten - der friends, And those who love not me;
5. What - ev - er falls of good or ill, Thy hand, Thy care I see,
6. And when my eyes close for the last, Still this my prayer shall be:

LIFE IN CHRIST: HOPE AND ASPIRATION

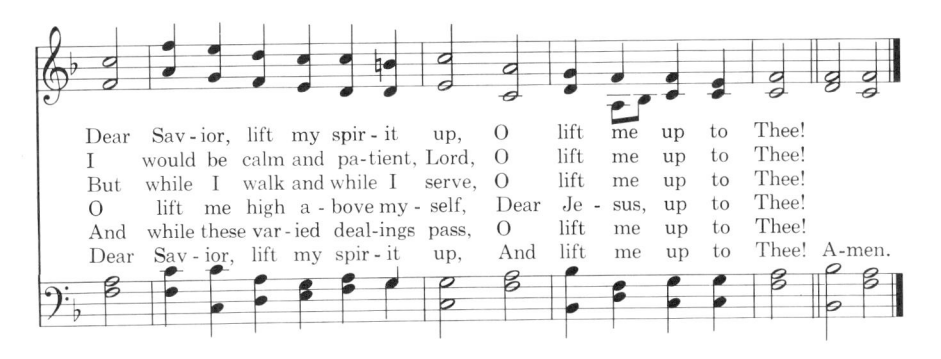

Dear Sav-ior, lift my spir-it up, O lift me up to Thee!
I would be calm and pa-tient, Lord, O lift me up to Thee!
But while I walk and while I serve, O lift me up to Thee!
O lift me high a-bove my-self, Dear Je-sus, up to Thee!
And while these var-ied deal-ings pass, O lift me up to Thee!
Dear Sav-ior, lift my spir-it up, And lift me up to Thee! A-men.

ALL MY HOPE ON GOD IS FOUNDED 291

MEINE HOFFNUNG 8.7.8.7.3.3.7.

Joachim Neander, 1680
Meine Hoffnung stehet feste
Paraphrase by Robert Bridges, 1899

Joachim Neander, 1680

1. All my hope on God is found-ed; He doth still my trust re-new.
2. Pride of man and earth-ly glo-ry, Sword and crown be-tray his trust;
3. God's great good-ness aye en-dur-eth, Deep His wis-dom pass-ing thought:
4. Dai-ly doth th' al-might-y Giv-er Boun-teous gifts on us be-stow.
5. Still from man to God e-ter-nal Sac-ri-fice of praise be done,

Me through change and chance He guid-eth, On-ly good and on-ly true.
What with care and toil he build-eth, Tower and tem-ple fall to dust.
Splen-dor, light and life at-tend Him, Beau-ty spring-eth out of nought.
His de-sire our soul de-light-eth, Plea-sure leads us where we go.
High a-bove all prais-es prais-ing For the gift of Christ His Son.

God un-known, He a-lone Calls my heart to be His own.
But God's power Hour by hour, Is my tem-ple and my tower.
Ev-er-more From His store New-born worlds rise and a-dore.
Love doth stand At His hand; Joy doth wait on His com-mand.
Christ doth call One and all: Ye who fol-low shall not fall. A-men.

LIFE IN CHRIST: HOPE AND ASPIRATION

292 THE SANDS OF TIME ARE SINKING

RUTHERFORD 7.6.7.6.7.6.7.5.

Annie Ross Cousin†, 1857 — Edward Francis Rimbault, 1867

1. O the sands of time are sinking, The dawn of heaven breaks,
The summer morn I've sighed for, The fair sweet morn awakes:
Dark, dark hath been the midnight, But day-spring is at hand,
And glory, glory dwelleth In Emmanuel's land.

2. O Christ! He is the fountain, The deep sweet well of love!
The streams on earth I've tasted, More deep I'll drink above:
There, to an ocean fullness, His mercy doth expand,
And glory, glory dwelleth In Emmanuel's land.

3. I've wrestled on towards heaven, 'Gainst storm, and wind, and tide;
Now, like a weary traveler, That leaneth on his guide,
Amid the shades of evening, While sinks life's lingering sand,
I hail the glory dawning In Emmanuel's land.

4. With mercy and with judgment My web of time He wove,
And aye the dews of sorrow Were lustred by His love;
I'll bless the hand that guided, I'll bless the heart that planned,
When throned where glory dwelleth In Emmanuel's land.

5. O! I am my Beloved's, And my Beloved is mine!
He brings a poor vile sinner Into His house of wine;
I stand upon His merit, I know no other stand,
Not e'en where glory dwelleth In Emmanuel's land.

6. The bride eyes not her garment, But her dear bride-groom's face;
I will not gaze at glory, But on my King of grace;
Not at the crown He giveth, But on His pierced hand:
The Lamb is all the glory Of Emmanuel's land.

LIFE IN CHRIST: HOPE AND ASPIRATION

LORD, I WANT TO BE A CHRISTIAN 293

LORD, I WANT TO BE A CHRISTIAN Irregular

Negro Spiritual
Traditional Melody

1. Lord, I want to be a Christian In my heart, in my heart;
2. Lord, I want to be more loving In my heart, in my heart;
3. Lord, I want to be more holy In my heart, in my heart;
4. Lord, I want to be like Jesus In my heart, in my heart;

Lord, I want to be a Christian In my heart.
Lord, I want to be more loving In my heart.
Lord, I want to be more holy In my heart.
Lord, I want to be like Jesus In my heart.

In my heart, In my heart,
In my heart, In my heart,

Lord, I want to be a Christian In my heart.
Lord, I want to be more loving In my heart.
Lord, I want to be more holy In my heart.
Lord, I want to be like Jesus In my heart.

LIFE IN CHRIST: HOPE AND ASPIRATION

294 ON JORDAN'S STORMY BANKS I STAND

BOUND FOR THE PROMISED LAND C.M. with Refrain

Samuel Stennett, 1787

Folk Hymn
W. Walker's *Southern Harmony*, 1835
Harmony by J. Harold Moyer, 1965

1. On Jordan's stormy banks I stand, And cast a wishful eye,
To Canaan's fair and happy land, Where my possessions lie.

2. There generous fruits that never fail, On trees immortal grow;
There rocks and hills and brooks and vales, With milk and honey flow.

3. All o'er those wide extended plains Shines one eternal day:
There God the sun forever reigns, And scatters night away.

4. When shall I reach that happy place, And be forever blest?
When shall I see my Father's face, And in His bosom rest?

5. Filled with delight, my raptured soul Can here no longer stay:
Though Jordan's waves around me roll, Fearless I'd launch away.

Refrain
I'm bound for the promised land, I'm bound for the promised land;
O who will come and go with me, I'm bound for the promised land.

LIFE IN CHRIST: HOPE AND ASPIRATION

HOPE OF THE WORLD 295
GENEVA 12 (DONNE SECOURS, SEIGNEUR) 11.10.11.10.

Pseaumes octante trois . . . . , Geneva, 1551
Harmony adapted from Claude Goudimel, 1565

Georgia Harkness, 1953

1. Hope of the world, Thou Christ of great compassion,
Speak to our fearful hearts by conflict rent;
Save us, Thy people, from consuming passion,
Who by our own false hopes and aims are spent.

2. Hope of the world, God's gift from highest heaven,
Bringing to hungry souls the bread of life,
Still let Thy Spirit unto us be given
To heal earth's wounds and end her bitter strife.

3. Hope of the world, afoot on dusty highways,
Showing to wandering souls the path of light;
Walk Thou beside us lest the tempting byways
Lure us away from Thee to endless night.

4. Hope of the world, who by Thy cross didst save us
From death and dark despair, from sin and guilt;
We render back the love Thy mercy gave us;
Take Thou our lives and use them as Thou wilt.

5. Hope of the world, O Christ, o'er death victorious,
Who by this sign didst conquer grief and pain,
We would be faithful to Thy gospel glorious:
Thou art our Lord! Thou dost forever reign! A-men.

LIFE IN CHRIST: HOPE AND ASPIRATION

296 SWEET HOUR OF PRAYER

SWEET HOUR L.M.D.

Anonymous, c. 1840
William Batchelder Bradbury, c. 1861

1. Sweet hour of prayer, sweet hour of prayer, That calls me from a world of care, And bids me at my Father's throne Make all my wants and wishes known; In seasons of distress and grief, My soul has often found relief; And oft escaped the tempter's snare, By thy return, sweet hour of prayer!

2. Sweet hour of prayer, sweet hour of prayer, The joys I feel, the bliss I share, Of those whose anxious spirits burn With strong desires for thy return! With such I hasten to the place Where God my Savior shows His face, And gladly take my station there, And wait for thee, sweet hour of prayer!

3. Sweet hour of prayer, sweet hour of prayer, Thy wings shall my petition bear To Him whose truth and faithfulness Engage the waiting soul to bless; And since He bids me seek His face, Believe His Word and trust His grace, I'll cast on Him my every care, And wait for thee, sweet hour of prayer!

LIFE IN CHRIST: PRAYER

PRAYER IS THE SOUL'S SINCERE DESIRE 297

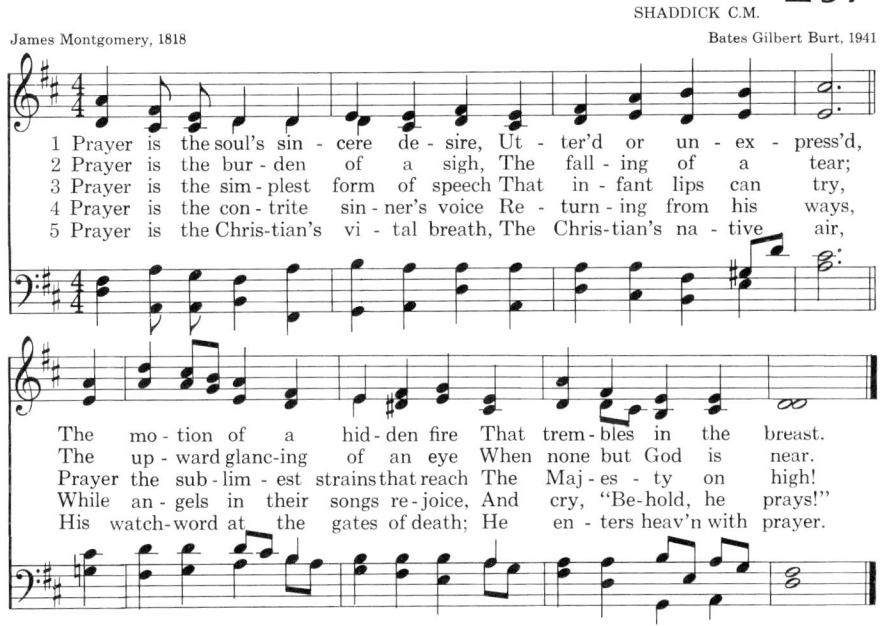

SHADDICK C.M.

James Montgomery, 1818
Bates Gilbert Burt, 1941

1. Prayer is the soul's sincere desire, Utter'd or unexpress'd,
   The motion of a hidden fire That trembles in the breast.
2. Prayer is the burden of a sigh, The falling of a tear;
   The upward glancing of an eye When none but God is near.
3. Prayer is the simplest form of speech That infant lips can try,
   Prayer the sublimest strains that reach The Majesty on high!
4. Prayer is the contrite sinner's voice Returning from his ways,
   While angels in their songs rejoice, And cry, "Behold, he prays!"
5. Prayer is the Christian's vital breath, The Christian's native air,
   His watchword at the gates of death; He enters heav'n with prayer.

O GOD OF MERCY! HEARKEN NOW 298

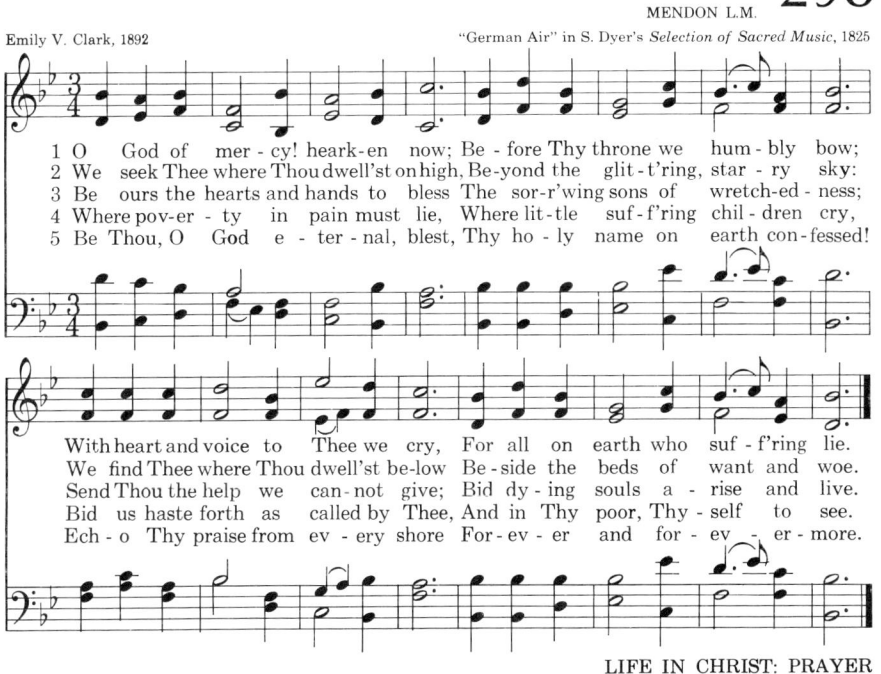

MENDON L.M.

Emily V. Clark, 1892
"German Air" in S. Dyer's *Selection of Sacred Music*, 1825

1. O God of mercy! hearken now; Before Thy throne we humbly bow;
   With heart and voice to Thee we cry, For all on earth who suff'ring lie.
2. We seek Thee where Thou dwell'st on high, Beyond the glitt'ring, starry sky:
   We find Thee where Thou dwell'st below Beside the beds of want and woe.
3. Be ours the hearts and hands to bless The sor'rwing sons of wretchedness;
   Send Thou the help we cannot give; Bid dying souls arise and live.
4. Where poverty in pain must lie, Where little suff'ring children cry,
   Bid us haste forth as called by Thee, And in Thy poor, Thyself to see.
5. Be Thou, O God eternal, blest, Thy holy name on earth confessed!
   Echo Thy praise from ev'ry shore Forever and for evermore.

LIFE IN CHRIST: PRAYER

299 LORD, WHAT A CHANGE WITHIN US
FFIGYSBREN 10.10.10.10.

Richard C. Trench, c. 1856
Arranged by William Pierson Merrill, 1907

Welsh Hymn Melody

1 Lord, what a change with-in us one short hour
2 We kneel, and all a-round us seems to lower;
3 Why should we ev-er weak or heart-less be,

Spent in Thy pres-ence will pre-vail to make;
We rise, and all, the dis-tant and the near,
Why are we ev-er o-ver-borne with care,

What heav-y bur-dens from our bos-oms take,
Stands forth in sun-ny out-line, brave and clear;
Anx-ious or trou-bled, when with us is prayer,

What parch-ed fields re-fresh as with a shower!
We kneel, how weak; we rise, how full of power.
And joy, and strength, and cour-age are with Thee?

LIFE IN CHRIST: PRAYER

BE THOU MY VISION 300
SLANE 10.10.9.10.

Ancient Irish
Rob tu mo bhoile, a Comdi cride
Tr. Mary Byrne, 1905
Versified by Eleanor Hull, 1912

Irish Traditional Melody
Harmony by Martin Shaw, 1925
Arrangement slightly altered

1. Be Thou my vi-sion, O Lord of my heart;
   Naught be all else to me save that Thou art,
   Thou my best thought, by day or by night,
   Wak-ing or sleep-ing, Thy pres-ence my light.

2. Be Thou my wis-dom, be Thou my true word;
   I ev-er with Thee, and Thou with me, Lord;
   Thou my great Fa-ther, I Thy true son;
   Thou in me dwell-ing, and I with Thee one.

3. Be Thou my buck-ler, my sword for the fight,
   Be Thou my dig-ni-ty, Thou my de-light,
   Thou my soul's shel-ter, Thou my high tower;
   Raise Thou me heav'n-ward, O power of my power.

4. Rich-es I heed not, nor man's emp-ty praise;
   Thou my in-her-it-ance, now and al-ways:
   Thou and Thou on-ly, first in my heart,
   High King of heav-en, my trea-sure Thou art.

5. High King of heav-en, when vic-t'ry is won
   May I reach heav-en's joys, O bright heav'n's sun!
   Heart of my heart, what-ev-er be-fall,
   Still be my vi-sion, O rul-er of all. A-men.

LIFE IN CHRIST: PRAYER

301 TEACH ME, MY GOD AND KING
ST. MICHAEL (OLD 134th) S.M.

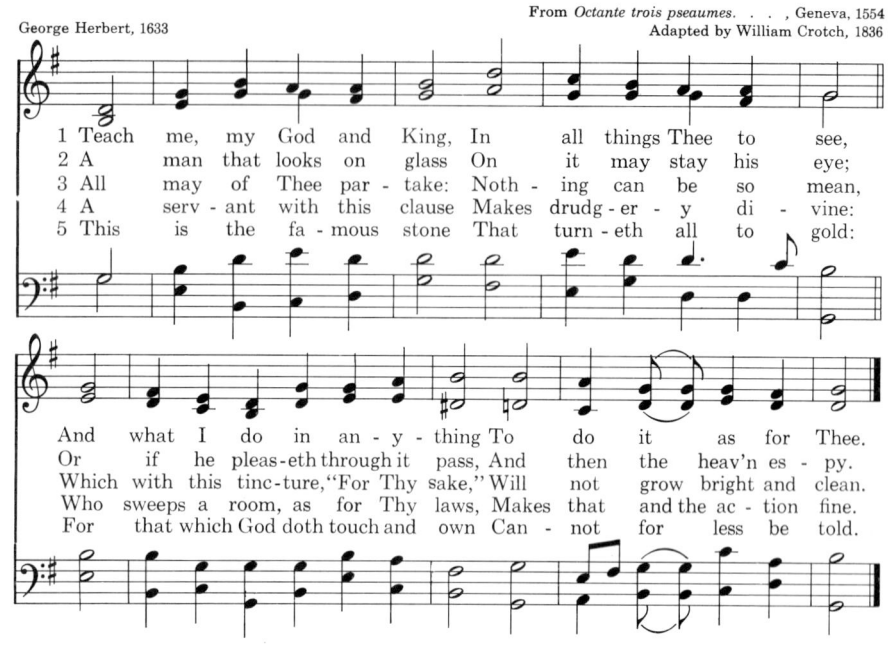

George Herbert, 1633

From *Octante trois pseaumes*. . . , Geneva, 1554
Adapted by William Crotch, 1836

1. Teach me, my God and King, In all things Thee to see,
   And what I do in an-y-thing To do it as for Thee.
2. A man that looks on glass On it may stay his eye;
   Or if he pleas-eth through it pass, And then the heav'n es-py.
3. All may of Thee par-take: Noth-ing can be so mean,
   Which with this tinc-ture, "For Thy sake," Will not grow bright and clean.
4. A serv-ant with this clause Makes drudg-er-y di-vine:
   Who sweeps a room, as for Thy laws, Makes that and the ac-tion fine.
5. This is the fa-mous stone That turn-eth all to gold:
   For that which God doth touch and own Can-not for less be told.

302 I WAITED FOR THE LORD MY GOD
ABBEY C.M.

Based on Psalm 40: 1-5
Scottish Psalter, 1650

Scottish Psalter, 1615

1. I wait-ed for the Lord my God, And pa-tient-ly did bear;
   At length to me He did in-cline My voice and cry to hear.
2. He took me from a fear-ful pit, And from the mir-y clay,
   And on a rock He set my feet, Es-tab-lish-ing my way.
3. He put a new song in my mouth, Our God to mag-ni-fy:
   Man-y shall see it, and shall fear, And on the Lord re-ly.
4. O bless-ed is the man whose trust Up-on the Lord re-lies;
   Re-spect-ing not the proud, nor such As turn a-side to lies.
5. O Lord my God, full man-y are The won-ders Thou hast done;
   Thy gra-cious thoughts to us-ward far A-bove all thoughts are gone. A-men.

LIFE IN CHRIST: PRAYER

WE WOULD SEE JESUS 303
HENLEY 11.10.11.10.

Anna Bartlett Warner, 1852
Lowell Mason, 1854

1. We would see Jesus; for the shadows lengthen
Across this little landscape of our life;
We would see Jesus, our weak faith to strengthen
For the last weariness, the final strife.

2. We would see Jesus, the great rock foundation,
Whereon our feet were set by sov'reign grace:
Not life nor death, with all their agitation,
Can thence remove us if we see His face.

3. We would see Jesus! Other lights are paling
Which for long years we have rejoiced to see:
The blessings of our pilgrimage are failing;
We would not mourn them, for we go to Thee!

4. We would see Jesus! This is all we're needing,
Strength, joy, and willingness come with the sight,
We would see Jesus, dying, risen, pleading;
Then welcome day and farewell mortal night! A-men.

LIFE IN CHRIST: COMMUNION WITH CHRIST

304 THOU TRUE VINE, THAT HEALS
PLEADING SAVIOR 8.7.8.7.D.

"T.S.N." in *Songs of Praise*, 1925

Folk Hymn
J. Leavitt's *Christian Lyre*, 1831
Harmony by R. Vaughan Williams, 1906

1 Thou true vine, that heals the na-tions, Tree of life, Thy branch-es we.
They who leave Thee fade and with-er, None bear fruit ex-cept in Thee.
Cleanse us, make us sane and sim-ple, Till we merge our lives in Thine,
Gain our-selves in Thee, the vint-age, Give our-selves through Thee, the vine.

2 Noth-ing can we do with-out Thee; On Thy life de-pends each one;
If we keep Thy words and love Thee, All we ask for shall be done.
May we, lov-ing one an-oth-er, Ra-diant in Thy light a-bide;
So through us, made fruit-ful by Thee, Shall our God be glo-ri-fied.

LIFE IN CHRIST: COMMUNION WITH CHRIST

O FOR A CLOSER WALK WITH GOD 305

ELIZABETHTOWN C.M.

William Cowper, 1772
George Kingsley, 1838

1. O for a clos-er walk with God, A calm and heav'n-ly frame. A light to shine up-on the road That leads me to the Lamb.
2. Where is the bless-ed-ness I knew When first I saw the Lord? Where is the soul re-fresh-ing view Of Je-sus and His Word?
3. The dear-est i-dol I have known, What-e'er that i-dol be, Help me to tear it from Thy throne, And wor-ship on-ly Thee.
4. So shall my walk be close with God, Calm and se-rene my frame; So pur-er light shall mark the road That leads me to the Lamb.

O LOVE DIVINE 306

HESPERUS L.M.

Oliver Wendell Holmes, 1849
Henry Baker, 1854

1. O Love di-vine, that stooped to share Our sharp-est pang, our bit-t'rest tear, On Thee we cast each earth-born care, We smile at pain while Thou art near.
2. Though long the wea-ry way we tread, And sor-row crown each lin-g'ring year, No path we shun, no dark-ness dread, Our hearts still whis-p'ring, Thou art near.
3. When droop-ing plea-sure turns to grief, And trem-bling faith is changed to fear, The murm'ring wind, the quiv-'ring leaf, Shall soft-ly tell us Thou art near.
4. On Thee we fling our bur-d'ning woe, O Love di-vine, for-ev-er dear, Con-tent to suf-fer, while we know, Liv-ing and dy-ing, Thou art near.

LIFE IN CHRIST: COMMUNION WITH CHRIST

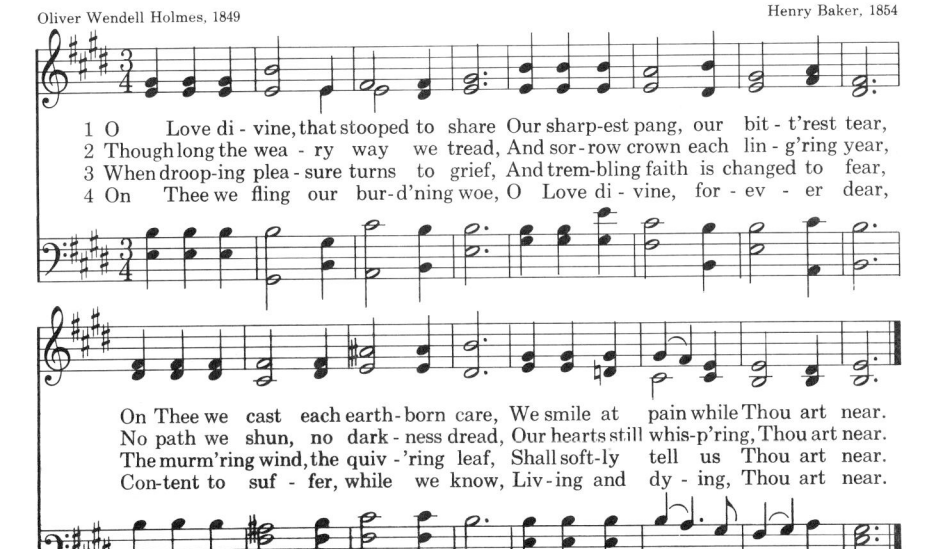

307 DRAW THOU MY SOUL, O CHRIST

ST. EDMUND 6.4.6.4.6.6.6.4.

Lucy Larcom, 1892
Arthur Seymour Sullivan, 1872

1 Draw Thou my soul, O Christ, Clos-er to Thine; Breathe in-to ev-ery wish Thy will di-vine: Raised my low self a-bove, Won by Thy deathless love, Ev - er, O Christ, through mine Let Thy life shine.

2 Lead forth my soul, O Christ, One with Thine own, Joy-ful to fol-low Thee Through paths un-known: In Thee my strength re-new; Give me Thy work to do: Through me Thy truth be shown, Thy love made known.

3 Not for my-self a-lone May my prayer be; Lift Thou Thy world, O Christ, Clos-er to Thee: Cleanse it from guilt and wrong, Teach it sal-va-tion's song, Make it a-live in Thee, Per-fect in Thee! A-men.

308 ABIDE, O DEAREST JESUS

CHRISTUS, DER IST MEIN LEBEN 7.6.7.6.

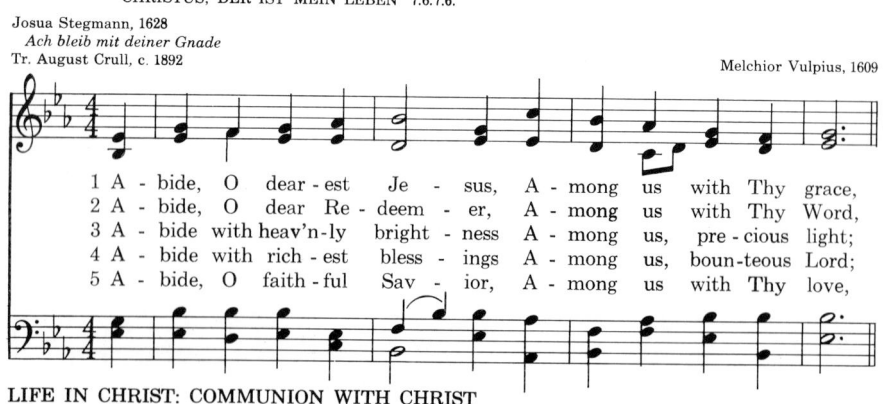

Josua Stegmann, 1628
Ach bleib mit deiner Gnade
Tr. August Crull, c. 1892

Melchior Vulpius, 1609

1 A-bide, O dear-est Je - sus, A-mong us with Thy grace,
2 A-bide, O dear Re-deem - er, A-mong us with Thy Word,
3 A-bide with heav'n-ly bright - ness A-mong us, pre-cious light;
4 A-bide with rich-est bless - ings A-mong us, boun-teous Lord;
5 A-bide, O faith-ful Sav - ior, A-mong us with Thy love,

LIFE IN CHRIST: COMMUNION WITH CHRIST

That Satan may not harm us, Nor we to sin give place.
And thus now and hereafter True peace and joy afford.
Thy truth direct, and keep us From error's gloomy night.
Let us in grace and wisdom Grow daily through Thy Word.
Grant steadfastness, and help us To reach our home above. A-men.

DEAR LORD, WHO SOUGHT AT DAWN 309

ANGELUS L.M.

Harry Webb Farrington, 1928

Scheffler's *Heilige Seelenlust*, 1657
and *Cantica Spiritualia*, 1847

1. Dear Lord, who sought at dawn of day The solitary woods to pray, In quietness we come to ask Thy guidance for the daily task.

2. O Master, who with kindly face At noonday trod the market place, We crave a brother's smile and song While mingling in the lonely throng.

3. Thou wearied Christ, at eventide Communing on the mountain-side, In mystic stillness now we seek Thy presence for the coming week.

4. Strong Pilot, who at midnight hour Could calm the sea with gentle power, Grant us the skill to aid the bark Of those who drift in storm and dark. A-men.

LIFE IN CHRIST: COMMUNION WITH CHRIST

310 COME, THOU FOUNT
NETTLETON 8.7.8.7.D.

Robert Robinson†, 1758

Folk Hymn
John Wyeth's *Repository of Sacred Music, Part Second*, 1813

1. Come, Thou Fount of ev-ery bless-ing, Tune my heart to sing Thy grace;
Streams of mer-cy, nev-er ceas-ing, Call for songs of loud-est praise.
Teach me some me-lo-dious son-net, Sung by flam-ing tongues a-bove;
Praise the mount; I'm fixed up-on it, Mount of God's un-chang-ing love.

2. Here I raise my Eb-en-e-zer; Hith-er by Thy help I'm come;
And I hope, by Thy good plea-sure, Safe-ly to ar-rive at home.
Je-sus sought me when a stran-ger, Wan-d'ring from the fold of God;
He, to res-cue me from dan-ger, In-ter-posed with pre-cious blood.

3. O to grace how great a debt-or Dai-ly I'm con-strained to be!
Let that grace now, like a fet-ter, Bind my wan-d'ring heart to Thee:
Prone to wan-der, Lord, I feel it, Prone to leave the God I love;
Here's my heart, O take and seal it; Seal it for Thy courts a-bove. A-men.

LIFE IN CHRIST: COMMUNION WITH CHRIST

GUIDE ME, O THOU GREAT JEHOVAH 311
CWM RHONDDA 8.7.8.7.8.7.

William Williams, 1745
Arglwydd arwain trwy'r anialwch
Tr. Peter Williams and Others, 1771-2

John Hughes, 1907

1. Guide me, O Thou great Jehovah, Pilgrim through this barren land; I am weak, but Thou art mighty; Hold me with Thy powerful hand; Bread of heaven, bread of heaven, Feed me now and evermore, Feed me now and evermore.

2. Open now the crystal fountain, Whence the healing streams do flow; Let the fiery cloudy pillar Lead me all my journey through; Strong deliverer, strong deliverer, Be Thou still my strength and shield, Be Thou still my strength and shield.

3. When I tread the verge of Jordan, Bid my anxious fears subside; Death of death, and hell's destruction, Land me safe on Canaan's side; Songs of praises, songs of praises, I will ever give to Thee, I will ever give to Thee. A-men.

LIFE IN CHRIST: PILGRIMAGE AND GUIDANCE

312 COME, COME, YE SAINTS

ALL IS WELL 10.6.10.6.8.8.8.6.

William Clayton, 1846
Altered by Joseph F. Green, 1960

Folk Hymn
Adapted from J. T. White's
Sacred Harp, 1844

1. Come, come, ye saints, no toil nor labor fear; But with joy wend your way. Though hard to you the journey may appear, Grace shall be as your day. We have a living Lord to guide, And we can trust Him to provide; Do

2. The world of care is with us every day; Let it not this obscure: Here we can serve the Master on the way, And in Him be secure. Gird up your loins; fresh courage take; Our God will never us forsake; And

3. We'll find the rest which God for us prepared, When at last He will call; Where none will come to hurt or make afraid, He will reign over all. We will make the air with music ring, Shout praise to God our Lord and King: O

LIFE IN CHRIST: PILGRIMAGE AND GUIDANCE

this, and joy your hearts will swell: All is well! All is well!
so our song no fear can quell; All is well! All is well!
how we'll make the cho - rus swell: All is well! All is well!

ETERNAL ONE, THOU LIVING GOD 313

WINCHESTER NEW L.M.

From *Musicalisch Hand-buch*, published
by George Rebelein's Widow, 1690
Arranged by William Henry Havergal, 1847

Samuel Longfellow, 1875

1. E - ter - nal one, Thou liv - ing God, Whom chang - ing years un - chang'd re - veal, With Thee their way our fa - thers trod; The hand they held, in ours we feel.
2. The same our trust, the same our need, In sor - row's stress, in du - ty's hour; We keep their faith, by Thee de - creed, That faith the fount of all our power.
3. We bless Thee for the grow - ing light, Th' ad - vanc - ing thought, the wid - 'ning view, The larg - er free - dom, clear - er sight, Which from the old un - folds the new.
4. With wid - er view, come loft - ier goal; With full - er light, more good to see; With free - dom, tru - er self - con - trol, With knowl - edge, deep - er rev - 'rence be.
5. A - new we pledge our - selves to Thee, To fol - low where Thy truth shall lead; A - float up - on its bound - less sea, Who sails with God is safe in - deed!

LIFE IN CHRIST: PILGRIMAGE AND GUIDANCE

314 IF THOU BUT SUFFER GOD TO GUIDE
WER NUR DEN LIEBEN GOTT LÄSST WALTEN 9.8.9.8.8.8.

Georg Neumark, 1641
Wer nur den lieben Gott lässt walten
Tr. Catherine Winkworth†, 1863

Georg Neumark, 1641

1. If thou but suffer God to guide thee, And hope in Him through all thy ways, He'll give thee strength what-e'er betide thee, And bear thee through the evil days. Who trusts in God's unchanging love Builds on a rock that nought can move.

2. Only be still and wait His leisure In cheerful hope, with heart content To take what-e'er thy Father's pleasure And all-deserving love hath sent, Nor doubt our inmost wants are known To Him who chose us for His own.

3. He knows the time for joy, and truly Will send it when He sees it meet, When He has tried and purged thee throughly And finds thee free from all deceit, He comes to thee all unaware And makes thee own His loving care.

4. Sing, pray, and keep His ways unswerving, So do thine own part faithfully, And trust His Word, though undiscerning Thou yet shall find it true for thee; God never yet forsook at need The soul that trusted Him indeed. A-men.

LIFE IN CHRIST: PILGRIMAGE AND GUIDANCE

1 Wer nur den lieben Gott lässt walten
  und hoffet auf ihn allezeit,
  den wird er wunderbar erhalten
  in aller Not und Traurigkeit.
  Wer Gott, dem Allerhöchsten, traut,
  der hat auf keinen Sand gebaut.

2 Man halte nur ein wenig stille
  und sei doch in sich selbst vergnügt,
  wie unsers Gottes Gnadenwille,
  wie sein Allwissenheit es fügt.
  Gott, der uns ihm hat auserwählt,
  der weiss am besten, was uns fehlt.

3 Er kennt die rechten Freudenstunden,
  er weiss wohl, was uns nützlich sei:
  Wenn er uns nur hat treu erfunden
  und merket keine Heuchelei,
  so kommt Gott, eh wir's uns versehn,
  und lässet uns viel Guts geschehn.

4 Sing, bet und geh auf Gottes Wegen,
  verricht das Deine nur getreu
  und trau des Himmels reichem Segen,
  so wird er bei dir werden neu;
  denn welcher seine Zuversicht
  auf Gott setzt, den verlässt er nicht.

TEACH ME THE MEASURE OF MY DAYS 315

ST. FLAVIAN C.M.

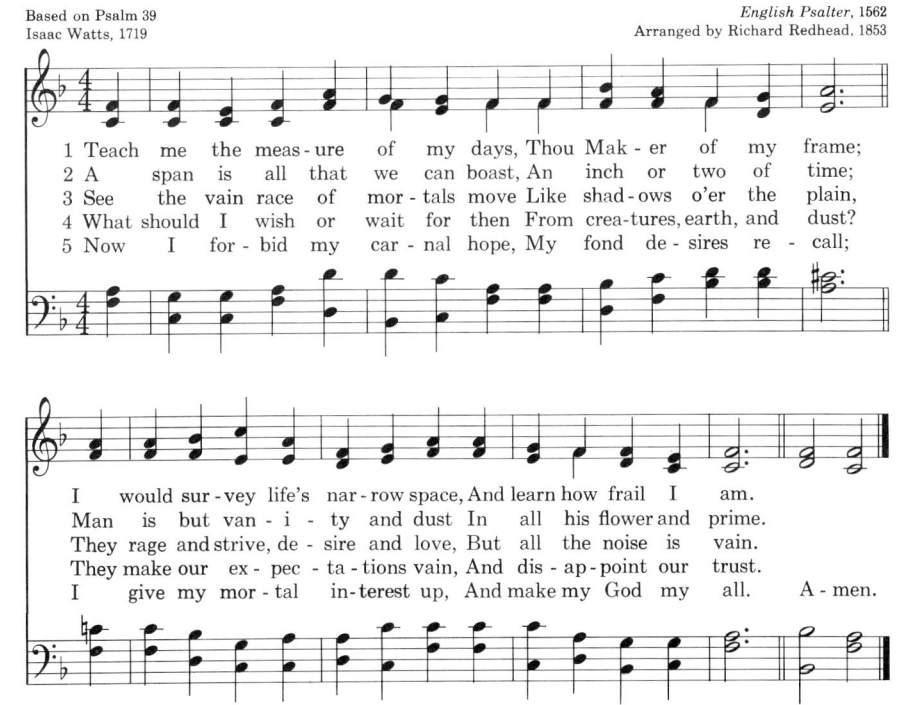

Based on Psalm 39
Isaac Watts, 1719

English Psalter, 1562
Arranged by Richard Redhead, 1853

1 Teach me the meas-ure of my days, Thou Mak-er of my frame;
  I would sur-vey life's nar-row space, And learn how frail I am.

2 A span is all that we can boast, An inch or two of time;
  Man is but van-i-ty and dust In all his flower and prime.

3 See the vain race of mor-tals move Like shad-ows o'er the plain,
  They rage and strive, de-sire and love, But all the noise is vain.

4 What should I wish or wait for then From crea-tures, earth, and dust?
  They make our ex-pec-ta-tions vain, And dis-ap-point our trust.

5 Now I for-bid my car-nal hope, My fond de-sires re-call;
  I give my mor-tal in-terest up, And make my God my all. A-men.

LIFE IN CHRIST: PILGRIMAGE AND GUIDANCE

316 LEAD, KINDLY LIGHT
SANDON 10.4.10.4.10.10.

John Henry Newman, 1833
Charles Henry Purday, 1860

1. Lead, kindly Light, amid th' encircling gloom, Lead Thou me on;
The night is dark, and I am far from home; Lead Thou me on.
Keep Thou my feet; I do not ask to see
The distant scene, one step enough for me.

2. I was not ever thus, nor prayed that Thou Shouldst lead me on;
I loved to choose and see my path, but now Lead Thou me on;
I loved the garish day, and, spite of fears,
Pride ruled my will. Remember not past years.

3. So long Thy power hath blest me, sure it still Will lead me on,
O'er moor and fen, o'er crag and torrent, till The night is gone,
And with the morn those angel faces smile,
Which I have loved long since, and lost awhile. A-men.

LIFE IN CHRIST: PILGRIMAGE AND GUIDANCE

LEAD US, O FATHER 317

LONGWOOD 10.10.10.10.

William Henry Burleigh, 1859
Joseph Barnby, 1872

1. Lead us, O Father, in the paths of peace;
   Without Thy guiding hand we go astray,
   And doubts appall, and sorrows still increase;
   Lead us through Christ, the true and living way.

2. Lead us, O Father, in the paths of truth;
   Unhelped by Thee, in error's maze we grope,
   While passion stains and folly dims our youth,
   And age comes on uncheered by faith and hope.

3. Lead us, O Father, in the paths of right:
   Blindly we stumble when we walk alone,
   Involv'd in shadows of a moral night;
   Only with Thee we journey safely on.

4. Lead us, O Father, to Thy heav'nly rest,
   However rough and steep the path may be,
   Through joy or sorrow, as Thou deemest best,
   Until our lives are perfected in Thee. A-men.

LIFE IN CHRIST: PILGRIMAGE AND GUIDANCE

318 TAKE THOU MY HAND, O FATHER
SO NIMM DENN MEINE HÄNDE 7.4.7.4.D.

Julie Katharina Hausmann, 1862
So nimm denn meine Hände
Tr. Herman Brückner, d. 1942

Friedrich Silcher, 1842

1. Take Thou my hand, O Father, And lead Thou me, Until my journey endeth, Eternally. Alone I will not wander One single day; Be Thou my true companion And with me stay.

2. O cover with Thy mercy My poor, weak heart! Let every thought rebellious From me depart. Permit Thy child to linger Here at Thy feet, And blindly trust Thy goodness With faith complete.

3. Though naught of Thy great power May move my soul, With Thee through night and darkness I reach the goal. Take, then, my hands, O Father, And lead Thou me Until my journey endeth Eternally. A-men.

1. So nimm denn meine Hände
 und führe mich
 bis an mein selig Ende
 und ewiglich!
 Ich kann allein nicht gehen,
 nicht einen Schritt;
 wo du wirst gehn und stehen,
 da nimm mich mit.

2. In deine Gnade hülle
 mein schwaches Herz,
 und mach es endlich stille
 in Freud und Schmerz.
 Lass ruhn zu deinen Füssen
 dein schwaches Kind;
 es will die Augen schliessen
 und folgen blind.

3. Wenn ich auch gar nichts fühle
 von deiner Macht,
 du bringst mich doch zum Ziele
 auch durch die Nacht.
 So nimm denn meine Hände
 und führe mich
 bis an mein selig Ende
 und ewiglich!

LIFE IN CHRIST: PILGRIMAGE AND GUIDANCE

JESUS, STILL LEAD ON 319
SEELENBRÄUTIGAM 5.5.8 8.5.5.

Nikolaus Ludwig von Zinzendorf, 1778
Jesu, geh' voran
Tr. Jane L. Borthwick†, 1846

Adam Drese, 1698

1. Jesus, still lead on, Till our rest be won, And, although the way be cheerless, We will follow, calm and fearless; Guide us by Thy hand To our fatherland.

2. If the way be drear, If the foe be near, Let not faithless fears o'ertake us, Let not faith and hope forsake us; For, through many a woe, To our home we go.

3. When we seek relief From a long-felt grief, When oppressed by new temptations, Lord, increase and perfect patience; Show us that bright shore Where we weep no more.

4. Jesus, still lead on, Till our rest be won; Heav'nly leader, still direct us, Still support, console, protect us, Till we safely stand In our fatherland. A-men.

---

1. Jesu, geh voran
auf der Lebensbahn,
und wir wollen nicht verweilen,
dir getreulich nachzueilen;
führ uns an der Hand
bis ins Vaterland.

2. Soll's uns hart ergehn,
lass uns feste stehn
und auch in den schwersten Tagen
niemals über Lasten klagen;
denn durch Trübsal hier
geht der Weg zu dir.

3. Rühret eigner Schmerz
irgend unser Herz,
kümmert uns ein fremdes Leiden,
o so gib Geduld zu beiden;
richte unsern Sinn
auf das Ende hin!

4. Ordne unsern Gang,
Jesu, lebenslang.
Führst du uns durch rauhe Wege,
gib uns auch die nötge Pflege;
tu uns nach dem Lauf
deine Türe auf.

LIFE IN CHRIST: PILGRIMAGE AND GUIDANCE

320 SHEPHERD OF SOULS, REFRESH
WINDSOR C.M.

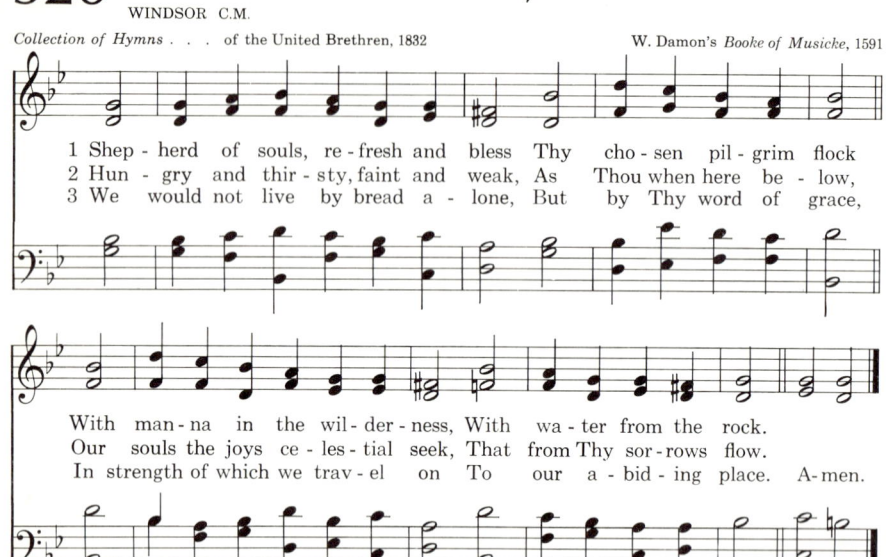

Collection of Hymns . . . of the United Brethren, 1832 W. Damon's *Booke of Musicke*, 1591

1 Shepherd of souls, refresh and bless Thy chosen pilgrim flock
With manna in the wilderness, With water from the rock.

2 Hungry and thirsty, faint and weak, As Thou when here below,
Our souls the joys celestial seek, That from Thy sorrows flow.

3 We would not live by bread alone, But by Thy word of grace,
In strength of which we travel on To our abiding place. A-men.

321 MY SOUL, BE ON THY GUARD
LABAN S.M.

George Heath, 1781 Lowell Mason, 1830

1 My soul, be on thy guard; Ten thousand foes arise;
The hosts of sin are pressing hard To draw thee from the skies.

2 O watch, and fight, and pray; The battle ne'er give o'er;
Renew it boldly every day, And help divine implore.

3 Ne'er think the vict'ry won, Nor lay thine armor down;
Thy arduous work will not be done, Till thou obtain thy crown.

4 Fight on, my soul, till death Shall bring thee to thy God;
He'll take thee, at thy parting breath, To His divine abode. A-men.

LIFE IN CHRIST: CONFLICT AND VICTORY

COME, O THOU TRAVELER UNKNOWN 322

VERNON 8.8.8.8.8.8.
Folk Hymn
J. Ingall's *Christian Harmony*, 1805
Version from Joseph Funk's *Genuine Church Music*, 1832
Harmony by J. Harold Moyer, 1965

Charles Wesley†, 1742

1. Come, O Thou Traveler unknown, Whom still I hold, but cannot see, My company before is gone, And I am left alone with Thee, With Thee all night I mean to stay, And wrestle till the break of day.
2. Wilt Thou not yet to me reveal Thy new, unutterable name? Tell me, I still beseech Thee, tell, To know it now resolved I am; Wrestling I will not let Thee go, Till I Thy name, Thy nature know.
3. 'Tis Love! tis' Love! Thou diedst for me, I hear Thy whisper in my heart. The morning breaks, the shadows flee: Pure universal love Thou art, To me, to all Thy mercies move, Thy nature, and Thy name is Love.
4. My prayer hath power with God; the grace Unspeakable I now receive, Through faith I see Thee face to face, I see Thee face to face and live: In vain I have not wept and strove, Thy nature, and Thy name is Love.

LIFE IN CHRIST: CONFLICT AND VICTORY

323 HE WHO WOULD VALIANT BE

ST. DUNSTANS 6.5.6.5.6.6.6.5.

Based on John Bunyan's
Who Would True Valor See, 1684
Percy Dearmer, 1906

Winfred Douglas, 1918

1. He who would valiant be 'Gainst all disaster,
Let him in constancy Follow the Master.
There's no discouragement Shall make him once relent
His first avowed intent To be a pilgrim.

2. Who so beset him round With dismal stories,
Do but themselves confound, His strength the more is.
No foes shall stay his might, Though he with giants fight;
He will make good his right To be a pilgrim.

3. Since, Lord, Thou dost defend Us with Thy Spirit,
We know we at the end Shall life inherit.
Then fancies flee away! I'll fear not what men say,
I'll labor night and day To be a pilgrim.

LIFE IN CHRIST: CONFLICT AND VICTORY

IN THE HOUR OF TRIAL 324

PENITENCE 6.5.6.5.D.

James Montgomery, 1834 — Spencer Lane, 1875

1. In the hour of trial, Jesus, pray for me;
Lest by base denial I depart from Thee;
When Thou seest me waver, With a look recall,
Nor for fear or favor Suffer me to fall.

2. With its witching pleasures Would this vain world charm,
Or its sordid treasures Spread to work me harm,
Bring to my remembrance Sad Gethsemane,
Or in darker semblance, Cross-crowned Calvary.

3. If with sore affliction Thou in love chastise,
Pour Thy benediction On the sacrifice;
Then, upon Thine altar Freely offered up,
Though the flesh may falter, Faith shall drink the cup.

4. When in dust and ashes To the grave I sink,
While heav'n's glory flashes O'er the shelving brink,
On Thy truth relying Through that mortal strife,
Lord, receive me, dying, To eternal life. A-men.

LIFE IN CHRIST: CONFLICT AND VICTORY

325 A MIGHTY FORTRESS IS OUR GOD

EIN FESTE BURG 8.7.8.7.6.6.6.6.7.

Based on Psalm 46
Martin Luther, 1527 or 1528
Ein feste Burg ist unser Gott
Tr. Frederich H. Hedge, 1852

Martin Luther, 1529

1. A mighty fortress is our God, A bulwark never failing;
Our helper He amid the flood Of mortal ills prevailing;
For still our ancient foe Doth seek to work us woe;
His craft and pow'r are great, And arm'd with cruel hate,
On earth is not His equal.

2. Did we in our own strength confide, Our striving would be losing;
Were not the right man on our side, The man of God's own choosing;
Dost ask who that may be? Christ Jesus, it is He!
Lord Sabaoth, His name, From age to age the same;
And He must win the battle.

3. And though this world, with devils filled, Should threaten to undo us,
We will not fear, for God hath willed His truth to triumph through us;
The prince of darkness grim, We tremble not for him;
His rage we can endure; For lo, his doom is sure;
One little word shall fell him.

4. That word above all earthly powers, No thanks to them, abideth;
The Spirit and the gifts are ours, Through Him who with us sideth;
Let goods and kindred go, This mortal life also;
The body they may kill, God's truth abideth still;
His kingdom is forever.

Another setting of this hymn may be found at No. 597.

LIFE IN CHRIST: CONFLICT AND VICTORY

GOD IS THE REFUGE OF HIS SAINTS 326
WARRINGTON L.M.

Based on Psalm 46
Isaac Watts, 1719

Ralph Harrison, 1784

1. God is the ref - uge of His saints, When storms of sharp dis - tress in - vade; Ere we can of - fer our com - plaints, Be - hold Him pres - ent with His aid!
2. Let moun - tains from their seats be hurled Down to the deep, and bur - ied there, Con - vul - sions shake the sol - id world, Our faith shall nev - er yield to fear.
3. Loud may the trou - bled o - cean roar; In sa - cred peace our souls a - bide; While ev - ery na - tion, ev - ery shore, Trem - bles, and dreads the swell - ing tide.
4. There is a stream, whose gen - tle flow Sup - plies the cit - y of our God, Life, love, and joy still glid - ing through, And wa - t'ring our di - vine a - bode. A - men.

5 That sacred stream, Thy holy Word,
    That all our raging fear controls;
Sweet peace Thy promises afford,
    And give new strength to fainting souls.

6 Zion enjoys her Monarch's love,
    Secure against a threatening hour;
Nor can her firm foundations move,
    Built on His truth and armed with power.

LIFE IN CHRIST: CONFLICT AND VICTORY

327 SO LET OUR LIPS AND LIVES EXPRESS
UXBRIDGE L.M.

Isaac Watts, c. 1707
Lowell Mason, 1830

1. So let our lips and lives express
The holy gospel we profess;
So let our works and virtues shine,
To prove the doctrine all divine.

2. Thus shall we best proclaim abroad
The honor of our Savior God;
When the salvation reigns within,
And grace subdues the power of sin.

3. Our flesh and sense must be denied;
Passion and envy, lust and pride;
While justice, temp'rance, truth and love
Our inward piety approve.

4. Religion bears our spirits up,
While we expect that blessed hope,
The bright appearance of the Lord,
And faith stands leaning on His Word.

328 STRIVE ARIGHT WHEN GOD DOTH CALL
RINGE RECHT 8.7.8.7.

Johann Joseph Winckler, 1714
Ringe recht wenn Gottes Gnade
Tr. Catherine Winkworth, 1855

J. Thommen's *Erbaulicher*
Musicalischer Christen-Schatz, 1745

1. Strive aright when God doth call thee,
When He draws thee by His grace,

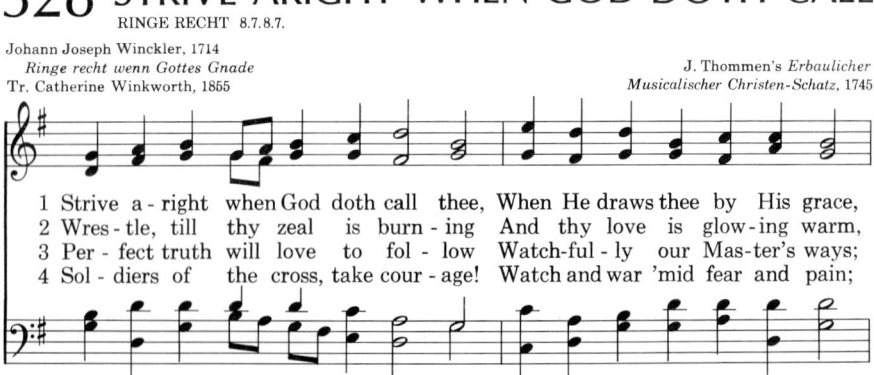

2. Wrestle, till thy zeal is burning
And thy love is glowing warm,

3. Perfect truth will love to follow
Watchfully our Master's ways;

4. Soldiers of the cross, take courage!
Watch and war 'mid fear and pain;

LIFE IN CHRIST: CONFLICT AND VICTORY

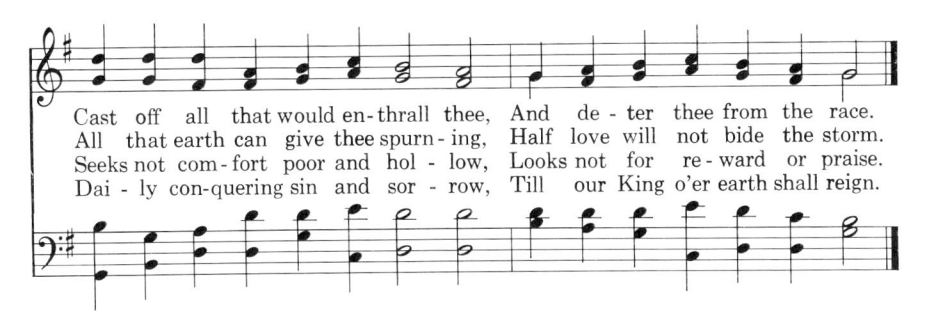

Cast off all that would en-thrall thee, And de-ter thee from the race.
All that earth can give thee spurn-ing, Half love will not bide the storm.
Seeks not com-fort poor and hol-low, Looks not for re-ward or praise.
Dai-ly con-quering sin and sor-row, Till our King o'er earth shall reign.

I AM THE LORD, O HEAR 329

MACH'S MIT MIR 8.7.8.7.8.8.8.

Johann Scheffler, 1668
Mir nach, spricht Christus, unser Held
Tr. Joanna Sudermann Andres, 1940

Johann Hermann Schein, 1628

1. I am the Lord, O hear My voice, A-rise, ye Chris-tians, fol-low!
2. I am the light, I light the way Un-to a life vic-to-rious.
3. Fear not, I am your con-stant stay Though strong the foe as-sail-eth;
4. Dear Lord, we rise to fol-low Thee, In Thee is grace suf-fi-cient;

De-ny your-self, for-sake the world, My name a-lone to hal-low.
He that will come and fol-low Me Shall find his path-way glo-rious.
I am your vic-tor in the fight, No foe o'er Me pre-vail-eth.
In Thee is strength, is vic-to-ry, In Thee is love om-nis-cient.

Take up your cross, your bur-dens bear And fol-low Me, My life to share.
I am the way, the heav'n-ly light By which the soul may walk a-right.
Woe un-to him that stand-eth still And fol-lows not to do My will.
Help us to tri-umph in the strife And grant to us the crown of life. A-men.

LIFE IN CHRIST: CONFLICT AND VICTORY

330 SOLDIERS OF CHRIST, ARISE
SILVER STREET S.M.

Charles Wesley, 1749 — Isaac Smith, 1770

1. Soldiers of Christ, arise, And put your armor on, Strong in the strength which God supplies Through His eternal Son;
2. Strong in the Lord of Hosts, And in His mighty power, Who in the strength of Jesus trusts Is more than conqueror.
3. Stand then in His great might, With all His strength endued, And take, to arm you for the fight, The panoply of God;
4. That having all things done, And all your conflicts past, Ye may o'ercome through Christ alone, And stand entire at last.

5. From strength to strength go on,
   Wrestle, and fight, and pray,
   Tread all the powers of darkness down,
   And win the well-fought day;

6. Still let the Spirit cry
   In all His soldiers, "Come";
   Till Christ the Lord descends from high
   And takes the conqu'rors home.

331 FROM EVERY STORMY WIND
RETREAT L.M.

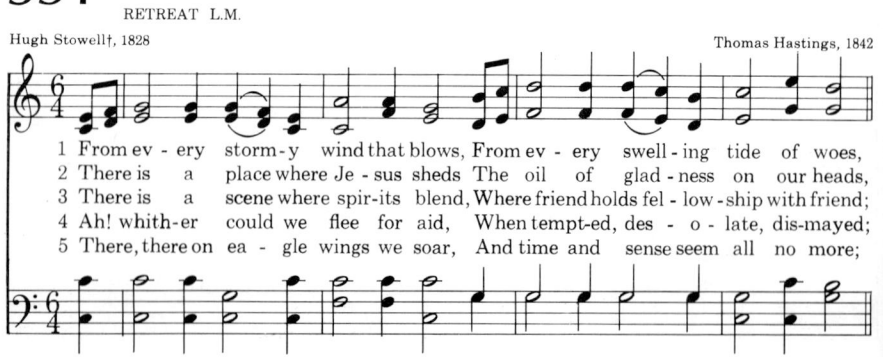

Hugh Stowell†, 1828 — Thomas Hastings, 1842

1. From every stormy wind that blows, From every swelling tide of woes,
2. There is a place where Jesus sheds The oil of gladness on our heads,
3. There is a scene where spirits blend, Where friend holds fellowship with friend;
4. Ah! whither could we flee for aid, When tempted, desolate, dismayed;
5. There, there on eagle wings we soar, And time and sense seem all no more;

LIFE IN CHRIST: CONFLICT AND VICTORY

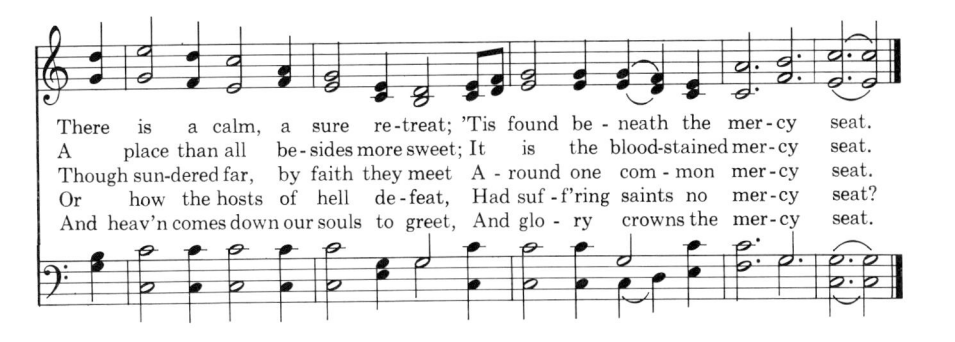

There is a calm, a sure re-treat; 'Tis found be-neath the mer-cy seat.
A place than all be-sides more sweet; It is the blood-stained mer-cy seat.
Though sun-dered far, by faith they meet A-round one com-mon mer-cy seat.
Or how the hosts of hell de-feat, Had suf-f'ring saints no mer-cy seat?
And heav'n comes down our souls to greet, And glo-ry crowns the mer-cy seat.

AWAKE, MY SOUL, STRETCH EVERY NERVE 332

CHRISTMAS C.M.

Philip Doddridge, 1755 — Arranged from George Frideric Handel, 1728

1. A-wake, my soul, stretch ev-ery nerve, And press with vig-or on; A heav'n-ly race de-mands thy zeal, And an im-mor-tal crown, And an im-mor-tal crown.

2. A cloud of wit-ness-es a-round Hold thee in full sur-vey: For-get the steps al-read-y trod, And on-ward urge thy way, And on-ward urge thy way.

3. 'Tis God's all-an-i-mat-ing voice, That calls thee from on high; 'Tis His own hand pre-sents the prize To thine as-pir-ing eye, To thine as-pir-ing eye.

4. Blest Sav-ior, in-tro-duced by Thee Have I my race be-gun; And crowned with vic-t'ry at Thy feet I'll lay my hon-ors down, I'll lay my hon-ors down.

LIFE IN CHRIST: CONFLICT AND VICTORY

333 COME, YE DISCONSOLATE

CONSOLATOR 11.10.11.10.

Thomas Moore and Thomas Hastings, 1824 and 1831

Samuel Webbe, 1792

1. Come, ye dis-con-so-late, wher-e'er ye lan-guish;
   Come to the mer-cy-seat, fer-vent-ly kneel;
   Here bring your wound-ed hearts, here tell your an-guish;
   Earth has no sor-row that heav'n can-not heal.

2. Joy of the des-o-late, light of the stray-ing,
   Hope of the pen-i-tent, fade-less and pure,
   Here speaks the Com-fort-er, ten-der-ly say-ing,
   "Earth has no sor-row that heav'n can-not cure."

3. Here see the bread of life, see wa-ters flow-ing
   Forth from the throne of God, pure from a-bove;
   Come to the feast of love, come, ev-er know-ing,
   Earth has no sor-row but heav'n can re-move.

LIFE IN CHRIST: COURAGE AND COMFORT

I LOOK TO THEE IN EVERY NEED 334

O JESU, WARUM LEGST DU MIR 8.6.8.6.8.8.

Samuel Longfellow, 1864
Gesangbuch, Hirschberg, 1741

1. I look to Thee in every need, And never look in vain; I feel Thy strong and tender love, And all is well again: The thought of Thee is mightier far Than sin and pain and sorrow are.

2. Discouraged in the work of life, Disheartened by its load, Shamed by its failures or its fears, I sink beside the road; But let me only think of Thee And then new heart springs up in me.

3. Thy calmness bends serene above, My restlessness to still; Around me flows Thy quickening life, To nerve my faltering will: Thy presence fills my solitude; Thy providence turns all to good.

4. Enfolded deep in Thy dear love, Held in Thy law, I stand; Thy hand in all things I behold, And all things in Thy hand; Thou leadest me by unsought ways, And turn'st my mourning into praise. A-men.

LIFE IN CHRIST: COURAGE AND COMFORT

335 CHILDREN OF THE HEAVENLY FATHER
SANDELL L.M.

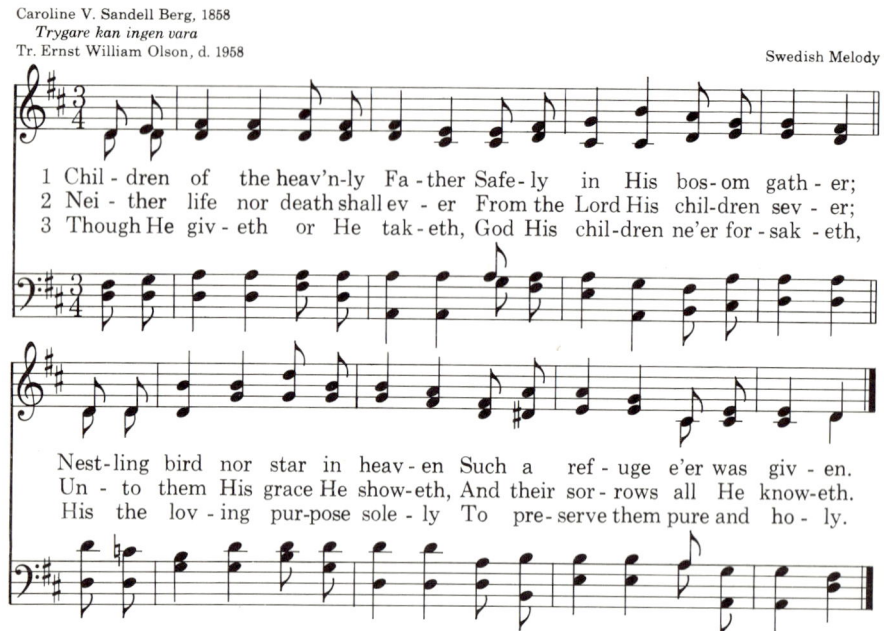

Caroline V. Sandell Berg, 1858
Trygare kan ingen vara
Tr. Ernst William Olson, d. 1958

Swedish Melody

1 Chil-dren of the heav'n-ly Fa-ther Safe-ly in His bos-om gath-er;
2 Nei-ther life nor death shall ev-er From the Lord His chil-dren sev-er;
3 Though He giv-eth or He tak-eth, God His chil-dren ne'er for-sak-eth,

Nest-ling bird nor star in heav-en Such a ref-uge e'er was giv-en.
Un-to them His grace He show-eth, And their sor-rows all He know-eth.
His the lov-ing pur-pose sole-ly To pre-serve them pure and ho-ly.

336 FATHER, WHATE'ER OF EARTHLY BLISS
NAOMI C.M.

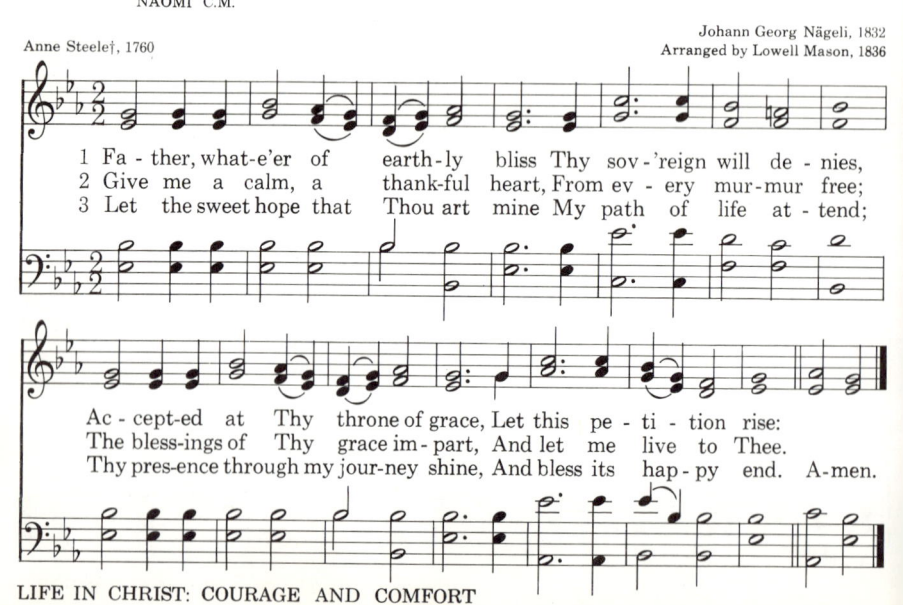

Anne Steele†, 1760

Johann Georg Nägeli, 1832
Arranged by Lowell Mason, 1836

1 Fa-ther, what-e'er of earth-ly bliss Thy sov-'reign will de-nies,
2 Give me a calm, a thank-ful heart, From ev-ery mur-mur free;
3 Let the sweet hope that Thou art mine My path of life at-tend;

Ac-cept-ed at Thy throne of grace, Let this pe-ti-tion rise:
The bless-ings of Thy grace im-part, And let me live to Thee.
Thy pres-ence through my jour-ney shine, And bless its hap-py end. A-men.

LIFE IN CHRIST: COURAGE AND COMFORT

WHAT A FRIEND WE HAVE IN JESUS 337

ERIE 8 7.8.7.D.

Joseph Medlicott Scriven†, 1855

Charles Crozat Converse, 1868

1 What a friend we have in Jesus, All our sins and griefs to bear;
What a privilege to carry Everything to God in prayer!
O what peace we often forfeit, O what needless pain we bear,
All because we do not carry Everything to God in prayer.

2 Have we trials and temptations? Is there trouble anywhere?
We should never be discouraged: Take it to the Lord in prayer!
Can we find a friend so faithful, Who will all our sorrows share?
Jesus knows our every weakness; Take it to the Lord in prayer!

3 Are we weak and heavy laden, Cumbered with a load of care?
Precious Savior, still our refuge, Take it to the Lord in prayer!
Do thy friends despise, forsake thee? Take it to the Lord in prayer!
In His arms He'll take and shield thee, Thou wilt find a solace there.

LIFE IN CHRIST: COURAGE AND COMFORT

338 THY WAY AND ALL THY SORROWS
BEFIEHL DU DEINE WEGE 7.6.7.6.D.

Paul Gerhardt, 1656
Befiehl du deine Wege
Tr. Arthur Tozer Russell, 1851

Johann Michael Haydn, d. 1806

1 Thy way and all thy sorrows, Give thou into His hand,
His gracious care unfailing, Who doth the heav'ns command.
Their course and path He giveth To clouds and air and wind;
A way thy feet may follow, He too for thee will find.

2 On Him be thy reliance, As thou wouldst prosper well;
To make thy work enduring Thy mind on His must dwell.
God yieldeth nought to sorrow And self-tormenting care;
Nought, nought with Him availeth; No power save that of prayer.

3 Leave all to His direction; In wisdom He doth reign;
Thy wonder far exceeding, He will His course maintain;
So He as Him beseemeth, With wonder-working skill,
Shall put away the sorrows That now thy spirit fill.

4 Give, Lord, the consummation To all our hearts' distress;
Our hands, our feet, O strengthen; In death our spirits bless.
Thy truth and Thy protection For evermore we pray:
With these in heav'nly glory Shall end our certain way.

LIFE IN CHRIST: COURAGE AND COMFORT

JESUS MERCIFUL 339

HUBBARD 5.5.5.5.

Tzu-ch'en Chao, 1931
Tr. Frank W. Price, 1952

Chinese Traditional Melody
Arranged by Bliss Wiant, 1936

1. Jesus merciful, Jesus pitying,
Melt my stony heart, Comfort to me bring.

2. Jesus valorous, Jesus wise and good,
Save me by Thy blood, Feed me with Thy food.

3. Jesus, brother man, Jesus, friend who knows,
Sharing all my load, Bearing all my woes.

4. Jesus, holy Lord, Jesus, Master true,
Re-inspire me now, Thy great work to do. A-men.

GIVE TO THE WINDS THY FEARS 340

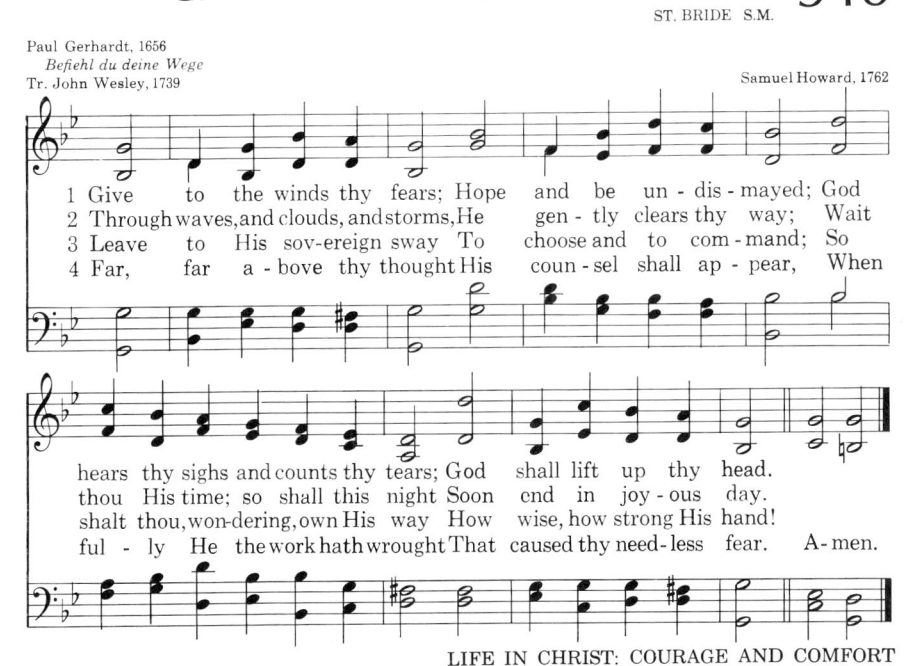

ST. BRIDE S.M.

Paul Gerhardt, 1656
Befiehl du deine Wege
Tr. John Wesley, 1739

Samuel Howard, 1762

1. Give to the winds thy fears; Hope and be undismayed; God hears thy sighs and counts thy tears; God shall lift up thy head.

2. Through waves, and clouds, and storms, He gently clears thy way; Wait thou His time; so shall this night Soon end in joyous day.

3. Leave to His sovereign sway To choose and to command; So shalt thou, wondering, own His way How wise, how strong His hand!

4. Far, far above thy thought His counsel shall appear, When fully He the work hath wrought That caused thy needless fear. A-men.

LIFE IN CHRIST: COURAGE AND COMFORT

341 THY WAY, NOT MINE, O LORD
QUAM DILECTA 6.6.6.6.

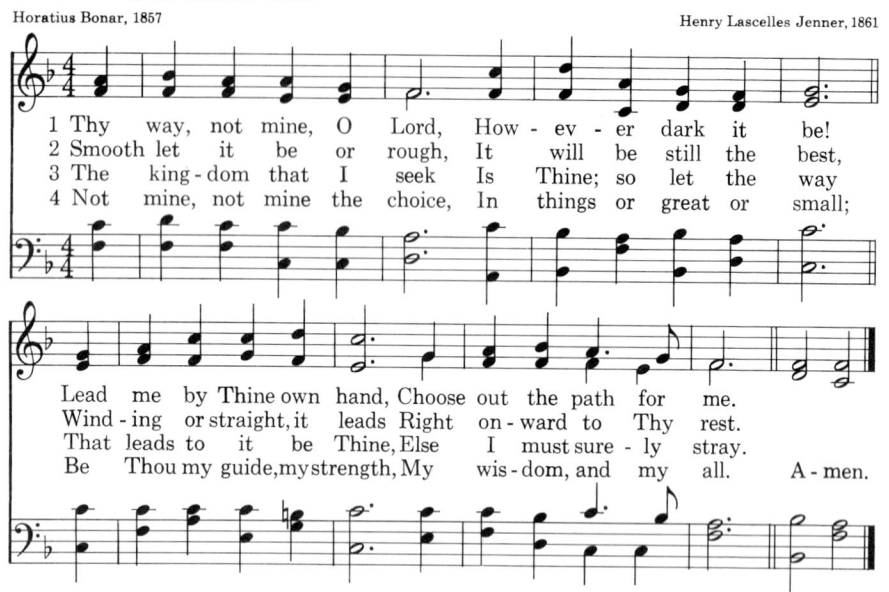

Horatius Bonar, 1857 — Henry Lascelles Jenner, 1861

1. Thy way, not mine, O Lord, However dark it be!
Lead me by Thine own hand, Choose out the path for me.

2. Smooth let it be or rough, It will be still the best,
Winding or straight, it leads Right onward to Thy rest.

3. The kingdom that I seek Is Thine; so let the way
That leads to it be Thine, Else I must surely stray.

4. Not mine, not mine the choice, In things or great or small;
Be Thou my guide, my strength, My wisdom, and my all. A-men.

342 GOD IS MY STRONG SALVATION
CHRISTUS, DER IST MEIN LEBEN 7.6.7.6.

James Montgomery, 1822 — Melchior Vulpius, 1609

1. God is my strong salvation; What foe have I to fear?
In darkness and temptation My light, my help, is near.

2. Though hosts encamp around me, Firm to the fight I stand;
What terror can confound me, With God at my right hand?

3. Place on the Lord reliance, My soul, with courage wait;
His truth be thine affiance, When faint and desolate.

4. His might thine heart shall strengthen, His love thy joy increase;
Mercy thy days shall lengthen; The Lord will give thee peace. A-men.

LIFE IN CHRIST: COURAGE AND COMFORT

O JESUS, I HAVE PROMISED 343

ANGEL'S STORY 7.6.7.6.D.

John Ernest Bode, 1869
Arthur H. Mann, 1881

1. O Jesus, I have promised To serve Thee to the end;
   Be Thou forever near me, My Master and my friend;
   I shall not fear the battle If Thou art by my side,
   Nor wander from the pathway If Thou wilt be my guide.

2. O let me feel Thee near me, The world is ever near;
   I see the sights that dazzle, The tempting sounds I hear:
   My foes are ever near me, Around me and within;
   But, Jesus, draw Thou nearer, And shield my soul from sin.

3. O let me hear Thee speaking In accents clear and still;
   Above the storms of passion, The murmurs of self-will.
   O speak to reassure me, To hasten or control;
   O speak, and make me listen, Thou guardian of my soul.

4. O Jesus, Thou hast promised To all who follow Thee
   That where Thou art in glory There shall Thy servant be;
   And, Jesus, I have promised To serve Thee to the end;
   O give me grace to follow, My Master and my friend. A-men.

LIFE IN CHRIST: OBEDIENCE AND CONSECRATION

344 HE WHO WOULD FOLLOW CHRIST

WARUM BETRÜBST DU DICH, MEIN HERZ 8.8.6.8.6.

Jörg Wagner, 1527, in the *Ausbund*, 1564
Wer Christo jetzt will folgen nach
Tr. David Augsburger, 1962

Bartholomeus Monoetius, 1565
Harmony by J. Harold Moyer, 1965

1. He who would follow Christ in life Must scorn the world's insult and strife, And bear his cross each day. For this alone leads to the throne; Christ is the only way.
2. Christ's servants follow Him to death, And give their body, life and breath On cross and rack and pyre. As gold is tried and purified They stand the test of fire.
3. Renouncing all, they choose the cross, And claiming it, count all as loss, E'en home and child and wife. Forsaking gain, forgetting pain, They enter into life.

345 MUST JESUS BEAR THE CROSS ALONE

MAITLAND C.M.

Thomas Shepherd, 1693, and Others

George Nelson Allen, 1844

1. Must Jesus bear the cross alone, And all the world go free?
2. Disowned on earth, 'mid griefs and cares He led His toilsome way;
3. The consecrated cross I'll bear, Till from the cross set free,

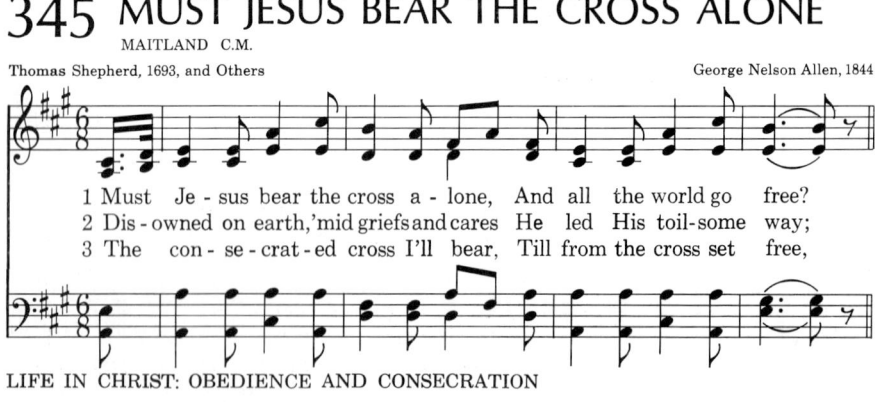

LIFE IN CHRIST: OBEDIENCE AND CONSECRATION

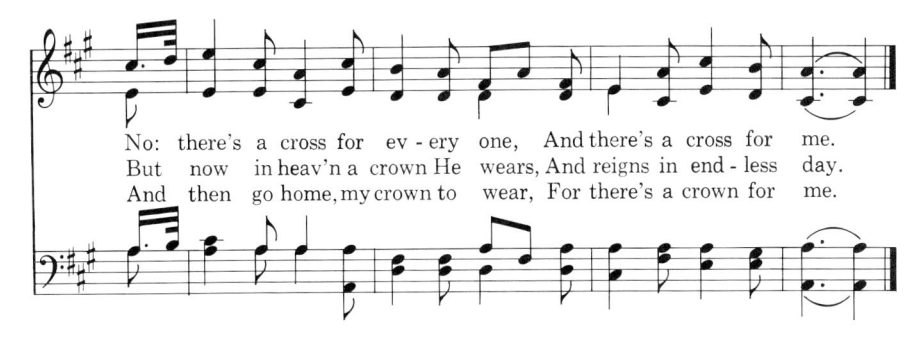

No: there's a cross for ev-ery one, And there's a cross for me.
But now in heav'n a crown He wears, And reigns in end-less day.
And then go home, my crown to wear, For there's a crown for me.

LORD OF OUR LIFE 346

LOUVAN L.M.

Samuel Francis Smith, 1891
Virgil C. Taylor, 1846

1. Lord of our life, God whom we fear, Un-known, yet known; un-seen, yet near; Breath of our breath, in Thee we live; Life of our life, our praise re-ceive.
2. Thine eye de-tects the spar-row's fall; Thy heart of love ex-pands for all; Our throb-bing life is full of Thee, Throned in Thy vast in-fin-i-ty.
3. Shine in our dark-ness, Light of light, Our minds il-lume, dis-perse our night; Make us re-spon-sive to Thy will, Our souls with all Thy full-ness fill.
4. We love Thy name, we heed Thy rod, Thy Word, our law, O gra-cious God! We wait Thy will; on Thee we call; Our light, our life, our love, our all. A-men.

LIFE IN CHRIST: OBEDIENCE AND CONSECRATION

347 MASTER, SPEAK! THY SERVANT HEARETH
AMEN, JESUS HAN SKAL RAADE 8.7.8.7.7.7.

Frances Ridley Havergal, 1867   Anton P. Berggreen, 1849

1. Mas-ter, speak! Thy ser-vant hear-eth, Wait-ing for Thy gra-cious word,
2. Speak to me by name, O Mas-ter, Let me know it is to me;
3. Mas-ter, speak! Though least and low-est, Let me not un-heard de-part;
4. Mas-ter, speak! And make me read-y, When Thy voice is tru-ly heard,

Long-ing for Thy voice that cheer-eth; Mas-ter, let it now be heard.
Speak, that I may fol-low fast-er, With a step more firm and free,
Mas-ter, speak! For, O Thou know-est All the yearn-ing of my heart,
With o-be-dience glad and stead-y Still to fol-low ev-ery word.

I am list'ning, Lord, for Thee: What hast Thou to say to me?
Where the shep-herd leads the flock, In the shad-ow of the rock.
Know-est all its tru-est need; Speak, and make me blest in-deed.
I am list'ning, Lord, for Thee: Mas-ter, speak, O speak to me!

348 AM I A SOLDIER OF THE CROSS
ARLINGTON C.M.

Isaac Watts, c. 1721   From Thomas A. Arne, 1762
                               Arranged by Ralph Harrison, 1784

1. Am I a sol-dier of the cross, A fol-l'wer of the Lamb?
2. Must I be car-ried to the skies On flow-'ry beds of ease,
3. Are there no foes for me to face? Must I not stem the flood?
4. Sure I must fight, if I would reign; In-crease my cour-age, Lord;
5. Thy saints in all this glo-rious war Shall con-quer, though they die:
6. When that il-lus-trious day shall rise, And all Thy ar-mies shine

LIFE IN CHRIST: OBEDIENCE AND CONSECRATION

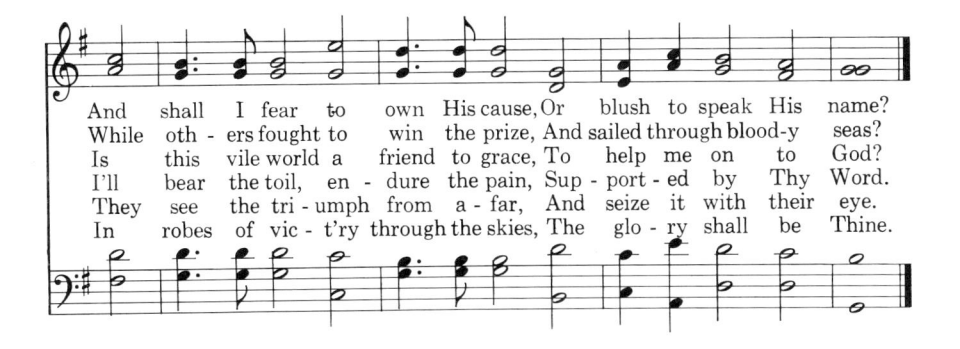

And shall I fear to own His cause, Or blush to speak His name?
While oth-ers fought to win the prize, And sailed through blood-y seas?
Is this vile world a friend to grace, To help me on to God?
I'll bear the toil, en-dure the pain, Sup-port-ed by Thy Word.
They see the tri-umph from a-far, And seize it with their eye.
In robes of vic-t'ry through the skies, The glo-ry shall be Thine.

HOW SHALL I FOLLOW HIM 349

GERMANY L.M.

Josiah Conder†, 1836

W. Gardiner's *Sacred Melodies*, 1815

1 How shall I fol-low Him I serve? How shall I learn of Him I love? Nor from those bless-ed foot-steps swerve, Which lead me to His seat a-bove?
2 Lord, should my path through suf-f'ring lie, For-bid it I should e'er re-pine; Still let me turn to Cal-va-ry, Nor heed my griefs, re-mem-b'ring Thine.
3 O let me think how Thou didst leave Un-tast-ed ev-ery pure de-light, To fast, to faint, to watch, to grieve, The toil-some day, the home-less night:
4 To faint, to grieve, to die for me! Thou cam-est not Thy-self to please: And, dear as earth-ly com-forts be, Shall I not love Thee more than these?
5 Yes! I would count them all but loss To gain the no-tice of Thine eye: Flesh shrinks and trem-bles at the cross, But Thou canst give the vic-to-ry.

LIFE IN CHRIST: OBEDIENCE AND CONSECRATION

350 A CHARGE TO KEEP I HAVE
BOYLSTON S.M.

Charles Wesley†, 1762 — Lowell Mason, 1832

1. A charge to keep I have, A God to glorify;
A never-dying soul to save, And fit it for the sky;
2. To serve the present age, My calling to fulfill,
O may it all my powers engage To do my Master's will!
3. Arm me with zealous care, As in Thy sight to live;
And O! Thy servant, Lord, prepare A strict account to give.
4. Help me to watch and pray, And on Thyself rely;
Assured, if I my trust betray, I shall forever die. A-men.

351 A CHARGE TO KEEP I HAVE
FERGUSON S.M.

Charles Wesley†, 1762 — George Kingsley, 1842

1. A charge to keep I have, A God to glorify;
A never-dying soul to save, And fit it for the sky.
2. To serve the present age, My calling to fulfill,
O, may it all my powers engage To do my Master's will!
3. Arm me with zealous care, As in Thy sight to live;
And O, Thy servant, Lord, prepare A strict account to give.
4. Help me to watch and pray, And on Thyself rely;
Assured, if I my trust betray, I shall forever die. A-men.

LIFE IN CHRIST: OBEDIENCE AND CONSECRATION

O GOD, THOU FAITHFUL GOD 352
O GOTT, DU FROMMER GOTT 6.7.6.7.6.6.6.6.

Johann Heermann, 1630
O Gott, du frommer Gott
Tr. Catherine Winkworth‡, 1858

A. Fritzsch's *Himmels-Lust*, 1679
Harmony by Johann Sebastian Bach, c. 1740

1. O God, Thou faithful God, Thou fountain ever flowing, Without whom nothing is, All perfect gifts bestowing, Grant me a healthy frame, And give me, Lord, within, A conscience free from blame, A soul unhurt by sin.
2. And grant me, Lord, to do, With ready heart and willing, Whate'er Thou shalt command, My calling here fulfilling; And do it when I ought, With zeal and joyfulness; And bless the work I've wrought, For Thou must give success.
3. If dangers gather round, Still keep me calm and fearless; Help me to bear the cross When life is dark and cheerless, To overcome my foe With words and actions kind; When counsel I would know, Good counsel let me find. A-men.

LIFE IN CHRIST: OBEDIENCE AND CONSECRATION

353 I BIND MY HEART THIS TIDE
UNION 6.7.7.7.

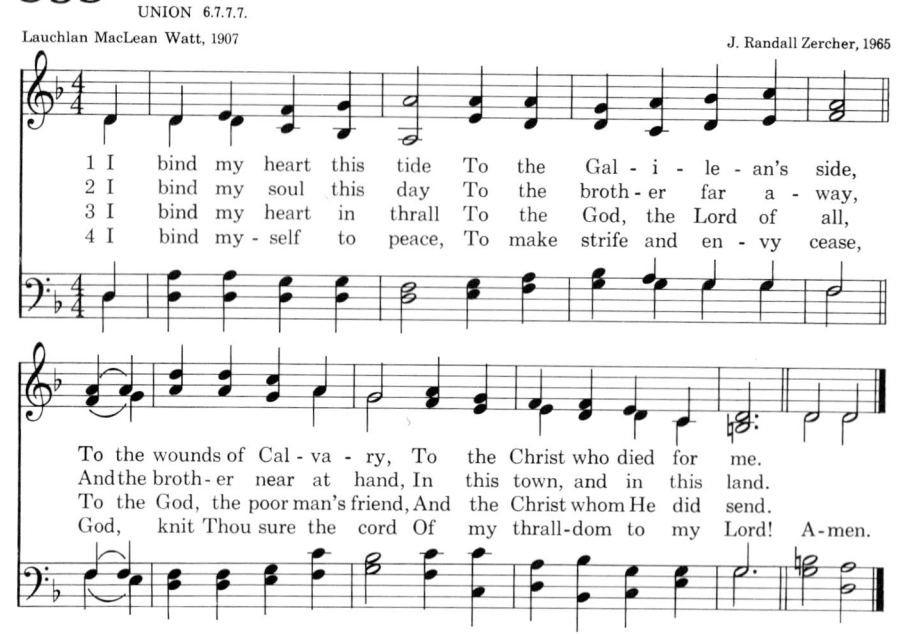

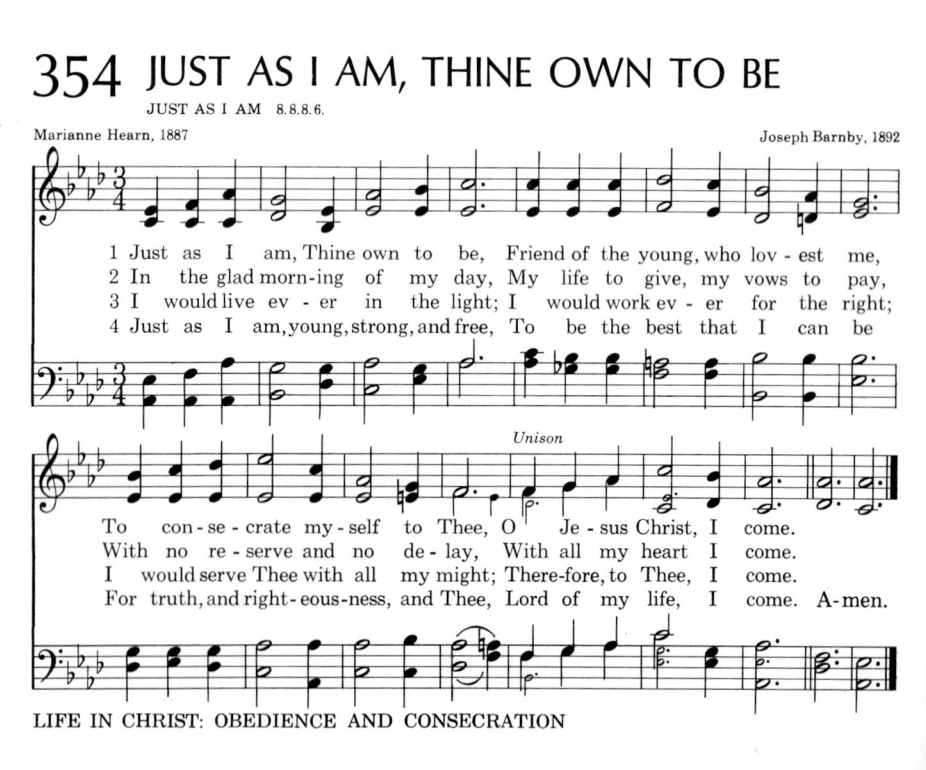

Lauchlan MacLean Watt, 1907 — J. Randall Zercher, 1965

1. I bind my heart this tide To the Galilean's side,
To the wounds of Calvary, To the Christ who died for me.

2. I bind my soul this day To the brother far away,
And the brother near at hand, In this town, and in this land.

3. I bind my heart in thrall To the God, the Lord of all,
To the God, the poor man's friend, And the Christ whom He did send.

4. I bind myself to peace, To make strife and envy cease,
God, knit Thou sure the cord Of my thralldom to my Lord! A-men.

354 JUST AS I AM, THINE OWN TO BE
JUST AS I AM 8.8.8.6.

Marianne Hearn, 1887 — Joseph Barnby, 1892

1. Just as I am, Thine own to be, Friend of the young, who lovest me,
To consecrate myself to Thee, O Jesus Christ, I come.

2. In the glad morning of my day, My life to give, my vows to pay,
With no reserve and no delay, With all my heart I come.

3. I would live ever in the light; I would work ever for the right;
I would serve Thee with all my might; Therefore, to Thee, I come.

4. Just as I am, young, strong, and free, To be the best that I can be
For truth, and righteousness, and Thee, Lord of my life, I come. A-men.

LIFE IN CHRIST: OBEDIENCE AND CONSECRATION

SAVIOR, THY DYING LOVE 355

SOMETHING FOR THEE 6.4.6.4.6.6.6.4.

Sylvanus D. Phelps, 1862
Robert Lowry, 1871

1. Savior, Thy dying love Thou gavest me, / Nor should I aught withhold, Dear Lord, from Thee; / In love my soul would bow, My heart fulfill its vow, / Some off'ring bring Thee now, Something for Thee.

2. At the blest mercy-seat, Pleading for me; / My feeble faith looks up, Jesus, to Thee. / Help me the cross to bear, Thy wondrous love declare, / Some song to raise, or prayer, Something for Thee.

3. Give me a faithful heart, Likeness to Thee, / That each departing day Henceforth may see / Some work of love begun, Some deed of kindness done, / Some wand'rer sought and won, Something for Thee.

4. All that I am and have, Thy gifts so free, / In joy, in grief, through life, Dear Lord, for Thee! / And when Thy face I see, My ransomed soul shall be, / Through all eternity, Something for Thee. A-men.

LIFE IN CHRIST: OBEDIENCE AND CONSECRATION

356 TEACH ME, O LORD
BISHOP L.M.

Based on Psalm 119: 33-40
Psalter, 1912

Joseph P. Holbrook, c. 1878

1. Teach me, O Lord, Thy way of truth, And from it I will not depart; That I may steadfastly obey, Give me an understanding heart.
2. In Thy commandments make me walk, For in Thy law my joy shall be; Give me a heart that loves Thy will, From discontent and envy free.
3. Turn Thou my eyes from vanity, And cause me in Thy ways to tread; O let Thy servant prove Thy Word, And thus to godly fear be led.
4. Turn Thou away reproach and fear, Thy righteous judgments I confess; To know Thy precepts I desire, Revive me in Thy righteousness. A-men.

357 TAKE UP THY CROSS, THE SAVIOR SAID
KEDRON L.M.

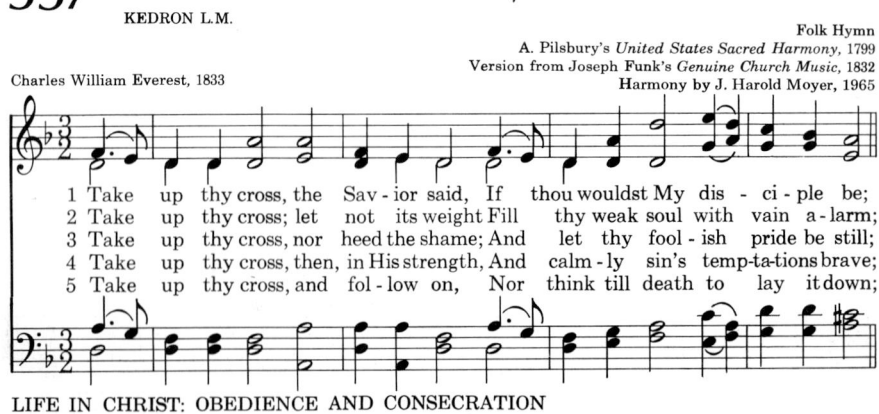

Folk Hymn
A. Pilsbury's *United States Sacred Harmony*, 1799
Version from Joseph Funk's *Genuine Church Music*, 1832
Harmony by J. Harold Moyer, 1965

Charles William Everest, 1833

1. Take up thy cross, the Savior said, If thou wouldst My disciple be;
2. Take up thy cross; let not its weight Fill thy weak soul with vain alarm;
3. Take up thy cross, nor heed the shame; And let thy foolish pride be still;
4. Take up thy cross, then, in His strength, And calmly sin's temptations brave;
5. Take up thy cross, and follow on, Nor think till death to lay it down;

LIFE IN CHRIST: OBEDIENCE AND CONSECRATION

Take up thy cross with willing heart, And humbly follow after Me.
His strength shall bear thy spirit up, And brace thy heart, and nerve thine arm.
The Lord refused not e'en to die Upon a cross on Cal'v'ry's hill.
'Twill guide thee to a better home; And point to glory o'er the grave.
For only he who bears the cross May hope to wear the glorious crown.

TAKE MY LIFE AND LET IT BE CONSECRATED 358
HENDON 7.7.7.7.

Frances Ridley Havergal, 1874

Henri Alexander César Malan, 1827
Arranged by Lowell Mason, c. 1827

1. Take my life and let it be Consecrated, Lord, to Thee; Take my moments and my days; Let them flow in ceaseless praise, Let them flow in ceaseless praise.
2. Take my hands, and let them move At the impulse of Thy love. Take my feet, and let them be Swift and beautiful for Thee, Swift and beautiful for Thee.
3. Take my voice, and let me sing, Always, only, for my King. Take my lips, and let them be Filled with messages from Thee, Filled with messages from Thee.
4. Take my silver and my gold; Not a mite would I withhold. Take my intellect and use Ev'ry power as Thou shalt choose, Ev'ry power as Thou shalt choose.
5. Take my will and make it Thine, It shall be no longer mine: Take my heart, it is Thine own, It shall be Thy royal throne, It shall be Thy royal throne.
6. Take my love; my Lord, I pour At Thy feet its treasure store; Take myself, and I will be Ever, only, all for Thee, Ever, only, all for Thee. A-men.

LIFE IN CHRIST: OBEDIENCE AND CONSECRATION

359 SON OF GOD, ETERNAL SAVIOR
IN BABILONE 8.7.8.7.D.

Somerset Corry Lowry, 1893

Dutch Traditional Melody
Oude en Nieuwe Hollantse Boerenlilies, c. 1710

1. Son of God, e-ter-nal Sav-ior, Source of life and truth and grace,
Son of man, whose birth a-mongst us Hal-lows all our hu-man race,
Thou, our head, who, throned in glo-ry, For Thine own dost ev-er plead,
Fill us with Thy love and pit-y,

2. As Thou, Lord, hast lived for oth-ers, So may we for oth-ers live,
Free-ly have Thy gifts been grant-ed, Free-ly may Thy serv-ants give.
Thine the gold and Thine the sil-ver, Thine the wealth of land and sea,
We but stew-ards of Thy boun-ty,

LIFE IN CHRIST: STEWARDSHIP

Heal our wrongs, and help our need.
Held in solemn trust for Thee. A-men.

GOD OF THE FERTILE FIELDS 360

ITALIAN HYMN 6.6.4.6.6.6.4.

Georgia Harkness, 1953 — Felice de Giardini, 1769

1 God of the fertile fields, Lord of the earth that yields
2 We would Thy stewards be, Holding in trust from Thee
3 As grows the hidden seed To fruit that serves men's need,
4 God of the countryside, Dear to our Lord who died

Our daily bread; Forth from Thy bounteous hand Come gifts Thy
All Thou dost give; Help us in love to share, Teach us like
Thy kingdom grows. So let our toil be used, No gift of
To make men one; We pledge our lives to Thee, To serve Thee

love has planned, That men through all the land Be clothed and fed.
Thee to care, That earth may all be fair, And men may live.
Thine abused, No humblest task refused, Thy love bestows.
faithfully Till in eternity Our day is done. A-men.

LIFE IN CHRIST: STEWARDSHIP

361 LORD, THOU DOST LOVE THE CHEERFUL GIVER

PLEADING SAVIOR 8.7.8.7.D.

Robert Murray†, d. 1910

J. Leavitt's *Christian Lyre*, 1831
Harmony by Ralph Vaughan Williams, 1906

1. Lord, Thou dost love the cheerful giver, Who with open heart and hand
Blesses freely, as a river That refreshes all the land;
Grant us, then, the grace of giving With a spirit large and free,
That our life and all our living We may consecrate to Thee.

2. We are Thine, Thy mercy sought us, Found us in death's dreadful way,
To the fold in safety brought us, Nevermore from Thee to stray.
Thine own life Thou freely gavest As an offering on the cross
For each sinner whom Thou savest From eternal shame and loss.

3. Blest by Thee with gifts and graces, May we heed Thy church's call;
Gladly in all times and places Give to Thee who givest all.
Thou hast bought us, and no longer Can we claim to be our own;
Ever free and ever stronger, We shall serve Thee, Lord, alone.

4. Savior, Thou hast freely given All the blessings we enjoy,
Earthly store and bread of heaven, Love and peace without alloy;
Humbly now we bow before Thee, And our all to Thee resign;
For the kingdom, power, and glory Are, O Lord, forever Thine. Amen.

LIFE IN CHRIST: STEWARDSHIP

HEART AND MIND, POSSESSIONS, LORD 362
TANA MANA DHANA Irregular

Krishnarao Rathnaji Sangle, d. 1908
Tr. Alden H. Clark, b. 1878, and Others

Ancient Indian Melody
Adapted by Marion Jean Chute, b. 1901

1. Heart and mind, pos-ses-sions, Lord, I of-fer un-to Thee;
All these were Thine, Lord; Thou didst give them all to me.
Won-drous are Thy do-ings un-to me. Plans and my thoughts and
ev-ery-thing I ev-er do are de-pend-ent on Thy
will and love a-lone. I com-mit my spir-it un-to Thee.

2. Heart and mind, pos-ses-sions, Lord, I of-fer un-to Thee;
Thou art the way, the truth; Thou art the life.
Sin-ful, I com-mit my-self to Thee. Je-sus Christ is fill-ing
all the heart of me. He can give me vic-t'ry o'er
all that threat-ens me. Je-sus Christ is fill-ing all my heart.

LIFE IN CHRIST: STEWARDSHIP

363 GOD, WHOSE GIVING

HYFRYDOL 8.7.8.7.D.

Robert Lansing Edwards, 1961

Rowland Hugh Pritchard, c. 1830
Harmony by Ralph Vaughan Williams, 1951

1. God, whose giving knows no ending, All our life is from Thy store:
Nature's wonder, Jesus' wisdom, Costly cross, grave's shattered door.
Gifted by Thee, turn we to Thee, Offering up ourselves in praise;
Thankful song shall rise forever; Gracious donor of our days.

2. Skills and time are ours for pressing Toward the goals of Christ, Thy Son:
Men at peace in health and freedom, Races joined, the church made one.
Now direct our daily labor, Lest we strive for self alone;
Born with talents make us servants Fit to answer at Thy throne.

3. Treasure, too. Thou hast entrusted, Gain through powers Thy grace conferred;
Ours to use for home and kindred, And to spread the gospel Word.
Open wide our hands in sharing, As we heed Christ's ageless call,
Healing, teaching, and reclaiming, Serving Thee who lovest all.

4. Lend Thy joy to all our giving, Let it light our pilgrim way;
From the dark of anxious keeping, Loose us into generous day.
Then when years on earth are over, Rich toward Thee and fellow man,
Lord, fulfill beyond our dreaming All our steward life began. A-men.

LIFE IN CHRIST: STEWARDSHIP

WE GIVE THEE BUT THINE OWN 364

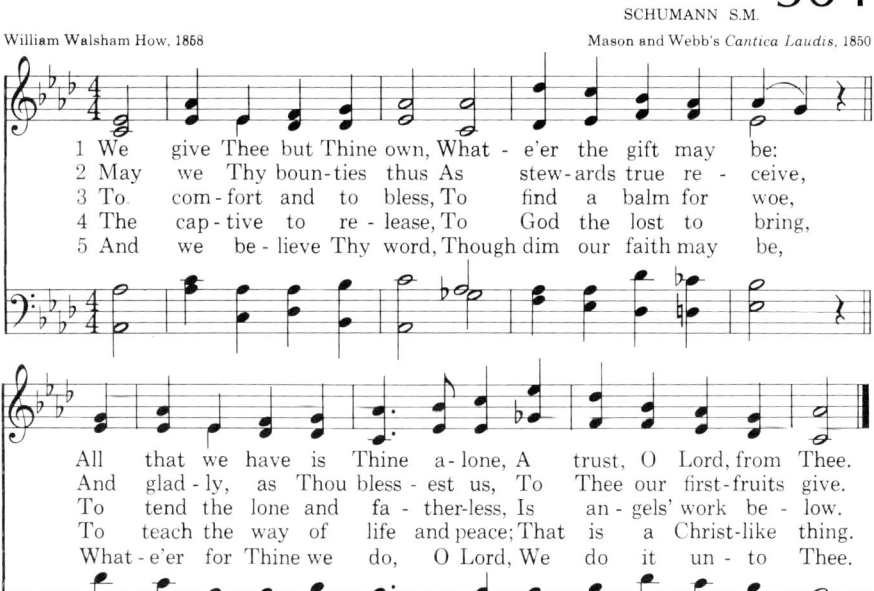

SCHUMANN S.M.

William Walsham How, 1858   Mason and Webb's *Cantica Laudis*, 1850

1 We give Thee but Thine own, What-e'er the gift may be:
All that we have is Thine a-lone, A trust, O Lord, from Thee.

2 May we Thy boun-ties thus As stew-ards true re-ceive,
And glad-ly, as Thou bless-est us, To Thee our first-fruits give.

3 To com-fort and to bless, To find a balm for woe,
To tend the lone and fa-ther-less, Is an-gels' work be-low.

4 The cap-tive to re-lease, To God the lost to bring,
To teach the way of life and peace; That is a Christ-like thing.

5 And we be-lieve Thy word, Though dim our faith may be,
What-e'er for Thine we do, O Lord, We do it un-to Thee.

ALL THINGS ARE THINE 365

O JESU CHRISTE, WAHRES LICHT L.M.

John Greenleaf Whittier, 1873   *Gesangbuch*, Nürnberg, 1676

1 All things are Thine; no gift have we, Lord of all gifts, to of-fer Thee;
And hence with grate-ful hearts to-day, Thine own be-fore Thy feet we lay.

2 Thy will was in the build-ers' thought; Thy hand un-seen a-midst us wrought;
Through mor-tal mo-tive, scheme, and plan, Thy wise e-ter-nal pur-pose ran.

3 In weak-ness and in want we call On Thee for whom the heav'ns are small;
Thy glo-ry is Thy chil-dren's good, Thy joy Thy ten-der fa-ther-hood.

4 O Fa-ther, deign these walls to bless; Fill with Thy love their emp-ti-ness;
And let their door a gate-way be To lead us from our-selves to Thee. A-men.

LIFE IN CHRIST: STEWARDSHIP

366 I HEARD A SOUND OF VOICES
PATMOS 7.6.8.6.D

Godfrey Thring, 1886
Henry Johnson Storer, 1891

1. I heard a sound of voices Around the great white throne,
With harpers harping on their harps To Him that sat thereon:
"Salvation, glory, honor!" I heard the song arise,
As through the courts of heav'n it rolled In wondrous harmonies.

2. From ev'ry clime and kindred, And nations from afar,
As serried ranks returning home In triumph from a war,
I heard the saints upraising, The myriad hosts among,
In praise of Him who died and lives, Their one glad triumph song.

3. O great and glorious vision! The Lamb upon His throne;
O wondrous sight for man to see! The Savior with His own:
To drink the living waters And stand upon the shore,
Where neither sorrow, sin, nor death Shall ever enter more.

4. And there no sun was needed, Nor moon to shine by night,
God's glory did enlighten all, The Lamb Himself the light;
And there His servants serve Him, And, life's long battle o'er,
Enthroned with Him, their Savior, King, They reign forevermore.

LIFE IN CHRIST: LIFE ETERNAL

NOW IS ETERNAL LIFE 367

EASTVIEW 6.6.6.6.8.8.

George Wallace Briggs, 1951
Vernon Lee, 1951

1. Now is eternal life, If risen with Christ we stand, In Him to life reborn, And holden in His hand; No more we fear death's ancient dread, In Christ arisen from the dead.

2. Man long in bondage lay, Brooding o'er life's brief span; Was it, O God, for nought, For nought, Thou madest man? Thou art our hope, our vital breath; Shall hope undying end in death?

3. And God, the living God, Stooped down to man's estate; By death destroying death Christ opened wide life's gate; He lives, who died; He reigns on high; Who live in Him shall never die.

4. Unfathomed love divine, Reign Thou within my heart; From Thee nor depth nor height, Nor life nor death can part; My life is hid in God with Thee, Now and through all eternity.

5. Thee will I love and serve Now in time's passing day; Thy hand shall hold me fast When time is done away, In God's unknown eternal spheres To serve Him through eternal years.

LIFE IN CHRIST: LIFE ETERNAL

368 SING WE THE SONG
NATIVITY C.M.

James Montgomery, 1824 *Henry Lahee, 1855*

1. Sing we the song of those who stand A-round th'e-ternal throne, Of ev-ery kin-dred, clime, and land, A mul-ti-tude un-known.
2. Toil, tri-al, suf-fering, still a-wait On earth the pil-grim throng, Yet learn we, in our low es-tate, The church tri-um-phant's song.
3. "Wor-thy the Lamb for sin-ners slain," Cry the re-deem'd a-bove, "Bless-ing and hon-or to ob-tain, And ev-er-last-ing love."
4. "Wor-thy the Lamb!" on earth we sing, "Who died our souls to save; Hence-forth, O death! where is thy sting? Thy vic-to-ry, O grave?"
5. Then, Al-le-lu-ia! power and praise To God in Christ be given; May all who now this an-them raise Re-new the strain in heav'n!

369 ALMIGHTY MAKER OF MY FRAME
WINSCOTT L.M.

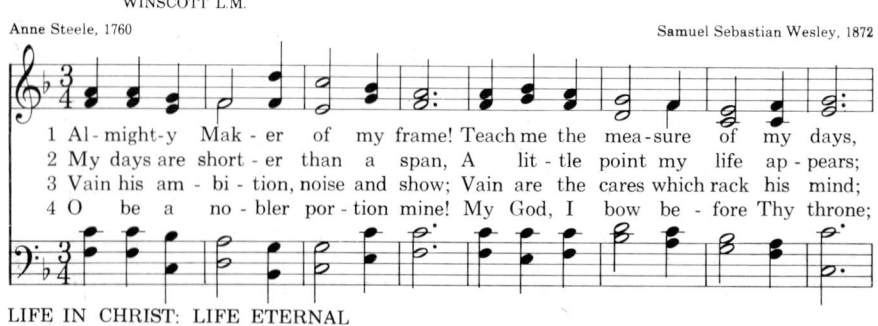

Anne Steele, 1760 *Samuel Sebastian Wesley, 1872*

1. Al-might-y Mak-er of my frame! Teach me the mea-sure of my days,
2. My days are short-er than a span, A lit-tle point my life ap-pears;
3. Vain his am-bi-tion, noise and show; Vain are the cares which rack his mind;
4. O be a no-bler por-tion mine! My God, I bow be-fore Thy throne;

LIFE IN CHRIST: LIFE ETERNAL

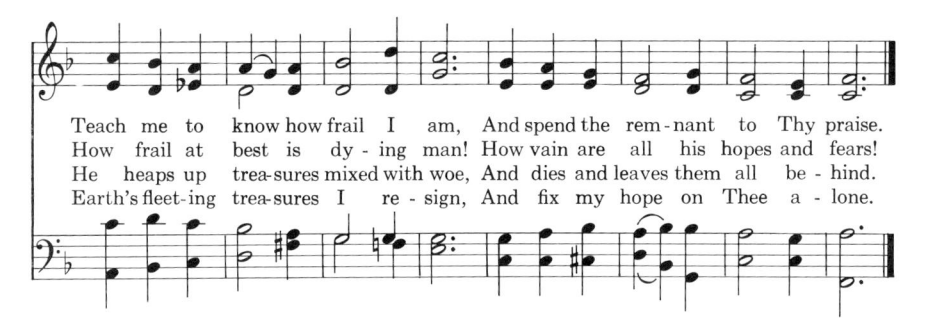

Teach me to know how frail I am, And spend the remnant to Thy praise.
How frail at best is dying man! How vain are all his hopes and fears!
He heaps up treasures mixed with woe, And dies and leaves them all behind.
Earth's fleeting treasures I resign, And fix my hope on Thee alone.

JERUSALEM! MY HAPPY HOME 370

LAND OF REST C.M.

Folk Hymn
Adapted from J. James' *Original Sacred Harp*, 1911
Harmony by J. Harold Moyer, 1965

Joseph Bromehead, 1795

1. Jerusalem! my happy home, Name ever dear to me! When shall my labors have an end In joy, and peace, and thee?
2. When shall these eyes thy heav'n-built walls And pearly gates behold; Thy bulwarks with salvation strong, And streets of shining gold!
3. O when, thou city of my God, Shall I thy courts ascend; Where congregations ne'er break up, And Sabbaths have no end?
4. Apostles, martyrs, prophets there, Around my Savior stand; And soon my friends in Christ below, Will join the glorious band.
5. Jerusalem! my happy home, My soul still pants for thee; Then shall my labors have an end, When I thy joys shall see.

LIFE IN CHRIST: LIFE ETERNAL

371 LORD, IT BELONGS NOT TO MY CARE
COLESHILL C.M.

Richard Baxter‡, 1681
W. Barton's *Psalms*, 1706

1. Lord, it belongs not to my care
Whether I die or live;
To love and serve Thee is my share,
And this Thy grace must give.

2. If life be long, I will be glad,
That I may long obey;
If short, yet why should I be sad
To welcome endless day?

3. Christ leads me through no darker rooms
Than He went through before;
He that into God's kingdom comes
Must enter by this door.

4. Come, Lord, when grace hath made me meet
Thy blessed face to see;
For, if Thy work on earth be sweet,
What will Thy glory be!

5. My knowledge of that life is small,
The eye of faith is dim;
But it's enough that Christ knows all,
And I shall be with Him. A-men.

LIFE IN CHRIST: LIFE ETERNAL

372 JESUS, FROM WHOM ALL BLESSINGS
DUKE STREET L.M.

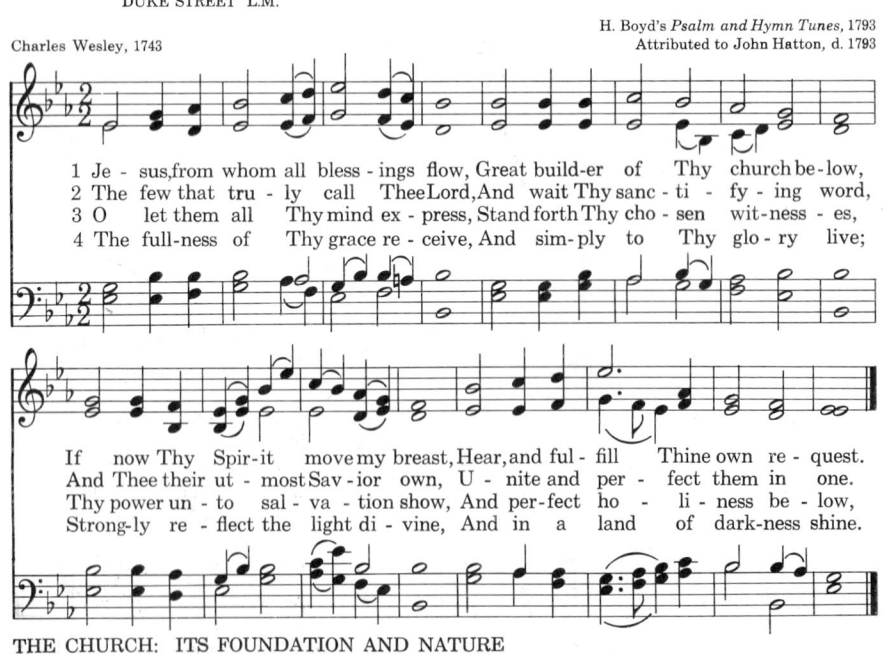

Charles Wesley, 1743
H. Boyd's *Psalm and Hymn Tunes*, 1793
Attributed to John Hatton, d. 1793

1. Jesus, from whom all blessings flow,
Great builder of Thy church below,
If now Thy Spirit move my breast,
Hear, and fulfill Thine own request.

2. The few that truly call Thee Lord,
And wait Thy sanctifying word,
And Thee their utmost Savior own,
Unite and perfect them in one.

3. O let them all Thy mind express,
Stand forth Thy chosen witnesses,
Thy power unto salvation show,
And perfect holiness below,

4. The fullness of Thy grace receive,
And simply to Thy glory live;
Strongly reflect the light divine,
And in a land of darkness shine.

THE CHURCH: ITS FOUNDATION AND NATURE

CHRIST IS MADE THE SURE FOUNDATION 373

REGENT SQUARE 8.7.8.7.8.7.

Anonymous Latin
Angularis fundamentum lapis
Tr. J. M. Neale and Compilers
of *Hymns Ancient and Modern*, 1861

Henry Smart, 1867

1. Christ is made the sure foundation, Christ the head and cornerstone, Chosen of the Lord and precious, Binding all the church in one, Holy Zion's help forever, And her confidence alone.

2. To this temple, where we call Thee, Come, O Lord of hosts, today: With Thy wonted lovingkindness Hear Thy people as they pray, And Thy fullest benediction Shed within its walls alway.

3. Here vouchsafe to all Thy servants What they ask of Thee to gain, What they gain from Thee forever With the blessed to retain, And hereafter in Thy glory Evermore with Thee to reign.

4. Praise and honor to the Father, Praise and honor to the Son, Praise and honor to the Spirit, Ever three, and ever one, One in might and one in glory, While eternal ages run. A-men.

THE CHURCH: ITS FOUNDATION AND NATURE

374 CHRIST IS OUR CORNERSTONE

DARWALL 148 6.6.6.6.8.8.

Anonymous Latin
Angularis fundamentum lapis
Tr. John Chandler†, 1837

John Darwall, 1770

1. Christ is our cor-ner-stone, On Him a-lone we build; With His true saints a-lone The courts of heav'n are filled: On His great love our hopes we place Of pres-ent grace and joys a-bove.

2. O then with hymns of praise These hal-low'd courts shall ring; Our voic-es we will raise The three in one to sing; And thus pro-claim in joy-ful song Both loud and long that glo-rious name.

3. Here, gra-cious God, do Thou For ev-er-more draw nigh; Ac-cept each faith-ful vow, And mark each sup-pliant sigh; In co-pious shower on all who pray Each ho-ly day Thy bless-ings pour!

4. Here may we gain from heav'n The grace which we im-plore; And may that grace, once given, Be with us ev-er-more, Un-til that day when all the blest To end-less rest are called a-way! A-men.

THE CHURCH: ITS FOUNDATION AND NATURE

THE CHURCH'S ONE FOUNDATION 375

AURELIA 7.6.7.6.D.

Samuel John Stone, 1868
Samuel Sebastian Wesley, 1864

1. The church's one foundation Is Jesus Christ her Lord;
   She is His new creation By water and the word:
   From heav'n He came and sought her To be His holy bride;
   With His own blood He bought her, And for her life He died.

2. Elect from every nation Yet one o'er all the earth,
   Her charter of salvation One Lord, one faith, one birth;
   One holy name she blesses, Partakes one holy food;
   And to one hope she presses, With every grace endued.

3. Though with a scornful wonder Men see her sore oppressed,
   By schisms rent asunder, By heresies distressed,
   Yet saints their watch are keeping, Their cry goes up, "How long?"
   And soon the night of weeping Shall be the morn of song.

4. 'Mid toil and tribulation, And tumult of her war,
   She waits the consummation Of peace for evermore;
   Till with the vision glorious Her longing eyes are blest,
   And the great church victorious Shall be the church at rest.

5. Yet she on earth hath union With God the three in one,
   And mystic sweet communion With those whose rest is won:
   O happy ones and holy! Lord, give us grace that we,
   Like them the meek and lowly, On high may dwell with Thee. A-men.

THE CHURCH: ITS FOUNDATION AND NATURE

376 GLORIOUS THINGS OF THEE ARE SPOKEN
AUSTRIAN HYMN 8.7.8.7.D.

John Newton, 1779 — Franz Joseph Haydn, 1797

1. Glorious things of thee are spoken, Zion, city of our God;
He whose word cannot be broken Formed thee for His own abode:
On the rock of ages founded, What can shake thy sure repose?
With salvation's walls surrounded, Thou mayst smile at all thy foes.

2. See the streams of living waters, Springing from eternal love,
Well supply thy sons and daughters, And all fear of want remove:
Who can faint while such a river Ever flows their thirst to assuage;
Grace which, like the Lord the giver, Never fails from age to age?

3. Round each habitation hov'ring, See the cloud and fire appear
For a glory and a cov'ring, Showing that the Lord is near:
Thus deriving from their banner Light by night and shade by day,
Safe they feed upon the manna Which He gives them when they pray.

4. Savior, if of Zion's city I, through grace, a member am,
Let the world deride or pity, I will glory in Thy name:
Fading is the worldling's pleasure, All his boasted pomp and show;
Solid joys and lasting treasure None but Zion's children know.

THE CHURCH: ITS FOUNDATION AND NATURE

HERE, O LORD, THY SERVANTS GATHER 377

TOKYO 7.5.7.5.D.

Tokuo Yamaguchi, 1958
Sekai no tomo to te o tsunagi
Tr. Everett M. Stowe†, 1958

Japanese Melody
Isao Koizumi, 1958
Altered by permission

1. Here, O Lord, Thy serv-ants gath-er, Hand we link with hand;
Look-ing toward our Sav-ior's cross, Joined in love we stand.
As we seek the realm of God, We u-nite to pray:
Je-sus, Sav-ior, guide our steps, For Thou art the way.

2. Man-y are the tongues we speak, Scat-tered are the lands,
Yet our hearts are one in God And His love's de-mands.
E'en in dark-ness hope ap-pears, Call-ing age and youth:
Je-sus, teach-er, dwell with us, For Thou art the truth.

3. Na-ture's se-crets o-pen wide, Chang-es nev-er cease;
Where, O where, can wea-ry men Find the source of peace?
Un-to all those sore dis-tressed, Torn by end-less strife:
Je-sus, heal-er, bring Thy balm, For Thou art the life.

4. Grant, O God, an age re-newed, Filled with death-less love,
Help us as we work and pray, Send us from a-bove
Truth and cour-age, faith and power Need-ed in our strife:
Je-sus Christ, Thou art our way, Thou our truth, our life.

THE CHURCH: ITS FOUNDATION AND NATURE

378 O WHERE ARE KINGS AND EMPIRES
ST. ANNE C.M.

Arthur Cleveland Coxe, 1839

William Croft (?) 1708

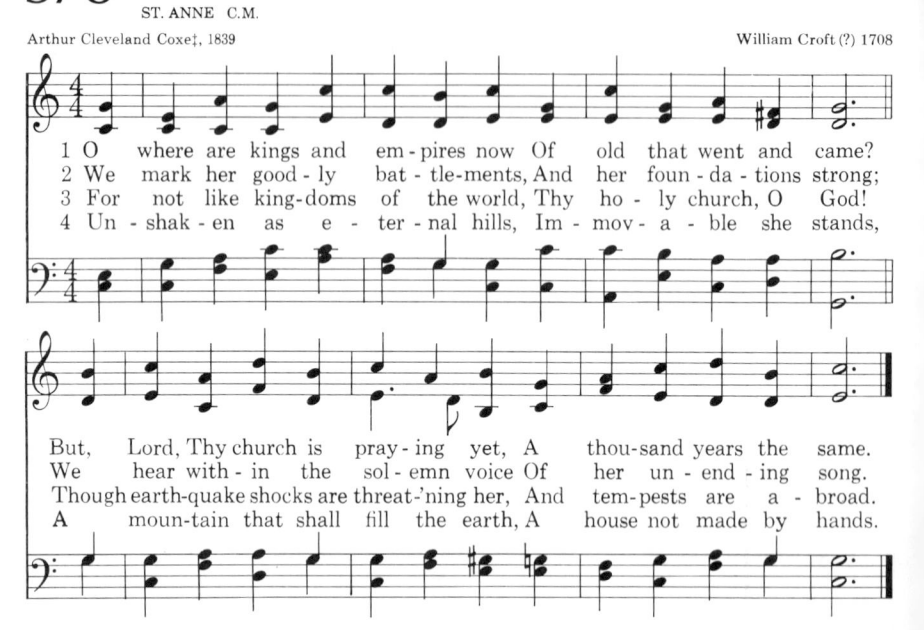

1. O where are kings and empires now Of old that went and came?
   But, Lord, Thy church is praying yet, A thousand years the same.
2. We mark her goodly battlements, And her foundations strong;
   We hear within the solemn voice Of her unending song.
3. For not like kingdoms of the world, Thy holy church, O God!
   Though earthquake shocks are threat'ning her, And tempests are abroad.
4. Unshaken as eternal hills, Immovable she stands,
   A mountain that shall fill the earth, A house not made by hands.

379 JESUS, WITH THY CHURCH ABIDE
HERVEY'S LITANY 7.7.7.6.

Thomas Benson Pollock, 1871

Frederick A. J. Hervey, 1875
Harmony from *The Hymnal*, 1940

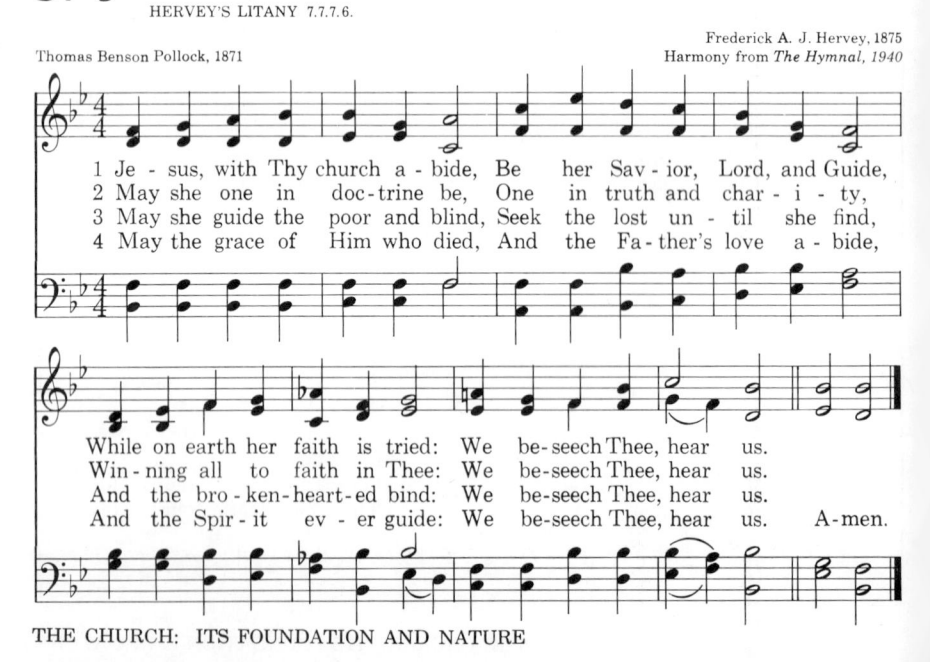

1. Jesus, with Thy church abide, Be her Savior, Lord, and Guide,
   While on earth her faith is tried: We beseech Thee, hear us.
2. May she one in doctrine be, One in truth and charity,
   Winning all to faith in Thee: We beseech Thee, hear us.
3. May she guide the poor and blind, Seek the lost until she find,
   And the brokenhearted bind: We beseech Thee, hear us.
4. May the grace of Him who died, And the Father's love abide,
   And the Spirit ever guide: We beseech Thee, hear us. A-men.

THE CHURCH: ITS FOUNDATION AND NATURE

I LOVE THY KINGDOM, LORD 380

BEALOTH S.M.D.

Timothy Dwight, 1800
Lowell Mason, d. 1872

1. I love Thy kingdom, Lord, The house of Thine abode, The church our blest Redeemer saved With His own precious blood.
2. For her my tears shall fall, For her my prayers ascend; To her my cares and toils be giv'n Till toils and cares shall end.
3. Jesus, Thou friend divine, Our Savior and our King, Thy hand from ev'ry snare and foe Shall great deliv'rance bring.

I love Thy church, O God, Her walls before Thee stand, Dear as the apple of Thine eye, And graven on Thy hand.

Beyond my highest joy I prize her heav'nly ways, Her sweet communion, solemn vows, Her hymns of love and praise.

Sure as Thy truth shall last, To Zion shall be giv'n The brightest glories earth can yield, And brighter bliss of heav'n.

THE CHURCH: ITS FOUNDATION AND NATURE

381 JESUS, WHERE'ER THY PEOPLE MEET
SHELTERING WING L.M.

William Cowper, 1779
Joseph Barnby, 1872

1. Jesus, where'er Thy people meet, There they behold Thy mercy seat; Where'er they seek Thee, Thou art found, And every place is hallowed ground.
2. For Thou, within no walls confined, Inhabitest the humble mind; Such ever bring Thee where they come, And, going, take Thee to their home.
3. Dear Shepherd of Thy chosen few, Thy former mercies here renew; Here, to our waiting hearts, proclaim The sweetness of Thy saving name.
4. Here may we prove the power of prayer To strengthen faith and sweeten care; To teach our faint desires to rise, And bring all heav'n before our eyes.

382 LO, WHAT A PLEASING SIGHT
GERAR S.M.

Based on Psalm 133
Isaac Watts, 1719, and Others
Lowell Mason, 1836

1. Lo, what a pleasing sight Are brethren that agree! How
2. All in their stations move, And each performs his part In
3. Formed for the purest joys, By one desire possessed, One
4. No bliss can equal theirs, Where such affections meet; While
5. 'Tis the same pleasure fills The breast in worlds above, Where

THE CHURCH: FELLOWSHIP OF BELIEVERS

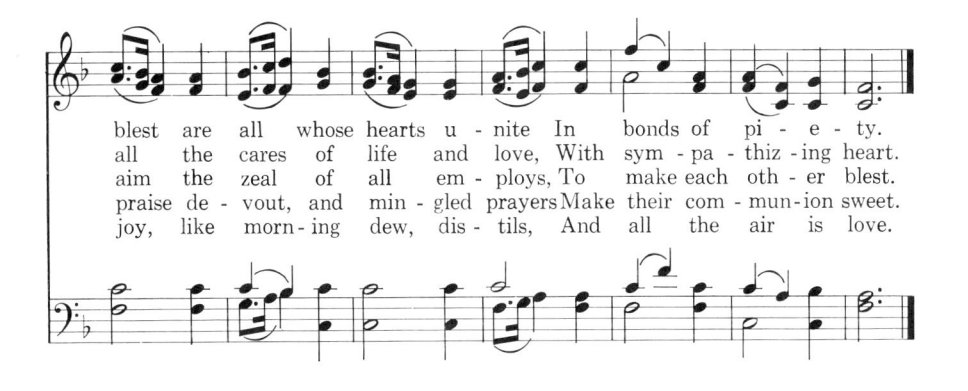

blest are all whose hearts u-nite In bonds of pi-e-ty.
all the cares of life and love, With sym-pa-thiz-ing heart.
aim the zeal of all em-ploys, To make each oth-er blest.
praise de-vout, and min-gled prayers Make their com-mun-ion sweet.
joy, like morn-ing dew, dis-tils, And all the air is love.

ALL PRAISE TO OUR REDEEMING LORD 383
DEDHAM C.M.

Charles Wesley, 1747, Sts. 1 to 4
Supplement to Church and Sunday School Hymnal, 1911, St. 5

L. Mason's *Boston Handel and Haydn Society* . . . , 1822

1. All praise to our re-deem-ing Lord, Who joins us by His grace,
2. He bids us build each oth-er up; And, gath-ered in-to one,
3. The gift which He on one be-stows, We all de-light to prove;
4. We all par-take the joy of one; The com-mon peace we feel;

And bids us, each to each re-stored, To-geth-er seek His face.
To our high call-ing's glo-rious hope, We hand in hand go on.
The grace through ev-ery ves-sel flows, In pur-est streams of love.
A peace to world-ly minds un-known, A joy un-speak-a-ble.

5. The kiss of peace to each we give,
A pledge of Christian love;
In love, while here on earth we'll live,
In love we'll dwell above.

THE CHURCH: FELLOWSHIP OF BELIEVERS

384 OUR FATHER GOD, THY NAME
NUN FREUT EUCH 8.7.8.7.8.8.7.

Leenaerdt Clock, c. 1590
O Gott, Vater, wir loben dich
Tr. Ernest A. Payne, 1956 and 1962

J. Klug's *Geistliche Lieder*, 1535

1. Our Father God, Thy name we praise, To Thee our hymns addressing,
And joyfully our voices raise Thy faithfulness confessing:
Assembled by Thy grace, O Lord, We seek fresh guidance from Thy Word;
Now grant anew Thy blessing.

2. Touch, Lord, the lips that speak for Thee; Set words of truth before us,
That we may grow in constancy, The light of wisdom o'er us.
Give us this day our daily bread; May hungry souls again be fed;
May heav'nly food restore us.

3. Lord, make Thy pilgrim people wise, The gospel message knowing,
That we may walk with light-ened eyes In grace and goodness growing.
The righteous must Thy precepts heed; Thy Word alone supplies their need,
From heav'n their succor flowing.

4. As with our brethren here we meet, Thy grace alone can feed us,
As here we gather at Thy feet We pray that Thou wilt heed us.
The power is Thine, O Lord divine, The kingdom and the rule are Thine.
May Jesus Christ still lead us!

THE CHURCH: FELLOWSHIP OF BELIEVERS

1 O Gott Vater, wir loben dich
  und deine Güte preisen,
  die du, o Herr, so gnädiglich
  an uns neu hast bewiesen;
  und hast uns, Herr, zusammeng'führt,
  uns zu ermahnen durch dein Wort.
    Gib uns Genad zu diesem!

2 Öffne den Mund, Herr, deiner Knecht,
  gib ihn'n Weisheit daneben,
  dass sie dein Wort mög'n sprechen recht,
  was dient zum frommen Leben
  und nützlich ist zu deinem Preis.
  Gib uns Hunger nach solcher Speis,
    das ist unser Begehren.

3 Gib unserm Herzen auch Verstand,
  Erleuchtung hier auf Erden,
  dass dein Wort in uns werd bekannt,
  dass wir fromm mögen werden
  und leben in Gerechtigkeit,
  achten auf dein Wort allezeit.
    So bleib'n wir unbetrogen.

4 Dein, o Herr, ist das Reich allein
  und auch die Macht zusammen.
  Wir loben dich in der Gemein
  und danken deinem Namen
  und bitten dich aus Herzens Grund,
  wollst bei uns sein zu dieser Stund,
    durch Jesum Christum, Amen.

BLEST BE THE TIE THAT BINDS 385

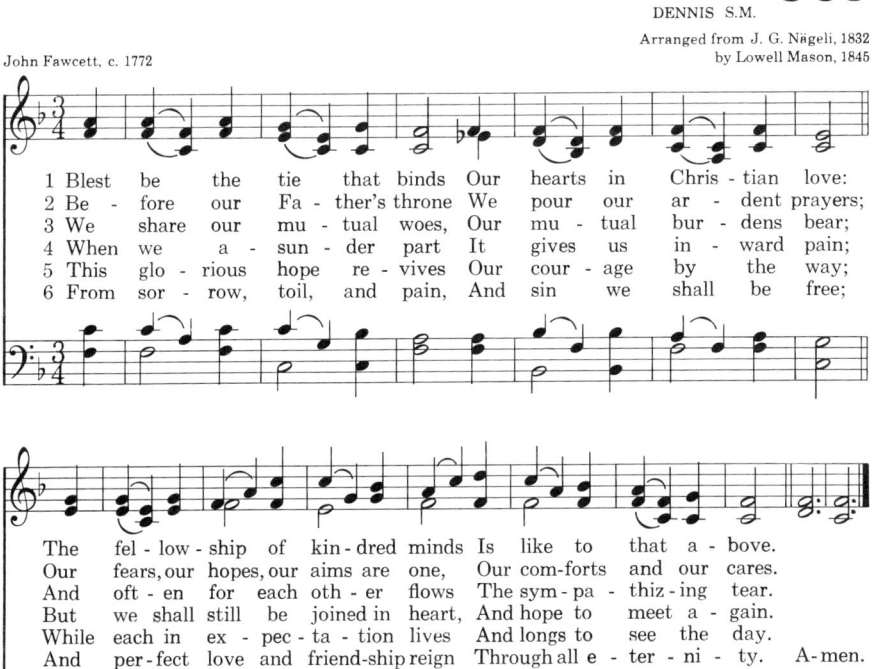

DENNIS S.M.

John Fawcett, c. 1772

Arranged from J. G. Nägeli, 1832
by Lowell Mason, 1845

1 Blest be the tie that binds Our hearts in Chris-tian love:
  The fel-low-ship of kin-dred minds Is like to that a-bove.

2 Be-fore our Fa-ther's throne We pour our ar-dent prayers;
  Our fears, our hopes, our aims are one, Our com-forts and our cares.

3 We share our mu-tual woes, Our mu-tual bur-dens bear;
  And oft-en for each oth-er flows The sym-pa-thiz-ing tear.

4 When we a-sun-der part It gives us in-ward pain;
  But we shall still be joined in heart, And hope to meet a-gain.

5 This glo-rious hope re-vives Our cour-age by the way;
  While each in ex-pec-ta-tion lives And longs to see the day.

6 From sor-row, toil, and pain, And sin we shall be free;
  And per-fect love and friend-ship reign Through all e-ter-ni-ty. A-men.

THE CHURCH: FELLOWSHIP OF BELIEVERS

386 HEART WITH LOVING HEART UNITED

O DU LIEBE MEINER LIEBE 8.7.8.7.D.

Nikolaus Ludwig von Zinzendorf, 1723
Herz und Herz vereint zusammen
Tr. Walter Klaassen, 1965

Manuscript Chorale Book,
Herrnhaag, 1735

1. Heart with lov-ing heart u-nit-ed, Met to know God's ho-ly will.
   Let His love in us ig-nit-ed More and more our spir-its fill.
   He the head, we are His mem-bers; We re-flect the light He is.
   He the Mas-ter, we the broth-ers, He is ours and we are His.

2. May we all so love each oth-er And all self-ish claims de-ny,
   That the broth-er for the broth-er Will not hes-i-tate to die.
   E-ven so our Lord has loved us; For our lives He shed His blood.
   Still He grieves and still He suf-fers When we mar the broth-er-hood.

3. Since, O Lord, You have de-mand-ed That our lives Your love should show,
   So we wait to be com-mand-ed Forth in-to Your world to go.
   Kin-dle in us love's com-pas-sion So that ev-ery-one may see
   In our fel-low-ship the prom-ise Of the new hu-man-i-ty. A-men.

THE CHURCH: FELLOWSHIP OF BELIEVERS

IN CHRIST THERE IS NO EAST OR WEST 387
ST. PETER C.M.

John Oxenham, 1908
Alexander Robert Reinagle, c. 1836

1 In Christ there is no East or West, In Him no South or North;
2 In Him shall true hearts ev-ery-where Their high com-mun-ion find;
3 Join hands, then, broth-ers of the faith, What-e'er your race may be.
4 In Christ now meet both East and West, In Him meet South and North;

But one great fel-low-ship of love Through-out the whole wide earth.
His serv-ice is the gold-en cord Close bind-ing all man-kind.
Who serves my Fa-ther as a son Is sure-ly kin to me.
All Christ-ly souls are one in Him Through-out the whole wide earth. A-men.

THE CHURCH: THE FELLOWSHIP OF BELIEVERS

POUR OUT THY SPIRIT FROM ON HIGH 388
MENDON L.M.

James Montgomery, 1833
"German Air" in Samuel Dyer's *Selection of Sacred Music*, 1825

1 Pour out Thy Spir-it from on high; Lord, Thine as-sem-bled serv-ants bless;
2 With-in Thy tem-ple when we stand, To teach the truth, as taught by Thee,
3 Wis-dom and zeal and faith im-part, Firm-ness with meek-ness from a-bove,
4 To watch and pray, and nev-er faint; By day and night strict guard to keep;
5 Then, when our work is fin-ished here, In hum-ble hope our charge re-sign:

Grac-es and gifts to each sup-ply, And clothe Thy priests with right-eous-ness.
Sav-ior, like stars in Thy right hand The an-gels of the church-es be!
To bear Thy peo-ple on our heart, And love the souls whom Thou dost love;
To warn the sin-ner, cheer the saint, Nour-ish Thy lambs, and feed Thy sheep;
When the Chief Shepherd shall appear, O God, may they and we be Thine. A-men.

THE MINISTRY: PASTORS AND TEACHERS

389 LORD, SPEAK TO ME
CANONBURY L.M.

Frances Ridley Havergal, 1872

Arranged from Robert Schumann, 1839

1. Lord, speak to me, that I may speak In liv-ing ech-oes of Thy tone;
As Thou hast sought, so let me seek Thy err-ing chil-dren lost and lone.
2. O lead me, Lord, that I may lead The wan-d'ring and the wav-'ring feet;
O feed me, Lord, that I may feed Thy hun-g'ring ones with man-na sweet.
3. O strength-en me, that while I stand Firm on the Rock, and strong in Thee,
I may stretch out a lov-ing hand To wres-tlers with the trou-bled sea.
4. O teach me, Lord, that I may teach The pre-cious things Thou dost im-part;
And wing my words, that they may reach The hid-den depths of many a heart.
5. O fill me with Thy full-ness, Lord, Un-til my ver-y heart o'er-flow
In kin-dling thought and glow-ing word, Thy love to tell, Thy praise to show. A-men.

THE MINISTRY: PASTORS AND TEACHERS

390 TO THY TEMPLE I REPAIR
GUISBOROUGH 7.7.7.7.

James Montgomery, 1812

C. T. Bowen, b. 1833

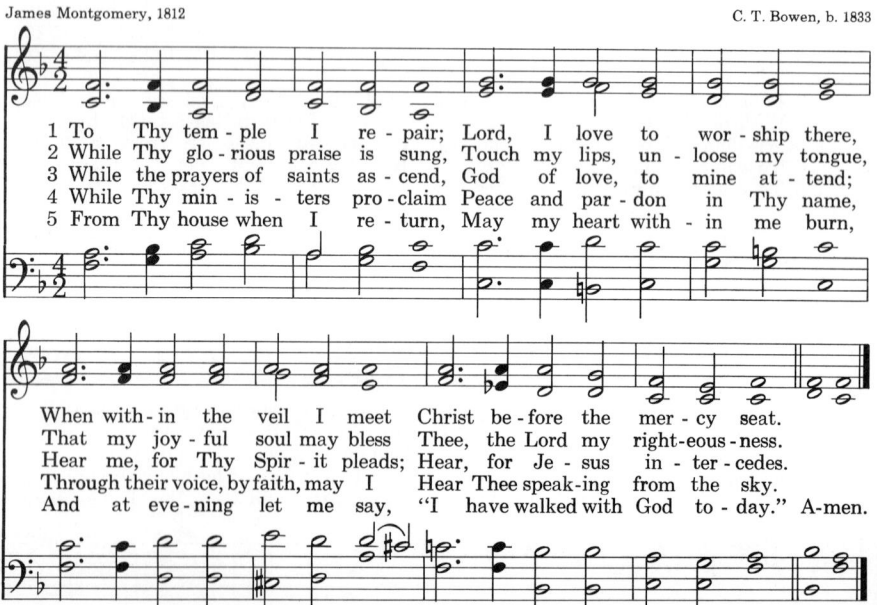

1. To Thy tem-ple I re-pair; Lord, I love to wor-ship there,
When with-in the veil I meet Christ be-fore the mer-cy seat.
2. While Thy glo-rious praise is sung, Touch my lips, un-loose my tongue,
That my joy-ful soul may bless Thee, the Lord my right-eous-ness.
3. While the prayers of saints as-cend, God of love, to mine at-tend;
Hear me, for Thy Spir-it pleads; Hear, for Je-sus in-ter-cedes.
4. While Thy min-is-ters pro-claim Peace and par-don in Thy name,
Through their voice, by faith, may I Hear Thee speak-ing from the sky.
5. From Thy house when I re-turn, May my heart with-in me burn,
And at eve-ning let me say, "I have walked with God to-day." A-men.

THE CHURCH: THE LORD'S HOUSE

BLESSED JESUS, AT THY WORD 391
LIEBSTER JESU, WIR SIND HIER 7.8.7.8.8.8.

Tobias Clausnitzer, 1663
Liebster Jesu, wir sind hier
Tr. Catherine Winkworth†, 1858

Johann Rudolph Ahle, 1664

1. Bless-ed Jesus, at Thy word We are gath-ered all to hear Thee; Let our hearts and souls be stirred Now to seek and love and fear Thee; By Thy teach-ings true and holy Drawn from earth to love Thee sole-ly.
2. All our knowl-edge, sense, and sight Lie in deep-est dark-ness shroud-ed, Till Thy Spir-it breaks our night With the beams of truth un-cloud-ed; Thou a-lone to God canst win us, Thou must work all good with-in us.
3. Glo-rious Lord, Thy-self im-part! Light of light from God pro-ceed-ing, O-pen Thou our ears and heart, Help us by Thy Spir-it's plead-ing, Hear the cry Thy peo-ple rais-es, Hear, and bless our prayers and prais-es! A-men.

THE CHURCH: THE LORD'S HOUSE

392 LORD OF THE WORLDS ABOVE

DARWALL 148 6.6.6.6.8.8.

Based on Psalm 84
Isaac Watts, 1719

John Darwall, 1770

1. Lord of the worlds above, How pleasant and how fair
The dwellings of Thy love, Thy earthly temples, are!
To Thine abode my heart aspires, With warm desires to see my God.

2. O happy souls that pray Where God appoints to hear!
O happy men that pay Their constant service there!
They praise Thee still; and happy they That love the way to Zion's hill.

3. They go from strength to strength, Through this dark vale of tears,
Till each arrives at length, Till each in heav'n appears:
O glorious seat, when God, our King, Shall thither bring our willing feet!

4. God is our sun and shield, Our light and our defense,
With gifts His hands are filled: We draw our blessings thence.
Thrice happy he, O God of hosts, Whose spirit trusts alone in Thee! A-men.

THE CHURCH: THE LORD'S HOUSE

HOW LOVELY ARE THY DWELLINGS FAIR 393

Based on Psalm 84
John Milton, 1648
WINCHESTER OLD C.M.
T. Est's *Whole Booke of Psalmes*, 1592

1. How love-ly are Thy dwell-ings fair! O Lord of hosts, how dear
   The pleas-ant tab-er-na-cles are Where Thou dost dwell so near!
2. Hap-py, who in Thy house re-side, Where Thee they ev-er praise,
   Hap-py, whose strength in Thee doth bide, And in their hearts Thy ways.
3. They pass through Ba-ca's thirst-y vale, That dry and bar-ren ground,
   As through a fruit-ful wa-ter-y dale Where springs and show'rs a-bound.
4. They jour-ney on from strength to strength With joy and glad-some cheer,
   Till all be-fore our God at length In Zi-on do ap-pear.
5. Lord God of hosts that reign'st on high, That man is tru-ly blest
   Who on-ly on Thee doth re-ly, And in Thee on-ly rest. A-men.

THE CHURCH: THE LORD'S HOUSE

COME, LET US JOIN OUR FRIENDS 394

Charles Wesley†, 1759
DUNDEE C.M.
Scottish Psalter, 1615

1. Come, let us join our friends a-bove Who have ob-tained the prize,
   And on the ea-gle wings of love To joy ce-les-tial rise.
2. Let saints on earth u-nite and sing, With those to glo-ry gone;
   For all the serv-ants of our King, In earth and heav'n, are one.
3. One fam-i-ly we dwell in Him, One church, a-bove, be-neath,
   Though now di-vid-ed by the stream, The nar-row stream of death:
4. One ar-my of the liv-ing God, To His com-mand we bow;
   Part of His host have crossed the flood, And part are cross-ing now.
5. E'en now by faith we join our hands With those that went be-fore,
   And greet the blood-re-deem-ed bands On the e-ter-nal shore.

THE CHURCH: COMMUNION OF SAINTS

395 FOR ALL THE SAINTS
SINE NOMINE 10.10.10. with Alleluias

William Walsham How, 1864 — Ralph Vaughan Williams, 1906

In unison

1. For all the saints, who from their la-bors rest, Who
2. Thou wast their rock, their for-tress, and their might:
3. O may Thy sol-diers, faith-ful, true, and bold,
7. But lo! there breaks a yet more glo-rious day; The
8. From earth's wide bounds, from o-cean's far-thest coast, Through

Thee by faith be-fore the world con-fessed,
Thou, Lord, their cap-tain in the well-fought fight;
Fight as the saints who no-bly fought of old,
saints tri-um-phant rise in bright ar-ray;
gates of pearl streams in the count-less host,

Thy name, O Je-sus, be for ev-er blest.
Thou, in the dark-ness drear, the one true light.
And win, with them, the vic-tor's crown of gold.
The King of glo-ry pass-es on His way.
Sing-ing to Fa-ther, Son, and Ho-ly Ghost,

THE CHURCH: COMMUNION OF SAINTS

Al - le - lu - ia, al - le - lu - ia! A-men.

4 O blest com-mun-ion, fel-low-ship di-vine! We fee-bly strug-gle, they in glo-ry shine; Yet all are one in Thee, for all are Thine.

5 And when the strife is fierce, the war-fare long, Steals on the ear the dis-tant tri-umph song, And hearts are brave a-gain, and arms are strong. Al-le-lu-ia, al-le-lu-ia!

6 The gold-en eve-ning bright-ens in the west; Soon, soon to faith-ful war-riors com-eth rest; Sweet is the calm of pa-ra-dise the blest.

THE CHURCH: COMMUNION OF SAINTS

396 WE COME UNTO OUR FATHERS' GOD

NUN FREUT EUCH 8.7.8.7.8.8.7.

Thomas Hornblower Gill, 1868

J. Klug's *Geistliche Lieder*, 1535

1 We come un-to our fa-thers' God; Their rock is our sal-va-tion;
 Th'e-ter-nal arms, their dear a-bode, We make our hab-i-ta-tion.
 We bring Thee, Lord, the praise they brought, We seek Thee as Thy
 saints have sought In ev-ery gen-er-a-tion.

2 Their joy un-to their Lord we bring; Their song to us de-scend-eth;
 The Spir-it who in them did sing To us His mu-sic lend-eth:
 His song in them, in us, is one; We raise it high, we
 send it on, The song that nev-er end-eth.

3 Ye saints to come, take up the strain, The same sweet theme en-deav-or;
 Un-bro-ken be the gold-en chain! Keep on the song for-ev-er!
 Safe in the same dear dwell-ing place, Rich with the same e-
 ter-nal grace, Bless the same bound-less giv-er.

THE CHURCH: COMMUNION OF SAINTS

HE WANTS NOT FRIENDS 397

SONG XXXIV L.M.

Richard Baxter†, 1663
Orlando Gibbons, 1623

1. He wants not friends that hath Thy love, And may converse and walk with Thee, And with Thy saints here and above, With whom for ever I must be.

2. In the communion of the saints Is wisdom, safety and delight; And, when my heart declines and faints, It's raised by their heat and light.

3. As for my friends, they are not lost; The several vessels of Thy fleet, Though parted now, by tempests tossed, Shall safely in the haven meet.

4. Still we are centered all in Thee, Members, though distant, of one head; In the same family we be, By the same faith and Spirit led.

5. Before Thy throne we daily meet
As joint-petitioners to Thee;
In spirit we each other greet,
And shall again each other see.

6. The heav'nly hosts, world without end,
Shall be my company above;
And Thou, my best and surest friend,
Who shall divide me from Thy love?

THE CHURCH: COMMUNION OF SAINTS

398 O HAPPY DAY, THAT FIXED MY CHOICE
ROCKINGHAM NEW L.M.

Philip Doddridge, 1755 *Lowell Mason, 1830*

1. O happy day, that fixed my choice On Thee, my Savior and my God! Well may this glowing heart rejoice, And tell its raptures all abroad.
2. O happy bond, that seals my vows, To Him who merits all my love! Let cheerful anthems fill His house, While to that sacred shrine I move.
3. 'Tis done! the great transaction's done; I am my Lord's, and He is mine; He drew me, and I followed on, Charmed to confess the voice divine.
4. High heav'n, that heard the solemn vow, That vow renewed shall daily hear, Till in life's latest hour I bow, And bless in death a bond so dear.

399 MY GOD, ACCEPT MY HEART
GLENLUCE C.M.

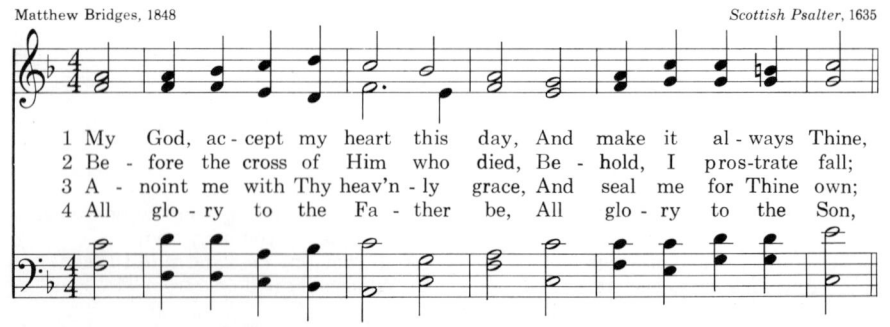

Matthew Bridges, 1848 *Scottish Psalter, 1635*

1. My God, accept my heart this day, And make it always Thine,
2. Before the cross of Him who died, Behold, I prostrate fall;
3. Anoint me with Thy heav'nly grace, And seal me for Thine own;
4. All glory to the Father be, All glory to the Son,

THE CHURCH: SACRAMENTS—BAPTISM

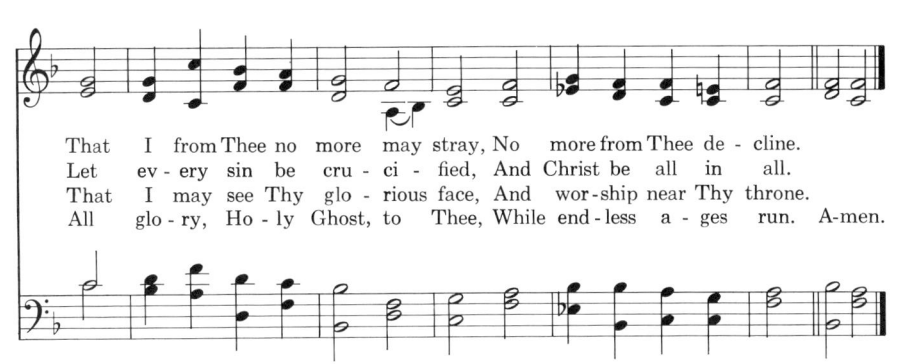

That I from Thee no more may stray, No more from Thee de - cline.
Let ev - ery sin be cru - ci - fied, And Christ be all in all.
That I may see Thy glo - rious face, And wor - ship near Thy throne.
All glo - ry, Ho - ly Ghost, to Thee, While end - less a - ges run. A-men.

See Topical Index for other suitable hymns on "Baptism."

ACCORDING TO THY GRACIOUS WORD 400

ST. FLAVIAN C.M.

James Montgomery, 1825

English Psalter, 1562

1 Ac - cord - ing to Thy gra - cious Word, In meek hu - mil - i - ty,
2 Thy bod - y, bro - ken for my sake, My bread from heav'n shall be;
3 Geth - sem - a - ne can I for - get? Or there Thy con - flict see,
4 When to the cross I turn my eyes, And rest on Cal - va - ry,
5 Re - mem - ber Thee, and all Thy pains, And all Thy love to me:
6 And when these fail - ing lips grow dumb, And mind and mem - 'ry flee,

This will I do, my dy - ing Lord, I will re - mem - ber Thee.
Thy tes - ta - men - tal cup I take, And thus re - mem - ber Thee.
Thine ag - o - ny and blood - y sweat, And not re - mem - ber Thee?
O Lamb of God, my sac - ri - fice, I must re - mem - ber Thee.
Yea, while a breath, a pulse re - mains Will I re - mem - ber Thee.
When Thou shalt in Thy king - dom come, Je - sus, re - mem - ber me. A-men.

THE CHURCH: SACRAMENTS — THE LORD'S SUPPER

401 BREAD OF HEAVEN! ON THEE WE FEED
O DU LIEBE MEINER LIEBE 7.7.7.7.7.7.

Josiah Conder, 1824 *Manuscript Chorale Book, Herrnhaag, 1735*

1. Bread of heav'n! on Thee we feed, For Thy flesh is meat indeed.
Ever may our souls be fed With this true and living bread;
Day by day with strength supplied, Through the life of Him who died.

2. Vine of heav'n! Thy blood supplies This blest cup of sacrifice.
'Tis Thy wounds our healing give: To Thy cross we look, and live.
Thou our life! O let us be Rooted, grafted, built on Thee. Amen.

402 BE KNOWN TO US IN BREAKING BREAD
DUNFERMLINE C.M.

James Montgomery, 1825 *Scottish Psalter, 1615*

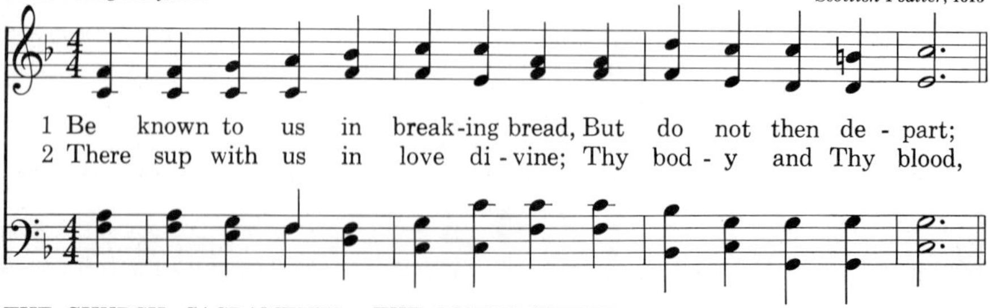

1. Be known to us in breaking bread, But do not then depart;

2. There sup with us in love divine; Thy body and Thy blood,

THE CHURCH: SACRAMENTS — THE LORD'S SUPPER

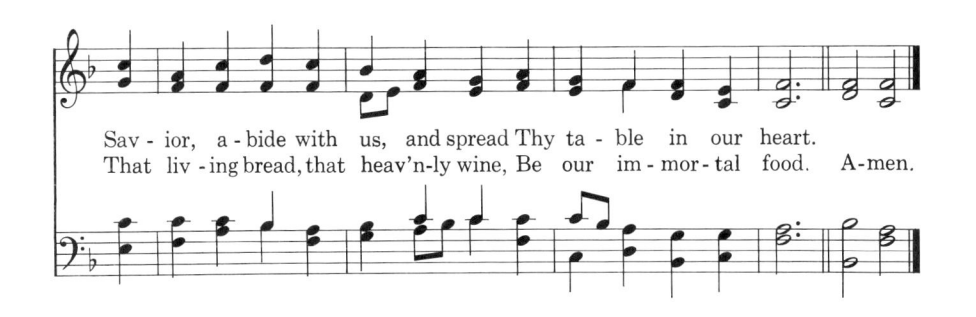

Sav - ior, a - bide with us, and spread Thy ta - ble in our heart.
That liv - ing bread, that heav'n-ly wine, Be our im - mor - tal food. A-men.

COME, RISEN LORD, AND DEIGN 403

BIRMINGHAM (CUNNINGHAM) 10.10.10.10.

George Wallace Briggs, 1926 and 1957

F. Cunningham's, *Selection of Psalm Tunes*, 1834

1 Come, ris - en Lord, and deign to be our guest; Nay, let us be Thy guests; the feast is Thine; Thy-self at Thine own board make man-i - fest, In Thine own sac - ra - ment of bread and wine.

2 We meet, as in that up - per room they met, Thou at the ta - ble, bless-ing, yet dost stand: "This is My bod - y": so Thou giv-est yet: Faith still re-ceives the cup as from Thy hand.

3 One bod - y we, one bod - y who par - take, One church u - nit - ed in com - mun - ion blest; One name we bear, one bread of life we break, With all Thy saints on earth and saints at rest.

4 One with each oth - er, Lord, for one in Thee, Who art one Sav - ior and one liv - ing head; Then o - pen Thou our eyes, that we may see; Be known to us in break - ing of the bread. A-men.

THE CHURCH: SACRAMENTS — THE LORD'S SUPPER

404 SING, MY TONGUE
PANGE LINGUA 8.7.8.7.8.7.

Thomas Aquinas, 1263
Pange lingua gloriosi
Tr. *New Congregational Hymn Book*, 1859

Sarum Plainsong

1. Sing, my tongue, the Savior's glo - ry, Of His cross the mys-tery sing;
2. Born for us and for us giv - en, Son of man, like us be - low,
3. Word made flesh! His word life-giv - ing, Gives His flesh our meat to be,
4. Low in ad - o - ra - tion bend - ing, Now our hearts our God re - vere;
5. Praise for ev - er, thanks and bless - ing Thine, O gra-cious Fa - ther, be:

Lift on high the won-drous tro - phy, Tell the tri - umph of the King;
He as man with men a - bid - ing Dwells, the seed of life to sow,
Bids us drink His blood be - liev - ing, Through His death, we life shall see:
Faith her aid to sight is lend - ing, Though un-seen the Lord is near;
Praise be Thine, O Christ, who bring - est Life and im - mor - tal - i - ty;

He, the world's Re-deem-er, con-quers Death, thro' death now van-quish-ing.
He, our heav - y griefs par-tak-ing, Thus ful-fills His life of woe.
Bless - ed they who thus re-ceiv-ing Are from death and sin set free.
An - cient types and shad-ows end-ing, Christ our pas-chal Lamb is here.
Praise be Thine, Thou quick-ening Spir-it, Praise through all e - ter - ni - ty. A - men.

THE CHURCH: SACRAMENTS — THE LORD'S SUPPER

HERE, O MY LORD, I SEE THEE 405

LANGRAN 10.10.10.10.

Horatius Bonar, 1855 — James Langran, 1861

1. Here, O my Lord, I see Thee face to face;
   Here would I touch and handle things unseen;
   Here grasp with firmer hand th'eternal grace,
   And all my weariness upon Thee lean.

2. Here would I feed upon the bread of God;
   Here drink with Thee the royal wine of heav'n;
   Here would I lay aside each earthly load,
   Here taste afresh the calm of sin forgiven.

3. Too soon we rise; the symbols disappear;
   The feast, though not the love, is passed and gone;
   The bread and wine remove, but Thou art here;
   Nearer than ever; still my shield and sun.

4. Feast after feast thus comes and passes by;
   Yet, passing, points to the glad feast above,
   Giving sweet foretaste of the festal joy,
   The Lamb's great bridal feast of bliss and love. A-men.

THE CHURCH: SACRAMENTS — THE LORD'S SUPPER

406 DECK THYSELF WITH JOY
SCHMÜCKE DICH, O LIEBE SEELE L.M.D.

Johann Franck, 1649
Schmücke dich, O liebe Seele
Tr. John Casper Mattes†, 1913

Johann Crüger, 1649

1. Deck thy-self with joy and gladness, Dwell no more, my soul, in sadness;
Let the day-light shine up-on thee, Put thy wed-ding gar-ment on thee,
For the Lord of life un-end-ing Un-to thee His call is send-ing,
Come, for now the King most gracious

2. Has-ten, then, my soul, to meet Him, Ea-ger-ly and glad-ly greet Him.
As with-out He stand-eth knock-ing, Quick-ly, thy soul's gate un-lock-ing,
O-pen wide the fast-closed por-tal, Say-ing to the Lord im-mor-tal,
"Come, and leave Thy serv-ant

3. Je-sus, source of life and plea-sure, Tru-est friend and dear-est trea-sure,
Joy, the sweet-est man e'er know-eth; Fount, whence all my be-ing flow-eth;
Hum-bly now I bow be-fore Thee, And in pen-i-tence a-dore Thee;
Wor-thi-ly let me re-

THE CHURCH: SACRAMENTS — THE LORD'S SUPPER

ho - ly Stoops to thee in like-ness low - ly.
nev - er, Dwell with - in my heart for - ev - er."
ceive Thee, Per - fect peace and par - don give me. A-men.

BREAD OF THE WORLD IN MERCY 407
LES COMMANDEMENS DE DIEU 9.8.9.8.

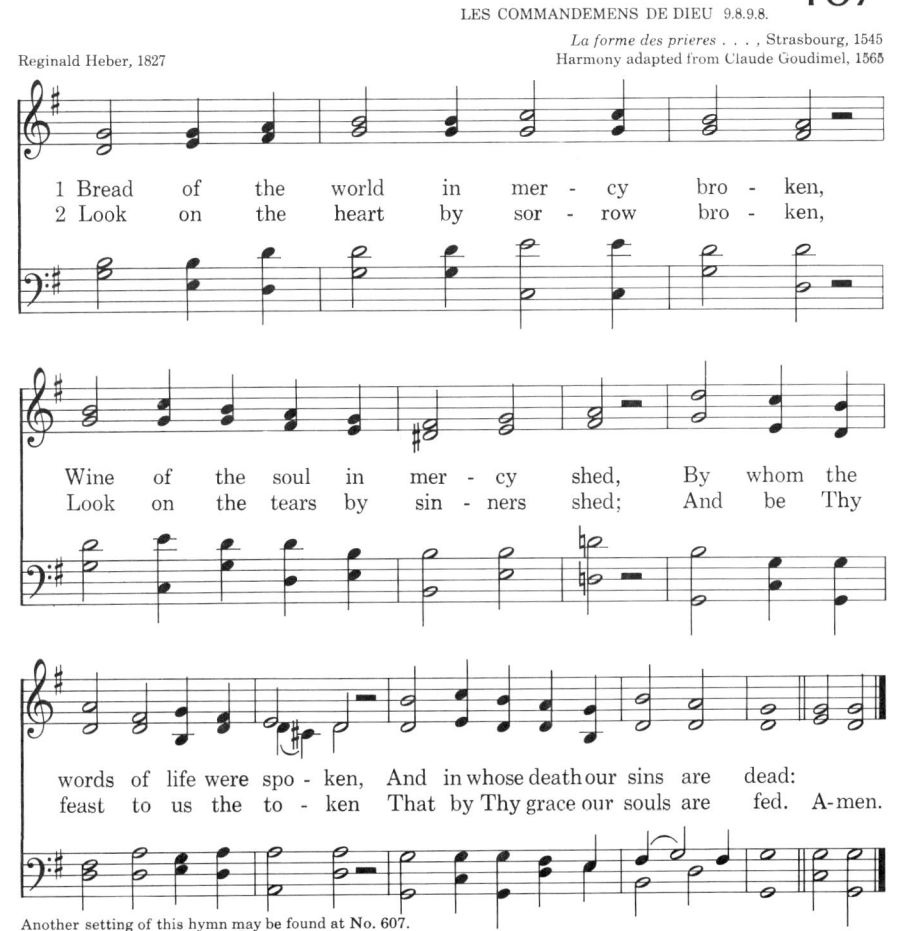

Reginald Heber, 1827

La forme des prieres . . . , Strasbourg, 1545
Harmony adapted from Claude Goudimel, 1565

1 Bread of the world in mer - cy bro - ken,
2 Look on the heart by sor - row bro - ken,

Wine of the soul in mer - cy shed, By whom the
Look on the tears by sin - ners shed; And be Thy

words of life were spo - ken, And in whose death our sins are dead:
feast to us the to - ken That by Thy grace our souls are fed. A-men.

Another setting of this hymn may be found at No. 607.

THE CHURCH: SACRAMENTS—THE LORD'S SUPPER

408 'TWAS ON THAT NIGHT

ROCKINGHAM OLD L.M.

Based on Matthew 26:26-29
Scottish Paraphrases, 1781

A. Williams' *Supplement to Psalmody*, c. 1780
Adapted by Edward Miller, 1790

1. 'Twas on that night when doomed to know The eager rage of every foe, That night in which He was betrayed The Savior of the world took bread;

2. And, after thanks and glory given To Him that rules in earth and heav'n, That symbol of His flesh He broke, And thus to all His followers spoke:

3. "My broken body thus I give For you, for all; take, eat, and live: And oft the sacred rite renew That brings My wondrous love to view."

4. Then in His hands the cup He raised, And God anew He thanked and praised, While kindness in His bosom glowed, And from His lips salvation flowed. A-men.

5. "My blood I thus pour forth," He cries,
"To cleanse the soul in sin that lies;
In this the covenant is sealed,
And heav'n's eternal grace revealed.

6. "With love to man this cup is fraught,
Let all partake the sacred draught;
Through latest ages let it pour
In memory of My dying hour."

THE CHURCH: SACRAMENTS—THE LORD'S SUPPER

BY CHRIST REDEEMED 409
IN MEMORIAM 8.8.8.4.

George Rawson, 1857
Frederick Charles Maker, 1876

1. By Christ redeemed, in Christ restored, We keep the memory adored, And show the death of our dear Lord Until He come.

2. His body broken in our stead Is shown in this memorial bread, And so our feeble love is fed Until He come.

3. The streams of His dread agony, His lifeblood shed for us, we see; The wine shall tell the mystery Until He come.

4. And thus that dark betrayal night With the last advent we unite By one blest chain of loving rite Until He come. A-men.

5. Until the trump of God be heard,
Until the ancient graves be stirred,
And, with the great commanding word,
The Lord shall come,

6. O blessed hope! with this elate
Let not your hearts be desolate,
But, strong in faith, in patience wait
Until He come.

THE CHURCH: SACRAMENTS—THE LORD'S SUPPER

410 EXTOL THE LOVE OF CHRIST

ELLACOMBE C.M.D.

Samuel Frederick Coffman, 1925 — Adapted from *Gesangbuch* ..., Württemberg, 1784

1. Extol the love of Christ, ye saints, And sing His wondrous worth, Whose love, like God, eternal is In heaven and on earth. From God He brought His blessing rare; To God He did ascend; And

2. Extol the love which sought to show The Father's boundless grace; The Son, from Father's bosom come, Beheld the Father's face: In servile garments clothed upon, With humble service meet, The

3. The Lord and Master humbly served To glorify the meek; His heav'nly glory shared with those Who would His favor seek. Lord, teach Thy saints in Example, worthy, Thee to know The fullness of Thy love, The

4. Let poor, vain man example take And from his pride repent; For Christ far greater is than man, Or servant that is sent. Example, worthy, Christ has giv'n, And happy shall they be Who

THE CHURCH: FOOTWASHING

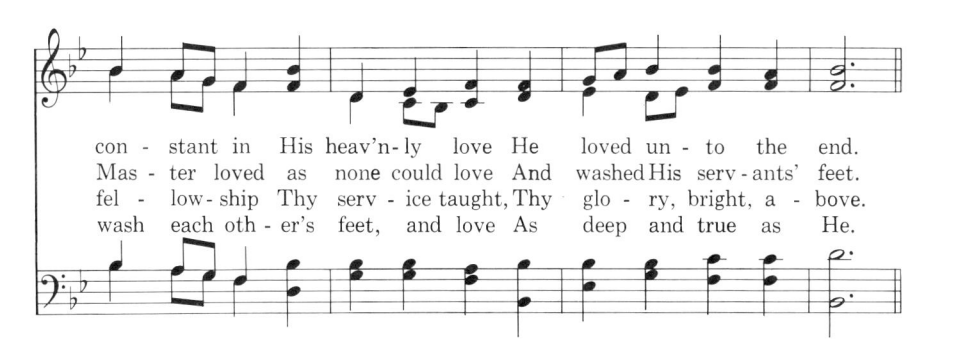

con - stant in His heav'n-ly love He loved un - to the end.
Mas - ter loved as none could love And washed His serv - ants' feet.
fel - low-ship Thy serv - ice taught, Thy glo - ry, bright, a - bove.
wash each oth - er's feet, and love As deep and true as He.

LOVE CONSECRATES THE HUMBLEST ACT   411
LOVE'S CONSECRATION C.M.

S. B. McManus, 1902　　　　　　　　　　　　　　　　　　　　Abram Bowman Kolb, 1902

1 Love con - se - crates the hum - blest act, And
2 When in the shad - ow of the cross, Christ
3 "As I have done this un - to you, My
4 Love serves, yet will - ing stoops to serve, What

sanc - ti - fies each deed; It sheds a ben - e -
bowed and washed the feet Of His dis - ci - ples,
breth - ren, here this night, Thus would I have you
Christ in love so true, Hath free - ly done for

dic - tion sweet, And hal - lows ev - ery need.
'twas a sign Of His great love com - plete.
do to each When I have passed from sight."
one and all, Shall we not glad - ly do?

THE CHURCH: FOOTWASHING

412 O PERFECT LOVE
SANDRINGHAM 11.10.11.10.

Dorothy F. Blomfield Gurney, 1883
Doxology by John Ellerton, 1875

Joseph Barnby, 1889

1. O perfect Love, all human thought transcending,
Lowly we kneel in prayer before Thy throne,
That theirs may be the love which knows no ending,
Whom Thou forevermore dost join in one.

2. O perfect Life, be Thou their full assurance
Of tender charity and steadfast faith,
Of patient hope, and quiet, brave endurance,
With childlike trust that fears nor pain nor death.

3. Grant them the joy which brightens earthly sorrow;
Grant them the peace which calms all earthly strife,
And to life's day the glorious, unknown morrow
That dawns upon eternal love and life.

4. Hear us, O Father, gracious and forgiving,
Through Jesus Christ Thy co-eternal Word,
Who, with the Holy Ghost, by all things living
Now and to endless ages art adored. A-men.

THE CHURCH: MARRIAGE

SHEPHERD OF TENDER YOUTH 413

BRAUN 6.6.4.6.6.6.4.

Clement of Alexandria, d.c. 220
Στομίον πώλων ἀδαῶν
Tr. Henry Martyn Dexter, 1846

Johann G. Braun, 1675

1. Shepherd of tender youth, Guiding in love and truth, Through devious ways: Christ, our triumphant King, We come Thy name to sing; And here our children bring, To shout Thy praise.
2. Thou art our holy Lord, The all-subduing Word, Healer of strife: Thou didst Thyself abase, That from sin's deep disgrace Thou mightest save our race, And give us life.
3. Thou art our soul's high priest, Thou hast prepared the feast Of holy love: And in our mortal pain, None calls on Thee in vain; Help Thou dost not disdain, Help from above.
4. Ever be Thou our guide, Our Shepherd and our pride, Our staff and song: Jesus, Thou Christ of God, By Thy perennial Word, Lead us where Thou hast trod; Make our faith strong.
5. So now and till we die, Sound we Thy praises high, And joyful sing: Infants, and the glad throng Who to Thy church belong, Unite and swell the song To Christ our King. A-men.

THE CHURCH: CONSECRATION OF CHILDREN AND PARENTS

414 JESUS, FRIEND, SO KIND
SICILIAN MARINERS 8.7.8.7.8.7.

Philip E. Gregory, b. 1886 — Tattersall's *Psalmody*, 1794

1. Jesus, friend, so kind and gentle, Little ones we bring to Thee; Grant to them Thy dearest blessing, Let Thine arms around them be; Now enfold them in Thy goodness, From all danger keep them free.

2. Thou who didst receive the children To Thyself so tenderly, Give to all who teach and guide them, Wisdom and humility, Vision true to keep them noble, Love to serve them faithfully. A-men.

THE CHURCH: CONSECRATION OF CHILDREN AND PARENTS

O JESUS CHRIST, OUR LORD MOST DEAR 415
VOM HIMMEL HOCH L.M.

Heinrich von Laufenburg, 1429
Ach lieber Herre Jesu Christ
Tr. Catherine Winkworth†, 1869

V. Schumann's *Geistliche Lieder*, 1539

1. O Jesus Christ, our Lord most dear, As Thou wast once an infant here, So give this child of Thine, we pray, Thy grace and blessing day by day.

2. As in Thy heav'nly kingdom, Lord, Thy messengers obey Thy Word, Send forth the succor of Thy might To shield this child both day and night.

3. And all his life, let angels keep Him safe from harm, awake, asleep; May he not bear the cross in vain, But with Thy saints a crown attain.

THE CHURCH: CONSECRATION OF CHILDREN AND PARENTS

416 JERUSALEM, THE GOLDEN
EWING 7.6.7.6.D.

Bernard of Cluny, c. 1140
Urbs Syon aurea
Tr. John Mason Neale†, 1858, Sts. 1-3
Hymns Ancient and Modern, 1861, St. 4

Alexander Ewing, 1853

1. Je-ru-sa-lem the gold-en, With milk and hon-ey blest,
Beneath thy con-tem-pla-tion Sink heart and voice op-pressed.
I know not, O I know not, What joys a-wait us there,
What ra-dian-cy of glo-ry, What bliss be-yond com-pare!

2. They stand, those halls of Zi-on, All ju-bi-lant with song,
And bright with man-y an an-gel, And all the mar-tyr throng.
The Prince is ev-er in them; The day-light is se-rene;
The pas-tures of the bless-ed Are decked in glo-rious sheen.

3. There is the throne of Da-vid, And there, from care re-leased,
The shout of them that tri-umph, The song of them that feast;
And they, who with their lead-er, Have con-quered in the fight,
For-ev-er and for-ev-er Are clad in robes of white.

4. O sweet and bless-ed coun-try, The home of God's e-lect!
O sweet and bless-ed coun-try, That ea-ger hearts ex-pect!
Je-sus, in mer-cy bring us To that dear land of rest,
Who art, with God the Fa-ther And Spir-it, ev-er blest!

THE CHURCH: BURIAL OF THE DEAD

THIS BODY IN THE GRAVE WE LAY 417

NUN LASST UNS DEN LEIB L.M.

Michael Weisse, 1531, Sts. 1-7
Anonymous St. 8
Nun lasst uns den Leib begraben
Tr. William M. Czamanske, 1938

G. Rhau's *Newe Deudsche Geistliche Gesenge*, 1544

1. This body in the grave we lay
There to await that solemn day
When God Himself shall bid it rise
To mount triumphant to the skies.

2. And so to earth we now entrust
What came from dust and turns to dust
And from the dust shall rise that day
In glorious triumph o'er decay.

3. The soul forever lives with God,
Who freely hath His grace bestowed
And through His Son redeemed it here
From every sin, from every fear.

4. All trials and all griefs are past,
A blessed end has come at last.
Christ's yoke was borne with ready will;
Who dieth thus is living still. A-men.

5. We have no cause to mourn or weep;
Securely shall this body sleep
Till Christ Himself shall death destroy
And raise the blessed dead to joy.

6. For they who with Him suffered here
Shall there be healed from woe and fear;
And when eternal bliss is won,
They'll shine in glory like the sun.

7. Then let us leave this place of rest
And homeward turn, for they are blest
Who heed God's warning and prepare
Lest death should find them unaware.

8. So help us, Jesus, ground of faith;
Thou hast redeemed us by Thy death
From endless death and set us free.
We laud and praise and worship Thee.

THE CHURCH: BURIAL OF THE DEAD

418 O LORD OF LIFE, WHERE'ER THEY BE
VICTORY 8.8.8. with Alleluia

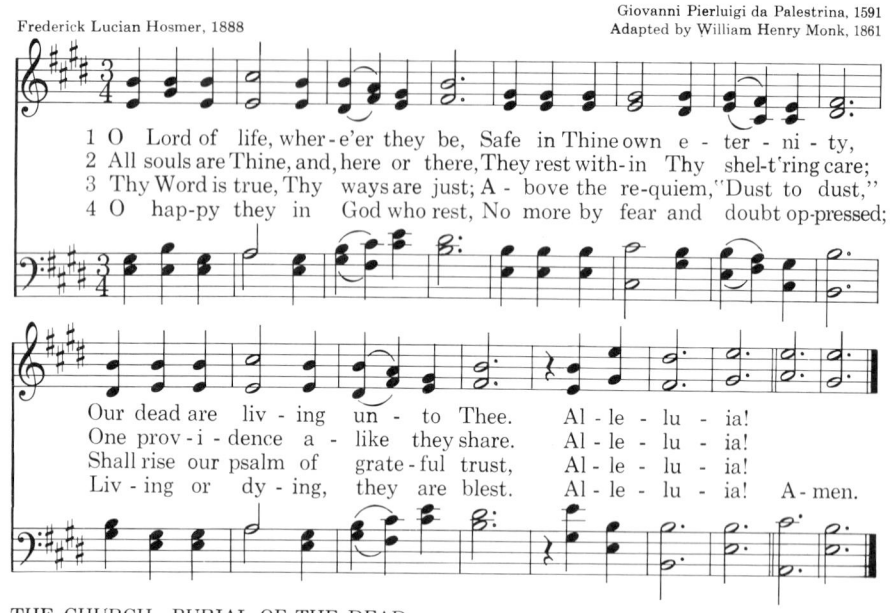

Frederick Lucian Hosmer, 1888

Giovanni Pierluigi da Palestrina, 1591
Adapted by William Henry Monk, 1861

1 O Lord of life, wher-e'er they be, Safe in Thine own e-ter-ni-ty,
2 All souls are Thine, and, here or there, They rest with-in Thy shel-t'ring care;
3 Thy Word is true, Thy ways are just; A-bove the re-quiem, "Dust to dust,"
4 O hap-py they in God who rest, No more by fear and doubt op-pressed;

Our dead are liv-ing un-to Thee. Al-le-lu-ia!
One prov-i-dence a-like they share. Al-le-lu-ia!
Shall rise our psalm of grate-ful trust, Al-le-lu-ia!
Liv-ing or dy-ing, they are blest. Al-le-lu-ia! A-men.

THE CHURCH: BURIAL OF THE DEAD

419 LORD, BLESS AND PITY US
GOLDEN HILL S.M.

Based on Psalm 67
Psalter, 1912

Folk Hymn
A. Davisson's *Kentucky Harmony*, 1816
Version from Joseph Funk's *Harmonia Sacra*, 1851

1 Lord, bless and pit-y us, Shine on us with Thy face,
2 Thy praise, O gra-cious God, Let all the na-tions sing;
3 The na-tions Thou wilt judge And lead them in Thy ways;
4 The earth her fruit shall yield, For God, our God, will bless;

That all the earth Thy way may know And men may see Thy grace.
Let all men wor-ship Thee with joy And songs of glad-ness bring.
Let all men praise Thy name, O God, Let all the peo-ple praise.
We shall be blest, and all the world His glo-ry shall con-fess.

MISSION OF THE CHURCH: EVANGELISM AND MISSIONS

HERALDS OF CHRIST 420

NATIONAL HYMN 10.10.10.10.

Laura S. Copenhaver, 1894
George William Warren, c. 1892

1. Her-alds of Christ, who bear the King's com-mands,
Im-mor-tal ti-dings in your mor-tal hands,
Pass on and car-ry swift the news ye bring;
Make straight, make straight the high-way of the King.

2. Through des-ert ways, dark fen, and deep mor-ass,
Through jun-gles, slug-gish seas, and moun-tain pass,
Build ye the road, and fal-ter not nor stay;
Pre-pare a-cross the earth the King's high-way.

3. Lord, give us faith and strength the road to build,
To see the prom-ise of the day ful-filled,
When war shall be no more and strife shall cease
Up-on the high-way of the Prince of Peace. A-men.

MISSION OF THE CHURCH: EVANGELISM AND MISSIONS

421 O SPIRIT OF THE LIVING GOD
ALSTONE L.M.

James Montgomery, 1823 — Christopher Edwin Willing, 1868

1. O Spirit of the living God, In all Thy plenitude of grace, Where'er the foot of man hath trod, Descend on our apostate race.
2. Give tongues of fire and hearts of love, To preach the reconciling word; Give power and unction from above, When e'er the joyful sound is heard.
3. Be darkness, at Thy coming, light; Confusion order, in Thy path; Souls without strength inspire with might; Bid mercy triumph over wrath.
4. O Spirit of the Lord, prepare All the round earth her God to meet; Breathe Thou abroad like morning air, Till hearts of stone begin to beat.
5. Baptize the nations; far and nigh The triumphs of the cross record; The name of Jesus glorify, Till every kindred call Him Lord. A-men.

422 FATHER, WHOSE WILL IS LIFE
TALLIS' ORDINAL C.M.

Hardwick Drummond Rawnsley, 1922 — Thomas Tallis, c. 1567

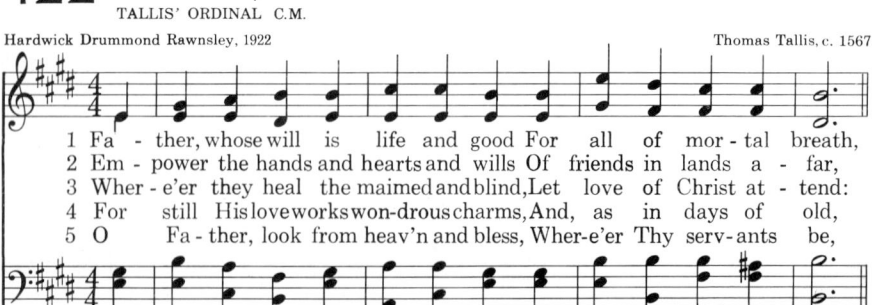

1. Father, whose will is life and good For all of mortal breath,
2. Empower the hands and hearts and wills Of friends in lands afar,
3. Wher-e'er they heal the maimed and blind, Let love of Christ attend:
4. For still His love works won-drous charms, And, as in days of old,
5. O Father, look from heav'n and bless, Wher-e'er Thy servants be,

MISSION OF THE CHURCH: EVANGELISM AND MISSIONS

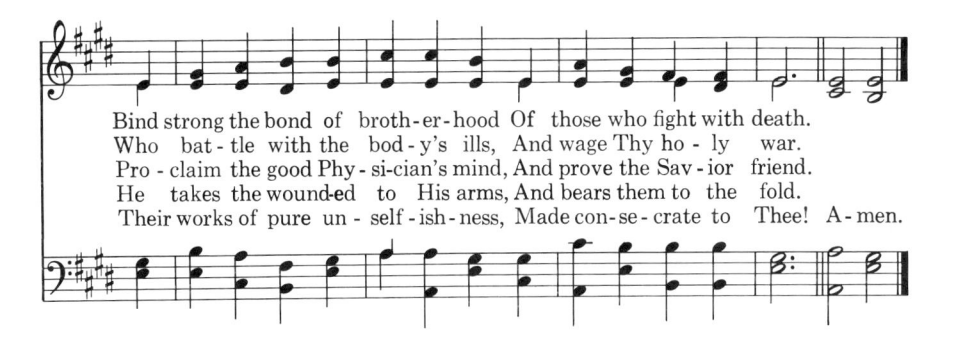

(continued from previous hymn)

Bind strong the bond of brotherhood Of those who fight with death.
Who battle with the body's ills, And wage Thy holy war.
Proclaim the good Physician's mind, And prove the Savior friend.
He takes the wounded to His arms, And bears them to the fold.
Their works of pure unselfishness, Made consecrate to Thee! A-men.

HAIL TO THE BRIGHTNESS 423

WESLEY 11.10.11.10.

Thomas Hastings, 1830
Lowell Mason, 1830

1. Hail to the brightness of Zion's glad morning, Joy to the lands that in darkness have lain! Hushed be the accents of sorrow and mourning, Zion in triumph begins her mild reign.
2. Hail to the brightness of Zion's glad morning, Long by the prophets of Israel foretold; Hail to the millions from bondage returning, Gentiles and Jews the blest vision behold.
3. Lo, in the desert rich flowers are springing, Streams ever copious are gliding along; Loud from the mountain-tops echoes are ringing, Wastes rise in verdure and mingle in song.
4. See, from all lands, from the isles of the ocean, Praise to Jehovah ascending on high; Fall'n are the engines of war and commotion, Shouts of salvation are rending the sky. A-men.

MISSION OF THE CHURCH: EVANGELISM AND MISSIONS

424 CHRIST FOR THE WORLD WE SING

MALVERN (DORCHESTER) 6.6.4.6.6.6.4.

Samuel Wolcott, 1869

Gauntlett and Waite's *Hallelujah*, 1849

1. Christ for the world we sing; The world to Christ we bring With loving zeal; The poor and them that mourn, The faint and overborne, Sin-sick and sorrow-worn, Whom Christ doth heal.

2. Christ for the world we sing; The world to Christ we bring With fervent prayer; The wayward and the lost, By restless passions tossed, Redeemed at countless cost From dark despair.

3. Christ for the world we sing; The world to Christ we bring With one accord; With us the work to share, With us reproach to dare, With us the cross to bear, For Christ our Lord.

4. Christ for the world we sing; The world to Christ we bring With joyful song; The new-born souls whose days, Reclaimed from error's ways, Inspired with hope and praise, To Christ belong.

MISSION OF THE CHURCH: EVANGELISM AND MISSIONS

CHRIST FOR THE WORLD WE SING 425

MILTON ABBAS 6.6.4.6.6.6.4.

Samuel Wolcott, 1869
Eric Harding Thiman, 1953

1 Christ for the world we sing; The world to Christ we bring With loving zeal; The poor and them that mourn, The faint and o-ver-borne, Sin-sick and sor-row-worn, Whom Christ doth heal.

2 Christ for the world we sing; The world to Christ we bring With fervent prayer; The way-ward and the lost, By rest-less pas-sions tossed, Re-deemed at count-less cost From dark de-spair.

3 Christ for the world we sing; The world to Christ we bring With one ac-cord; With us the work to share, With us re-proach to dare, With us the cross to bear, For Christ our Lord.

4 Christ for the world we sing; The world to Christ we bring With joy-ful song; The new-born souls whose days, Re-claimed from er-ror's ways, In-spired with hope and praise, To Christ be-long.

MISSION OF THE CHURCH: EVANGELISM AND MISSIONS

426 THE WORK IS THINE, O CHRIST

DIE SACH IST DEIN 8.6.8.6 8.8.8.8.4.6.

Samuel Preiswerk, 1829, Sts. 1, 2, and
Felician von Zaremba, d. 1874, St. 3
Die Sach ist dein
Tr. Julius Henry Horstmann, 1908

Johann Michael Haydn, late 18th century

1 The work is Thine, O Christ our Lord, The cause for which we stand;
2 Through suff'ring Thou, O Christ, didst go Unto Thy throne above,
3 Thou hast, O Savior, led the way Through agony and death;

And being Thine, 'twill overcome Its foes on every hand.
And leadest now the self-same way Those true in faith and love;
O give, we pray, yet more and more Thy Spirit's living breath!

Yet grains of wheat, before they grow, Are buried in the earth below;
So lead us, then, though suff'rings wait, To share Thy kingdom's heav'nly state,
Send messengers o'er land and sea To bring Thy children all to Thee;

All that is old doth perish there To form a life both new and fair:
Thy death has broken Satan's might, And leads the faithful to the light;
Thy name can save, Thy name makes free; We consecrate ourselves to Thee

MISSION OF THE CHURCH: EVANGELISM AND MISSIONS

So too are we From self and sin made free.
E-ter-nal light, From dark-ness in-to light.
As serv-ants true, As war-riors brave and true. A-men.

1 Die Sach ist dein, Herr Jesu Christ,
  die Sach, an der wir stehn,
und weil es deine Sache ist,
  kann sie nicht untergehn.
Allein das Weizenkorn, bevor
es fruchtbar sprosst zum Licht empor,
muss sterben in der Erde Schoss
zuvor vom eignen Wesen los.
  Durch Sterben los,
vom eignen Wesen los.

2 Du gingst, o Jesus, unser Haupt,
  durch Leiden himmelan
und führest jeden, der da glaubt,
  mit dir die gleiche Bahn.
Wohlan, so nimm uns allzugleich
zum Teil am Leiden und am Reich.
Führ uns durch deines Todes Tor
samt deiner Sach zum Licht empor,
  zum Licht empor,
durch Nacht zum Licht empor.

FORGET THEM NOT, O CHRIST 427
ELSENHAM 8.8.

Margaret Sangster, d. 1912
J. D. Macey, 1916

1 For-get them not, O Christ, who stand
2 In flood, in flame, in dark, in dread,
3 Ex-alt them o-ver ev-ery fear,
4 Thine is the work they strive to do,
5 Be with Thine own, Thy loved, who stand,

Thy van-guard in the dis-tant land.
Sus-tain, we pray, each lift-ed head.
In per-il come Thy-self more near.
Their foes so man-y, they so few.
Christ's van-guard in the storm-swept land. A-men.

MISSION OF THE CHURCH: EVANGELISM AND MISSIONS

428 O ZION, HASTE

TIDINGS 11.10.11.10. with Refrain

Mary Ann Thomson, 1868
James Walch, 1875

1. O Zion, haste, thy mission high fulfilling,
2. Behold how many thousands still are lying
3. Proclaim to every people, tongue, and nation
4. Give of thy sons to bear the message glorious;
5. He comes again: O Zion, ere thou meet Him,

To tell to all the world that God is light;
Bound in the darksome prison-house of sin,
That God, in whom they live and move, is love:
Give of thy wealth to speed them on their way;
Make known to every heart His saving grace;

That He who made all nations is not willing
With none to tell them of the Savior's dying
Tell how He stooped to save His lost creation,
Pour out thy soul for them in prayer victorious,
Let none whom He hath ransomed fail to greet Him,

Refrain

One soul should perish, lost in shades of night.
Or of the life He died for them to win.
And died on earth that man might live above.
And all thou spendest Jesus will repay.
Through thy neglect, unfit to see His face.

Publish glad tidings,

MISSION OF THE CHURCH: EVANGELISM AND MISSIONS

ti - dings of peace, Ti - dings of Je - sus, re - demp-tion and re - lease.

THOU, WHOSE ALMIGHTY WORD 429

SERUG 6.6.4.6.6.6.4.

John Marriott†, c. 1813
S. S. Wesley's *European Psalmist*, 1872

1. Thou, whose al - might - y word Cha - os and dark - ness heard,
2. Thou who didst come to bring On Thy re - deem - ing wing,
3. Spir - it of truth and love, Life - giv - ing, ho - ly dove,
4. Ho - ly and bless - ed Three, Glo - ri - ous Trin - i - ty,

And took their flight; Hear us, we hum - bly pray, And where the
Heal - ing and sight, Health to the sick in mind, Sight to the
Speed forth Thy flight; Move o'er the wa - ters' face Bear - ing the
Wis - dom, love, might; Bound - less as o - cean's tide Roll - ing in

gos - pel day Sheds not its glo - rious ray, Let there be light!
in - ly blind; O now, to all man-kind, Let there be light!
lamp of grace; And in earth's dark - est place, Let there be light!
full - est pride, Through the world far and wide, Let there be light! A - men.

MISSION OF THE CHURCH: EVANGELISM AND MISSIONS

430 FORTH IN THY NAME
INTERCESSION L.M.

Charles Wesley, 1749 — *Easy Music for Church Choirs*, 1853

1. Forth in Thy name, O Lord, I go, My daily labor to pursue, Thee, only Thee, resolved to know In all I think, or speak, or do.
2. The task Thy wisdom hath assigned, O let me cheerfully fulfill; In all my works Thy presence find, And prove Thy good and perfect will.
3. Thee may I set at my right hand, Whose eyes my inmost substance see, And labor on at Thy command, And offer all my works to Thee.
4. For Thee delightfully employ What-e'er Thy bounteous grace hath giv'n, And run my course with even joy, And closely walk with Thee to heav'n. Amen.

431 GO, LABOR ON
ERNAN L.M.

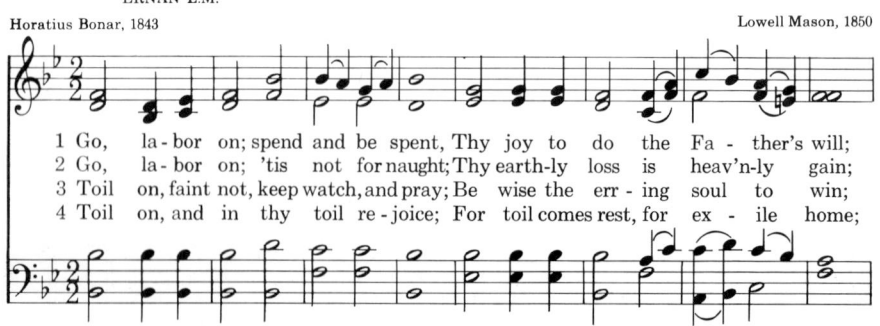

Horatius Bonar, 1843 — Lowell Mason, 1850

1. Go, labor on; spend and be spent, Thy joy to do the Father's will;
2. Go, labor on; 'tis not for naught; Thy earthly loss is heav'nly gain;
3. Toil on, faint not, keep watch, and pray; Be wise the erring soul to win;
4. Toil on, and in thy toil rejoice; For toil comes rest, for exile home;

MISSION OF THE CHURCH: SERVICE AND WITNESS

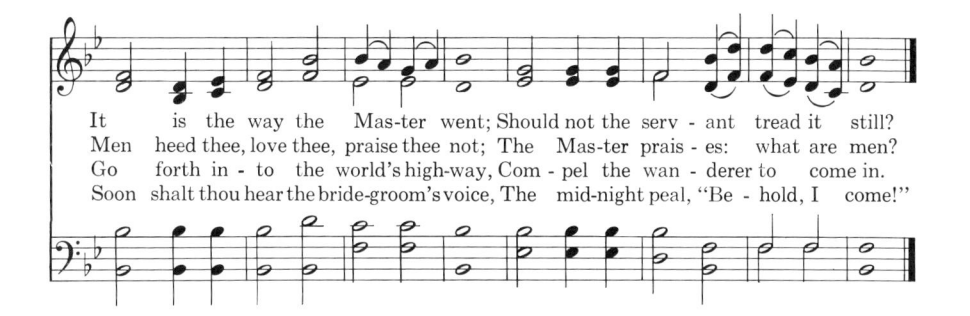

It is the way the Master went; Should not the servant tread it still?
Men heed thee, love thee, praise thee not; The Master praises: what are men?
Go forth into the world's highway, Compel the wanderer to come in.
Soon shalt thou hear the bridegroom's voice, The midnight peal, "Behold, I come!"

FORTH IN THY NAME 432
SONG XXXIV L.M.

Charles Wesley, 1749 — Orlando Gibbons, 1623

1 Forth in Thy name, O Lord, I go, My daily labor to pursue, Thee, only Thee, resolved to know In all I think, or speak, or do.
2 The task Thy wisdom hath assigned, O let me cheerfully fulfill; In all my works Thy presence find, And prove Thy good and perfect will.
3 Thee may I set at my right hand, Whose eyes my inmost substance see, And labor on at Thy command, And offer all my works to Thee.
4 For Thee delightfully employ What'er Thy bounteous grace hath giv'n, And run my course with even joy, And closely walk with Thee to heav'n. A-men.

MISSION OF THE CHURCH: SERVICE AND WITNESS

433 JESUS, THOU DIVINE COMPANION

HYFRYDOL 8.7.8.7.D.

Henry van Dyke, 1909

Rowland Hugh Pritchard, c. 1830
Harmony by Ralph Vaughan Williams, 1951

1. Jesus, Thou divine companion, By Thy lowly human birth
Thou hast come to join the workers, Burden-bearers of the earth.
Thou, the carpenter of Nazareth, Toiling for Thy daily food,
By Thy patience and Thy courage, Thou hast taught us toil is good.

2. They who tread the path of labor Follow where Thy feet have trod;
They who work without complaining Do the holy will of God.
Thou, the peace that passeth knowledge, Dwellest in the daily strife;
Thou, the bread of heav'n, art broken In the sacrament of life.

3. Every task, however simple, Sets the soul that does it free;
Every deed of love and kindness Done to man is done to Thee.
Jesus, Thou divine companion, Help us all to work our best;
Bless us in our daily labor, Lead us to our Sabbath rest. A-men.

MISSION OF THE CHURCH: SERVICE AND WITNESS

GOD OF GRACE AND GOD OF GLORY 434

CWM RHONDDA 8.7.8.7.8.7.

Harry Emerson Fosdick, 1930　　　　　　　　　　　　　　　　John Hughes, 1907

1. God of grace and God of glory, On Thy people pour Thy power; Crown Thine ancient church's story; Bring her bud to glorious flower. Grant us wisdom, Grant us courage, For the facing of this hour, For the facing of this hour.

2. Lo! the hosts of evil round us Scorn Thy Christ, assail His ways! From the fears that long have bound us, Free our hearts to faith and praise. Grant us wisdom, Grant us courage, For the living of these days, For the living of these days.

3. Cure Thy children's warring madness; Bend our pride to Thy control; Shame our wanton, selfish gladness, Rich in things and poor in soul. Grant us wisdom, Grant us courage, Lest we miss Thy kingdom's goal, Lest we miss Thy kingdom's goal.

4. Set our feet on lofty places; Gird our lives that they may be Armored with all Christ-like graces In the fight to set men free. Grant us wisdom, Grant us courage, That we fail not man nor Thee, That we fail not man nor Thee.

5. Save us from weak resignation To the evils we deplore; Let the search for Thy salvation Be our glory evermore. Grant us wisdom, Grant us courage, Serving Thee whom we adore, Serving Thee whom we adore. A-men.

MISSION OF THE CHURCH: SERVICE AND WITNESS

435 O BROTHER MAN, FOLD TO THY HEART
INTERCESSOR 11.10.11.10.

John Greenleaf Whittier, 1847 — Charles Hubert Hastings Parry, 1904

1. O brother man, fold to thy heart thy brother:
Where pity dwells, the peace of God is there;
To worship rightly is to love each other,
Each smile a hymn, each kindly deed a prayer.

2. For he whom Jesus loved hath truly spoken;
The holier worship which He deigns to bless
Restores the lost, and binds the spirit broken,
And feeds the widow and the fatherless!

3. Follow with reverent steps the great example
Of Him whose holy work was doing good:
So shall the wide earth seem our Father's temple,
Each loving life a psalm of gratitude.

4. Then shall all shackles fall: the stormy clangor
Of wild war music o'er the earth shall cease;
Love shall tread out the baleful fire of anger,
And in its ashes plant the tree of peace. A-men.

MISSION OF THE CHURCH: SERVICE AND WITNESS

LORD OF LIGHT, WHOSE NAME 436

TANTUM ERGO 8.7.8.7.D.

Howell Elvet Lewis, 1916

S. Webbe's *Essay on the Church Plain-Chant*, 1782

1. Lord of light, whose name out-shin-eth All the stars and suns of space,
Deign to make us Thy co-work-ers In the king-dom of Thy grace;
Use us to ful-fill Thy pur-pose In the gift of Christ Thy Son:
Fa-ther, as in high-est heav-en So on earth Thy will be done.

2. By the toil of low-ly work-ers In some far out-ly-ing field;
By the cour-age where the ra-diance Of the cross is still re-vealed;
By the vic-to-ries of meek-ness Through re-proach and suf-f'ring won:
Fa-ther, as in high-est heav-en So on earth Thy will be done.

3. Grant that knowl-edge, still in-creas-ing, At Thy feet may low-ly kneel;
With Thy grace our tri-umphs hal-low, With Thy char-i-ty our zeal;
Lift the na-tions from the shad-ows To the glad-ness of the sun:
Fa-ther, as in high-est heav-en So on earth Thy will be done.

4. By the prayers of faith-ful watch-men, Nev-er si-lent day or night;
By the cross of Je-sus bring-ing Peace to men, and heal-ing light;
By the love that pass-eth knowl-edge, Mak-ing all Thy chil-dren one:
Fa-ther, as in high-est heav-en So on earth Thy will be done. A-men.

MISSION OF THE CHURCH: SERVICE AND WITNESS

437 THOU, LORD OF LIFE

HESPERUS L.M.

Samuel Longfellow, c. 1886 — Henry Baker, 1854

1. Thou, Lord of life, our saving health, Who mak'st Thy suff'ring ones our care, Our gifts are still our truest wealth, To serve Thee our sincerest prayer.
2. As on the river's rising tide Flow strength and coolness from the sea, So through the ways our hands provide, May quick'ning life flow in from Thee;
3. To heal the wound, to still the pain, And strength to failing pulses bring, Till the lame feet shall leap again, And the parched lips with gladness sing.
4. Bless Thou the gifts our hands have brought! Bless Thou the work our hearts have planned, Ours is the faith, the will, the thought; The rest, O God, is in Thy hand. A-men.

438 TEACH ME THY TRUTH, O MIGHTY ONE

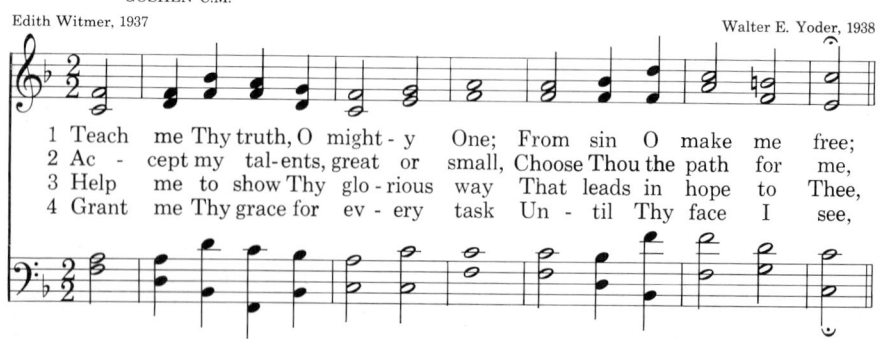

GOSHEN C.M.

Edith Witmer, 1937 — Walter E. Yoder, 1938

1. Teach me Thy truth, O mighty One; From sin O make me free;
2. Accept my talents, great or small, Choose Thou the path for me,
3. Help me to show Thy glorious way That leads in hope to Thee;
4. Grant me Thy grace for ev'ry task Until Thy face I see,

MISSION OF THE CHURCH: SERVICE AND WITNESS

Pre - pare my life to fill its place In ser-vice, Lord, for Thee.
Where I shall la - bor joy - ous - ly In ser-vice, Lord, for Thee.
Till oth - er souls their joy shall find, In ser-vice, Lord, for Thee.
Then ev - er new shall be that joy In ser-vice, Lord, for Thee. A-men.

WHERE CROSS THE CROWDED WAYS 439

GERMANY L.M.

Frank Mason North, 1903
W. Gardiner's *Sacred Melodies*, 1815

1 Where cross the crowd - ed ways of life, Where sound the
2 In haunts of wretch - ed - ness and need, On shad - owed
3 From ten - der child - hood's help - less - ness, From wom - an's
4 The cup of wa - ter given for Thee Still holds the
5 O Mas - ter, from the moun - tain side, Make haste to
6 Till sons of men shall learn Thy love, And fol - low

cries of race and clan, A - bove the noise of
thresh - olds dark with fears, From paths where hide the
grief, man's bur - dened toil, From fam - ished souls, from
fresh - ness of Thy grace; Yet long these mul - ti -
heal these hearts of pain; A - mong these rest - less
where Thy feet have trod; Till glo - rious from Thy

self - ish strife, We hear Thy voice, O Son of man!
lures of greed, We catch the vi - sion of Thy tears.
sor - row's stress, Thy heart has nev - er known re - coil.
tudes to see The sweet com - pas - sion of Thy face.
throngs a - bide, O tread the cit - y's streets a - gain;
heav'n a - bove Shall come the cit - y of our God. A - men.

MISSION OF THE CHURCH: SERVICE AND WITNESS

440 O MASTER, LET ME WALK WITH THEE
MARYTON L.M.

Washington Gladden, 1879
Henry Percy Smith, 1874

1. O Master, let me walk with Thee In lowly paths of service free; Tell me Thy secret, help me bear The strain of toil, the fret of care.
2. Help me the slow of heart to move By some clear, winning word of love; Teach me the wayward feet to stay, And guide them in the homeward way.
3. Teach me Thy patience; still with Thee In closer, dearer company, In work that keeps faith sweet and strong, In trust that triumphs over wrong.
4. In hope that sends a shining ray Far down the future's broad'ning way, In peace that only Thou canst give; With Thee, O Master, let me live. A-men.

441 RISE UP, O MEN OF GOD
FESTAL SONG S.M.

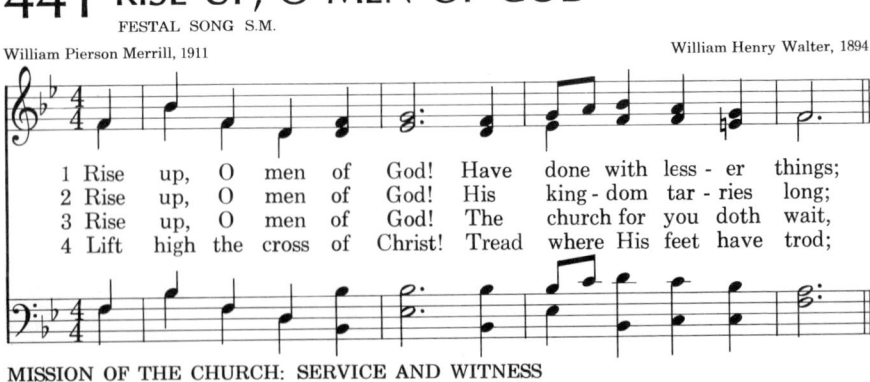

William Pierson Merrill, 1911
William Henry Walter, 1894

1. Rise up, O men of God! Have done with lesser things;
2. Rise up, O men of God! His kingdom tarries long;
3. Rise up, O men of God! The church for you doth wait,
4. Lift high the cross of Christ! Tread where His feet have trod;

MISSION OF THE CHURCH: SERVICE AND WITNESS

Give heart and soul and mind and strength To serve the King of kings.
Bring in the day of broth-er-hood, And end the night of wrong.
Her strength un-e-qual to her task, Rise up, and make her great!
As broth-ers of the Son of man, Rise up, O men of God!

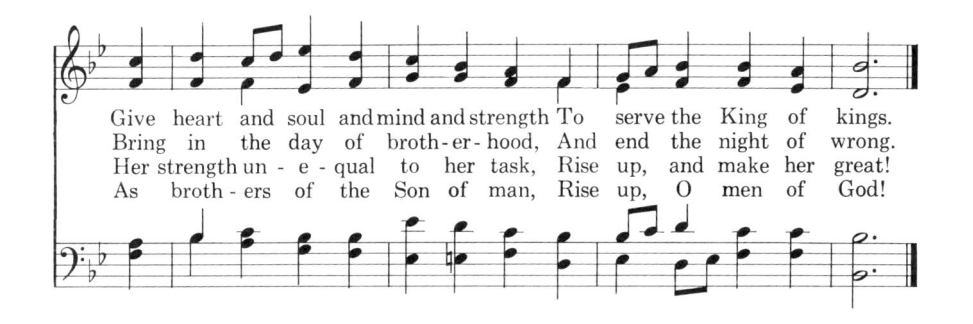

STRONG SON OF GOD 442

ROCKINGHAM OLD L.M.

Alfred Tennyson, 1850

A. Williams' *Supplement to Psalmody*, c. 1780
Adapted by Edward Miller, 1790

1 Strong Son of God, im-mor-tal love, Whom we, that have not seen Thy face, By faith, and faith a-lone, em-brace, Be-liev-ing where we can-not prove.
2 Thou seem-est hu-man and di-vine, The high-est, ho-liest man-hood, Thou: Our wills are ours, we know not how; Our wills are ours, to make them Thine.
3 Our lit-tle sys-tems have their day; They have their day and cease to be; They are but bro-ken lights of Thee, And Thou, O Lord, art more than they.
4 Let knowl-edge grow from more to more, But more of rev-'rence in us dwell; That mind and soul, ac-cord-ing well, May make one mu-sic as be-fore. A-men.

MISSION OF THE CHURCH: EDUCATION

443 LEAD ON, O KING ETERNAL

LANCASHIRE 7.6.7.6.D.

Ernest Warburton Shurtleff, 1887

Henry Thomas Smart, 1835

1. Lead on, O King eternal, The day of march has come;
Henceforth in fields of conquest Thy tents shall be our home:
Through days of preparation Thy grace has made us strong,
And now, O King eternal, We lift our battle song.

2. Lead on, O King eternal, Till sin's fierce war shall cease,
And holiness shall whisper The sweet amen of peace;
For not with swords, loud clashing, Nor roll of stirring drums,
But deeds of love and mercy, The heav'nly kingdom comes.

3. Lead on, O King eternal, We follow, not with fears,
For gladness breaks like morning Where'er Thy face appears:
Thy cross is lifted o'er us; We journey in its light;
The crown awaits the conquest; Lead on, O God of might. Amen.

MISSION OF THE CHURCH: EDUCATION

O GRANT US LIGHT 444

CANONBURY L.M.

Lawrence Tuttiett, 1885

Arranged from Robert Schumann, 1839

1. O grant us light, that we may know The wisdom Thou alone canst give;
That truth may guide wher-e'er we go, And virtue bless wher-e'er we live.

2. O grant us light, that we may see Where error lurks in human lore,
And turn our doubting minds to Thee, And love Thy simple Word the more.

3. O grant us light, that we may learn How dead is life from Thee apart,
How sure is joy for all who turn To Thee an undivided heart. A-men.

COME, MY WAY, MY TRUTH, MY LIFE 445

FREUEN WIR UNS ALL IN EIN 7.7.7.7.

Bohemian Melody, 15th century
Michael Weisse, 1531
Harmony by George Ratcliffe Woodward, 1910

George Herbert, 1633

1. Come, my Way, my Truth, my Life: Such a way as gives us breath:
Such a truth as ends all strife: Such a life as killeth death.

2. Come, my Light, my Feast, my Strength: Such a light as shows a feast:
Such a feast as mends in length: Such a strength as makes his guest.

3. Come, my Joy, my Love, my Heart: Such a joy as none can move:
Such a love as none can part: Such a heart as joys in love.

MISSION OF THE CHURCH: EDUCATION

446 JUDGE ETERNAL, THRONED

ZEUCH MICH, ZEUCH MICH (ALL SAINTS) 8.7.8.7.8.7.

Henry Scott Holland†, 1902
Geistreiches Gesangbuch, Darmstadt, 1698

1. Judge eternal, throned in splendor, Lord of lords and King of kings, With Thy living fire of judgment Purge this land of bitter things; Solace all its wide dominion With the healing of Thy wings.

2. Still the weary folk are pining For the hour that brings release; And the city's crowded clangor Cries aloud for sin to cease; And the homesteads and the woodlands Plead in silence for their peace.

3. Crown, O God, Thine own endeavor; Cleave our darkness with Thy sword; Feed the faint and hungry peoples With the richness of Thy Word; Cleanse the body of this nation Through the glory of the Lord. A-men.

MISSION OF THE CHURCH: CHRISTIAN CITIZENSHIP

FATHER ETERNAL, RULER OF CREATION 447

GENEVA 124 11.10.11.10.10.

Laurence Housman, 1919 — *Pseaumes octante trois . . .*, Geneva, 1551

1. Father eternal, ruler of creation, Spirit of life, which moved ere form was made; Through the thick darkness cov'ring every nation Light to man's blindness, O be Thou our aid: Thy kingdom come, O Lord, Thy will be done.

2. Races and peoples, lo we stand divided, And sharing not our griefs, no joys can share; By wars and tumults love is mocked, derided, His conqu'ring cross no kingdom wills to bear; Thy kingdom come, O Lord, Thy will be done.

3. Envious of heart, blind-eyed, with tongues confounded, Nation by nation still goes unforgiv'n; In wrath and fear, by jealousies surrounded, Building proud tow'rs which shall not reach to heav'n: Thy kingdom come, O Lord, Thy will be done.

4. Lust of possession worketh desolations; There is no meekness in the sons of earth; Led by no star, the rulers of the nations Still fail to bring us to the blissful birth. Thy kingdom come, O Lord, Thy will be done.

5. How shall we love Thee, holy hidden Being, If we love not the world which Thou hast made? O give us brotherlove for better seeing Thy Word made flesh, and in a manger laid: Thy kingdom come, O Lord, Thy will be done. A-men.

MISSION OF THE CHURCH: CHRISTIAN CITIZENSHIP

448 GOD OF OUR FATHERS
NATIONAL HYMN 10.10.10.10.

Daniel Crane Roberts, 1876
George William Warren, c. 1892

1. God of our fathers, whose almighty hand
Leads forth in beauty all the starry band
Of shining worlds in splendor through the skies,
Our grateful songs before Thy throne arise.

2. Thy love divine hath led us in the past,
In this free land by Thee our lot is cast;
Be Thou our ruler, guardian, guide and stay,
Thy Word our law, Thy paths our chosen way.

3. From war's alarms, from deadly pestilence,
Be Thy strong arm our ever sure defense;
Thy true religion in our hearts increase,
Thy bounteous goodness nourish us in peace.

4. Refresh Thy people on their toilsome way,
Lead us from night to never-ending day;
Fill all our lives with love and grace divine,
And glory, laud and praise be ever Thine. A-men.

MISSION OF THE CHURCH: CHRISTIAN CITIZENSHIP

PEACE IN OUR TIME, O LORD 449

DIADEMATA S.M.D.

John Oxenham, 1936
George Job Elvey, 1868

1. Peace in our time, O Lord, To all the peo-ples, Peace!
Peace sure-ly based up-on Thy will And built in right-eous-ness.
Thy power a-lone can break The fet-ters that en-chain
The sore-ly strick-en soul of life, And make it live a-gain.

2. Too long mis-trust and fear Have held our souls in thrall;
Sweep through the earth, keen breath of heav'n, And sound a no-bler call!
Come, as Thou didst of old, In love so great that men
Shall cast a-side all oth-er gods And turn to Thee a-gain!

3. O shall we nev-er learn The truth all time has taught,
That with-out God as ar-chi-tect Our build-ing comes to naught?
O liv-ing Christ, who still Dost all our bur-dens share,
Come now and dwell with-in the hearts Of all men ev-ery-where! A-men.

MISSION OF THE CHURCH: PEACE AND NON-RESISTANCE

450 O HOLY CITY, SEEN OF JOHN
CONSOLATION (MORNING SONG) 8.6.8.6.8.6.

Walter Russell Bowie, 1909

Folk Hymn
J. Wyeth's *Repository of Sacred Music,*
Part Second, 1813

1. O holy city, seen of John, Where Christ, the Lamb, doth reign,
   Within whose four-square walls shall come No night, nor need, nor pain,
   And where the tears are wiped from eyes That shall not weep again,
2. O shame to us who rest content While lust and greed for gain
   In street and shop and tenement Wring gold from human pain,
   And bitter lips in blind despair Cry, "Christ hath died in vain!"
3. Give us, O God, the strength to build The city that hath stood
   Too long a dream, whose laws are love, Whose ways are brotherhood,
   And where the sun that shineth is God's grace for human good.
4. Already in the mind of God That city riseth fair:
   Lo, how its splendor challenges The souls that greatly dare,
   Yea, bids us seize the whole of life And build its glory there.

451 LORD, AS TO THY DEAR CROSS WE FLEE
GREEN HILL C.M.

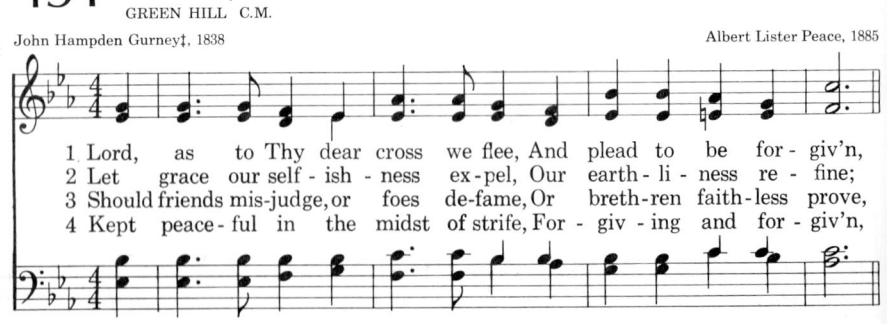

John Hampden Gurney‡, 1838

Albert Lister Peace, 1885

1. Lord, as to Thy dear cross we flee, And plead to be forgiv'n,
2. Let grace our selfishness expel, Our earthliness refine;
3. Should friends misjudge, or foes defame, Or brethren faithless prove,
4. Kept peaceful in the midst of strife, Forgiving and forgiv'n,

MISSION OF THE CHURCH: PEACE AND NONRESISTANCE

So let Thy life our pat-tern be, And form our souls for heav'n.
And kind-ness in our bos-oms dwell, As free and true as Thine.
Then, as Thine own, be this our aim To win them all by love.
O may we lead the pil-grim's life, And fol-low Thee to heav'n. A-men.

POUR DOWN THY SPIRIT 452

BIRLING L.M.

William Romanis, 1878

Early 19th century
Arranged by Geoffrey Shaw, 1919

1. Pour down Thy Spir-it from a-bove, And bid all strife and dis-cord cease; Join heart to heart in mu-tual love, O reign a-mong us, Prince of Peace.
2. If in the souls where love should be A-rise the storms of fierce self-will, Calm Thou that trou-bled, an-gry sea, Speak to the tem-pest, "Peace, be still."
3. If rude re-proach be o'er us flung, And slan-der wound as with a sword, Rule Thou the' un-ru-ly an-swering tongue, And si-lence ev-ery venge-ful word.
4. When-e'er in this wild world we meet Un-kind-ly deeds that an-ger move, Teach us for-give-ness, tri-umph sweet, To con-quer e-vil will with love.
5. In ev-ery land, in ev-ery home, In ev-ery heart let love in-crease; Let love pro-claim Thy king-dom come, O reign a-mong us, Prince of Peace. A-men.

MISSION OF THE CHURCH: PEACE AND NONRESISTANCE

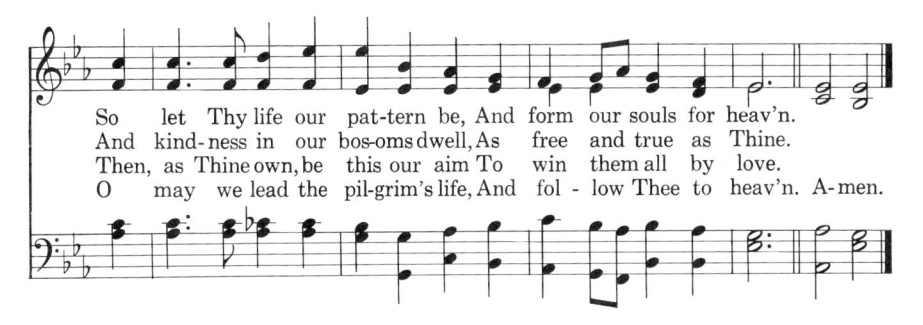

453 DEAR FATHER, WHOM WE CANNOT SEE
LOBT GOTT, IHR CHRISTEN 8.6.8.8.6.6.

Roderic Dunkerley

Nicolaus Herman, 1554
Harmony by Johann Sebastian Bach, c. 1735-1740

1 Dear Father, whom we cannot see, We know that Thou art near;
  With longing hearts we turn to Thee, And ask that Thou wilt set us free From war and hate and fear.
2 Dear Father, King of love and peace, We know that Thou art strong;
  Make conflicts everywhere to cease, Let mercy everywhere increase, And kindness conquer wrong.
3 Dear Father, Lord of sea and land, We know that Thou art wise;
  O make the nations understand That only by Thy guiding hand Can lasting peace arise. A-men.

454 O GOD OF LOVE, O KING OF PEACE
ROCKINGHAM OLD L.M.

Henry Williams Baker, 1860

A. Williams' *Supplement to Psalmody*, c. 1780
Adapted by Edward Miller, 1790

1 O God of love, O King of peace, Make wars throughout the world to cease;
2 Remember, Lord, Thy works of old, The wonders that our fathers told;
3 Whom shall we trust but Thee, O Lord? Where rest but on Thy faithful Word?
4 Where saints and angels dwell above, All hearts are knit in holy love;

MISSION OF THE CHURCH: PEACE AND NONRESISTANCE

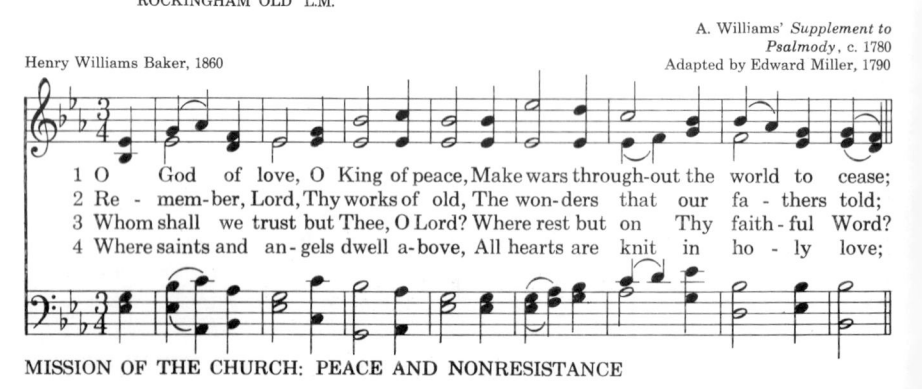

The wrath of sin-ful man re-strain; Give peace, O God, give peace a-gain!
Re-mem-ber not our sin's dark stain; Give peace, O God, give peace a-gain!
None ev-er called on Thee in vain; Give peace, O God, give peace a-gain!
O bind us in that heav'n-ly chain; Give peace, O God, give peace a-gain! A-men.

LET THERE BE LIGHT 455

MISSIONARY CHANT L.M.

William Merrill Vories, 1908 Charles Zeuner, 1832

1 Let there be light, Lord God of hosts! Let there be wis-dom on the earth! Let there be deeds, in-stead of boasts.
2 With-in our pas-sioned hearts in-still The calm that end-eth strain and strife; Make us Thy min-is-ters of life; Purge us from lusts that curse and kill!
3 Give us the peace of vi-sion clear To see our broth-ers' good our own, To joy and suf-fer not a-lone: The love that cast-eth out all fear!
4 Let woe and waste of war-fare cease, That use-ful la-bor yet may build Its homes with love and laugh-ter filled! God, give Thy way-ward chil-dren peace! A-men.

MISSION OF THE CHURCH: PEACE AND NONRESISTANCE

456 LORD OF OUR LIFE, AND GOD
ISTE CONFESSOR (ROUEN) 11.11.11.5.

Matthäus Apelles von Löwenstern, 1644
Christe, du Beistand deiner Kreuzgemeine
Paraphrase by Philip Pusey, 1834

Poitiers Antiphoner, 1746

1. Lord of our life, and God of our salvation, Star of our night, and hope of every nation, Hear and receive Thy church's supplication, Lord God almighty.

2. Lord, Thou canst help when earthly armor faileth; Lord, Thou canst save when sin itself assaileth; Lord, o'er Thy rock nor death nor hell prevaileth; Grant us Thy peace, Lord:

3. Peace, in our hearts, our evil thoughts assuaging; Peace, in Thy church, where brothers are engaging; Peace, when the world its busy war is waging; Calm Thy foes' raging! A-men.

4. Grant us Thy help till backward they are driven;
Grant them Thy truth, that they may be forgiven;
Grant peace on earth, or after we have striven,
Peace in Thy heaven.

MISSION OF THE CHURCH: PEACE AND NONRESISTANCE

O GOD OF EARTH AND ALTAR 457

KING'S LYNN 7.6.7.6.D.

English Traditional Melody
Harmony by Ralph Vaughan Williams, 1906
Arrangement Altered

Gilbert Keith Chesterton, c. 1906

1. O God of earth and altar, Bow down and hear our cry, Our earthly rulers falter, Our people drift and die; The walls of gold entomb us, The swords of scorn divide, Take not Thy thunder from us, But take away our pride.

2. From all that terror teaches, From lies of tongue and pen, From all the easy speeches That comfort cruel men, From sale and profanation Of honor, and the sword, From sleep and from damnation, Deliver us, good Lord!

3. Tie in a living tether The prince and priest and thrall, Bind all our lives together, Smite us and save us all; In ire and exultation Aflame with faith, and free, Lift up a living nation, A single sword to Thee.

MISSION OF THE CHURCH: SOCIAL JUSTICE

458 O MASTER WORKMAN OF THE RACE
BETHLEHEM C.M.D.

Jay T. Stocking, 1912
Gottfried Wilhelm Fink, 1842

1. O master Workman of the race, Thou Man of Galilee,
Who with the eyes of early youth Eternal things did see:
We thank Thee for Thy boyhood faith That shone Thy whole life through;
"Did ye not know it is My work, My Father's work to do?"

2. O Carpenter of Nazareth, Builder of life divine,
Who shapest man to God's own law, Thyself the fair design;
Build us a tower of Christ-like height, That we the land may view,
And see, like Thee, our noblest work, Our Father's work to do.

3. O Thou who didst the vision send And gives to each his task,
And with the task sufficient strength: Show us Thy will, we ask;
Give us a conscience bold and good, Give us a purpose true,
That it may be our highest joy, Our Father's work to do. A-men.

MISSION OF THE CHURCH: SOCIAL JUSTICE

O YOUNG AND FEARLESS PROPHET 459

LLANGLOFFAN 7.6.7.6.D.

S. Ralph Harlow, 1930 and 1935

Welsh Hymn Melody
Hymnau a Thonau, 1865

1. O young and fearless Prophet of ancient Galilee:
Thy life is still a summons to serve humanity,
To make our thoughts and actions less prone to please the crowd,
To stand with humble courage for truth with hearts uncowed.

2. We marvel at the purpose that held Thee to Thy course
While ever on the hilltop before Thee loomed the cross;
Thy steadfast face set forward where love and duty shone,
While we betray so quickly and leave Thee there alone.

3. O help us stand unswerving against war's bloody way,
Where hate and lust and falsehood hold back Christ's holy sway;
Forbid false love of country, that blinds us to His call
Who lifts above the nation the brotherhood of all.

4. Create in us the splendor that dawns when hearts are kind,
That knows not race nor color as boundaries of the mind;
That learns to value beauty, in heart, or brain, or soul,
And longs to bind God's children into one perfect whole.

5. O young and fearless Prophet, we need Thy presence here,
Amid our pride and glory to see Thy face appear;
Once more to hear Thy challenge above our noisy day,
Again to lead us forward along God's holy way. A-men.

MISSION OF THE CHURCH: SOCIAL JUSTICE

460 GRACIOUS SAVIOR, WHO DIDST HONOR
KOMM, O KOMM 8.7.8.7.7.7.

Emily L. Shirreff

Neu-vermehrtes . . . Gesangbuch,
Meiningen, 1693

1. Gracious Savior, who didst honor Womankind as woman's son;
Very man, though God begotten, And with God the Father one,
Grant that womanhood may be Consecrated, Lord, to Thee.

2. Jesus, Son of human mother, Bless our motherhood, we pray;
Give us grace to lead our children, Draw them to Thee day by day;
May our sons and daughters be Dedicated, Lord, to Thee.

3. Thou who didst with Joseph labor, Nor didst humble work disdain,
Grant we may Thy footsteps follow Patiently through toil or pain;
May our quiet home-life be Lived, O Lord, in Thee, to Thee.

4. Thou who didst go forth in sorrow, Toiling for the souls of men,
Thou who shalt draw all men to Thee, Though despised, rejected then;
Humble though our influence be, Use it in the world for Thee. A-men.

461 HAPPY THE HOME WHEN GOD
ST. AGNES C.M.

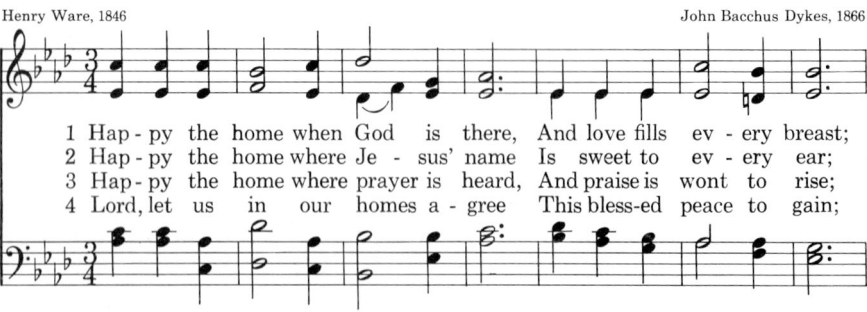

Henry Ware, 1846

John Bacchus Dykes, 1866

1. Happy the home when God is there, And love fills every breast;
2. Happy the home where Jesus' name Is sweet to every ear;
3. Happy the home where prayer is heard, And praise is wont to rise;
4. Lord, let us in our homes agree This blessed peace to gain;

HOME AND FAMILY: THE CHRISTIAN HOME

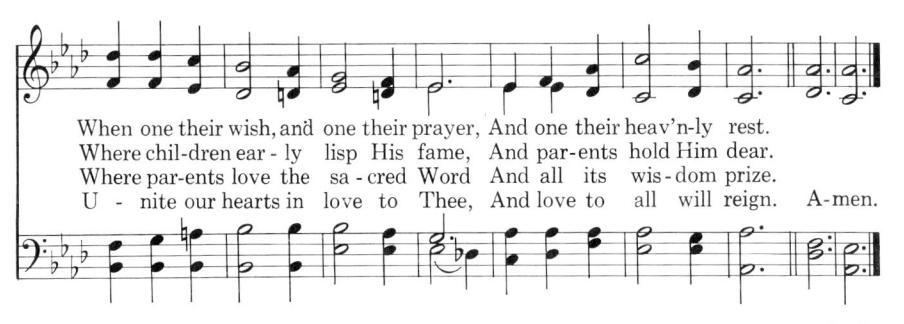

When one their wish, and one their prayer, And one their heav'n-ly rest.
Where chil-dren ear-ly lisp His fame, And par-ents hold Him dear.
Where par-ents love the sa-cred Word And all its wis-dom prize.
U-nite our hearts in love to Thee, And love to all will reign. A-men.

LORD OF THE HOME 462

PHILIPPINE L.M.

Albert Frederick Bayly, 1947

Robert Edwin Roberts, 1925
Arrangement Altered

1. Lord of the home, Thine on-ly Son Re-ceived a moth-er's ten-der love; And from an earth-ly fa-ther won His vi-sion of Thy home a-bove.
2. Help us, O Lord, our homes to make Thy Ho-ly Spir-it's dwell-ing place; Our hands and hearts' de-vo-tion take To be the ser-vants of Thy grace.
3. Pray we that all who with us dwell, Thy love and joy and peace may know; And while our lips Thy prais-es tell, May faith-ful lives Thy glo-ry show.
4. Teach us to keep our homes so fair, That were our Lord a child once more, He might be glad our hearth to share, And find a wel-come at our door.
5. Lord, may Thy Spir-it sanc-ti-fy Each house-hold du-ty we ful-fill, May we our Mas-ter glo-ri-fy In glad o-be-dience to Thy will. A-men.

HOME AND FAMILY: THE CHRISTIAN HOME

463 O HAPPY HOME, WHERE THOU ART
HENLEY 11.10.11.10.

Carl Johann Philipp Spitta, 1833
O selig Haus, wo man dich aufgenommen
Tr. Sarah B. Findlater, 1858, and Others

Lowell Mason, 185

1. O happy home, where Thou art loved the dearest,
   Thou loving Friend and Savior of our race,
   And where among the guests there never cometh
   One who can hold such high and honored place.

2. O happy home, where each one serves Thee, lowly,
   Whatever his appointed work may be,
   Till every common task seems great and holy,
   When it is done, O Lord, as unto Thee.

3. O happy home, where Thou art not forgotten
   When joy is overflowing, full, and free;
   O happy home, where every wounded spirit
   Is brought, Physician, Comforter, to Thee.

4. Until at last, when earth's day's work is ended,
   All meet Thee in the blessed home above,
   From whence Thou camest, where Thou hast ascended,
   Thy everlasting home of peace and love! A-men.

HOME AND FAMILY: THE CHRISTIAN HOME

A GLADSOME HYMN OF PRAISE 464

CANAAN 8.7.8.7. with Refrain

Ambrose N. Blatchford, 1876
Composer Unknown

1. A gladsome hymn of praise we sing, And thankfully we gather
To bless the love of God above, Our everlasting Father.

2. From shades of night He calls the light, And from the sod the flower;
From every cloud His blessings break In sunshine or in shower.

3. Full in His sight His children stand, By His strong arm defended,
And He whose wisdom guides the world, Our footsteps hath attended.

4. For nothing falls unknown to Him, Or care or joy or sorrow,
And He whose mercy ruled the past Will be our stay tomorrow.

5. Then praise the Lord with one accord, To His great name give glory,
And of His never-changing love Repeat the wondrous story.

Refrain
In Him rejoice with heart and voice Whose glory fadeth never,
Whose providence is our defense, Who lives and loves forever.

HOME AND FAMILY: HYMNS FOR CHILDREN

465 EACH LITTLE FLOWER THAT OPENS

DANISH TUNE 7.6.7.6. with Refrain

Cecil Frances Alexander†, 1848

Danish Traditional Melody

1. Each little flower that opens, Each little bird that sings:
   God made their glowing colors, He made their tiny wings.
2. The purple-headed mountain, The river running by,
   The sunset, and the morning That brightens up the sky,
3. The cold wind in the winter, The pleasant summer sun,
   The ripe fruits in the garden: He made them every one.
4. He gave us eyes to see them, And lips that we might tell
   How great is God almighty, Who has made all things well.

Refrain:
Yes, all things bright and beautiful, All creatures great and small,
And all things wise and wonderful: The Lord God made them all.

HOME AND FAMILY: HYMNS FOR CHILDREN

ONCE IN ROYAL DAVID'S CITY 466
IRBY 8.7.8.7.7.7.

Cecil Frances Alexander, 1848
Henry John Gauntlett, 1849

1. Once in royal David's city Stood a lowly cattle shed, Where a mother laid her Baby, In a manger for His bed: Mary was that mother mild, Jesus Christ her little Child.

2. He came down to earth from heaven Who is God and Lord of all, And His shelter was a stable, And His cradle was a stall; With the poor, and mean, and lowly, Lived on earth our Savior holy.

3. And, through all His wondrous childhood, He would honor and obey, Love and watch the lowly maiden In whose gentle arms He lay; Christian children all must be Mild, obedient, good as He.

4. And our eyes at last shall see Him, Through His own redeeming love; For that Child so dear and gentle Is our Lord in heav'n above: And He leads His children on To the place where He is gone.

5. Not in that poor lowly stable, With the oxen standing by, We shall see Him; but in heaven, Set at God's right hand on high: When like stars His children crowned, All in white shall wait around.

HOME AND FAMILY: HYMNS FOR CHILDREN

467 I LOVE TO THINK THAT JESUS SAW
CHILDHOOD 8.8.8.6.

Ada Skemp, d. 1927
H. Walford Davies, b. 1869

1. I love to think that Jesus saw The same bright sun that shines today; It gave Him light to do His work, And smiled upon His play.
2. The same white moon with silver face That sails across the sky at night, He used to see in Galilee, And watch it with delight.
3. The same great God that hears my prayers Heard His, when Jesus knelt to pray; He is my Father, who will keep His child through every day.

468 WISE MEN SEEKING JESUS
GLENFINLAS 6.5.6.5.

James Thomas East, 1926
Kenneth George Finlay, 1925

1. Wise men seeking Jesus Traveled from afar,
2. But if we desire Him, He is close at hand;
3. Prayerful souls may find Him By our quiet lakes,

HOME AND FAMILY: HYMNS FOR CHILDREN

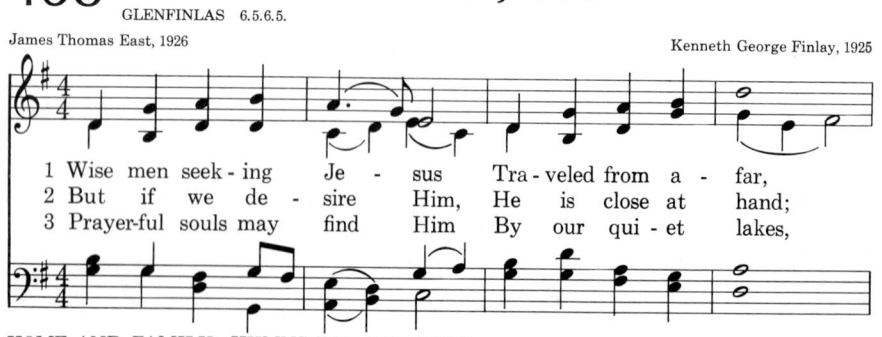

Guid - ed on their jour - ney By a beau - teous star.
For our na - tive coun - try Is our ho - ly land.
Meet Him on our hill - sides When the morn - ing breaks.

4 In our fertile cornfields
   While the sheaves are bound,
   In our busy markets,
   Jesus may be found.

5 Fishermen talk with Him
   By the great north sea,
   As the first disciples
   Did in Galilee.

6 Every peaceful village
   In our land might be
   Made by Jesus' presence
   Like sweet Bethany.

7 He is more than near us,
   If we love Him well;
   For He seeketh ever
   In our hearts to dwell.

LONG AGO WHEN JESUS 469

GLENFINLAS 6.5.6.5.

Albert Frederick Bayly, 1954 — Kenneth George Finlay, 1925

1 Long a - go when Je - sus Walked in Gal - i - lee,
2 Now He gives the chil - dren Born in ev - ery land,
3 Red - skin, white and yel - low, Black and brown draw near.

Chil - dren found a wel - come At the Sav - ior's knee.
Dark and fair, a bless - ing From His lov - ing hand.
Then, since He re - ceives them, We too hold them dear.

HOME AND FAMILY: HYMNS FOR CHILDREN

470 O COME, ALL YE CHILDREN
IHR KINDERLEIN, KOMMET 11.11.11.11.

Christian von Schmid
Ihr Kinderlein, kommet
Tr. Unknown

Johann Abraham Peter Schulz, d. 1800

1. O come, all ye children, O come, one and all,
To Bethlehem haste to the manger so small,
God's Son for a gift has been sent you this night
To be your Redeemer, your joy and delight.

2. He's born in a stable for you and for me,
Draw near by the bright gleaming starlight to see,
In swaddling clothes lying so meek and so mild,
And purer than angels the heavenly Child;

3. See Mary and Joseph with love-beaming eyes
Are gazing upon the rude bed where He lies,
The shepherds are kneeling with hearts full of love,
While angels sing loud alleluias above.

4. Kneel down and adore Him with shepherds today,
Lift up little hands now and praise Him as they;
Rejoice that a Savior from sin you can boast,
And join in the song of the heavenly host.

5. Dear Christ Child, what gifts can we children bestow
By which our affection and gladness to show?
No riches and treasures of value can be,
But hearts that believe are accepted with Thee.

6. Our hearts, then, to Thee we will offer today,
We offer them gladly; accept them, we pray,
And make them so spotless and pure that we may
Abide in Thy presence in heaven for aye.

HOME AND FAMILY: HYMNS FOR CHILDREN

FOR GOD SO LOVED US 471

GOTT IST DIE LIEBE 10.9. with Refrain

August Rische, d. 1906
Gott ist die Liebe
Paraphrase Composite, 1956 and 1960

Thüringer Melody, c. 1840

1 For God so loved us, He sent the Savior: For God so loved us, And loves me too.
2 He sent the Savior, The blest Redeemer; He sent the Savior To set me free.
3 He bade me welcome, O word of mercy; He bade me welcome, O voice divine.
4 Glory and honor, O Love eternal, To Thee be given While life shall last.

REFRAIN
Love so unending! I'll sing Thy praises, God loves His children, Loves even me.

1 Gott ist die Liebe, lässt mich erlösen;
  Gott ist die Liebe, er liebt auch mich.

2 Ich lag in Banden der schnöden Sünde;
  ich lag in Banden und konnt nicht los.

3 Er sandte Jesum, den treuen Heiland;
  er sandte Jesum und macht mich los.

4 Jesus, mein Heiland, gab sich zum Opfer;
  Jesus, mein Heiland, büsst meine Schuld.

REFRAIN Drum sag ich noch einmal:
Gott ist die Liebe,
Gott ist die Liebe,
er liebt auch mich.

HOME AND FAMILY: HYMNS FOR CHILDREN

472 AWAY IN A MANGER

AWAY IN A MANGER 11.11.11.11.

Little Children's Book . . . †, 1885, Sts. 1 and 2
St. 3 somewhat later

James R. Murray (?), 1887

1. A-way in a man-ger, no crib for His bed, The lit-tle Lord Je-sus laid down His sweet head, The stars in the sky looked down where He lay, The lit-tle Lord Je-sus, a-sleep on the hay.
2. The cat-tle are low-ing, the poor ba-by wakes, The lit-tle Lord Je-sus, no cry-ing He makes. I love Thee, Lord Je-sus, look down from the sky, And stay by my side un-til morn-ing is nigh.
3. Be near me, Lord Je-sus; I ask Thee to stay Close by me for ev-er and love me I pray. Bless all the dear chil-dren in Thy ten-der care And fit us for heav-en to live with Thee there.

473 THERE IS A GREEN HILL FAR AWAY

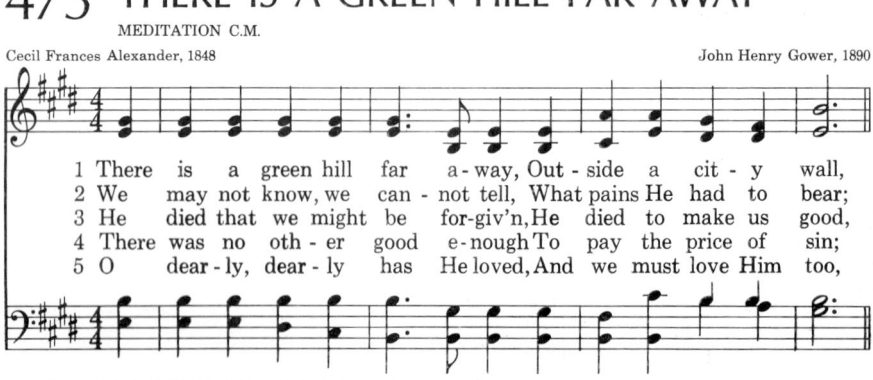

MEDITATION C.M.

Cecil Frances Alexander, 1848

John Henry Gower, 1890

1. There is a green hill far a-way, Out-side a cit-y wall,
2. We may not know, we can-not tell, What pains He had to bear;
3. He died that we might be for-giv'n, He died to make us good,
4. There was no oth-er good e-nough To pay the price of sin;
5. O dear-ly, dear-ly has He loved, And we must love Him too,

HOME AND FAMILY: HYMNS FOR CHILDREN

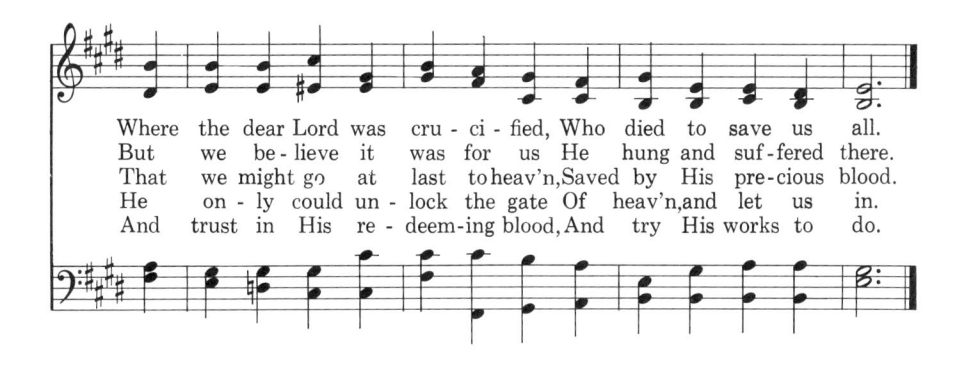

Where the dear Lord was cru-ci-fied, Who died to save us all.
But we be-lieve it was for us He hung and suf-fered there.
That we might go at last to heav'n, Saved by His pre-cious blood.
He on-ly could un-lock the gate Of heav'n, and let us in.
And trust in His re-deem-ing blood, And try His works to do.

WE WELCOME GLAD EASTER 474

ST. DENIO 11.11.11.11.

Anonymous
Welsh Hymn Melody, 1839

1 We wel-come glad Eas-ter when Je-sus a-rose And won a great vic-to-ry o-ver His foes.
2 And tell how three Mar-ys came ear-ly that day And there at the tomb found the stone rolled a-way.
3 And sing of the an-gel who said: "Do not fear! Your Sav-ior is ris'n a-gain; He is not here."
4 So think of the prom-ise which Je-sus did give, That he who be-lieves in Him al-so shall live.

REFRAIN

Then raise your glad voic-es, ye chil-dren, and sing, Bring sweet Eas-ter prais-es to Je-sus, our King.

HOME AND FAMILY: HYMNS FOR CHILDREN

475 FATHER, WE THANK THEE FOR THE NIGHT
ONSLOW L.M.

Rebecca J. Weston, late nineteenth century
Daniel Batchellor, 1885

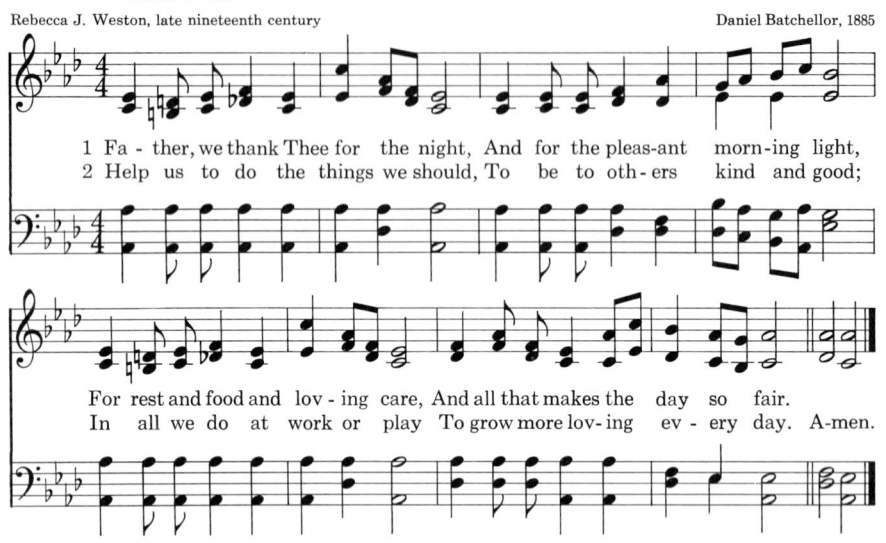

1. Fa-ther, we thank Thee for the night, And for the pleas-ant morn-ing light,
For rest and food and lov-ing care, And all that makes the day so fair.
2. Help us to do the things we should, To be to oth-ers kind and good;
In all we do at work or play To grow more lov-ing ev-er-y day. A-men.

476 GOD MY FATHER, LOVING ME
INNOCENTS 7.7.7.7.

George Wallace Briggs, 1930
The Parish Choir, 1850

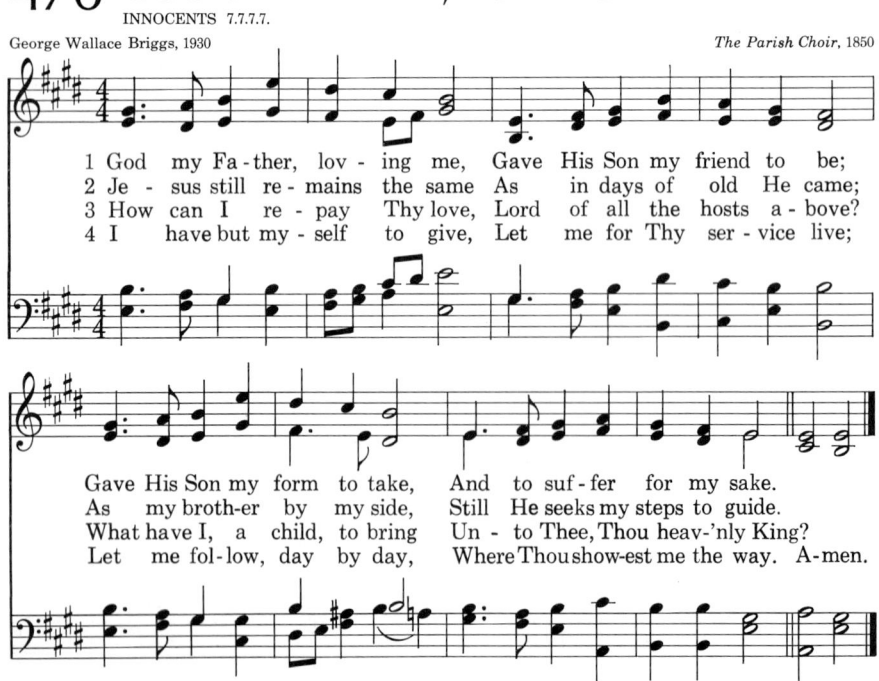

1. God my Fa-ther, lov-ing me, Gave His Son my friend to be;
Gave His Son my form to take, And to suf-fer for my sake.
2. Je-sus still re-mains the same As in days of old He came;
As my broth-er by my side, Still He seeks my steps to guide.
3. How can I re-pay Thy love, Lord of all the hosts a-bove?
What have I, a child, to bring Un-to Thee, Thou heav-'nly King?
4. I have but my-self to give, Let me for Thy ser-vice live;
Let me fol-low, day by day, Where Thou show-est me the way. A-men.

HOME AND FAMILY: HYMNS FOR CHILDREN

COME, MY SOUL, THOU MUST BE 477

HAYDN 8.4.7.D.

Frederich R. L. von Canitz, 1700
Seele, du musst munter werden
Tr. Henry J. Buckoll, 1838

Arranged from Franz Joseph Haydn, 1791

1. Come, my soul, thou must be wak-ing, Now is break-ing O'er the earth an-oth-er day; Come, to Him who made this splen-dor, See thou ren-der All thy fee-ble powers can pay.
2. Thou too hail the light re-turn-ing, Read-y burn-ing Be the in-cense of thy powers! For the night is safe-ly end-ed; God hath tend-ed With His care thy help-less hours.
3. Pray that He may pros-per ev-er Each en-deav-or, When thine aim is good and true; But that He may ev-er thwart thee, And con-vert thee, When thou e-vil wouldst pur-sue.
4. On-ly God's free gifts a-buse not, Light re-fuse not, But His Spir-it's voice o-bey; Thou with Him shalt dwell, be-hold-ing Light en-fold-ing All things in un-cloud-ed day.

TIMES AND SEASONS: MORNING

478 CHRIST, WHOSE GLORY FILLS THE SKIES
LUX PRIMA 7.7.7.7.7.7.

Charles Wesley, 1740   Charles F. Gounod, 1872

1. Christ, whose glo-ry fills the skies, Christ, the true, the on-ly light,
Sun of right-eous-ness, a-rise, Tri-umph o'er the shades of night;
Day-spring from on high, be near; Day-star, in my heart ap-pear.

2. Dark and cheer-less is the morn Un-ac-com-pan-ied by Thee;
Joy-less is the day's re-turn Till Thy mer-cy's beams I see
Till they in-ward light im-part, Glad my eyes and warm my heart.

3. Vis-it, then, this soul of mine; Pierce the gloom of sin and grief;
Fill me, ra-dian-cy di-vine; Scat-ter all my un-be-lief;
More and more Thy-self dis-play, Shin-ing to the per-fect day. A-men.

479 I OWE THE LORD A MORNING SONG
GRATITUDE C.M.

Amos Herr, 1890   Amos Herr, 1890

1. I owe the Lord a morn-ing song Of grat-i-tude and praise,
2. He kept me safe an-oth-er night; I see an-oth-er day;
3. Keep me from dan-ger and from sin: Help me Thy will to do,
4. Keep me till Thou wilt call me hence, Where nev-er night can be;

TIMES AND SEASONS: MORNING

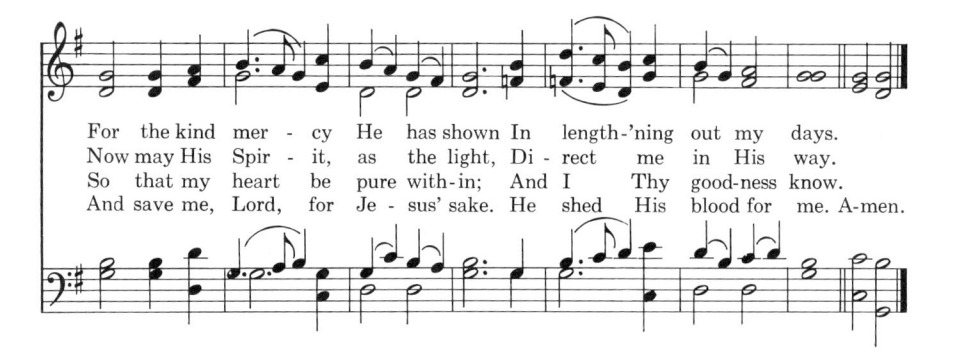

For the kind mer - cy He has shown In length-'ning out my days.
Now may His Spir - it, as the light, Di - rect me in His way.
So that my heart be pure with-in; And I Thy good-ness know.
And save me, Lord, for Je - sus' sake. He shed His blood for me. A-men.

FATHER, WE PRAISE THEE 480
CHRISTE SANCTORUM 11.11.11.5.

Ascribed to Gregory the Great, d. 604
Nocte surgentes vigilemus omnes
Tr. Percy Dearmer, 1906

Paris Antiphoner, 1681

1 Fa - ther, we praise Thee, now the night is o - ver; Ac - tive and
2 Mon-arch of all things, fit us for Thy man - sions; Ban - ish our
3 All - ho - ly Fa - ther, Son and e - qual Spir - it, Trin - i - ty

watch - ful, stand we all be - fore Thee; Sing - ing, we of - fer
weak - ness, health and whole-ness send - ing; Bring us to heav - en,
bless - ed, send us Thy sal - va - tion; Thine is the glo - ry,

prayer and med - i - ta - tion: Thus we a - dore Thee.
where Thy saints u - nit - ed Joy with-out end - ing.
gleam - ing and re - sound-ing Through all cre - a - tion. A-men.

TIMES AND SEASONS: MORNING

481 LORD GOD OF MORNING
MACH'S MIT MIR, L.M.

Francis Turner Palgrave, 1862 — Johann Hermann Schein, 1628

1. Lord God of morning and of night, We thank Thee for Thy gift of light; As in the dawn the shadows fly, We seem to find Thee now more nigh.
2. Fresh hopes have wakened in our hearts, Fresh energy to do our parts; Thy thousand sleeps our strength restore, A thousand-fold to serve Thee more.
3. O Lord of lights! 'tis Thou alone Canst make our darkened hearts Thine own; Though this new day with joy we see, O dawn of God! we cry for Thee!
4. Praise God, our Maker and our Friend! Praise Him through time, till time shall end! Till psalm and song His name adore Through heav'n's great day of evermore! A-men.

482 LORD, THOU SHALT EARLY HEAR
WARWICK C.M.

Based on Psalm 5
Scottish Psalter‡, 1650 — Samuel Stanley, 1802

1. Lord, Thou shalt early hear my voice: I early will direct
2. For Thou art not a God that doth In wickedness delight;
3. But I into Thy house will come In Thine abundant grace;
4. Let all that trust in Thee be glad, With joy lift up their voice;

TIMES AND SEASONS: MORNING

My prayer to Thee; and, look-ing up, An an-swer will ex-pect.
Nei-ther shall e-vil dwell with Thee, Nor fools stand in Thy sight.
And I will wor-ship in Thy fear To-ward Thy ho-ly place.
Be-cause Thou sav-est them; let all That love Thy name re-joice. A-men.

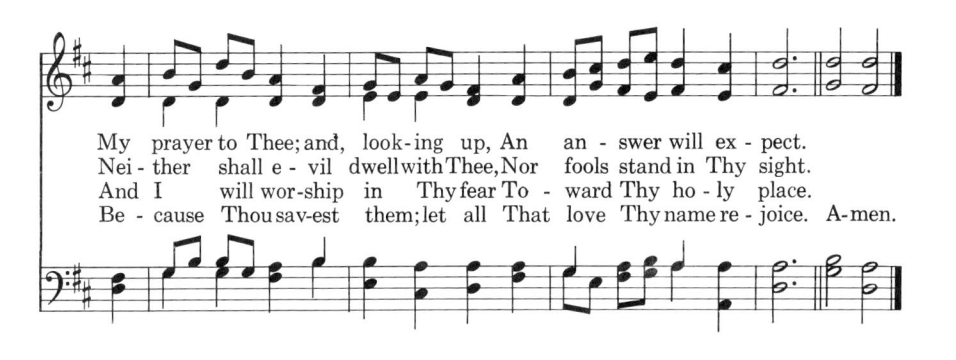

NEW EVERY MORNING IS THY LOVE 483
MELCOMBE L.M.

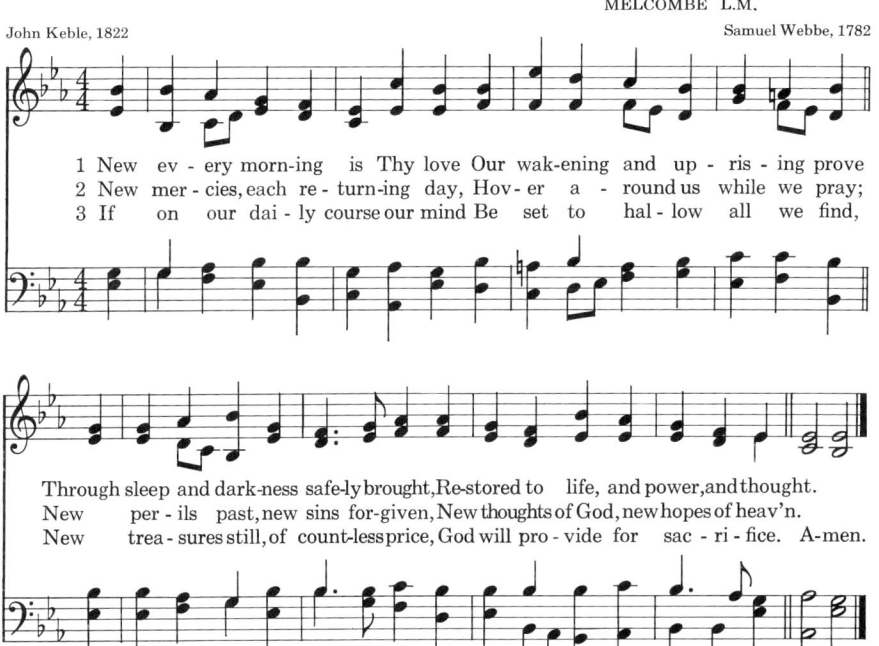

John Keble, 1822

Samuel Webbe, 1782

1 New ev-ery morn-ing is Thy love Our wak-ening and up-ris-ing prove
2 New mer-cies, each re-turn-ing day, Hov-er a-round us while we pray;
3 If on our dai-ly course our mind Be set to hal-low all we find,

Through sleep and dark-ness safe-ly brought, Re-stored to life, and power, and thought.
New per-ils past, new sins for-given, New thoughts of God, new hopes of heav'n.
New trea-sures still, of count-less price, God will pro-vide for sac-ri-fice. A-men.

4 The trivial round, the common task,
 Will furnish all we ought to ask,
 Room to deny ourselves, a road
 To bring us daily nearer God.

5 Only, O Lord, in Thy dear love,
 Fit us for perfect rest above,
 And help us, this and every day,
 To live more nearly as we pray.

TIMES AND SEASONS: MORNING

484 DAYSPRING OF ETERNITY
MORGENGLANZ DER EWIGKEIT 7.8.7.8.7.3.

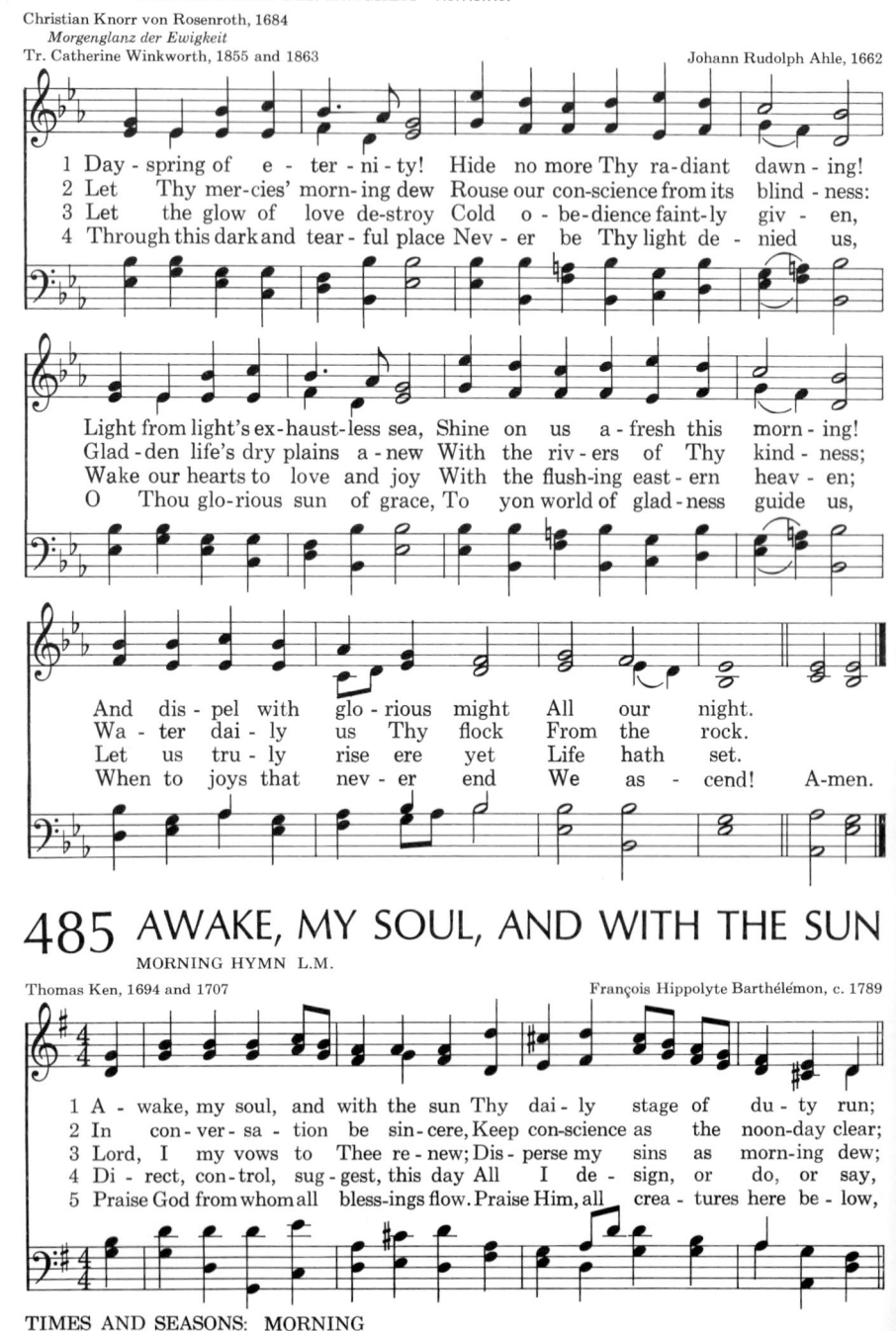

Christian Knorr von Rosenroth, 1684
Morgenglanz der Ewigkeit
Tr. Catherine Winkworth, 1855 and 1863

Johann Rudolph Ahle, 1662

1. Day-spring of e - ter - ni - ty! Hide no more Thy ra-diant dawn - ing!
   Light from light's ex-haust-less sea, Shine on us a-fresh this morn - ing!
   And dis - pel with glo - rious might All our night.

2. Let Thy mer-cies' morn-ing dew Rouse our con-science from its blind - ness:
   Glad - den life's dry plains a-new With the riv - ers of Thy kind - ness;
   Wa - ter dai - ly us Thy flock From the rock.

3. Let the glow of love de-stroy Cold o - be-dience faint-ly giv - en,
   Wake our hearts to love and joy With the flush-ing east - ern heav - en;
   Let us tru - ly rise ere yet Life hath set.

4. Through this dark and tear - ful place Nev - er be Thy light de - nied us,
   O Thou glo - rious sun of grace, To yon world of glad - ness guide us,
   When to joys that nev - er end We as - cend! A-men.

485 AWAKE, MY SOUL, AND WITH THE SUN
MORNING HYMN L.M.

Thomas Ken, 1694 and 1707

François Hippolyte Barthélémon, c. 1789

1. A - wake, my soul, and with the sun Thy dai - ly stage of du - ty run;
2. In con - ver - sa - tion be sin - cere, Keep con-science as the noon-day clear;
3. Lord, I my vows to Thee re - new; Dis - perse my sins as morn-ing dew;
4. Di - rect, con-trol, sug - gest, this day All I de - sign, or do, or say,
5. Praise God from whom all bless-ings flow. Praise Him, all crea - tures here be - low,

TIMES AND SEASONS: MORNING

Shake off dull sloth, and joy-ful rise To pay thy morn-ing sac-ri-fice.
Think how all-see-ing God thy ways And all thy se-cret thoughts sur-veys.
Guard my first springs of thought and will And with Thy-self my spir-it fill.
That all my powers, with all their might, In Thy sole glo-ry may u-nite.
Praise Him a-bove, ye heav'n-ly host, Praise Fa-ther, Son, and Ho-ly Ghost. A-men.

LIGHT OF LIGHT, ENLIGHTEN ME 486

MEINEM JESUM (MEINHOLD) 7.8.7.8.7.7.

Benjamin Schmolck, 1714
Licht von Licht, erleuchte mich
Tr. Catherine Winkworth, 1858

Gesangbuch, Lüneburg, 1686

1 Light of light, en-light-en me, Now a-new the day is dawn-ing;
2 Fount of all our joy and peace, To Thy liv-ing wa-ters lead me;
3 Kin-dle Thou the sac-ri-fice That up-on my lips is ly-ing;
4 Let me with my heart to-day, Ho-ly, ho-ly, ho-ly, sing-ing

Sun of grace, the shad-ows flee, Bright-en Thou my Sab-bath morn-ing;
Thou from earth my soul re-lease, And with grace and mer-cy feed me;
Clear the shad-ows from my eyes, That from ev-ery er-ror fly-ing,
Rapt a-while from earth a-way, All my soul to Thee up-spring-ing,

With Thy joy-ous sun-shine blest, Hap-py is my day of rest.
Bless Thy Word, that it may prove Rich in fruits that Thou dost love.
No strange fire may in me glow That Thine al-tar doth not know.
Have a fore-taste in-ly given How they wor-ship Thee in heav'n.

TIMES AND SEASONS: MORNING

487 THE DUTEOUS DAY NOW CLOSETH
O WELT, ICH MUSS DICH LASSEN (INNSBRUCK) 7.7.6.7.7.8.

Paul Gerhardt, 1648
Nun ruhen alle Wälder
Tr. Robert Bridges, 1899

German Melody; Sacred use by 1505
Harmony by Johann Sebastian Bach, 1729

1. The duteous day now closeth, Each flower and tree reposeth, Shade creeps o'er wild and wood: Let us, as night is falling, On God our maker calling, Give thanks to Him the giver good.

2. Now all the heav'nly splendor Breaks forth in star-light tender From myriad worlds unknown; And man, the marvel seeing, Forgets his selfish being, For joy of beauty not his own.

3. His care he drowneth yonder, Lost in th' abyss of wonder; To heav'n his soul doth steal: This life he disesteemeth, The day it is that dreameth, That doth from truth his vision seal.

4. Awhile his mortal blindness May miss God's loving kindness, And grope in faithless strife: But when life's day is over Shall death's fair night discover The fields of everlasting life.

TIMES AND SEASONS: EVENING

THE DAY THOU GAVEST, LORD 488

LES COMMANDEMENS DE DIEU 9.8.9.8.

John Ellerton, 1870

La forme des prieres . . . , Strasbourg, 1545
Harmony adapted from Claude Goudimel, 1565

1. The day Thou gavest, Lord, is ended,
The darkness falls at Thy behest;
To Thee our morning hymns ascended,
Thy praise shall sanctify our rest.

2. We thank Thee that Thy church, unsleeping
While earth rolls onward into light,
Through all the world her watch is keeping,
And rests not now by day or night.

3. As o'er each continent and island
The dawn leads on another day,
The voice of prayer is never silent,
Nor dies the strain of praise away.

4. The sun that bids us rest is waking
Our brethren 'neath the western sky,
And hour by hour fresh lips are making
Thy wondrous doings heard on high.

5. So be it, Lord; Thy throne shall never,
Like earth's proud empires, pass away;
Thy kingdom stands, and grows forever,
Till all Thy creatures own Thy sway. A-men.

TIMES AND SEASONS: EVENING

489 O GLADSOME LIGHT, O GRACE
NUNC DIMITTIS 6.6.7.D.

Anonymous, 3rd century (?)
Φῶς ἱλαρὸν ἁγίας δόξης
Tr. Robert Bridges, 1899

Pseaumes octante trois, Geneva, 1551
Harmony adapted from Claude Goudimel, 1565

1. O gladsome light, O grace Of God the Father's face, Th' eternal splendor wearing; Celestial, holy, blest, Our Savior Jesus Christ, Joyful in Thine appearing.
2. Now, ere day fadeth quite, We see the evening light, Our wonted hymn out-pouring; Father of might unknown, Thee, His incarnate Son, And Holy Spirit adoring.
3. To Thee of right belongs All praise of holy songs, O Son of God, life-giver; Thee therefore, O Most High, The world doth glorify, And shall exalt forever.

490 NOW THE DAY IS OVER
MERRIAL 6.5.6.5.

Sabine Baring-Gould, 1865

Joseph Barnby, 1868

1. Now the day is over, Night is drawing nigh;
2. Jesus, give the weary Calm and sweet repose;
3. Grant to little children Visions bright of Thee;
4. Through the long night watches May Thine angels spread
5. When the morning wakens, Then may I arise

TIMES AND SEASONS: EVENING

Shadows of the evening   Steal across the sky.
With Thy tend'rest blessing   May our eyelids close.
Guard the sailors tossing   On the deep, blue sea.
Their white wings above me,   Watching round my bed.
Pure, and fresh, and sinless   In Thy holy eyes.   A-men.

SUN OF MY SOUL, THOU SAVIOR DEAR 491

HURSLEY L.M.

Arranged from *Grosser Gott, wir loben dich*
From *Katholisches Gesanghuch*, Vienna, 1776

John Keble, 1820

1 Sun of my soul, Thou Savior dear, It is not night if Thou be near; O may no earth-born cloud arise To hide Thee from Thy servant's eyes.
2 Abide with me, from morn till eve, For without Thee I cannot live; Abide with me when night is nigh, For without Thee I dare not die.
3 Watch by the sick; enrich the poor With blessings from Thy boundless store; Be every mourner's sleep tonight, Like infants' slumbers, pure and light.
4 Come near and bless us when we wake, Ere through the world our way we take, Till in the ocean of Thy love We lose ourselves in heav'n above.   A-men.

TIMES AND SEASONS: EVENING

492 NOW, ON LAND AND SEA DESCENDING

VESPER HYMN 8.7.8.7.8.6.8.7.

Samuel Longfellow‡, 1859 — John Andrew Stevenson, 1818

1. Now, on land and sea de-scend-ing, Brings the night its peace pro-found;
2. Soon as dies the sun-set glo-ry, Stars of heav'n shine out a-bove,
3. Now, our wants and bur-dens leav-ing To His care who cares for all,
4. As the dark-ness deep-ens o'er us, Lo! e-ter-nal stars a-rise;

Let our ves-per hymn be blend-ing With the ho-ly calm a-round.
Tell-ing still the an-cient sto-ry, Their Cre-a-tor's change-less love.
Cease we fear-ing, cease we griev-ing: At His touch our bur-dens fall.
Hope and faith and love rise glo-rious, Shin-ing in the spir-it's skies.

Ju-bi-la-te! Ju-bi-la-te! Ju-bi-la-te! A-men!

Let our ves-per hymn be blend-ing With the ho-ly calm a-round.
Tell-ing still the an-cient sto-ry, Their Cre-a-tor's change-less love.
Cease we fear-ing, cease we griev-ing: At His touch our bur-dens fall.
Hope and faith and love rise glo-rious, Shin-ing in the spir-it's skies.

TIMES AND SEASONS: EVENING

DAY IS DYING IN THE WEST 493

CHAUTAUQUA 7.7.7.7.4. with Refrain

Mary A. Lathbury†, 1877 and 1890

William F. Sherwin, 1877

1. Day is dy-ing in the west; Heav'n is touch-ing earth with rest; Wait and wor-ship while the night Sets her eve-ning lamps a-light Through all the sky.
2. Lord of life, be-neath the dome Of the u-ni-verse, Thy home, Gath-er us who seek Thy face To the fold of Thy em-brace, For Thou art nigh.
3. While the deep-ening shad-ows fall, Heart of love, en-fold-ing all, Through the glo-ry and the grace Of the stars that veil Thy face, Our hearts as-cend.
4. When for-ev-er from our sight Pass the stars, the day, the night, Lord of an-gels, on our eyes Let e-ter-nal morn-ing rise, And shad-ows end.

Refrain
Ho-ly, ho-ly, ho-ly, Lord God of hosts! Heav'n and earth are full of Thee; Heav'n and earth are prais-ing Thee, O Lord most high!

TIMES AND SEASONS: EVENING

494 AT EVEN, ERE THE SUN WAS SET
ANGELUS L.M.

Henry Twells, 1868

Scheffler's *Heilige Seelenlust*, 1657

1 At even, ere the sun was set, The sick, O Lord, around Thee lay; O in what divers pains they met! O with what joy they went away!

2 Once more 'tis eventide, and we, Oppressed with various ills, draw near; What if Thy form we cannot see? We know and feel that Thou art here.

3 O Savior Christ, our woes dispel: For some are sick, and some are sad, And some have never loved Thee well, And some have lost the love they had.

4 And none, O Lord, have perfect rest, For none are wholly free from sin; And they who fain would serve Thee best Are conscious most of wrong within. A-men.

5 O Savior Christ, Thou too art man;
  Thou hast been troubled, tempted, tried;
Thy kind but searching glance can scan
  The very wounds that shame would hide.

6 Thy touch has still its ancient power;
  No word from Thee can fruitless fall:
Hear in this solemn evening hour,
  And in Thy mercy heal us all.

TIMES AND SEASONS: EVENING

ABIDE WITH ME 495

EVENTIDE 10.10.10.10.

Henry Francis Lyte, 1847
William Henry Monk, 1861

1. A-bide with me: fast falls the e-ven-tide; The dark-ness deep-ens; Lord, with me a-bide: When oth-er help-ers fail, and com-forts flee, Help of the help-less, O a-bide with me.

2. Swift to its close ebbs out life's lit-tle day; Earth's joys grow dim, its glo-ries pass a-way; Change and de-cay in all a-round I see; O Thou who chang-est not, a-bide with me.

3. I need Thy pres-ence ev-ery pass-ing hour; What but Thy grace can foil the temp-ter's power? Who like Thy-self my guide and stay can be? Through cloud and sun-shine, O a-bide with me.

4. I fear no foe, with Thee at hand to bless: Ills have no weight, and tears no bit-ter-ness. Where is death's sting? where, grave, thy vic-to-ry? I tri-umph still, if Thou a-bide with me. A-men.

5. Hold then Thy cross before my closing eyes;
Shine through the gloom, and point me to the skies:
Heav'n's morning breaks, and earth's vain shadows flee:
In life and death, O Lord, abide with me.

TIMES AND SEASONS: EVENING

496 ALL PRAISE TO THEE, MY GOD
TALLIS' CANON L.M.

Thomas Ken, 1709
Thomas Tallis, c. 1567

1. All praise to Thee, my God, this night,
For all the blessings of the light:
Keep me, O keep me, King of kings,
Beneath Thine own almighty wings.

2. Forgive me, Lord, for Thy dear Son,
The ill that I this day have done;
That with the world, myself, and Thee,
I, ere I sleep, at peace may be.

3. O may my soul on Thee repose,
And with sweet sleep my eyelids close;
Sleep that shall me more vig'rous make
To serve my God when I awake. A-men.

*Tenor is in canon beginning here.

4. When in the night I sleepless lie,
My soul with heav'nly thoughts supply!
Let no ill dreams disturb my rest,
No powers of darkness me molest!

5. Praise God, from whom all blessings flow;
Praise Him, all creatures here below;
Praise Him above, ye heav'nly host:
Praise Father, Son, and Holy Ghost.

TIMES AND SEASONS: EVENING

O DAY OF SACRED REST 497

LISCHER 6.6.6.6.8.8.

"Hayward" in John Dobell's, *Collection*, 1806, and Others

Friedrich Schneider, d. 1853
Arranged by Lowell Mason, 1841

1. O day of sacred rest, We welcome thee anew;
Lord, make these moments blest, Send Thy refreshing dew;
From fleeting pleasures and delights, I soar to reach immortal heights, I soar to reach immortal heights.

2. To heav'n our prayers we send, O Son of God most high;
Thy scepter, Lord, extend, As humbly we draw nigh;
May sinful hearts now contrite be, Teach all to know and follow Thee, Teach all to know and follow Thee.

3. Descend, celestial Dove, With all Thy quick'ning powers;
Disclose a Savior's love, And bless the sacred hours:
Then shall my soul new life obtain, Nor Sabbaths be enjoyed in vain, Nor Sabbaths be enjoyed in vain.

TIMES AND SEASONS: THE LORD'S DAY

498 PRAISE OUR FATHER FOR THIS SUNDAY
P'UT'O 8.8.7.8.

Tzu-ch'en Chao, 1931
Tr. Frank W. Price, 1952

Chinese Melody
Hymns of Universal Praise, 1936

1 Praise our Father for this Sunday, Praise His goodness now and alway.
2 After toiling through the long week Now we gather to hear Thee speak.
3 Sometimes we bear pain and sorrow, Sometimes darkness hides the morrow;
4 Sometimes we find peace and gladness, Calm and hope in joy and sadness;
5 Here we come our lives to offer, Hearts and minds we humbly proffer.

Praise His grace that loves men thus, Praise His mercy that forgives us.
In Thy house may all be blest, Here may all gain strength and find rest.
Father, Father, leave us not When sore trouble becomes our lot.
On our way God sheds His light, Loves us ever, day and dark night.
Father, hear us while we pray, And receive us, now and for aye. A-men.

499 THIS IS THE DAY THE LORD HATH MADE
ARLINGTON C.M.

Based on Psalm 118
Isaac Watts, 1719

Thomas Augustine Arne, 1762
Arranged by Ralph Harrison, 1784

1 This is the day the Lord hath made; He calls the hours His own;
2 Today He rose and left the dead, And Satan's empire fell;
3 Blest be the Lord who comes to men With messages of grace;
4 Hosanna in the highest strains The church on earth can raise!

Let heav'n rejoice, let earth be glad, And praise surround the throne.
Today the saints His triumphs spread, And all His wonders tell.
Who comes in God His Father's name To save our sinful race.
The highest heav'ns in which He reigns Shall give Him nobler praise. A-men.

TIMES AND SEASONS: THE LORD'S DAY

THIS IS THE DAY OF LIGHT 500

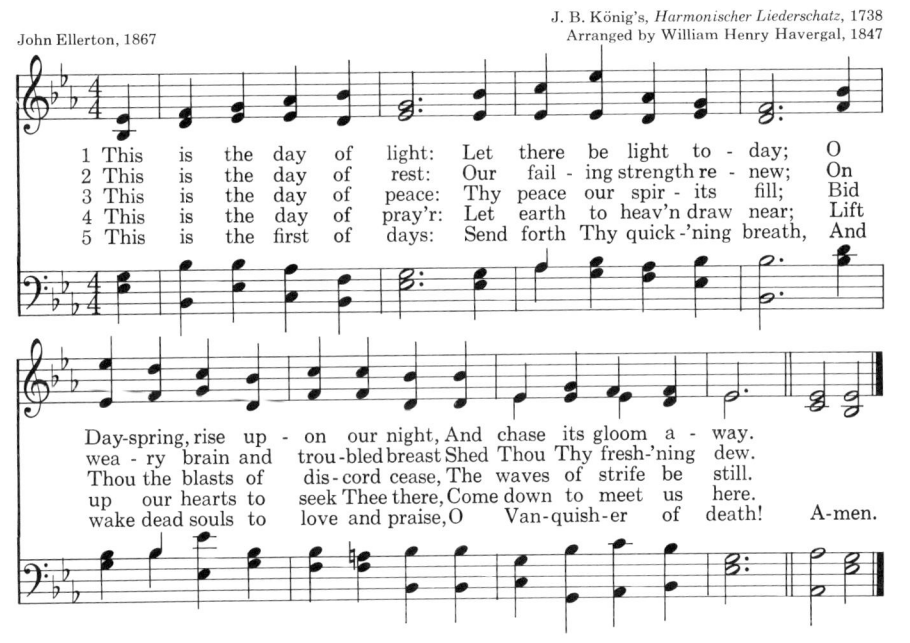

FRANCONIA S.M.

John Ellerton, 1867

J. B. König's, *Harmonischer Liederschatz*, 1738
Arranged by William Henry Havergal, 1847

1. This is the day of light: Let there be light to-day; O Day-spring, rise up-on our night, And chase its gloom a-way.
2. This is the day of rest: Our fail-ing strength re-new; On wea-ry brain and trou-bled breast Shed Thou Thy fresh-'ning dew.
3. This is the day of peace: Thy peace our spir-its fill; Bid Thou the blasts of dis-cord cease, The waves of strife be still.
4. This is the day of pray'r: Let earth to heav'n draw near; Lift up our hearts to seek Thee there, Come down to meet us here.
5. This is the first of days: Send forth Thy quick-'ning breath, And wake dead souls to love and praise, O Van-quish-er of death! A-men.

COME, LET US JOIN WITH ONE ACCORD 501

RICHMOND C.M.

Charles Wesley, 1763

Thomas Haweis, 1792

1. Come, let us join with one ac-cord In hymns a-round the throne! This is the day our ris-ing Lord Hath made and called His own.
2. This is the day which God hath blest, The bright-est of the sev'n, Type of that ev-er-last-ing rest The saints en-joy in heav'n.
3. Then let us in His name sing on, And has-ten to that day When our Re-deem-er shall come down, And shad-ows pass a-way.
4. Not one, but all our days be-low, Let us in hymns em-ploy; And in our Lord re-joic-ing, go To His e-ter-nal joy.

TIMES AND SEASONS: THE LORD'S DAY

502 LORD, DISMISS US WITH THY BLESSING
SICILIAN MARINERS 8.7.8.7.8.7.

Attributed to John Fawcett‡, 1773 — Tattersall's *Psalmody*, 1794

1. Lord, dismiss us with Thy blessing; Fill our hearts with joy and peace; Let us each, Thy love possessing, Triumph in redeeming grace: O refresh us, O refresh us, Trav-'ling through this wilderness.

2. Thanks we give and adoration For Thy gospel's joyful sound: May the fruits of Thy salvation In our hearts and lives abound: Ever faithful, Ever faithful To the truth may we be found;

3. So that when Thy love shall call us, Savior, from the world away, Let no fear of death appall us, Glad Thy summons to obey: May we ever, May we ever Reign with Thee in endless day. A-men.

TIMES AND SEASONS: CLOSE OF WORSHIP

GOD BE WITH YOU TILL WE MEET 503

RANDOLPH 9.8.8.8.9.

Jeremiah Eames Rankin, 1880

Ralph Vaughan Williams, 1906
Arrangement Altered

1 God be with you till we meet a-gain; By His coun-sels guide, up-hold you,
2 God be with you till we meet a-gain; 'Neath His wings pro-tect-ing hide you,
3 God be with you till we meet a-gain; When life's per-ils thick con-found you,
4 God be with you till we meet a-gain; Keep love's ban-ner float-ing o'er you,

With His sheep se-cure-ly fold you: God be with you till we meet a-gain.
Dai-ly man-na still pro-vide you: God be with you till we meet a-gain.
Put His arms un-fail-ing round you: God be with you till we meet a-gain.
Smite death's threat-'ning wave be-fore you: God be with you till we meet a-gain. A-men.

GOD BE WITH YOU TILL WE MEET 504

GOD BE WITH YOU 9.8.8.8.9.

Jeremiah Eames Rankin, 1880

William Gould Tomer, 1880

1 God be with you till we meet a-gain; By His coun-sels guide, up-hold you,
2 God be with you till we meet a-gain; 'Neath His wings pro-tect-ing hide you,
3 God be with you till we meet a-gain; When life's per-ils thick con-found you,
4 God be with you till we meet a-gain; Keep love's ban-ner float-ing o'er you,

With His sheep se-cure-ly fold you: God be with you till we meet a-gain.
Dai-ly man-na still pro-vide you: God be with you till we meet a-gain.
Put His arms un-fail-ing round you: God be with you till we meet a-gain.
Smite death's threat-'ning wave be-fore you: God be with you till we meet a-gain. A-men.

TIMES AND SEASONS: CLOSE OF WORSHIP

505 SAVIOR, AGAIN TO THY DEAR NAME
ELLERS 10.10.10.10.

John Ellerton, 1868 — Edward John Hopkins, 1869

1. Savior, again to Thy dear name we raise
With one accord our parting hymn of praise;
We stand to bless Thee ere our worship cease;
Then, lowly kneeling, wait Thy word of peace.

2. Grant us Thy peace upon our homeward way;
With Thee began, with Thee shall end the day:
Guard Thou the lips from sin, the hearts from shame,
That in this house have called upon Thy name.

3. Grant us Thy peace, Lord, through the coming night;
Turn Thou for us its darkness into light;
From harm and danger keep Thy children free,
For dark and light are both alike to Thee.

4. Grant us Thy peace throughout our earthly life,
Our balm in sorrow, and our stay in strife;
Then, when Thy voice shall bid our conflict cease,
Call us, O Lord, to Thine eternal peace. A-men.

TIMES AND SEASONS: CLOSE OF WORSHIP

NOW MAY HE, WHO FROM THE DEAD 506

INNOCENTS 7.7.7.7.

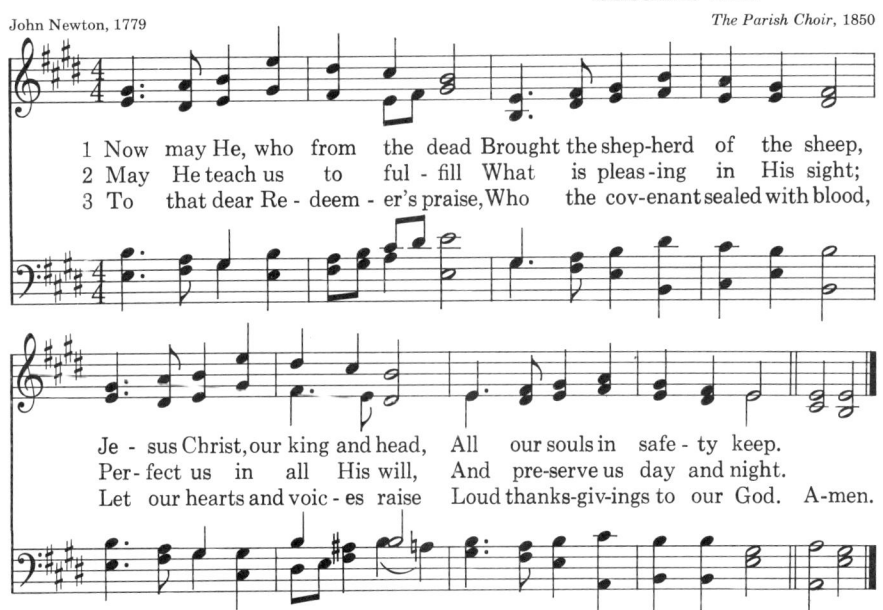

John Newton, 1779

The Parish Choir, 1850

1 Now may He, who from the dead Brought the shep-herd of the sheep,
2 May He teach us to ful - fill What is pleas-ing in His sight;
3 To that dear Re - deem - er's praise, Who the cov-enant sealed with blood,

Je - sus Christ, our king and head, All our souls in safe - ty keep.
Per - fect us in all His will, And pre-serve us day and night.
Let our hearts and voic - es raise Loud thanks-giv-ings to our God. A-men.

TO GOD THE ONLY WISE 507

ST. MICHAEL (OLD 134) S.M.

From *Pseaumes octante trois*, Geneva, 1551
Adapted by William Crotch, 1836

Isaac Watts, 1707

1 To God the on - ly wise, Our Sav - ior, and our King, Let all the
2 'Tis His al-might - y love, His coun - sel, and His care, Pre - serve us

saints be - low the skies Their hum - ble prais - es bring.
safe from sin and death, And ev - ery hurt - ful snare. A - men.

TIMES AND SEASONS: CLOSE OF WORSHIP

508 GREAT GOD, WE SING THAT MIGHTY

WAREHAM L.M.

Philip Doddridge, 1755 — William Knapp, 1738

1. Great God, we sing that mighty hand By which supported still we stand; The opening year Thy mercy shows; That mercy crowns it, till it close.
2. By day, by night, at home, abroad, Still are we guarded by our God; By His incessant bounty fed, By His unerring counsel led.
3. With grateful hearts the past we own; The future, all to us unknown, We to Thy guardian care commit, And, peaceful, leave before Thy feet.
4. In scenes exalted or depressed, Thou art our joy, and Thou our rest; Thy goodness all our hopes shall raise, Adored through all our changing days. A-men.

509 FOR THY MERCY AND THY GRACE

UNIVERSITY COLLEGE 7.7.7.7.

Henry Downton, 1841 — Henry John Gauntlett, 1852

1. For Thy mercy and Thy grace, Constant through another year,
2. Lo! our sins on Thee we cast, Thee our perfect sacrifice,
3. In our weakness and distress, Rock of strength, be Thou our stay;
4. Keep us faithful, keep us pure, Keep us evermore Thine own,

TIMES AND SEASONS: OLD AND NEW YEAR

Hear our song of thank-ful-ness; Fa-ther and Re-deem-er, hear.
And, for-get-ting all the past, Press to-wards our glo-rious prize.
In the path-less wil-der-ness Be our true and liv-ing way.
Help, O help us to en-dure; Fit us for the prom-ised crown. A-men.

ANOTHER YEAR IS DAWNING 510
CHRISTUS, DER IST MEIN LEBEN 7.6.7.6.

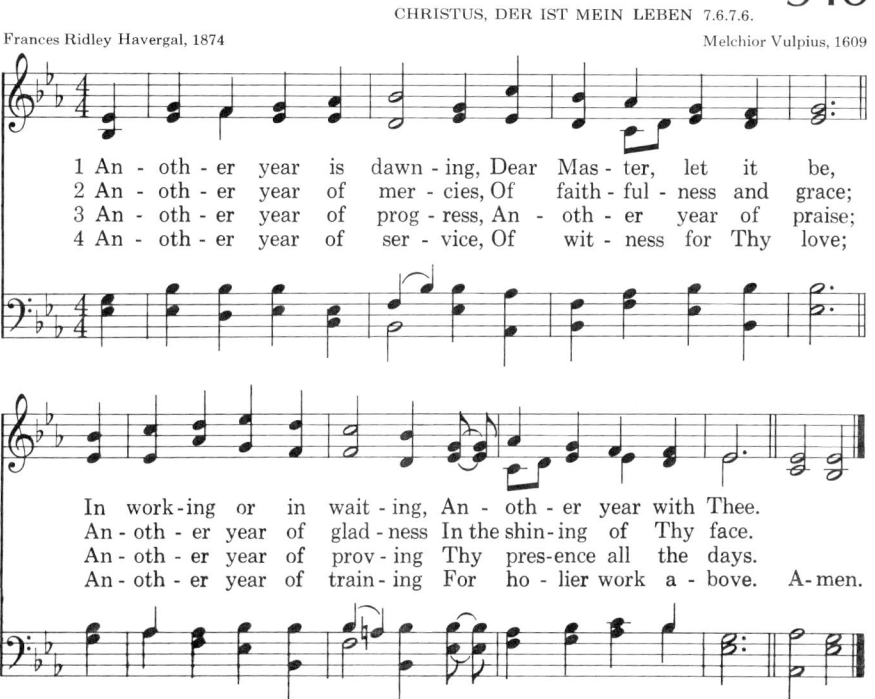

Frances Ridley Havergal, 1874
Melchior Vulpius, 1609

1 An-oth-er year is dawn-ing, Dear Mas-ter, let it be,
2 An-oth-er year of mer-cies, Of faith-ful-ness and grace;
3 An-oth-er year of prog-ress, An-oth-er year of praise;
4 An-oth-er year of ser-vice, Of wit-ness for Thy love;

In work-ing or in wait-ing, An-oth-er year with Thee.
An-oth-er year of glad-ness In the shin-ing of Thy face.
An-oth-er year of prov-ing Thy pres-ence all the days.
An-oth-er year of train-ing For ho-lier work a-bove. A-men.

5 Another year is dawning,
Dear Master, let it be,
On earth, or else in heaven,
Another year for Thee!

TIMES AND SEASONS: OLD AND NEW YEAR

511 ACROSS THE SKY THE SHADES
NUN FREUT EUCH 8.7.8.7.8.8.7.

James Hamilton‡, 1882 — J. Klug's *Geistliche Lieder*, 1535

1. A-cross the sky the shades of night This win-ter's eve are fleet-ing.
We come to Thee, the life and light, In sol-emn wor-ship meet-ing.
And as the year's last hours go by We lift to Thee our ear-nest cry,
Once more Thy love en-treat-ing.

2. Be-fore the cross sub-dued we bow, To Thee our prayers ad-dress-ing;
Re-count-ing all Thy mer-cies now, And all our sins con-fess-ing;
Be-seech-ing Thee, this com-ing year, To hold us in Thy faith and fear,
And crown us with Thy bless-ing.

3. We gath-er up in this brief hour The mem-'ry of Thy mer-cies;
Thy won-drous good-ness, love, and power Our grate-ful song re-hears-es;
For Thou hast been our strength and stay In man-y a dark and drear-y day
Of sor-row and re-vers-es.

4. Then, O great God, in years to come, What-ev-er fate be-tide us,
Right on-ward through our jour-ney home Be Thou at hand to guide us;
Nor leave us till, at close of life, Safe from all per-il, toil, and strife,
Heav'n shall re-ceive and hide us. A-men.

TIMES AND SEASONS: OLD AND NEW YEAR

'TIS WINTER NOW 512

MELROSE L.M.

Samuel Longfellow, 1864
Frederick Charles Maker, d. 1927

1. 'Tis winter now; the fallen snow
   Has left the heav'ns all coldly clear;
   Through leafless boughs the sharp winds blow,
   And all the earth lies dead and drear.

2. And yet God's love is not withdrawn;
   His life within the keen air breathes,
   His beauty paints the crimson dawn,
   And clothes the boughs with glittering wreaths.

3. And though abroad the sharp winds blow,
   And skies are chill, and frosts are keen,
   Home closer draws her circle now,
   And warmer glows her light within.

4. O God! who giv'st the winter's cold,
   As well as summer's joyous rays,
   Us warmly in Thy love enfold,
   And keep us through life's wintry days. A-men.

TIMES AND SEASONS: THE SEASONS

513 THE GLORY OF THE SPRING
KING'S LANGLEY C.M.

Thomas Hornblower Gill, 1867

Melody, Lucy Broadwood
Arranged and harmonized by
Ralph Vaughan Williams, 1906

1 The glory of the spring how sweet! The new-born life how glad!
What joy the happy earth to greet, In new, bright raiment clad!

2 Divine Renewer, Thee I bless; I greet Thy going forth;
I love Thee in the loveliness Of Thy renewed earth.

3 But O these wonders of Thy grace, These nobler works of Thine,
These marvels sweeter far to trace, These new births more divine:

4 This new-born glow of faith so strong, This bloom of love so fair,
This new-born ecstasy of song, And fragrancy of prayer! A-men.

5 Creator Spirit, work in me
These wonders sweet of Thine;
Divine Renewer, graciously
Renew this heart of mine.

6 Still let new life and strength upspring,
Still let new joy be giv'n;
And grant the glad new song to ring
Through the new earth and heav'n.

514 KINDLY SPRING AGAIN IS HERE
ORIENTIS PARTIBUS 7.7.7.7.

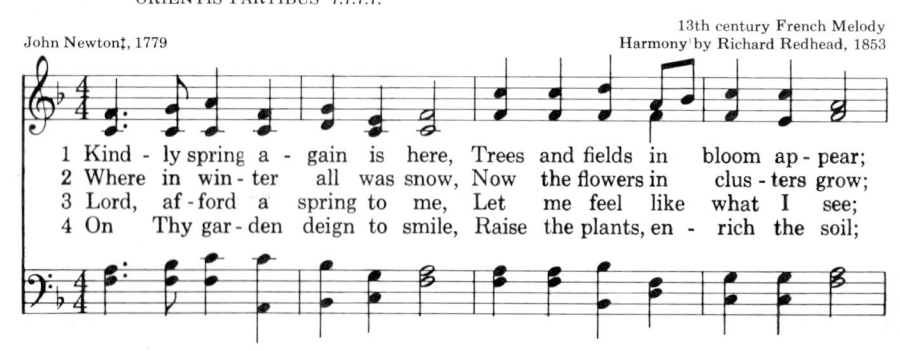

John Newton‡, 1779

13th century French Melody
Harmony by Richard Redhead, 1853

1 Kindly spring again is here, Trees and fields in bloom appear;
2 Where in winter all was snow, Now the flowers in clusters grow;
3 Lord, afford a spring to me, Let me feel like what I see;
4 On Thy garden design to smile, Raise the plants, enrich the soil;

TIMES AND SEASONS: THE SEASONS

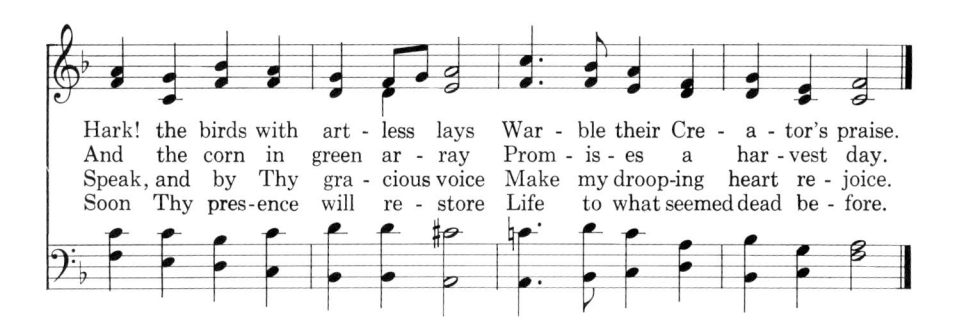

Hark! the birds with art - less lays War - ble their Cre - a - tor's praise.
And the corn in green ar - ray Prom - is - es a har - vest day.
Speak, and by Thy gra - cious voice Make my droop-ing heart re - joice.
Soon Thy pres-ence will re - store Life to what seemed dead be - fore.

WITH SONGS AND HONORS 515
BROMSGROVE C.M.

Based on Psalm 147
Isaac Watts, 1719

Psalmodia Evangelica, 1789

1. With songs and hon - ors sound-ing loud, Ad - dress the Lord on high; O - ver the heav'ns He spreads His cloud, And wa - ters veil the sky, And wa - ters veil the sky.
2. He sends His showers of bless-ing down To cheer the plains be - low; He makes the grass the moun - tains crown, And corn in val - leys grow, And corn in val - leys grow.
3. His hoar - y frost, His fleec - y snow, De - scend and clothe the ground; The liq - uid streams for - bear to flow, In i - cy fet - ters bound, In i - cy fet - ters bound.
4. He sends His word, and melts the snow; The fields no lon - ger mourn; He calls the warm - er gales to blow, And bids the spring re - turn, And bids the spring re - turn.
5. The chang-ing wind, the fly - ing cloud, O - bey His might-y word: With songs and hon - ors sound - ing loud Praise ye the sov - 'reign Lord, Praise ye the sov - 'reign Lord.

TIMES AND SEASONS: THE SEASONS

516 SUMMER SUNS ARE GLOWING
RUTH 6.5.6.5.D.

William Walsham How, 1871 — Samuel Smith, 1865

1. Sum-mer suns are glow-ing O-ver land and sea,
   Hap-py light is flow-ing Boun-ti-ful and free;
   Ev-ery-thing re-joic-es In the mel-low rays:
   All earth's thou-sand voic-es Swell the psalm of praise.

2. God's free mer-cy stream-eth O-ver all the world,
   And His ban-ner gleam-eth Ev-ery-where un-furled:
   Broad and deep and glo-rious, As the heav'n a-bove,
   Shines in might vic-to-rious His e-ter-nal love.

3. Lord, up-on our blind-ness Thy pure ra-diance pour;
   For Thy lov-ing-kind-ness Make us love Thee more;
   And when clouds are drift-ing, Dark a-cross our sky,
   Then, the veil up-lift-ing, Fa-ther, be Thou nigh.

4. We will nev-er doubt Thee Though Thou veil Thy light;
   Life is dark with-out Thee; Death with Thee is bright.
   Light of light! shine o'er us On our pil-grim way,
   Go Thou still be-fore us To the end-less day. A-men.

TIMES AND SEASONS: THE SEASONS

THE YEAR IS SWIFTLY WANING 517
WAS KANN ES SCHÖN'RES GEBEN 7.6.7.6.

William Walsham How, 1871

German Folk Melody
Gesangbuch mit Noten, Berne, Indiana, 1890

1. The year is swift-ly wan-ing, The sum-mer days are past;
And life, brief life, is speed-ing; The end is near-ing fast.
2. The ev-er-chang-ing sea-sons In si-lence come and go,
But Thou, e-ter-nal Fa-ther, No time or change canst know.
3. O pour Thy grace up-on us, That we may wor-thier be,
Each year that pass-es o'er us, To dwell in heav'n with Thee.
4. O by each mer-cy sent us, And by each grief and pain,
By bless-ings like the sun-shine, And sor-rows like the rain,
5. Our bar-ren hearts make fruit-ful With ev-ery good-ly grace,
That we Thy name may hal-low, And see at last Thy face. A-men.

TIMES AND SEASONS: THE SEASONS:

PRAISE, O PRAISE OUR GOD AND KING 518
MONKLAND 7.7.7.7.

Henry Williams Baker, 1861

John Bernard Wilkes, 1861

1. Praise, O praise our God and King! Hymns of ad-o-ra-tion sing;
2. Praise Him that He made the sun Day by day his course to run;
3. Praise Him that He gave the rain To ma-ture the swell-ing grain;
4. And hath bid the fruit-ful field Crops of pre-cious in-crease yield;
5. Glo-ry to our boun-teous King! Glo-ry let cre-a-tion sing!

For His mer-cies still en-dure Ev-er faith-ful, ev-er sure.
For His mer-cies still en-dure Ev-er faith-ful, ev-er sure.
For His mer-cies still en-dure Ev-er faith-ful, ev-er sure.
For His mer-cies still en-dure Ev-er faith-ful, ev-er sure.
Glo-ry to the Fa-ther, Son, And blest Spir-it, three in One. A-men.

TIMES AND SEASONS: HARVEST AND THANKSGIVING

519 COME, YE THANKFUL PEOPLE, COME
ST. GEORGE'S WINDSOR 7.7.7.7.D.

Henry Alford, 1844
Altered in *Hymns Ancient and Modern*, 1861

George Job Elvey, 1858

1. Come, ye thankful people, come, Raise the song of harvest-home:
All is safely gathered in, Ere the winter storms begin;
God, our Maker, doth provide For our wants to be supplied:
Come to God's own temple, come, Raise the song of harvest-home.

2. All the world is God's own field, Fruit unto His praise to yield;
Wheat and tares together sown, Unto joy or sorrow grown;
First the blade, and then the ear, Then the full corn shall appear:
Lord of harvest, grant that we Wholesome grain and pure may be.

3. For the Lord our God shall come, And shall take His harvest home;
From His field shall in that day All offenses purge away;
Give His angels charge at last In the fire the tares to cast,
But the fruitful ears to store In His garner evermore.

4. Even so, Lord, quickly come To Thy final harvest home;
Gather Thou Thy people in, Free from sorrow, free from sin;
There forever purified, In Thy presence to abide:
Come, with all Thine angels, come, Raise the glorious harvest-home. A-men.

TIMES AND SEASONS: HARVEST AND THANKSGIVING

SING TO THE LORD OF HARVEST 520
WIE LIEBLICH IST DER MAIEN 7.6.7.6.D.

John Samuel Bewley Monsell, 1866

German Folk Melody, 1581
Setting by Healey Willan, 1959

1. Sing to the Lord of harvest, Sing songs of love and praise;
With joyful hearts and voices Your alleluias raise!
By Him the rolling seasons In fruitful order move;
Sing to the Lord of harvest A song of happy love.

2. By Him the clouds drop fatness, The deserts bloom and spring,
The hills leap up in gladness, The valleys laugh and sing.
He filleth with His fullness All things with large increase;
He crowns the year with goodness, With plenty, and with peace.

3. Heap on His sacred altar The gifts His goodness gave,
The golden sheaves of harvest, The souls He died to save.
Your hearts lay down before Him When at His feet ye fall,
And with your lives adore Him Who gave His life for all.

4. To God the gracious Father, Who made us "very good,"
To Christ, who, when we wandered, Restored us with His blood,
And to the Holy Spirit, Who doth upon us pour
His blessed dews and sunshine, Be praise for evermore. A-men.

TIMES AND SEASONS: HARVEST AND THANKSGIVING

521 WE PLOW THE FIELDS, AND SCATTER

WIR PFLÜGEN 7.6.7.6.D. with Refrain

Matthias Claudius, 1782
Wir pflügen und wir streuen
Tr. Jane Montgomery Campbell, 1861

Lieder für Volksschulen mit Musik, Hannover, 1800

1. We plow the fields, and scatter The good seed on the land,
But it is fed and watered By God's almighty hand;
He sends the snow in winter, The warmth to swell the grain,
The breezes and the sunshine, And soft refreshing rain.

2. He only is the Maker Of all things near and far;
He paints the wayside flower, He lights the evening star;
The winds and waves obey Him, By Him the birds are fed;
Much more to us, His children, He gives our daily bread.

3. We thank Thee, then, O Father, For all things bright and good,
The seed-time and the harvest, Our life, our health, our food;
No gifts have we to offer, For all Thy love imparts,
But that which Thou desirest, Our humble, thankful hearts.

Refrain
All good gifts around us Are sent from heav'n above;

TIMES AND SEASONS: HARVEST AND THANKSGIVING

Then thank the Lord, O thank the Lord For all His love.

THE GOD OF HARVEST PRAISE 522

PERKINS 6.6.4.6.6.6.6.4.

James Montgomery†, 1840
Edward A. Perkins, mid 19th century

1 The God of har - vest praise; In loud thanks - giv - ing raise
2 Yes, bless His ho - ly name, And pur - est thanks pro-claim
3 The God of har - vest praise; Hands, hearts, and voic - es raise

Hand, heart and voice; The val - leys smile and sing, For - ests and
Through all the earth; To glo - ry in your lot Is come - ly,
With one ac - cord; From field to gar - ner throng, Bear - ing your

moun-tains ring; The plains their trib - ute bring; The streams re - joice.
but be not God's ben - e - fits for-got, A - midst your mirth.
sheaves a-long, And, in your har - vest song, Bless ye the Lord. A-men.

TIMES AND SEASONS: HARVEST AND THANKSGIVING

523 O LORD OF HEAVEN AND EARTH

ES IST KEIN TAG 8.8.8.4.

Christopher Wordsworth‡, 1863   J. D. Meyer's *Geistliche Seelenfreud*, 1692

1. O Lord of heav'n and earth and sea, To Thee all praise and glory be; How shall we show our love to Thee, Who givest all?

2. The golden sunshine, vernal air, Sweet flowers and fruit Thy love declare; When harvests ripen, Thou art there, Who givest all.

3. For peaceful homes and healthful days, For all the blessings earth displays, We owe Thee thankfulness and praise, Who givest all.

4. Thou didst not spare Thine only Son, But gav'st Him for a world undone, And freely with that blessed One, Thou givest all. Amen.

5. Thou giv'st the Spirit's blessed dower,
   Spirit of life and love and power,
   And dost His sevenfold graces shower
       Upon us all.

6. For souls redeemed, for sins forgiven,
   For means of grace and hopes of heaven,
   Father, all praise to Thee be given,
       Who givest all. Amen.

TIMES AND SEASONS: HARVEST AND THANKSGIVING

PRAISE TO GOD, IMMORTAL PRAISE 524

PRAYER 7.7.7.7.

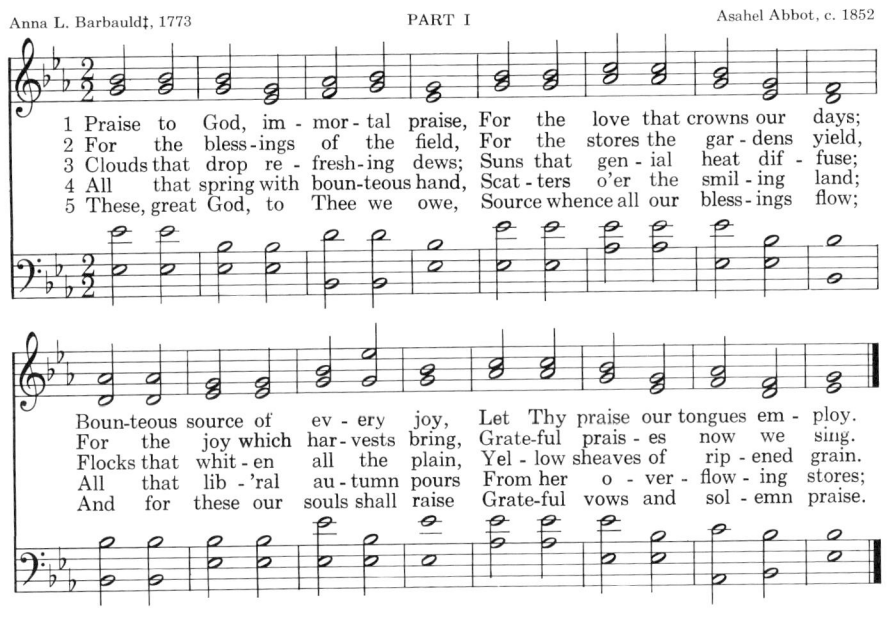

Anna L. Barbauld‡, 1773   PART I   Asahel Abbot, c. 1852

1. Praise to God, immortal praise, For the love that crowns our days; Bounteous source of every joy, Let Thy praise our tongues employ.
2. For the blessings of the field, For the stores the gardens yield, For the joy which harvests bring, Grateful praises now we sing.
3. Clouds that drop refreshing dews; Suns that genial heat diffuse; Flocks that whiten all the plain, Yellow sheaves of ripened grain.
4. All that spring with bounteous hand, Scatters o'er the smiling land; All that lib'ral autumn pours From her o'erflowing stores;
5. These, great God, to Thee we owe, Source whence all our blessings flow; And for these our souls shall raise Grateful vows and solemn praise.

LORD, SHOULD RISING WHIRLWINDS 525

ORIENTIS PARTIBUS 7.7.7.7

Anna L. Barbauld†, 1773   PART II   13th century French Melody
Harmony by Richard Redhead, 1853

6. Lord, should rising whirlwinds tear From its stem the ripening ear; Should the fig-tree's blasted shoot Drop her green untimely fruit;
7. Should the vine put forth no more, Nor the olive yield her store; Though the sick'ning flocks should fall, And the herds desert the stall;
8. Should Thine altered hand restrain Th' early and the latter rain, Blast each op'ning bud of joy, And the rising year destroy;
9. Yet to Thee my soul should raise Grateful vows and solemn praise; And, when ev'ry blessing's flown, Love Thee for Thyself alone!

TIMES AND SEASONS: HARVEST AND THANKSGIVING

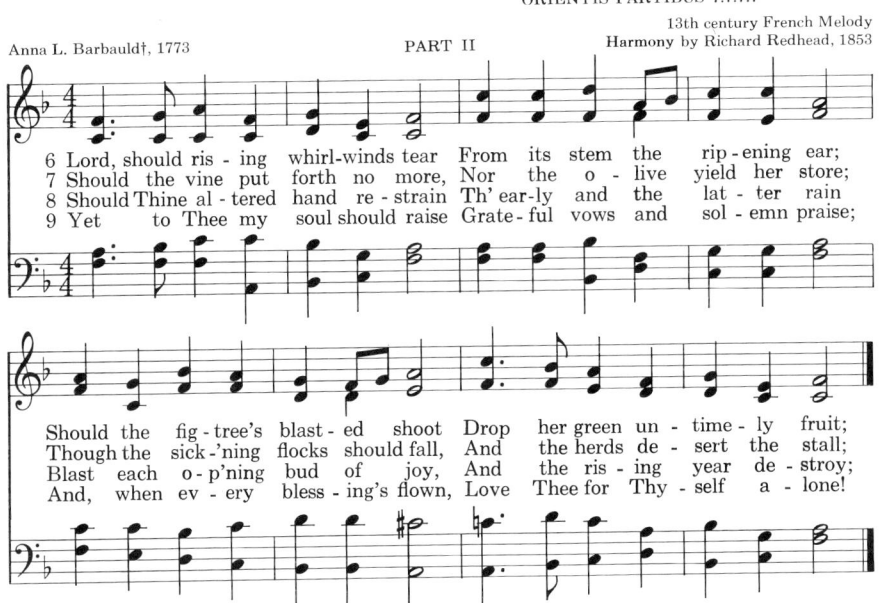

526 WE THANK THEE, LORD
SONG XXXIV L.M.

George Edward Lynch Cotton, 1856
Orlando Gibbons, 1623

1. We thank Thee, Lord, for this fair earth, The glittering sky, the silver sea; For all their beauty, all their worth, Their light and glory, come from Thee.

2. Thine are the flowers that clothe the ground, The trees that wave their arms above, The hills that gird our dwellings round As Thou dost gird Thine own with love.

3. Yet teach us still how far more fair, More glorious, Father, in Thy sight, Is one pure deed, one holy prayer, One heart that owns Thy Spirit's might.

4. So, while we gaze with thoughtful eye On all the gifts Thy love has giv'n, Help us in Thee to live and die, By Thee to rise from earth to heav'n.

TIMES AND SEASONS: HARVEST AND THANKSGIVING

WE PRAISE THEE, O GOD 527

REVIVE US AGAIN 11.11. with Refrain

William Paton Mackay, 1863 and 1867

"English Melody" in Bliss and Sankey's *Gospel Hymns* ..., 1875

1. We praise Thee, O God, for the Son of Thy love,
For Jesus who died, and is now gone above.
2. We praise Thee, O God, for Thy Spirit of light,
Who has shown us our Savior and scattered our night.
3. All glory and praise to the Lamb that was slain,
Who has borne all our sins, and doth cleanse every stain.
4. We praise Thee, O God, for the joy Thou hast giv'n
To Thy saints in communion these foretastes of heav'n.
5. Revive us again, fill each heart with Thy love;
May each soul be rekindled with fire from above.

REFRAIN

Hallelujah! Thine the glory, Hallelujah! Amen!
Hallelujah! Thine the glory, Revive us again.

GOSPEL SONGS

528 COME, LET US ALL UNITE

GOD IS LOVE 8.3.8.3.8.8.8.4. with Refrain

Ascribed to Howard Kingsbury

Edmund S. Lorenz, 1886

1. Come, let us all unite to sing, God is love; Let heav'n and earth their praises bring, God is love; Let every soul from sin awake, Each in his heart sweet music make, And sing with us for Jesus' sake, For God is love.

2. O tell to earth's remotest bound, God is love; In Christ we have redemption found, God is love; His blood has washed our sins away, His Spirit turned our night to day, And now we can rejoice to say, That God is love.

3. How happy is our portion here, God is love; His promises our spirits cheer, God is love; He is our sun and shield by day, Our help, our hope, our strength and stay, He will be with us all the way, Our God is love.

Refrain
God is love! God is love! Come, let us all unite to sing That God is love.

GOSPEL SONGS

COME, WE THAT LOVE THE LORD 529
WE'RE MARCHING TO ZION S.M. with Refrain

Isaac Watts†, 1707
Refrain added by Robert Lowry

Robert Lowry, 1867

1. Come, we that love the Lord, And let our joys be known; Join in a song with sweet ac-cord, Join in a song with sweet ac-cord, And thus sur-round the throne, And thus sur-round the throne.
2. Let those re-fuse to sing Who nev-er knew our God; But chil-dren of the heav'n-ly King, But chil-dren of the heav'n-ly King May speak their joys a-broad, May speak their joys a-broad,
3. The hill of Zi-on yields A thou-sand sa-cred sweets, Be-fore we reach the heav'n-ly fields, Be-fore we reach the heav'n-ly fields, Or walk the gold-en streets, Or walk the gold-en streets.
4. Then let our songs a-bound, And ev-ery tear be dry; We're march-ing through Im-man-uel's ground, We're march-ing through Im-man-uel's ground, To fair-er worlds on high, To fair-er worlds on high.

REFRAIN

We're march-ing to Zi-on, Beau-ti-ful, beau-ti-ful Zi-on; We're march-ing up-ward to Zi-on, The beau-ti-ful cit-y of God.

We're march-ing on to Zi-on, Zi-on, Zi-on,

GOSPEL SONGS

530 PRAISE HIM! PRAISE HIM!

ALLEN Irregular with Refrain

Fanny Crosby, 1869, and Others
Chester G. Allen, 1869

1. Praise Him! praise Him! Jesus, our blessed Redeemer! Sing, O earth, His wonderful love proclaim! Hail Him! hail Him! highest archangels in glory; Strength and honor give to His holy name! Like a shepherd, Jesus will guard His children, In His arms He carries them all day long:

2. Praise Him! praise Him! Jesus, our blessed Redeemer! For our sins He suffered, and bled, and died; He our Rock, our hope of eternal salvation, Hail Him! hail Him! Jesus the crucified. Sound His praises! Jesus who bore our sorrows, Love unbounded, wonderful, deep and strong:

3. Praise Him! praise Him! Jesus, our blessed Redeemer! Heav'nly portals, loud with hosannas ring! Jesus, Savior, reigneth forever and ever; Crown Him! crown Him! Prophet, and Priest, and King! Christ is coming, over the world victorious; Power and glory unto the Lord belong:

REFRAIN: Praise Him! praise Him! tell of His excellent greatness. Praise Him! praise Him! ever in joyful song.

GOSPEL SONGS

O MY SOUL, BLESS THOU JEHOVAH 531
CLOSE TO THEE 8.7.8.7. with Refrain

Based on Psalm 103
United Presbyterian Book of Psalms, 1871

Silas Jonas Vail, 1874

1. O my soul, bless thou Je-ho-vah, All with-in me bless His name;
   Bless Je-ho-vah, and for-get not All His mer-cies to pro-claim.
2. Who for-gives all thy trans-gres-sions, Thy dis-eas-es all who heals;
   Who re-deems thee from de-struc-tion, Who with thee so kind-ly deals;
3. Who with ten-der mer-cies crowns thee, Who with good things fills thy mouth,
   So that e-ven like the ea-gle Thou hast been re-stored to youth.
4. In His right-eous-ness, Je-ho-vah Will de-liv-er those dis-tressed;
   He will ex-e-cute just judg-ment In the cause of all op-pressed.
5. For as high as is the heav-en, Far a-bove the earth be-low,
   Ev-er great to them that fear Him Is the mer-cy He will show.

REFRAIN
Bless Je-ho-vah, all His crea-tures Ev-er un-der His con-trol,
All through-out His vast do-min-ion; Bless Je-ho-vah, O my soul.

GOSPEL SONGS

532 TO GOD BE THE GLORY

TO GOD BE THE GLORY 11.11.11.11. with Refrain

Fanny Crosby, 1875 — William Howard Doane, 1875

1. To God be the glory, great things He hath done, So loved He the world that He gave us His Son, Who yielded His life an atonement for sin, And opened the Life-gate that all may go in.
2. O perfect redemption, the purchase of blood, To every believer the promise of God; The vilest offender who truly believes, That moment from Jesus a pardon receives.
3. Great things He hath taught us, great things He hath done, And great our rejoicing through Jesus the Son; But purer, and higher, and greater will be Our wonder, our transport, when Jesus we see.

Refrain
Praise the Lord, praise the Lord, Let the earth hear His voice! Praise the Lord, praise the Lord, Let the people rejoice! O come to the Father, through Jesus the Son, And give Him the glory, great things He hath done.

GOSPEL SONGS

Je - sus the Son, And give Him the glo - ry, great things He hath done.

GOD OF OUR STRENGTH 533

GOD OF OUR STRENGTH L.M. with Refrain

Fanny Crosby, 1882
William Howard Doane, 1883

1 God of our strength, en-throned a-bove, The source of life, the fount of love;
2 To Thee we lift our joy - ful eyes, To Thee on wings of faith we rise,
3 God of our strength, from day to day Di - rect our thoughts and guide our way;
4 God of our strength, on Thee we call; God of our hope, our light, our all,

O let de - vo - tion's sa - cred flame Our souls a - wake to praise Thy name.
Come Thou, and let Thy courts on earth Ring out Thy praise in days of mirth.
O may our hearts u - nit - ed be In sweet com-mun - ion, Lord, with Thee.
Thy name we praise, Thy love a - dore, Our rock, our shield, for - ev - er - more.

REFRAIN

God of our strength, we wait on Thee, Our sure de - fense for - ev - er be.

GOSPEL SONGS

534 GREAT IS THY FAITHFULNESS

FAITHFULNESS 11.10.11.10. with Refrain

Thomas O. Chisholm, 1923
William M. Runyan, 1923

1. Great is Thy faith-ful-ness, O God my Fa-ther, There is no shad-ow of turn-ing with Thee; Thou chang-est not, Thy com-pas-sions, they fail not; As Thou hast been Thou for-ev-er wilt be.
2. Sum-mer and win-ter, and spring-time and har-vest, Sun, moon, and stars in their cours-es a-bove, Join with all na-ture in man-i-fold wit-ness To Thy great faith-ful-ness, mer-cy, and love.
3. Par-don for sin and a peace that en-dur-eth, Thy own dear pres-ence to cheer and to guide; Strength for to-day and bright hope for to-mor-row, Bless-ings all mine, with ten thou-sand be-side!

Refrain

Great is Thy faith-ful-ness! Great is Thy faith-ful-ness! Morn-ing by morn-ing new mer-cies I see; All I have need-ed Thy hand hath pro-vid-ed, Great is Thy faith-ful-ness! Lord un-to me!

GOSPEL SONGS © Copyright 1923, 1958. Assigned to Hope Publishing Co. See page 610, No. 534.

HOW GREAT THOU ART 535

O STORE GUD 11.10.11.10. with Refrain

Carl Boberg, 1859-1940
Tr. by Stuart K. Hine, b. 1899

Swedish Folk Melody
Arranged by Manna Music, Inc.

1. O Lord my God! When I in awe-some won-der Con-sid-er all the worlds thy hands have made, I see the stars, I hear the roll-ing thun-der, thy pow'r through-out the un-i-verse dis-played.

2. When through the woods and for-est glades I wan-der And hear the birds sing sweet-ly in the trees; When I look down from loft-y moun-tain gran-deur And hear the brook and feel the gen-tle breeze;

3. And when I think that God, his Son not spar-ing, Sent him to die, I scarce can take it in; That on the cross, my bur-den glad-ly bear-ing, He bled and died to take a-way my sin;

4. When Christ shall come with shout of ac-cla-ma-tion And take me home, what joy shall fill my heart! Then I shall bow in hum-ble ad-o-ra-tion And there pro-claim, my God, how great thou art!

REFRAIN

Then sings my soul, my Sav-ior God to thee; How great thou art, how great thou art! Then sings my soul, my Sav-ior God to thee; How great thou art, How great thou art!

© Copyright 1955 by Manna Music, Inc., Hollywood 28, California. International copyright secured. All rights reserved. Used by permission. *Translator's original words are "works" and "mighty."

GOSPEL SONGS

536 HOLY, HOLY, HOLY IS THE LORD

HOLY IS THE LORD 9.10.9.9.10.9. with Refrain

Fanny Crosby, 1869 William Batchelder Bradbury, 1869

1. Ho-ly, ho-ly, ho-ly is the Lord! Sing, O ye peo-ple, glad-ly a-dore Him; Let the moun-tains trem-ble at His Word, Let the hills be joy-ful be-fore Him; Might-y in wis-dom, bound-less in mer-cy, Great is Je-ho-vah, King o-ver all.

2. Praise Him, praise Him, shout a-loud for joy! Watch-man of Zi-on, her-ald the sto-ry; Sin and death, His king-dom shall de-stroy, All the earth shall sing of His glo-ry; Praise Him, ye an-gels, ye who be-hold Him Robed in His splen-dor, match-less, di-vine.

3. King e-ter-nal, bless-ed be His name! So may His chil-dren glad-ly a-dore Him; When in heav'n we join the hap-py strain, When we cast our bright crowns be-fore Him; There in His like-ness, joy-ful a-wak-ing, There we shall see Him, there we shall sing.

GOSPEL SONGS

REFRAIN

Ho - ly, ho - ly, ho - ly is the Lord, Let the hills be joy - ful be - fore Him.

'TIS THE PROMISE OF GOD 537
HALLELUJAH, 'TIS DONE 12.12. with Refrain

Philip Paul Bliss, 1874

1. 'Tis the prom-ise of God, full sal - va - tion to give Un - to him who on Je - sus, His Son, will be - lieve.
2. Though the path-way be lone - ly, and dan - ger - ous too, Sure - ly Je - sus is a - ble to car - ry me through.
3. Man - y loved ones have I in yon heav - en - ly throng, They are safe now in glo - ry, and this is their song:
4. There's a part in that cho - rus for you and for me, And the theme of our prais - es for - ev - er will be:

REFRAIN

Hal - le - lu - jah, 'tis done! I be - lieve on the Son; I am saved by the blood of the cru - ci - fied One; cru - ci - fied One.

GOSPEL SONGS

538 THE LOVE OF GOD

LOVE OF GOD 8.8.8.8.8.8.6.8.6. with Refrain

F. M. Lehman, c. 1917
Arranged by Claudia Lehman Mays

F. M. Lehman, c. 1917

1. The love of God is greater far Than tongue or pen can ever tell;
2. When hoary time shall pass away, And earthly thrones and kingdoms fall;
3. Could we with ink the ocean fill And were the skies of parchment made;

It goes beyond the highest star, And reaches to the lowest hell.
When men who here refuse to pray, On rocks and hills and mountains call;
Were every stalk on earth a quill, And every man a scribe by trade;

The guilty pair, bowed down with care, God gave His Son to win;
God's love, so sure, shall still endure, All measureless and strong;
To write the love of God above Would drain the ocean dry;

His erring child He reconciled, And pardoned from his sin.
Redeeming grace to Adam's race The saints' and angels' song.
Nor could the scroll contain the whole, Though stretched from sky to sky.

REFRAIN

O love of God, how rich and pure! How measureless and strong!

GOSPEL SONGS

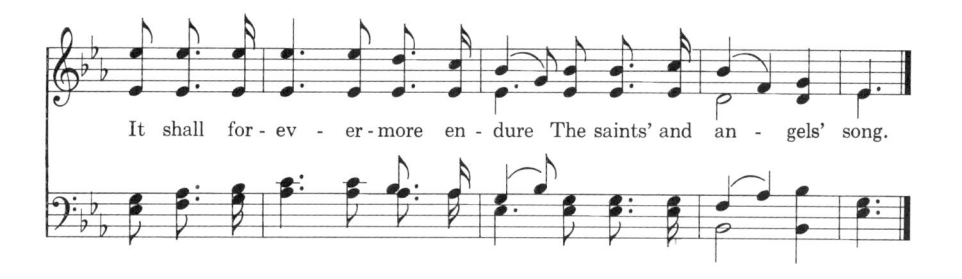

It shall for-ev-er-more en-dure The saints' and an-gels' song.

MORE LOVE TO THEE, O CHRIST 539

MORE LOVE TO THEE 6.4.6.4.6.6.4.4.

Elizabeth Payson Prentiss, 1856

William Howard Doane, 1870

1. More love to Thee, O Christ, More love to Thee! Hear Thou the prayer I make, On bend-ed knee; This is my ear-nest plea, More love, O Christ, to Thee, More love to Thee, More love to Thee!
2. Once earth-ly joy I craved, Sought peace and rest; Now Thee a-lone I seek, Give what is best: This all my prayer shall be, More love, O Christ, to Thee, More love to Thee, More love to Thee!
3. Let sor-row do its work, Send grief and pain; Sweet are Thy mes-sen-gers, Sweet their re-frain, When they can sing with me, More love, O Christ, to Thee, More love to Thee, More love to Thee!
4. Then shall my lat-est breath Whis-per Thy praise; This be the part-ing cry My heart shall raise, This still its prayer shall be, More love, O Christ, to Thee, More love to Thee, More love to Thee!

GOSPEL SONGS

540 I STAND AMAZED IN THE PRESENCE

HOW MARVELOUS 8.7.8.7. with Refrain

Charles H. Gabriel, 1905
Source of St. 4 unknown

Charles H. Gabriel, 1905

1. I stand a-mazed in the pres-ence Of Je-sus the Naz-a-rene,
And won-der how He could love me, A sin-ner con-demned, un-clean.

2. For me it was in the gar-den He prayed, "Not My will, but Thine;"
He had no tears for His own griefs, But sweat drops of blood for mine.

3. In pit-y an-gels be-held Him, And came from the world of light
To com-fort Him in the sor-row He bore for my soul that night.

4. He took my sins and my sor-rows, He made them His ver-y own;
He bore the bur-den to Cal-vary, And suf-fered and died a-lone.

5. When with the ran-somed in glo-ry His face I at last shall see,
'Twill be my joy through the a-ges To sing of His love for me.

REFRAIN

How mar-vel-ous! How won-der-ful!
O how mar-vel-ous! O how won-der-ful! And my song shall ev-er be:
How mar-vel-ous! How won-der-ful!
O how mar-vel-ous! O how won-der-ful Is my Sav-ior's love for me!

GOSPEL SONGS

MARVELOUS GRACE 541

MARVELOUS GRACE 9.9.9.9. with Refrain

Julia H. Johnson, c. 1910   Daniel Brink Towner, 1910

1. Mar-vel-ous grace of our lov-ing Lord, Grace that ex-ceeds our sin and our guilt, Yon-der on Cal-va-ry's mount out-poured, There where the blood of the Lamb was spilt.
2. Sin and de-spair like the sea waves cold, Threat-en the soul with in-fi-nite loss; Grace that is great-er, yes, grace un-told, Points to the re-fuge, the might-y cross.
3. Dark is the stain that we can-not hide, What can a-vail to wash it a-way? Look! there is flow-ing a crim-son tide; Whit-er than snow you may be to-day.
4. Mar-vel-ous, in-fi-nite, match-less grace, Free-ly be-stowed on all who be-lieve; You that are long-ing to see His face, Will you this mo-ment His grace re-ceive?

Refrain

Grace, grace, Mar-vel-ous grace, God's grace, Grace that will par-don and cleanse with-in; Grace, grace, Mar-vel-ous grace, in-fi-nite grace, God's grace, in-fi-nite grace, Grace that is great-er than all our sin.

© Copyright 1910, 1938. Assigned to Hope Publishing Co. See page 610, No. 541.   GOSPEL SONGS

542 I'VE FOUND A FRIEND

FRIEND 8.7.8.7.D.

James G. Small, 1863 — George C. Stebbins, 1878

1. I've found a Friend, O such a Friend! He loved me ere I knew Him;
He drew me with the cords of love, And thus He bound me to Him.
And 'round my heart still close-ly twine Those ties which naught can sev-er,
For I am His, and He is mine, For-ev-er and for-ev-er.

2. I've found a Friend, O such a Friend! He bled, He died to save me;
And not a-lone the gift of life, But His own self He gave me.
Naught that I have my own I call, I hold it for the giv-er;
My heart, my strength, my life, my all Are His, and His for-ev-er.

3. I've found a Friend, O such a Friend! So kind, and true, and tender,
So wise a coun-se-lor and guide, So might-y a de-fend-er!
From Him who loves me now so well, What power my soul can sev-er?
Shall life or death, shall earth or hell? No! I am His for-ev-er.

GOSPEL SONGS

HE LEADETH ME, O BLESSED THOUGHT 543

HE LEADETH ME L.M. with Refrain

Joseph H. Gilmore†, 1862
William Batchelder Bradbury, 1864

1. He lead-eth me, O bless-ed thought! O words with heav'n-ly com-fort fraught!
What-e'er I do, wher-e'er I be, Still 'tis God's hand that lead-eth me.

2. Some-times 'mid scenes of deep-est gloom, Some-times where E-den's bow-ers bloom,
By wa-ters calm, o'er trou-bled sea, Still 'tis His hand that lead-eth me.

3. Lord, I would clasp Thy hand in mine, Nor ev-er mur-mur nor re-pine;
Con-tent, what-ev-er lot I see, Since 'tis my God that lead-eth me.

4. And when my task on earth is done, When by Thy grace, the vic-t'ry's won,
E'en death's cold wave I will not flee, Since God through Jor-dan lead-eth me.

Refrain
He lead-eth me, He lead-eth me; By His own hand He lead-eth me:
His faith-ful fol-lower I would be, For by His hand He lead-eth me.

GOSPEL SONGS

544 BLESSED ASSURANCE

BLESSED ASSURANCE 9.10.9.9. with Refrain

Fanny Crosby, 1873
Mrs. Joseph F. Knapp, 1873

1. Bless-ed as-sur-ance, Je-sus is mine! O what a fore-taste of glo-ry di-vine! Heir of sal-va-tion, pur-chased of God, Born of His Spir-it, washed in His blood;
2. Per-fect sub-mis-sion, per-fect de-light, Vi-sions of rap-ture burst on my sight; An-gels de-scend-ing bring from a-bove Ech-oes of mer-cy, whis-pers of love.
3. Per-fect sub-mis-sion, all is at rest, I in my Sav-ior am hap-py and blest; Watch-ing and wait-ing, look-ing a-bove, Filled with His good-ness, lost in His love.

REFRAIN

This is my sto-ry, this is my song, Prais-ing my Sav-ior all the day long; This is my sto-ry, this is my song, Prais-ing my Sav-ior all the day long.

GOSPEL SONGS

BLESSED SAVIOR, WE ADORE THEE 545

GLORIOUS NAME 8.7.8.7. with Refrain

Benjamin Baylus McKinney, 1942 Benjamin Baylus McKinney, 1942

1. Bless-ed Sav-ior, we a-dore Thee, We Thy love and grace pro-claim;
2. Great Re-deem-er, Lord and Mas-ter, Light of all e-ter-nal days;
3. From the throne of heav-en's glo-ry To the cross of sin and shame,
4. Come, O come, im-mor-tal Sav-ior, Come and take Thy roy-al throne;

Thou art might-y, Thou art ho-ly, Glo-rious is Thy match-less name!
Let the saints of ev-ery na-tion Sing Thy just and end-less praise!
Thou didst come to die a ran-som, Guilt-y sin-ners to re-claim!
Come, and reign, and reign for-ev-er, Be the king-dom all Thine own!

Refrain

Glo - - - rious, Glo - - - rious,
Glo-rious is Thy name, O Lord! Glo-rious is Thy name, O Lord!
Glo-rious is Thy name, O Lord! Glo - - - rious,
Glo-rious is Thy name, O Lord!
Glo - - - ri-ous, Glo-rious is Thy name, O Lord!
Glo-rious is Thy name, O Lord!

GOSPEL SONGS

546 A WONDERFUL SAVIOR IS JESUS

KIRKPATRICK 11.8.11.8. Refrain

Fanny Crosby, 1890   William J. Kirkpatrick, 1890

1. A wonderful Savior is Jesus my Lord, A wonderful Savior to me; He hideth my soul in the cleft of the rock, Where rivers of pleasure I see.
2. A wonderful Savior is Jesus my Lord, He taketh my burden away; He holdeth me up, and I shall not be moved, He giveth me strength as my day.
3. With numberless blessings each moment He crowns, And filled with His fullness divine, I sing in my rapture, O glory to God For such a Redeemer as mine!
4. When clothed in His brightness, transported I rise To meet Him in clouds of the sky, His perfect salvation, His wonderful love I'll shout with the millions on high.

Refrain
He hideth my soul in the cleft of the rock That shadows a dry, thirsty land; He hideth my life in the depths of His love, And covers me there with His hand, And covers me there with His hand.

GOSPEL SONGS

IN LOVING KINDNESS JESUS CAME 547
HE LIFTED ME 8.8.8.6. with Refrain

Charles H. Gabriel, 1905   Charles H. Gabriel, 1905

1 In loving kindness Jesus came My soul in mercy to reclaim,
And from the depths of sin and shame Through grace He lifted me.

2 He called me long before I heard, Before my sinful heart was stirred,
But when I took Him at His word, Forgiv'n, He lifted me.

3 His brow was pierced with many a thorn, His hands by cruel nails were torn,
When from my guilt and grief, forlorn, In love He lifted me.

4 Now on a higher plane I dwell, And with my soul I know 'tis well;
Yet how or why I cannot tell He should have lifted me.

REFRAIN
From sinking sand He lifted me, With tender hand He lifted me,
From shades of night to plains of light, O praise His name, He lifted me!

GOSPEL SONGS

548 COME WITH THY SINS

COME TO THE FOUNTAIN 8.7.8.7. with Refrain

Fanny Crosby, 1883
George C. Stebbins, 1883

1. Come with thy sins to the Fountain, Come with thy burden of grief;
Bury them deep in its waters, There thou wilt find a relief.

2. Come as thou art to the Fountain, Jesus is waiting for thee;
What though thy sins be like crimson, White as the snow they shall be.

3. These are the words of the Savior; They who repent and believe,
They who are willing to trust Him, Life at His hand shall receive.

4. Come and be healed at the Fountain, List to the peace-speaking voice;
Over a sinner returning Now let the angels rejoice.

Refrain:
Haste thee away, why wilt thou stay? Risk not thy soul on a moment's delay;
Jesus is waiting to save thee, Mercy is pleading today.

GOSPEL SONGS

I HEAR THY WELCOME VOICE 549

WELCOME VOICE S.M. with Refrain

Lewis Hartsough, 1872 Lewis Hartsough, 1872

1. I hear Thy welcome voice, That calls me, Lord, to Thee, For cleansing in Thy precious blood That flowed on Calvary.
2. Though coming weak and vile, Thou dost my strength assure; Thou dost my vileness fully cleanse, Till spotless all and pure.
3. 'Tis Jesus calls me on To perfect faith and love, To perfect hope, and peace, and trust, For earth and heav'n above.

Refrain
I am coming, Lord! Coming now to Thee! Wash me, cleanse me in the blood That flowed on Calvary.

GOSPEL SONGS

550 SINNERS JESUS WILL RECEIVE

NEUMEISTER 7.7.7.7. with Refrain

Erdmann Neumeister, 1718
Jesus nimmt die Sünder an!
Tr. Emma F. Bevan, 1858
Arranged by James McGranahan

James McGranahan, 1883

1. Sinners Jesus will receive: Sound this word of grace to all
Who the heav'nly pathway leave, All who linger, all who fall.
2. Come, and He will give you rest; Trust Him, for His word is plain;
He will take the sinfulest; Christ receiveth sinful men.
3. Now my heart condemns me not, Pure before the law I stand;
He who cleansed me from all spot. Satisfied His last demand.
4. Christ receiveth sinful men, Even me with all my sin;
Purged from every spot and stain, Heav'n with Him I enter in.

REFRAIN

Sing it o'er and o'er again: Christ receiveth sinful men;
Sing it o'er again, Sing it o'er again: Christ receiveth sinful men, Christ receiveth sinful men;
Make the message clear and plain: Christ receiveth sinful men.
Make the message plain, Make the message plain:

GOSPEL SONGS

I WILL SING THE WONDROUS STORY 551

WONDROUS STORY 8.7.8.7. with Refrain

Francis H. Rowley, 1886
Altered by Ira D. Sankey, 1887

Peter P. Bilhorn, 1886

1. I will sing the wondrous story Of the Christ who died for me,
2. I was lost, but Jesus found me, Found the sheep that went astray,
3. I was bruised, but Jesus healed me; Faint was I from many a fall;
4. Days of darkness still come o'er me, Sorrow's paths I often tread,
5. He will keep me till the river Rolls its waters at my feet;

How He left His home in glory For the cross of Calvary.
Threw His loving arms around me, Drew me back into His way.
Sight was gone, and fears possessed me, But He freed me from them all.
But the Savior still is with me; By His hand I'm safely led.
Then He'll bear me safely o-ver, Where the loved ones I shall meet.

REFRAIN

Yes, I'll sing the wondrous story Of the
Yes, I'll sing the wondrous story

Christ who died for me, Sing it with the saints in
Of the Christ who died for me, Sing it with

glory, Gathered by the crystal sea.
the saints in glory, Gathered by the crystal sea.

GOSPEL SONGS

552 THERE WERE NINETY AND NINE

NINETY AND NINE Irregular

Elizabeth C. Clephane, 1868 · Ira D. Sankey, 1874

1. There were ninety and nine that safely lay In the shelter of the fold, But one was out on the hills away, Far off from the gates of gold, A-way on the mountains wild and bare, A-way from the tender

2. "Lord, Thou hast here Thy ninety and nine; Are they not enough for Thee?" But the Shepherd made answer: "This of Mine Has wandered away from Me; And although the road be rough and steep I go to the desert to

3. But none of the ransomed ever knew How deep were the waters crossed; Nor how dark was the night that the Lord passed through Ere He found His sheep that was lost. Out in the desert He heard its cry, Sick and so helpless and

4. "Lord, whence are those blood-drops all the way That mark out the mountain's track?" "They were shed for one who had gone astray Ere the Shepherd could bring him back." "Lord, whence are Thy hands so rent and torn?" "They are pierced tonight by

5. But all through the mountains, thunder-riv'n, And up from the rocky steep, There arose a glad cry to the gate of heav'n, "Rejoice! I have found My sheep!" And the angels echoed around the throne, "Rejoice, for the Lord brings

GOSPEL SONGS

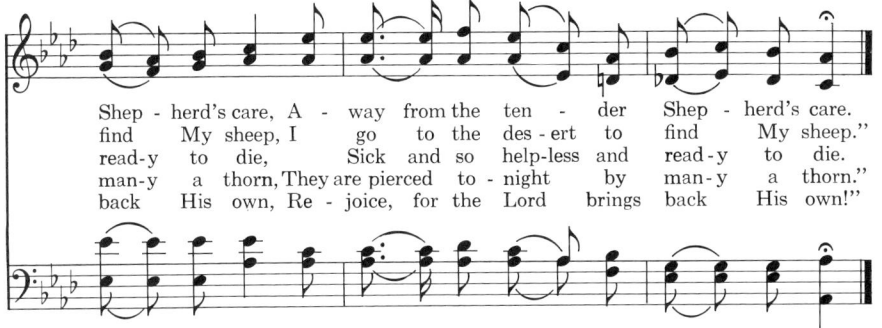

Shep - herd's care, A - way from the ten - der Shep - herd's care.
find My sheep, I go to the des - ert to find My sheep."
read-y to die, Sick and so help-less and read-y to die.
man-y a thorn, They are pierced to - night by man-y a thorn."
back His own, Re - joice, for the Lord brings back His own!"

COME, EVERY SOUL BY SIN OPPRESSED 553

STOCKTON C.M. with Refrain

John Hart Stockton, 1874 — John Hart Stockton, 1874

1 Come, ev - ery soul by sin op-pressed, There's mer-cy with the Lord, And He will
2 For Je - sus shed His pre-cious blood Rich bless-ings to be - stow; Come now un-
3 Yes, Je - sus is the truth, the way, That leads you in - to rest; Be - lieve in
4 Come then, and join this ho - ly band, And on to glo - ry go, To dwell in

Refrain

sure - ly give you rest, By trust-ing in His Word.
to that fount which flowed That wash-es white as snow.
Him with - out de - lay, And you are ful - ly blest.
that ce - les - tial land, Where joys im-mor-tal flow.

Come to Je - sus, Come to Je - sus, Come to Je - sus now; He will save you, He will save you, He will save you now.

GOSPEL SONGS

554 I WILL SING OF MY REDEEMER

MY REDEEMER 8.7.8.7. with Refrain

Philip Paul Bliss, 1876 — James McGranahan, 1877

1. I will sing of my Redeemer, And His wondrous love to me;
On the cruel cross He suffered From the curse to set me free.

2. I will tell the wondrous story, How my lost estate to save,
In His boundless love and mercy, He the ransom freely gave.

3. I will praise my dear Redeemer, His triumphant power I'll tell,
How the victory He giveth Over sin and death and hell.

4. I will sing of my Redeemer, And His heav'nly love to me;
He from death to life hath brought me, Son of God, with Him to be.

Refrain:
Sing, O sing of my Redeemer, With His blood He purchased me;
On the cross He sealed my pardon, Paid the debt and made me free.

GOSPEL SONGS

WOULD YOU BE FREE 555

THERE IS POWER IN THE BLOOD 10.9.10.8. with Refrain

Lewis E. Jones, c. 1899
Lewis E. Jones, 1899

1. Would you be free from your bur-den of sin? There's power in the blood, power in the blood; Would you o'er e-vil a vic-to-ry win? There's wonderful power in the blood.
2. Would you be free from your pas-sion and pride? There's power in the blood, power in the blood; Come for a cleans-ing to Cal-va-ry's tide: There's wonderful power in the blood.
3. Would you be whit-er, much whit-er than snow? There's power in the blood, power in the blood; Sin-stains are lost in its life-giv-ing flow; There's wonderful power in the blood.
4. Would you do ser-vice for Je-sus your King? There's power in the blood, power in the blood; Would you live dai-ly His prais-es to sing? There's wonderful power in the blood.

Refrain

There is power, power, Won-der-work-ing power In the blood of the Lamb; There is power, power, Won-der-work-ing power In the pre-cious blood of the Lamb.

GOSPEL SONGS

556 O HAVE YOU NOT HEARD

THE BEAUTIFUL RIVER 11.7.11.7. with Refrain

R. Torry, Jr.†, c. 1862
Asa Hull, c. 1862

1. O have you not heard of that beau-ti-ful stream That flows through our Fa-ther's land? Its wa-ters gleam bright in the heav-en-ly light, And rip-ple o'er gold-en sand.
2. Its foun-tains are deep and its wa-ters are pure; And sweet to the wea-ry soul; It flows from the throne of Je-ho-vah a-lone! O come where its bright waves roll.
3. This beau-ti-ful stream is the riv-er of life! It flows for all na-tions free! A balm for each wound in its wa-ter is found; O sin-ner, it flows for thee!
4. O will you not drink of this beau-ti-ful stream, And dwell on its peace-ful shore? The Spir-it says, Come, all ye wea-ry ones, home, And wan-der in sin no more.

REFRAIN

O seek that beau-ti-ful stream, O seek that beau-ti-ful stream; Its wa-ters, so free, are flow-ing for thee, O seek that beau-ti-ful stream.

GOSPEL SONGS

1 Ich weiss einen Strom, dessen herrliche Flut
  fliesst wunderbar stille durchs Land,
  doch strahlet und glänzt er wie feurige Glut,
  wem ist dieses Wässer bekannt?

2 Wohin dieser Strom sich nur immer ergiesst,
  da jubelt und jauchzet das Herz,
  das nunmehr den köstlichsten Segen geniesst,
  erlöset von Sorgen und Schmerz.

3 Der Strom ist gar tief und sein Wasser ist klar,
  es schmecket so lieblich und fein;
  es heilet die Kranken und stärkt wunderbar,
  ja machet die Unreinsten rein.

4 Wen dürstet, der komme und trinke sich satt,
  so rufet der Geist und die Braut,
  nur wer in dem Strome gewaschen sich hat,
  das Angesicht Gottes einst schaut.

REFRAIN: O Seele, ich bitte dich: Komm!
  Und such diesen herrlichen Strom!
  Sein Wasser fliesst frei und mächtiglich,
  o glaub's, es fliesset für dich!

THY LIFE WAS GIVEN FOR ME 557

SACRIFICE 6.6.6.6.6.6.

Frances Ridley Havergal, 1871

Philip Paul Bliss, 1874

1. Thy life was given for me; Thy blood, O Lord, was shed,
   That I might ran-somed be, And quick-ened from the dead:
   Thy life, Thy life was given for me; What have I given for Thee?

2. Long years were spent for me In wea-ri-ness and woe,
   That through e-ter-ni-ty Thy glo-ry I might know:
   Long years, long years were spent for me; Have I spent one for Thee?

3. And Thou hast brought to me, Down from Thy home a-bove,
   Sal-va-tion full and free, Thy par-don and Thy love:
   Great gifts, great gifts Thou brought-est me; What have I brought to Thee?

4. O let my life be given, My years for Thee be spent,
   World fet-ters all be riven, And joy with suf-fering blent!
   Thou gav'st, Thou gav'st Thy-self for me; I give my-self to Thee.

GOSPEL SONGS

558 MY HOPE IS BUILT ON NOTHING LESS

SOLID ROCK L.M. with Refrain

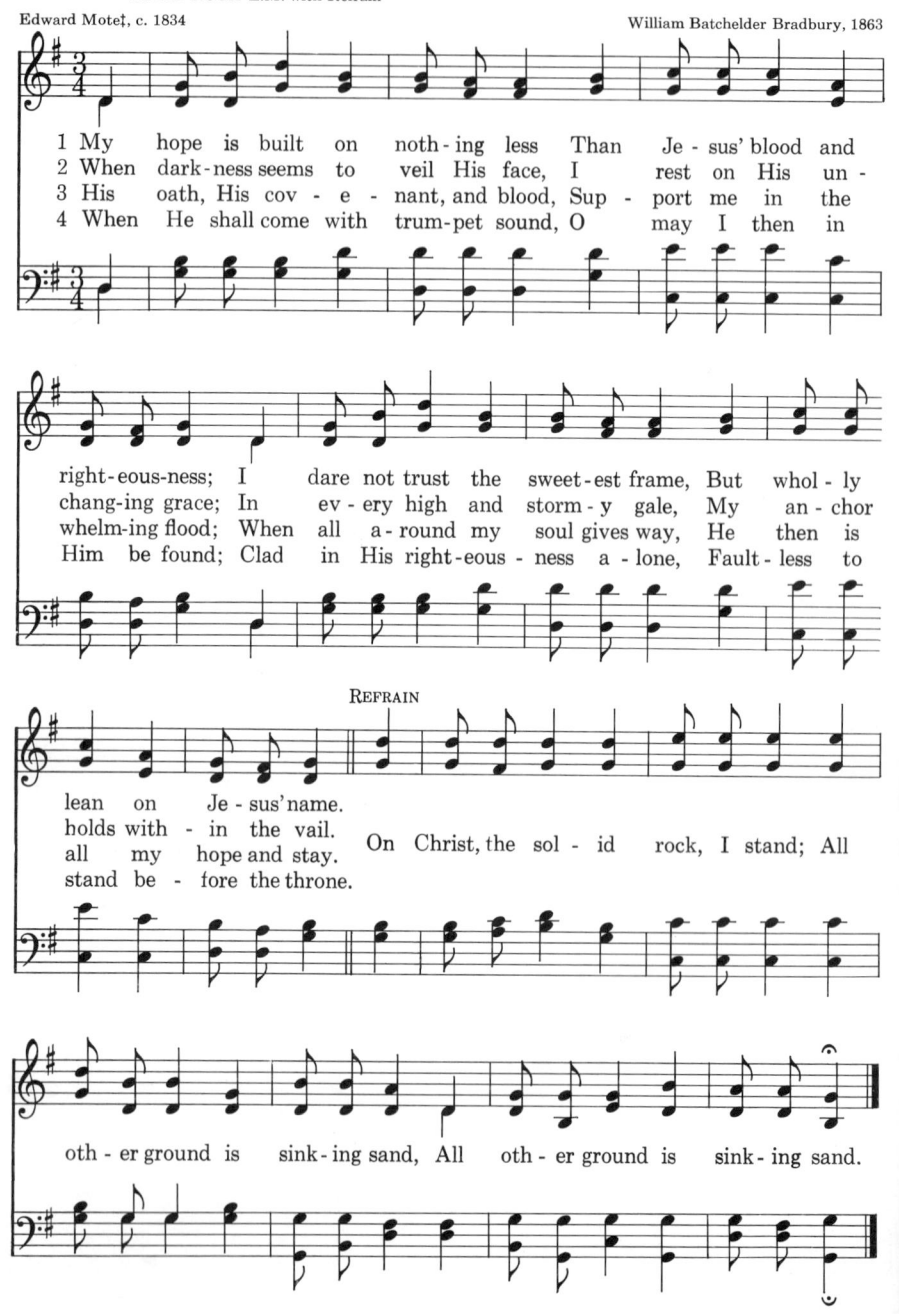

Edward Mote, c. 1834 — William Batchelder Bradbury, 1863

1. My hope is built on nothing less Than Jesus' blood and righteousness; I dare not trust the sweetest frame, But wholly lean on Jesus' name.
2. When darkness seems to veil His face, I rest on His unchanging grace; In every high and stormy gale, My anchor holds within the vail.
3. His oath, His covenant, and blood, Support me in the whelming flood; When all around my soul gives way, He then is all my hope and stay.
4. When He shall come with trumpet sound, O may I then in Him be found; Clad in His righteousness alone, Faultless to stand before the throne.

Refrain
On Christ, the solid rock, I stand; All other ground is sinking sand, All other ground is sinking sand.

GOSPEL SONGS

WONDERFUL SAVIOR, REDEEMER 559

WONDERFUL SAVIOR 8.5.8.5. with Refrain

Wellington K. Jacobs, 1902   Wellington K. Jacobs, 1902

1. Won-der-ful Sav-ior, Re-deem-er, Thou in ten-d'rest love
Watch-est o'er ev-ery be-liev-er, From Thy throne a-bove.

2. Thou hast in great-est com-pas-sion Died our souls to save:
Pur-chased for us our re-demp-tion, Hope be-yond the grave.

3. O-pen my heart e'er to hear Thee, Quick to hear Thy voice;
Fill Thou my soul with Thy prais-es, Let my heart re-joice.

REFRAIN

Won-der-ful Sav-ior! Mer-ci-ful Sav-ior!
Je-sus, won-der-ful Sav-ior! Je-sus, mer-ci-ful Sav-ior!
My hope and Re-deem-er, Who shed His blood for me. (for me.)

GOSPEL SONGS

560 JESUS, KEEP ME NEAR THE CROSS

NEAR THE CROSS 7.6.7.6. with Refrain

Fanny Crosby, 1869
William Howard Doane, 1869

1. Je-sus, keep me near the cross, There a pre-cious foun-tain, Free to all, a heal-ing stream, Flows from Cal-vary's moun-tain.
2. Near the cross, a trem-bling soul, Love and mer-cy found me; There the bright and morn-ing star Shed its beams a-round me.
3. Near the cross! O Lamb of God, Bring its scenes be-fore me; Help me walk from day to day, With its shad-ow o'er me.
4. Near the cross I'll watch and wait, Hop-ing, trust-ing ev-er, Till I reach the gold-en strand, Just be-yond the riv-er.

REFRAIN

In the cross, in the cross, Be my glo-ry ev-er; Till my rap-tured soul shall find Rest be-yond the riv-er.

561 MAN OF SORROWS, WHAT A NAME

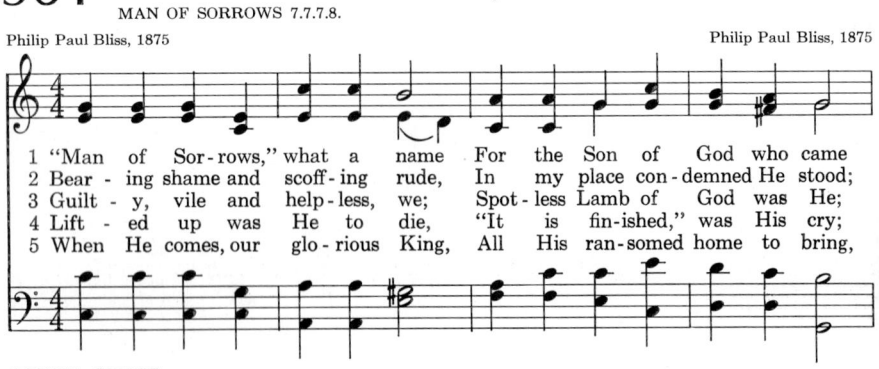

MAN OF SORROWS 7.7.7.8.

Philip Paul Bliss, 1875
Philip Paul Bliss, 1875

1. "Man of Sor-rows," what a name For the Son of God who came
2. Bear-ing shame and scoff-ing rude, In my place con-demned He stood;
3. Guilt-y, vile and help-less, we; Spot-less Lamb of God was He;
4. Lift-ed up was He to die, "It is fin-ished," was His cry;
5. When He comes, our glo-rious King, All His ran-somed home to bring,

GOSPEL SONGS

Ru - ined sin - ners to re - claim! Al - le - lu - ia! what a Sav - ior!
Sealed my par - don with His blood; Al - le - lu - ia! what a Sav - ior!
"Full a - tone - ment!" can it be? Al - le - lu - ia! what a Sav - ior!
Now in heav'n ex - alt - ed high; Al - le - lu - ia! what a Sav - ior!
Then a new this song we'll sing: Al - le - lu - ia! what a Sav - ior!

CHRIST HAS FOR SIN ATONEMENT MADE 562

BENTON HARBOR (HOFFMAN) 8.7.8.7. with Refrain

Elisha A. Hoffman, 1891   Elisha A. Hoffman, 1891

1 Christ has for sin a-tone-ment made, What a won - der - ful Sav - ior! We are re -
2 I praise Him for the cleans-ing blood, What a won - der - ful Sav - ior! That rec - on -
3 He cleansed my heart from all its sin, What a won - der - ful Sav - ior! And now He
4 He gives me o - ver-com-ing power, What a won - der - ful Sav - ior! And tri-umph

REFRAIN

deemed! the price is paid; What a won-der-ful Sav - ior!
ciled my soul to God; What a won-der-ful Sav - ior!   What a won-der-ful Sav-ior
reigns and rules there-in; What a won-der-ful Sav - ior!
in each try-ing hour; What a won-der-ful Sav - ior!

is Je - sus, my Je - sus! What a won-der-ful Sav - ior is Je - sus, my Lord!

GOSPEL SONGS

563 THOU DIDST LEAVE THY THRONE

ROOM FOR THEE Irregular

Emily E. S. Elliott‡, 1864
Ira David Sankey, 1876

1. Thou didst leave Thy throne, and Thy kingly crown, When Thou camest to earth for me; But in Bethlehem's home there was found no room, For Thy holy nativity.

2. Heav'n's arches rang when the angels sang, Of Thy birth and Thy royal decree; But in lowly birth didst Thou come to earth, And in greatest humility.

3. Foxes found their rest, and the birds had their nests, In the shade of the cedar tree; But Thy couch was the sod, O Thou Son of God, In the deserts of Galilee.

4. Thou camest, O Lord, with Thy living word, That should set Thy people free; But with mocking and scorn and with crown of thorn, Did they bear Thee to Calvary.

5. Heav'n's arches shall ring, and its choirs shall sing, At Thy coming to victory, Thou wilt call me home, saying "Yet there is room," There is room at My side for thee.

REFRAIN

O come to my heart, Lord Jesus! There is room in my heart for Thee.
O come to my heart, Lord Jesus, come! There is room in my heart for Thee.

GOSPEL SONGS

IF YE THEN WITH CHRIST BE RISEN 564

IF YE THEN BE RISEN 8.5.8.5.8.7.8.7. with Refrain

Grant Colfax Tullar, 1926
I. H. Meredith, 1926

1 If ye then with Christ be ris-en, Seek those things a-bove; Let His glo-ry shine a-round thee, Show-ing forth His love. Once up-on the cross He suf-fered, Gave His life a ran-som free, Yet the grave could not re-tain Him, And He lives e-ter-nal-ly.

2 If ye then with Christ be ris-en, And the vic-t'ry won, Let your thoughts on Him be cen-tered Till the race is run; Let no anx-ious thought per-plex thee, Or temp-ta-tion still dis-may, Think when-e'er the clouds sur-round thee, Soon shall dawn a bright-er day.

3 If ye then with Christ be ris-en, Let thy soul re-joice; Let con-tin-ual praise be sound-ing, With glad heart and voice. He who died to be your Sav-ior Rose a-gain to be your King; If ye then with Him be ris-en, Let your joy-ous prais-es ring.

Refrain
If ye then be ris-en With the King of love, Look not to the things that per-ish, Seek those things a-bove.

GOSPEL SONGS

565 I KNOW THAT MY REDEEMER LIVETH

FILLMORE 9.8.9.8. with Refrain

Jessie Brown Pounds, 1893
James H. Fillmore, 1893

1. I know that my Redeemer liveth, And on the earth again shall stand; I know eternal life He giveth, That grace and power are in His hand.
2. I know His promise never faileth, The word He speaks, it cannot die; Though cruel death my flesh assaileth, Yet I shall see Him by and by.
3. I know my mansion He prepareth, That where He is there I may be; O wondrous thought, for me He careth, And He at last will come for me.

REFRAIN
I know, I know that Jesus liveth, And on the earth again shall stand; I know, I know that life He giveth,

GOSPEL SONGS

giv - eth, That grace and power are in His hand.
That grace and power

CHRIST WHO LEFT HIS HOME IN GLORY 566

CHRIST IS RISEN 8.7.8.7. with Refrain

Abram Bowman Kolb, 1896 — Abram Bowman Kolb, 1896

1 Christ who left His home in glo - ry, And up - on the cross was slain,
2 While the world in peace was sleep-ing, Ear - ly on that East - er day,
3 Christ, our lov - ing Me - di - a - tor, Now with God for you and me

Now is ris'n! O tell the sto - ry That the Sav - ior lives a - gain.
Came the faith - ful wom - en, weep-ing, But the stone was rolled a - way.
In - ter-cedes, and our Cre - a - tor Hears and an - swers ev - ery plea.

REFRAIN
Hail Him! Hail Him! Tell the sto - ry;
Hail to the King, the might-y Re-deem-er! Hail Him who robbed the grave of its power!

Hail! all hail! Je - sus lives for - ev - er - more.
Tell ev - ery na - tion, all is well,

GOSPEL SONGS

567 LOW IN THE GRAVE HE LAY

CHRIST AROSE 11.10. with Refrain

Robert Lowry, 1874   Robert Lowry, 1874

1. Low in the grave He lay, Jesus, my Savior! Waiting the coming day, Jesus, my Lord!
2. Vainly they watch His bed, Jesus, my Savior! Vainly they seal the dead, Jesus, my Lord!
3. Death cannot keep his prey, Jesus, my Savior! He tore the bars away, Jesus, my Lord!

Refrain

Up from the grave He arose, With a mighty triumph o'er His foes! He arose a victor from the dark domain, And He lives forever with His saints to reign; He arose! He arose! Alleluia! Christ arose!

GOSPEL SONGS

AS LIVES THE FLOWER WITHIN THE SEED 568

CHRIST LIVETH IN ME C.M. with Refrain

Daniel Webster Whittle, c. 1891 — James McGranahan, 1891

1 As lives the flower with-in the seed, As in the cone the tree,
2 Once far from God and dead in sin, No light my heart could see;
3 As rays of light from yon-der sun The flowers of earth set free,
4 With long-ing all my heart is filled, That like Him I may be,

So, praise the God of truth and grace, His Spir-it dwell-eth in me.
But in God's Word the light I found, Now Christ liv-eth in me.
So life and light and love came forth From Christ liv-ing in me.
As on the won-drous thought I dwell, That Christ liv-eth in me.

REFRAIN

Christ liv-eth in me, Christ liv-eth in me,
Christ liv-eth in me, Christ liv-eth in me, O
O what a sal-va-tion this, That Christ liv-eth in me!

GOSPEL SONGS

569 HE IS COMING, THE MAN OF SORROWS

NEWCASTLE 9.6.9.6. with Refrain

Fanny Crosby, 1887
Ira David Sankey, 1887

1. He is coming, the Man of Sorrows, Now exalted on high;
   He is coming with loud hosannas, In the clouds of the sky.
2. He is coming, our loving Savior, Blessed Lamb that was slain;
   In the glory of God the Father, On the earth He shall reign.
3. He is coming, our Lord and Master, Our Redeemer and King;
   We shall see Him in all His beauty, And His praise we shall sing.
4. He shall gather His chosen people, Who are called by His name;
   And the ransomed of every nation For His own He shall claim.

Refrain
Alleluia! Alleluia! He is coming again;
And with joy we shall gather round Him, At His coming to reign.

GOSPEL SONGS

IT MAY BE AT MORN 570

CHRIST RETURNETH 12.12.12.7. with Refrain

H. L. Turner, 1878 — James McGranahan, 1878

1. It may be at morn, when the day is a-wak-ing, When sun-light through dark-ness and shad-ow is break-ing, That Je-sus will come in the full-ness of glo-ry, To re-ceive from the world "His own."
2. It may be at mid-day, it may be at twi-light, It may be, per-chance, that the black-ness of mid-night Will burst in-to light in the blaze of His glo-ry, When Je-sus re-ceives "His own."
3. While its hosts cry, "Ho-san-na," from heav-en de-scend-ing, With glo-ri-fied saints and the an-gels at-tend-ing, With grace on His brow, like a ha-lo of glo-ry, Will Je-sus re-ceive "His own."
4. O joy! O de-light! should we go with-out dy-ing, No sick-ness, no sad-ness, no dread and no cry-ing, Caught up through the clouds with our Lord in-to glo-ry, When Je-sus re-ceives "His own."

REFRAIN

O Lord Je-sus, how long, How long ere we shout the glad song, Christ re-turn-eth! Al-le-lu-ia! Al-le-lu-ia! A-men, Al-le-lu-ia! A-men.

GOSPEL SONGS

571 JUDGE ME, GOD OF MY SALVATION

AMARA 8.7.8.7. with Refrain

Based on Psalm 43
Psalter, 1912

William O. Perkins, d. 1902

1. Judge me, God of my salvation, Plead my cause, for Thee I trust;
   Hear my earnest supplication, Save me from my foes unjust.
2. On Thy strength alone relying, Why am I cast off by Thee,
   In my helpless sorrow sighing, While the foe oppresses me?
3. Light and truth, my way attending, Send Thou forth to be my guide,
   Till Thy holy mount ascending, I within Thy house abide.
4. At Thy sacred altar bending, God, my God, my boundless joy,
   Harp and voice, in worship blending, For Thy praise will I employ.

REFRAIN

O my soul, why art thou grieving? What disquiets and dismays?
Hope in God; His help receiving, I shall yet my Savior praise.

GOSPEL SONGS

SAVIOR, LIKE A SHEPHERD LEAD US 572

BRADBURY 8.7.8.7.8.7.

D. Thrupp's *Hymns for the Young*, 1836

William Batchelder Bradbury, 1859

1. Savior, like a shepherd lead us, Much we need Thy tend'rest care;
In Thy pleasant pastures feed us, For our use Thy folds prepare;
Blessed Jesus! Blessed Jesus! Thou hast bought us, Thine we are,
Blessed Jesus! Blessed Jesus! Thou hast bought us, Thine we are.

2. We are Thine, do Thou befriend us, Be the guardian of our way;
Keep Thy flock, from sin defend us, Seek us when we go astray:
Blessed Jesus! Blessed Jesus! Hear, O hear us, when we pray,
Blessed Jesus! Blessed Jesus! Hear, O hear us, when we pray.

3. Thou hast promised to receive us, Poor and sinful though we be;
Thou hast mercy to relieve us, Grace to cleanse, and power to free:
Blessed Jesus! Blessed Jesus! We will early turn to Thee,
Blessed Jesus! Blessed Jesus! We will early turn to Thee.

4. Early let us seek Thy favor, Early let us do Thy will;
Blessed Lord and only Savior, With Thy love our bosoms fill:
Blessed Jesus! Blessed Jesus! Thou hast loved us, love us still,
Blessed Jesus! Blessed Jesus! Thou hast loved us, love us still. A-men.

GOSPEL SONGS

573 ALL THE WAY MY SAVIOR LEADS ME

ALL THE WAY 8.7.8.7.D.

Fanny Crosby, 1875 — Robert Lowry, 1875

1. All the way my Savior leads me; What have I to ask beside?
Can I doubt His tender mercy, Who through life has been my guide?
Heav'nly peace, divinest comfort, Here by faith in Him to dwell!
For I know, what-e'er befall me, Jesus doeth all things well;
For I know, what-e'er befall me, Jesus doeth all things well.

2. All the way my Savior leads me; Cheers each winding path I tread;
Gives me grace for every trial; Feeds me with the living bread;
Though my weary steps may falter, And my soul a-thirst may be,
Gushing from the rock before me, Lo! a spring of joy I see;
Gushing from the rock before me, Lo! a spring of joy I see.

3. All the way my Savior leads me; O the fullness of His love!
Perfect rest to me is promised In my Father's house above;
When my spirit, clothed immortal, Wings its flight to realms of day,
This my song through endless ages, Jesus led me all the way;
This my song through endless ages, Jesus led me all the way.

GOSPEL SONGS

BE NOT DISMAYED WHATE'ER BETIDE 574

GOD CARES C.M. with Refrain

Civilla D. Martin, 1904

Walter Stillman Martin, 1904

1 Be not dis-mayed what-e'er be-tide, God will take care of you;
2 Through days of toil when heart doth fail, God will take care of you;
3 All you may need He will pro-vide, God will take care of you;
4 No mat-ter what may be the test, God will take care of you;

Be-neath His wings of love a-bide, God will take care of you.
When dan-gers fierce your path as-sail, God will take care of you.
Noth-ing you ask will be de-nied, God will take care of you.
Lean, wea-ry one, up-on His breast, God will take care of you.

REFRAIN

God will take care of you, Through ev-ery day, O'er all the way;

He will take care of you, God will take care of you.

GOSPEL SONGS

575 UNDER HIS WINGS I AM SAFELY ABIDING

UNDER HIS WINGS 11.10.11.10. with Refrain

William Orcutt Cushing, c. 1896   Ira David Sankey, 1896

1. Un-der His wings I am safe-ly a-bid-ing; Though the night deep-ens and tem-pests are wild, Still I can trust Him; I know He will keep me; He has re-deemed me, and I am His child.

2. Un-der His wings, what a ref-uge in sor-row! How the heart yearn-ing-ly turns to His rest! Oft-en when earth has no balm for my heal-ing, There I find com-fort, and there I am blest.

3. Un-der His wings, O what pre-cious en-joy-ment! There will I hide till life's tri-als are o'er; Shel-tered, pro-tect-ed, no e-vil can harm me; Rest-ing in Je-sus I'm safe ev-er-more.

Refrain

Un-der His wings, un-der His wings, Who from His love can sev-er? Un-der His wings my soul shall a-bide, Safe-ly a-bide for-ev-er.

GOSPEL SONGS

WHEN PEACE, LIKE A RIVER 576

IT IS WELL 11.8.11.9. with Refrain

Horatio G. Spafford, 1873
Philip Paul Bliss, 1876

1. When peace, like a river, at-tend-eth my way, When sor-rows like sea-bil-lows roll; What-ev-er my lot, Thou hast taught me to say, It is well, it is well with my soul.
2. Though Satan should buf-fet, though tri-als should come, Let this blest as-sur-ance con-trol, That Christ hath re-gard-ed my help-less es-tate, And hath shed His own blood for my soul.
3. My sin! O the bliss of this glo-ri-ous thought, My sin! not in part, but the whole, Is nailed to His cross and I bear it no more, Praise the Lord, praise the Lord, O my soul!
4. And, Lord, haste the day when the faith shall be sight, The clouds be rolled back as a scroll, The trump shall re-sound and the Lord shall de-scend, "E-ven so," it is well with my soul.

Refrain

It is well with my soul, It is well, it is well with my soul.

GOSPEL SONGS

577 WHEN WE WALK WITH THE LORD

TRUST AND OBEY 6.6.9.D. with Refrain

John H. Sammis, 1887
Daniel Brink Towner, 1887

1. When we walk with the Lord In the light of His Word, What a glory He sheds on our way! While we do His good will, He abides with us still, And with all who will trust and obey.

2. Not a burden we bear, Not a sorrow we share, But our toil He doth richly repay; Not a grief nor a loss, Not a frown nor a cross, But is blest if we trust and obey.

3. But we never can prove The delights of His love, Until all on the altar we lay, For the favor He shows, And the joy He bestows, Are for them who will trust and obey.

4. Then in fellowship sweet We will sit at His feet, Or we'll walk by His side in the way; What He says we will do, Where He sends we will go, Never fear, only trust and obey.

Refrain:
Trust and obey, for there's no other way To be happy in Jesus, but to trust and obey.

GOSPEL SONGS

I NEED THEE EVERY HOUR 578

NEED 6.4.6.4. with Refrain

Annie S. Hawks, 1872   Robert Lowry, 1872

1. I need Thee ev-ery hour, Most gra-cious Lord;
2. I need Thee ev-ery hour, Stay Thou near by;
3. I need Thee ev-ery hour, In joy or pain;
4. I need Thee ev-ery hour, Teach me Thy will;
5. I need Thee ev-ery hour, Most ho-ly One;

No ten-der voice like Thine Can peace af-ford.
Temp-ta-tions lose their power When Thou art nigh.
Come quick-ly and a-bide, Or life is vain.
And Thy rich prom-is-es In me ful-fill.
O make me Thine in-deed, Thou bless-ed Son.

Refrain

I need Thee, O I need Thee, Ev-ery hour I need Thee;
O bless me now, my Sav-ior, I come to Thee. A-men.

GOSPEL SONGS

579 NEARER, STILL NEARER

MORRIS 9.10.9.10.

Leila Naylor Morris, 1898 *Leila Naylor Morris, 1898*

1. Nearer, still nearer, close to Thy heart, Draw me, my Savior, so precious Thou art; Fold me, O fold me close to Thy breast, Shelter me safe in that haven of rest, Shelter me safe in that haven of rest.

2. Nearer, still nearer, nothing I bring, Naught as an off'ring to Jesus my King, Only my sinful, now contrite heart; Grant me the cleansing Thy blood doth impart, Grant me the cleansing Thy blood doth impart.

3. Nearer, still nearer, Lord, to be Thine, Sin, with its follies, I gladly resign, All of its pleasures, pomp and its pride; Give me but Jesus, my Lord crucified, Give me but Jesus, my Lord crucified.

4. Nearer, still nearer, while life shall last, Till safe in glory my anchor is cast, Through endless ages, ever to be, Nearer, my Savior, still nearer to Thee, Nearer, my Savior, still nearer to Thee.

GOSPEL SONGS

HELP ME TO BE HOLY 580

TOWNER 11.11.11.11.

Adoniram J. Gordon, c. 1894 — Daniel Brink Towner, 1894

1. Help me to be holy, O Father of light;
Guilt-burdened and lowly, I bow in Thy sight;
How shall a stained conscience Dare gaze on Thy face,
E'en though in Thy presence Thou grant me a place?

2. Help me to be holy, O Savior divine;
Why conquer so slowly This nature of mine?
Stamp deeply Thy likeness Where Satan's hath been;
Expel with Thy brightness My darkness and sin!

3. Help me to be holy, O Spirit divine;
Come, sanctify wholly This temple of Thine;
Now cast out each idol. Here set up Thy throne.
Reign, reign without rival, Supreme and alone! A-men.

GOSPEL SONGS

581 I AM THINE, O LORD
DRAW ME NEARER 10.7.10.7. with Refrain

Fanny Crosby, 1875   William Howard Doane, 1875

1. I am Thine, O Lord, I have heard Thy voice, And it told Thy love to me; But I long to rise in the arms of faith, And be clos-er drawn to Thee.
2. Con-se-crate me now to Thy ser-vice, Lord, By the power of grace di-vine; Let my soul look up with a stead-fast hope, And my will be lost in Thine.
3. O the pure de-light of a sin-gle hour That be-fore Thy throne I spend, When I kneel in prayer, and with Thee, my God, I com-mune as friend with friend!
4. There are depths of love that I can-not know Till I cross the nar-row sea; There are heights of joy that I may not reach Till I rest in peace with Thee.

Refrain

Draw me near-er, near-er, near-er, bless-ed Lord, To the cross where Thou hast died; Draw me near-er, near-er, near-er, bless-ed Lord, To Thy pre-cious bleed-ing side.

GOSPEL SONGS

I'M PRESSING ON THE UPWARD WAY 582

HIGHER GROUND L.M. with Refrain

Johnson Oatman, Jr., d. 1922   Charles H. Gabriel, 1892

1. I'm press-ing on the up-ward way, New heights I'm gain-ing ev-ery day;
Still pray-ing as I on-ward bound, "Lord, plant my feet on high-er ground."

2. My heart has no de-sire to stay Where doubts a-rise and fears dis-may;
Tho' some may dwell where these a-bound, My prayer, my aim is high-er ground.

3. I want to live a-bove the world, Though Sa-tan's darts at me are hurled;
For faith has caught the joy-ful sound, The song of saints on high-er ground.

4. I want to scale the ut-most height, And catch a gleam of glo-ry bright;
But still I'll pray till heav'n I've found, "Lord, lead me on to high-er ground."

REFRAIN

Lord, lift me up and let me stand, By faith, on heav-en's ta-ble-land,
A high-er plane than I have found; Lord, plant my feet on high-er ground.

GOSPEL SONGS

583 LORD JESUS, I LONG TO BE PERFECTLY

WHITER THAN SNOW 11.11.11.11. with Refrain

James L. Nicholson†, 1872   William Gustavus Fischer, 1872

1. Lord Jesus, I long to be perfectly whole;
   I want Thee forever, to live in my soul;
   Break down every idol, cast out every foe;

2. Lord Jesus, come down from Thy throne in the skies,
   And help me to make a complete sacrifice;
   I give up myself and whatever I know,

3. Lord Jesus, Thou seest I patiently wait;
   Come now, and within me a new heart create;
   To those who have sought Thee, Thou never saidst No,

4. The blessing by faith, I receive from above;
   O glory! My soul is made perfect in love;
   My prayer has prevailed, and this moment I know,

Refrain

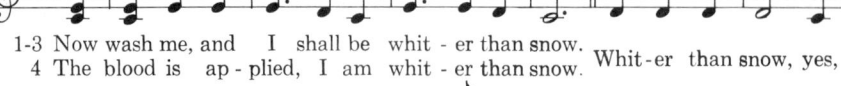

1-3 Now wash me, and I shall be whiter than snow.
4 The blood is applied, I am whiter than snow. Whiter than snow, yes, whiter than snow; Now wash me, and I shall be whiter than snow.

GOSPEL SONGS

O LIFE IN WHOM IS LIFE INDEED 584

BAPTISTE L.M. with Refrain

Jesse Brown Pounds, d. 1921   "From Baptiste," c. 1920

1. O Life in whom is life indeed, Through whom our best desires are freed. Stir Thou that life in us, we plead; We come to Thee, we come to Thee!

2. O Light beyond men's highest thought, Beyond all wisdom seers have wrought, Ne'er yet that light in vain was sought; We come to Thee, we come to Thee!

3. O Good beyond the dreams of men, Who makest stained lives white again, Thou Christ, bestow Thy pureness when We come to Thee, we come to Thee!

REFRAIN
Come to Thee, Come to Thee, Come to Thee, We come to Thee.
We come to Thee, We come to Thee, We come to Thee, We come to Thee.

GOSPEL SONGS

585 LORD, I AM FONDLY, EARNESTLY

OPEN THE WELLS 10.9.10.9. with Refrain

Elisha Albright Hoffman, c. 1902 — Charles Edward Pollock, c. 1902

1. Lord, I am fondly, earnestly longing Into Thy holy likeness to grow; Thirsting for more and deeper communion, Yearning Thy love more fully to know.
2. Dead to the world would I be, O Father! Dead unto sin, alive unto Thee; Crucify all the earthly within me, Emptied of sin and self may I be.
3. I would be Thine, and serve Thee forever, Filled with Thy Spirit, lost in Thy love; Come to my heart, Lord, come with anointing, Showers of grace send down from above.

Refrain:
Open the wells of grace and salvation, Pour the rich streams deep into my heart; Cleanse and refine my

GOSPEL SONGS

thought and af-fec-tion, Seal me and make me pure as Thou art.
thought and af-fec-tion, Seal me and make me pure as Thou art.

I KNOW NOT WHY GOD'S WONDROUS 586

EL NATHAN C.M. with Refrain

Daniel W. Whittle, 1883　　　　　　　　　　　　　　　　James McGranahan, 1883

1. I know not why God's won-drous grace To me He hath made known,
2. I know not how this sav-ing faith To me He did im-part,
3. I know not how the Spir-it moves, Con-vinc-ing men of sin,
4. I know not when my Lord may come, At night or noon-day fair,

Nor why, un-wor-thy, Christ in love Re-deemed me for His own.
Nor how be-liev-ing in His Word Wrought peace with-in my heart.
Re-veal-ing Je-sus through the Word, Cre-at-ing faith in Him.
Nor if I'll walk the vale with Him, Or meet Him in the air.

REFRAIN

But I know whom I have be-liev-ed, and am per-suad-ed that He is
a-ble To keep that which I've com-mit-ted Un-to Him a-gainst that day.

GOSPEL SONGS

587 O WONDERFUL, WONDERFUL WORD

WONDERFUL WORD 11.8.11.8.11.8.12.8.

J. L. Sterling, c. 1886　　　　　　　　　　　　　　　　　　　　　　Ira David Sankey, 1886

1. O wonderful, wonderful Word of the Lord! True wisdom its pages unfold; And though we may read them a thousand times o'er, They never, no never, grow old! Each line hath a treasure, each promise a pearl, That all if they will may secure; And we know that when time and the

2. O wonderful, wonderful Word of the Lord! The lamp that our Father above So kindly has lighted to teach us the way That leads to the arms of His love! Its warnings, its counsels, are faithful and just; Its judgments are perfect and pure; And we know that when time and the

3. O wonderful, wonderful Word of the Lord! Our only salvation is there; It carries conviction down deep in the heart, And shows us ourselves as we are. It tells of a Savior, and points to the cross, Where pardon we now may secure, For we know that when time and the

4. O wonderful, wonderful Word of the Lord! The hope of our friends in the past; Its truth, where so firmly they anchored their trust, Through ages eternal shall last. O wonderful, wonderful Word of the Lord! Unchanging, abiding and sure; For we know that when time and the

GOSPEL SONGS

world pass a-way, God's Word shall for-ev-er en-dure.

IN THE LAND OF STRANGERS 588
WELCOME, WANDERER, WELCOME 6.5.6.4. with Refrain

Horatius Bonar, 1874
Refrain added by Ira David Sankey

Ira David Sankey, 1884

1. In the land of stran-gers Whith-er thou art gone,
2. From the land of hun-ger, Faint-ing, fam-ished, lone,
3. See the door still o-pen: Thou art still My own;
4. See the well-spread ta-ble, Un-for-got-ten one!
5. Thou art friend-less, hope-less, Hope-less and un-done;

Hear a far voice call-ing, My son, My son!
Come to love and glad-ness, My son, My son!
Eyes of love are on thee, My son, My son!
Here is rest and plen-ty, My son, My son!
Mine is love un-chang-ing, My son, My son!

REFRAIN
Wel-come, wan-d'rer, wel-come, Wel-come back to home;
Thou hast wan-dered far a-way: Come home, come home.

GOSPEL SONGS

589 ENCAMPED ALONG THE HILLS
FAITH IS THE VICTORY C.M.D. with Refrain

John H. Yates, 1891   Ira David Sankey, 1891

1. En-camped a-long the hills of light, Ye Chris-tian sol-diers, rise, And press the bat-tle ere the night Shall veil the glow-ing skies. A-gainst the foe in vales be-low Let all our strength be hurled; Faith is the vic-to-ry, we know, That o-ver-comes the world.

2. His ban-ner o-ver us is love, Our sword the Word of God; We tread the road the saints a-bove With shouts of tri-umph trod. By faith, they like a whirl-wind's breath, Swept on o'er ev-ery field; The faith by which they con-quered death Is still our shin-ing shield.

3. On ev-ery hand the foe we find Drawn up in dread ar-ray; Let tents of ease be left be-hind, And on-ward to the fray. Sal-va-tion's hel-met on each head, With truth all girt a-bout, The earth shall trem-ble 'neath our tread, And ech-o with our shout.

4. To him that o-ver-comes the foe, White rai-ment shall be giv'n; Be-fore the an-gels he shall know His name con-fessed in heav'n. Then on-ward from the hills of light, Our hearts with love a-flame; We'll van-quish all the hosts of night, In Je-sus' con-qu'ring name.

Refrain

Faith is the vic-to-ry! Faith is the vic-to-ry! Faith is the

GOSPEL SONGS

vic - to - ry! O glo - ri - ous vic - to - ry, That o - ver-comes the world.
vic - to - ry!

O LORD, WITHIN MY SOUL 590
FULL SALVATION FREE 6.6.6.4. with Refrain

Elisha Albright Hoffman, c. 1900   Elisha Albright Hoffman, c. 1900

1 O Lord, with - in my soul I long for pu - ri - ty,
2 I bend be - fore Thy cross, And know my heart can be
3 I pray at Thy dear feet, Sal - va - tion full en - treat,
4 My faith Thy Word be - lieves, The prom - ise made to me,

REFRAIN

To be com - plete and whole A - lone through Thee.
Cleansed from its sin and dross A - lone through Thee. There is no
And want to feel my love In Thee com - plete.
And per - fect peace re - ceives A - lone through Thee.

oth - er hope, There is no oth - er plea;
There is no oth - er hope, There is no oth - er plea;

Sal - va - tion, full sal - va - tion free, Must come a - lone through Thee.

GOSPEL SONGS

591 ONWARD, CHRISTIAN SOLDIERS

ST. GERTRUDE 6.5.6.5.D. with Refrain

Sabine Baring-Gould, 1865 — Arthur Seymour Sullivan, 1871

1. On-ward, Christian soldiers, Marching as to war, With the cross of Jesus Going on before; Christ the royal Master Leads against the foe; Forward into battle, See, His banners go.

2. Like a mighty army Moves the church of God; Brothers, we are treading Where the saints have trod; We are not divided, All one body we, One in hope and doctrine, One in charity.

3. Crowns and thrones may perish, Kingdoms rise and wane, But the church of Jesus Constant will remain; Gates of hell can never 'Gainst that church prevail; We have Christ's own promise, And that cannot fail.

4. Onward, then, ye people! Join our happy throng! Blend with ours your voices In the triumph song; Glory, laud, and honor, Unto Christ the King; This through countless ages Men and angels sing.

Refrain: Onward, Christian soldiers, Marching as to war, With the cross of Jesus, Going on before.

GOSPEL SONGS

STAND UP! STAND UP FOR JESUS 592

WEBB 7.6.7.6.D.

George Duffield, Jr., 1858
George James Webb, 1830

1. Stand up! stand up for Jesus! Ye soldiers of the cross;
Lift high His royal banner, It must not suffer loss.
From vict'ry unto vict'ry His army He shall lead
Till every foe is vanquished, And Christ is Lord indeed.

2. Stand up! stand up for Jesus! The trumpet call obey;
Forth to the mighty conflict, In this His glorious day.
Ye that are men now serve Him, Against unnumbered foes;
Let courage rise with danger, And strength to strength oppose.

3. Stand up! stand up for Jesus! Stand in His strength alone;
The arm of flesh will fail you, Ye dare not trust your own.
Put on the gospel armor, Each piece put on with prayer;
Where duty calls or danger, Be never wanting there!

4. Stand up! stand up for Jesus! The strife will not be long;
This day the noise of battle, The next the victor's song.
To him that overcometh, A crown of life shall be;
He with the King of glory Shall reign eternally!

GOSPEL SONGS

593 I LOVE TO TELL THE STORY

HANKEY 7.6.7.6.D. with Refrain

Catherine Hankey, 1866
Refrain by William G. Fischer, 1869

William G. Fischer, 1869

1. I love to tell the story Of unseen things above, Of Jesus and His glory, Of Jesus and His love. I love to tell the story, Because I know it's true; It satisfies my longings As nothing else would do.

2. I love to tell the story; More wonderful it seems Than all the golden fancies Of all our golden dreams. I love to tell the story, It did so much for me; And that is just the reason I tell it now to thee.

3. I love to tell the story; 'Tis pleasant to repeat What seems, each time I tell it, More wonderfully sweet. I love to tell the story, For some have never heard The message of salvation From God's own holy Word.

4. I love to tell the story; For those who know it best Seem hungering and thirsting To hear it, like the rest. And when, in scenes of glory, I sing the new, new song, 'Twill be the old, old story That I have loved so long.

Refrain: I love to tell the story, 'Twill be my theme in glory, To tell the old, old story Of Jesus and His love.

GOSPEL SONGS

WE HAVE HEARD A JOYFUL SOUND 594

JESUS SAVES 7.6.7.6.7.7.7.6.

Priscilla J. Owens, c. 1882
William J. Kirkpatrick, 1882

1. We have heard a joy-ful sound: Jesus saves! Jesus saves!
2. Waft it on the roll-ing tide: Jesus saves! Jesus saves!
3. Sing a-bove the bat-tle strife, Jesus saves! Jesus saves!
4. Give the winds a might-y voice: Jesus saves! Jesus saves!

Spread the ti-dings all a-round: Jesus saves! Jesus saves!
Tell to sin-ners far and wide: Jesus saves! Jesus saves!
By His death and end-less life, Jesus saves! Jesus saves!
Let the na-tions now re-joice, Jesus saves! Jesus saves!

Bear the news to ev-ery land; Climb the steeps and cross the waves;
Sing, ye is-lands of the sea; Ech-o back, ye o-cean caves;
Sing it soft-ly through the gloom, When the heart for mer-cy craves;
Shout sal-va-tion full and free, High-est hills and deep-est caves;

On-ward! 'tis our Lord's com-mand: Jesus saves! Jesus saves!
Earth shall keep her ju-bi-lee: Jesus saves! Jesus saves!
Sing in tri-umph o'er the tomb, Jesus saves! Jesus saves!
This our song of vic-to-ry, Jesus saves! Jesus saves!

GOSPEL SONGS

595 WHEN MORNING GILDS THE SKIES

GENEVA 3 (O SEIGNEUR) 6.6.7.6.6.7.D.

Katholisches Gesangbuch, Würzburg, 1828
Beim frühen Morgenlicht
Tr. Edward Caswall†, 1854

Pseaumes octante trois . . . , Geneva, 1551
Harmony from *The Yattendon Hymnal*, 1899

1. When morn-ing gilds the skies, My heart a-wak-ing cries: May Je-sus Christ be prais-ed! A - like at work or prayer To Je-sus I re-pair: May Je-sus Christ be prais-ed! Does sad-ness fill my mind, A sol-ace here I find: May Je-sus Christ be prais-ed! Or fades my earth-ly bliss, My com-fort still is this! May Je-sus Christ be prais-ed!

2. The night be-comes as day, When from the heart we say; May Je-sus Christ be prais-ed! In heav'n's e-ter-nal bliss, The love-liest strain is this: May Je-sus Christ be prais-ed! Be this, while life is mine, My can-ti-cle di-vine, May Je-sus Christ be prais-ed! Be this th' e-ter-nal song, Through all the a-ges long: May Je-sus Christ be prais-ed!

CHORAL HYMNS

O PRAISE YE THE LORD 596
OLD 104th 5.5.5.5.6.5.6.5.

Based on Psalm 150
Henry Williams Baker, 1875

Ravenscroft's *Psalter*, 1621

1. O praise ye the Lord! Praise Him in the height; Rejoice in His Word, Ye angels of light; Ye heavens, adore Him By whom ye were made, And worship before Him, In brightness arrayed.

2. O praise ye the Lord! Praise Him upon earth, In tuneful accord, Ye sons of new birth; Praise Him who hath brought you His grace from above, Praise Him who hath taught you To sing of His love.

3. O praise ye the Lord! All things that give sound; Each jubilant chord, Re-echo around; Loud organs, His glory Forth tell in deep tone, And sweet harp, the story Of what He hath done.

4. O praise ye the Lord! Thanksgiving and song To Him be outpoured All ages along: For love in creation, For heaven restored, For grace of salvation, O praise ye the Lord!

CHORAL HYMNS

597 EIN FESTE BURG IST UNSER GOTT

EIN FESTE BURG 8.7.8.7.6.5.5.6.7.

Based on Psalm 46
Martin Luther, 1527 or 1528

Martin Luther, 1529

1 Ein fe-ste Burg ist un-ser Gott, ein gu-te Wehr und Waf-fen.
2 Mit un-srer Macht ist nichts ge-tan, wir sind gar bald ver-lo-ren.
3 Und wenn die Welt voll Teu-fel wär und wollt uns gar ver-schling-en,
4 Das Wort sie sol-len las-sen stahn und kein Dank da-zu ha-ben.

Er hilft uns frei aus al-ler Not, die uns jetzt hat be-trof-fen.
Es streit für uns der rech-te Mann, den Gott hat selbst er-ko-ren.
So fürch-ten wir uns nicht so sehr; es soll uns doch ge-ling-en.
Er ist bei uns wohl auf dem Plan mit sei-nem Geist und Ga-ben.

Der alt bö-se Feind mit Ernst er's jetzt meint; gross Macht und viel List
Fragst du, wer der ist? Er heisst Je-sus Christ, der Herr Ze-ba-oth,
Der Fürst die-ser Welt, wie saur er sich stellt, tut er uns doch nichts;
Neh-men sie den Leib, Gut, Ehr, Kind und Weib; lass fah-ren da-hin,

sein grau-sam Rü-stung ist; auf Erd ist nicht seins-glei-chen.
und ist kein an-drer Gott; das Feld muss er be-hal-ten.
das macht, er ist ge-richt, ein Wört-lein kann ihn fäl-len.
sie ha-ben's kein Ge-winn; das Reich muss uns doch blei-ben. A-men.

CHORAL HYMNS

Tr. Thomas Carlyle‡, 1831

1. A safe stronghold our God is still,
A trusty shield and weapon;
He'll help us clear from all the ill
That hath us now o'ertaken.
The ancient prince of hell,
Doth show purpose fell;
His mail, craft, and power,
He weareth in this hour,
On earth is not his fellow.

2. With force of arms we nothing can,
Full soon were we down-ridden;
But for us fights the proper man,
Whom God Himself hath bidden.
Ask ye, Who is this same?
Christ Jesus His name,
Lord Sabaoth's Son,
He and no other one
Shall conquer in the battle.

3. And were this world all devils o'er
And watching to devour us,
We lay it not to heart so sore,
Not they can overpower us.
And let the prince of ill
Look grim as he will,
He harms not a whit,
For why? His doom is writ,
A word shall quickly slay him.

4. God's Word, for all their craft and force,
One moment will not linger,
But spite of hell, shall have its course,
'Tis written by His finger.
And though they take our life,
Goods, fame, children, wife,
Their profit is small;
These things shall vanish all,
The city of God remaineth.

NOW PRAISE WE CHRIST 598

Based on Latin of Coelius Sedulius, c. 450
Tr. Martin Luther, 1524
Christum wir sollen loben schon
Tr. Richard Massie‡, 1854

CHRISTUM WIR SOLLEN LOBEN SCHON L.M.

Enchiridion, Erfurt, 1524

1. Now praise we Christ, the holy One, The bless-ed vir-gin Ma-ry's Son, Far as the glo-rious sun doth shine E'en to the world's re-mote con-fine.
2. He who Him-self all things did make A ser-vant's form vouch-safed to take, That He as man man-kind might win And save His crea-tures from their sin.
3. The grace and power of God the Lord Up-on the moth-er was out-poured; A vir-gin pure and un-de-filed In won-drous wise con-ceived a child.
4. The heav'n-ly choirs re-joice and raise Their voice to God in songs of praise. To hum-ble shep-herds is pro-claimed The Shep-herd who the world hath framed.
5. All hon-or un-to Christ be paid, Pure off-spring of the fa-vored maid, With Fa-ther and with Ho-ly Ghost, Till time in end-less time be lost. A-men.

CHORAL HYMNS

599 JESUS, JOY OF MAN'S DESIRING
WERDE MUNTER 8.7.8.7.8.8.7.7.

Martin Janus, 1661
Jesu, meiner Seelen Wonne
Tr. Unknown

Johann Schop, 1642
Harmony by Johann Sebastian Bach, c. 1727

1 Jesus, joy of man's desiring, Holy wisdom, love most bright,
Drawn by Thee, our souls aspiring, Soar to uncreated light.
Word of God, our flesh that fashioned, With the fire of life impassioned,
Striving still to truth unknown, Soaring, dying round Thy throne.

2 Through the way, where hope is guiding, Hark, what peaceful music rings,
Where the flock, in Thee confiding, Drink of joy from deathless springs.
Theirs is beauty's fairest pleasure; Theirs is wisdom's holiest treasure;
Thou dost ever lead Thine own In the love of joys unknown.

(Numbers in parentheses indicate measures of rest if Bach's accompaniment is used.)

CHORAL HYMNS

JESUS, PRICELESS TREASURE 600
JESU, MEINE FREUDE 6.6.5.6.6.5.7.8.6.

Johann Franck, 1653
Jesu, meine Freude
Tr. Catherine Winkworth, 1853 and 1869

Johann Crüger, 1653
Harmony by Johann Sebastian Bach, 1723

1 Je - sus, price-less trea - sure, Source of pur-est plea - sure, Tru-est friend to me;
2 In Thine arm I rest me; Foes who would mo-lest me Can-not reach me here.
3 Hence, all thoughts of sad-ness! For the Lord of glad-ness, Je - sus, en - ters in:

Long my heart hath pant - ed, Till it well-nigh faint - ed, Thirst-ing af - ter Thee.
Though the earth be shak - ing, Ev - ery heart be quak - ing, Je - sus calms my fear;
Those who love the Fa - ther, Though the storms may gath-er, Still have peace with-in;

Thine I am, O spot - less Lamb, I will suf - fer
Sin and hell in con - flict fell With their heav - iest
Yea, what-e'er we here must bear, Still in Thee lies

naught to hide Thee, Ask for naught be - side Thee.
storms as - sail me: Je - sus will not fail me.
pur - est plea - sure, Je - sus, price - less trea - sure!

CHORAL HYMNS

601 ALL HAIL THE POWER OF JESUS' NAME
DIADEM C.M.

Edward Perronet, 1779 and 1780
Altered by John Rippon

James Ellor, c. 1838

1. All hail the power of Jesus' name! Let angels prostrate fall, Let angels prostrate fall; Bring forth the royal diadem, And crown Him, And crown Him, crown Him, crown Him, crown Him, crown Him, crown Him, crown Him, And crown Him Lord of all. A-men.

2. Ye chosen seed of Israel's race, Ye ransomed of the fall, Ye ransomed of the fall; Hail Him who saves you by His grace,

3. Let every kindred, every tribe, On this terrestrial ball, On this terrestrial ball, To Him all majesty ascribe,

4. O that with yonder sacred throng We at His feet may fall, We at His feet may fall! We'll join the everlasting song,

Another setting of this hymn may be found at No. 95.

CHORAL HYMNS

GOD, THE LORD, A KING REMAINETH 602

Based on Psalm 93   BRYN CALFARIA 8.7.8.7.4.7.
John Keble, 1839   William Owen, 1850

1. God, the Lord, a King remaineth, Robed in His own glorious light;
God hath robed Him and He reigneth; He hath girded Him with might.
Alleluia! Alleluia! Alleluia!
God is King in depth and height! God is King in depth and height!

2. In her everlasting station Earth is poised, to swerve no more;
Thou hast laid Thy throne's foundation From all time where thought can soar.
Alleluia! Alleluia! Alleluia!
Lord, Thou art forevermore! Lord, Thou art forevermore!

3. With all tones of waters blending, Glorious is the breaking deep;
Glorious, beauteous, without ending, God, who reigns on heav'n's high steep.
Alleluia! Alleluia! Alleluia!
Songs of ocean never sleep. Songs of ocean never sleep.

4. Lord, the words Thy lips are telling Are the perfect verity;
Of Thine high eternal dwelling, Holiness shall inmate be:
Alleluia! Alleluia! Alleluia!
Pure is all that lives with Thee. Pure is all that lives with Thee. A-men.

CHORAL HYMNS

603 GOD OF OUR LIFE

YATTENDON 11 10.4.10.4.10.10.

Hugh Thomson Kerr, 1916

H. Ellis Wooldridge, 1890

1. God of our life, through all the cir-cling years, We trust in Thee; In all the past, through all our hopes and fears, Thy hand we see. With each new day, when morn-ing lifts the veil, We own Thy mer-cies, Lord, which nev-er fail.

2. God of the past, our times are in Thy hand; With us a-bide. Lead us by faith to hope's true prom-ised land; Be thou our guide. With Thee to bless, the dark-ness shines as light. And faith's fair vi-sion chang-es in-to sight.

3. God of the com-ing years, through paths un-known We fol-low Thee; When we are strong, Lord, leave us not a-lone; Our ref-uge be. Be Thou for us in life our dai-ly bread, Our heart's true home when all our years have sped.

CHORAL HYMNS

LOVE OF THE FATHER 604

SONG XXII 10.10.10.10.

Anonymous, 12th century
Amor patris et filii
Tr. Robert Bridges, 1899

Orlando Gibbons, 1623
Harmony from *The Yattendon Hymnal*, 1899

1. Love of the Father, love of God the Son,
From whom all came, in whom was all begun;
Who formest heav'nly beauty out of strife,
Creation's whole desire and breath of life.

2. Thou the all holy, Thou supreme in might,
Thou dost give peace, Thy presence maketh right;
Thou with Thy favor all things dost enfold,
With Thine all-kindness free from harm wilt hold.

3. Eternal glory, all men Thee adore,
Who art and shalt be worshiped evermore;
Us whom Thou madest, comfort with Thy might,
And lead us to enjoy Thy heav'nly light. A-men.

CHORAL HYMNS

605 GOD IS WORKING HIS PURPOSE OUT

PURPOSE Irregular

Arthur Campbell Ainger, 1894

Martin Shaw, 1931

1. God is working His purpose out As year succeeds to year: God is working His purpose out, And the time is drawing near; Nearer and
2. From utmost east to utmost west, Where'er man's foot hath trod, By the mouth of many messengers Goes forth the voice of God; Give ear to
3. March we forth in the strength of God, With the banner of Christ unfurled, That the light of the glorious gospel of truth May shine throughout the world: Fight we the
4. All we can do is nothing worth Unless God blesses the deed; Vainly we hope for the harvest-tide Till God gives life to the seed; Yet nearer and

Octaves to the end

CHORAL HYMNS

near-er draws the time, The time that shall sure-ly be,
me, ye con-ti-nents, Ye isles, give ear to me,
fight with sor-row and sin To set their cap-tives free,
near-er draws the time, The time that shall sure-ly be,

When the earth shall be filled with the glo-ry of God
That the earth may be filled with the glo-ry of God
That the earth may be filled with the glo-ry of God
When the earth shall be filled with the glo-ry of God

As the wa-ters cov-er the sea.
As the wa-ters cov-er the sea.
As the wa-ters cov-er the sea.
As the wa-ters cov-er the sea.

CHORAL HYMNS

606 PRAISE GOD FROM WHOM
DOXOLOGY (DEDICATION ANTHEM)

Thomas Ken, 1709

Lowell Mason's *Boston Handel and Haydn Society* . . . , 1830
Possibly Samuel Stanley, d. 1822

Praise God from whom all bless-ings flow,
Praise Him all crea-tures here be-low,
Praise Him a-bove, Praise Him a-bove,

CHORAL HYMNS

Soprano and tenor voices exchanged as in *Harmonia Sacra*, 1876

CHORAL HYMNS

CHORAL HYMNS

BREAD OF THE WORLD 607

GENEVA 118 (RENDEZ A DIEU) 9.8.9.8.D.

La forme des prieres . . ., Strasbourg, 1545
(Second line, Geneva, 1551)
Harmony adapted from Claude Goudimel, 1565

Reginald Heber, 1827

Bread of the world in mer-cy bro-ken, Wine of the soul in mer-cy shed,

By whom the words of life were spo-ken, And in whose death our sins are dead;

Look on the heart by sor-row bro-ken, Look on the tears by sin-ners shed;

And be Thy feast to us a to-ken That by Thy grace our souls are fed.

Another setting of this text may be found at No. 407.

CHORAL HYMNS

608 LORD, ALL MY HEART IS FIXED ON THEE
HERZLICH LIEB HAB' ICH DICH, O HERR 8.8.7 8.8.7.8.8.8.8.4.8.8.

Martin Schalling, 1567
Herzlich lieb hab' ich dich, O Herr
Tr. Catherine Winkworth, 1863

B. Schmid's *Orgeltabulatur-Buch*, 1577
Harmony from *Chorale Book for England*, 1863

1. Lord, all my heart is fixed on Thee, I pray Thee, be not far from me, With tender grace uphold me. The whole wide world delights me not, Of heav'n or earth, Lord, ask I not, If but Thy love enfold me.
2. Rich are Thy gifts! 'Twas God that gave Body and soul and all I have In this poor life of labor; O grant that I may through Thy grace Use all my powers to show Thy praise, And serve and help my neighbor;

CHORAL HYMNS

Yea, though my heart be like to break, Thou art my trust that nought can shake, My por-tion and my hid-den joy, Whose cross could all my bonds de-stroy; Lord Je-sus Christ! My God and Lord! My God and Lord! For-sake me not who trust Thy Word!

From all false doc-trine keep me, Lord; All lies and mal-ice from me ward; In ev-ery cross up-hold Thou me, That I may bear it pa-tient-ly; Lord Je-sus Christ! My God and Lord! My God and Lord! In death Thy com-fort still af-ford. A-men.

CHORAL HYMNS

609 BREAK FORTH, O BEAUTEOUS HEAVENLY LIGHT
ERMUNTRE DICH 8.7.8.7.8.8.7.7.

Johann Rist, 1641
Ermuntre dich, mein schwacher Geist
Tr. St. 1 composite
Sts. 2, 3 Arthur Tozer Russell, 1851

Johann Schop, 1641
Harmony by Johann Sebastian Bach, 1734

1 Break forth, O beau-teous heav'n-ly light, And ush - er in the morn - ing;
2 O won-drous work! O won-drous night, All else so far ex - cell - ing!
3 All bless - ing, thanks, and praise to Thee, Lord Je - sus Christ, be giv - en:

Ye shep-herds, shrink not with af-fright, But hear the an - gel's warn - ing.
The Sav - ior now, un - veiled to sight, On earth as man is dwell - ing:
Our broth - er Thou hast deign'd to be, Our foes in sun - der riv - en.

This Child, now born in in - fan - cy, Our con - fi - dence and
That man to whom a - lone is given Power o'er the lights, the
O grant us through our day of grace With con - stant praise to

joy shall be, The power of Sa - tan break - ing, Our
clouds of heav'n! The trem-bling heav'ns a - dore Him! The
seek Thy face. Grant us ere long in glo - ry With

CHORAL HYMNS

peace e - ter - nal mak - ing.
moun - tains shake be - fore Him!
prais - es to a - dore Thee. A - men.

O SONS AND DAUGHTERS, LET US SING 610
GELOBT SEI GOTT 8.8.8. with Alleluia

Jean Tisserand (?), 15th century
O Filii et Filiae
Tr. John Mason Neale, 1851
Altered by Compilers of *Hymns Ancient and Modern*, 1861

Melchior Vulpius, 1609

1 O sons and daugh-ters, let us sing! The King of heav'n, the
2 That Sun-day morn, at break of day, The faith-ful wom - en
3 An an - gel clad in white they see, Who sat and spake un -
4 How blest are they who have not seen, And yet whose faith hath
5 On this most ho - ly day of days, To God your hearts and

glo - rious King, O'er death to - day rose tri - umph - ing.
went their way To seek the tomb where Je - sus lay.
to the three, "Your Lord doth go to Gal - i - lee."
con - stant been; For they e - ter - nal life shall win.
voic - es raise In laud, and ju - bi - lee, and praise.

Al - le - lu - ia! Al - le - lu - ia! Al - le - lu - ia!

CHORAL HYMNS

611 CHRIST LAY AWHILE IN DEATH'S STRONG BANDS
CHRIST LAG IN TODESBANDEN 8.7.8.7.7.8.7.4.

Martin Luther, 1524
Christ lag in Todesbanden
Tr. Richard Massie, 1854

Melody adapted from *Christ ist erstanden* in 1524
Version of Johann Sebastian Bach, c. 1740

1 Christ lay a-while in death's strong bands, For our of - fenc - es giv - en;
2 It was a strange and dread-ful strife, When life and death con - tend - ed;
3 So let us keep the fes - ti - val, Where-to the Lord in - vites us;
4 Then let us feast this Ea - ster day On the true bread of heav - en;

But now at God's right hand He stands, And brings us life from heav - en:
The vic - to - ry re-mained with life, The reign of death was end - ed:
Christ is Him-self the joy of all, The sun which warms and lights us;
The Word of grace hath purged a - way The old and wick - ed leav - en:

Where-fore let us joy - ful be, And sing to God right thank - ful - ly
Ho - ly Scrip - tures plain - ly saith, That death is swal - lowed up by death,
By His grace He doth im - part E - ter - nal sun - shine to the heart;
Christ a - lone our souls will feed, He is our meat and drink in - deed;

Loud songs of Al - le - lu - ia! Al - le - lu - ia!
Made hence-forth a de - ri - sion. Al - le - lu - ia!
The night of sin is end - ed. Al - le - lu - ia!
Faith lives up - on no oth - er. Al - le - lu - ia!

CHORAL HYMNS

CHRIST IS ARISEN 612
CHRIST IST ERSTANDEN

German Hymn, c. 1100
Christ ist erstanden, von der Marter alle
Tr. William Gustave Polack, 1939

Germany Melody, 12th century
Version, Wittenberg, 1529

Christ is a-ris-en From the grave's dark pris-on. We now re-joice with glad-ness;

Christ will end all sad-ness. Lord, have mer-cy. All our hopes were end-ed

Had Je-sus not as-cend-ed From the grave tri-um-phant-ly. For this, Lord Christ,

we wor-ship Thee. Lord, have mer-cy. Al-le-lu-ia! Al-le-lu-ia! Al-le-lu-ia!

We now re-joice with glad-ness; Christ will end all sad-ness. Lord, have mer-cy. A-men.

CHORAL HYMNS

613 THE LORD IS RISEN INDEED
EASTER ANTHEM

"Words from Scripture and Dr. Young"
William Billings, 1786

Hal - le - lu - jah. The Lord is ris'n in - deed. Hal - le - lu - jah.

The Lord is ris'n in - deed.

Now is Christ ris - en from the dead and be - come the first fruits of them that slept.

Now is Christ ris - en from the dead and be - come the first fruits of them that slept.

Hal - le - lu - jah, Hal - le - lu - jah.
Hal - le - lu - jah,

CHORAL HYMNS

CHORAL HYMNS

Then first hu-man-i-ty tri-um-phant passed the crys-tal ports of light and seized e-ter-nal youth. youth. Man all im-mor-tal, hail, hail, Hea-ven all lav-ish of strange gifts to man. Thine all the glo-ry, Man's the bound-less bliss. Thine all the glo-ry, Man's the bound-less bliss.

CHORAL HYMNS

THIS JOYFUL EASTERTIDE 614

VRUECHTEN 6.7.6.7. with Refrain

George Ratcliffe Woodward, 1902

David's Psalmen, Amsterdam, 1685
Harmony by Alice Parker, 1966

1. This joyful Eastertide A-way with sin and sorrow!
My love, the Crucified, Hath sprung to life this morrow.
2. My flesh in hope shall rest, And for a season slumber:
Till trump from east to west Shall wake the dead in number,
3. Death's flood hath lost its chill, Since Jesus crossed the river:
Lover of souls, from ill My passing soul deliver.

Had Christ, that once was slain, Ne'er burst His three-day prison, Our faith had been in vain: But now hath Christ arisen, a-risen, a-risen, a-ris - - - en.

CHORAL HYMNS

615 BUILT ON THE ROCK
KIRKEN DEN ER ET 8.8.8.8.8.8.8.8.

Nicolai F. S. Grundtvig, 1837
Kirken den er et gammelt Hus
Tr. Carl Döving†, 1909

Ludvig M. Lindeman, 1840

1 Built on the Rock the church doth stand, E-ven when stee-ples are fall-ing; Crum-bled have spires in ev-ery land, Bells still are chim-ing and call-ing, Call-ing the young and old to rest, But a-bove all the soul dis-trest, Long-ing for rest ev-er-last-ing.

2 Sure-ly in tem-ples made with hands, God, the most high, is not dwell-ing; High a-bove earth His tem-ple stands, All earth-ly tem-ples ex-cell-ing. Yet He whom heav'ns can-not con-tain Chose to a-bide on earth with men, Built in our bod-ies His tem-ple.

3 Now we may gath-er with our King E'en in the low-li-est dwell-ing; Prais-es to Him we there may bring, His won-drous mer-cy forth-tell-ing. Je-sus His grace to us ac-cords; Spir-it and life are all His words; His truth doth hal-low the tem-ple.

CHORAL HYMNS

O JESUS CHRIST, TO THEE MAY HYMNS 616
CITY OF GOD 11.10.11.10.

Bradford Gray Webster, 1954 — Daniel Moe, 1957

1. O Jesus Christ, to Thee may hymns be rising,
In every city for Thy love and care;
Inspire our worship, grant the glad surprising
That Thy blest Spirit brings men everywhere.

2. Grant us new courage, sacrificial, humble,
Strong in Thy strength to venture and to dare;
To lift the fallen, guide the feet that stumble,
Seek out the lonely and God's mercy share.

3. Show us Thy Spirit, brooding o'er each city,
As Thou didst weep above Jerusalem,
Seeking to gather all in love and pity,
And healing those who touch Thy garment's hem.

CHORAL HYMNS

617 I LOVE THE LORD
GELINEAU 114

Based on Psalm 116
Gelineau *Psalms*, 1953
Tr. Ladies of the Grail, 1955

Joseph Gelineau, 1953, and Others

1. I love the Lord, for He has heard the cry of my ap-peal;
2. They sur-rounded me, the snares of death, with the anguish of the tomb;
3. How gracious is the Lord, and just; our God has com-passion.
4. Turn back, my soul, to your rest for the Lord has been good,
5. I will walk in the presence of the Lord in the land of the living.

1. for He turned His ear to me, in the day when I called Him.
2. they caught me, sorrow and dis-tress. I called on the Lord's name.
3. The Lord pro-tects the simple hearts, I was helpless, so He saved me.
4. He has kept my soul from death, and my feet from stum-bling.
5. Praise the Father, the Son, and Holy Spirit, for-ever and ev - er.

Antiphon 1
Obligatory
after verse 2

O Lord, my God, de-liv-er me!

A. G. Murray

Antiphon 2

When I cry to the Lord, He hears my prayer.

C. W. Howell

Antiphon 3

I will walk in the pres-ence of the Lord in the land of the liv - ing.

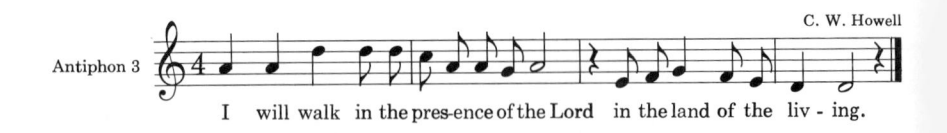

One Antiphon should be sung following each stanza. The Psalm may be sung by a soloist (soloists) and the Antiphon by choir or congregation.

CHORAL HYMNS

CRY OUT WITH JOY 618

GELINEAU 99

Based on Psalm 100
Gelineau *Psalms*, 1953
Tr. Ladies of the Grail, 1955

Joseph Gelineau, 1953
and A. Gregory Murray

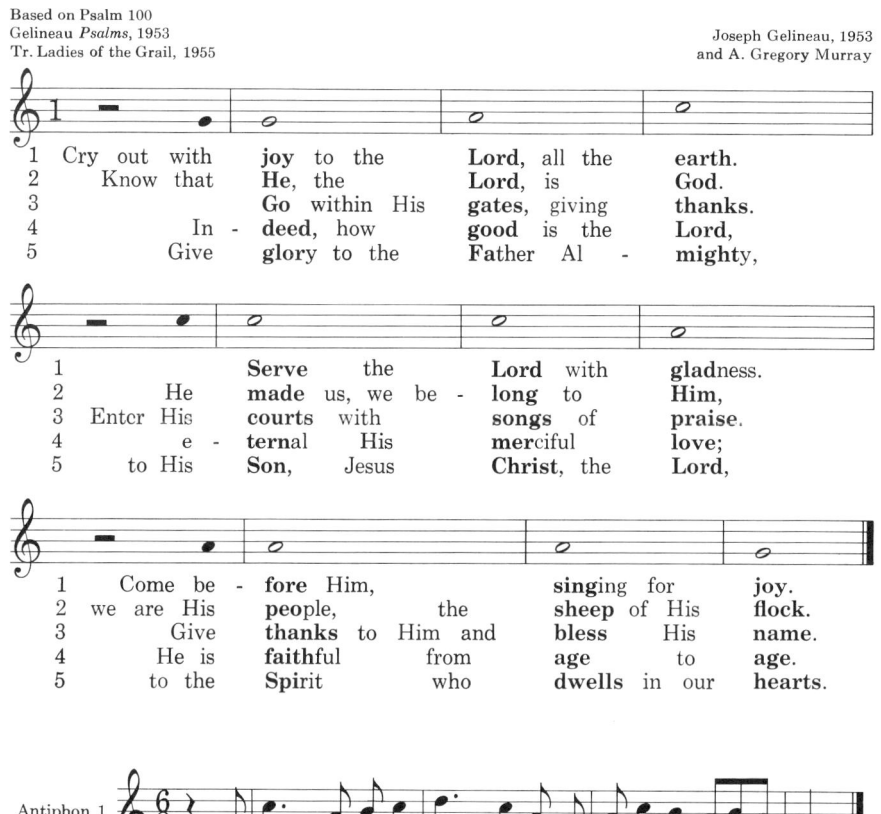

1. Cry out with joy to the Lord, all the earth.
   Serve the Lord with gladness.
   Come before Him, singing for joy.
2. Know that He, the Lord, is God.
   He made us, we belong to Him,
   we are His people, the sheep of His flock.
3. Go within His gates, giving thanks.
   Enter His courts with songs of praise.
   Give thanks to Him and bless His name.
4. Indeed, how good is the Lord,
   eternal His merciful love;
   He is faithful from age to age.
5. Give glory to the Father Almighty,
   to His Son, Jesus Christ, the Lord,
   to the Spirit who dwells in our hearts.

Antiphon 1: A-rise, come to your God, sing Him your songs of re-joic - ing.

Antiphon 2: Glo-ry to You, O God!

Antiphon 3 (A. G. Murray): Al-le-lu-ia, al-le-lu-ia, al-le-lu-ia.

One Antiphon should be sung following each stanza. The Psalm may be sung by a soloist (soloists) and the Antiphon by choir or congregation.

CHORAL HYMNS

619 LORD, THOU HAST SEARCHED ME
TENDER THOUGHT L.M.

Based on Psalm 139
The Psalter Hymnal, 1927

Folk Hymn
A. Davisson's *Kentucky Harmony*, 1816

1. Lord, Thou hast searched me and dost know
Wher-e'er I rest, wher-e'er I go;
Thou knowest all that I have planned,
And all my ways are in Thy hand.

2. My words from Thee I cannot hide;
I feel Thy power on every side;
O wondrous knowledge, awful might,
Unfathomed depth, unmeasured height!

3. Where can I go apart from Thee,
Or whither from Thy presence flee?
In heav'n? It is Thy dwelling fair;
In death's abode? Lo, Thou art there.

4. If I the wings of morning take,
And far away my dwelling make,
The hand that leadeth me is Thine,
And my support Thy power divine.

5. If deepest darkness cover me,
The darkness hideth not from Thee;
To Thee both night and day are bright,
The darkness shineth as the light.

CHORAL HYMNS

THE LORD IS IN HIS HOLY TEMPLE 620

Habakkuk 2:20
George Frederick Root, d. 1895

The Lord is in His ho-ly tem-ple, The Lord is in His ho-ly tem-ple, Let all the earth keep si-lence, Let all the earth keep si-lence be-fore Him, Keep si-lence, keep si-lence be-fore Him. A-men.

THE LORD IS IN HIS HOLY TEMPLE 621

Habakkuk 2:20
Edwin Othello Excell, c. 1902

The Lord is in His ho-ly tem-ple, Let all the earth keep si-lence, keep si-lence be-fore Him. A-men.

MUSICAL AIDS TO WORSHIP

622 HOLY, HOLY, HOLY, LORD GOD

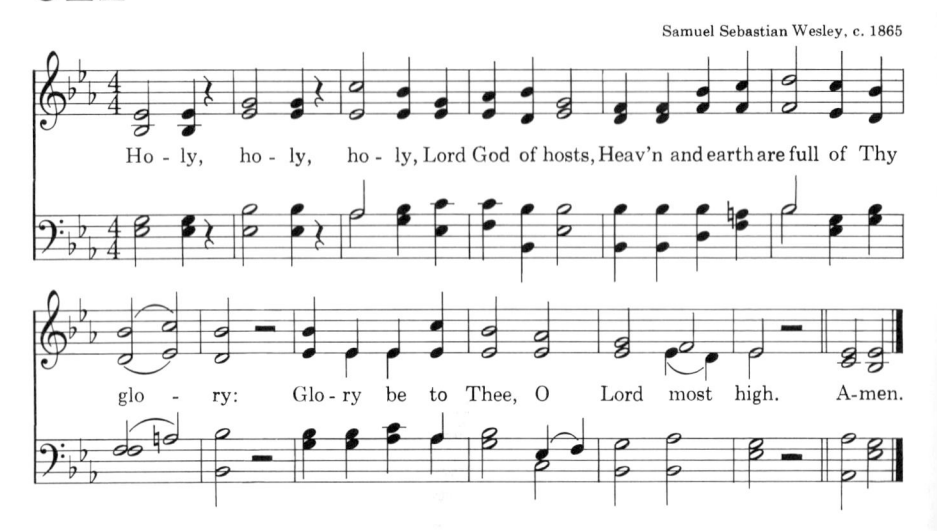

Samuel Sebastian Wesley, c. 1865

Ho-ly, ho-ly, ho-ly, Lord God of hosts, Heav'n and earth are full of Thy glo-ry: Glo-ry be to Thee, O Lord most high. A-men.

623 NOW TO THE KING OF HEAVEN

ST. JOHN 6.6.6.6.8.8.

Philip Doddridge, 1755 and Isaac Watts, 1719

The Parish Choir, 1851

Now to the King of heav'n Your cheer-ful voic-es raise; To Him be glo-ry giv'n, Power, maj-es-ty and praise; Wide as He reigns His name be sung By ev-ery tongue in end-less strains. A-men.

MUSICAL AIDS TO WORSHIP

JESUS, STAND AMONG US 624
WEM IN LEIDENSTAGEN 6.5.6.5.

William Pennefather, 1855
Friedrich Filitz, 1847

1 Jesus, stand among us In Thy risen power;
Let this time of worship Be a hallowed hour.

2 Breathe the Holy Spirit Into every heart;
Bid the fears and sorrows From each soul depart. A-men.

O LORD OF LOVE, THOU LIGHT DIVINE 625
VICTORY 8.8.8. with Alleluia

Giovanni Pierluigi da Palestrina, 1591
Adapted by William Henry Monk, 1861

O Lord of love, Thou light divine, O'er all the world Thy glories shine;
Thee we adore, for we are Thine. Alleluia!

MUSICAL AIDS TO WORSHIP

626 O COME, LET US WORSHIP

Psalm 95: 6,7
J. Harold Moyer, 1964

O come, let us wor-ship and bow down; Let us kneel be-fore the Lord our Mak-er. For He is our God, And we are the peo-ple of His pas-ture and the sheep of His hand.

627 OUR FATHER WHO ART IN HEAVEN

Matthew 6: 9-13

1 Our Father who art in heaven, Hallowed be Thy name.
2 Give us this day our dai-ly bread.
3 And lead us not into temptation, but deliver us from evil:

Thy kingdom come. Thy will be done in earth, as it is in heaven.
And forgive us our trespasses, as we forgive them that trespass a-gainst us.
For Thine is the kingdom, and the power, and the glory, for-ever. A-men.

MUSICAL AIDS TO WORSHIP

CREATE IN ME A CLEAN HEART 628

Psalm 51: 10-12

1. Create in me a clean heart, O God; and renew a right spirit within me.
2. Cast me not away from Thy presence; and take not Thy Holy Spirit from me.
3. Restore unto me the joy of Thy salvation; and uphold me with Thy free spirit.

ALMIGHTY FATHER, HEAR OUR PRAYER 629

Arranged from Felix Mendelssohn, 1846

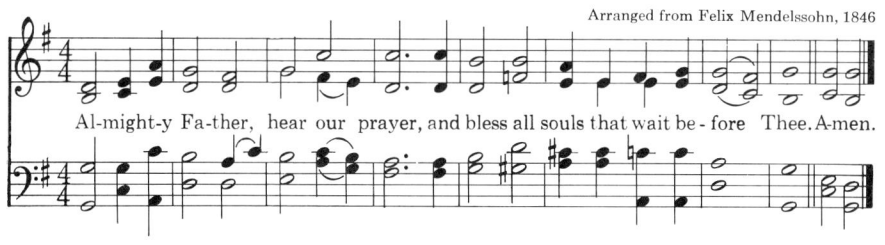

Almighty Father, hear our prayer, and bless all souls that wait before Thee. Amen.

HEAR THOU OUR PRAYER 630

Nelson T. Huffman, b. 1901

Hear Thou our prayer, Lord, and bless all souls that wait before Thee. Amen.

MUSICAL AIDS TO WORSHIP

631 SEND OUT THY LIGHT AND THY TRUTH
LUX FIAT

Psalm 43: 3
Charles F. Gounod, d. 1893

Send out Thy light and Thy truth, let them lead me; O let them bring me to Thy ho-ly hill. Send out Thy light and Thy truth, let them lead me; O let them bring me to Thy ho-ly hill. O let them lead me, O let them lead me; O let them bring me to Thy ho-ly hill. A-men.

MUSICAL AIDS TO WORSHIP

GLORY BE TO GOD ON HIGH 632

Before 500, A.D.
Gloria in excelsis Deo

Scottish Chant

1 Glory be to God on high: and on earth peace, good will towards men.
2 We praise Thee, worship Thee: we glorify Thee, we bless Thee, we give thanks to Thee for Thy great glory.

3 O Lord God, heavenly King: God the Father Almighty.
4 O Lord, the only-begotten Son Jesus Christ: O Lord God, Lamb of God, Son of the Father,

5 That takest away the sins of the world: have mercy upon us.
6 Thou that takest away the sins of the world: receive our prayer.
7 Thou that sittest at the right hand of God the Father: have mercy upon us.

8 For Thou only art holy: Thou only art the Lord.
9 Thou only, O Christ, with the Holy Ghost: art most high in the glory of God the Father. Amen.

MUSICAL AIDS TO WORSHIP

633 LET THE WORDS OF MY MOUTH

Psalm 19: 14
Adolph Baumbach, 1862

Let the words of my mouth and the med-i-ta-tions of my heart be ac-cept-a-ble in Thy sight, O Lord, my strength and my Re-deem-er. A-men.

634 BLESS THOU THE GIFTS
CANONBURY L.M.

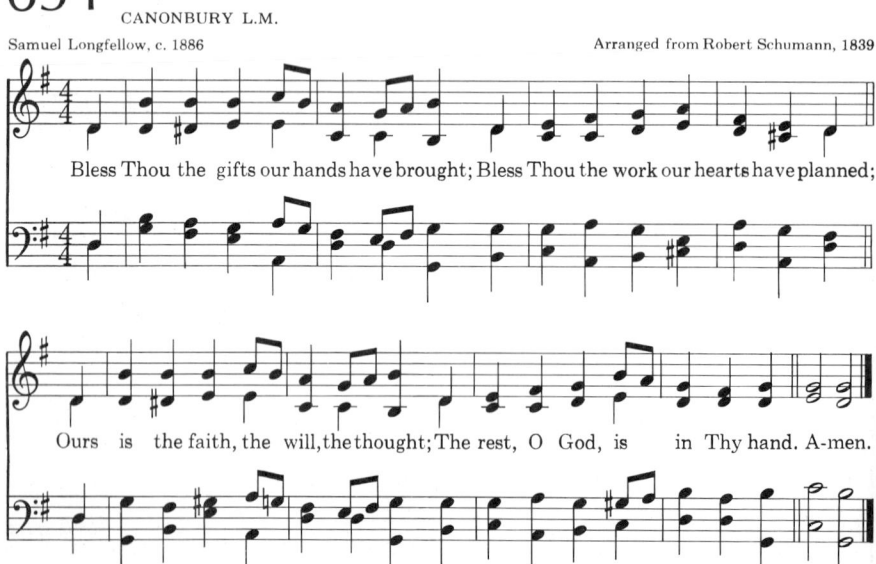

Samuel Longfellow, c. 1886
Arranged from Robert Schumann, 1839

Bless Thou the gifts our hands have brought; Bless Thou the work our hearts have planned;
Ours is the faith, the will, the thought; The rest, O God, is in Thy hand. A-men.

MUSICAL AIDS TO WORSHIP

GRANT US, LORD, THE GRACE OF GIVING 635
STUTTGART 8.7.8.7.

C. F. Witt, 1715
Adapted by Henry John Gauntlett, 1861

Grant us, Lord, the grace of giv-ing, With a spir-it large and free,

That our-selves and all our liv-ing We may of-fer un-to Thee. A-men.

ALL THINGS COME OF THEE 636

I Chronicles 29: 14b

All things come of Thee, O Lord; and of Thine own have we giv-en Thee. A-men.

GREAT GOD, THOU GIVER OF ALL 637
RETREAT L.M.

James Skinner, d. 1881

Thomas Hastings, 1842

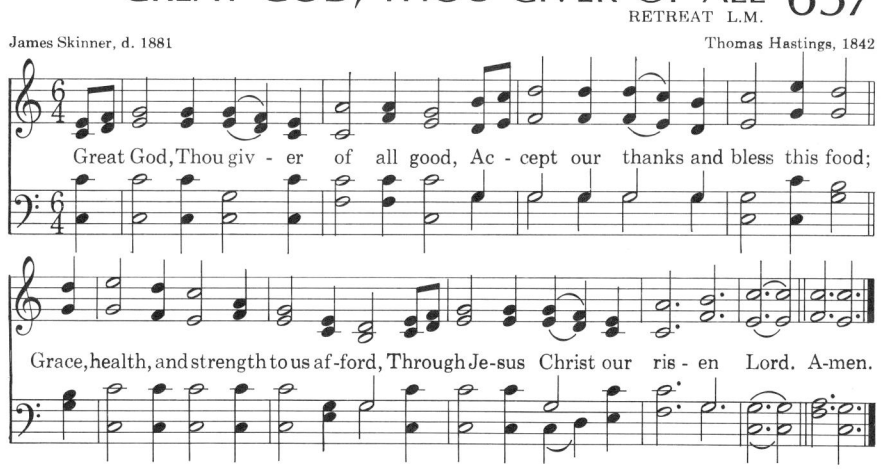

Great God, Thou giv-er of all good, Ac-cept our thanks and bless this food;

Grace, health, and strength to us af-ford, Through Je-sus Christ our ris-en Lord. A-men.

MUSICAL AIDS TO WORSHIP

638 PRAISE GOD FROM WHOM ALL BLESSINGS FLOW
OLD HUNDREDTH L.M.

Thomas Ken, 1709 — *Pseaumes octante trois . . . , Geneva, 1551*

Praise God, from whom all bless-ings flow; Praise Him, all crea-tures here be-low;

Praise Him a-bove, ye heav'n-ly host; Praise Fa-ther, Son, and Ho-ly Ghost. A-men.

639 BE PRESENT AT OUR TABLE, LORD
OLD HUNDREDTH L.M.

John Cennick, 1741 — *Pseaumes octante trois . . . , Geneva, 1551* — English form of final line

Be pres-ent at our ta-ble, Lord; Be here, and ev-ery-where a-dored;

Thy crea-tures bless, and grant that we May feast in par-a-dise with Thee. A-men.

MUSICAL AIDS TO WORSHIP — Other forms of Old Hundredth may be found at Numbers 2 and 3.

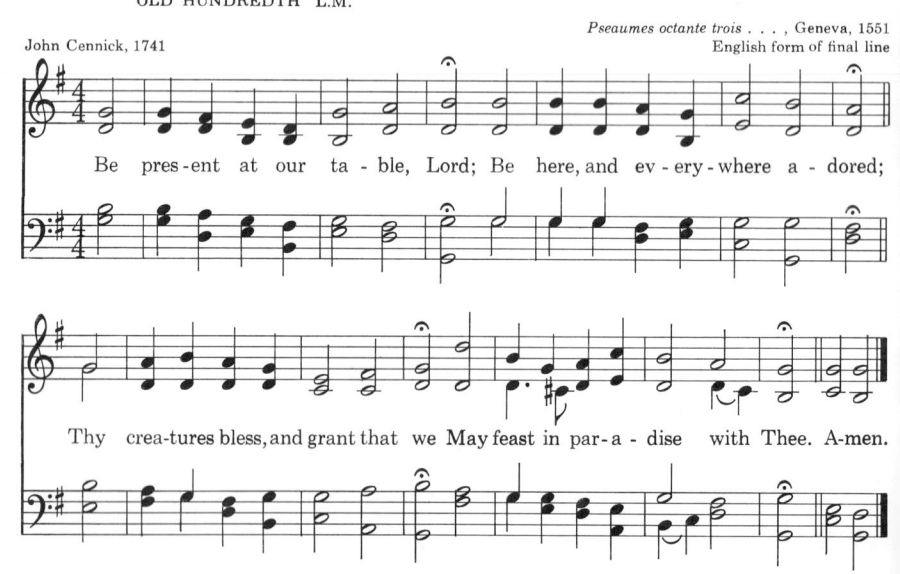

GLORY BE TO THE FATHER 640

Early Christian Doxology
Gloria Patri

From H. W. Greatorex' *Collection*, 1851

Glo-ry be to the Fa-ther, and to the Son, and to the Ho-ly Ghost; As it was in the be-gin-ning, is now, and ev-er shall be, world with-out end. A-men, A-men.

GLORY BE TO THE FATHER 641

Early Christian Doxology
Gloria Patri

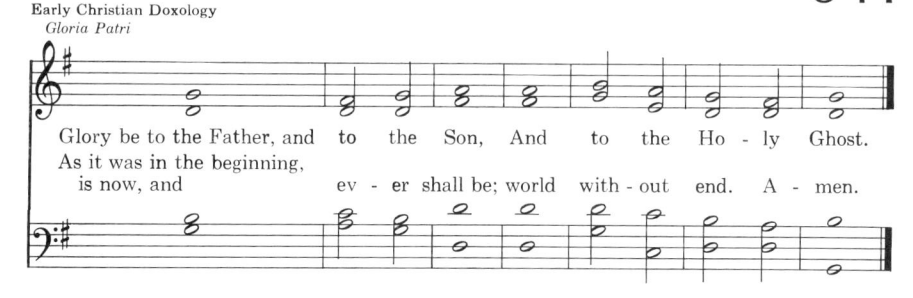

Glory be to the Father, and to the Son, And to the Ho-ly Ghost. As it was in the beginning, is now, and ev-er shall be; world with-out end. A-men.

GLORY BE TO THE FATHER 642

Early Christian Doxology
Gloria Patri

Christopher Meineke, 1844

Glo-ry be to the Fa-ther, and to the Son, and to the Ho-ly Ghost; As it was in the be-gin-ning, is now, and ev-er shall be, world with-out end. A-men, A-men.

MUSICAL AIDS TO WORSHIP

643 CAST THY BURDEN UPON THE LORD
BIRMINGHAM (MENDELSSOHN)

Julius Schubring, b. 1806
Wirf dein Anliegen auf den Herrn
Tr. William Bartholomew, 1846

Felix Mendelssohn, 1846

Cast thy bur-den up-on the Lord, And He shall sus-tain thee: He nev-er will suf-fer the right-eous to fall; He is at thy right hand. Thy mer-cy, Lord, is great, and far a-bove the heav'ns; Let none be made a-sham-ed, that wait up-on Thee. A-men.

MUSICAL AIDS TO WORSHIP

CHRIST, WE DO ALL ADORE THEE 644

Adoramus Te Christe   Theodore Dubois, 1867

Christ, we do all adore Thee, And we do praise Thee forever, Christ, we do all adore Thee, And we do praise Thee forever, For on the holy cross Thou hast the world from sin redeemed. Christ, we do all adore Thee, And we do praise Thee forever. Christ, we do all adore Thee.

MUSICAL AIDS TO WORSHIP

645 GOD BE IN MY HEAD
GOD BE IN MY HEAD

Book of Hours†, 1514 H. Walford Davies, 1910

God be in my head, and in my un-der-stand-ing;
God be in mine eyes and in my look-ing; God be in my mouth, and in my speak-ing; God be in my heart, and in my think-ing;
God be at mine end, and at my de-part-ing.

MUSICAL AIDS TO WORSHIP

GRACE TO YOU AND PEACE 646

Romans 1:7
Alice Parker, 1962

Grace to you and peace from God the Father, and the Lord Jesus Christ, A - men.

Grace to you and peace from God the Father, and the Lord Jesus Christ, A - men.

Grace to you and peace from God the Father, and the Lord Jesus Christ, A - men.

MAY THE GRACE OF CHRIST 647

RINGE RECHT 8.7.8.7.

John Newton, 1779
J. Thommen's *Erbaulicher Musicalischer Christen-Schatz*, 1745

1 May the grace of Christ our Savior, And the Father's boundless love,
With the Holy Spirit's favor Rest upon us from above.

2 Thus may we abide in union With each other and the Lord,
And possess, in sweet communion, Joys which earth cannot afford. A-men.

MUSICAL AIDS TO WORSHIP

648 DRESDEN AMEN

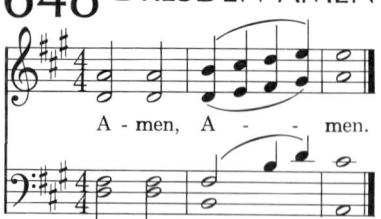

649 TWOFOLD AMEN

650 THREEFOLD AMEN

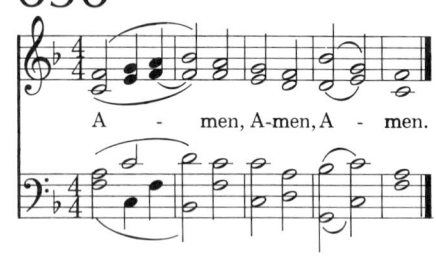

651 THREEFOLD AMEN

652 FOURFOLD AMEN
John Stainer

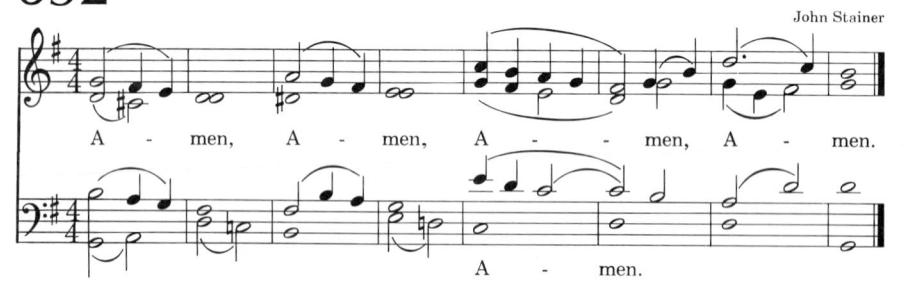

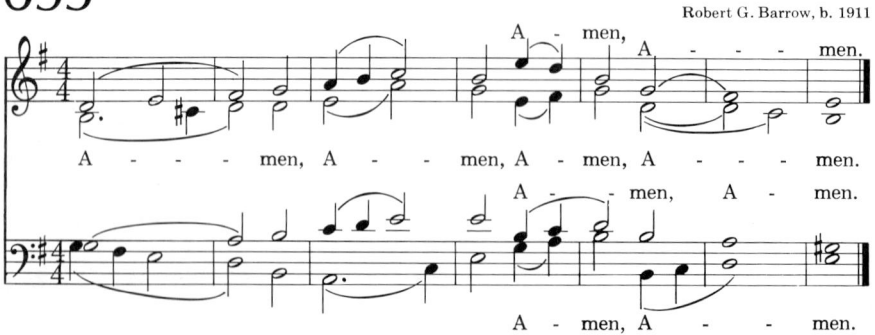

653 FOURFOLD AMEN
Robert G. Barrow, b. 1911

MUSICAL AIDS TO WORSHIP

Additional Worship Resources

INTRODUCTION

Recently all churches have recognized a need for greater congregational participation in Christian worship. In many churches the only corporate expression has been the singing of hymns. If there is to be greater congregational involvement, materials must be available. This section of *The Mennonite Hymnal* is an attempt to meet that need. Materials are provided only for worship forms which can be used corporately by the congregation. Texts for other forms, such as calls to worship, pastoral prayers, etc., can be obtained elsewhere.

Scripture Readings

Scripture readings represent all portions of salvation history, from the song of Moses to the final songs of hope in the Book of Revelation. All readings are *units* of Scripture, not collections of verses from several chapters. Five English translations are represented, although most of the selections are from the *Revised Standard Version*. In selecting the translations to be used, each passage was studied for clarity of thought and for ease in group reading as well as accuracy of translation.

The format suggests that these readings can be read in three different ways: in unison, responsively, or antiphonally. For antiphonal passages the congregation will need to be divided into two groups for alternate reading. Where several suggestions are listed for one reading, they are given in order of preference, determined largely by the nature of the text. All readings can, of course, be in unison. Each worshiping group will need to decide how a Scripture passage is to be read. This choice will depend on the size of the group, the nature of the service, the preference of the worship leader, and other factors.

A topical index for Scripture readings has been incorporated in the Topical Index for Hymns. This encourages a close coordination of hymns and Scripture readings in worship services. Worship leaders may wish to develop their own topical index.

Affirmations of Faith

Four affirmations of faith are given to provide an opportunity for congregations to express unitedly and in summary form the essentials of Christian belief. These affirmations do not represent official documents of any church body; but they are, in a sense, the church's answer to the Word of God. No one statement covers the entire range of Christian doctrine. The Nicene Creed and the Apostles' Creed are confessions that were developed from the fourth to the eighth centuries. A contemporary Affirmation of Faith (No. 723) was created by several church leaders for *The Mennonite Hymnal* and was completed in 1967.

Every hymn that a congregation sings is, in a sense, an affirmation of faith. Scripture readings can also be used as confessions of faith.

Congregational Responses

Congregational responses offer opportunities for congregations to participate more actively in the many special services in the life of the church. Material given here is not the complete service, but can be included at the appropriate time.

Prayers

When congregations pray, they usually think about specific concerns at certain times and places. But there are also needs and conditions of a universal nature that find expression in the prayers of Christians everywhere. A need to confess, a desire to praise, a concern for the church and for the world—these and many more find expression in all congregations of Christian people. To enable churches to give corporate expression in prayer, several prayers from both ancient and contemporary sources are included. Scripture readings, such as No. 670 (Psalm 51) and No. 686 (Daniel 9), can also be used as prayers. Worship leaders may wish to supplement this collection with other prayers.

CONTENTS

Section 1. Scripture Readings 654-719
(Listed by subjects in Topical Index of hymns, pages 625-633, and at end of this section, pages 606 and 607.)

Section 2. Affirmations of Faith..............................720-723

    An Affirmation of Faith from the Writings of John..........720
    Apostles' Creed, The 721
    Nicene Creed, The 722
    An Affirmation of Faith (Contemporary) 723

Section 3. Congregational Responses 724-733

    Baptism 724, 725
    Pledge of Faith and Love (Lord's Supper) 726
    Reception of New Members, On.........................727
    Newly Married, To the................................728
    Dedication of Children, At the.........................729
    Installation or Ordination of a Minister, On.............730
    Restoration, Statement of 731
    Commissioning Workers, In 732
    Benediction, A 733

Section 4. Prayers 734-752

    Opening 734-736
    Thanksgiving 737, 738
    Confession 739, 740
    Supplication and Intercession 741-748
    Offering 749
    Closing 750-752

SECTION I
Scripture Readings

654 Exodus 15:1-12, 15b-18
(Responsively or Antiphonally)

Then Moses and the people of Israel sang this song to the Lord, saying,

I will sing to the Lord, for he has triumphed gloriously; the horse and his rider he has thrown into the sea.

The Lord is my strength and my song, and he has become my salvation;

This is my God, and I will praise him, my father's God, and I will exalt him.

The Lord is a man of war; the Lord is his name.

Pharaoh's chariots and his host he cast into the sea; and his picked officers are sunk in the Red Sea.

The floods cover them; they went down into the depths like a stone.

Thy right hand, O Lord, glorious in power, thy right hand, O Lord, shatters the enemy.

In the greatness of thy majesty thou overthrowest thy adversaries; thou sendest forth thy fury, it consumes them like stubble.

At the blast of thy nostrils the waters piled up, the floods stood up in a heap; the deeps congealed in the heart of the sea.

The enemy said, "I will pursue, I will overtake, I will divide the spoil, my desire shall have its fill of them. I will draw my sword, my hand shall destroy them."

Thou didst blow with thy wind, the sea covered them; they sank as lead in the mighty waters.

Who is like thee, O Lord, among the gods? Who is like thee, majestic in holiness, terrible in glorious deeds, doing wonders?

Thou didst stretch out thy right hand, the earth swallowed them.

All the inhabitants of Canaan have melted away. Terror and dread fall upon them; because of the greatness of thy arm, they are as still as a stone,

Till thy people, O Lord, pass by, till the people pass by whom thou hast purchased.

Thou wilt bring them in, and plant them on thy own mountain, the place, O Lord, which thou hast made for thy abode, the sanctuary, O Lord, which thy hands have established.

The Lord will reign for ever and ever.

655 Exodus 20:2-17
(Antiphonally)

I am the Lord your God, who brought you out of the land of Egypt, out of the house of bondage.

You shall have no other gods before me.

You shall not make for yourself a graven image, or any likeness of anything that is in heaven above, or that is in the earth beneath, or that is in the water under the earth;

You shall not bow down to them or serve them; for I the Lord your God am a jealous God, visiting the iniquity of the fathers upon the children to the third and the fourth generation of those who hate me, but showing steadfast love to thousands of those who love me and keep my commandments.

You shall not take the name of the Lord your God in vain; for the Lord

SCRIPTURE READINGS

will not hold him guiltless who takes his name in vain.

Remember the sabbath day, to keep it holy. Six days you shall labor, and do all your work, but the seventh day is a sabbath to the Lord your God;

In it you shall not do any work, you, or your son, or your daughter, your manservant, or your maidservant, or your cattle, or the sojourner who is within your gates;

For in six days the Lord made heaven and earth, the sea, and all that is in them, and rested the seventh day; therefore the Lord blessed the sabbath day and hallowed it.

Honor your father and your mother, that your days may be long in the land which the Lord your God gives you.

You shall not kill.

You shall not commit adultery.

You shall not steal.

You shall not bear false witness against your neighbor.

You shall not covet your neighbor's house; you shall not covet your neighbor's wife, or his manservant, or his maidservant, or his ox, or his ass, or anything that is your neighbor's.

656   Deuteronomy 6:4-15
(Antiphonally)

(Unison)
Hear, O Israel: The Lord our God is one Lord; and you shall love the Lord your God with all your heart, and with all your soul, and with all your might.
(Antiphonally)
And these words which I command you this day shall be upon your heart; and you shall teach them diligently to your children, and shall talk of them when you sit in your house, and when you walk by the way, and when you lie down, and when you rise.

And you shall bind them as a sign upon your hand, and they shall be as frontlets between your eyes. And you shall write them on the doorposts of your house and on your gates.

And when the Lord your God brings you into the land which he swore to your fathers, to Abraham, to Isaac, and to Jacob, to give you, with great and goodly cities, which you did not build, and houses full of all good things, which you did not fill, and cisterns hewn out, which you did not hew, and vineyards and olive trees, which you did not plant, and when you eat and are full,

Then take heed lest you forget the Lord, who brought you out of the land of Egypt, out of the house of bondage.

You shall fear the Lord your God; you shall serve him, and swear by his name.

You shall not go after other gods, of the gods of the peoples who are round about you; for the Lord your God in the midst of you is a jealous God; lest the anger of the Lord your God be kindled against you, and he destroy you from off the face of the earth.

657   2 Samuel 22:2-7, 17-25
(Responsively, Antiphonally, or Unison)
The Lord is my rock, and my fortress, and my deliverer, my God, my rock, in whom I take refuge,

My shield and the horn of my salvation, my stronghold and my

SCRIPTURE READINGS

refuge, my savior; thou savest me from violence.

I call upon the Lord, who is worthy to be praised, and I am saved from my enemies.

For the waves of death encompassed me, the torrents of perdition assailed me;

The cords of Sheol entangled me, the snares of death confronted me.

In my distress I called upon the Lord; to my God I called.

From his temple he heard my voice, and my cry came to his ears.

He reached from on high, he took me, he drew me out of many waters.

He delivered me from my strong enemy, from those who hated me; for they were too mighty for me.

They came upon me in the day of my calamity; but the Lord was my stay.

He brought me forth into a broad place; he delivered me, because he delighted in me.

The Lord rewarded me according to my righteousness; according to the cleanness of my hands he recompensed me.

For I have kept the ways of the Lord, and have not wickedly departed from my God.

For all his ordinances were before me, and from his statutes I did not turn aside.

I was blameless before him, and I kept myself from guilt.

Therefore the Lord has recompensed me according to my righteousness, according to my cleanness in his sight.

658   1 Chronicles 16:23-34
(Responsively, Antiphonally, or Unison)

Sing to the Lord, all the earth! Tell of his salvation from day to day.

Declare his glory among the nations, his marvelous works among all the peoples!

For great is the Lord, and greatly to be praised, and he is to be held in awe above all gods.

For all the gods of the peoples are idols; but the Lord made the heavens.

Honor and majesty are before him; strength and joy are in his place.

Ascribe to the Lord, O families of the peoples, ascribe to the Lord glory and strength!

Ascribe to the Lord the glory due his name; bring an offering, and come before him!

Worship the Lord in holy array; tremble before him, all the earth; yea, the world stands firm, never to be moved.

Let the heavens be glad, and let the earth rejoice, and let them say among the nations, "The Lord reigns!"

Let the sea roar, and all that fills it, let the field exult, and everything in it!

Then shall the trees of the wood sing for joy before the Lord, for he comes to judge the earth.

O give thanks to the Lord, for he is good; for his steadfast love endures for ever!

659   Job 28:12-15, 20-21, 23-28
(Antiphonally or Responsively)

But where shall wisdom be found? And where is the place of under-

SCRIPTURE READINGS

standing?

Man does not know the way to it, and it is not found in the land of the living.

The deep says, "It is not in me," and the sea says, "It is not with me."

It cannot be gotten for gold, and silver cannot be weighed as its price.

Whence then comes wisdom? And where is the place of understanding?

It is hid from the eyes of all living, and concealed from the birds of the air.

God understands the way to it, and he knows its place.

For he looks to the ends of the earth, and sees everything under the heavens.

When he gave to the wind its weight, and meted out the waters by measure;

When he made a decree for the rain, and a way for the lightning of the thunder;

Then he saw it and declared it; he established it, and searched it out.

And he said to man, "Behold, the fear of the Lord, that is wisdom; and to depart from evil is understanding."

660   Psalm 1:1-6
(Antiphonally or Unison)

Blessed is the man who walks not in the counsel of the wicked,

Nor stands in the way of sinners, nor sits in the seat of scoffers;

But his delight is in the law of the Lord, and on his law he meditates day and night.

He is like a tree planted by streams of water, that yields its fruit in its season, and its leaf does not wither.

In all that he does, he prospers.

The wicked are not so, but are like chaff which the wind drives away.

Therefore the wicked will not stand in the judgment, nor sinners in the congregation of the righteous;

For the Lord knows the way of the righteous, but the way of the wicked will perish.

661   Psalm 8:1-9
(Responsively, Antiphonally, or Unison)

O Lord, our Lord, how majestic is thy name in all the earth!

Thou whose glory above the heavens is chanted by the mouth of babes and infants, thou hast founded a bulwark because of thy foes, to still the enemy and the avenger.

When I look at thy heavens, the work of thy fingers, the moon and the stars which thou hast established;

What is man that thou art mindful of him, and the son of man that thou dost care for him?

Yet thou hast made him little less than God, and dost crown him with glory and honor.

Thou hast given him dominion over the works of thy hands; thou hast put all things under his feet,

All sheep and oxen, and also the beasts of the field, the birds of the air, and the fish of the sea, whatever passes along the paths of the sea.

O Lord, our Lord, how majestic is thy name in all the earth!

662   Psalm 19:1-14
(Responsively, Antiphonally, or Unison)

The heavens are telling the glory of God;

SCRIPTURE READINGS

And the firmament proclaims his handiwork.

Day to day pours forth speech, and night to night declares knowledge.

There is no speech, nor are there words; their voice is not heard;

Yet their voice goes out through all the earth,

And their words to the end of the world.

In them he has set a tent for the sun which comes forth like a bridegroom leaving his chamber,

And like a strong man runs its course with joy.

Its rising is from the end of the heavens, and its circuit to the end of them;

And there is nothing hid from its heat.

The law of the Lord is perfect, reviving the soul;

The testimony of the Lord is sure, making wise the simple;

The precepts of the Lord are right, rejoicing the heart;

The commandment of the Lord is pure, enlightening the eyes;

The fear of the Lord is clean, enduring for ever;

The ordinances of the Lord are true, and righteous altogether.

More to be desired are they than gold, even much fine gold;

Sweeter also than honey and drippings of the honeycomb.

Moreover by them is thy servant warned;

In keeping them there is great reward.

But who can discern his errors?

Clear thou me from hidden faults.

Keep back thy servant also from presumptuous sins;

Let them not have dominion over me!

Then I shall be blameless, and innocent of great transgression.

Let the words of my mouth and the meditation of my heart be acceptable in thy sight, O Lord, my rock and my redeemer.

663 Psalm 23:1-6
(Unison)

The Lord is my shepherd; I shall not want. He maketh me to lie down in green pastures: he leadeth me beside the still waters. He restoreth my soul: he leadeth me in the paths of righteousness for his name's sake. Yea, though I walk through the valley of the shadow of death, I will fear no evil; for thou art with me; thy rod and thy staff they comfort me. Thou preparest a table before me in the presence of mine enemies: thou anointest my head with oil; my cup runneth over. Surely goodness and mercy shall follow me all the days of my life: and I will dwell in the house of the Lord for ever.

664 Psalm 24:1-10
(Responsively, Antiphonally, or Unison)

The earth is the Lord's and the fulness thereof, the world and those who dwell therein;

For he has founded it upon the seas, and established it upon the rivers.

Who shall ascend the hill of the Lord? And who shall stand in his holy place?

He who has clean hands and a pure heart, who does not lift up his soul to what is false, and does not swear deceitfully.

He will receive blessing from the Lord, and vindication from the God of his salvation.

Such is the generation of those who seek him, who seek the face of the God of Jacob.

Lift up your heads, O gates! and be lifted up, O ancient doors!

That the King of glory may come in.

Who is the King of glory?

The Lord, strong and mighty, the Lord, mighty in battle!

Lift up your heads, O gates! and be lifted up, O ancient doors!

That the King of glory may come in!

Who is this King of glory?

The Lord of hosts, he is the King of glory!

665   Psalm 27:1-5, 11-14
(Antiphonally or Unison)

The Lord is my light and my salvation; whom shall I fear?

The Lord is the stronghold of my life; of whom shall I be afraid?

When evildoers assail me, uttering slanders against me,

My adversaries and foes, they shall stumble and fall.

Though a host encamp against me, my heart shall not fear;

Though war arise against me, yet I will be confident.

One thing have I asked of the Lord, that will I seek after;

That I may dwell in the house of the Lord all the days of my life, to behold the beauty of the Lord, and to inquire in his temple.

For he will hide me in his shelter in the day of trouble;

He will conceal me under the cover of his tent, he will set me high upon a rock.

Teach me thy way, O Lord; and lead me on a level path because of my enemies.

Give me not up to the will of my adversaries; for false witnesses have risen against me, and they breathe out violence.

I believe that I shall see the goodness of the Lord in the land of the living!

Wait for the Lord; be strong, and let your heart take courage; yea, wait for the Lord!

666   Psalm 32:1-11
(Responsively, Antiphonally, or Unison)

Blessed is he whose transgression is forgiven, whose sin is covered.

Blessed is the man to whom the Lord imputes no iniquity, and in whose spirit there is no deceit.

When I declared not my sin, my body wasted away through my groaning all day long.

For day and night thy hand was heavy upon me; my strength was dried up as by the heat of summer.

I acknowledged my sin to thee, and I did not hide my iniquity; I said, "I will confess my transgressions to the Lord";

Then thou didst forgive the guilt of my sin.

Therefore let everyone who is godly offer prayer to thee;

At a time of distress, in the rush of great waters, they shall not reach him.

Thou art a hiding place for me, thou preservest me from trouble;

Thou dost encompass me with deliverance.

I will instruct you and teach you the way you should go; I will counsel you with my eye upon you.

Be not like a horse or a mule, without understanding, which must be curbed with bit and bridle, else it will not keep with you.

Many are the pangs of the wicked; but steadfast love surrounds him who trusts in the Lord.

Be glad in the Lord, and rejoice, O righteous, and shout for joy, all you upright in heart!

667   Psalm 34:1-10, 15-18

(Responsively, Antiphonally, or Unison)

I will bless the Lord at all times; his praise shall continually be in my mouth.

My soul makes its boast in the Lord; let the afflicted hear and be glad.

O magnify the Lord with me, and let us exalt his name together!

I sought the Lord, and he answered me, and delivered me from all my fears.

Look to him, and be radiant; so your faces shall never be ashamed.

This poor man cried, and the Lord heard him, and saved him out of all his troubles.

The angel of the Lord encamps around those who fear him, and delivers them.

O taste and see that the Lord is good! Happy is the man who takes refuge in him!

O fear the Lord, you his saints, for those who fear him have no want!

The young lions suffer want and hunger; but those who seek the Lord lack no good thing.

The eyes of the Lord are toward the righteous, and his ears toward their cry.

The face of the Lord is against evildoers, to cut off the remembrance of them from the earth.

When the righteous cry for help, the Lord hears, and delivers them out of all their troubles.

The Lord is near to the brokenhearted, and saves the crushed in spirit.

668   Psalm 42:1-11

(Responsively, Antiphonally, or Unison)

As a hart longs for flowing streams, so longs my soul for thee, O God.

My soul thirsts for God, for the living God.

When shall I come and behold the face of God?

My tears have been my food day and night, while men say to me continually, "Where is your God?"

These things I remember, as I pour out my soul:

How I went with the throng, and led them in procession to the house of God, with glad shouts and songs of thanksgiving, a multitude keeping festival.

Why are you cast down, O my soul, and why are you disquieted within me?

SCRIPTURE READINGS

Hope in God; for I shall again praise him, my help and my God.

My soul is cast down within me, therefore I remember thee from the land of Jordan and of Hermon, from Mount Mizar.

Deep calls to deep at the thunder of thy cataracts; all thy waves and thy billows have gone over me.

By day the Lord commands his steadfast love;

And at night his song is with me, a prayer to the God of my life.

I say to God, my rock: "Why hast thou forgotten me? Why go I mourning because of the oppression of the enemy?"

As with a deadly wound in my body, my adversaries taunt me, while they say to me continually, "Where is your God?"

Why are you cast down, O my soul, and why are you disquieted within me?

Hope in God; for I shall again praise him, my help and my God.

669   Psalm 46:1-11
(Responsively, Antiphonally, or Unison)

God is our refuge and strength, a very present help in trouble.

Therefore we will not fear though the earth should change, though the mountains shake in the heart of the sea;

Though its waters roar and foam, though the mountains tremble with its tumult.

There is a river whose streams make glad the city of God, the holy habitation of the Most High.

God is in the midst of her, she shall not be moved; God will help her right early.

The nations rage, the kingdoms totter;

He utters his voice, the earth melts.

The Lord of hosts is with us; the God of Jacob is our refuge.

Come, behold the works of the Lord, how he has wrought desolations in the earth.

He makes wars cease to the end of the earth; he breaks the bow, and shatters the spear, he burns the chariots with fire!

"Be still, and know that I am God. I am exalted among the nations, I am exalted in the earth!"

The Lord of hosts is with us; the God of Jacob is our refuge.

670   Psalm 51:1-17
(Responsively, Antiphonally, or Unison)

Have mercy on me, O God, according to thy steadfast love; according to thy abundant mercy blot out my transgressions.

Wash me thoroughly from my iniquity, and cleanse me from my sin!

For I know my transgressions, and my sin is ever before me.

Against thee, thee only, have I sinned, and done that which is evil in thy sight, so that thou art justified in thy sentence and blameless in thy judgment.

Behold, I was brought forth in iniquity, and in sin did my mother conceive me.

Behold, thou desirest truth in the inward being; therefore teach me wisdom in my secret heart.

SCRIPTURE READINGS

Purge me with hyssop, and I shall be clean; wash me, and I shall be whiter than snow.

Fill me with joy and gladness; let the bones which thou hast broken rejoice.

Hide thy face from my sins, and blot out all my iniquities.

Create in me a clean heart, O God, and put a new and right spirit within me.

Cast me not away from thy presence, and take not thy Holy Spirit from me.

Restore to me the joy of thy salvation, and uphold me with a willing spirit.

Then I will teach transgressors thy ways, and sinners will return to thee.

Deliver me from bloodguiltiness, O God, thou God of my salvation, and my tongue will sing aloud of thy deliverance.

O Lord, open thou my lips, and my mouth shall show forth thy praise.

For thou hast no delight in sacrifice; were I to give a burnt offering, thou wouldst not be pleased.

The sacrifice acceptable to God is a broken spirit;

A broken and contrite heart, O God, thou wilt not despise.

671 Psalm 84:1-12

(Responsively, Antiphonally, or Unison)

How lovely is thy dwelling place, O Lord of hosts!

My soul longs, yea, faints for the courts of the Lord; my heart and flesh sing for joy to the living God.

Even the sparrow finds a home, and the swallow a nest for herself, where she may lay her young, at thy altars, O Lord of hosts, my King and my God.

Blessed are those who dwell in thy house, ever singing thy praise!

Blessed are the men whose strength is in thee, in whose heart are the highways to Zion.

As they go through the valley of Baca they make it a place of springs; the early rain also covers it with pools.

They go from strength to strength; the God of gods will be seen in Zion.

O Lord God of hosts, hear my prayer; give ear, O God of Jacob!

Behold our shield, O God; look upon the face of thine anointed!

For a day in thy courts is better than a thousand elsewhere.

I would rather be a doorkeeper in the house of my God than dwell in the tents of wickedness.

For the Lord God is a sun and shield; he bestows favor and honor.

No good thing does the Lord withhold from those who walk uprightly.

O Lord of hosts, blessed is the man who trusts in thee!

672 Psalm 90:1-12

(Responsively, Antiphonally, or Unison)

Lord, thou hast been our dwelling place in all generations.

Before the mountains were brought forth, or ever thou hadst formed the earth and the world, from everlasting to everlasting thou art God.

Thou turnest man back to the dust, and sayest, "Turn back, O children of men!"

For a thousand years in thy sight are but as yesterday when it is past, or as a watch in the night.

Thou dost sweep men away; they are like a dream, like grass which is renewed in the morning:

In the morning it flourishes and is renewed; in the evening it fades and withers.

For we are consumed by thy anger; by thy wrath we are overwhelmed.

Thou hast set our iniquities before thee, our secret sins in the light of thy countenance.

For all our days pass away under thy wrath, our years come to an end like a sigh.

The years of our life are threescore and ten, or even by reason of strength fourscore; yet their span is but toil and trouble; they are soon gone, and we fly away.

Who considers the power of thy anger, and thy wrath according to the fear of thee?

So teach us to number our days that we may get a heart of wisdom.

673   Psalm 91:1-16

(Responsively, Antiphonally, or Unison)

He who dwells in the shelter of the Most High, who abides in the shadow of the Almighty, will say to the Lord, "My refuge and my fortress; my God, in whom I trust."

For he will deliver you from the snare of the fowler and from the deadly pestilence;

He will cover you with his pinions, and under his wings you will find refuge;

His faithfulness is a shield and buckler.

You will not fear the terror of the night,

Nor the arrow that flies by day,

Nor the pestilence that stalks in darkness,

Nor the destruction that wastes at noonday.

A thousand may fall at your side, ten thousand at your right hand; but it will not come near you.

You will only look with your eyes and see the recompense of the wicked.

Because you have made the Lord your refuge, the Most High your habitation, no evil shall befall you, no scourge come near your tent.

For he will give his angels charge of you to guard you in all your ways.

On their hands they will bear you up, lest you dash your foot against a stone.

You will tread on the lion and the adder, the young lion and the serpent you will trample under foot.

Because he cleaves to me in love, I will deliver him;

I will protect him, because he knows my name.

When he calls to me, I will answer him; I will be with him in trouble, I will rescue him and honor him.

With long life I will satisfy him, and show him my salvation.

674   Psalm 95:1-7a

(Responsively, Antiphonally, or Unison)

O come, let us sing to the Lord;

Let us make a joyful noise to the rock of our salvation!

Let us come into his presence with thanksgiving;

Let us make a joyful noise to him with songs of praise!

SCRIPTURE READINGS

For the Lord is a great God,

And a great King above all gods.

In his hand are the depths of the earth;

The heights of the mountains are his also.

The sea is his, for he made it;

For his hands formed the dry land.

O come, let us worship and bow down, let us kneel before the Lord, our Maker!

For he is our God, and we are the people of his pasture, and the sheep of his hand.

675   Psalm 100:1-5
(Unison)

Make a joyful noise to the Lord, all the lands! Serve the Lord with gladness! Come into his presence with singing!

Know that the Lord is God! It is he that made us, and we are his; we are his people, and the sheep of his pasture.

Enter his gates with thanksgiving, and his courts with praise! Give thanks to him, bless his name!

For the Lord is good; his steadfast love endures for ever, and his faithfulness to all generations.

676   Psalm 103:1-22
(Responsively, Antiphonally, or Unison)

Bless the Lord, O my soul; and all that is within me, bless his holy name!

Bless the Lord, O my soul, and forget not all his benefits,

Who forgives all your iniquity,

Who heals all your diseases,

Who redeems your life from the Pit,

Who crowns you with steadfast love and mercy,

Who satisfies you with good as long as you live so that your youth is renewed like the eagle's.

The Lord works vindication and justice for all who are oppressed.

He made known his ways to Moses, his acts to the people of Israel.

The Lord is merciful and gracious, slow to anger and abounding in steadfast love.

He will not always chide, nor will he keep his anger for ever.

He does not deal with us according to our sins, nor requite us according to our iniquities.

For as the heavens are high above the earth, so great is his steadfast love toward those who fear him;

As far as the east is from the west, so far does he remove our transgressions from us.

As a father pities his children, so the Lord pities those who fear him.

For he knows our frame; he remembers that we are dust.

As for man, his days are like grass; he flourishes like a flower of the field;

For the wind passes over it, and it is gone, and its place knows it no more.

But the steadfast love of the Lord is from everlasting to everlasting upon those who fear him,

And his righteousness to children's children,

To those who keep his covenant and remember to do his commandments.

SCRIPTURE READINGS

The Lord has established his throne in the heavens, and his kingdom rules over all.

Bless the Lord, O you his angels, you mighty ones who do his word, hearkening to the voice of his word!

Bless the Lord, all his hosts, his ministers that do his will!

Bless the Lord, all his works, in all places of his dominion.

Bless the Lord, O my soul!

677   Psalm 121:1-8
(Responsively, Antiphonally, or Unison)

I lift up my eyes to the hills. From whence does my help come?

My help comes from the Lord, who made heaven and earth.

He will not let your foot be moved, he who keeps you will not slumber.

Behold, he who keeps Israel will neither slumber nor sleep.

The Lord is your keeper; the Lord is your shade on your right hand.

The sun shall not smite you by day, nor the moon by night.

The Lord will keep you from all evil; he will keep your life.

The Lord will keep your going out and your coming in from this time forth and for evermore.

678   Psalm 136:1-26
(Responsively)

O give thanks to the Lord, for he is good,

For his steadfast love endures for ever.

O give thanks to the God of gods,

For his steadfast love endures for ever.

O give thanks to the Lord of lords,

For his steadfast love endures for ever;

To him who alone does great wonders,

For his steadfast love endures for ever;

To him who by understanding made the heavens,

For his steadfast love endures for ever;

To him who spread out the earth upon the waters,

For his steadfast love endures for ever;

To him who made the great lights,

For his steadfast love endures for ever;

The sun to rule over the day,

For his steadfast love endures for ever;

The moon and stars to rule over the night,

For his steadfast love endures for ever;

To him who smote the first-born of Egypt,

For his steadfast love endures for ever;

And brought Israel out from among them,

For his steadfast love endures for ever;

With a strong hand and an outstretched arm,

For his steadfast love endures for ever;

To him who divided the Red Sea in sunder,

For his steadfast love endures for ever;

And made Israel pass through the midst of it,

For his steadfast love endures for ever;

But overthrew Pharaoh and his host in the Red Sea,

For his steadfast love endures for ever;

To him who led his people through the wilderness,

For his steadfast love endures for ever;

To him who smote great kings,

For his steadfast love endures for ever;

And slew famous kings,

For his steadfast love endures for ever;

Sihon, king of the Amorites,

For his steadfast love endures for ever;

And Og, king of Bashan,

For his steadfast love endures for ever;

And gave their land as a heritage,

For his steadfast love endures for ever;

A heritage to Israel his servant,

For his steadfast love endures for ever.

It is he who remembered us in our low estate,

For his steadfast love endures for ever;

And rescued us from our foes,

For his steadfast love endures for ever;

He who gives food to all flesh,

For his steadfast love endures for ever.

O give thanks to the God of heaven,

For his steadfast love endures for ever.

679 Isaiah 9:2-7

(Unison)

The people who walked in darkness have seen a great light;

Those who dwelt in a land of deep darkness, on them has light shined.

Thou hast multiplied the nation, thou hast increased its joy;

They rejoice before thee as with joy at the harvest, as men rejoice when they divide the spoil.

For the yoke of his burden, and the staff for his shoulder, the rod of his oppressor, thou hast broken as on the day of Midian.

For every boot of the tramping warrior in battle tumult and every garment rolled in blood will be burned as fuel for the fire.

For to us a child is born, to us a son is given;

And the government will be upon his shoulder, and his name will be called "Wonderful Counselor, Mighty God, Everlasting Father, Prince of Peace."

Of the increase of his government and of peace there will be no end,

Upon the throne of David, and over his kingdom, to establish it, and to uphold it

With justice and with righteousness from this time forth and for evermore.

The zeal of the Lord of hosts will do this.

SCRIPTURE READINGS

680   Isaiah 11:1-9
(Antiphonally or Responsively)

There shall come forth a shoot from the stump of Jesse,

And a branch shall grow out of his roots.

And the Spirit of the Lord shall rest upon him, the spirit of wisdom and understanding, the spirit of counsel and might, the spirit of knowledge and the fear of the Lord.

And his delight shall be in the fear of the Lord.

He shall not judge by what his eyes see, or decide by what his ears hear;

But with righteousness he shall judge the poor, and decide with equity for the meek of the earth;

And he shall smite the earth with the rod of his mouth, and with the breath of his lips he shall slay the wicked.

Righteousness shall be the girdle of his waist, and faithfulness the girdle of his loins.

The wolf shall dwell with the lamb, and the leopard shall lie down with the kid,

And the calf and the lion and the fatling together, and a little child shall lead them.

The cow and the bear shall feed; their young shall lie down together; and the lion shall eat straw like the ox.

The sucking child shall play over the hole of the asp, and the weaned child shall put his hand on the adder's den.

They shall not hurt or destroy in all my holy mountain;

For the earth shall be full of the knowledge of the Lord as the waters cover the sea.

681   Isaiah 40:1-11
(Unison or Antiphonally)

Comfort, comfort my people, says your God. Speak tenderly to Jerusalem, and cry to her that her warfare is ended, that her iniquity is pardoned, that she has received from the Lord's hand double for all her sins.

A voice cries:
"In the wilderness prepare the way of the Lord, make straight in the desert a highway for our God. Every valley shall be lifted up, and every mountain and hill be made low; the uneven ground shall become level, and the rough places a plain. And the glory of the Lord shall be revealed, and all flesh shall see it together, for the mouth of the Lord has spoken."

A voice says, "Cry!" And I said, "What shall I cry?" All flesh is grass, and all its beauty is like the flower of the field. The grass withers, the flower fades, when the breath of the Lord blows upon it; surely the people is grass. The grass withers, the flower fades; but the word of our God will stand for ever.

Get you up to a high mountain, O Zion, herald of good tidings, lift up your voice with strength, O Jerusalem, herald of good tidings, lift it up, fear not; say to the cities of Judah, "Behold your God!" Behold, the Lord God comes with might, and his arm rules for him; behold, his reward is with him, and his recompense before him. He will feed his flock like a shepherd, he will gather the lambs in his arms, he will carry them in his bosom, and gently lead those that are with young.

SCRIPTURE READINGS

682 Isaiah 40:27-31
(Unison)

Why do you say, O Jacob, and speak, O Israel, "My way is hid from the Lord, and my right is disregarded by my God"? Have you not known? Have you not heard? The Lord is the everlasting God, the Creator of the ends of the earth. He does not faint or grow weary, his understanding is unsearchable. He gives power to the faint, and to him who has no might he increases strength. Even youths shall faint and be weary, and young men shall fall exhausted; but they who wait for the Lord shall renew their strength, they shall mount up with wings like eagles, they shall run and not be weary, they shall walk and not faint.

683 Isaiah 53:1-12
(Antiphonally)

Who has believed what we have heard? And to whom has the arm of the Lord been revealed?

For he grew up before him like a young plant, and like a root out of dry ground;

He had no form or comeliness that we should look at him, and no beauty that we should desire him.

He was despised and rejected by men; a man of sorrows, and acquainted with grief;

And as one from whom men hide their faces he was despised, and we esteemed him not.

Surely he has borne our griefs and carried our sorrows;

Yet we esteemed him stricken, smitten by God, and afflicted.

But he was wounded for our transgressions, he was bruised for our iniquities;

Upon him was the chastisement that made us whole, and with his stripes we are healed.

All we like sheep have gone astray; we have turned every one to his own way;

And the Lord has laid on him the iniquity of us all.

He was oppressed, and he was afflicted, yet he opened not his mouth;

Like a lamb that is led to the slaughter, and like a sheep that before its shearers is dumb, so he opened not his mouth.

By oppression and judgment he was taken away; and as for his generation, who considered that he was cut off out of the land of the living, stricken for the transgression of my people?

And they made his grave with the wicked and with a rich man in his death, although he had done no violence, and there was no deceit in his mouth.

Yet it was the will of the Lord to bruise him; he has put him to grief;

When he makes himself an offering for sin, he shall see his offspring, he shall prolong his days;

The will of the Lord shall prosper in his hand; he shall see the fruit of the travail of his soul and be satisfied;

By his knowledge shall the righteous one, my servant, make many to be accounted righteous; and he shall bear their iniquities.

Therefore I will divide him a portion with the great, and he shall divide the spoil with the strong;

Because he poured out his soul to death, and was numbered with the transgressors;

Yet he bore the sin of many, and made intercession for the transgressors.

684   Jeremiah 31:31-34
(Unison)

Behold, the days are coming, says the Lord, when I will make a new covenant with the house of Israel and the house of Judah, not like the covenant which I made with their fathers when I took them by the hand to bring them out of the land of Egypt, my covenant which they broke, though I was their husband, says the Lord. But this is the covenant which I will make with the house of Israel after those days, says the Lord: I will put my law within them, and I will write it upon their hearts; and I will be their God, and they shall be my people. And no longer shall each man teach his neighbor and each his brother, saying, "Know the Lord," for they shall all know me, from the least of them to the greatest, says the Lord; for I will forgive their iniquity, and I will remember their sin no more.

685   Lamentations 3:22-27, 31-42
(Antiphonally)

The steadfast love of the Lord never ceases, his mercies never come to an end; they are new every morning; great is thy faithfulness. "The Lord is my portion," says my soul, "therefore I will hope in him."

The Lord is good to those who wait for him, to the soul that seeks him. It is good that one should wait quietly for the salvation of the Lord. It is good for a man that he bear the yoke in his youth.

For the Lord will not cast off for ever, but, though he cause grief, he will have compassion according to the abundance of his steadfast love; for he does not willingly afflict or grieve the sons of men.

To crush under foot all the prisoners of the earth, to turn aside the right of a man in the presence of the Most High, to subvert a man in his cause, the Lord does not approve.

Who has commanded and it came to pass, unless the Lord has ordained it? Is it not from the mouth of the Most High that good and evil come? Why should a living man complain, a man, about the punishment of his sins?

Let us test and examine our ways, and return to the Lord! Let us lift up our hearts and hands to God in heaven: "We have transgressed and rebelled, and thou hast not forgiven."

686   Daniel 9:4b-7a, 8b-10, 12, 13, 15, 18, 19
(Unison)

O Lord, the great and terrible God, who keepest covenant and steadfast love with those who love him and keep his commandments,

(Unison or Antiphonal)

We have sinned and done wrong and acted wickedly and rebelled, turning aside from thy commandments and ordinances;

We have not listened to thy servants the prophets, who spoke in thy name to our kings, our princes, and our fathers, and to all the people of the land.

To thee, O Lord, belongs righteousness, but to us confusion of face, to our kings, to our princes, and to our fathers, because we have sinned against thee.

To the Lord our God belong mercy and forgiveness; because we have rebelled against him, and have not obeyed the voice of the Lord our God by following his laws, which he set before us by his servants the prophets.

He has confirmed his words, which he spoke against us and against our rulers who ruled us, by bringing upon us a great calamity.

As it is written in the law of Moses, all this calamity has come upon us, yet we have not entreated the favor of the Lord our God, turning from our iniquities and giving heed to thy truth.

And now, O Lord our God, who didst bring thy people out of the land of Egypt with a mighty hand, and hast made thee a name, as at this day, we have sinned, we have done wickedly.

O my God, incline thy ear and hear; open thy eyes and behold our desolations, and the city which is called by thy name; for we do not present our supplications before thee on the ground of our righteousness, but on the ground of thy great mercy.

(Unison)

O Lord, hear; O Lord, forgive; O Lord, give heed and act; delay not, for thy own sake, O my God, because thy city and thy people are called by thy name.

687 Micah 4:1-4

(Unison)

It shall come to pass in the latter days that the mountain of the house of the Lord
Shall be established as the highest of the mountains, and shall be raised up above the hills;
And peoples shall flow to it, and many nations shall come, and say:
"Come, let us go up to the mountain of the Lord, to the house of the God of Jacob;
That he may teach us his ways and we may walk in his paths."
For out of Zion shall go forth the law, and the word of the Lord from Jerusalem.
He shall judge between many peoples, and shall decide for strong nations afar off;
And they shall beat their swords into plowshares, and their spears into pruning hooks;
Nation shall not lift up sword against nation, neither shall they learn war any more;
But they shall sit every man under his vine and under his fig tree, and none shall make them afraid; for the mouth of the Lord of hosts has spoken.

688 Micah 6:1-8

(Antiphonally)

Hear what the Lord says: Arise, plead your case before the mountains, and let the hills hear your voice. **Hear, you mountains, the controversy of the Lord, and you enduring foundations of the earth; for the Lord has a controversy with his people, and he will contend with Israel.**

"O my people, what have I done to you? In what have I wearied you? Answer me! For I brought you up from the land of Egypt, and redeemed you from the house of bondage; and I sent before you Moses, Aaron, and Miriam. O my people, remember what Balak king of Moab devised, and what Balaam the son of Beor answered him, and what happened from Shittim to Gilgal, that you may know the saving acts of the Lord."

"With what shall I come before the Lord, and bow myself before God on high? Shall I come before him with burnt offerings, with calves a year old? Will the Lord be pleased with thousands of rams, with ten thousands of rivers of oil? Shall I give my first-born for my transgression, the fruit of my body for the sin of my soul?"

He has showed you, O man, what is good; and what does the Lord require of you but to do justice, and to love kindness, and to walk humbly with your God?

689   Matthew 6:1-18
(Antiphonally)

Beware of practicing your piety before men in order to be seen by them; for then you will have no reward from your Father who is in heaven.

Thus, when you give alms, sound no trumpet before you, as the hypocrites do in the synagogues and in the streets, that they may be praised by men. Truly, I say to you, they have their reward. But when you give alms, do not let your left hand know what your right hand is doing, so that your alms may be in secret; and your Father who sees in secret will reward you.

And when you pray, you must not be like the hypocrites; for they love to stand and pray in the synagogues and at the street corners, that they may be seen by men. Truly, I say to you, they have their reward. But when you pray, go into your room and shut the door and pray to your Father who is in secret; and your Father who sees in secret will reward you.

And in praying do not heap up empty phrases as the Gentiles do; for they think that they will be heard for their many words. Do not be like them, for your Father knows what you need before you ask him. Pray then like this:

(Unison)

Our Father who art in heaven, Hallowed be thy name. Thy kingdom come, Thy will be done, On earth as it is in heaven. Give us this day our daily bread; And forgive us our debts, As we also have forgiven our debtors; And lead us not into temptation, But deliver us from evil.

For if you forgive men their trespasses, your heavenly Father also will forgive you; but if you do not forgive men their trespasses, neither will your Father forgive your trespasses.

And when you fast, do not look dismal, like the hypocrites, for they disfigure their faces that their fasting may be seen by men. Truly, I say to you, they have their reward. But when you fast, anoint your head and wash your face, that your fasting may not be seen by men but by your Father who is in secret; and your Father who sees in secret will reward you.

690   Matthew 6:25-33
(Antiphonally)

Therefore I bid you put away anxious thoughts about food and drink to keep you alive, and clothes to cover your body.

Surely life is more than food, the body more than clothes.

Look at the birds of the air; they do not sow and reap and store in barns, yet your heavenly Father feeds them. You are worth more than the birds!

Is there a man of you who by anxious thought can add a foot to his height? And why be anxious about clothes?

Consider how the lilies grow in the fields; they do not work, they do not spin; and yet, I tell you, even Solomon in all his splendour was not attired like one of these.

But if that is how God clothes the grass in the fields, which is there today, and tomorrow is thrown on the stove, will he not all the more clothe you? How little faith you have!

No, do not ask anxiously, "What are we to eat? What are we to drink? What shall we wear?"

All these are things for the heathen to run after, not for you, because your heavenly Father knows that you need them all.

Set your mind on God's kingdom and his justice before everything else, and all the rest will come to you as well.

So do not be anxious about tomorrow; tomorrow will look after itself. Each day has troubles enough of its own.

691   Matthew 13:31-33, 44-52

(Unison or Antiphonally)

Another parable he put before them, saying, "The kingdom of heaven is like a grain of mustard seed which a man took and sowed in his field; it is the smallest of all seeds, but when it has grown it is the greatest of shrubs and becomes a tree, so that the birds of the air come and make nests in its branches."

He told them another parable. "The kingdom of heaven is like leaven which a woman took and hid in three measures of meal, till it was all leavened."

"The kingdom of heaven is like treasure hidden in a field, which a man found and covered up; then in his joy he goes and sells all that he has and buys that field.

"Again, the kingdom of heaven is like a merchant in search of fine pearls, who, on finding one pearl of great value, went and sold all that he had and bought it.

"Again, the kingdom of heaven is like a net which was thrown into the sea and gathered fish of every kind; when it was full, men drew it ashore and sat down and sorted the good into vessels but threw away the bad. So it will be at the close of the age. The angels will come out and separate the evil from the righteous, and throw them into the furnace of fire; there men will weep and gnash their teeth.

"Have you understood all this?" They said to him, "Yes." And he said to them, "Therefore every scribe who has been trained for the kingdom of heaven is like a householder who brings out of his treasure what is new and what is old."

692   Matthew 18:10-22

(Antiphonally)

Never despise one of these little ones; I tell you, they have their guardian angels in heaven, who look continually on the face of my heavenly Father.

What do you think? Suppose a man has a hundred sheep. If one of them strays, does he not leave the other ninety-nine on the hillside and go in search of the one that strayed?

And if he should find it, I tell you this: he is more delighted over that sheep than over the ninety-nine that never strayed. In the same way, it is not your heavenly Father's will that one of these little ones should be lost.

If your brother commits a sin, go and take the matter up with him, strictly between yourselves, and if he listens to you, you have won your brother over.

If he will not listen, take one or two others with you, so that all facts may be duly established on the evidence of two or three witnesses.

If he refuses to listen to them, report the matter to the congregation; and if he will not listen even to the congregation, you must then treat him as you would a pagan or a tax-gatherer.

I tell you this: whatever you forbid on earth shall be forbidden in heaven, and whatever you allow on earth shall be allowed in heaven.

Again I tell you this: if two of you agree on earth about any request you have to make, that request will be granted by my heavenly Father. For where two or three have met together in my name, I am there among them.

693   Matthew 25:31-46
(Antiphonally)

When the Son of man comes in his glory, and all the angels with him, then he will sit on his glorious throne. Before him will be gathered all the nations, and he will separate them one from another as a shepherd separates the sheep from the goats, and he will place the sheep at his right hand, but the goats at the left.

Then the King will say to those at his right hand, "Come, O blessed of my Father, inherit the kingdom prepared for you from the foundation of the world; for I was hungry and you gave me food, I was thirsty and you gave me drink, I was a stranger and you welcomed me, I was naked and you clothed me, I was sick and you visited me, I was in prison and you came to me."

Then the righteous will answer him, "Lord, when did we see thee hungry and feed thee, or thirsty and give thee drink? And when did we see thee a stranger and welcome thee, or naked and clothe thee? And when did we see thee sick or in prison and visit thee?"

And the King will answer them, "Truly, I say to you, as you did it to one of the least of these my brethren, you did it to me."

Then he will say to those at his left hand, "Depart from me, you cursed, into the eternal fire prepared for the devil and his angels; for I was hungry and you gave me no food, I was thirsty and you gave me no drink, I was a stranger and you did not welcome me, naked and you did not clothe me, sick and in prison and you did not visit me."

Then they also will answer, "Lord, when did we see thee hungry or thirsty or a stranger or naked or sick or in prison, and did not minister to thee?"

Then he will answer them, "Truly, I say to you, as you did it not to one of the least of these, you did it not to me."

And they will go away into eternal punishment, but the righteous into eternal life.

694   Mark 14:32-42
(Unison)

And they went to a place which was called Gethsemane; and he said to his

SCRIPTURE READINGS

disciples, "Sit here, while I pray." And he took with him Peter and James and John, and began to be greatly distressed and troubled. And he said to them, "My soul is very sorrowful, even to death; remain here, and watch." And going a little farther, he fell on the ground and prayed that, if it were possible, the hour might pass from him. And he said, "Abba, Father, all things are possible to thee; remove this cup from me; yet not what I will, but what thou wilt."

And he came and found them sleeping, and he said to Peter, "Simon, are you asleep? Could you not watch one hour? Watch and pray that you may not enter into temptation; the spirit indeed is willing, but the flesh is weak." And again he went away and prayed, saying the same words. And again he came and found them sleeping, for their eyes were very heavy; and they did not know what to answer him.

And he came the third time, and said to them, "Are you still sleeping and taking your rest? It is enough; the hour has come; the Son of man is betrayed into the hands of sinners. Rise, let us be going; see, my betrayer is at hand."

695 Luke 1:46b-55
(Unison)

My soul magnifies the Lord, and my spirit rejoices in God my Savior, for he has regarded the low estate of his handmaiden.

For behold, henceforth all generations will call me blessed; for he who is mighty has done great things for me, and holy is his name.

And his mercy is on those who fear him from generation to generation.

He has shown strength with his arm, he has scattered the proud in the imagination of their hearts, he has put down the mighty from their thrones, and exalted those of low degree; he has filled the hungry with good things, and the rich he has sent empty away.

He has helped his servant Israel, in remembrance of his mercy, as he spoke to our fathers, to Abraham and to his posterity for ever.

696 Luke 6:20b-36
(Antiphonally or Unison)

Blessed are you poor, for yours is the kingdom of God. Blessed are you that hunger now, for you shall be satisfied. Blessed are you that weep now, for you shall laugh. Blessed are you when men hate you, and when they exclude you and revile you, and cast out your name as evil, on account of the Son of man! Rejoice in that day, and leap for joy, for behold, your reward is great in heaven; for so their fathers did to the prophets.

But woe to you that are rich, for you have received your consolation. Woe to you that are full now, for you shall hunger. Woe to you that laugh now, for you shall mourn and weep. Woe to you, when all men speak well of you, for so their fathers did to the false prophets.

But I say to you that hear, Love your enemies, do good to those who hate you, bless those who curse you, pray for those who abuse you. To him who strikes you on the cheek, offer the other also; and from him who takes away your cloak do not withhold your coat as well. Give to every one who begs from you; and of him who takes away your goods do not ask them again. And as you wish that men would do to you, do so to them.

If you love those who love you, what credit is that to you? For even sinners love those who love them. And if you do good to those who do good to you, what credit is that to you? For even sinners do the same. And if you lend to those from whom you hope to receive, what credit is that to you? Even sinners lend to sinners, to receive as much again. But love your enemies, and do good, and lend, expecting nothing in return; and your reward will be great, and you will be sons of the Most High; for he is kind to the ungrateful and the selfish. Be merciful, even as your Father is merciful.

697 John 1:1-14

(Antiphonally)

In the beginning was the Word, and the Word was with God, and the Word was God. He was in the beginning with God; all things were made through him, and without him was not anything made that was made. In him was life, and the life was the light of men. The light shines in the darkness, and the darkness has not overcome it.

There was a man sent from God, whose name was John. He came for testimony, to bear witness to the light, that all might believe through him. He was not the light, but came to bear witness to the light.

The true light that enlightens every man was coming into the world. He was in the world, and the world was made through him, yet the world knew him not. He came to his own home, and his own people received him not.

But to all who received him, who believed in his name, he gave power to become children of God; who were born, not of blood nor of the will of the flesh nor of the will of man, but of God.

(Unison)
And the Word became flesh and dwelt among us, full of grace and truth; we have beheld his glory, glory as of the only Son from the Father.

698 John 3:3b-21

(Antiphonally or Unison)

"Truly, truly, I say to you, unless one is born anew, he cannot see the kingdom of God."

Nicodemus said to him, "How can a man be born when he is old? Can he enter a second time into his mother's womb and be born?"

Jesus answered, "Truly, truly, I say to you, unless one is born of water and the Spirit, he cannot enter the kingdom of God. That which is born of the flesh is flesh, and that which is born of the Spirit is spirit. Do not marvel that I said to you, 'You must be born anew.' The wind blows where it wills, and you hear the sound of it, but you do not know whence it comes or whither it goes; so it is with every one who is born of the Spirit."

Nicodemus said to him, "How can this be?"

Jesus answered him, "Are you a teacher of Israel, and yet you do not understand this? Truly, truly, I say to you, we speak of what we know, and bear witness to what we have seen; but you do not receive our testimony. If I have told you earthly things and you do not believe, how can you believe if I tell you heavenly things? No one has ascended into heaven but he who descended from heaven, the Son of man. And as Moses lifted up the serpent in the wilderness, so must the Son of man be lifted up, that whoever believes in him may have eternal life."

For God so loved the world that he gave his only Son, that whoever believes in him should not perish but have eternal life. For God sent the Son into the world, not to condemn the world, but that the world might be saved through him.

He who believes in him is not condemned; he who does not believe is condemned already, because he has not believed in the name of the only Son of God. And this is the judgment, that the light has come into the world, and men loved darkness rather than light, because their deeds were evil.

For every one who does evil hates the light, and does not come to the light, lest his deeds should be exposed. But he who does what is true comes to the light, that it may be clearly seen that his deeds have been wrought in God.

699 John 6:35-40, 47-58
(Unison or Antiphonally)

Jesus said to them, "I am the bread of life; he who comes to me shall not hunger, and he who believes in me shall never thirst. But I said to you that you have seen me and yet do not believe.

All that the Father gives me will come to me; and him who comes to me I will not cast out. For I have come down from heaven, not to do my own will, but the will of him who sent me; and this is the will of him who sent me, that I should lose nothing of all that he has given me, but raise it up at the last day.

For this is the will of my Father, that every one who sees the Son and believes in him should have eternal life; and I will raise him up at the last day."

"Truly, truly, I say to you, he who believes has eternal life. I am the bread of life. Your fathers ate the manna in the wilderness, and they died. This is the bread which comes down from heaven, that a man may eat of it and not die.

I am the living bread which came down from heaven; if any one eats of this bread, he will live for ever; and the bread which I shall give for the life of the world is my flesh."

The Jews then disputed among themselves, saying, "How can this man give us his flesh to eat?"

So Jesus said to them, "Truly, truly, I say to you, unless you eat the flesh of the Son of man and drink his blood, you have no life in you; he who eats my flesh and drinks my blood has eternal life, and I will raise him up at the last day. For my flesh is food indeed, and my blood is drink indeed.

He who eats my flesh and drinks my blood abides in me, and I in him. As the living Father sent me, and I live because of the Father, so he who eats me will live because of me. This is the bread which came down from heaven, not such as the fathers ate and died; he who eats this bread will live for ever."

700 John 15:1-11
(Unison)

"I am the true vine, and my Father is the vinedresser. Every branch of mine that bears no fruit, he takes away, and every branch that does bear fruit he prunes, that it may bear more fruit. You are already made clean by the word which I have spoken to you.

"Abide in me, and I in you. As the branch cannot bear fruit by itself, unless it abides in the vine, neither can you, unless you abide in me. I am the vine, you are the branches. He who abides in me, and I in him, he it is that bears much fruit, for apart from me you can do nothing.

"If a man does not abide in me, he is cast forth as a branch and withers; and the branches are gathered, thrown into the fire and burned. If you abide in me, and my words abide in you, ask whatever you will, and it shall be done for you. By this my Father is glorified, that you bear much fruit, and so prove to be my disciples.

"As the Father has loved me, so have I loved you; abide in my love. If you keep my commandments, you will abide in my love, just as I have kept my Father's commandments and abide in his love. These things I have spoken to you, that my joy may be in you, and that your joy may be full."

701 John 17:3-6, 16-26
(Unison)

"And this is eternal life, that they know thee the only true God, and Jesus Christ whom thou hast sent. I glorified thee on earth, having accomplished the work which thou gavest me to do; and now, Father, glorify thou me in thy own presence with the glory which I had with thee before the world was made.

"I have manifested thy name to the men whom thou gavest me out of the world; thine they were, and thou gavest them to me, and they have kept thy word. They are not of the world, even as I am not of the world. Sanctify them in the truth; thy word is truth. As thou didst send me into the world, so I have sent them into the world. And for their sake I consecrate myself, that they also may be consecrated in truth.

"I do not pray for these only, but also for those who believe in me through their word, that they may all be one; even as thou, Father, art in me, and I in thee, that they also may be in us, so that the world may believe that thou hast sent me. The glory which thou hast given me I have given to them, that they may be one even as we are one, I in them and thou in me, that they may become perfectly one, so that the world may know that thou hast sent me and hast loved them even as thou hast loved me.

"Father, I desire that they also, whom thou hast given me, may be with me where I am, to behold my glory which thou hast given me in thy love for me before the foundation of the world. O righteous Father, the world has not known thee, but I have known thee; and these know that thou hast sent me. I made known to them thy name, and I will make it known, that the love with which thou hast loved me may be in them, and I in them."

702 Romans 8:1-11
(Unison or Antiphonally)

There is therefore now no condemnation for those who are in Christ Jesus. For the law of the Spirit of life in Christ Jesus has set me free from the law of sin and death.

For God has done what the law, weakened by the flesh, could not do: sending his own Son in the likeness of sinful flesh and for sin, he condemned sin in the flesh, in order that the just requirement of the law might be fulfilled in us, who walk not according to the flesh but according to the Spirit.

For those who live according to the flesh set their minds on the things of the flesh, but those who live according to the Spirit set their minds on the things of the Spirit.

To set the mind on the flesh is death, but to set the mind on the Spirit is life and peace.

For the mind that is set on the flesh is hostile to God; it does not submit to God's law, indeed it cannot; and those who are in the flesh cannot please God.

But you are not in the flesh, you are in the Spirit, if the Spirit of God really dwells in you. Any one who does not have the Spirit of Christ does not belong to him.

But if Christ is in you, although your bodies are dead because of sin, your spirits are alive because of righteousness.

If the Spirit of him who raised Jesus from the dead dwells in you, he who raised Christ Jesus from the dead will give life to your mortal bodies also through his Spirit which dwells in you.

703   Romans 8:28-39

(Unison)

Moreover we know that to those who love God, who are called according to his plan, everything that happens fits into a pattern for good. God, in his foreknowledge, chose them to bear the family likeness of his Son, that he might be the eldest of a family of many brothers. He chose them long ago; when the time came he called them, he made them righteous in his sight and then lifted them to the splendor of life as his own sons.

(Unison or Antiphonally)
In face of all this, what is there left to say? If God is for us, who can be against us?

He that did not spare his own Son but gave him up for us all—can we not trust such a God to give us, with him, everything else that we can need?

Who dares accuse us now? The Judge himself has declared us free from sin. Who is in a position to condemn?

Only Christ, and Christ died for us, Christ rose for us, Christ reigns in power for us, Christ prays for us!

Can anything separate us from the love of Christ?

Can trouble, pain or persecution? Can lack of clothes and food, danger to life and limb, the threat of force of arms?

Indeed some of us know the truth of that ancient text: For thy sake we are killed all the day long; We were accounted as sheep for the slaughter.

(Unison)
No, in all these things we win an overwhelming victory through him who has proved his love for us. I have become absolutely convinced that neither death nor life, neither messenger of Heaven nor monarch of earth, neither what happens today nor what happens tomorrow, neither a power from on high nor a power from below, nor anything else in God's whole world has any power to separate us from the love of God in Jesus Christ our Lord!

704   Romans 12:1, 2, 9-21

(Unison)
Therefore, my brothers, I implore you by God's mercy to offer your very selves to him: a living sacrifice, dedi-

cated and fit for his acceptance, the worship offered by mind and heart. Adapt yourselves no longer to the pattern of this present world, but let your minds be remade and your whole nature thus transformed. Then you will be able to discern the will of God, and to know what is good, acceptable, and perfect.

(Unison or Antiphonally)
Love in all sincerity, loathing evil and clinging to the good. Let love for our brotherhood breed warmth of mutual affection. Give pride of place to one another in esteem.

With unflagging energy, in ardour of spirit, serve the Lord.

Let hope keep you joyful; in trouble stand firm; persist in prayer.

Contribute to the needs of God's people, and practise hospitality.

Call down blessings on your persecutors—blessings, not curses.

With the joyful be joyful, and mourn with the mourners.

Have equal regard for one another. Do not be haughty, but go about with humble folk. Do not keep thinking how wise you are.

Never pay back evil for evil. Let your aims be such as all men count honourable.

If possible, so far as it lies with you, live at peace with all men.

My dear friends, do not seek revenge, but leave a place for divine retribution; for there is a text which reads, 'Justice is mine, says the Lord, I will repay.'

But there is another text: 'If your enemy is hungry, feed him; if he is thirsty, give him a drink; by doing this you will heap live coals on his head.'

(Unison)
Do not let evil conquer you, but use good to defeat evil.

705   1 Corinthians 13:1-13

(Unison)
If I speak in the tongues of men and of angels, but have not love, I am a noisy gong or a clanging cymbal. And if I have prophetic powers, and understand all mysteries and all knowledge, and if I have all faith, so as to remove mountains, but have not love, I am nothing. If I give away all I have, and if I deliver my body to be burned, but have not love, I gain nothing.

Love is patient and kind; love is not jealous or boastful; it is not arrogant or rude. Love does not insist on its own way; it is not irritable or resentful; it does not rejoice at wrong, but rejoices in the right. Love bears all things, believes all things, hopes all things, endures all things.

Love never ends; as for prophecies, they will pass away; as for tongues, they will cease; as for knowledge, it will pass away. For our knowledge is imperfect and our prophecy is imperfect; but when the perfect comes, the imperfect will pass away. When I was a child, I spoke like a child, I thought like a child, I reasoned like a child; when I became a man, I gave up childish ways. For now we see in a mirror dimly, but then face to face. Now I know in part; then I shall understand fully, even as I have been fully understood. So faith, hope, love abide, these three; but the greatest of these is love.

706   1 Corinthians 15:20b-26, 51-58

(Responsively, Antiphonally, or Unison)
Christ has been raised from the dead, the first fruits of those who have fallen asleep.

SCRIPTURE READINGS

For as by a man came death, by a man has come also the resurrection of the dead. For as in Adam all die, so also in Christ shall all be made alive. But each in his own order: Christ the first fruits, then at his coming those who belong to Christ.

Then comes the end, when he delivers the kingdom to God the Father after destroying every rule and every authority and power.

For he must reign until he has put all his enemies under his feet. The last enemy to be destroyed is death.

Lo! I tell you a mystery. We shall not all sleep, but we shall all be changed, in a moment, in the twinkling of an eye, at the last trumpet.

For the trumpet will sound, and the dead will be raised imperishable, and we shall be changed.

For this perishable nature must put on the imperishable, and this mortal nature must put on immortality. When the perishable puts on the imperishable, and the mortal puts on immortality, then shall come to pass the saying that is written:

"Death is swallowed up in victory."
"O death, where is thy victory?
O death, where is thy sting?"

The sting of death is sin, and the power of sin is the law. But thanks be to God, who gives us the victory through our Lord Jesus Christ.

Therefore, my beloved brethren, be steadfast, immovable, always abounding in the work of the Lord, knowing that in the Lord your labor is not in vain.

707 2 Corinthians 9:6b-15
(Antiphonally or Unison)

Sow bountifully, and you will reap bountifully. Each person should give as he has decided for himself; there should be no reluctance, no sense of compulsion; God loves a cheerful giver.

And it is in God's power to provide you richly with every good gift; thus you will have ample means in yourselves to meet each and every situation, with enough and to spare for every good cause.

Scripture says of such a man: 'He has lavished his gifts on the needy, his benevolence stands fast for ever.'

Now he who provides seed for sowing and bread for food will provide the seed for you to sow; he will multiply it and swell the harvest of your benevolence, and you will always be rich enough to be generous.

Through our action such generosity will issue in thanksgiving to God, for as a piece of willing service this is not only a contribution towards the needs of God's people; more than that, it overflows in a flood of thanksgiving to God.

For through the proof which this affords, many will give honour to God when they see how humbly you obey him and how faithfully you confess the gospel of Christ; and will thank him for your liberal contribution to their need and to the general good.

And as they join in prayer on your behalf, their hearts will go out to you because of the richness of the grace which God has imparted to you.

(Unison)

Thanks be to God for his gift beyond words!

708 Philippians 2:1-11
(Unison)

Does your life in Christ make you

strong? Does his love comfort you? Do you have fellowship with the Spirit? Do you feel kindness and compassion for one another? I urge you, then, make me completely happy by having the same thoughts, sharing the same love, and being one in soul and mind. Don't do anything from selfish ambition, or from a cheap desire to boast; but be humble toward each other, never thinking you are better than others. And look out for each other's interests, not for just your own. The attitude you should have is the one that Christ Jesus had:

> He always had the very nature of God,
> But he did not think that by force he should try to become equal with God.
> Instead, of his own free will he gave it all up,
> And took the nature of a servant.
> He was born like man, he appeared in human likeness;
> He was humble and walked the path of obedience to death—his death on the cross.
> For this reason God raised him to the highest place above.
> And gave him the name that is greater than any other name,
> So that all beings in heaven, and on earth, and in the world below
> Will fall on their knees,
> In honor of the name of Jesus,
> And all will openly proclaim that Jesus Christ is the Lord,
> To the glory of God the Father.

709   Philippians 4:4-13
(Unison)

Rejoice in the Lord always; again I will say, Rejoice. Let all men know your forbearance. The Lord is at hand. Have no anxiety about anything, but in everything by prayer and supplication with thanksgiving let your requests be made known to God. And the peace of God, which passes all understanding, will keep your hearts and your minds in Christ Jesus.

Finally, brethren, whatever is true, whatever is honorable, whatever is just, whatever is pure, whatever is lovely, whatever is gracious, if there is any excellence, if there is anything worthy of praise, think about these things. What you have learned and received and heard and seen in me, do; and the God of peace will be with you.

I rejoice in the Lord greatly that now at length you have revived your concern for me; you were indeed concerned for me, but you had no opportunity. Not that I complain of want; for I have learned, in whatever state I am, to be content. I know how to be abased, and I know how to abound; in any and all circumstances I have learned the secret of facing plenty and hunger, abundance and want. I can do all things in him who strengthens me.

710   Colossians 3:1-17
(Antiphonally, Responsively, or Unison)

If then you have been raised with Christ, seek the things that are above, where Christ is, seated at the right hand of God.

Set your minds on things that are above, not on things that are on earth.

For you have died, and your life is hid with Christ in God.

When Christ who is our life appears, then you also will appear with him in glory.

Put to death therefore what is earthly in you: immorality, impurity, passion, evil desire, and covetousness, which is idolatry.

SCRIPTURE READINGS

On account of these the wrath of God is coming.

In these you once walked, when you lived in them.

But now put them all away: anger, wrath, malice, slander, and foul talk from your mouth.

Do not lie to one another, seeing that you have put off the old nature with its practices and have put on the new nature, which is being renewed in knowledge after the image of its creator.

Here there cannot be Greek and Jew, circumcised and uncircumcised, barbarian, Scythian, slave, free man, but Christ is all, and in all.

Put on then, as God's chosen ones, holy and beloved, compassion, kindness, lowliness, meekness, and patience, forbearing one another and, if one has a complaint against another, forgiving each other; as the Lord has forgiven you, so you also must forgive.

And above all these put on love, which binds everything together in perfect harmony.

And let the peace of Christ rule in your hearts, to which indeed you were called in the one body. And be thankful.

Let the word of Christ dwell in you richly, as you teach and admonish one another in all wisdom, and as you sing psalms and hymns and spiritual songs with thankfulness in your hearts to God.

(Unison)
And whatever you do, in word or deed, do everything in the name of the Lord Jesus, giving thanks to God the Father through him.

711 1 Thessalonians 4:13-18
(Unison)

But we would not have you ignorant, brethren, concerning those who are asleep, that you may not grieve as others do who have no hope. For since we believe that Jesus died and rose again, even so, through Jesus, God will bring with him those who have fallen asleep. For this we declare to you by the word of the Lord, that we who are alive, who are left until the coming of the Lord, shall not precede those who have fallen asleep.

For the Lord himself will descend from heaven with a cry of command, with the archangel's call, and with the sound of the trumpet of God. And the dead in Christ will rise first; then we who are alive, who are left, shall be caught up together with them in the clouds to meet the Lord in the air; and so we shall always be with the Lord. Therefore comfort one another with these words.

712 1 Timothy 6:7-12, 17-19
(Unison)

We brought nothing into the world, because when we leave it we cannot take anything with us either, but if we have food and covering we may rest content. Those who want to be rich fall into temptations and snares and many foolish harmful desires which plunge men into ruin and perdition. The love of money is the root of all evil things, and there are some who in reaching for it have wandered from the faith and spiked themselves on many thorny griefs.

But you, man of God, must shun all this, and pursue justice, piety, fidelity, love, fortitude, and gentleness. Run the great race of faith and take hold of eternal life. For to this you were called; and you confessed your faith nobly before many witnesses.

Instruct those who are rich in this world's goods not to be proud, and not to fix their hopes on so uncertain a thing as money, but upon God, who endows us richly with all things to enjoy. Tell them to hoard a wealth of noble actions by doing good, to be ready to give away and to share, and so acquire a treasure which will form a good foundation for the future. Thus they will grasp the life which is life indeed.

713   Hebrews 11:1-6, 13-16, 39, 40; 12:1, 2

(Antiphonally)

Now faith is the assurance of things hoped for, the conviction of things not seen. For by it the men of old received divine approval.

By faith we understand that the world was created by the word of God, so that what is seen was made out of things which do not appear.

By faith Abel offered to God a more acceptable sacrifice than Cain, through which he received approval as righteous, God bearing witness by accepting his gifts; he died, but through his faith he is still speaking.

By faith Enoch was taken up so that he should not see death; and he was not found, because God had taken him. Now before he was taken he was attested as having pleased God.

And without faith it is impossible to please him. For whoever would draw near to God must believe that he exists and that he rewards those who seek him.

These all died in faith, not having received what was promised, but having seen it and greeted it from afar, and having acknowledged that they were strangers and exiles on the earth.

For people who speak thus make it clear that they are seeking a homeland. If they had been thinking of that land from which they had gone out, they would have had opportunity to return. But as it is, they desire a better country, that is, a heavenly one.

Therefore God is not ashamed to be called their God, for he has prepared for them a city.

And all these, though well attested by their faith, did not receive what was promised, since God had foreseen something better for us, that apart from us they should not be made perfect.

(Unison)

Therefore, since we are surrounded by so great a cloud of witnesses, let us also lay aside every weight, and sin which clings so closely, and let us run with perseverance the race that is set before us, looking to Jesus the pioneer and perfecter of our faith, who for the joy that was set before him endured the cross, despising the shame, and is seated at the right hand of the throne of God.

714   James 1:12-27

(Unison)

Blessed is the man who endures trial, for when he has stood the test he will receive the crown of life which God has promised to those who love him. Let no one say when he is tempted, "I am tempted by God"; for God cannot be tempted with evil and he himself tempts no one; but each person is tempted when he is lured and enticed by his own desire. Then desire when it has conceived gives birth to sin; and sin when it is full-grown brings forth death.

Do not be deceived, my beloved brethren. Every good endowment and every perfect gift is from above, coming down from the Father of lights with whom there is no variation or shadow due to change. Of his own will he brought us forth by the word of truth that we should be a kind of first fruits of his creatures.

Know this, my beloved brethren. Let every man be quick to hear, slow to speak, slow to anger, for the anger of man does not work the righteousness of God. Therefore put away all filthiness and rank growth of wickedness and receive with meekness the implanted word, which is able to save your souls.

But be doers of the word, and not hearers only, deceiving yourselves. For if any one is a hearer of the word and not a doer, he is like a man who observes his natural face in a mirror; for he observes himself and goes away and at once forgets what he was like. But he who looks into the perfect law, the law of liberty, and perseveres, being no hearer that forgets but a doer that acts, he shall be blessed in his doing.

If any one thinks he is religious, and does not bridle his tongue but deceives his heart, this man's religion is vain. Religion that is pure and undefiled before God and the Father is this: to visit orphans and widows in their affliction, and to keep oneself unstained from the world.

715   1 John 1:1—2:2

(Antiphonally)

It was there from the beginning; we have heard it; we have seen it with our own eyes; we looked upon it, and felt it with our own hands; and it is of this we tell. Our theme is the word of life.

This life was made visible; we have seen it and bear our testimony; we here declare to you the eternal life which dwelt with the Father and was made visible to us. What we have seen and heard we declare to you, so that you and we together may share in a common life, that life which we share with the Father and his Son Jesus Christ. And we write this in order that the joy of us all may be complete.

Here is the message we heard from him and pass on to you: that God is light, and in him there is no darkness at all.

If we claim to be sharing in his life while we walk in the dark, our words and our lives are a lie;

But if we walk in the light as he himself is in the light, then we share together a common life, and we are being cleansed from every sin by the blood of Jesus his Son.

If we claim to be sinless, we are self-deceived and strangers to the truth.

If we confess our sins, he is just, and may be trusted to forgive our sins and cleanse us from every kind of wrong;

But if we say we have committed no sin, we make him out to be a liar, and then his word has no place in us.

My children, in writing thus to you my purpose is that you should not commit sin.

But should anyone commit a sin, we have one to plead our cause with the Father, Jesus Christ, and he is just.

(Unison)

He is himself the remedy for the defilement of our sins, not our sins only but the sins of all the world.

SCRIPTURE READINGS

716   1 John 4:7-21
(Unison)

Beloved, let us love one another; for love is of God, and he who loves is born of God and knows God. He who does not love does not know God; for God is love. In this the love of God was made manifest among us, that God sent his only Son into the world, so that we might live through him. In this is love, not that we loved God but that he loved us and sent his Son to be the expiation for our sins. Beloved, if God so loved us, we also ought to love one another. No man has ever seen God; if we love one another, God abides in us and his love is perfected in us.

By this we know that we abide in him and he in us, because he has given us of his own Spirit. And we have seen and testify that the Father has sent his Son as the Savior of the world. Whoever confesses that Jesus is the Son of God, God abides in him, and he in God. So we know and believe the love God has for us.

God is love, and he who abides in love abides in God, and God abides in him. In this is love perfected with us, that we may have confidence for the day of judgment, because as he is so are we in this world. There is no fear in love, but perfect love casts out fear. For fear has to do with punishment, and he who fears is not perfected in love. We love, because he first loved us. If any one says, "I love God," and hates his brother, he is a liar; for he who does not love his brother whom he has seen, cannot love God whom he has not seen. And this commandment we have from him, that he who loves God should love his brother also.

717   Revelation 5:1-14
(Antiphonally)

And I saw in the right hand of him who was seated on the throne a scroll written within and on the back, sealed with seven seals; and I saw a strong angel proclaiming with a loud voice, "Who is worthy to open the scroll and break its seals?"

And no one in heaven or on earth or under the earth was able to open the scroll or to look into it, and I wept much that no one was found worthy to open the scroll or to look into it.

Then one of the elders said to me, "Weep not; lo, the Lion of the tribe of Judah, the Root of David, has conquered, so that he can open the scroll and its seven seals."

And between the throne and the four living creatures and among the elders, I saw a Lamb standing, as though it had been slain, with seven horns and with seven eyes, which are the seven spirits of God sent out into all the earth; and he went and took the scroll from the right hand of him who was seated on the throne.

And when he had taken the scroll, the four living creatures and the twenty-four elders fell down before the Lamb, each holding a harp, and with golden bowls full of incense, which are the prayers of the saints; and they sang a new song, saying,

"Worthy art thou to take the scroll and to open its seals, for thou wast slain and by thy blood didst ransom men for God from every tribe and tongue and people and nation, and hast made them a kingdom and priests to our God, and they shall reign on earth."

Then I looked, and I heard around

the throne and the living creatures and the elders the voice of many angels, numbering myriads of myriads and thousands of thousands, saying with a loud voice, "Worthy is the Lamb who was slain, to receive power and wealth and wisdom and might and honor and glory and blessing!"

And I heard every creature in heaven and on earth and under the earth and in the sea, and all therein, saying, "To him who sits upon the throne and to the Lamb be blessing and honor and glory and might for ever and ever!" And the four living creatures said, "Amen!" and the elders fell down and worshiped.

718 Revelation 7:9-17
(Unison)

After this I looked, and behold, a great multitude which no man could number, from every nation, from all tribes and peoples and tongues, standing before the throne and before the Lamb, clothed in white robes, with palm branches in their hands, and crying out with a loud voice, "Salvation belongs to our God who sits upon the throne, and to the Lamb!"

And all the angels stood round the throne and round the elders and the four living creatures, and they fell on their faces before the throne and worshiped God, saying, "Amen! Blessing and glory and wisdom and thanksgiving and honor and power and might be to our God for ever and ever! Amen."

Then one of the elders addressed me, saying, "Who are these, clothed in white robes, and whence have they come?" I said to him, "Sir, you know." And he said to me, "These are they who have come out of the great tribulation; they have washed their robes and made them white in the blood of the Lamb.

"Therefore are they before the throne of God, and serve him day and night within his temple; and he who sits upon the throne will shelter them with his presence. They shall hunger no more, neither thirst any more; the sun shall not strike them, nor any scorching heat. For the Lamb in the midst of the throne will be their shepherd, and he will guide them to springs of living water; and God will wipe away every tear from their eyes."

719 Revelation 21:1-4; 22:1-5
(Unison)

Then I saw a new heaven and a new earth; for the first heaven and the first earth had passed away, and the sea was no more. And I saw the holy city, new Jerusalem, coming down out of heaven from God, prepared as a bride adorned for her husband; and I heard a great voice from the throne saying,

"Behold, the dwelling of God is with men. He will dwell with them, and they shall be his people, and God himself will be with them; he will wipe away every tear from their eyes, and death shall be no more, neither shall there be mourning nor crying nor pain any more, for the former things have passed away."

Then he showed me the river of the water of life, bright as crystal, flowing from the throne of God and of the Lamb through the middle of the street of the city; also, on either side of the river, the tree of life with its twelve kinds of fruit, yielding its fruit each month; and the leaves of the tree were for the healing of the nations.

There shall no more be anything accursed, but the throne of God and of the Lamb shall be in it, and his servants shall worship him; they shall see his face, and his name shall be on their foreheads. And night shall be no more; they need no light of lamp or sun, for the Lord God will be their light, and they shall reign for ever and ever.

SECTION II

Affirmations of Faith

720 An Affirmation of Faith from the Writings of John

We believe that God is Spirit, and they that worship Him must worship Him in spirit and in truth.

That God is Light, and that if we walk in the light, as He is in the light, we have fellowship one with another.

That God is Love, and that every one that loves is born of God and knows God.

We believe that Jesus Christ is the Son of God, and that God has given to us eternal life, and this life is in His Son.

That He is the Resurrection and the Life, and that whoever believes on Him, though he were dead, yet shall he live.

We believe that the Holy Spirit has come and convinces the world of sin, and of righteousness, and of judgment; that He guides us into all truth.

We believe that we are children of God, and that He has given us of His Spirit.

We believe that if we confess our sins He is faithful and just to forgive us our sins, and to cleanse us from all unrighteousness.

We believe that the world passes away and the lust thereof, but he that does the will of God abides forever.

721 The Apostles' Creed

I believe in God the Father Almighty, maker of heaven and earth: and in Jesus Christ His only Son our Lord, who was conceived by the Holy Spirit, born of the Virgin Mary, suffered under Pontius Pilate, was crucified, dead, and buried. He descended into hell;* the third day He arose again from the dead. He ascended into heaven, and sitteth on the right hand of God the Father Almighty; from thence He shall come to judge the quick and the dead. I believe in the Holy Spirit; the holy catholic** church; the communion of saints; the forgiveness of sins; the resurrection of the body; and the life everlasting. Amen.

*"Hades," meaning realm of the dead.
**Meaning "universal."

722 The Nicene Creed

I believe in one God the Father Almighty, maker of heaven and earth, and of all things visible and invisible: and in one Lord Jesus Christ, the only-begotten Son of God, begotten of His Father before all worlds, God of God, Light of Light, very God of very God, begotten, not made, being of one substance with the Father, by whom all things were made: who for us men and for our salvation came down from heaven, and was incarnate by the Holy Spirit of the Virgin Mary, and was made man, and was crucified also for us under Pontius Pilate. He suffered and was buried, and the third day

AFFIRMATIONS OF FAITH

He rose again according to the Scriptures, and ascended into heaven, and sitteth on the right hand of the Father. And He shall come again with glory to judge both the quick and the dead: whose kingdom shall have no end. And I believe in the Holy Spirit, the Lord and giver of life, who proceedeth from the Father and the Son, who with the Father and the Son together is worshiped and glorified, who spoke by the prophets. And I believe in one catholic* and apostolic church; I acknowledge one baptism for the remission of sins, and I look for the resurrection of the dead, and the life of the world to come. Amen.

*Meaning "universal."

723 An Affirmation of Faith *(Contemporary)*

We believe in Jesus Christ the Lord,
    Who was promised to the people of Israel,
    Who came in the flesh to dwell among us,
    Who announced the coming of the rule of God,
    Who gathered disciples and taught them,
    Who died on the cross to free us from sin,
    Who rose from the dead to give us life and hope,
    Who reigns in heaven at the right hand of God,
    Who comes to judge and bring justice to victory.

We believe in God His Father,
    Who raised Him from the dead,
    Who created and sustains the universe,
    Who acts to deliver His people in times of need,
    Who desires all men everywhere to be saved,
    Who rules over the destinies of men and nations,
    Who continues to love men even when they reject Him.

We believe in the Holy Spirit,
    Who is the form of God present in the church,
    Who moves men to faith and obedience,
    Who is the guarantee of our deliverance,
    Who leads us to find God's will in the Word,
    Who assists those whom He renews in prayer,
    Who guides us in discernment,
    Who impels us to act together.

We believe God has made us His people,
    To invite others to follow Christ,
    To encourage one another to deeper commitment,
    To proclaim forgiveness of sins and hope,
    To reconcile men to God through word and deed,
    To bear witness to the power of love over hate,
    To proclaim Jesus the Lord over all,
    To meet the daily tasks of life with purpose,
    To suffer joyfully for the cause of right,
        To the ends of the earth,
        To the end of the age,
        To the praise of His glory. Amen.

SECTION III
Congregational Responses

724 Response to Baptism (No. 1)

Congregation: As we now receive you into the fellowship of Christ's body, the church, we pledge that we will uphold and strengthen you in the Christian life, and that we will endeavor to grow together in the knowledge of Christ, that we may advance His kingdom throughout the world.

725 Response to Baptism (No. 2)

Congregation: As we now receive you into the fellowship of the church, we make a covenant with you as we renew our own covenant with our Lord:
    To bear one another's burdens,
    To share mutually in the forgiving or the retaining of our sins,
    To share in the abundance of this world's goods,
    To assist each other in times of need,
    To share our joys and our sorrows,
    And in all things to work for the common good,
Thus manifesting God's presence among us to His glory. As we unite with each other now, may we all be joined with Christ our Lord.

726 A Pledge of Faith and Love *(In preparation for the Lord's Supper)*

In token of the faith which binds us to God and of the love in which we are united,

We join in voicing our trust in God as our Father, in Christ as our Savior and Lord, and in the Holy Spirit as our Divine Strengthener.

We acknowledge our inclination to sin, both in what we do and in what we leave undone.

We ask for divine forgiveness for all our failure to glorify our Father, and we pledge ourselves to forsake and disown all conduct and attitudes which are unworthy of Christ.

We declare our love for the church, our belief in her principles, and our desire to practice them in all of life.

We pledge to the church our support in prayers, counsels, and gifts, so that she might become stronger in both her inward life and her outward witness.

We will strive by God's grace to remove from our lives all unlove, and cause of disharmony, so that our mutual love may lead men to know true discipleship.

We engage to watch over one another with Christian discernment, to counsel those who are weak, to seek in meekness to restore any who fall.

We will give ourselves to self-examination in preparation for the Lord's Supper, so that the Lord's table may be honored, and that we who gather around it may, by faith, eat and drink richly of Christ.

CONGREGATIONAL RESPONSES

(A Prayer)

O God, who searchest the thoughts and triest the hearts of all men, enable us to prepare ourselves to approach Thy table; cleanse us from all unlove, that being pure in heart, we may without fear of condemnation commune in the body and blood of our Lord. Amen.

727 On Reception of New Members

Minister: These persons now presented to you, have witnessed to their faith in Jesus Christ, and offer themselves as companions in our obedience to Christ. It is our privilege and joy to welcome them into our family of faith.

Congregation: Your expressed faith and Christian intention compels us to renew our own covenant with Christ. In your coming to us, we are newly summoned to become a community in which the wholeness of Christ is realized.

We freely receive you, even as Christ has received us. We open ourselves to fellowship with you in worship, study, service, and discipline. We commit ourselves to watch over you and one another with a heart of concern and caring. We pledge our willingness to offer and to receive forgiveness in the redeemed community. We joyfully accept you as partners, both in the care of our spiritual family, and in our mission to the world.

728 To the Newly Married

Congregation: With joy we identify with you in this high moment of commitment and covenant. The vows you have taken compel us to weigh the purity of our love and to strengthen the relationships of our homes. We pledge that, as you follow Christ, we will join you in seeking to apprehend Him as our true life, and in serving Him by our love.

We offer our prayers that your lives may become increasingly rich in understanding, in common loyalties, and in useful vocation. We thank God for the home you now establish, and anticipate its strength, influence, and support of the church in its mission.

729 At the Dedication of Children

Congregation: You have offered your child to the strong and tender providence of God, and to the nurture of the church. We accept with humility of spirit and seriousness of purpose our responsibility for the spiritual well-being of this child. By our example and our words, we will support your parental role, in disposing this child to respond to the fullness that is in Christ. We earnestly pray that the life and witness of each of us will make your task both joyful and fruitful.

730 On Installation or Ordination of a Minister

Congregation: The charge to you becomes a charge to all of us, for we are all members one of another. As you exercise your gifts in equipping God's people for their work of ministering, we also will exercise our Spirit-given gifts. They are His to use even as your gifts are at His disposal. In common vocation with you as servants, we pledge to you our ungrudging support that you might freely exercise the ministries of leadership committed to you. Our material gifts, our prayers, our counsel, and our encouragement will be freely shared to support you. We are fellow servants, and seek to have you and ourselves realize the true fulfillment of the people of God. We earnestly desire that for us and for all whom you will serve, you will be a "good minister of Jesus Christ."

731 Statement of Restoration

Congregation: In your confession of failure to fulfill your Christian commitment, we are involved with you. We have failed to provide the supporting community which keeps the conscience alert, and the will strong to resist temptation. Forgive us for our failure to surround you with sufficient resources to draw you from the mastery of sin. We assure you that we are now, and will be, a forgiving community in which you are loved, accepted, and encouraged. We promise to be a caring, healing fellowship, forgetting the past in our continuing quest of following Christ. Having been freely pardoned ourselves, and having received your confession, we declare you forgiven in the name and for the sake of Christ. We therefore commend you to the strength and guardianship of the Holy Spirit.

732 In Commissioning Workers

Minister: God gives His people many gifts, all of which are useful in building His church. He calls all of us to serve in the ministry of reconciliation. Each of us thus participates in the servanthood of each. Of this vocation we are again reminded as these representatives leave us for service assignments elsewhere. Their task becomes our task. We, therefore, join in this commissioning charge.

Congregation: As God's Spirit calls and the church commissions, the servants of Christ are scattered in places of need throughout the world. We accept your service as an extension of this congregation, and pledge our support in ways which will make your ministry effective. We join with you in affirming the priority of Christ's kingdom. We urge you to consider your assignment as God's occasion to work through you in ministering to human need. We pray that you may be given a deep love for those whom you will serve. May Christ express Himself through you in word and deed. Our prayers will constantly support you while you are absent from us.

733 A Benediction *(For Congregational Use in Unison)*

Congregation: May the grace of Christ which daily renews our lives, and the love of God which enables us to love all men, and the fellowship of the Holy Spirit which unites us in one body, make us keen to discern and prompt to obey the complete will of God until we meet again, through Jesus Christ our Lord. Amen.

SECTION IV
Prayers

734   **Opening Prayers**

Our God, how great You are! On the first day of the week we commemorate
Your creation of the world and all that is in it.
Thank You for the light which wakes us morning by morning
and for that greater light which shines in Jesus Christ.

Our God, how great You are! On the first day of the week You raised
Jesus from the dead.
Raise us with Him to a new quality of faith and life.

Our God, how great You are! Again on the first day of the week
You sent Your Spirit on Your disciples.
Do not deprive us of Your Spirit,
but renew Him in us day by day. Amen.

735

Lord, You are our God.
We want to realize how much we depend upon You.
You have not only given us life,
    You have made us able to think about its meaning
    And to choose and work for what is good.
In the world much is confusing;
    Many voices strive to be heard.
Yet we have Your word to guide us,
    The life and teaching of Your Son,
    The example of many faithful Christians.
We have known Your hand holding us fast,
    Your steps marking out the way for us:
    We long to know You still.
Your presence transforms even the darker times:
    With You we need not be afraid.
Nothing can separate us from Your love.
Draw out from us such an answering love
    That in our time of testing we may not fall away. Amen.

736

    Come, O Holy Spirit.
    Come as Holy Fire and burn in us,
    Come as Holy Wind and cleanse us within,
    Come as Holy Light and lead us in the darkness,
    Come as Holy Truth and dispel our ignorance,
    Come as Holy Power and enable our weakness,
    Come as Holy Life and dwell in us.

Convict us, convert us, consecrate us until we are set free from the service of ourselves to be Thy servants to the world.

O Holy God, place us humbly at the feet of Thy Son Jesus Christ, that looking steadfastly up unto Him we may both learn and receive from Him those things that belong to the world's true peace and salvation and do Thou make us such faithful interpreters of His life that our fellowmen may return unto Thee and be saved through the same Jesus Christ our Lord. Amen.

737 Thanksgiving Prayers

Lord Jesus Christ, our great High Priest, merciful and faithful, we are glad that You were made like us, that You passed through the test of suffering, that You were made perfect through suffering.

Humbly and joyfully we thank You for offering Yourself to God as the perfect sacrifice, to cleanse our consciences and make us fit to serve God.

We thank You that by dying You broke the power of death, and that You live to intercede on our behalf.

Grant our request that today and throughout our lives we may approach God through You with confidence, and hold fast to the faith we profess. Amen.

738

Thou, O Lord, art the giver of every good and perfect gift. Thou hast called us to the adventure of life, sustained us by Thy providence, chastened us by Thy discipline, and redeemed us by Thy love.

We thank Thee for life with its mystery and wonder, its friendships and activities, its splendor and satisfactions.

We thank Thee for food, raiment, shelter, and all the material benefits of Thy providence.

We thank Thee for burdens which increase our strength, for hindrances that turn our steps away from evil, and for all discipline that brings us closer to Thee.

We thank Thee for the divine light that shone in the face of Jesus, the divine spirit that showed in His teachings, and the divine love that made Him obedient unto death, even the death of the cross.

Our tribute of praise we offer in the name of our Savior. Amen.

739 Prayers of Confession

We confess to You, Lord, what we are: we are not the people we like others to think we are; we are afraid to admit even to ourselves what lies in the depths of our souls. But we do not want to hide our true selves from You. We believe that You know us as we are, and yet You love us. Help us not to shrink from self-knowledge; teach us to respect ourselves for Your sake; give us the courage to put our trust in Your guiding and power.

We also confess to You, Lord, the unrest of the world, to which we contribute and in which we share. Forgive us that so many of us are indifferent to the needs of our fellowmen.

Forgive our reliance on weapons of terror, our discrimination against people of different race, and our preoccupation with material standards. And forgive us Christians for being so unsure of our good news and so unready to tell it.

Raise us out of the paralysis of guilt into the freedom and energy of forgiven people. And for those who through long habit find forgiveness hard to accept, we ask You to break their bondage and set them free. Through Jesus Christ our Lord. Amen.

740

Almighty and most merciful God, we acknowledge and confess that we have sinned against Thee in thought and word and deed, that we have not loved Thee with all our heart and soul, with all our mind and strength, and that we have not loved our neighbor as ourselves.

We beseech Thee, O God, to be forgiving to what we have been, to help us to amend what we are, and by Thy mercy to direct what we shall be, so that the love of goodness may ever be first in our hearts, that we may always walk in Thy commandments and ordinances blameless, and follow unto our life's end in the steps of Jesus Christ our Lord. Amen.

741 Supplication and Intercession

Lord, make me an instrument of Thy peace.
    Where there is hatred, let me sow love;
    Where there is injury, pardon;
    Where there is doubt, faith;
    Where there is despair, hope;
    Where there is darkness, light;
    Where there is sadness, joy.
O Divine Master, grant that I may not so much seek
    To be consoled, as to console;
    To be understood, as to understand;
    To be loved, as to love.
For it is in giving that we receive;
It is in pardoning that we are pardoned;
It is in dying that we are born to eternal life.

742

Lord Jesus, when You have drawn all men to Yourself, there will be peace on earth.

When we try to get things for ourselves, and have things our own way, we fight and push, and are angry and cruel, and everything is made less happy than it was meant to be, and Your kingdom does not come.

So give us Your Spirit, to make us people who build Your kingdom, not people who pull it down.

Help us to want things Your way, not our way.

Take our strength and our energy, and help us to put all we have into the struggle for Your goodness and Your truth.

Yours be the power and the victory for ever and ever. Amen.

743

O Thou who rulest the world from end to end and from everlasting to everlasting, make us to know that Thou art God and that in Thee alone is our hope.

Grant us grace to repent of our sins and to yield our wills to Thine, that Thou mayest forgive all our iniquities and heal all our diseases and redeem our lives from destruction.

Bring us more and more into fellowship with Thee, O God of peace, that we may have peace within our hearts and that Thou, O Lord, mayest work through us to give peace to the world; through Jesus Christ our Lord. Amen.

744

Lord God, the story of Your love for us makes us realize that there are many others as well as ourselves who need Your help and Your grace.
So we bring our prayers to You:
> For those who suffer pain;
> For those whose minds are disturbed, or have never matured;
> For those who have not had the opportunity to realize their potentialities;
> For those who are satisfied with something less than the life for which they were made;
> For those who know their guilt, their shallowness, their need, but who do not know of Jesus;
> For those who know that they must shortly die;
> For those who cannot wait to die.

Lord God, Your Son has taken all our sufferings upon Himself and has transformed them.

Help us, who offer these prayers, to take the sufferings of others upon ourselves, and so, by Your grace, become the agents of Your transforming love.

Through Jesus Christ our Lord. Amen.

745

Thou Father of our Lord Jesus Christ, who is head of the church, give us grace to lay to heart the great dangers we are in by our unhappy divisions. Take away all hatred and prejudice, and whatsoever else may hinder us from godly union and concord, that as there is but one body, and one spirit, and one hope of our calling, one Lord, one faith, one baptism, one God and Father of us all, so we may henceforth be all of one heart, and of one soul, united in one holy bond of truth and peace, of faith and charity, and may with one mind and one mouth glorify Thee, through Jesus Christ our Lord. Amen.

746

O Lord, we know not what to ask of Thee.
Thou alone knowest what are our true needs.
Thou lovest us more than we ourselves know how to love.
Help us to see our real needs which are concealed from us.
We dare not ask either a cross or consolation.
We can only wait on Thee. Our hearts are open unto Thee.
> Visit and help us, for Thy great mercy's sake.
> Strike us and heal us.
> Cast us down and raise us up.

We worship in silence Thy holy will and Thine inscrutable ways.
We offer ourselves as a sacrifice unto Thee.
We put all our trust in Thee.
We have no other desire than to fulfill Thy will.
> Teach us how to pray.
> Pray Thou Thyself in us. Amen.

747

O Master, lover of mankind, kindle within our hearts the clear light of Thy divine knowledge, and open the eyes of our understanding, that we may understand the preaching of Thy gospel: graft in us also the fear of Thy blessed commandments, that having trodden underfoot all fleshly lusts, and thinking and doing always such things as please Thee, we may continue in a spiritual manner of life.

For Thou art the light, O Christ our God, both of our souls and bodies, and we give glory to Thee, together with Thine unbegotten Father, and Thy most holy and gracious and life-giving Spirit, now and for ever and world without end. Amen.

748

Heavenly Father, give us Your Holy Spirit that He may enable us to make known to You our needs by our prayers and supplications; that He Himself may intercede for us with groanings which cannot be uttered, sanctifying us and keeping our hearts, our thoughts, and our desires; and that in these days particularly, He will grant us to know ourselves and to manifest to the world Your light in Jesus Christ, Your Son, our Lord, who lives and reigns with You in the unity of the Holy Spirit, one God, now and always and unto ages of ages. Amen.

749   **Offering**

Father, we give back to You in thankfulness what You have given to us in Your kindness. We acknowledge that the world and its resources are not ours but Yours, and that You have put us in charge as Your trustees. Help us to exercise responsibly the authority You give us in Your world.

Let Jesus Your Son be the pattern for all our dealings with one another, and with the rest of creation. He is truth: so help us to take our quest for truth seriously, whether in the research laboratories, or in the dialectic of philosophy and politics. He is life: so give us reverence for life, whether on the poultry farms or on the roads.

Yet with His care give us also His joy in life. With His compassion give us also His strength. So that in everything He may be everything to us. Praise and victory be to Him from all, and in all, for ever and ever. Amen.

750 Closing

Father, as we go to our homes and our work this coming week, we ask You to send the Holy Spirit into our lives.

Open our ears—To hear what You are saying to us in the things that happen to us and in the people we meet.
Open our eyes—To see the needs of the people round us.
Open our hands—To do our work well. To help when help is needed.
Open our lips—To tell others the good news of Jesus and bring comfort, happiness, and laughter to other people.
Open our minds—To discover new truth about You and the world.
Open our hearts—To love You and our fellowmen as You have loved us in Jesus.

To Him, with You our Father and the Holy Spirit, one God, all honor and praise shall be given now and for ever. Amen.

751

Lord Jesus, Word of the Father, spoken in mercy and power to mankind, may all power serve You, all mercy follow Your lead.

Word of pity, let men find in You an example to inspire them without daunting them, and a love to reassure them without smothering them.

Word of life, let men find in You the key to all the riddles of existence, and the door to an eternal hope.

Word of command, may we go now, refreshed by Your presence, and put Your plans into action and Your energy to good use.

For Your name's sake. Amen.

752

Lord God, You have come near to us and shown us something of Your patience, something of Your sympathy, something of Your love.

Give us, Lord, as we go about our life in the world, patience when men are indifferent to Your claims, sympathy for the needs of all Your creatures, a love which reflects Your forgiving love for men.

Through Jesus Christ our Lord. Amen.

Topical Index of Worship Resources

Adoration and Praise of Christ, 717
Adoration and Praise of God, 654, 658, 667, 668, 670, 674, 676, 718, 719
Affliction, 668, 672, 683, 703 (see Comfort)
Angels, 673, 676, 692, 693, 717, 718
Anniversaries, 656, 672
Anxiety, 690, 709
Aspiration, 668, 671
Assurance, 663, 665

Beatitudes, 696
Beauty, 661, 665, 671, 690
Benevolence, 696, 707, 712
Bereavement (see Comfort)
Bible, The, 660, 662
Brotherhood, 692, 701, 704, 708, 710, 716

Call to Worship, 658, 667, 668, 671, 674, 675, 676
Children, 656, 692
Christ—Advent, 664, 679, 680, 681, 695
Christ—Ascension, 717
Christ—Communion with, 699, 700, 701, 702, 703, 709, 710
Christ—Cross of, 683, 694
Christ—Incarnation, 695, 697, 708, 715
Christ—His Intercession, 683, 701, 703, 715
Christ—Kingdom of, 679, 680, 693, 706, 717
Christ—Love of, 700, 703
Christ—Person and Work, 683, 694, 699, 701, 703, 708, 713
Christ—His Resurrection, 702, 706, 711
Christ—Second Coming, 693, 706, 711
Christ—Sufferings of, 683, 694
Christian Life, 689, 690, 691, 692, 693, 696, 699, 700, 702, 704, 709, 710, 712, 714, 715
Christmas, 679, 695, 697, 708
Church, The (see Brotherhood)
Church, The—Body of Christ, 691
Church, The—Dedication (see Dedication, Building)
Church, The—Unity of, 692, 701, 708, 710
Church, The—Worship of (see Worship)
City of God, 713, 719
Comfort, 657, 663, 677, 681, 682, 683, 711, 718, 719
Communion, Holy, 699, 700, 703
Compassion, Divine, 685
Confession, 670, 685, 686, 715, 716
Confidence, 663, 665
Consecration—Personal, 704, 710
Courage, 665
Covenant, 656, 676, 684, 686
Creation (see God—as Creator)
Cross Bearing, 694

Day of Rest, 655
Death, 706, 711, 714, 719
Dedication Services—Church Building, 671
Deliverance, 656, 657, 667
Discipleship, 689, 690, 692, 693, 696, 700, 714
Discipline, 692, 700
Duty, 656

Easter (see Christ—His Resurrection)
Education, 656
Enemies, 654, 665, 678, 696, 704
Evangelistic Hymns (Evangelism), 667, 691, 697, 698, 699

Faith, 663, 665, 690, 698, 699, 705, 712, 713, 716
Faithfulness—of God, 685, 686, 695
Fasting, 689
Fellowship (see Brotherhood)
Forgiveness, 666, 670, 676, 684, 686, 689, 710, 715
Freedom—Spiritual, 702, 703, 714
Funeral Services, 663, 669, 672 (see Resurrection of the Body)

God—As Creator, 659, 661, 662, 664, 672, 674, 675, 678, 682
God—As Deliverer, 654, 657, 669, 673, 678 (see God—Our Refuge)
God—As Father, 676

God—Divine Shepherd, 663, 674, 675, 681, 692, 718
God—Eternal, 672, 682, 717
God—His Glory and Majesty, 658, 661, 662, 663, 669, 681
God—Hearer of Prayer, 666
God—Helper in Trouble, 657, 663, 666, 669, 670, 673, 677
God—His Holiness, 695
God—His Justice, 655, 658, 667, 672, 676, 680, 685, 704
God—His Law, 655, 657, 660, 662, 687, 702
God—His Love, 658, 668, 673, 675, 676, 678, 685, 692, 698, 701, 703, 716
God—His Mercy, 662, 666, 670, 675, 676, 678, 684, 685, 686, 695, 696
God—His Power, 654, 664, 682, 695
God—His Presence, 663, 669, 672
God—His Providence, 663, 665, 673, 676, 677, 681, 689, 690
God—His Unchangeableness, 672, 677, 678, 681, 682
God—His Wisdom, 659, 678
God—Our Refuge, 654, 665, 669, 672, 673
Good Friday (see Christ—Cross of, and Christ—Sufferings of)
Grace, 707
Gratitude (see Thanksgiving)
Guidance, 663, 665, 666, 677

Healing, 665, 667, 673, 676, 682, 683, 719
Heaven, 663
Holy Scriptures, The (see Bible, The)
Holy Spirit, 698, 702, 716
Home, Christian, 656
Hope, 668, 679, 685, 704, 705, 711
Hospitals, 693
Humility, 671, 688, 704, 708, 710
Hypocrisy, 689, 715

Inner Life, The, 700 (see Christ—Communion with)
Instruction, 656, 666, 687
International Relations (see Peace—Among Men)

Joy, 658, 666, 670, 671, 675, 679, 692, 695, 696, 700, 704, 709, 713, 715
Judgment, 691, 693, 698, 716 (see God—His Law)
Justice, 688

Kingdom of God, The, 690, 696, 698
Kingdom of Heaven, 691

Lamb of God, 683, 717, 718
Laws of God, 655, 684, 686 (see God—His Justice, His Law)
Lent (see Christ—Cross of)
Life, Eternal, 663, 693, 697, 698, 699, 701, 702, 712, 713, 715, 718, 719
Life—Transience of, 660, 672, 676
Light, 665, 697, 698, 715, 719
Litany, 678
Lord's Day, The, 655
Lord's Prayer, The, 689
Lord's Supper, The (see Communion, Holy)
Love—For God, 656
Love—For Man, 696, 704, 705, 708, 716

Magnificat, 695
Man, 660, 661
Man—His Need for Redemption, 662, 664, 666, 670, 685, 702, 715
Ministry, The, 656
Missions, 680, 701
Mother (see Home, Christian)
Music—Singing, 658, 674, 675, 692, 695, 710, 717

Nature, 661, 662, 690
New Birth, 697, 698, 702
Nonresistance (see Enemies)

Obedience, 655, 662, 693, 699, 702, 710, 714
Offering, 658, 686, 689, 704, 707, 709, 712
Opening of Worship (see Call to Worship. See also Adoration and Praise)

TOPICAL INDEX OF WORSHIP RESOURCES

Parables, 691, 692
Patience, 665, 685, 713
Peace—Among Men, 669, 679, 680, 681, 687, 696, 704
Peace—Inner, 663, 673, 690, 709, 710
Penitence (*see* Repentance)
Pentecost (*see* Holy Spirit)
Persecution, 696, 703, 704, 718
Perseverance, 706, 713, 714
Praise (*see* Adoration and Praise)
Prayer, 662, 668, 671, 686, 689, 692, 694, 701, 709
Prophecy, 683, 684, 687, 693
Purity, 714

Redemption, 654, 657, 676, 678, 683, 688, 702, 716, 717
Repentance, 670, 686, 692
Resurrection of the Body, 699, 702, 706, 711
Reward, 662, 681, 689, 693, 696, 713
Riches, 696, 712
Righteousness, 657, 664, 680, 685, 686, 702, 703, 713

Salvation, 657, 658, 664, 665, 670, 673, 683, 698, 714, 715, 718
Service, 656, 675, 693, 704
Shepherd, The Divine (*see* God—Divine Shepherd)
Sick, For the, 663, 665, 667
Sin, 662, 666, 670, 672, 702, 710, 714, 715, 716 (*see* Man His Need for Redemption)
Sorrow (*see* Comfort)
Spirit, 680 (*see* Holy Spirit)
Stewardship, 707, 709, 712
Submission, 663, 669, 689, 694
Suffering, 663, 666, 696, 703

Sunday (*see* Lord's Day, The)

Teachers, 656, 659, 698, 710
Teaching of Christ, 689, 690, 691, 692, 693, 696, 698, 699, 700
Temptation, 689, 712, 714
Ten Commandments, 655
Thanksgiving, 658, 674, 675, 676, 678, 706, 707, 709, 710
Travelers, 677
Trials, 694, 696, 714
Trinity, 701
Trust, 663, 665, 666, 669, 671, 673, 682, 690
Truth, 670, 701

Unity (*see* Church, The—Unity of)

Victory, 659, 669, 673, 703, 706, 717

Waiting for God, 665, 682, 685
Walking with God, 663, 677, 715
Warning, 655, 662
Watchfulness, 694
Whitsunday (*see* Holy Spirit)
Wisdom, 659
Witnessing, 670, 691, 697, 712, 716
Word of God, 655, 681, 686, 697, 713, 714 (*see* Bible, The)
World Friendship and Peace (*see* Peace—Among Men)
Worship, 658, 664, 665, 671, 674, 675, 688, 689, 692, 708, 717, 718, 719 (*see* Adoration and Praise)

Acknowledgments

With sincere gratefulness and deep appreciation the publishers wish to acknowledge all persons, publishers, and trustees of estates for permission to use the copyrighted matter in this *Hymnal*. Numerous correspondents were especially helpful in providing addresses difficult to locate and in giving information on copyright material. To these, too, we wish to express our gratitude. Every effort was made to locate and write to copyright owners for permissions. If we have inadvertently omitted securing permission or have used material which we had thought to be in public domain, you will be doing the publishers a favor by giving them the correct information. Proper acknowledgment can then be made in future editions.

THE HYMNS

9. Music from *Gesangbuch der Mennoniten* by permission of Faith and Life Press. International copyright, 1965.
10. Music by permission of Verein zur Herausgabe des Gesangbuches der Evangelisch-Reformierten Kirchen der Deutschsprachigen Schweiz.
13. Words by permission of J. Curwen & Sons, Ltd.
17. Harmonization from *Songs of Syon*, Schott & Co., London; by permission of J. Meredith Tatton, copyright owner.
20. Translation by permission of Lester Hostetler. Music from *Gesangbuch der Mennoniten* by permission of Faith and Life Press. International copyright, 1965.
22. Music by permission of Public Trustee Office, London.
23. Words from the *Scottish Metrical Psalter* by Nichol Grieve by permission of T. & T. Clark, Edinburgh.
24, 26. Music from *Gesangbuch der Mennoniten* by permission of Faith and Life Press. International copyright, 1965.
28. Music by permission of Public Trustee Office, London.
31. Music from *Gesangbuch der Mennoniten* by permission of Faith and Life Press. International copyright, 1965.
33. Words and music copyright 1941 by Eden Publishing House. Used by permission.
38. Music by permission of Verein zur Herausgabe des Gesangbuches der Evangelisch-Reformierten Kirchen der Deutschsprachigen Schweiz.
40. Translation by permission of Marion Wenger. Music from *Gesangbuch der Mennoniten*. International copyright, 1965.
51. Words by permission of J. Curwen & Sons, Ltd. Music from *The English Hymnal* by permission of Oxford University Press. Arrangement altered with permission.
52. Words by permission of J. Curwen & Sons, Ltd.
55. Words and music from the *EACC Hymnal*. Copyright by Christian Audio Visual Center, Tokyo.
59. Music from *Gesangbuch der Mennoniten* by permission of Faith and Life Press. International copyright, 1965.
60. Music from Layriz from *Eine Sammlung der gangbarsten Chorale der evang.-Lutherischen Kirchen.*
62. Words by permission of Lord Brooke of Cumnor, Hampstead, England.
68. Words from *The Mennonite Hymnary* by permission of the Board of Publication of the General Conference of the Mennonite Church of North America. Music from *Gesangbuch der Mennoniten* by permission of Faith and Life Press. International copyright, 1965.
71. Words from *The English Hymnal* by permission of Oxford University Press.
73. Melody by permission of the original publisher, Breitkopf and Hartel, Wiesbaden. Arrangement of music copyright 1933, 1961, by Presbyterian Board of Education. Used by permission.
76. Music copyright by Mary B. Rowlands. Used by permission.
77. Music by permission of Verein zur Herausgabe des Gesangbuches der Evangelisch-Reformierten Kirchen der Deutschsprachigen Schweiz.
82. Words from the *Scottish Metrical Psalter* by Nichol Grieve by permission of T. & T. Clark, Edinburgh.
88. Words by permission of Robert B. Y. Scott. Music by permission of James Hopkirk.
92. Music by permission of The Church Pension Fund.
94. Music from *Enlarged Songs of Praise* by permission of Oxford University Press.
115. Music from *The BBC Hymn Book* by permission of Oxford University Press.
116. Translation by permission of Martin L. Seltz. Music from *Gesangbuch der Mennoniten* by permission of Faith and Life Press. International copyright, 1965.
118. Music from the *Service Book and Hymnal* (Lutheran) by permission of the Commission on the Liturgy and the Hymnal.
119. Words and music from the *Hymnal for Colleges and Schools* by permission of Yale University Press.
124. Words and music from the *Service Book and Hymnal* (Lutheran) by permission of the Commission on the Liturgy and the Hymnal.
131. Words for stanza 3 from the *Service Book and Hymnal* (Lutheran) by permission of the Commission on the Liturgy and the Hymnal. Words for stanzas 1 and 2 by permission of G. Schirmer, Inc., New York and E. C. Shirmer Music Co., Boston.
134. Music altered from Layriz by permission from *Eine Sammlung der gangbarsten Chorale der evang.-Lutherischen Kirchen.*
141. Music from the *Service Book and Hymnal* (Lutheran) by permission of the Commission on the Liturgy and the Hymnal.
145. Words copyright 1927 by Calvin W. Laufer; renewed 1955 by E. B. Laufer; from *Hymns for Junior Worship*. Used by permission.
153. Music from the *Service Book and Hymnal* (Lutheran) by permission of the Commission on the Liturgy and the Hymnal.
158. Words copyright. From *The Yattendon Hymnal* by permission of Oxford University Press. Stanza 3 omitted with permission.
163. Harmony by permission of Alice Parker.
172. Words from the *Service Book and Hymnal* (Lutheran) by permission of the Commission on the Liturgy and the Hymnal. The tune is copyright and reprinted by permission of the executors of the late Dr. John Ireland.
173. Music by permission of Verein zur Herausgabe des Gesangbuches der Evangelisch-Reformierten Kirchen der Deutschsprachigen Schweiz.
175. Music from *Choralbuch zum Einheitsgesangbuch* by permission of Gutersloher Verlagshaus Gerd Mohn, Gutersloh, Germany.
180. Words from *Cantate Domino*. By permission of the Word Student Christian Federation, Geneva.
182. Words and music from the *Service Book and Hymnal* (Lutheran) by permission of the Commission on the Liturgy and the Hymnal.
196. Words from *Hymns of the Russian Church* by permission of Oxford University Press.
198. Words from *Enlarged Songs of Praise* by permission of Oxford University Press.
200. Words by permission of Independent Press, Ltd., London.
204. Words and music from *The Hymnbook* of the Mennonite Brethren Church of Canada.
205. Words from *The Common Service Book of the United Lutheran Church of America*. Used by permission. Music by permission of Verein zur Herausgabe des Gesangbuches der Evangelisch-Reformierten Kirchen der Deutschsprachigen Schweiz.

ACKNOWLEDGMENTS

207. Music by permission of Alice Parker.
209. Translation copyright, 1953, by Frank W. Price. Used by permission. Music by permission of The United Church of Christ in Japan, Tokyo.
210. Music from *The English Hymnal* by permission of Oxford University Press.
211. Words copyright. From *The Yattendon Hymnal* by permission of Oxford University Press. Stanzas 3 and 5 omitted with permission. Music from the *Hymnal for Colleges and Schools* by permission of Yale University Press.
212. Words from the *Service Book and Hymnal* (Lutheran) by permission of the Commission on the Liturgy and the Hymnal. Music by permission of Verein zur Herausgabe des Gesangbuches der Evangelisch-Reformierten Kirchen der Deutschsprachigen Schweiz.
218. Words and music from the *Service Book and Hymnal* (Lutheran) by permission of the Commission on the Liturgy and the Hymnal.
223. Music from *Gesangbuch der Mennoniten* by permission of Faith and Life Press. International copyright, 1965.
224. Words from *Enlarged Songs of Praise* by permission of Oxford University Press. Music from *Gesangbuch der Mennoniten* by permission of Faith and Life Press. International copyright, 1965.
228. Music by permission of J. Harold Moyer.
231. Music from *The English Hymnal* by permission of Oxford University Press.
232. Music from the *Church Hymnal*. Copyright 1927 by the Mennonite Publishing House.
235. Words from the *Service Book and Hymnal* (Lutheran) by permission of the Commission on the Liturgy and the Hymnal. Music by permission of Verein zur Herausgabe des Gesangbuches der Evangelisch-Reformierten Kirchen der Deutschsprachigen Schweiz.
247. Words by permission of Walter Russell Bowie.
250. Music from Layriz from *Eine Sammlung der gangbarsten Chorale der evang.-Lutherischen Kirchen*.
252. Music from *Revised Church Hymnary* by permission of Oxford University Press.
253. Words from the *Service Book and Hymnal* (Lutheran) by permission of the Commission on the Liturgy and the Hymnal. Tune copyright reprinted by permission of the Executors of the late Professor David Evans.
255. Words copyright and used by permission of Bryn A. Rees.
256. Music from the *Hymnal for Colleges and Schools* by permission of Yale University Press.
264. Music by permission of Verein zur Herausgabe des Gesangbuches der Evangelisch-Reformierten Kirchen der Deutschsprachigen Schweiz.
274. Words by permission of Houghton Mifflin Co. Music copyright. Used by permission of the Psalms and Hymns Trust.
278. Words from the *Scottish Metrical Psalter* by Nichol Grieve by permission of T. & T. Clark, Edinburgh.
281. Music by permission of Novello & Co., Ltd.
286. Words from the *Service Book and Hymnal* (Lutheran) by permission of the Commission on the Liturgy and the Hymnal.
291. Words copyright. From *The Yattendon Hymnal* by permission of Oxford University Press.
295. Words from *Eleven Ecumenical Hymns*, copyright 1954 by The Hymn Society of America. Used by permission.
297. Music by permission of The Church Pension Fund.
299. Words by permission of Ernest Merrill.
300. Stanzas 1, 2, 4, 5 from "A Prayer" in *The Poem Book of the Gael*, edited by Eleanor Hull by permission of Editor's Literary Estate, and Chatto and Windus, Ltd., London. Music from *Enlarged Songs of Praise* by permission of Oxford University Press. Harmonization altered by permission.
304. Words from *Enlarged Songs of Praise* and music from *The English Hymnal*, both by permission of Oxford University Press.
308. Words from *The Lutheran Hymnal*, copyright 1941. Reprinted by permission of Concordia Publishing House.
309. Words copyright by Harry Webb Farrington and used by permission of The Hymn Society of America.
311. Music under international copyright of Mrs. Dilys Webb through Mechanical-Copyright Protection Society, Ltd., and reproduced by permission of the legal representatives of the composer who reserve all rights therein.
312. Words © Copyright 1960, Broadman Press. All rights reserved. International copyright secured. Used by permission.
319. Music from *Gesangbuch der Mennoniten* by permission of Faith and Life Press. International copyright, 1965.
323. Words from *The English Hymnal* by permission of Oxford University Press. Music by permission of The Church Pension Fund.
329. Translation by permission of Joanna S. Andres.
335. Words and music from the *Service Book and Hymnal* (Lutheran) by permission of the Commission on the Liturgy and the Hymnal.
338. Words and music from *The Hymnbook* of the Mennonite Brethren Church of Canada.
339. Translation copyright, 1953, by Frank W. Price. Used by permission. Music from *Hymns of Universal Praise*. Copyright 1965 by Bliss Wiant. Used by permission.
341. Music by permission of Verein zur Herausgabe des Gesangbuches der Evangelisch-Reformierten Kirchen der Deutschsprachigen Schweiz.
344. Translation by permission of David Augsburger.
352. Words and music from *Hymnal for Colleges and Schools* by permission of Yale University Press.
353. Music by permission of J. Randall Zercher.
359. Words by permission of Oxford University Press.
360. Words from *Fourteen New Rural Hymns*, copyright 1955 by The Hymn Society of America. Used by permission.
361. Music from *The English Hymnal* by permission of Oxford University Press.
362. Words and music from the *Pilgrim Hymnal*. Copyright 1958, The Pilgrim Press. Used by permission.
363. Words from *Ten Stewardship Hymns*, copyright 1961 by The Hymn Society of America. Used by permission. Music from *The BBC Hymn Book* by permission of Oxford University Press.
365. Music by permission of Verein zur Herausgabe des Gesangbuches der Evangelisch-Reformierten Kirchen der Deutschsprachigen Schweiz.
367. Words by permission of Oxford University Press. Music by permission of Independent Press, Ltd., London.
377. Words and music by permission of The United Church of Christ in Japan, Tokyo. Bass stave added by permission.
384. Words by permission of Ernest A. Payne. Music from Layriz from *Eine Sammlung der gangbarsten Chorale der evang.-Lutherischen Kirchen*.
386. Translation by permission of Walter Klaassen.
387. Words by permission of Theo. Oxenham.
391. Music by permission of Verein zur Herausgabe des Gesangbuches der Evangelisch-Reformierten Kirchen der Deutschsprachigen Schweiz.
395. Music from *The English Hymnal* by permission of Oxford University Press.
396. Music from Layriz from *Eine Sammlung der gangbarsten Chorale der evang.-Lutherischen Kirchen*.
403. Words from *Enlarged Songs of Praise* by permission of Oxford University Press.
404. Music by permission of The Church Pension Fund.
406. Words and music from the *Service Book and Hymnal* (Lutheran) by permission of the Commission on the Liturgy and the Hymnal.
414. Words by permission of Philip E. Gregory.
415. Music from Layriz from *Eine Sammlung der gangbarsten Chorale der evang.-Lutherischen Kirchen*.
417. Words and music from *The Lutheran Hymnal*, copyright 1941. Reprinted by permission of Concordia Publishing House.
420. Words from the *Service Book and Hymnal* (Lutheran) by permission of the Commission on the Liturgy and the Hymnal.
425. Music by permission of Independent Press, Ltd., London.
426. Words and music copyright 1941 by Eden Publishing House. Used by permission.

ACKNOWLEDGMENTS

427. Music by permission of Independent Press, Ltd., London.
433. Words from *The Toiling of Felix and Other Poems* by Henry van Dyke. Charles Scribner's Sons (1900). Music from *The BBC Hymn Book* by permission of Oxford University Press.
434. Words by permission of Harry Emerson Fosdick. Music under international copyright of Mrs. Dilys Webb through Mechanical-Copyright Protection Society, Ltd., and reproduced by permission of the legal representatives of the composer who reserve all rights therein.
435. Music by permission of the Proprietors of *Hymns Ancient and Modern*.
438. Words and music from *Life Songs II*. Copyright 1938 by Mennonite Publishing House. Words by permission of Edith Witmer.
441. Words by permission of Ernest Merrill and *The Presbyterian Outlook*.
445. Music by permission of Schott & Co., Ltd., London.
446, 447. Words by permission of Oxford University Press.
449. Words by permission of Theo. Oxenham.
450. Words by permission of Walter Russell Bowie. Music from *Hymnal for Colleges and Schools* by permission of Yale University Press.
452. Music by permission of Oxford University Press.
453. Words by permission of Elispeth Dunkerley.
455. Words by permission of The American Peace Society.
457. Words and music by permission of Oxford University Press. Arrangement altered with permission.
459. Words by permission of S. Ralph Harlow.
462. Words by permission of Albert Frederick Bayly. Music from *Songs of Praise* (1925) by permission of Oxford University Press. Arrangement altered with permission.
466. Words and music from the *Service Book and Hymnal* (Lutheran) by permission of the Commission on the Liturgy and the Hymnal.
467. Words by permission of the National Sunday School Union. Music from *A Student's Hymnal* by permission of Oxford University Press.
468. Words copyright. By permission of the Methodist Youth Department. Music by permission of Kenneth G. Finlay.
469. Words by permission of Albert Frederick Bayly. Music by permission of Kenneth G. Finlay.
470. Words copyright 1946 by the Westminster Press; from *Hymns for Primary Worship*. Used by permission.
471. Words for stanzas 1, 2, and 3 from *Youth Hymnary* by permission of Faith and Life Press. Copyright 1956. Words for stanza 4 and refrain from *The Hymnbook* of the Mennonite Brethren Church of Canada.
476. Words from *Songs of Praise for Boys and Girls* by permission of Oxford University Press.
479. Words and music from the *Church Hymnal*. Copyright 1927 by Mennonite Publishing House.
480. Words from *The English Hymnal* by permission of Oxford University Press. Music from *Hymnal for Colleges and Schools* by permission of Yale University Press.
484. Words and music from the *Service Book and Hymnal* (Lutheran) by permission of the Commission on the Liturgy and the Hymnal.
486. Music from *Gesangbuch der Mennoniten* by permission of Faith and Life Press. International copyright, 1965.
487, 489. Words copyright. From *The Yattendon Hymnal* by permission of Oxford University Press.
497. Words and music from *The Hymnbook* of the Mennonite Brethren Church of Canada.
498. Words by permission of Frank W. Price. Music from *Hymns of Universal Praise*. Copyright 1965 by Bliss Wiant. Used by permission.
503. Music from *The English Hymnal* by permission of Oxford University Press. Arrangement altered with permission.
511. Music from Layriz from *Eine Sammlung der gangbarsten Chorale der evang.-Lutherischen Kirchen*.
513. Music from *The English Hymnal* by permission of Oxford University Press.
520. Music from *The Church Choir Book*; setting by Healey Willan. Reprinted by permission of Concordia Publishing House.
523. Words and music from the *Service Book and Hymnal* (Lutheran) by permission of the Commission on the Liturgy and the Hymnal.
534. Words and music copyright, 1923. Renewal, 1951, by W. M. Runyan. Assigned to Hope Publishing Co. All rights reserved. Used by permission.
535. Copyright 1955 by Manna Music, Inc., Hollywood, Calif. International copyright secured. All rights reserved. Used by permission.
538. Words and music copyright 1917. Renewed 1945 by Nazarene Publishing House. Used by permission.
541. Words and music copyright, 1910. Renewal, 1938, by A. P. Towner. Assigned to Hope Publishing Co. All rights reserved. Used by permission.
545. Words and music copyright 1942 by Broadman Press. Used by permission.
548. Words and music from *The Hymnbook* of the Mennonite Brethren Church of Canada.
584. Words and music by permission of Carl Fischer, Inc., New York.
595. Music by permission of Oxford University Press.
597. German words and music from *Harvard University Hymn Book* by permission of Harvard University Press. English words from *Hymnal for Colleges and Schools* by permission of Yale University Press.
603. Words copyright 1928, renewed 1956 by Board of Christian Education of the Presbyterian Church in the U.S.A.; from *The Hymnal*; used by permission. Music copyright. From *The Yattendon Hymnal* by permission of Oxford University Press.
604. Words copyright. From *The Yattendon Hymnal* by permission of Oxford University Press. Music from *Hymnal for Colleges and Schools* by permission of Yale University Press.
605. Words by permission of Major E. Ainger and S.P.C.K. Music from *Enlarged Songs of Praise* by permission of Oxford University Press.
609. Words for first stanza from the *Service Book and Hymnal* (Lutheran) by permission of the Commission on the Liturgy and the Hymnal.
610. Music from Layriz from *Eine Sammlung der gangbarsten Chorale der evang.-Lutherischen Kirchen*.
612. Words from *The Lutheran Hymnal*, copyright 1941. Reprinted by permission of Concordia Publishing House.
614. Words by permission of A. R. Mowbray & Co., Ltd., London. Harmony by permission of Alice Parker.
615. Words and music from the *Service Book and Hymnal* (Lutheran) by permission of the Commission on the Liturgy and the Hymnal.
616. Words from *Five New Hymns on the City*, copyright 1954 by The Hymn Society of America. Used by permission. Original hymn tune: "City of God" by Daniel Moe. Reprinted from ACL 1193, "O Jesus Christ to Thee May Hymns be Rising." Copyright 1957. By permission of Augsburg Publishing House, Minneapolis, Minn., copyright owners.
617, 618. Words and music by permission of The Grail, London.
619. Music from *Hymnal for Colleges and Schools* by permission of Yale University Press.
626. Music by permission of J. Harold Moyer.
630. Words and music by permission of the Brethren Press.
645. Music from *The Clarendon Hymnbook* by permission of the Trustees of the late Sir Walford Davies.
646. Music by permission of Alice Parker.
653. Music from *Pilgrim Hymnal*. Copyright, 1958, The Pilgrim Press. Used by permission.

The following material is covered by the publisher's copyright:
Translations and Words: 40, 284, 344, 386.
Altered Words: 158, 211.
Music and Harmonizations: 163, 207, 228, 273, 353, 615, 626, 646.
Altered Music: 51, 134, 300, 377, 457, 462, 503.

ACKNOWLEDGMENTS 611

ADDITIONAL WORSHIP RESOURCES

654-662, 664-689, 691, 693-702, 705, 706, 709-711, 713, 714, 716-719. These readings are from the *Revised Standard Version* of the Bible. Copyrighted 1946 and 1952. Used by permission.
663. From the *King James Version* of the Bible.
690, 692, 704, 707, 712, 715. From *The New English Bible.* © the Delegates of the Oxford University Press and the Syndics of the Cambridge University Press 1961. Used by permission.
703. From *The New Testament in Modern English.* © J. B. Phillips, 1958. Used by permission of The Macmillan Company. Changes in the text of verses 32 and 33 by permission of J. B. Phillips.
708. From *Good News for Modern Man* copyright © 1966 by American Bible Society. Used by permission.
720. From *Book of Common Worship* by Bishop Wilbur P. Thirkield and Dr. Oliver Huckle. Copyright, 1932, by E. P. Dutton & Co., Inc. Renewal, © 1960 by Gilbert H. Thirkield. Reprinted by permission of the publishers.
723. By Committee on Worship Aids for *The Mennonite Hymnal*, 1967.
725. Patterned after the baptismal vows made at an Anabaptist congregation in Strasbourg in 1557.
726-733. By John H. Mosemann, 1967.
734, 735, 737, 739, 742, 744, 749-752. From *Contemporary Prayers for Public Worship* ed. by Caryl Micklem. Copyright 1967 by Wm. B. Eerdmans Publishing Co. Used by permission.
736. By Charles F. Whiston from *A Prayer Companion.*
738. From *Prayers for Christian Service* by Carl A. Glover. Copyright © 1959 by Abingdon Press. Used by permission.
740. From the book *Devotional Services* by Rev. John Hunter, DD. Reprinted by permission of the publishers, E. P. Dutton & Co., Inc.
741. From St. Francis of Assisi.
743. From *A Book of Pastoral Prayers* by Ernest Fremont Tittle. Copyright 1951 by Pierce and Smith (Abingdon Press). Used by permission.
745. From the *Book of Common Worship*, Eden Publishing House. Used by permission.
746. From *A Manual of Eastern Orthodox Prayers.* Published by the S.P.C.K. for the Fellowship of St. Alban and St. Regius. Used by permission.
747. From *The Orthodox Liturgy*, Published by the S.P.C.K. for the Fellowship of St. Alban and St. Regius. Used by permission.
748. From Old Catholic Liturgy.

Index of Authors, Translators, and Sources

Adams, Sarah (1805-1848), 289
Addison, Joseph (1672-1719), 56, 74
Ainger, Arthur Campbell (1841-1919), 605
Albert, Heinrich (1604-1651), 60
Alexander, Cecil Frances (1818-1895), 229, 465, 466, 473
Alexander, James Waddell (1804-1859), 159
Alford, Henry (1810-1871), 250, 519
Allen, James (1734-1804), 101
Ambrose of Milan (340-397), 44, 45
Anderson, Boris (c. 1961), 55
Anderson, Clare (c. 1961), 55
Andres, Joanna Sudermann (b. 1903), 329
Anonymous, 4, 53, 296, 474, 625, 629, 635
  American, 163, 164, 293
  English, 137
  French, 127
  German, 131, 417, 612
  Greek, 196, 489
  Hebrew, 11
  Irish, 300
  Latin, 1, 111, 132, 181, 183, 211, 288, 373, 374, 604, 622, 632, 640, 641, 642, 644
  Taiwanese, 55
Aquinas, Thomas (1227-1274), 404
Augsburger, David (b. 1938), 344
Ausbund, 40, 344, 384

Babcock, Maltbie D. (1858-1901), 49
Bacon, Leonard (1802-1881), 199
Bahnmaier, Jonathan Friedrich (1774-1841), 224
Baker, Henry Williams (1821-1877), 65, 92, 221, 454, 518, 596
Baker, Theodore (1851-1934), 131
Barbauld, Anna L. (1743-1825), 524, 525
Barber, Mary Ann Serrett (1801-1864), 276
Baring-Gould, Sabine (1834-1924), 490, 591
Bartholomew, William (1793-1867), 643
Barton, Bernard (1784-1849), 223, 282
Bathurst, William Hiley (1796-1877), 259
Baxter, Richard (1615-1691), 371, 397
Bayly, Albert Frederick (b. 1901), 462, 469
Bede, The Venerable (d. 735), 190
Benson, Louis F. (1855-1930), 44, 45
Berg, Caroline V. Sandell (1832-1903), 335
Bergen, Esther (c. 1959), 89
Bernard of Clairvaux ? (1091-1153), 98, 108
Bernard of Cluny (c. 1140), 416
Bevan, Emma F. (1827-1909), 550
Bianco da Siena (d. 1434), 210
Bickersteth, Edward Henry (1825-1906), 42, 271
Blackie, John Stuart (1809-1895), 30
Blacklock, Thomas (1721-1791), 53

Blatchford, Ambrose Nichols (1842-1924), 464
Bliss, Philip Paul (1838-1876), 537, 554, 561
Bliss, P. P., *Gospel Songs* (1874), 243
Boberg, Carl (1859-1940), 535
Bode, John Ernest (1816-1874), 343
Bonar, Horatius (1808-1889), 64, 231, 232, 248, 287, 341, 405, 431, 588
Book of Hours (1514), 645
Borthwick, Jane Laurie (1813-1897), 73, 319
Bowie, Walter Russell (b. 1882), 247, 450
Bowring, John (1792-1872), 71, 169
Bridges, Matthew (1800-1894), 188, 191, 399
Bridges, Robert (1844-1930), 158, 211, 291, 487, 489, 604
Briggs, George Wallace (1875-1959), 198, 367, 403, 476
Bromehead, Joseph (1747-1826), 370
Brooke, Stopford Augustus (1832-1916), 62
Brooks, Phillips (1835-1893), 133
Browne, Simon (c. 1680-1732), 215
Brownlie, John (1857-1925), 196
Brückner, Herman (1866-1942), 106, 318
Buckoll, Henry James (1803-1871), 477
Bundry, Edmond (1854-1932), 180
Bunyan, John, *Who Would True Valor See* (1628-1688), 323
Burleigh, William Henry (1812-1871), 317
Byrne, Mary Elizabeth (1880-1931), 300
Byrom, John (1691 or 1692-1763), 123

Campbell, Jane Montgomery (1817-1878), 521
Campbell, John (1845-1914), 257
Canitz, Frederick R. L. von (1654-1699), 477
Cantionale sacrum, Gotha (1651), 91
Carlyle, Thomas (1795-1881), 597
Caswall, Edward (1814-1878), 107, 108, 595
Cennick, John (1718-1755), 192, 639
Chandler, John (1806-1876), 288, 374
Chao, Tzu-ch'en (b. 1888), 209, 339, 498
Chatfield, Allen W. (1808-1896), 246
Chesterton, Gilbert Keith (1874-1936), 457
Chisholm, Thomas O. (1866-1960), 534
Chorley, Henry Fothergill (1808-1872), 86
Church and Sunday School Hymnal, Supplement (1911), 383
Clark, Alden H. (1878-1960), 362
Clark, Emily V. (1892), 298
Clark, W. H. (c. 1888), 32
Claudius, Matthias (1740-1815), 521
Clausnitzer, Tobias (1619-1684), 391
Clayton, William (1814-1879), 312
Clemens, Christian G. (1743-1815), 24
Clement of Alexandria (d. c. 220), 413
Clephane, Elizabeth C. (1830-1869), 171, 552

INDEX OF AUTHORS, TRANSLATORS, AND SOURCES

Clock, Leenaerdt (c. 1590), 384
Coffman, Samuel Frederick (1872-1954), 410
Collection of Hymns . . . of the United Brethren (1832), 320
Conder, Eustace R. (1830-1892), 146
Conder, Josiah (1789-1855), 204, 349, 401
Copenhaver, Laura Scherer (1868-1940), 420
Cory, Julia Bulkey Cady (b. 1882), 12
Cotterill, Thomas (1779-1823), 254
Cotton, George Edward Lynch (1813-1866), 526
Cousin, Annie Ross (1824-1906), 292
Cowper, William (1731-1800), 80, 253, 305, 381
Cox, Frances Elizabeth (1812-1897), 21, 59, 77
Coxe, Arthur Cleveland (1818-1896), 103, 378
Cramer, Johann A. (1723-1788), 26
Crasselius, Bartholomäus (1667-1724), 8
Croly, George (1780-1860), 217
Crosby, Fanny (1820-1915), 96, 530, 532, 533, 536, 544, 546, 548, 560, 569, 573, 581
Crossman, Samuel (c. 1624-1684), 172
Crull, August (1845-1923), 308
Curtis, Christine Turner (b. c. 1891), 284
Cushing, William Orcutt (1823-1902), 575
Czamanske, William M. (b. 1873), 417

Davison, Fannie Estelle (1851-1887), 280
Dearmer, Percy (1867-1936), 224, 323, 480
Decius, Nicolaus (d. 1541), 38, 173
Dexter, Henry Martyn (1821-1890), 413
Dix, William Chatterton (1837-1898), 129, 142, 226
Doane, George Washington (1799-1859), 149
Dobell, John, *Collection* (1806), 497
Doddridge, Philip (1702-1751), 83, 112, 332, 398, 508, 623
Doving, Carl (1867-1937), 615
Downton, Henry (1818-1885), 509
Draper, William Henry (1855-1933), 51, 52
Duffield, George, Jr. (1818-1888), 592
Dunkerly, Roderic (dates unknown) 453
Dunkerly, William Arthur (*see* John Oxenham)
Dwight, Timothy (1752-1817), 380

E. A. C. C. Hymnal (1964), 55
East, James Thomas (1860-1937), 468
Eber, Paul (1511-1569), 264
Edwards, Robert Lansing (c. 1961), 363
Ellerton, John (1826-1893), 86, 162, 412, 488, 500, 505
Elliott, Charlotte (1789-1871), 235, 263
Elliott, Emily E. S. (1836-1897), 563
Elliott, Norman (b. 1893), 200
Everest, Charles William (1814-1877), 357

Faber, Frederick William (1814-1863), 78, 262
Fallersleben, Heinrich August Hoffmann von (1798-1874), 97
Farrington, Harry Webb (1879-1930), 309
Fawcett, John (1739 or 1740-1817), 385, 502
Featherston, William Ralph (1846-1873), 265
Findlater, Sarah Borthwick (1823-1907), 194, 463
Fischer, William G. (1835-1912), 593
Fosdick, Harry Emerson (b. 1878), 434
Foster, Frederick William (1760-1835), 24
Foundling Hospital Collection (c. 1796), 27
Francis of Assisi (1182-1226), 51, 52
Franck, Johann (1618-1677), 406, 600

Gabriel, Charles H. (1856-1932), 540, 547
Ganse, Hervey Doddridge (1822-1891), 37
Garve, Carl Bernhard (1763-1841), 218
Gelineau Psalms (1953), 617, 618
Gerhardt, Paul (1607-1676), 17, 119, 124, 159, 266, 338, 340, 487
Gesangbuch, Münster (1677), 307
Gill, Thomas Hornblower (1819-1906), 396, 513
Gilmore, Joseph H. (1834-1918), 543
Gladden, Washington (1836-1918), 440
Gordon, Adoniram Judson (1836-1895), 580
Gospel Mazazine (1777), 206
Gotter, Ludwig Andreas (1661-1735), 33
Grant, Robert H. (1779-1838), 15
Green, Joseph F. (b. 1924), 312
Gregor, Christian (1723-1801), 24
Gregory, Philip E. (b. 1886), 414
Gregory the Great (c. 540-604), 480
Grieve, Nichol (1868-1954), 23, 82, 278
Groves, Alexander (1843-1909), 222
Grundtvig, Nicolai Frederik Severin (1783-1872), 615

Gurney, Dorothy F. Blomfield (1858-1932), 412
Gurney, John Hampden (1802-1862), 451

Hamilton, James (1819-1896), 511
Hankey, Catherine (1834-1911), 593
Harkness, Georgia (b. 1891), 295, 360
Harlow, S. Ralph (b. 1885), 459
Hart, Joseph (1712-1768), 214
Hartsough, Lewis (1828-1919), 549
Hastings, Thomas (1784-1872), 333, 423
Hatch, Edwin (1835-1889), 216
Hausmann, Julie Katharina (1825-1901), 318
Havergal, Frances Ridley (1836-1879), 347, 358, 389, 510, 557
Hawks, Annie S. (1835-1918), 578
"Hayward" in John Dobell's *Collection* (1806), 497
Hearn, Marianne (1834-1909), 354
Heath, George (1750-1822), 321
Heber, Reginald (1783-1826), 5, 143, 407, 607
Hedge, Frederick Henry (1805-1890), 325
Heermann, Johann (1585-1647), 158, 352
Held, Heinrich (d. 1659), 212
Hengstenberg, Ernst William (1802-1869), 85
Hengstenberg, Johann Heinrich Karl (1770-1834), 85
Herbert, George (1593-1632), 22, 301, 445
Herbert, Petrus (d. 1571), 249
Herman, Nicolaus (c. 1485-1561), 136
Herr, Amos (1816-1897), 419
Herrnschmidt, Johann Daniel (1675-1723), 20
Hiller, Philipp Friedrich (1699-1769), 68
Hine, Stuart K. (b. 1889), 535
Hoffman, Elisha Albright (1839-1929), 562, 585, 590
Holland, Henry Scott (1847-1918), 446
Holmes, Oliver Wendell (1809-1894), 57, 306
Homburg, Ernst Christoph (1605-1681), 168
Horn, Edward Traill III (b. 1909), 212, 234
Horstmann, Julius Henry (b. 1908), 426
Hosmer, Frederick Lucian (1840-1929), 153, 418
Hostetler, Lester (b. 1892), 20
Housman, Laurence (1865-1959), 447
How, William Walsham (1823-1897), 219, 227, 364, 395, 516, 517
Hoyle, Richard Birch (1875-1939), 180
Huffman, Nelson T. (b. 1901), 630
Hull, Eleanor Henrietta (1860-1935), 300
Hymnal, 1940, 7
Hymnary, 1872, 181
Hymnbook, 1955, 238
Hymns Ancient and Modern, 1861, 111, 373, 416, 519, 610

Jacobi, Johann Christian (1670-1750), 17
Jacobs, Wellington K. (b. 1876), 559
Janus, Martin (c. 1620-c. 1682), 599
John of Damascus (c. 750), 174, 178
John, Rudolph A. (1859-1938), 33
Johnson, Julia H. (1849-1919), 541
Jones, Lewis E. (1865-1936), 555

"K" in J. Rippon's *Selection of Hymns* (1787), 260, 261
Katholisches Gesangbuch, Würzburg (1828), 107, 595
Kaufman, Frieda (1883-1944), 68
Keble, John (1792-1866), 279, 483, 491, 602
Kelly, Thomas (1769-1855), 176, 186, 189, 201
Ken, Thomas (1637-1710), 485, 496, 606, 638
Kerr, Hugh Thomson (1872-1950), 603
Kethe, William (d. 1594), 2, 3
Kingsbury, Howard (dates unknown), 528
Klaassen, Walter (b. 1926), 386
Kolb, Abram Bowman (1862-1925), 566

Larcom, Lucy (1826-1893), 307
Lathbury, Mary Artemia (1841-1913), 222, 493
Laufenburg, Heinrich von (c. 1385-1460), 415
Laufer, Calvin W. (1874-1938), 145
Laurenti, Laurentius (1660-1722), 194
Lehman, F. M. (c. 1917), 538
Lewis, Howell Elvet (1860-1953), 436
Lindemann, Johann (c. 1550-c. 1634), 90
Little Children's Book (1885), 472
Littledale, Richard Frederick (1833-1890), 210
Liturgy of St. James, 117
Logan, John (1748-1788), 83
Longfellow, Samuel (1819-1892), 54, 207, 313, 334, 437, 492, 512, 634
Löwenstern, Matthäus Apelles von (1594-1648), 456

INDEX OF AUTHORS, TRANSLATORS, AND SOURCES

Lowry, Robert (1826-1899), 529, 567
Lowry, Somerset Corry (1855-1932), 359
Loy, Matthias (1828-1915), 195
Luther, Martin (1483-1546), 134, 234, 325, 597, 598, 611
Lyte, Henry Francis (1793-1847), 16, 61, 495

MacDuff, John Ross (1818-1895), 193
Mackay, William Paton (1839-1885), 527
Madan, Martin (1726-1790), 192
Manz, Felix (c. 1498-1527), 40
Marlatt, Earl (b. 1892), 127
Marriott, John (1780-1825), 429
Martin, Civilla D. (1866-1948), 574
Massie, Richard (1800-1887), 60, 598, 611
Matheson, George (1842-1906), 269
Mattes, John Caspar (1876-1948), 205, 406
McGranahan, James (1840-1907), 550
McKinney, Benjamin Baylus (1886-1952), 545
McManus, S. B. (c. 1902), 411
Medley, Samuel (1738-1799), 99, 110
Mentzer, Johann (1658-1734), 10
Mercer, J., *Cluster of Spiritual Songs* (1836), 163
Mercer, William (1811-1873), 132, 141
Merrill, William Pierson (1867-1954), 299, 441
Milman, Henry Hart (1791-1868), 156
Milton, John (1608-1674), 70, 393
Mohr, Joseph (1792-1848), 130
Monsell, John Samuel Bewley (1811-1875), 139, 520
Montgomery, James (1771-1854), 29, 113, 128, 160, 297, 324, 342, 368, 388, 390, 400, 402, 421, 522
Moore, Thomas (1779-1852), 333
Morison, John (1749-1798), 125
Morris, Leila Naylor (Mrs. Charles H.) (1862-1929), 579
Mote, Edward (1797-1874), 558
Moultrie, Gerard (1829-1885), 117
Murray, Robert (1832-1910), 361

Neale, John Mason (1818-1866), 92, 111, 154, 157, 174, 178, 230, 373, 416, 610
Neander, Joachim (1650-1680), 9, 59, 291
Neumark, Georg (1621-1681), 314
Neumeister, Erdmann (1671-1756), 550
New Congregational Hymn Book (1859), 404
Newman, John Henry (1801-1890), 316
Newton, John (1725-1807), 102, 239, 242, 376, 506, 514, 647
Nicholson, James L. (1828-1876), 583
Nicolai, Philipp (1556-1608), 118, 141
Niedling, Johann (1602-1668), 205
Noel, Caroline Maria (1817-1877), 94
North, Frank Mason (1850-1935), 439

Oakeley, Frederick (1802-1880), 132
Oatman, Johnson, Jr. (1856-1922), 582
Olearius, Johann (1635-1711), 121
Olivers, Thomas (1725-1799), 11
Olson, Ernst William (1870-1958), 335
Osler, Edward (1798-1863), 27
Owens, Priscilla J. (1829-1907), 594
Oxenham, John (Pseud. for W. A. Dunkerly) (1852-1951), 387, 449

Palgrave, Francis Turner (1824-1897), 481
Palmer, Ray (1808-1887), 98, 251
Payne, Ernest A. (b. 1902), 384
Pennefather, William (1816-1873), 624
Pensum sacrum, Altenberg (1648), 91
Perronet, Edward (1726-1792), 95, 601
Phelps, Sylvanus D. (1816-1895), 355
Pierpoint, Folliott Sanford (1835-1917), 58
Pilgrim Hymnal, The (1904), 228
Plumptre, Adelaide M. (c. 1908), 281
Plumptre, Edward Hayes (1821-1891), 152, 277
Polack, William Gustave (b. 1890), 612
Pollock, Thomas Benson (1836-1896), 379
Pott, Francis (1832-1909), 144, 183
Pounds, Jessie Brown (1861-1921), 565, 584
Preiswerk, Samuel (1799-1871), 426
Prentiss, Elizabeth Payson (1818-1878), 539
Price, Anna L. (c. 1837-1924), 209
Price, Frank W. (b. 1895), 209, 339, 498
Procter, Adelaide Anne (1825-1864), 267
Prudentius, Aurelius Clemens (348-413), 92
Psalter (1912), 47, 202, 238, 356, 571
Psalter Hymnal (1927), 619

Pusey, Philip (1799-1855), 456

Rankin, Jeremiah Eames (1828-1904), 503, 504
Rawnsley, Hardwick Drummond (1851-1920), 422
Rawson, George (1807-1889), 409
Rees, Bryn A. (b. 1911), 255
Rights, Douglas LeTell (b. 1891), 114
Rinckart, Martin (1586-1649), 31
Rippon, John (1751-1836), 95, 601
Rippon, J., *Selection of Hymns* (1787), 260, 261
Rische, August (d. 1906), 471
Rist, Johann (1607-1667), 609
Roberts, Daniel Crane (1841-1907), 448
Robinson, Robert (1735-1790), 310
Romanis, William (1824-1899), 452
Rosenroth, Christian Knorr von (1636-1689), 484
Rowley, Francis H. (1854-1952), 551
Runge, C., *Praxis pietatis melica* (1653), 182
Russell, Arthur Tozer (1806-1874), 119, 136, 173, 338, 609

Sammis, John H. (1846-1919), 577
Sangle, Krishnarao Rathnaji (1834-1908), 362
Sangster, Margaret (1838-1912), 427
Sankey, Ira David (1840-1908), 551, 588
Schalling, Martin (1532-1608), 608
Scheffler, Johann (1624-1677), 329
Schirmer, Michael (1606-1673), 208
Schlegel, Catharina Amalia Dorothea von (b. 1697), 73
Schmid, Christian von (dates unknown), 470
Schmolck, Benjamin (1672-1737), 6, 77, 486
Schubring, Julius (b. 1806), 643
Schütz, Johann Jacob (1640-1690), 21
Scott, Robert B. Y. (b. 1899), 88
Scott, Walter (1771-1832), 87
Scottish Paraphrases (1781), 81, 83, 125, 268, 408
Scottish Psalter (1650), 2, 3, 67, 82, 241, 258, 302, 482
Scriven, Joseph Medlicott (1819-1886), 337
Sears, Edmund Hamilton (1810-1876), 126
Sedulius, Coelius (c. 450), 598
Seltz, Martin L. (c. 1965), 116
Shepherd, Thomas (1665-1739), 345
Shirreff, Emily L. (dates unknown), 460
Shurtleff, Ernest Warburton (1862-1917), 443
Sidebotham, Mary Ann (1833-1913), 240
Simpson, William John Sparrow (1859-1952), 166
Skemp, Ada (1857-1927), 467
Skinner, James (1818-1881), 637
Small, James G. (1817-1888), 542
Smith, Samuel Francis (1808-1895), 213, 346
Smith, Walter Chalmers (1824-1908), 43
Smyttan, George Hunt (1822-1870), 144
Songs of Praise (1925), 304
Spaeth, Harriett R. (1845-1925), 26, 131
Spafford, Horatio G. (1828-1888), 576
Spitta, Carl Johann Philipp (1801-1859), 463
Steele, Anne (1717-1778), 69, 275, 336, 369
Stegmann, Josua (1588-1632), 308
Stennett, Samuel (1727-1795), 187, 294
Sterling, J. L. (c. 1886), 587
"Stocker, J." in *Gospel Magazine* (1777), 206
Stocking, Jay T. (1870-1936), 458
Stockton, John Hart (1813-1877), 553
Stone, Samuel John (1839-1900), 375
Stowe, Everett M. (1958), 377
Stowell, Hugh (1799-1865), 331
Swain, Joseph (1762-1796), 273
Swertner, John (1746-1813), 24
Synesius of Cyrene (c. 410), 246

"T. S. N." in *Songs of Praise* (1925), 304
Tappan, William Bingham (1794-1849), 161
Tate, Nahum (1652-1715), 138
Tate and Brady, *New Version of the Psalms* (1696), 14
(1696 and 1698), 41, 285
Supplement (1700), 28
Tennyson, Alfred (1809-1892), 442
Tersteegen, Gerhard (1697-1769), 7, 106
Theodulph of Orleans (c. 820), 154
Thomas of Celano (13th century), 87
Thomson, Mary Ann (1834-1923), 428
Threlfall, Jeannette (1821-1880), 155
Thring, Godfrey (1823-1903), 140, 148, 151, 197, 366
Thrupp, Dorothy, *Hymns for the Young* (1836), 572
Tisserand, Jean (15th century), 610
Toplady, Augustus Montague (1740-1778), 254

614 INDEX OF AUTHORS, TRANSLATORS, AND SOURCES

Torry, R., Jr. (c. 1862), 556
Trench, Richard Chenevix (1807-1886), 299
Tullar, Grant Colfax (1869-1950), 564
Turner, H. L. (c. 1878), 570
Tuttiett, Lawrence (1825-1897), 444
Twells, Henry (1823-1900), 494

United Presbyterian Book of Psalms (1871), 531

Van Dyke, Henry (1852-1933), 13, 433
Vories, William Merrill (b. 1880), 455

Wagner, Jörg (d. 1527), 344
Walther, Johann (1496-1570), 195
Walworth, Clarence Augustus (1820-1900), 1
Wardlaw, Ralph (1779-1853), 286
Ware, Henry (1794-1843), 175, 461
Waring, Anna Laetita (1823-1910), 252
Warner, Anna Bartlett (1820-1915), 303
Watt, Lauchlan MacLean (1867-1957), 353
Watts, Isaac (1674-1748), 18, 19, 25, 34, 35, 36, 39, 46, 48, 50, 63, 66, 72, 79, 81, 84, 105, 109, 122, 147, 165, 167, 170, 203, 220, 245, 315, 326, 327, 348, 382, 392, 499, 507, 515, 529, 623
Webb, Benjamin (1820-1885), 190
Webster, Bradford Gray (1954), 616
Weisse, Michael (c. 1480-1534), 177, 417
Weissel, Georg (1590-1635), 120
Wenger, Marion M. (b. 1932), 40
Wesley, Charles (1707-1788), 75, 76, 100, 104, 115, 135, 179, 184, 185, 192, 233, 236, 237, 244, 256, 272, 283, 322, 330, 350, 351, 372, 383, 394, 430, 432, 478, 501
Wesley, John (1703-1791), 48, 266, 340
West, Robert Athow (1809-1865), 93
Weston, Rebecca J. (dates unknown), 475
Whittier, John Greenleaf (1807-1892), 150, 274, 365, 435
Whittle, Daniel Webster (1840-1901), 568, 586
Wigner, John M. (1844-1911), 225
Williams, Peter (1723-1796), 311
Williams, William (1717-1791), 311
Willis, R. S., *Church Chorals* (1850), 97
Winckler, Johann Joseph (1670-1722), 328
Winkworth, Catherine (1827-1878), 6, 8, 9, 10, 31, 38, 59, 60, 90, 91, 118, 120, 121, 124, 134, 168, 177, 182, 208, 218, 264, 314, 328, 352, 391, 415, 484, 486, 600, 608
Witmer, Edith (b. 1902), 438
Wolcott, Samuel (1813-1886), 424, 425
Woodward, George Ratcliffe (1848-1934), 614
"Words from Scripture and Dr. Young," 613
Wordsworth, Christopher (1807-1885), 270, 523

Yamaguchi, Tokuo (c. 1958), 377
Yates, John Henry (1840-1908), 589
Young, John Freeman (1820-1885), 130

Zaremba, Felician von (1794-1874), 426
Zinzendorf, Nikolaus Ludwig von (1700-1760), 89, 319, 386

Index of Composers, Arrangers, and Sources

A und Ω Glaub-und Liebesübung, Bremen (1680), 7
Abbot, Asahel (c. 1852), 524
Ahle, Johann Rudolph (1625-1673), 85, 391, 484
Albert, Heinrich (1604-1651), 60
Allen, Chester G. (1838-1878), 530
Allen, George Nelson (1812-1877), 345
Alte Catholische Geistliche Kirkengeseng, Köln (1599), 131
Anonymous, 452, 464
  American (Folk Hymn), 63, 110, 112, 147, 163, 242, 243, 256, 260, 272, 273, 294, 304, 310, 312, 322, 357, 370, 419, 450, 608
  American (Negro), 164, 293
  Bohemian, 445
  Chinese, 209, 339, 498
  Danish, 218, 465
  Dutch, 12, 359
  English, 71, 129, 137, 190, 200, 457, 527
  Finnish, 252
  French, 117, 127, 514, 525
  German, 487, 517, 520, 612
  Hebrew, 11
  Indian, 362
  Irish, 300
  Japanese, 377
  Plainsong, 45, 92, 111, 211, 404
  Scottish, 632
  Swedish, 335, 535
  Thüringer, 471
  Welsh, 43, 299, 459, 474
Anton, Christoph (c. 1610-1658), 168
Arne, Thomas Augustine (1710-1778), 348, 499
Atkinson, Frederick Cook (1841-1897), 217

Bach, Johann Sebastian (1685-1750), 136, 159, 198, 352, 453, 487, 599, 600, 609, 611
Baker, Henry (1835-1910), 306, 437
Baker, Henry Williams (1821-1877), 230
"Baptiste, from" (c. 1920), 584
Barnby, Joseph (1838-1896), 54, 98, 107, 317, 354, 381, 412, 490
Barrow, Robert G. (b. 1911), 653
Barthelemon, Francois Hippolyte (1741-1808), 485
Barton, W., *Psalms* (1706), 371
Batchellor, Daniel (c. 1885), 475
Baumbach, Adolph (1830-1880), 633
Beastall, William (fl. 1820), 64
Beethoven, Ludwig van (1770-1827), 13

"Bentzenauer Ton," Nurnberg (1540), 40
Berggreen, Anton Peter (1801-1880), 347
Bilhorn, Peter P. (1865-1936), 551
Billings, William (1746-1800), 613
Bliss, Philip Paul (1838-1876), 537, 557, 561, 576
Bliss and Sankey's *Gospel Hymns and Sacred Songs* (1875), 527
Bohemian Brethren's *Kirchengesang . . . ,* Berlin (1566), 21, 247
Bonner's *Vollkommenes . . . Choral-Buch* (1715), 151
Bortniansky, Dimitri S. (1751-1825), 106
Bowen, C. T. (b. 1833), 390
Boyd, H., *Psalm and Hymn Tunes* (1793), 69, 203, 372
Boyd, William (c. 1847-1928), 281
Bradbury, William Batchelder (1816-1868), 161, 215, 235, 276, 296, 536, 543, 558, 572
Braun, Johann G. (c. 1675), 413
Broadwood, Lucy (c. 1893), 231, 513
Brunk, John David (1872-1926), 35, 48, 232
Burt, Bates Gilbert (1878-1948), 297

Caldbeck, George Thomas (1852-1918), 271
Cantica Spiritualia (1847), 309
Cantionale Germanicum, Gochsheim (1628), 91
Carr, Benjamin (1769-1831), 162
Cent cinquante pseaumes, Les, Geneva (1562), 70
Choralbuch der Mennoniten Gemeinden Russlands, Halbstadt (1914), 89
Chorale Book for England (1863), 608
"Christopher" in W. Hauser's *Hesperian Harp* (1848), 163
Chute, Marion Jean (b. 1901), 362
Clark, Jeremiah (1659-1707), 81, 189
Cole, John (1774-1855), 74
Collection of Hymns and Sacred Poems, A, Dublin (1749), 41
Conkey, Ithamar (1815-1867), 169
Converse, Charles Crozat (1832-1918), 337
Croft, William (1678-1727), 84, 100, 152, 378
Crotch, William (1775-1846), 301, 507
Crüger, Johann (1598-1662), 31, 113, 153, 158, 223, 406, 600
Cunningham, Francis, *Selection of Psalm Tunes* (1834), 403

Damon, W., *Booke of Musicke* (1591), 46, 320
Damon, W., *Psalms* (1579), 246, 255

INDEX OF COMPOSERS, ARRANGERS, AND SOURCES

Darwall, John (1731-1789), 374, 392
David's Psalmen, Amsterdam (1685), 614
Davies, H. Walford (1869-1941), 467, 645
Davisson, A., *Kentucky Harmony* (1816), 419, 619
Decius, Nicolaus (d. 1541), 38, 173
Doane, William Howard (1832-1915), 96, 532, 533, 539, 560, 581
Dougall, Neil (1776-1862), 283
Douglas, Winfred (1867-1944), 92, 323
Drese, Adam (1620-1701), 319
Dubois, Theodore (1837-1924), 644
Dyer, Samuel, *Selection of Sacred Music* (1825), 298, 388
Dykes, John Bacchus (1823-1876), 5, 65, 108, 148, 461

E. A. C. C. *Hymnal* (1964), 55, 209
Easy Music for Church Choirs (1853), 430
Easy Tunes for Catholic Schools (1852), 146, 266
Ebeling, Johann Georg (1637-1676), 114, 124
Edson, Lewis (1748-1820), 244
Ellor, James (1819-1899), 601
Elvey, George Job (1816-1893), 191, 449, 519
Emerson, Luther Orlando (1820-1915), 249
Enchiridion, Erfurt (1524), 598
English Psalter (1562), 315, 400
Est, Thomas, *Whole Booke of Psalmes* (1592), 241, 268, 393
Evans, David (1874-1948), 252
Ewing, Alexander (1830-1895), 416
Excell, Edwin Othello (1851-1921), 621

Fallersleben, H. A. Hoffman von, *Schlesische Volkslieder* (1842), 97
Filitz, Friedrich (1804-1876), 270, 624
Fillmore, James Henry (1849-1936), 280, 565
Fink, Gottfried Wilhelm (1783-1846), 458
Finlay, Kenneth George (b. 1882), 468, 469
Fischer, William Gustavus (1835-1912), 583, 593
Flemming, Friedrich F. (1778-1813), 263
Forme des prieres, La, Strasbourg (1545), 264, 407, 488, 609
Freylinghausen, J. A., *Neues Geistreiches Gesangbuch*, Halle (1704), 8, 24, 59, 120, 224
Fritsch, A., *Himmels-Lust...*, Jena (1679), 198, 352
Funk, Joseph, *Genuine Church Music (Harmonia Sacra)*, 63, 74, 242, 260, 272, 322, 357, 419

Gabriel, Charles Hutchison (1856-1932), 540, 547, 582
Gardiner, William, *Sacred Melodies* (1815), 15, 19, 349, 439
Gastoldi, Giovanni Giacomo (c. 1556-1622), 90
Gastorius, Severus (1649-1708), 77
Gauntlett, Henry John (1805-1876), 466, 509, 635
Gauntlett and Waite's *Hallelujah* (1849), 424
Gawler, W., *Hymns and Psalms* (1785-1788), 196
Geistliche Kirchengesang, Cologne (1623), 205
Geistreiches Gesangbuch, Darmstadt (1698), 446
Gelineau, Joseph (20th century), 617, 618
"German Air" in Samuel Dyer's *Selection of Sacred Music* (1825), 298, 388
Gesangbuch, Augsburg (1666), 116
Gesangbuch, Hirschberg (1741), 334
Gesangbuch, Lüneburg (1686), 486
Gesangbuch, Nürnberg (1676), 144, 365
Gesangbuch, Stralsund (1665), 9
Gesangbuch..., Württemberg (1784), 50, 155, 410
Gesangbuch mit Noten, Berne, Indiana (1890), 517
Giardini, Felice de (1716-1796), 4, 101, 360
Gibbons, Orlando (1583-1625), 286, 397, 432, 526, 604
Gläser, Carl Gotthelf (1784-1829), 104
Gordon, Adoniram Judson (1836-1895), 265
Goss, John (1800-1880), 16, 184, 197
Goudimel, Claude (1505-1572), 3, 23, 70, 121, 284, 295, 407, 488, 489, 607
Gould, John Edgar (1822-1875), 79, 175
Gounod, Charles F. (1818-1893), 478, 631
Gower, John Henry (1855-1922), 473
Greatorex, Henry W., *Collection* (1851), 640
Grenoble Antiphoner (1753), 36
Gruber, Franz (1787-1863), 130

"Handel, from," 122
Handel, George Frideric (1685-1759), 138, 180, 332
Harding, James Procktor (1850-1911), 143
Harmonia Sacra (see Funk, Joseph, *Genuine Church Music*)
Harrison, Ralph (1748-1810), 34, 326, 348, 499

Hartsough, Lewis (1828-1919), 549
Harwood, Basil (1859-1949), 22
Hassler, Hans Leo (1564-1612), 159
Hastings, Thomas (1784-1872), 187, 239, 254, 331, 637
Hatton, John (d. 1793), 69, 203, 372
Hauser, W., *Hesperian Harp* (1848), 163
Havergal, William Henry (1793-1870), 156, 259, 275, 279, 313, 500
Haweis, Thomas (1733-1820), 32, 149, 501
"Haydn" in Lowell Mason's *Boston Handel and Haydn Society Collection* (1822), 14
Haydn, Franz Joseph (1732-1809), 56, 176, 204, 376, 477
Haydn, Johann Michael (1737-1806), 42, 83, 194, 338, 426
Hayne, Leighton George (1836-1883), 206, 233
Hemy, Henri Frederick (1818-1888), 262
Herman, Nicolaus (c. 1485-1561), 136, 250, 453
Herr, Amos (1816-1897), 479
Hervey, Frederick Alfred John (1846-1910), 379
Hodges, Edward (1796-1867), 13
Hoffman, Elisha A. (1839-1929), 562, 590
Holbrook, Joseph Perry (1822-1888), 356
Holden, Oliver (1765-1844), 95
Hopkins, Edward John (1818-1901), 505
Hopkirk, James (b. 1908), 88
Horn, Johann (c. 1490-1547), 178
Howard, Samuel (1710-1782), 340
Huffman, Nelson T. (b. 1901), 630
Hughes, John (1873-1932), 311, 434
Hull, Asa (c. 1862), 556
Hundert... geistliche Arien, Dresden (1694), 177
Husband, Edward (1843-1908), 227, 248
Hymn Tunes of the United Brethren (1824), 29, 518
Hymnal, The (1933), 73
Hymnal, The (1940), 379
Hymnal Noted, The, Part II (1854), 111
Hymnau a Thonau (1865), 459
Hymnbook, The (1955), 94
Hymns and Songs of Praise (1874), 184
Hymns of Universal Praise (1936), 498

Ingalls, Jeremiah, *Christian Harmony* (1805), 147, 322
Ireland, John (1879-1962), 172
Irvine, Jessie Seymour (1836-1887), 67

Jackson, Robert (1842-1914), 216
Jacobs, Wellington K. (b. 1876), 559
James, J., *Original Sacred Harp* (1911), 370
Jenner, Henry Lascelles (1820-1898), 341
Jones, Joseph David (1827-1870), 61
Jones, Lewis E. (1865-1936), 555
Jones, William (1726-1800), 288
Jude, William Herbert (1851-1922), 229

Katholisches Gesangbuch, Vienna (1776), 1, 491
Kingsley, George (1811-1884), 105, 305, 351
Kirchenampt, Strassburg (1525), 234
Kirchengesangbuch, Köln (1623), 51, 52
Kirkpatrick, William James (1838-1921), 546, 594
Klug, J., *Geistliche Lieder* (1535), 384, 396, 511
Knapp, Mrs. Joseph Fairfield (1839-1908), 544
Knapp, William (1698-1768), 37, 508
Knecht, Justin Heinrich (1752-1817), 26, 33, 227, 248
Kocher, Conrad (1786-1872), 58, 142
Koizumi, Isao (c. 1958), 377
Kolb, Abram Bowman (1862-1925), 411, 566
König, Johann Balthasar (1691-1758), 10
König, J. B., *Harmonischer Liederschatz* (1738), 279, 500
"Kyrie," Mainz (1821), 93

Lahee, Henry (1826-1912), 368
Lane, Spencer (1843-1903), 324
Langran, James (1835-1909), 405
Leavitt, Joshua, *Christian Lyre* (1831), 110, 273, 304, 361
Lee, Vernon (1892-1959), 367
Lehman, F. M. (c. 1917), 538
Leoni, Meyer (c. 1770), 11
Lewis, F., *Beauties of Harmony* (c. 1828), 63
Lieder für Volksschulen mit Musik, Hanover (1800), 521
Lindeman, Ludvig M. (1812-1887), 616
Lloyd, William (1786-1852), 226
Lorenz, Edmund Simon (1854-after 1923), 528

616 INDEX OF COMPOSERS, ARRANGERS, AND SOURCES

Lowry, Robert (1826-1899), 355, 529, 567, 573, 578
Luther, Martin (1483-1546), 325, 597
Luther, Orlando Emerson (1820-1915), 249
Lvov, Alexis (1799-1870), 86
Lyra Davidica (1708), 179

Macey, J. D. (1860-1933), 427
Maker, Frederick Charles (1844-1927), 30, 171, 225, 267, 274, 409, 512
Malan, Henri Alexander César (1787-1864), 358
Mann, Arthur Henry (1850-1929), 343
Manuscript Choral Book, Herrnhaag (1735), 386, 401
Manuscript Chorale Book, Uttingen (1754), 139
Marsh, Simeon Butler (1798-1875), 236
Martin, Walter Stillman (1862-1935), 574
Mason, Lowell (1792-1872), 18, 25, 99, 104, 122, 125, 167, 188, 199, 201, 202, 213, 220, 251, 259, 289, 303, 321, 327, 336, 350, 358, 380, 382, 385, 398, 423, 431, 463, 497
Mason and Webb's *Cantica Laudis* (1850), 364
Mason, Lowell, *Boston Handel and Haydn Society* (1822), 14, 282, 383
Mason, Lowell, *Boston Handel and Haydn Society* (1830), 606
Mays, Claudia Lehman (dates unknown), 538
McGranahan, James (1840-1907), 550, 554, 568, 570, 586
McKinney, Benjamin Baylus (1886-1952), 545
Meineke, Christopher (1782-1850), 642
Mendelssohn, Felix (1809-1847), 135, 219, 629, 643
Meredith, I. H. (1872-1962), 564
Messiter, Arthur Henry (1834-1916), 277
Meyer, J. D., *Geistliche Seelenfreud* (1692), 523
Miller, Edward (1731-1807), 72, 165, 408, 442, 454
Moe, Daniel (b. 1926), 616
Monk, William Henry (1823-1889), 58, 113, 142, 183, 186, 221, 418, 495, 625
Monoetius, Bartholomeus (c. 1565), 344
Morris, Leila Naylor (Mrs. Charles H.) (1862-1929), 579
Moyer, J. Harold (b. 1927), 52, 63, 112, 147, 228, 272, 273, 294, 322, 344, 357, 370, 626
Mozart, Wolfgang Amadeus (1756-1791), 99
Murray, A. Gregory (20th century), 618
Murray, James R. (c. 1887), 472

Nägeli, Johann Georg (1773-1836), 213, 336, 385
Neander, Joachim (1650-1680), 6, 193, 291
Nederlandtsch Gedenekelanck (1626), 12
Neumark, Georg (1621-1681), 314
Neu-vermehrtes Gesangbuch, Meiningen (1693), 212, 219, 460
New-vermehrte Christliche Seelenharf, Ansbach (1664 or 1665), 20
Nicolai, Philipp (1556-1608), 118, 141, 208

Octante trois pseaumes..., Geneva (1554), 301
Oude en Nieuwe Hollantse Boerenlilies (c. 1710), 359
Owen, William (1813-1893), 602

Palestrina, Giovanni Pierluigi da (1525-1594), 183, 418, 625
Parish Choir, The (1850), 476, 506
Parish Choir, The (1851), 623
Paris Antiphoner (1681), 480
Paris Gradual (1689), 44
Parker, Alice (b. 1925), 163, 207, 614, 646
Parry, Charles Hubert Hastings (1848-1918), 435
Parry, John, *Peroriaeth Hyfryd* (**1837**), **253**
Parry, Joseph (1841-1903), 237
Peace, Albert Lister (1844-1912), **269, 451**
Perkins, Edward A. (19th century), **522**
Perkins, William Oscar (1831-1902), **571**
Piae Cantiones (1582), 181
Pilsbury, A., *United States Sacred Harmony* (1799), 357
Pitts, William (1829-1903), 140
Poitiers Antiphoner (1746), 456
Pollock, Charles Edward (c. 1902), 585
Praetorius, Michael (1560-1629), 131
Pritchard, Rowland Hugh (1811-1887), 115, 363, 433
Pseaumes..., Lyon (1547), 21, 247
Pseaumes octante trois . . ., Geneva (1551), 2, 3, 23, 121, 284, 295, 447, 489, 507, 595, 638, 639
Purday, Charles Henry (1799-1885), 257, 316

Ravenscroft, *Psalter* (1621), 596
Read, Daniel (1757-1836), 87
Rebelein, Widow of George, *Musicalisch Hand-buch* (1690), 156, 313
Redhead, Richard (1820-1901), 160, 238, 315, 514, 525
Redner, Lewis Henry (1830-1908), 133
Reinagle, Alexander Robert (1799-1877), 102, 387
Rhau, G., *Newe Deudsche Geistliche Gesenge* (1544), 417
Rimbault, Edward Francis (1816-1876), 292
Roberts, Robert Edwin (1878-1940), 462
"Robison" in J. Wyeth's *Repository of Sacred Music, Part Second* (1813), 112
Root, George Frederick (1820-1895), 620
Rowlands, William Penfro (1860-1937), 76
Runge, C., *Praxis pietatis melica* (1653), 182
Runyan, William Marion (1870-1957), 534

Sankey, Ira David (1840-1908), 552, 563, 569, 575, 587, 588, 589
Scheffler's *Heilige Seelenlust* (1657), 309, 494
Schein, Johann Hermann (1586-1630), 329, 481
Schicht, J. G., *Allgemeines Choral-Buch* (1819), 68
Schmid, B., *Orgeltabulatur-Buch* (1577), 608
Schneider, Friedrich (1786-1853), 497
Schop, Johann (c. 1590-1667), 599, 609
Schröter, Leonhart (1540-1602), 195
Schulz, Johann Abraham Peter (1747-1800), 470
Schumann, Robert (1810-1856), 389, 444, 634
Schumann, V., *Geistliche Lieder* (1539), 134, 415
"Scotch Tune," 18
Scottish Psalter (1615), 47, 80, 258, 278, 290, 302, 394, 399, 402
Selnecker, Nikolaus, *Christliche Psalmen* (1587), 17
Service Book and Hymnal (1958), 218
Shaw, Geoffrey (1879-1943), 452
Shaw, Martin (1875-1958), 300, 605
Sheppard, Franklin L. (1852-1930), 49
Sherwin, William Fiske (1826-1888), 222, 493
Sibelius, Jean (1865-1957), 73
Silcher, Friedrich (1789-1862), 318
Smart, Henry Thomas (1813-1879), 128, 174, 373, 443
Smith, Henry Percy (1825-1898), 103, 440
Smith, Isaac (c. 1725-c. 1800), 82, 145, 330
Smith, Robert Archibald (1780-1829), 170, 285
Smith, Samuel (1821-1917), 516
Spinney, Frank S. (1850-1888), 287
Stainer, John (1840-1901), 166, 652
Stanley, Samuel (1767-1822), 482, 606
Stebbins, George Coles (1846-1945), 542, 548
Stevenson, John Andrew (1761-1833), 492
Stockton, John Hart (1813-1877), 553
Storer, Henry Johnson (1860-1935), 366
Sullivan, Arthur Seymour (1842-1900), 307, 591

Tallis, Thomas (c. 1505-1585), 28, 422, 496
Tans'ur, William (c. 1706-1783), 109
Tattersall's *Psalmody* (1794), 414, 502
Taylor, Virgil Corydon (1817-1891), 57, 346
Teschner, Melchior (1584-1635), 119, 154
Thiman, Eric Harding (b. 1900), 425
Thommen, J., *Erbaulicher Musicalischer Christen-Schatz* (1745), 240, 328, 647
Toasia (Pepuhoan), 55
Tomer, William Gould (1833-1896), 504
Tourjée, Lizzie Shove (1858-1913), 78
Towner, Daniel Brink (1850-1919), 541, 577, 580

Unseld, Benjamin Carl (1843-1923), 66

Vail, Silas Jonas (1818-1884), 531
Vaughan Williams, Ralph (1872-1958), 51, 71, 94, 115, 210, 231, 304, 361, 363, 395, 433, 457, 503, 513
Venua, Frederick M. A. (1788-1872), 53
Vulpius, Melchior (1560-1616), 308, 342, 510, 610

Wade, John Francis (c. 1711-1786), 132, 192, 261
Wainwright, John (c. 1723-1768), 123
Walch, James (1837-1901), 428
Walker, W., *Southern Harmony* (1835), 243, 294
Wallace, William V. (1812-1865), 150
Walter, William Henry (1825-1893), 441
Walton, James G. (1821-1905), 262
Warren, George William (1828-1902), 420, 448
Webb, George James (1803-1887), 592
Webbe, Samuel (1740-1816), 333, 483
Webbe, S., *Essay on the Church Plain-Chant* (1782), 436
Weisse, Michael (1480-1534), 445
Weisse, Michael, *Gesengbuchlein* (1531), 221

INDEX OF COMPOSERS, ARRANGERS, AND SOURCES

Wellesley, Garret (1735-1781), 214
Wesley, Samuel Sebastian (1810-1876), 157, 369, 375, 622
Wesley, S. S., *European Psalmist* (1872), 429
White, J. T., *Sacred Harp* (1844), 312
Wiant, Bliss (b. 1895), 339
Wiebe, Esther (b. 1932), 116
Wilcox, John H. (1827-1875), 27
Wilkes, John Bernard (1785-1869), 29, 518
Willan, Healey (1880-1968), 520
Williams, Aaron (1731-1776), 245
Williams, A., *Supplement to Psalmody* (c. 1780), 72, 165, 408, 442, 454
Williams, Robert (c. 1781-1821), 62, 185
Williams, Thomas, *Psalmodia Evangelica* (1789), 39, 515
Willing, Christopher Edwin (1830-1904), 421

Willis, Richard Storrs (1819-1900), 97, 126
Wilson, Hugh (1766-1824), 170, 285
Witt, C. F. (c. 1660-1716), 635
Wittenberg (1529), 612
Wittenberg (1567), 264
Woodward, George Ratcliffe (1848-1934), 445
Wooldridge, Harry Ellis (1845-1917), 603
Wyeth, John, *Repository of Sacred Music, Part Second* (1813), 112, 256, 450

Y Llawlyfr Moliant (1890), 200
Yattendon Hymnal, The (1899), 595
Yoder, Walter E. (1889-1964), 438

Zercher, J. Randall (b. 1940), 353
Zeuner, Charles (1795-1857), 455
Zundel, John (1815-1882), 75

Metrical Index of Tunes

SHORT METER
S.M. 6 6 8.6.

Bellwoods, 88
Benjamin, 176
Boylston, 350
Dennis, 385
Ferguson, 351
Festal Song, 441
Franconia, 279, 500
Gerar, 382
Golden Hill, 419
Laban, 321
Mornington, 214
St. Bride, 340
St. Michael, 301, 507
St. Thomas, 245
Schumann, 364
Silver Street, 330
Southwell, 246, 255
Sweet Day, 66
Trentham, 216

SHORT METER
with Refrain

Marion, 277
Welcome Voice, 549
We're Marching to Zion, 529

SHORT METER DOUBLE
S.M.D. 6.6.8.6. D.

Bealoth, 380
Diademata, 191, 449
Terra Beata, 49

COMMON METER
C.M. 8.6.8.6.

Abbey, 302
Abridge, 82, 145
Antioch, 122
Arlington, 348, 499
Azmon, 104
Bromsgrove, 515
Byefield, 239
Cheshire, 241
Christmas, 138, 332
Coleshill, 371
Consolation, 256
Coronation, 95
Crimond, 67
Dedham, 282, 383
Diadem, 601
Dundee, 258, 290, 394
Dunfermline, 47, 80, 278, 402
Eden, 275
Elizabethtown, 305
Evan, 259
Geneva, 74
Glenluce, 399
Goshen, 438
Gratitude, 479
Green Hill, 451
Irish, 41

Kilmarnock, 283
King's Langley, 513
Land of Rest, 370
Lobt Gott, ihr Christen, 136, 250
Love's Consecration, 411
Maitland, 345
Martyrdom, 170, 285
Meditation, 473
Naomi, 213, 336
Nativity, 368
Newbold, 105
Nun danket all', 223
Ortonville, 187
Richmond, 32, 149, 501
St. Agnes, 108, 461
St. Anne, 84, 378
St. Flavian, 315, 400
St. Magnus, 81, 189
St. Martin's, 109
St. Peter, 102, 387
St. Stephen, 288
Salzburg, 83
Serenity, 150
Shaddick, 297
Solon, 242
Tallis' Ordinal, 28, 422
Warwick, 482
Wetherby, 157
Winchester Old, 268, 393
Windsor, 46, 320
Zerah, 125

COMMON METER
with Refrain

Bound for the Promised Land, 294
Christ Liveth in Me, 568
El Nathan, 586
God Cares, 574
Stockton, 553

COMMON METER DOUBLE
C.M.D. 8.6.8.6. D.

Bethlehem, 458
Bonar, 232
Carol, 126
Communion, 112
Ellacombe, 50, 155, 410
Kingsfold, 231
Release, 218
Resignation, 63
St. Matthew, 152
St. Michel's, 196

COMMON METER DOUBLE
with Refrain

Faith Is the Victory, 589

LONG METER
L.M. 8.8.8.8.

Alfreton, 64
Alstone, 421
Angelus, 309, 494

Baca, 215
Bera, 79
Birling, 452
Bishop, 356
Canonbury, 389, 444, 634
Christum wir sollen loben schon, 598
Creation, 204
Deo Gracias, 190
Deus tuorum militum, 36
Duke Street, 69, 203, 372
Ernan, 431
Germany, 19, 349, 439
Hagerstown, 35
Hamburg, 167
Herr Jesu Christ, dich zu uns wend, 91
Hesperus, 306, 437
Hursley, 491
Intercession, 430
Kedron, 357
Lob sei dem allmächtigen, 153
Louvan, 57, 346
Mach's mit mir, 481
Maryton, 103, 440
Melcombe, 483
Melrose, 512
Mendon, 298, 388
Missionary Chant, 455
Morning Hymn, 485
Mozart, 93
Nun lasst uns den Leib, 417
O Heiland, reiss die Himmel auf, 116
O Jesu Christe, wahres Licht, 365
Old Hundredth, 2, 3, 638, 639
Olive's Brow, 161
Onslow, 475
Park Street, 53
Pentecost, 281
Philippine, 462
Puer nobis nascitur, 181
Retreat, 331, 637
Rockingham New, 398
Rockingham Old, 72, 165, 408, 442, 454
Sandell, 335
Sessions, 249
Sheltering Wing, 54, 98, 381
So lange Jesus bleibt, 89
Solemnis haec Festivitas, 44
Song XXXIV, 397, 432, 526
Splendor paternae, 45
Tallis' Canon, 496
Tender Thought, 619
Truro, 39
Uxbridge, 202, 220, 327
Veni Creator Spiritus, 211
Vom Himmel hoch, 134, 415
Ward, 18
Wareham, 37, 508
Warrington, 34, 326

METRICAL INDEX OF TUNES

Watts, 48
Wenn wir in höchsten Nöten sein, 264
Winchester New, 156, 313
Windham, 87
Winscott, 369
Woodworth, 235

LONG METER with Alleluias
Lasst uns erfreuen, 51, 52

LONG METER with Refrain
Baptiste, 584
God of Our Strength, 533
He Leadeth Me, 543
Higher Ground, 582
Loving Kindness, 110
St. Catherine, 262
Salisbury, 14
Solid Rock, 558
Veni Emmanuel, 111

LONG METER DOUBLE L.M.D. 8.8.8.8. D.
Creation, 56
Schmücke dich, O liebe Seele, 406
Social Band, 147
Sweet Hour, 296

4.6.6.4.6.6.9.9.4.
Gott ist getreu, 85

5.5.5.5.
Hubbard, 339

5.5.5.5.6.5.6.5.
Old 104th, 596

5.5.7.D.5.5.5.5.9. D.
In Dir ist Freude, 90

5.5.8.8.5.5.
Seelenbräutigam, 319

5.6.8.5.5.8.
Crusaders' Hymn, 97

6.4.6.4. with Refrain
Need, 578

6.4.6.4. D.
Bread of Life, 222
Doane, 96

6.4.6.4.6.6.4.
Bethany, 289

6.4.6.4.6.6.4.4.
More Love to Thee, 539
Purer in Heart, 280

6.4.6.4.6.6.6.4.
St. Edmund, 307
Something for Thee, 355

6.5.6.4. with Refrain
Welcome, Wanderer, Welcome, 588

6.5.6.5.
Glenfinlas, 468, 469
Merrial, 490
Wem in Leidenstagen, 624

6.5.6.5. D.
Kingdom of God, 200
King's Weston, 94
Penitence, 324
Princethorpe, 140
Ruth, 516

6.5.6.5. D. with Refrain
St. Gertrude, 591

6.5.6.5.6.6.6.5.
St. Dunstans, 323

6.6.4.6.6.6.4.
Braun, 413
Dort, 188
Italian Hymn, 4, 101, 360
Malvern, 424
Milton Abbas, 425
Olivet, 251

Perkins, 522
Serug, 429

6.6.5.6.6.5.7.8.6.
Jesu meine Freude, 600

6.6.6.4. with Refrain
Full Salvation Free, 590

6.6.6.6.
Quam dilecta, 341
Ravenshaw, 221
St. Denys, 287

6.6.6.6. with Refrain
Arthur's Seat, 184

6.6.6.6.4.4.4.4.
Love Unknown, 172

6.6.6.6.6.6.
Laudes Domini, 107
Sacrifice, 557

6.6.6.6. D.
Invitation (Maker), 225

6.6.6.6.8.8.
Darwall, 148, 374, 392
Eastview, 367
Lenox, 244
Lischer, 497
St. John, 623

6.6.7. D.
Nunc dimittis, 489

6.6.7.6.6.7. D.
Geneva 3, 595

6.6.8.4. D.
Leoni, 11

6.6.8.6.6.8.3.3.6.6.
Wunderbarer König, 7

6.6.9.6.6.9.
New Concord, 272

6.6.9. D. with Refrain
Trust and Obey, 577

6.6.11.6.6.11.
Down Ampney, 210

6.7.6.7. with Refrain
Vruechten, 614

6.7.6.7.6.6.6.6.
Nun danket alle Gott, 31
O Gott, du frommer Gott, 198, 352

6.7.7.7.
Union, 353

6.7.8.7.8.9.6.
Fahre fort, 24

7.4.7.4. D.
So nimm denn meine Hände, 318

7.5.7.5. D.
Tokyo, 377

7.5.7.5.7.6.7.6.
Nun wend ihr hören sagen, 40

7.6.7.6.
Christus, der ist mein Leben, 308, 342, 510
Was kann es Schön'res geben, 517

7.6.7.6. with Refrain
Danish Tune, 465
Near the Cross, 560
Valet will ich dir geben, 154

7.6.7.6. D.
Angel's Story, 343
Aurelia, 375
Ave Virgo Virginum, 178
Befiehl du deine Wege, 338
Crüger, 113
Ewing, 416
Freut euch, ihr lieben, 195
Greenland, 42, 194
Herzlich tut mich verlangen, 159
King's Lynn, 457
Lancashire, 174, 443
Llangloffan, 459

Meirionydd, 226
Munich, 219
Nyland, 252
Rhyddid, 253
St. Hilda, 227, 248
Valet will ich dir geben, 119
Webb, 592
Wie lieblich ist der Maien, 520

7.6.7.6.6.7.6.
Es ist ein Ros', 131

7.6.7.6.7.6.7.5.
Rutherford, 292

7.6.7.6. D. with Refrain
Hankey, 593
Wir pflügen, 521

7.6.7.6.7.7.7.6.
Jesus Saves, 594

7.6.8.6. D.
Patmos, 366

7.6.8.6.8.6.8.6.
St. Christopher, 171

7.7.6.7.7.8.
O Welt, ich muss dich lassen, 487

7.7.7.5.
Capetown, 270

7.7.7.6.
Hervey's Litany, 379

7.7.7.7.
Aletta, 276
Aus der Tiefe, 144
Buckland, 206, 233
Freuen wir uns all in ein, 445
Geneva 136, 70
Gott sei Dank, 59, 224
Guisborough, 390
Hendon, 358
Innocents, 476, 506
Monkland, 29, 518
Orientis Partibus, 514, 525
Prayer, 524
Song XIII, 286
University College, 509
Wach auf, mein Herz, 17
West End, 207

7.7.7.7. with Alleluias
Easter Hymn, 179
Gwalchmai, 61
Llanfair, 62, 185

7.7.7.7. with Refrain
Gloria, 127
Neumeister, 550
Straf mich nicht in deinem Zorn, 177

7.7.7.7.4. with Refrain
Chautauqua, 493

7.7.7.7.7.7.
Dix, 58, 142
Ebeling, 114
Lux Prima, 478
O du Liebe meiner Liebe, 401
Redhead No. 76, 160, 238
Spanish Hymn, 162
Toplady, 254

7.7.7.7. D.
Aberystwyth, 237
Amboy, 199
Martyn, 236
St. George's Windsor, 519

7.7.7.7. D. with Refrain
Mendelssohn, 135

7.7.7.7.7.7.8.
O Lamm Gottes, 173

7.7.7.8.
Man of Sorrows, 561

7.8.7.8.3.
Morgenglanz der Ewigkeit, 484

7.8.7.8.7.7.
Grosser Gott, wir loben Dich, 1

METRICAL INDEX OF TUNES

Jesus, meine Zuversicht, 182
Meinem Jesum, 486

7.8.7.8.8.8.
Liebster Jesu, wir sind hier, 391

7.8.7.9.
Toasia, 55

7.9.7.10.4.10.
Ju Meng Ling, 209

8.3.3.6. D.
Warum sollt ich mich denn grämen, 124

8.3.8.3.8.8.8.4. with Refrain
God Is Love, 528

8.4.7. D.
Haydn, 477

8.4.8.4.8.4.
Wentworth, 267

8.5.8.3.
Stephanos, 230

8.5.8.5. with Refrain
Wonderful Savior, 559

8.5.8.5.8.7.8.7. with Refrain
If Ye Then Be Risen, 564

8.6.8.6.7.6.8.6.
St. Louis, 133

8.6.8.6.8.6.
Consolation, 450

8.6.8.6.8.8.
O Jesu, warum legst du mir, 334

8.6.8.6.8.8.8.8.4.6.
Die Sach' ist Dein, 426

8.6.8.8.8.6.
Lobt Gott, ihr Christen, 453
Rest, 274

8.7.8.7.
Cross of Jesus, 166
Dominus regit me, 65
Galilee, 229
Rathbun, 169
Ringe recht, 240, 328, 647
Stuttgart, 635
Sussex, 71
Wellesley, 78

8.7.8.7. with Refrain
Amara, 571
Benton Harbor, 562
Canaan, 464
Christ Is Risen, 566
Close to Thee, 531
Come to the Fountain, 548
Glorious Name, 545
Greensleeves, 129
How Marvelous, 540
My Redeemer, 554
Wondrous Story, 551

8.7.8.7.3.3.7.
Meine Hoffnung, 291

8.7.8.7.4.4.7.7.
Was Gott tut das ist wohlgetan, 77

8.7.8.7.4.7.
Bryn Calfaria, 602
Coronae, 186

8.7.8.7.6.5.5.6.7.
Ein feste Burg, 597

8.7.8.7.6.6.6.6.7.
Ein feste Burg, 325

8.7.8.7.7.7.
Amen, Jesus han skal raade, 347
Gott des Himmels, 60
Irby, 466
Jesus, Jesus, nichts als Jesus, 151
Komm, O komm, 212, 460
Unser Herrscher, 6

8.7.8.7.7.7. with Refrain
Harwell, 201

8.7.8.7.7.7.7.7.
Alle Menschen müssen sterben, 168

8.7.8.7.7.7.8.8.
Geneva 42, 121, 284

8.7.8.7.7.8.7.8.7.4.
Christ lag in Todesbanden, 611

8.7.8.7.8.6.8.7.
Vesper Hymn, 492

8.7.8.7.8.7.
Benedic Anima, 16, 197
Bradbury, 572
Cwm Rhondda, 311, 434
Pange Lingua, 404
Picardy, 117
Regent Square, 128, 373
St. Thomas, 192
Sicilian Mariners, 414, 502
Unser Herrscher, 193
Zeuch mich, zeuch mich, 446

8.7.8.7.8.7.7.
Divinum Mysterium, 92

8.7.8.7. D.
All the Way, 573
Austrian Hymn, 376
Beecher, 75
Blaenwern, 76
Erie, 337
Faben, 27
Friend, 542
Hyfrydol, 115, 363, 433
Hymn to Joy, 13
In Babilone, 359
Nettleton, 310
O du Liebe meiner Liebe, 386
Pleading Savior, 304, 361
Tantum ergo, 436

8.7.8.7.8.8.
Mach's mit mir, 329

8.7.8.7.8.8.7.
Allein Gott in der Höh, 38
Aus tiefer Not, 234
Mit Freuden zart, 21, 247
Nun freut euch, 384, 396, 511

8.7.8.7.8.8.7.7.
Ermuntre dich, 609
Werde munter, 599
Womit soll ich, 33

8.7.8.8.8.7.
Windermere, 30

8.8.
Elsenham, 427

8.8.6.8.6.
Warum betrübst du dich, mein Herz, 344

8.8.6.8.8.6.
Ariel, 99

8.8.7.8.
P'u T'o, 498

8.8.7.8.8.7.4.12.8.
Wie schön leuchtet der Morgenstern, 141, 208

8.8.7.8.8.7.8.8.8.8.4.8.8.
Herzlich lieb hab' ich dich, O Herr, 608

8.8.8. with Alleluias
Gelobt sei Gott, 610
Victory, 183, 418, 625

8.8.8.3.
St. Aelred, 148

8.8.8.4.
Es ist kein Tag, 523
In Memoriam, 409

8.8.8.6.
Childhood, 467
Integer Vitae, 263
Just as I Am, 354

8.8.8.6. with Refrain
He Lifted Me, 547

8.8.8.8.6.
St. Margaret, 269

8.8.8.8.8.6.8.6. with Refrain
Love of God, 538

8.8.8.8.8.8.
Nashville, 25
Stella, 146, 266
Vernon, 322

8.8.8.8.8.8.6.6.
Macht hoch die Tür, 120

8.8.8.8.8.8.8.8.
Kirken den er et, 615

8.9.8.8.9.8.6.6.4.8.8.
Wachet auf, ruft uns die Stimme, 118

9.6.9.6. with Refrain
Newcastle, 569

9.8.8.9.
God Be with You, 504
Randolph, 503

9.8.9.8.
Les Commandemens de Dieu, 407, 488

9.8.9.8. with Refrain
Fillmore, 565

9.8.9.8.8.8.
Mir ist Erbarmung, 68
O dass ich tausend Zungen, 10
Wer nur den lieben Gott lässt walten, 314

9.8.9.8. D.
Geneva 118, 607

9.8.9.8.9.9.
St. Petersburg, 106

9.9.8.9.9.8.9.8.
Herr, Dir ist niemand, 26

9.9.9.9. with Refrain
Marvelous Grace, 541

9.10.9.9. with Refrain
Blessed Assurance, 544

9.10.9.9.10.9. with Refrain
Holy Is the Lord, 536

9.10.9.10.
Morris, 579

9.10.9.10.10.10
Dir, dir Jehovah, 8

10.4.6.6.6.6.10.4.
Luckington, 22

10.4.10.4.10.10.
Sandon, 257, 316
Yattendon 11, 603

10.6.10.6.8.8.8.6.
All Is Well, 312

10.7.10.7. with Refrain
Draw Me Nearer, 581

10.8.8.8.8.10.
O Heiliger Geist, 205

10.8.10.8.8.8.
Lobe den Herren, O meine Seele, 20

10.9. with Refrain
Gott ist die Liebe, 471

10.9.10.8. with Refrain
There Is Power in the Blood, 555

10.9.10.9. with Refrain
Open the Wells, 585

10.10
Pax Tecum, 271

10.10.9.10.
Slane, 300

620   METRICAL INDEX OF TUNES

10.10.10. with Alleluias
Sine Nomine, 395
    10.10.10.6.
Faith, 228
    10.10.10.10.
Birmingham (Cunningham), 403
Ellers, 505
Eventide, 495
Ffigysbren, 299
Langran, 405
Longwood, 317
Morecambe, 217
National Hymn, 420, 448
Song XXII, 604
    10.10.10.10.10.
Geneva 124, 23
    10.10.10.10.10.10.
Finlandia, 73
Yorkshire, 123
    10.10.11.11.
Hanover, 100
Lyons, 15
    10.11.11.11. with Refrain
Judas Maccabeus, 180
    11.7.11.7. with Refrain
The Beautiful River, 556
    11.8.11.8. with Refrain
Kirkpatrick, 546
    11.8.11.8. D.
Zion's Pilgrim, 273
    11.8.11.8.11.8.12.8.
Wonderful Word, 587

11.8.11.9. with Refrain
It Is Well, 576
    11.10. with Refrain
Christ Arose, 567
    11.10.11.9.
Russian Hymn, 86
    11.10.11.10.
City of God, 616
Consolator, 333
Geneva 12, 295
Henley, 303, 463
Intercessor, 435
Morning Star, 143
Sandringham, 412
Wesley, 423
    11.10.11.10. with Refrain
Faithfulness, 534
How Great Thou Art, 535
Tidings, 428
Under His Wings, 575
    11.10.11.10.10.
Geneva 124, 447
    11.11. with Refrain
Revive Us Again, 527
    11.11.11.5.
Christe Sanctorum, 480
Herzliebster Jesu, 158
Iste Confessor, 456
    11.11.11.11.
Adeste Fideles, 261
Away in a Manger, 472
Bellevue, 260
Gordon, 265

Ihr Kinderlein, kommet, 470
St. Denio, 43, 474
Towner, 580
    11.11.11.11. with Refrain
To God Be the Glory, 532
Whiter Than Snow, 583
    11.12.12.10.
Nicaea, 5
    12.10.12.10.
Was lebet, was schwebet, 139
    12.11.12.11.
Kremser, 12
    12.12. with Refrain
Hallelujah, 'tis Done, 537
    12.12.12.7. with Refrain
Christ Returneth, 570
    14.14.4.7.8.
Lobe den Herren, 9

IRREGULAR

Adeste Fideles, 132
Allen, 530
Lord, I Want to Be, 293
Ninety and Nine, 552
Purpose, 605
Restoration, 243
Resurrection, 175
Room for Thee, 563
Silent Night, 130
Tana mana dhana, 362
The First Noel, 137
Were You There, 164
Wondrous Love, 163

Alphabetical Index of Tunes

Abbey, 302
Aberystwyth, 237
Abridge, 82, 145
Adeste Fideles, 132, 261
Ainsi que la biche ree (see Geneva 42)
Ajalon (see Redhead No. 76)
Aletta, 276
Alfreton, 64
All Is Well, 312
All Saints (see Zeuch mich, zeuch mich)
All the Way, 573
Alle Menschen müssen sterben, 168
Allein Gott in der Höh, 38
Allen, 530
Alstone, 421
Amara, 571
Amazing Grace (see Solon)
Amboy, 199
Amen, Jesus han skal raade, 347
Angels' Song (see Song XXXIV)
Angel's Story, 343
Angelus, 309, 494
Antioch, 122
Ariel, 99
Arlington, 348, 499
Arthur's Seat, 184
Aurelia, 375
Aus der Tiefe, 144
Aus tiefer Not, 234
Austrian Hymn, 376
Ave Virgo Virginum (Gaudeamus Pariter), 178
Away in a Manger, 472
Azmon, 104

Baca, 215
Baptiste, 584
Bealoth, 380
Beecher, 75

Befiehl du deine Wege (Haydn), 338
Bellevue (Foundation), 260
Bellwoods, 88
Benedic Anima, 16, 197
Benjamin, 176
Benton Harbor (Hoffman), 562
Bera, 79
Bethany, 289
Bethlehem, 458
Birling, 452
Birmingham (Cunningham), 403
Birmingham (Mendelssohn), 643
Bishop. 356
Blaenwern, 76
Blessed Assurance, 544
Bonar, 232
Bound for the Promised Land, 294
Boylston, 350
Bradbury, 572
Braun, 413
Bread of Life, 222
Bromsgrove, 515
Bryn Calfaria, 602
Buckland, 206, 263
Byefield, 239

Canaan, 464
Canonbury, 389, 444, 634
Capetown, 270
Carol, 126
Chautauqua, 493
Cheshire, 241
Childhood, 467
Christ Arose, 567
Christ Is Risen, 566
Christ ist erstanden, 612
Christ lag in Todesbanden, 611
Christ Liveth in Me, 568
Christ Returneth, 570
Christe Sanctorum, 480

Christmas, 138, 332
Christum wir sollen loben schon, 598
Christus, der ist mein Leben, 308, 342, 510
City of God, 616
Clamanda (see Social Band)
Close to Thee, 531
Coleshill (Dublin Tune), 371
Come to the Fountain, 548
Communion, 112
Consolation (Morning Song), 256, 450
Consolator, 333
Coronae, 186
Coronation, 95
Creation, 56, 204
Crimond, 67
Cross of Jesus, 166
Crüger, 113
Crusaders' Hymn, 97
Cunningham (see Birmingham)
Cwm Rhondda, 311, 434

Danish Tune, 465
Darwall 148, 374, 392
Dedham, 282, 383
Dedication Anthem (see Doxology)
Dennis, 385
Deo Gracias, 190
Deus tuorum militum, 36
Diadem, 601
Diademata, 191, 449
Die Sach ist dein, 426
Dir, dir Jehovah, 8
Divinum Mysterium, 92
Dix, 58, 142
Doane, 96
Dominus regit me, 65
Donne Secours, Seigneur (see Geneva 12)
Dorchester (see Malvern)

ALPHABETICAL INDEX OF TUNES

Dort, 188
Down Ampney, 210
Doxology (Dedication Anthem), 606
Draw Me Nearer, 581
Dublin Tune (see Coleshill)
Duke Street, 69, 203, 372
Dundee, 258, 290, 394
Dunfermline, 47, 80, 278, 402

Easter Anthem, 613
Easter Hymn, 179
Eastview, 367
Ebeling, 114
Eden (St. Nicholas), 275
Ein feste Burg, 325, 597
El Nathan, 586
Elizabethtown, 305
Ellacombe, 50, 155, 410
Ellers, 505
Elsenham, 427
Erie, 337
Ermuntre dich, 609
Ernan, 431
Es ist ein Ros', 131
Es ist kein Tag, 523
Evan, 259
Eventide, 495
Ewing, 416

Faben, 27
Fahre fort, 24
Faith, 228
Faith Is the Victory, 589
Faithfulness, 534
Ferguson, 351
Festal Song, 441
Ffigysbren, 299
Fillmore, 565
Finlandia, 73
Foundation (see Bellevue)
Franconia, 279, 500
Freuen wir uns all in ein, 445
Freut euch, ihr lieben, 195
Friend, 542
Full Salvation Free, 590

Galilee, 229
Gaudeamus Pariter (see Ave Virgo Virginum)
Gelineau 99, 618
Gelineau 114, 617
Gelobt sei Gott, 610
Geneva, 74
Geneva 3 (O Seigneur), 595
Geneva 12 (Donne Secours, Seigneur), 295
Geneva 42 (Ainsi que la biche ree), 121, 284
Geneva 118 (Rendez à Dieu), 607
Geneva 124 (Old 124th), 23, 447
Geneva 136 (Louez Dieu tout hautement), 70
Gerar, 382
Germany, 19, 349, 439
Glenfinlas, 468, 469
Glenluce, 399
Gloria, 127
Glorious Name, 545
God Be in My Head, 645
God Be with You, 504
God Cares, 574
God Is Love, 528
God of Our Strength, 533
Golden Hill, 419
Gordon, 265
Goshen, 438
Gott des Himmels, 60
Gott ist die Liebe, 471
Gott ist getreu, 85
Gott sei Dank, 59, 224
Gratitude, 479
Green Hill, 451
Greenland, 42, 194
Greensleeves, 129
Grosser Gott, wir loben Dich, 1
Guisborough, 390
Gwalchmai, 61

Hagerstown, 35
Hallelujah, 'tis Done, 537
Hamburg, 167
Hankey, 593
Hanover, 100
Harwell, 201
Haydn, 477
Haydn (see Befiel du deine Wege)
He Leadeth Me, 543
He Lifted Me, 547
Hendon, 358
Henley, 303, 463
Herr, Dir ist niemand, 26
Herr Jesu Christ, dich zu uns wend, 91
Hervey's Litany, 379
Herzlich lieb hab' ich dich, O Herr, 608
Herzlich tut mich verlangen, 159
Herzliebster Jesu, 158
Hesperus (Quebec), 306, 437
Higher Ground, 582
Hoffman (see Benton Harbor)
Holy Is the Lord, 536
Holywood (see St. Thomas)
How Great Thou Art (O Store Gud), 535
How Marvelous, 540
Hubbard, 339
Hursley, 491
Hyfrydol, 115, 363, 433
Hymn to Joy, 13

I Will Arise (see Restoration)
Ich weiss einen Strom (see The Beautiful River)
If Ye Then Be Risen, 564
Ihr Kinderlein, kommet, 470
In Babilone, 359
In Dir ist Freude, 90
In Memoriam, 409
Innocents, 476, 506
Innsbruck (see O Welt, ich muss dich lassen)
Integer Vitae, 263
Intercession, 430
Intercessor, 435
Invitation (Maker), 225
Irby, 466
Irish, 41
Iste Confessor (Rouen), 456
It Is Well, 576
Italian Hymn, 4, 101, 360

Jerusalem, Jerusalem (see St. Michel's)
Jesu, meine Freude, 600
Jesu, meines Lebens Leben, 168
Jesus, Jesus, nichts als Jesus, 151
Jesus, meine Zuversicht, 182
Jesus Saves, 594
Joanna (see St. Denio)
Ju Meng Ling, 209
Judas Maccabeus, 180
Just as I Am, 354

Kedron, 357
Kilmarnock, 283
Kingdom of God, 200
King's Langley, 513
King's Lynn, 457
King's Weston, 94
Kingsfold, 231
Kirken den er et, 615
Kirkpatrick, 546
Komm, O komm, 212, 460
Kremser, 12

Laban, 321
Lancashire, 174, 443
Land of Rest, 370
Langran, 405
Lasst uns erfreuen, 51, 52
Laudes Domini, 107
Lenox, 244
Leoni, 11

Les Commandemens de Dieu, 407, 488
Liebster Jesu, wir sind hier, 391
Lischer, 497
Llanfair, 62, 185
Llangloffan, 459
Lob sei dem allmächtigen, 153
Lobe den Herren, 9
Lobe den Herren, O meine Seele, 20
Lobt Gott, ihr Christen, 136, 250, 453
Longwood, 317
Lord, I Want to Be, 293
Louez Dieu tout hautement (see Geneva 136)
Louvan, 57, 346
Love of God, 538
Love Unknown, 172
Love's Consecration, 411
Loving Kindness, 110
Luckington, 22
Lux Fiat, 631
Lux Prima, 478
Lyons, 15

Mach's mit mir, 329, 481
Macht hoch die Tür, 120
Maitland, 345
Maker (see Invitation)
Malvern (Dorchester), 424
Man of Sorrows, 561
Marion, 277
Martyn, 236
Martyrdom, 170, 285
Marvelous Grace, 541
Maryton, 103, 440
Meditation, 473
Meine Hoffnung, 291
Meinem Jesum (Meinhold), 486
Meinhold (see Meinem Jesum)
Meirionydd, 226
Melcombe, 483
Melrose, 512
Mendelssohn, 135
Mendon, 298, 388
Merrial, 490
Milton Abbas, 425
Mir ist Erbarmung, 68
Missionary Chant, 455
Mit Freuden zart, 21, 247
Monkland, 29, 518
More Love to Thee, 539
Morecambe, 217
Morgenglanz der Ewigkeit, 484
Morning Hymn, 485
Morning Song (see Consolation)
Morning Star, 143
Mornington, 214
Morris, 579
Mozart, 93
Munich, 219
My Redeemer, 554

Naomi, 213, 336
Nashville, 25
National Hymn, 420, 448
Nativity, 368
Near the Cross, 560
Need, 578
Nettleton, 310
Neumeister, 550
New Concord (True Happiness), 272
Newbold, 105
Newcastle, 569
Newington (see St. Stephen)
Nicaea, 5
Ninety and Nine, 552
Nun danket all', 223
Nun danket alle Gott, 31
Nun freut euch, 384, 396, 511
Nun lasst uns den Leib, 417
Nun wend ihr hören sagen, 40
Nunc dimittis, 489
Nyland, 252

O dass ich tausend Zungen, 10

ALPHABETICAL INDEX OF TUNES

O du Liebe meiner Liebe, 386, 401
O Gott, du frommer Gott, 198, 352
O Heiland, reiss die Himmel auf, 116
O Heiliger Geist, 205
O Jesu Christe, wahres Licht, 365
O Jesu, warum legst du mir, 334
O Lamm Gottes, 173
O Seigneur (see Geneva 3)
O Store Gud (see How Great Thou Art)
O Welt, ich muss dich lassen (Innsbruck), 487
Old 100th, 2, 3, 638, 639
Old 104th, 596
Old 124th (see Geneva 124)
Old 134th (see St. Michael)
Olive's Brow, 161
Olivet, 251
Onslow, 475
Open the Wells, 585
Orientis Partibus, 514, 525
Ortonville, 187

Pange Lingua, 404
Park Street, 53
Patmos, 366
Pax Tecum, 271
Penitence, 324
Pentecost, 281
Perfect Love (see Sandringham)
Perkins, 522
Philippine, 462
Picardy, 117
Pleading Savior, 304, 361
Prayer, 524
Princethorpe, 140
P'u T'o, 498
Puer nobis nascitur, 181
Purer in Heart, 280
Purpose, 605

Quam dilecta, 341
Quebec (see Hesperus)

Randolph, 503
Rathbun, 169
Ravenshaw, 221
Redhead No. 76 (Ajalon), 160, 238
Regent Square, 128, 373
Release, 218
Rendez à Dieu (see Geneva 118), 607
Resignation, 63
Rest (Whittier), 274
Restoration (I Will Arise), 243
Resurrection, 175
Retreat, 331, 637
Revive Us Again, 527
Rhyddid, 253
Richmond, 32, 149, 501
Ringe recht, 240, 328, 647
Rockingham New, 398
Rockingham Old, 72, 165, 408, 442, 454
Room for Thee, 563
Rouen (see Iste Confessor)
Russian Hymn, 86
Ruth, 516
Rutherford, 292

Sacrifice, 557
St. Aelred, 148
St. Agnes, 108, 461
St. Anne, 84, 378
St. Bride, 340
St. Catherine, 262
St. Christopher, 171
St. Denio (Joanna), 43, 474
St. Denys, 287

St. Dunstans, 323
St. Edmund, 307
St. Flavian, 315, 400
St. George's Windsor, 519
St. Gertrude, 591
St. Hilda, 227, 248
St. John, 623
St. Louis, 133
St. Magnus, 81, 189
St. Margaret, 269
St. Martin's, 109
St. Matthew, 152
St. Michael (Old 134th), 301, 507
St. Michel's (Jerusalem, Jerusalem), 196
St. Nicholas (see Eden)
St. Peter, 102, 387
St. Petersburg, 106
St. Stephen (Newington), 288
St. Thomas, 245
St. Thomas (Holywood), 192
Salisbury, 14
Salzburg, 83
Samarantha (see Zion's Pilgrim)
Sandell, 335
Sandon, 257, 316
Sandringham (Perfect Love), 412
Schmücke dich, O liebe Seele, 406
Schumann, 364
Seelenbräutigam, 319
Serenity, 150
Serug, 429
Sessions, 249
Shaddick, 297
Sheltering Wing, 54, 98, 381
Sicilian Mariners, 414, 502
Silent Night, 130
Silver Street, 330
Sine Nomine, 395
Slane, 300
So lange Jesus bleibt, 89
So nimm denn meine Hände, 318
Social Band (Clamanda), 147
Solemnis haec Festivitas, 44
Solid Rock, 558
Solon (Amazing Grace), 242
Something for Thee, 355
Song XIII, 286
Song XXII, 604
Song XXXIV (Angels' Song), 397, 432, 526
Southwell, 246, 255
Spanish Hymn, 162
Splendor paternae, 45
Stella, 146, 266
Stephanos, 230
Stockton, 553
Straf mich nicht in deinem Zorn, 177
Stuttgart, 635
Sussex, 71
Sweet Day, 66
Sweet Hour, 296

Tallis' Canon, 496
Tallis' Ordinal, 28, 422
Tana mana dhana, 362
Tantum ergo, 436
Tender Thought, 619
Terra Beata, 49
The Beautiful River (Ich weiss einen Strom), 556
The First Noel, 137
There Is Power in the Blood, 555
Tidings, 428
To God Be the Glory, 532
Toasia, 55
Tokyo, 377
Toplady, 254
Towner, 580

Trentham, 216
True Happiness (see New Concord)
Truro, 39
Trust and Obey, 577

Under His Wings, 575
Union, 353
University College, 509
Unser Herrscher, 6, 193
Uxbridge, 202, 220, 327

Valet will ich dir geben, 119, 154
Veni Creator Spiritus, 211
Veni Emmanuel, 111
Vernon, 322
Vesper Hymn, 492
Victory, 183, 418, 625
Vom Himmel hoch, 134, 415
Vruechten, 614

Wach auf, mein Herz, 17
Wachet auf, ruft uns die Stimme, 118
Ward, 18
Wareham, 37, 508
Warrington, 34, 326
Warum betrübst du dich, mein Herz, 344
Warum sollt ich mich denn grämen, 124
Warwick, 482
Was Gott tut das ist wohlgetan, 77
Was kann es Schön'res geben, 517
Was lebet, was schwebet, 139
Watts, 48
Webb, 592
Welcome Voice, 549
Welcome, Wanderer, Welcome, 588
Wellesley, 78
Wem in Leidenstagen, 624
Wenn wir in höchsten Nöten sein, 264
Wentworth, 267
Wer nur den lieben Gott lässt walten, 314
Werde munter, 599
We're Marching to Zion, 529
Were You There, 164
Wesley, 423
West End, 207
Wetherby, 157
Whiter Than Snow, 583
Whittier (see Rest)
Wie lieblich ist der Maien, 520
Wie schön leuchtet der Morgenstern, 141, 208
Winchester New, 156, 313
Winchester Old, 268, 393
Windermere, 30
Windham, 87
Windsor, 46, 320
Winscott, 369
Wir pflügen, 521
Womit soll ich, 33
Wonderful Savior, 559
Wonderful Word, 587
Wondrous Love, 163
Wondrous Story, 551
Woodworth, 235
Wunderbarer König, 7

Yattendon 11, 603
Yorkshire, 123

Zerah, 125
Zeuch mich, zeuch mich (All Saints), 446
Zion's Pilgrim (Samarantha), 273

Index of Scriptural Allusions

GENESIS
1:1-3 447
1:3 . . . . 54, 429, 455
1:31 465
5:24 305
8:8 429
11:1-9 447
28:10-15 289
28:18-22 83
32:24-30 322

EXODUS
3:16 11
13:21, 22 . . 311, 316, 376
15:1-21 178
17:6 . . . . 254, 376
25:21, 22 . . . . 331, 333
33:21-23 . . . . 254, 546

LEVITICUS
8:35 . . . . 350, 351
25 112

NUMBERS
9:15 376

DEUTERONOMY
8:14-16 311
32:4 77
32:13 294
33:27 396
34:1-4 294

JOSHUA
1:5-9 . . . . 260, 261
1:9 . . . . 503, 504
3:7-17 311
10:25 . . . . 260, 261

1 SAMUEL
3:1-10 347
7:12 310

2 SAMUEL
23:4 . . . . 253, 478

1 KINGS
19:11, 12 274

1 CHRONICLES
29:14 . . . . 365, 636

2 CHRONICLES
15:12-15 398

JOB
19:25-27 . . . . 182, 565
33:4 216
38:7 13

PSALMS
1 278
2 202
3:5 491
5 482
5:7 390
8 47
10:16 204
16:8 . . . . 430, 432
17:8 . . . . 236, 237
18:2 . . . . 325, 597
19:1 53
19:1-4 . . . . 56, 59, 220
19:14 633
22:28 122
23 . . . . 63, 65, 66, 67
23:1, 2 . . . . . . 252, 572
23:1-4 273
23:2, 3 543
24:1 49
24:7 120
25:1 290
25:4, 5 . . . . . . 317, 389
27 342
27:1 85
29:11 505
30:5 139
33:5 58
34 41
36 39
36:5-9 43
36:9 57
37:4 273
37:5 . . . . . . 77, 338, 340
39:4-7 . . . . . . 315, 369
40 302
40:9, 10 593
42 . . . . 284, 285
42:5 334
43 571
43:3 . . . . 486, 631
46 326
46:1 . . . . 325, 597
46:6 378
46:9 454
46:10 73
47:8 48
51 238
51:7 583
51:10 283
51:10-12 . . . . 217, 628
55:18 576
55:22 . . . . 314, 643
57:8 . . . . 332, 485
57:8, 9 . . . 69, 110, 477
63 35
63:6, 7 496
65 82
65:9-13 . . . . . 520, 522
65:11 508
66:4 22
67 419
68:4 21
72 . . . . 113, 203
72:7 191
73:24 316
73:25 98
73:28 289
77:19 80
78:52, 53 319
79:9 456
84 . . . . 392, 393
84:2 6
87:1-3 376
90 . . . . 42, 84
90:1, 2 48
90:2 11
90:17 437
91:4 . . . . . 9, 496, 575
92:1, 2
. . . 107, 479, 480, 481, 595
93 602
95 14
95:6, 7 626
98 122
100 . . . . . 2, 3, 46, 618
100:4 6
103 . . . 16, 17, 245, 531
103:11 78
104 . . . . . . 15, 50, 55
104:1, 2 26
104:2 43
104:10-15 524
104:24 . . . . 49, 59, 267
104:30 513
105:39-41 376
107:1-3 387
107:28-31 12
111:1 9
113:3 488

PSALMS (cont.)
116 617
117 36
118:19 6
118:24 499
119:33-40 356
119:35 317
119:105 . . . . . . 221, 223
121 . . . . 257, 258
121:2 60
121:4 42
122:1 390
130 . . . . 234, 241
133 382
133:1 385
136 . . . . . . 34, 70, 518
136:3, 4 31
139 . . . . 79, 619
139:11, 12 505
139:17 108
143:10 485
145 23
145:4 396
145:17 77
146 . . . . 20, 25
147 515
147:1 30
147:16, 17 512
148 . . 10, 13, 27, 51, 52, 62
150 . . . . 61, 596
150:6 . . . . 9, 10

PROVERBS
3:24 . . . . 490, 496
18:24 337

SONG OF SOLOMON
1:7 273

ISAIAH
1:18 . . . . 248, 583
6:2, 3 . . . . . 1, 28, 117
6:3 . . . . . . 493, 536, 622
6:3-5 5
7:14 . . . . 111, 135
9:2 . . . . 429, 609
9:6, 7 . . 32, 96, 125, 191
11:1 . . . . 131, 141
11:9 605
11:10 111
12:3 583
26:3 . . . . 271, 276
26:4 254
28:5 . . . . 95, 601
30:15 . . . . 334, 492
32:2 171
32:15 388
33:20, 21 376
40 121
40:3 420
40:28 21
40:28-31 81
41:10 574
43:2 . . . . 260, 261
45:7 18
48:12 11
52:1 423
52:1, 8 118
53:3 . . . . 103, 561
53:4 248
53:5 . . 158, 159, 168, 170
54:7, 8 80
59:20 111
60:1-3 423
60:19 436
60:20 316
61:3 331
62:3 . . . . . 95, 189, 601
64:1 116

JEREMIAH
1:9 389

LAMENTATIONS
3:22, 23 . . 18, 483, 534

EZEKIEL
47:1-12 556

DANIEL
7:13, 14 4

MICAH
4:3 198
5:2 133

HABAKKUK
2:14 605
2:20 . . . . 620, 621
3:17, 18 . . . . . 253, 525

ZECHARIAH
4:6 443
9:9 156

MALACHI
1:11 488
3:1 128
4:2 . . . . 135, 253

MATTHEW
1:23 . . . . 111, 135
2:1, 2 . . . . . . 128, 468
2:1-12 . . 137, 140, 142, 143
2:6 133
2:9-11 . . . . . . 124, 137
2:11 139
4:1, 2 144
4:18-22 . . . . . . 229, 274
4:23, 24 . . . . . 151, 152
5:8 . . . . 279, 280
5:9 449
5:11, 12 431
6:9-13 627
6:10 . . . . 436, 447
6:13 60
6:25-32 . . . . . . 49, 253
6:33 200
8:20 563
8:26 343
9:20, 21 616
9:28, 29 235
9:35, 36 439
10:5-8 441
10:8-10 359
10:32, 33 324
10:42 439
11:28 . . . . 226, 230
. . . . . . 231, 232, 337, 553
11:28-30 492
13:24-30 519
13:31-33 200
13:44-46 200
14:13-21 222
16:18 . . . 378, 456, 615
16:24 . . . 329, 345, 357
16:24, 25 . . . . 230, 344
16:27 196
17:1-8 153
19:6 412
19:13-15 . . . . . 414, 469
20:28 557
21:1-11 . . . 154, 155, 156
21:8, 9 172
22:37 441
22:39 455
24:30, 31 569
24:35 29
25:1-13 . . . 118, 194, 195
25:6 431
25:31-40 298
25:40 . . . . 364, 439
26:26-29 . . . . 400, 408

623

INDEX OF SCRIPTURAL ALLUSIONS

26:36 160
26:39 . . . . . 341, 540
26:69-75 324
27:22 172
27:28, 29 . . . 159, 247
27:45 170
27:46 162
28:1-6 . . . . . 566, 567
28:1-7 610
28:6 . . . . . . 177, 179
28:9 174
28:18 100
28:18-20 . . . . 203, 224

MARK

1:32-34 494
1:35 309
4:36-41 . . 148, 309, 452
5:15 274
6:31 274
12:41-44 139
14:58 615
16:1-6 474
(Parallel passages are listed under Matthew)

LUKE

1:32, 33 115
1:68-79 . . . . . 111, 140
1:76-79 128
1:78, 79 484
2:7 . . . . 466, 472, 563
2:7-18 124
2:8-11 . . . . . . 137, 609
2:8-14 . . 123, 128, 135, 138
2:8-15 124
2:8-16 . . . . . . 129, 130
2:10, 11 . . . . 122, 133
2:10-15 . . . . . 127, 134
2:13, 14 126
2:13-15 132
2:14 . . . . 38, 114, 632
2:15, 16 470
2:25 115
2:49-52 458
2:51, 52 146
4:18, 19 . . . . 112, 113, 424, 425
6:12 274
7:22 104
10:27 217
12:35-38 . . . 406, 480
14:23 431
15:1, 2 550
15:3-7 552
15:11-32 . . . . 243, 588
15:18, 19 297
17:5 259
19:10 . . . . . . 228, 269
19:41, 42 . . . 439, 617
21:27 . . . . . . 192, 197
22:12-19 403
22:32 324
22:39-46 161
23:42, 43 246
24:28-35 403
24:29 . . . . . . 491, 495
24:30 . . . . . . 407, 607
24:34 . . 176, 177, 179, 613
24:35 402
24:36 624
24:39, 40 181
24:50-53 185
(Parallel passages are listed under Matthew)

JOHN

1:1-3, 14 19
1:1-4 . . . . . . 132, 219
1:1-9 . . . . 44, 45
1:4, 5 . . . 85, 346, 584
1:9 . . . 133, 489, 609
1:14 . . 4, 132, 135, 404
1:29 . . . . . . 173, 248
3:16 532
3:17 594
3:20, 21 485

4:12 453
4:13, 14 287
4:14 . . . . 98, 231, 232
            236, 237, 287, 486
4:24 7
5:25 418
6:31, 32 320
6:32, 33 401
6:35 . . . 98, 222, 333
6:37 . . . . . . 226, 235
6:51 . . . . . . 407, 607
7:37 . . . . . . 231, 232
8:12 . . . 231, 232, 329, 478, 491
10:11 . . . . . . 65, 572
10:27 347
12:20-23 303
12:24 426
12:26 . . 343, 349, 389, 440
12:36 269
13:3-5 410
13:12-15 411
13:35 207
14:2, 3 289
14:6 . . 149, 329, 445, 590
14:16-18 . . . . 216, 333
14:18 85
14:21 265
14:26, 27 38
14:27 . . . . 440, 505, 600
15:1-5 304
15:4-11 308
15:5 578
15:14 . . . . . . 337, 542
15:14, 15 73
16:7, 8 214
16:13 4
16:13-15 . . 207, 211, 215
16:22 269
17:10 395
17:24 371
19:17, 18 473
19:30 160
19:34 . . . 165, 167, 581
20:11-16 160
20:22 216
20:25-29 . . . . 181, 250
20:29 610
21:15 265
(Parallel passages are listed under Matthew)

ACTS

1:8 207
1:9-11 . . 185, 188, 190
1:11 196
2:1-4 . . 205, 210, 212, 421
2:17, 18 . . . . 388, 452
2:32, 33 174
4:32 383
7:38 111
7:59, 60 297
14:15 . . . . 54, 59
14:17 521
17:27, 28 54

ROMANS

1:7 646
1:16, 17 249
5:5 . . . . 213, 217
8:9-11 212
8:15 244
8:16 216
8:19-25 193
8:26 208
8:26, 27 297
8:28 . . . . . 71, 77, 80
8:35-39 . . 64, 268, 600
8:37 180
8:38, 39 . . . . . 90, 367
10:12 140
12:1 358
14:7-9 . . . . . 491, 495
14:9 191
16:16 383
16:27 507

1 CORINTHIANS

1:18 . . . . . . 171, 560
1:18-25 442
2:2 169
3:11 . . . . . . 260, 261
            373, 374, 375, 558
3:22, 23 544
5:7, 8 177
6:19 208
6:19, 20 . . 75, 76, 281
9:24 332
11:24-26 . . . 400, 409
13 270
13:8 538
13:12 . . . . 80, 371
15:17-20 614
15:20 . . . 182, 612, 613
15:20-22 175
15:24-27 193
15:51, 52 . . . 417, 614
15:54-57 . . . .
            180, 183, 495, 611
15:55 . . . . . . 179, 368
16:13 348

2 CORINTHIANS

1:21, 22 217
2:14 . . . . . . 443, 502
3:17, 18 . . . . 75, 76
4:6 . . . . 444, 478
4:14 178
5:7 . . 250, 251, 263, 442
5:10 . . . . . . 350, 351
5:15 359
5:17 . . . . 75, 76
5:18, 19 38
5:20 . . . . . . 424, 425
5:21 170
6:2 398
8:9 563
9:7 361
12:9, 10 266
13:12 383
13:14 647

GALATIANS

2:20 . . 165, 167, 168, 343
3:13, 14 122
3:14 140
3:26-28 387
4:6 244
5:25 217
6:14 . . . .
            165, 167, 169, 171, 560

EPHESIANS

1:7, 8 . . . . . . 473, 559
1:12 . . . . . . 107, 595
1:22, 23 379
2:19-22 . . . . . 373, 374
3:9, 10 19
3:17-19 . . . .
            106, 108, 150, 266, 389
4:1, 2 440
4:4-6 . . . . . 375, 403
4:23, 24 513
4:26 496
5:19, 20 29
5:20 267
6:10-13 . . . .
            321, 330, 591, 592
6:13-17 589
6:17 209

PHILIPPIANS

1:21 . . . . . . 371, 568
2:5 451
2:5-7 279
2:5-11 . . . . . 94, 598
2:7 136
2:8 166
2:8-11 . . . . . . 32, 177
2:9-11 . . . . . 95, 107
            185, 201, 595, 601
2:12 328
3:7, 8 . . . . . 165, 167

3:12-14 332
3:14 582
4:4 . . . . 184, 277
4:7 505
4:19 334

COLOSSIANS

1:15-17 . . . 19, 92, 191
2:6, 7 266
3:1, 2 564
3:11 387
3:15 456
4:12 592

1 THESSALONIANS

4:15-18 . . . . 192, 570
5:2 570
5:14 440

2 THESSALONIANS

3:11-13 433
3:13 431

1 TIMOTHY

1:12-14 68
1:17 . . . . 15, 43
3:15 380
6:6-8 336
6:14 . . . . 350, 351
6:14-16 . . . . . 113, 201
6:16 43

2 TIMOTHY

1:12 586
2:3 348
4:8 332

TITUS

2:11-14 327

HEBREWS

1:3, 4 . . . . . . 97, 187
2:9 . . . . . 161, 189, 611
2:12 . . . . 99, 379
2:20 7
4:14-16 371
4:16 . . 239, 244, 296, 299
6:4-6 227
7:22-25 244
10:22 581
12:1 . . . . 328, 395
12:1, 2 332
12:2 . . . . 165, 167, 303
12:22-24 416
13:8 495
13:12 473
13:20, 21 506

JAMES

1:12 443
1:27 . . . . 364, 435
3:18 . . . . 449, 454
4:8 . . . . 307, 579, 581

1 PETER

1:8, 9 442
1:21 291
2:4-8 . . . . . . 373, 374
2:24 171
4:12 . . . . . . 260, 261
5:7 . . . . 266, 296

2 PETER

1:19 478

1 JOHN

1:7 . . . 104, 282, 549
1:9 198
2:2 . . . . 424, 425
2:5, 6 305
2:24 308
3:14-18 386
4:8 . . . . 71, 454
4:8, 9 . . . . . . 471, 528
4:9, 10 . . . . . . 75, 76
            159, 172, 266, 269, 476
4:11, 12 435

INDEX OF SCRIPTURAL ALLUSIONS

4:18 . . . . . . 287, 455	3:7 111	7:13, 14 416	21:1 29
4:20 447	3:20 227	11:15-17 . 95, 186, 191, 601	21:1-4 . . . . . 439, 450
5:4 . . . . 259, 589	4:8 91	12:11 555	21:2 376
5:11 367	4:8-11 5	14:1-3 201	21:6 548
5:12 584	5:5 188	14:2, 3 118	21:10, 11 416
3 JOHN	5:6-12 109	14:12, 13 . 31, 375, 394, 395	21:10-21 370
2 576	5:9-14 368	15:3, 4 96	21:21 118
JUDE	5:11 104	19:6 . . . 177, 204, 395	22:1, 2 . . . . . 376, 556
3 262	5:11-13 . . . . . 105, 191	19:6-9 118	22:16 . . . . . . 141, 143
REVELATION	5:12 101	19:9 406	22:17 199
1:7 192	6:12-17 87	19:16	22:20 . . . . . . 193, 196
	7:9-12 . . 95, 100, 199, 601	95, 177, 186, 189, 601	

Topical Index

ADORATION AND PRAISE, 1-41
(See also JESUS CHRIST: Praise and Glory)
Scripture Readings, 654, 658, 667, 668, 670, 674, 676, 718, 719
A gladsome hymn, 464
All creatures, 51
All my hope on God, 291
Before Jehovah's aweful, 48
Bless, O my soul, 72
Come, let us join, 501
Come, my soul, 477
Cry out with joy, 618
Day is dying, 493
Father, we praise, 480
Glory be to God, 632
Glory be to the Father, 640, 641, 642
God of our strength, 533
Holy, holy, holy, 622
How great Thou art, 535
Let all together praise, 136
Let us, with a gladsome, 70
Lord of our life, 346
O for a heart, 283
O my soul, bless, 531
O Thou in whose presence, 273
Our Father, God, 384
Praise God from whom, 606
Praise, O praise, 518
Praise the Lord, 61
Praise to God, 524
Sing we the song, 368
The Lord is King, 204
To God be the glory, 532
To God the only wise, 507
To Thy temple, 390
We come, 396
We praise Thee, O God, 527
With songs and honors, 515

ADVENT
(See JESUS CHRIST: Advent)

AFFLICTION
(See also COMFORT)
Scripture Readings, 668, 672, 683, 703
In the hour of trial, 324
Lord, should rising, 525

ANGELS
Scripture Readings, 673, 676, 692, 693, 717, 718

ANNIVERSARIES
Scripture Readings, 656, 672

ANXIETY
Scripture Readings, 690, 709

ASCENSION
(See JESUS CHRIST: Ascension)

ASPIRATION
(See also Hope and Aspiration, 284-295)
Scripture Readings, 668, 671
Above the trembling, 290
As lives the flower, 568
As pants the hart, 285
As the hart, 284
Be Thou my vision, 300
I am Thine, O Lord, 581
I need Thee, 578
I'm pressing on, 582
Jesus, priceless, 600
Lord, I am fondly, 585
Lord, I want to be, 293
Lord Jesus, I long, 583
More love to Thee, 539
O for a closer walk, 305
O for a faith, 259
O Life in whom, 584
O Lord, within my soul, 590
O love that wilt not, 269
On Jordan's stormy banks, 294
Unto the hills around, 257
We would see Jesus, 303

ASSURANCE
(See also Faith and Assurance, 249-264)
Scripture Readings, 673, 665
A wonderful Savior, 546
Blessed assurance, 544
Come, come, ye saints, 312
I know not why, 586
I've found a friend, 542
Lord Jesus, I long, 583
My hope is built, 558
Under His wings, 575

ATONEMENT
(See also Passion, 157-173)
Arise, my soul, arise, 244
Bread of heaven, 401
Bread of the world, 407
Bread of the world, 607
Christ has for sin, 562
Christ the Lord, 177
Come, every soul, 553
Come with thy sins, 548
Create in me a clean, 628
For Thy mercy, 509
Glory be to God, 632
How great Thou art, 535
How shall I follow, 349
I hear Thy welcome, 549
I lay my sins, 248
I stand amazed, 540
Just as I am, 235
Marvelous grace, 541

My faith looks up, 251
O Christ, our hope, 288
O for a heart, 283
The church's one, 375
There is a green hill, 473
'Tis the promise, 537
To God be the glory, 532
When peace, 576
Would you be free, 555

AUTUMN
Come, ye thankful, 519
Praise to God, 524
Sing to the Lord, 520
The year is swiftly, 517

BAPTISM, 398, 399
I sing with exultation, 40

BEATITUDES
Scripture Reading, 696

BEAUTY
Scripture Readings, 661, 665, 671, 690

BENEDICTION
Grace to you, 646
May the grace, 647

BENEVOLENCE
Scripture Readings, 696, 707, 712

BEREAVEMENT
(See COMFORT)

BIBLE
(See also Holy Scriptures, 218-224)
Scripture Readings, 660, 662
How firm a foundation, 260, 261
I love to tell, 593
O grant us light, 444
O wonderful, wonderful, 587
Our Father, God, 384
Teach me, O Lord, 356
That man hath perfect, 278

BROTHERHOOD
(See also Fellowship of Believers, 381-387)
Scripture Readings, 692, 701, 704, 708, 710, 716
Christ is the world's, 198
Father eternal, 447
Father, whose will, 422
Here, O Lord, 377
I bind my heart, 353
Long ago when Jesus, 469
Lord of our life, 456
O brother man, 435
O holy city, 450
O young and fearless, 459

Rise up, O men of God, 441
Spirit of holiness, 213
The day Thou gavest, 488

CALL TO WORSHIP
Scripture Readings, 658, 667, 668, 671, 674, 675, 676
All people that, 2
God Himself is with us, 7
Holy, holy, holy, 622
Jesus, stand among us, 624
Now to the King, 623
O come, let us worship, 626
O come, loud anthems, 14
O Lord of love, 625
Open now the gates, 6
The Lord is in His, 620, 621

CHILDREN
Scripture Readings, 692, 656

CHILDREN'S HYMNS, 464-476
Children of the heavenly, 335
Come, Thou Almighty, 4
Fairest Lord Jesus, 97
Holy, holy, holy, 5
Now the day is over, 490
O little town, 133
Onward, Christian, 591
Praise the Lord, 27
Silent night, 130
This is my Father's, 49

CHRIST
(See JESUS CHRIST)

CHRISTIAN EDUCATION
(See EDUCATION)

CHRISTIAN LIFE
(See LIFE IN CHRIST, 225-371)
Scripture Readings, 689, 690, 691, 692, 693, 696, 699, 700, 702, 704, 709, 710, 712, 714, 715

CHRISTMAS
(See also Birth, 122-138)
Scripture Readings, 679, 695, 697, 708
Away in a manger, 472
Once in royal David's, 466
Wise men seeking, 468

CHURCH, 372-418
Built on the Rock, 615
Onward, Christian, 591
The day Thou gavest, 488

TOPICAL INDEX

Body of Christ
Scripture Reading, 691
He is coming, 569
Heart with loving, 386
The church's one, 375
  Communion of Saints,
  394-397
  Awake, my soul, 332
  Holy God, we praise, 1
  Jerusalem! my happy, 370
  O for a thousand, 104
  The bridegroom soon, 195
  O God, we praise Thee, 28
  The church's one, 375
  Dedication
  (See DEDICATION SERVICES)
  Lord's House, 390-393
  Lord, Thou shalt, 482
  Praise our Father, 498
  Unity of
  Scripture Readings, 692, 701, 708, 710
  All praise to our, 383
  Blest be the tie, 385
  By Christ redeemed, 409
  Christ is made, 373
  Come, let us join, 394
  Come, risen Lord, 403
  From every stormy, 331
  He wants not friends, 397
  Heart with loving, 386
  Here, O Lord, 377
  In Christ there is no, 387
  Jesus, from whom all, 372
  Jesus, with Thy church, 379
  Lo, what a pleasing, 382
  May the grace, 647
  The church's one, 375
  Worship of
  Across the sky, 511
  Blessed Jesus, 391
  Christ is our, 374
  Come, let us join, 501
  For the beauty, 58
  Here, O Lord, 377
  I love Thy kingdom, 380
  Jesus, stand among us, 624
  Jesus, where'er Thy, 381
  Let the words, 633
  Light of light, 486
  Lord of the worlds, 392
  O come, let us, 626
  O God, we praise Thee, 28
  O Word of God, 219
  Our Father, God, 384
  Pour out Thy Spirit, 388
  Shepherd of tender, 413
  Sing we the song, 368
  The Lord is in His, 620, 621
  To Thy temple, 390

CITY OF GOD
Scripture Readings, 713, 719
Dear Lord, who sought, 309
Judge eternal, 446
O God of mercy! 298
O holy city, 450
O Jesus Christ, 616
Where cross, 439

CLOSE OF WORSHIP,
502-507
(See also BENEDICTION)
Cast thy burden, 643
Christ, we do all, 644
God be in my head, 645

COMFORT
(See also Courage and Comfort, 333-342)

Scripture Readings, 657, 663, 677, 681, 682, 683, 711, 718, 719
All glory be to God, 38
Be still, my soul, 73
Come, gracious Spirit, 215
Comfort, comfort ye, 121
God is love, 71
How firm a foundation, 261
How lovely are Thy, 393
How sweet the name, 102
Jesus, still lead on, 319
Lord, Thy Word, 221
Love of the Father, 604
May the Holy Spirit's, 209
More love to Thee, 539
Now on land and sea, 492
O holy Savior, 263
Savior, again to Thy, 505
Sun of my soul, 491
The King of love, 65
'Tis the promise, 537
Under His wings, 575
When in the hour, 264
When morning gilds, 595

COMPASSION, DIVINE
Scripture Reading, 685

COMMUNION, HOLY
(See also The Lord's Supper, 400-409)
Scripture Readings, 699, 700, 703
Alas, and did my, 170
Blest be the tie, 385
Bread of the world, 607
Break Thou the bread, 222
Come, let us join, 394
Holy God, we praise, 1
I need Thee, 578
Immortal love, 150
In the cross, 169
Jesus, lover of my, 236, 237
Jesus, the very, 108
Jesus, Thou joy, 98
Just as I am, 235
Love divine, 75, 76
O holy Savior, 263
O Lamb of God, 173
Spirit of God, 217
The King of love, 65
The Lord my Shepherd, 66
The Lord's my Shepherd, 67
'Tis midnight, 161
When I survey, 165, 167
Ye servants of God, 100

COMMUNION OF SAINTS
(See CHURCH: Communion of Saints)

COMMUNION WITH CHRIST, 303-310
Scripture Readings, 699, 700, 701, 702, 703, 709, 710
As lives the flower, 568
Be known to us, 402
Blessed assurance, 544
Christ lay awhile, 611
Christ, of all my, 286
Come, risen Lord, 403
God of our strength, 533
Heart and mind, 362
I am Thine, O Lord, 581
I know not why, 586
I sought the Lord, 228
Immortal love, 150
I've found a friend, 542
Jesus, lover, 236, 237
Jesus, Thou Joy, 98
Jesus, where'er Thy, 381
Lift up your heads, 120

Lord, it belongs not, 371
Master, speak, 347
Nearer, still nearer, 579
O holy Savior, 263
O Jesus, I have, 343
O Master, let me walk, 440
The head that once, 189
Thou art the Way, 149
We praise Thee, O God, 527
When we walk, 577

CONFESSION
Scripture Readings, 670, 685, 686, 715, 716
Approach, my soul, 239
God, be merciful, 238
Lord, Thy mercy, 240
O God of earth, 457

CONFIDENCE
Scripture Readings, 663, 665

CONSCIENCE
At even, ere the sun, 494
Awake, my soul, 485
Help me to be holy, 580
O Master workman, 458
Sinners Jesus will, 550

CONSECRATION
  Of Children and Parents, 413-415
  Gracious Savior, 460
  Lord of the home, 462
  Personal
  (See also Obedience and Consecration, 343-358)
  Scripture Readings, 704, 710
  Alas, and did my, 170
  All things are Thine, 365
  Deck thyself with joy, 406
  Forth in Thy name, 430, 432
  God, whose giving, 363
  Grant us, Lord, 635
  Heart and mind, 362
  Help me to be holy, 580
  I am the Lord, O hear, 329
  I've found a friend, 542
  Lord Jesus, I long, 583
  Lord, Thou dost love, 361
  Praise our Father, 498
  Prince of Peace, 276
  Rise up, O men, 441
  Teach me Thy truth, 438
  Thy life was given, 557
  We give Thee but Thine, 364
  When I survey, 165, 167
  When we walk, 577

CORNERSTONE LAYING
Christ is made, 373
Christ is our, 374

COURAGE
(See also Courage and Comfort, 333-342)
Scripture Reading, 665
A mighty fortress, 325
Am I a soldier, 348
Come, come, ye saints, 312
Encamped along, 589
God of grace, 434
God moves, 80
He who would valiant, 323
Jesus Christ, my sure, 182
O Jesus Christ, 616
Strive aright, 328

COVENANT
Scripture Readings, 656, 676, 684, 686

CROSS
(See JESUS CHRIST: Cross of)

CROSS BEARING
Scripture Reading, 694
He who would follow, 344
I am the Lord, O hear, 329
Must Jesus bear, 345
O God, Thou faithful, 352
Take up thy cross, 357

DAY OF REST
(See also LORD'S DAY)
Scripture Reading, 655
Light of light, 486

DEATH
(See also Burial of the Dead, 416-418)
Scripture Readings, 706, 711, 714, 719
Abide with me, 495
Alleluia! The strife, 183
Christ lay awhile, 611
Christ the Lord, 179
Dayspring of eternity, 484
God be in my head, 645
Guide me, O Thou, 311
I will sing, 551
In the hour of trial, 324
Jesus Christ, my sure, 182
Jesus, Thy boundless, 266
Lift your glad voices, 175
Lord, dismiss us, 502
Low in the grave, 567
Majestic sweetness, 187
My Jesus, I love Thee, 265
Now is eternal life, 367
Rejoice, the Lord is, 184
Rock of ages, 254
Sing, my tongue, 404
Sing we the song, 368
The Lord's my Shepherd, 67
Thine is the glory, 180
This is the day, 500
This joyful Eastertide, 614
Thy way and all, 338
We would see Jesus, 303

DECISION FOR CHRIST
(See also Call of Christ, 225-232)
Beneath the cross, 171
Deck thyself with joy, 406
Father, I stretch, 256
He who would follow, 344
I hear Thy welcome, 549
Just as I am, 354
Just as I am, 235
Lord Jesus, I long, 583
My God, accept, 399
My Jesus, I love Thee, 265
Nearer, still nearer, 579
O happy day, 398
O Jesus, I have, 343
Stand up! stand up, 592
Thou didst leave, 563

DEDICATION SERVICES
  Church Building
  Scripture Reading, 671
  All things are Thine, 365
  Built on the Rock, 615
  Christ is made, 373
  Christ is our, 374
  Praise God from, 606

TOPICAL INDEX

Home
(See also Christian Home, 460-463)
God, whose giving, 363

DELIVERANCE
Scripture Readings, 656, 657, 667

DISCIPLESHIP
(See also Obedience and Consecration, 343-358)
Scripture Readings, 689, 690, 692, 693, 696, 700, 714
All my hope on God, 291
Art thou weary, 230
Blest are the pure, 279
Breathe on me, 216
Dear Lord and Father, 274
Draw Thou my soul, 307
Extol the love, 410
Gracious Savior, 460
He leadeth me, 543
How beauteous, 103
I am the Lord, O hear, 329
I lay my sins, 248
Jesus calls us, 229
Jesus Christ, my sure, 182
Lord, as to Thy dear, 451
Lord, I want to be, 293
My dear Redeemer, 147
New every morning, 483
Not always on the mount, 153
O brother man, fold, 435
O for a heart, 283
O happy day, 398
O Holy Spirit, enter, 208
O Master of the loving, 145
O young and fearless, 459
Purer in heart, O God, 280
Seek ye first, 200
So let our lips, 327
Strive aright, 328
Teach me, my God, 301
Teach me the measure, 315
Ye fair green hills, 146

DISCIPLINE
Scripture Readings, 692, 700

DOCTORS AND NURSES
God, whose giving, 363
Father, whose will, 422
Thou, Lord of life, 437

DOXOLOGIES
Awake, my soul, 485
Glory be to God, 632
Glory be to the Father, 640, 641, 642
Now to the King, 623
Praise God from, 638

DUTY
Scripture Reading, 656
Awake, my soul, 485
Forth in Thy name, 430, 432
Lord of the home, 462
Not always on the, 153
O Master workman, 458
Stand up! stand up, 592

EASTER
(See JESUS CHRIST: Resurrection)

EDUCATION, 442-445
Scripture Reading, 656

ENEMIES
Scripture Readings, 654, 665, 678, 696, 704

EPIPHANY, 139-143
Break forth, 609
Wise men seeking, 468

EVANGELISTIC HYMNS
(See GOSPEL SONGS, 527-594; INVITATION HYMNS)
Christ for the world, 424, 425
Go, labor on, 431
Heralds of Christ, 420
O Spirit of the living, 421

EVENING, 487-496

FAITH
(See also Faith and Assurance, 249-264)
Scripture Readings, 663, 665, 690, 698, 699, 705, 712, 713, 716
Come, O Thou Traveler, 322
Come with thy sins, 548
Encamped along, 589
Eternal One, 313
God of our life, 603
God moves, 80
Gracious Spirit, 270
I know not why, 586
I'm pressing on, 582
Jesus Christ, my sure, 182
Lead, kindly Light, 316
O day of God, 88
O Lord, within my soul, 590
Savior, Thy dying, 355
Sing, my tongue, 404
Strong Son of God, 442
Take Thou my hand, 318
'Tis the promise, 537

FAREWELL SERVICES
Forget them not, 427
God be with you, 503, 504
O Zion, haste, 428
The work is Thine, 426

FASTING
Scripture Reading, 689

FELLOWSHIP
(See BROTHERHOOD)

FOOT WASHING, 410-411

FORGIVENESS
(See also Repentance and Forgiveness, 233-248)
Scripture Readings, 666, 670, 676, 684, 686, 689, 710, 715
All praise to Thee, 496
Bless, O my soul, 72
Christ the Lord, 177
Comfort, comfort ye, 121
Great is Thy faithfulness, 534
Here, O my Lord, 405
I will sing, 554
In loving kindness, 547
Lord, as to Thy dear, 451
O my soul, bless thou, 531
Our Father who art, 627
Pour out Thy Spirit, 452
Praise waits for Thee, 82
The heavens declare, 220
The love of God, 538
To God be the glory, 532

FREEDOM—SPIRITUAL
Scripture Readings, 702, 703, 714

FUNERAL SERVICES
(See also Burial of the Dead, 416-418; Courage and Comfort, 333-342; RESURRECTION OF THE BODY)
Scripture Readings, 663, 669, 672
Above the trembling, 290
Be still, my soul, 73
For all the saints, 395
Jesus, still lead on, 319
Take Thou my hand, 318

GOD

Creator, as
(See also Creator of Heaven and Earth, 49-62)
Scripture Readings, 659, 661, 662, 664, 672, 674, 675, 678, 682
All people that, 2, 3
Almighty Maker, 369
Before Jehovah's awful, 48
Each little flower, 465
Father eternal, ruler, 447
How great Thou art, 535
I'll praise my Maker, 25
Love of the Father, 604
O Lord, our Lord, 47
Praise, O praise, 518

Deliverer, as
(See also GOD: Refuge, Our)
Scripture Readings, 654, 657, 669, 673, 678
A mighty fortress, 325
Abide with me, 495
From every stormy, 331
God is the refuge, 326
God the omnipotent, 86
My soul, awake, 17
Through all the changing scenes, 41

Divine Shepherd
Scripture Readings, 663, 674, 675, 681, 692, 718
All people that, 2, 3
Before Jehovah's awful, 48
Cry out with joy, 618
God be with you, 503, 504
I'll praise my Maker, 25
In heavenly love, 252
Jesus, joy of man's, 599
Jesus, where'er Thy, 381
Master, speak, 347
My Shepherd will, 63
Now may He, who, 506
O come, let us worship, 626
O Thou in whose, 273
Pour out Thy Spirit, 388
Praise Him, 530
Savior, like a shepherd, 572
Shepherd of souls, 320
The King of love, 65
The Lord my Shepherd is, 66
The Lord's my Shepherd, 67
There were ninety, 552

Eternal
Scripture Readings, 672, 682, 717

Faithfulness of
Scripture Readings, 685, 686, 695

Father, as
Scripture Reading, 676
All things are Thine, 365
Be Thou my vision, 300

Children of the heavenly Father, 335
Dear Lord and Father, 274
I love to think, 467
In Christ there is no, 387

Glory and Majesty of
Scripture Readings, 658, 661, 662, 663, 669, 681
Built on the Rock, 615
Come, O my soul, 53
Day is dying, 493
How great Thou art, 535
Lord of all being, 57
Now to the King, 623
O Lord, our Lord, 47
O splendor of God's, 44, 45

Hearer of Prayer
Scripture Reading, 666
Almighty Father, hear, 629
Be not dismayed, 574
Hear Thou our prayer, 630
I love the Lord, 617
I waited for the Lord, 302
Lord, Thou shalt early, 482
Lord, what a change, 299
Praise waits for Thee, 82

Helper in Trouble
Scripture Readings, 657, 663, 666, 669, 670, 673, 677
All glory be to God, 38
Be not dismayed, 574
God is my light, 85
God is my strong, 342
He leadeth me, 543
Judge me, God, 571
Praise our Father, 498
Unto the hills around, 257

Holiness of
Scripture Reading, 695
Cast thy burden, 643
God, the Lord, a King, 602
Holy, holy, holy, 5, 536, 622
Holy Lord, 24
The Lord is in, 620, 621

Justice of
(See also His Laws and Judgment, 86-88)
Scripture Readings, 655, 658, 667, 672, 676, 680, 685, 704
High in the heavens, 39
Judge eternal, throned, 446
Judge me, God, 571
O bless the Lord, 245
O my soul, bless thou, 531
There's a wideness, 78
To us a child, 125

Law of
(See also HOLY SCRIPTURES)
Scripture Readings, 655, 657, 660, 662, 687, 702
Lord of our life, 346
O Master workman, 458
Teach me, O Lord, 356
That man hath perfect, 278

Love of
(See also His Love and Mercy, 63-78)
Scripture Readings, 658, 668, 673, 675, 676, 678, 685, 692, 698, 701, 703, 716
Be not dismayed, 574
Come, let us all, 528
Come, O Thou Traveler, 322

TOPICAL INDEX

Come, Thou Fount, 310
Eternal Source, 275
Far, far away, 243
For God so loved us, 471
He wants not friends, 397
If thou but suffer God, 314
I look to Thee, 334
Immortal love, 150
Joyful, joyful, 13
Lord of our life, 346
Love of the Father, 604
May the grace, 647
My God, how endless, 18
O how shall I receive, 119
O love divine, 306
O love that casts, 287
O love that wilt not, 269
O perfect love, 412
O power of love, 106
Strong Son of God, 442
The love of God, 538
The sands of time, 292
'Tis winter now, 512
To God the only wise, 507
We plow the fields, 521

Majesty and Holiness of, 42-48

Mercy of
(See also His Love and Mercy, 63-78)
Scripture Readings, 662, 666, 670, 675, 676, 678, 684, 685, 686, 695, 696

All people that on, 2, 3
Approach, my soul, 239
Bread of the world, 607
Cast thy burden, 643
Come, every soul, 553
Depth of mercy, 233
Give to our God, 34
God of our life, 603
I love the Lord, 617
Lord, Thy mercy, 240
New every morning, 483
O bless the Lord, 245
O my soul, bless thou, 531
Out of the depths, 234
Praise, O praise, 518
Savior, like a shepherd, 572
Summer suns, 516
Thou to whom the sick, 151
We would extol Thee, 23

Power of
Scripture Readings, 654, 664, 682, 695

Glory be to God, 632
God the omnipotent, 86
Great God, we sing, 508
Hast thou not known, 81
Now to the King, 623
Soldiers of Christ, 330

Presence of
Scripture Readings, 663, 669, 672

Abide with me, 495
Another year, 510
Father, whate'er, 336
God be in my head, 645
God be with you, 503, 504
God is the refuge, 326
I look to Thee, 334
I sing the mighty, 50
Lord God of morning, 481
Lord, Thou hast, 79
O love divine, 306
O love that casts, 287
O Thou in whose, 273
Summer suns, 516
Sun of my soul, 491
Take Thou my hand, 318

Providence of
(See also His Providence and Care, 79-85)
Scripture Readings, 663, 665, 673, 676, 677, 681, 689, 690

A gladsome hymn, 464
All my hope on God, 291
All people that, 2, 3
Amazing grace, 242
Be not dismayed, 574
Be still, my soul, 73
Come, come, ye saints, 312
Come, my soul, 477
Come, ye thankful, 519
Glorious things, 376
God of our life, 603
God, the Lord, 55
Great God, we sing, 508
Great is Thy, 534
I look to Thee, 334
I'll praise my Maker, 25
Jehovah, let me now, 8
Lord of the worlds, 392
My Shepherd will, 63
O worship the King, 15
Our Father who art, 627
Praise the Lord, 61
Shepherd of souls, 320
Sing to the Lord, 520
Sometimes a light, 253
The Lord my Shepherd is, 66
We plow the fields, 521

Refuge, Our
Scripture Readings, 654, 665, 669, 672, 673

Children of the heavenly, 335
Come, let us all unite, 528
For all the saints, 395
Forget them not, 427
For Thy mercy, 509
Glorious things, 376
God of our strength, 533
He who would valiant, 323
High in the heavens, 39
How firm a foundation, 260, 261
I to the hills will, 258
Lord of our life, 456
O God, our help, 84
Praise to the Lord, 9
Rock of ages, 254
That day of wrath, 87
Under His wings, 575
When in the hour, 264

Unchangeableness of
Scripture Readings, 672, 677, 678, 681, 682

A gladsome hymn, 464
All people that, 2, 3
Cry out with joy, 618
Eternal One, 313
God is love, 71
God, the Lord, a King, 602
Great God, how infinite, 46
Great is Thy, 534
Hast thou not known, 81
If thou but suffer, 314
Immortal, invisible, 43
Now on land and sea, 492
O God, our help, 84
O God, the Rock, 42
The Lord is King, 89
The year is swiftly, 517
Unto the hills around, 257

Wisdom of
Scripture Readings, 659, 678

Be Thou my vision, 300
Give to the winds, 340
God is love, His mercy, 71
God the omnipotent, 86
Great God, how infinite, 46

Hast thou not known, 81
I sing the mighty, 50
Lord, Thou hast searched, 79
Lord, Thou hast, 619
O grant us light, 444
To God the only wise, 507

GOOD FRIDAY
(See JESUS CHRIST: Cross of; Sufferings of)

GRACE
Scripture Reading, 707

Amazing grace, 242
Bread of the world, 407
Come, Thou Fount, 310
Grace to you, 646
Jesus, from whom all, 372
Jesus, lover, 236, 237
Lord, I am fondly, 585
Marvelous grace, 541
May the grace, 647
My hope is built, 558
My God, accept my heart, 399
O praise ye the Lord, 596
Shepherd of souls, 320
Sinners Jesus will, 550
The love of God, 538
The year is swiftly, 517

GRADUATION
(See also EDUCATION; Obedience and Consecration, 343-358)
Soldiers of Christ, 330

GRATITUDE
(See also Harvest and Thanksgiving, 518-526; Love and Gratitude, 265-270)
Across the sky, 511
I owe the Lord, 479
The duteous day, 487

GUIDANCE
(See also Pilgrimage and Guidance, 311-320)
Scripture Readings, 663, 665, 666, 677

Across the sky, 511
All the way, 573
As with gladness, 142
Come, gracious Spirit, 215
Dear Lord, who sought, 309
From the eastern, 140
God of our life, 603
God of our strength, 533
He leadeth me, 543
I will sing, 551
Lamp of our feet, 223
Lead on, O King, 443
Lord Jesus, think, 246
O God of Bethel, 83
O Holy Spirit, 208
O Word of God, 219
Purer in heart, O God, 280
Send out Thy light, 631
Summer suns, 516
The heavens declare, 220
The Lord my Shepherd is, 66
Thy way, not mine, 341

HARVEST
(See also Harvest and Thanksgiving, 518-526)
God of the fertile, 360
Great is Thy, 534

HEALING
Scripture Readings, 665, 667, 673, 676, 682, 683, 719

At even, ere the sun, 494
Bread of heaven, 401
Faith is a living, 249
Father, we praise, 480
How sweet the name, 102
I lay my sins, 248
I will sing, 551
Immortal love, 150
Jesus, keep me near, 560
Jesus, Thy boundless, 266
O bless the Lord, 245
O Jesus Christ, 616
O Master of the loving, 145
O my soul, bless thou, 531
Sometimes a light, 253
There's a wideness, 78
Thine arm, O Lord, 152
Thou, Lord of life, 437
Thou to whom the sick, 151
Thou, whose almighty, 429

HEAVEN
(See also Burial of the Dead, 416-418; LIFE ETERNAL)
Scripture Reading, 663

Blest be the tie, 385
Come, gracious Spirit, 215
Come, we that love, 529
Come, ye disconsolate, 333
Come, ye thankful, 519
For all the saints, 395
Hail the day, 185
Hark, ten thousand, 201
Here, O my Lord, 405
Holy, holy, holy, 536
I will ever sing, 33
Lo, what a pleasing, 382
My Jesus, I love Thee, 265
My Shepherd will supply, 63
O could I speak, 99
O happy home, 463
O holy city, 450
On Jordan's stormy, 294
The bridegroom soon, 195
The sands of time, 292
Wake, awake, 118

HERITAGE
Eternal One, 313
Faith of our fathers, 262
We come unto our, 396

HOLY SCRIPTURES, 218-224
(See also BIBLE; His Laws and Judgment, 86-88)

HOLY SPIRIT, 205-217
Scripture Readings, 698, 702, 716

Blessed Jesus, 391
Create in me a clean, 628
Gracious Spirit, 270
I know not why, 586
I owe the Lord, 479
Jesus, stand among us, 624
Keep thyself pure, 281
Lamp of our feet, 223
May the grace, 647
O Lord of heaven, 523
The Lord is King, 89
We praise Thee, 527

HOLY WEEK
(See Passion, 157-173; Triumphal Entry, 154-156)

TOPICAL INDEX

HOME, CHRISTIAN,
460-463
Scripture Reading, 656
Jesus, friend so kind, 414
Once in royal David's, 466
'Tis winter now, 512

HOPE
(See also Hope and Aspiration, 284-295)
Scripture Readings, 668, 679, 685, 704, 705, 711
All the way, 573
Almighty Maker, 369
Be still, my soul, 73
Blest be the tie, 385
By Christ redeemed, 409
Christians, awake, 123
Father, whate'er, 336
God is working, 605
Gracious Spirit, 270
Great is Thy, 534
I am Thine, O Lord, 581
I'm pressing on, 582
In heavenly love, 252
Jesus, joy of man's, 599
Jesus, keep me near, 560
Jesus, Thy boundless, 266
Judge me, God, 571
Lead, kindly Light, 316
Lo! He comes, 192
Lord of our life, 456
Love divine, 75, 76
My hope is built, 558
Nearer, still nearer, 579
Now is eternal life, 367
So let our lips, 327
The Lord is King, 89

HOSPITALS
Scripture Reading, 693
Father, whose will, 422
Thou, Lord of life, 437

HUMILITY
Scripture Readings, 671, 688, 704, 708, 710
All creatures, 51, 52
Blest are the pure, 279
Come down, O Love, 210
Great God, how infinite, 46
How beauteous, 103
O Lord, our Lord, 47
Worship the Lord, 139

HYPOCRISY
Scripture Readings, 689, 715

INNER LIFE
(See also COMMUNION WITH CHRIST; HOLY SPIRIT)
Scripture Reading, 700
Abide, O dearest, 308
As lives the flower, 568
Blest are the pure, 279
Bread of heaven, 401
I heard the voice, 231, 232
If ye then with Christ, 564
Jesus, Thy boundless, 266
Lamp of our feet, 223
Light of light, 486
Lord, I want to be, 293
Nearer, my God, 289
Now is eternal life, 367
Prayer is the soul's, 297
Prince of Peace, 276
The glory of the spring, 513
Walk in the light, 282
We thank Thee, Lord, 526
Wise men seeking, 468

INSTALLATION SERVICES
(See Ministry—Pastors and Teachers, 388, 389; Obedience and Consecration, 343-358)

INSTRUCTION
Scripture Readings, 656, 666, 687

INTERNATIONAL RELATIONS
(See also PEACE AMONG MEN)
Father eternal, ruler, 447
In Christ there is no, 387
Long ago when Jesus, 469
Lord of light, 436
O Spirit of the living, 421
O young and fearless, 459

INVITATION HYMNS
(See also Call of Christ, 225-232)
Come, every soul, 553
Come with thy sins, 548
Depth of mercy, 233
I hear Thy welcome, 549
Just as I am, 235
Marvelous grace, 541
O have you not heard, 556
Thou didst leave, 563

JESUS CHRIST
Advent, 111-121
Scripture Readings, 664, 679, 680, 681, 695
Break forth, 609
Ascension, 184-191
Scripture Reading, 717
Birth, 122-138
Cross of
(See also Passion, 157-173)
Scripture Readings, 683, 694
According to Thy, 400
Approach, my soul, 239
Arise, my soul, arise, 244
Christ the Lord, 177
Christ, we do all, 644
How beauteous, 103
How great Thou art, 535
How shall I follow, 349
I am Thine, O Lord, 581
I will sing of my, 554
I will sing me, 551
Jesus, keep me near, 560
Lord Christ, when, 247
Lord of light, 436
Lord, Thou dost love, 361
Marvelous grace, 541
My God, my accept, 399
My Jesus, I love Thee, 265
O Lord, within my soul, 590
O love of God, 64
Onward, Christian, 591
Rock of ages, 254
Sing, my tongue, 404
Take up thy cross, 357
There is a green hill, 473
Thou didst leave Thy, 563
When peace, like a, 576
Incarnation
Scripture Readings, 695, 697, 708, 715
At even, ere the sun, 494
Break forth, 609
Christians, awake, 123
Ere the blue heavens, 19
Gracious Savior, 460
Hark! the herald, 135
How bright appears, 141
Jesus, Thou divine, 433
Let all mortal flesh, 117
Let all together, 136
Lo, how a rose, 131
My song is love, 172
Now praise we Christ, 598
O come, all ye, 132
O come, O come, 111
O how shall I receive, 119
Rise, glorious, 188
Sing, my tongue, 404
Son of God, eternal, 359
Strong Son of God, 442
Thou didst leave, 563
Intercession
Scripture Readings, 683, 701, 703, 715
Christ who left, 566
Glory be to God, 632
In the hour of trial, 324
Son of God, eternal, 359
The Savior died, 268
Kingdom of
(See also Reign and Kingdom, 198-204)
Scripture Readings, 679, 680, 693, 706, 717
All hail the power, 601
All praise to Him, 32
Angels from the realms, 128
Blessed Savior, 545
Christ is coming, 193
Christ is the world's, 198
Come, let us tune, 93
Come, Thou long-expected, 115
Crown Him with many, 191
Hail to the Lord's, 113
Hark, ten thousand, 201
He is coming, 569
Jesus shall reign, 203
Jesus, Thou mighty, 96
Joy to the world, 122
Lift up your heads, 120
Lo! He comes, 192
Look, ye saints, 186
Low in the grave, 567
Must Jesus bear, 345
Pour down Thy Spirit, 452
Rejoice, the Lord is, 184
Stand up! Stand up, 592
The first noel, 137
The King shall come, 196
This is my Father's, 49
Wake the song, 199
What child is this, 129
Ye servants of God, 100
Love of
Scripture Readings, 700, 703
Person and Work
(See also Life and Ministry, 144-153)
Scripture Readings, 683, 694, 699, 701, 703, 708, 713
A wonderful Savior, 546
At the name of Jesus, 94
Blessed Jesus, at Thy, 391
Dear Lord, who sought, 309
Hail to the Lord's, 113
Hark, the glad sound, 112
Here, O Lord, 377
How beauteous, 103
Jesus came, 197
Jesus, Thou joy, 98
Lo, how a rose, 131
Love divine, 75, 76
Majestic sweetness, 187
O come, O come, 111
O could I speak, 99
Of the Father's love, 92
O splendor of God's, 44, 45
Sinners Jesus will, 550
The Lord is risen, 176
There is a green hill, 473
What mercy and divine, 68
Wonderful Savior, 559
Praise and Glory, 89-110
Scripture Reading, 717
All glory, laud, 154
All hail the power, 601
Blessed Savior, 545
Brightest and best, 143
Christ, of all my, 286
Christ, we do all, 644
Crown Him with many, 191
Ere the blue heavens, 19
I heard a sound, 366
I sing with exultation, 40
I stand amazed, 108
Jesus, joy of man's, 599
Jesus, priceless, 600
Jesus shall reign, 203
Let all mortal flesh, 117
Man of sorrows, 561
Now praise we Christ, 598
O Christ, our hope, 288
O come, all ye, 132
O gladsome light, 489
O Savior, rend, 116
Praise Him, 530
Shepherd of tender, 413
Sing, my tongue, 404
When morning gilds, 595
Wonderful Savior, 559
Priesthood
Alas, and did my, 170
Arise, my soul, 244
Beneath the cross, 171
Christ lay awhile, 611
Christ, the like, 168
Christ who left His, 566
Cross of Jesus, 166
O Lamb of God, 173
O Thou who through, 157
Throned upon the awful, 162
'Tis midnight, 161
Resurrection, 174-183
Scripture Readings, 702, 706, 711
Christ is arisen, 612
Christ lay awhile, 611
Christ who left His, 566
Go to dark Gethsemane, 160
If ye then with Christ, 564
Jesus, stand among us, 624
Low in the grave, 567
O sons and daughters, 610
The Lord is risen, 613
This is the day, 499
This joyful Eastertide, 614
We welcome glad Easter, 474
Were you there, 164
Second Coming, 192-197
Scripture Readings, 693, 706, 711
At the name of Jesus, 94
By Christ redeemed, 409
Come, ye thankful, 519
Go, labor on, 431
Hark! ten thousand, 201
He is coming, the Man, 569
How great Thou art, 535

TOPICAL INDEX

I know not why God's, 586
I know that my, 565
It may be at morn, 570
Let all mortal flesh, 117
Man of sorrows, 561
My hope is built, 558
O how shall I receive, 119
O Savior, rend, 116
Praise Him, 530
Thou didst leave Thy, 563
Wake, awake, 118
Wake the song, 199
When peace, like a, 576

Sufferings of
(See also Passion, 157-173)

Scripture Readings, 683, 694

According to Thy, 400
Father, I stretch, 256
I stand amazed, 540
In loving kindness, 547
Lord Christ, when, 247
Man of sorrows, 561
Rise, glorious, 188
Sing, my tongue, 404
There were ninety, 552
Thy life was given, 557
We praise Thee, O God, 527

JOY
(See also Joy and Peace, 271-278)

Scripture Readings, 658, 666, 670, 671, 675, 679, 692, 695, 696, 700, 704, 709, 713, 715

All my heart, 124
All praise to our, 383
Angels we have heard, 127
Another year, 510
As with gladness, 142
Christ is arisen, 612
Christians, awake, 123
Come, come, ye saints, 312
Come, let us tune, 93
Come, Thou long-expected, 115
Come, we that love, 529
Come, ye faithful, 178
Create in me a clean, 628
Cry out with joy, 618
Dayspring of eternity, 484
Deck thyself with joy, 406
Eternal Source of joys, 275
From heaven above, 134
Glorious things, 376
God of our strength, 533
Hail to the brightness, 423
How lovely are Thy, 393
In the cross of Christ, 169
In Thee is gladness, 90
I stand amazed, 540
Jerusalem! My happy, 370
Jerusalem the golden, 416
Jesus, joy of man's, 599
Jesus, priceless, 600
Jesus, the very, 108
Jesus, Thou joy, 98
Joy to the world, 122
Joyful, joyful, 13
Lord, Thou shalt early, 482
Love divine, all loves, 75, 76
Majestic sweetness, 187
May the grace, 647
Nearer, my God, 289
O come, O come, 111
O happy day, 398
O how happy are they, 272
O love that wilt not, 269
Rejoice, the Lord is, 184
Rejoice, ye pure, 277

Teach me Thy truth, 438
The day of resurrection, 174
The glory of the spring, 513
There were ninety, 552
To God be the glory, 532
We welcome glad Easter, 474
When we walk, 577
While shepherds, 138

JUDGMENT
(See also His Laws and Judgment, 86-88)

Scripture Readings, 691, 693, 698, 716

Bless, O my soul, 72
Come, ye thankful, 519
God, who madest earth, 60
Judge eternal, 446
Lo! He comes, 192
Lord, bless and pity, 419
Lord Christ, when, 247
O wherefore do the, 202
That man hath perfect, 278
The Lord is King, 204
What mercy and divine, 68

JUSTICE
Scripture Reading, 688

KINGDOM OF GOD
(See also Reign and Kingdom, 198-204)

Scripture Readings, 690, 696, 698

A mighty fortress, 325
Father eternal, ruler, 447
God is my light, 85
God of the fertile, 360
God, the Lord, a King, 602
God, the omnipotent, 86
Hail to the brightness, 423
Holy, holy, holy, 536
I love Thy kingdom, 380
Lead on, O King, 443
Lord, dismiss us, 502
Lord of light, 436
Now to the King, 623
O where are kings, 378
Our Father who art, 627
The day Thou gavest, 488

KINGDOM OF HEAVEN
Scripture Reading, 691

KISS OF PEACE
All praise to our, 383

LABOR
Bless Thou the gifts, 634
Dear Lord, who sought, 309
Forth in Thy name, 430, 432
Go, labor on, 431
Gracious Savior, 460
Jesus, Thou divine, 433
Let there be light, 455
Lord of light, 436
New every morning, 483
O God, Thou faithful, 352
O happy home, 463
O Master workman, 458
Teach me, my God, 301
When morning gilds, 595

LAMB OF GOD
Scripture Readings, 683, 717, 718

LAWS OF GOD
Scripture Readings, 655, 684, 686

LENT
(See also JESUS CHRIST: Cross of; Sufferings of)
Forty days and forty, 144

LIFE ETERNAL, 366-371

Scripture Readings, 663, 693, 697, 698, 699, 701, 702, 712, 713, 715, 718, 719

Be known to us, 402
God of the earth, 54
God, the Lord, 55
Guide me, O Thou, 311
I know that my, 565
I will sing of my, 554
O Life in whom is life, 584
O Lord of life, 418
The duteous day, 487
Thy life was given, 557
We welcome glad Easter, 474

LIFE—TRANSIENCE OF
Scripture Readings, 660, 672, 676

All my hope on God, 291
Almighty Maker, 369
Great God, we sing, 508
Immortal, invisible, 43
Lord, it belongs not, 371
My faith looks up, 251
O God, our help, 84
O God, the Rock, 42
O wonderful, wonderful, 587
Strong Son of God, 442
Teach me the measure, 315
The year is swiftly, 517
We would see Jesus, 303

LIGHT
Scripture Readings, 665, 697, 698, 715, 719

Blessed Jesus, at Thy, 391
Christ, whose glory, 478
From the eastern, 140
God is my light, 85
God is my strong, 342
I am the Lord, O hear, 329
I heard the voice, 231, 232
In loving kindness, 547
Lead, kindly Light, 316
Let there be light, 455
Light of light, 486
Lord God of morning, 481
Lord of all being, 57
Lord of our life, 346
O gladsome light, 489
O grant us light, 444
O holy Savior, 263
O Life in whom is life, 584
O little town, 133
O Lord of love, 625
O love that wilt not, 269
O Word of God, 219
Send out Thy light, 631
Silent night, 130
Summer suns are, 516
The heavens declare, 220
This is the day of, 500
Thou, whose almighty, 429
Thy Word, O Lord, 218
Veiled in darkness, 114
Walk in the light, 282

LITANY
Scripture Reading, 678

LORD'S DAY, 497-501
Scripture Reading, 655
O sons and daughters, 610

LORD'S PRAYER
Scripture Reading, 689
Our Father who art, 627

LORD'S SUPPER
(See COMMUNION, HOLY)

LOVE
For God
Scripture Reading, 656

All my heart this, 124
Come, we that love, 529
Lord, should rising, 525
Love divine, all loves, 75, 76
O for a heart, 283
O Lord, within my soul, 590
O power of love, 106
For Man
Scripture Readings, 696, 704, 705, 708, 716

Above the trembling, 290
All creatures of our, 51, 52
Blest be the tie, 385
Dear Father, whom we, 453
Faith of our fathers, 262
Father, we thank Thee, 475
For the beauty, 58
Gracious Spirit, Holy, 270
Happy the home, 461
Hope of the world, 295
Joyful, joyful, 13
Love consecrates, 411
My God, I thank Thee, 267
O brother man, fold, 435
O God of mercy, 298
Thou to whom the sick, 151
Thou true vine, 304
Where cross the, 439

LOYALTY
Am I a soldier, 348
Lord, all my heart, 608
O grant us light, 444
Onward, Christian, 591
Peace in our time, 449

MAGNIFICAT
Scripture Reading, 695

MAN
Scripture Readings, 660, 661

MAN—HIS NEED FOR REDEMPTION
(See also Repentance and Forgiveness, 233-248)

Scripture Readings, 662, 664, 666, 670, 685, 702, 715

As lives the flower, 568
Help me to be holy, 580
I hear Thy welcome, 549
I love the Lord, 617
I will sing the, 551
Jesus, keep me near, 560
Marvelous grace, 541
O Spirit of the living, 421
Sinners Jesus will, 550
The sands of time, 292
There were ninety and, 552
What mercy and divine, 68

MARRIAGE HYMNS
(See also Marriage, 412)
Abide, O dearest Jesus, 308
Blessed Jesus, at Thy, 391

TOPICAL INDEX

God is love, His mercy, 71
Happy the home when, 461
If thou but suffer God, 314
Immortal love, 150
In heavenly love, 252
Jesus, joy of man's, 599
Love divine, all loves, 75, 76
Now thank we all, 31
O happy home, 463
O Holy Spirit, enter, 208
Praise to the Lord, 9
The King of love, 65
The Lord my Shepherd, 66
What God hath done, 77

MINISTRY

(See also Ministry—Pastors and Teachers, 388, 389)
Scripture Reading, 656
To Thy temple I repair, 390

MISSIONS

(See also Evangelism and Missions, 419-429)
Scripture Readings, 680, 701
God is working, 605
Spread, still spread, 224
Thou, Lord of life, 437
We have heard a joyful, 594

MORNING, 477-486

A gladsome hymn, 464
Holy, holy, holy, 5
When morning gilds, 107, 595

MOTHER

(See HOME—CHRISTIAN)

MUSIC—SINGING

Scripture Readings, 658, 674, 675, 695, 710, 717

NATION

(See also Christian Citizenship, 446-448)
Dear Father, whom we, 453
Lord, bless and pity, 419
O God of earth, 457
O young and fearless, 459
Thou true vine, 304

NATURE

Scripture Readings, 661, 662, 690
All creatures of our, 51, 52
Each little flower, 465
Fairest Lord Jesus, 97
For the beauty, 58
God of the earth, 54
God, the Lord, 55
Great is Thy, 534
Heaven and earth, 59
Holy, holy, holy, 536
How great Thou art, 535
I love to think that, 567
I sing the mighty, 50
Joyful, joyful, 13
Joy to the world, 122
My God, I thank Thee, 267
O that I had a thousand, 10
O worship the King, 15
Praise the Lord, 27
Praise to God, 524
The duteous day, 487
The glory of the, 513
The spacious firmament, 56

This is my Father's, 49
'Tis winter now, 512
With songs and honors, 515
We thank Thee, Lord, 526

NEW BIRTH

Scripture Readings, 697, 698, 702

NEW YEAR

(See Old and New Year, 508-511)

NONRESISTANCE

(See also Peace and Nonresistance, 449-456)
God of grace and God, 434
Heralds of Christ, 420
O brother man, fold, 435
O God, Thou faithful, 352

OBEDIENCE

(See also Obedience and Consecration, 343-358)
Scripture Readings, 655, 662, 693, 699, 702, 710, 714
Break Thou the bread, 222
Come, my soul, thou, 477
Dayspring of eternity, 484
God, who madest earth, 60
Jesus calls us, 229
Keep thyself pure, 281
Lord, Thou hast, 79
Love consecrates, 411
Master, speak, 347
May the Holy Spirit's, 209
Now may He, who from, 506
O day of God, 88
O how happy are they, 272
O splendor of God's, 44, 45
Once in royal David's, 466
Teach me, O Lord, 356
Thou, Lord of life, 437
When in the hour of, 264
When we walk with, 577
Worship the Lord, 139

OFFERING

(See also Stewardship, 359-365)
Scripture Readings, 658, 686, 689, 704, 707, 709, 712
All things come of, 636
Bless Thou the gifts, 634
Forth in Thy name, 430, 432
Grant us, Lord, 635
Take my life, 358
Thou, Lord of life, 437

OPENING OF WORSHIP

(See ADORATION AND PRAISE; CALL TO WORSHIP)

ORDINATION

(See Ministry—Pastors and Teachers, 388, 389)

PALM SUNDAY

(See also Triumphal Entry, 154-156)
O how shall I receive, 119

PARABLES

Scripture Readings, 691, 692

PARTING SONGS

(See CLOSE OF WORSHIP)

PATIENCE

Scripture Readings, 665, 685, 713
Above the trembling, 290
Be still, my soul, 73
By Christ redeemed, 409
Give to the winds, 340
I waited for the Lord, 302
It may be at morn, 570
Jesus, still lead on, 319
O Jesus, Thou art, 227
O Master, let me walk, 440
Rejoice, all ye, 194
Spirit of God, 217

PEACE—AMONG MEN

(See also Peace and Nonresistance, 449-456)
Scripture Readings, 669, 679, 680, 681, 687, 696, 704
Christ is the world's, 198
Christians, awake, 123
Glory be to God, 632
God is the refuge, 326
God of grace and God, 434
God the omnipotent, 86
Hail to the brightness, 423
Heralds of Christ, 420
Hope of the world, 295
I bind my heart, 353
It came upon the, 126
O brother man, fold, 435
O day of God, draw, 88
O grant us light, 444
To us a child of hope, 125
Veiled in darkness, 114

PEACE—INNER

(See also Joy and Peace, 271-278)
Scripture Readings, 663, 673,690,709,710
All praise to our, 383
All praise to Thee, 496
Christ has for sin, 562
Come unto Me, 226
Come, Ye faithful, 178
Deck thyself with joy, 406
Faith is a living, 249
Father, whate'er of, 336
Fierce raged the, 148
God is my strong, 342
Great is Thy, 534
Have faith in God, 255
Here, O my Lord, 405
Holy Spirit, truth, 207
I know not why God's, 586
In the cross of Christ, 169
Jesus, priceless, 600
Lead us, O Father, 317
O Lamb of God, 173
Savior, again to Thy, 505
This is the day, 500
What a friend we have, 337
When peace, like a, 576

PENITENCE

(See REPENTANCE)

PENTECOST

(See HOLY SPIRIT)

PERSECUTION

Scripture Readings, 696, 703, 704, 718

PERSEVERANCE

Scripture Readings, 706, 713, 714

PILGRIMAGE

(See also Pilgrimage and Guidance, 311-320)

God of our fathers, 448
He who would valiant, 323
How firm a foundation, 260
Lord, as to Thy dear, 451
Lord, dismiss us, 502
O God of Bethel, 83
O Word of God, 219
Our Father, God, 384
Rejoice, ye pure, 277
Sing we the song, 368
Summer suns are, 516
The Lord is King, 89
We would see Jesus, 303

PRAISE

(See ADORATION AND PRAISE)

PRAYER, 296-302

Scripture Readings, 662, 668, 671, 686, 689, 692, 694, 701, 709
Come, O Thou Traveler, 322
Come, ye disconsolate, 333
From every stormy, 331
I love to think, 467
Jesus, where'er Thy, 381
Thy way and all, 338
What a friend we have, 337
When morning gilds, 595

PROCESSIONAL HYMNS

All glory, laud, 154
As with gladness, 142
Christ the Lord, 179
Come, ye thankful, 519
For the beauty, 58
Glorious things, 376
God of our fathers, 448
Hail to the Lord's, 113
Holy, holy, holy, 5
How firm a foundation, 261
Joyful, joyful, 13
O come, all ye, 132
Onward, Christian, 591
Open now the gates, 6
Praise to the Lord, 9
Rejoice, ye pure, 277
Soldiers of Christ, 330
Stand up! stand up, 592

PROPHECY

Scripture Readings, 679, 680, 683, 689

PURITY

(See also Purity and Holiness, 279-283)
Scripture Reading, 714
Breathe on me, 216
Christ has for sin, 562
Come down, O Love, 210
Come, gracious Spirit, 215
Come, Holy Spirit, 214
Come, O come, 212
Create in me a clean, 628
Dear Lord and Father, 274
Help me to be holy, 580
Holy Spirit, truth, 207
I owe the Lord, 479
Jesus, from whom, 372
Lord, as to Thy dear, 451
Lord, I am fondly, 585
Lord, I want to be, 293
Lord Jesus, think, 246
Now the day is over, 490
O for a closer walk, 305
O Holy Spirit, enter, 208
O Life in whom is life, 584
O young and fearless, 459
Savior, again to Thy, 505
Thou true vine, 304

RACE RELATIONS

God, whose giving, 363

TOPICAL INDEX

In Christ there is no, 387
O brother man, fold, 435

RECESSIONAL HYMNS
For the beauty, 58
Glorious things, 376
God of grace and God, 434
Lead on, O King, 443
Lord, dismiss us, 502
Peace in our time, 449
Savior, again to Thy, 505

REDEMPTION
Scripture Readings, 654, 657, 676, 678, 683, 688, 702, 716, 717
All hail the power, 95, 601
All praise to Him, 32
Angels from the realms, 128
Arise, my soul, arise, 244
Awake, my soul, 110
Behold the glories, 109
Blessed Savior, 545
Bless, O my soul, 72
Christ, the life, 168
Christ the Lord, 179
Christ, we do all, 644
Come, let us all, 528
Come, let us join our, 394
Come, let us join, 501
Crown Him with many, 191
For God so loved us, 471
Glory to God on high, 101
Hark, the glad sound, 112
I know not why God's, 586
I will sing of my, 554
If ye then with Christ, 564
Joy to the world, 122
Let the words, 633
Lift your glad voices, 177
Lord, from the depths, 241
Man of sorrows, 561
My faith looks up, 251
Now may He, 506
O Christ, our hope, 288
O for a thousand, 104
O how happy are they, 272
Out of the depths, 234
Praise Him, 530
Prince of Peace, 276
Rejoice, all ye, 194
Savior, like a, 572
Silent night, 130
This body in the grave, 417
Thy life was given, 557
We praise Thee, O God, 12
Wonderful Savior, 559

REFORMATION DAY
A Mighty Fortress, 325

REPENTANCE
(See also Repentance and Forgiveness, 233-248)
Scripture Readings, 670, 686, 692
Bread of the world, 407, 607
Comfort, comfort ye, 121
Deck thyself with joy, 406
Nearer, still nearer, 579

RESPONSIBILITY
A charge to keep, 350, 351

RESURRECTION OF THE BODY
(See also JESUS CHRIST: Resurrection)
Scripture Readings, 699, 702, 706, 711
That day of wrath, 87

This body in the grave, 417
This joyful Eastertide, 614

REVIVAL
Teach me, O Lord, 356
We praise Thee, O God, 527

REWARD
Scripture Readings, 662, 681, 689, 693, 696, 713
Encamped along, 589
For Thy mercy, 509
Go, labor on, 431
Must Jesus bear, 345
Stand up! stand up, 592
Take up thy cross, 357

RICHES
Scripture Readings, 696, 712

RIGHTEOUSNESS
Scripture Readings, 657, 664, 680, 685, 686, 702, 703, 713

RURAL LIFE
God of the fertile, 360
We plow the fields, 521

SALVATION
Scripture Readings, 657, 658, 664, 665, 670, 673, 683, 698, 714, 715, 718
A wonderful Savior, 546
Ah, holy Jesus, 158
As lives the flower, 568
Christ for the world, 424, 425
Christ, the life, 168
Come, let us join, 105
Come, Thou Fount, 310
Create in me a clean, 628
Far, far away, 243
Glory to God on high, 101
God, be merciful, 238
God is my strong, 342
Gracious Spirit, 206
How bright appears, 141
I love the Lord, 617
I love to tell, 593
Jesus merciful, 339
Jesus, the very, 108
Judge me, God, 571
Lo! He comes, 192
Lord Christ, when, 247
Lord, dismiss us, 502
Lord, I am fondly, 585
Lord, Thy Word, 221
My song is love, 172
O Lord of heaven, 523
O Lord, within my soul, 590
O praise ye the Lord, 596
Rock of ages, 254
There is a green hill, 473
There were ninety, 552
This is the day, 499
Thy life was given, 557
'Tis the promise, 537
What child is this, 129
While shepherds, 138

SCHOOLS AND COLLEGES
(See also EDUCATION)
Eternal One, 313

SERVICE
(See also Service and Witness, 430-441)
Scripture Readings, 656, 675, 693, 704

A charge to keep, 350, 351
Another year, 510
Extol the love, 410
Father, whose will, 422
God, whose giving, 363
Hope of the world, 295
I bind my heart, 353
Jesus, with Thy church, 379
Just as I am, 354
Lead on, O King, 443
Lord God of morning, 481
Lord, speak to me, 389
O God of mercy, 298
O Jesus Christ, 616
Savior, Thy dying, 355
Son of God, eternal, 359
Take my life, 358
The work is Thine, 426
We give Thee but Thine, 364
Would you be free, 555

SHEPHERD, THE DIVINE
(See GOD: Divine Shepherd)

SICK, FOR THE
Scripture Readings, 663, 665, 667
O love divine, 306

SIN
(See MAN—HIS NEED FOR REDEMPTION)
Scripture Readings, 662, 666, 670, 672, 702, 710, 714, 715, 716

SORROW
(See also Courage and Comfort, 333-342)
As the hart, 284
Be still, my soul, 73
How firm a foundation, 260, 261
I lay my sins on Jesus, 248
My faith looks up, 251
O God of mercy, 298

SPIRIT
(See HOLY SPIRIT)

SPIRITUALS
Lord, I want to be, 293
Were you there, 164
What wondrous love, 163

SPRING
(See also The Seasons, 512-517)
Come, ye faithful, 178'
Great is Thy, 534
Praise to God, 524

STEWARDSHIP, 359-365
Scripture Readings, 707, 709, 712

SUBMISSION
Scripture Readings, 663, 669, 689, 694
Blessed assurance, 544
He leadeth me, 543
If thou but suffer, 314
O love that wilt not, 269
Thy way, not mine, 341

SUFFERING
Scripture Readings, 663, 666, 696, 703
All creatures of our, 51, 52
How shall I follow, 349

O love divine, 306
Thy way, not mine, 341
Where cross, 439

SUMMER
(See also The Seasons, 512-517)
Great is Thy, 534

SUNDAY
(See LORD'S DAY)

TABLE GRACES
Be present, 639
Great God, Thou Giver, 637

TEACHERS
(See also Ministry—Pastors and Teachers, 388, 389)
Scripture Readings, 656, 659, 698, 710
God, whose giving, 363
Jesus, friend so kind, 414
Shepherd of tender, 413

TEACHING OF CHRIST
Scripture Readings, 689, 690, 691, 692, 693, 696, 698, 699, 700

TEMPTATION
Scripture Readings, 689, 712, 714
Abide with me, 495
At the name of Jesus, 94
Come, O come, 212
Forty days and forty, 144
Hope of the world, 295
I need Thee every hour, 578
If ye then with Christ, 564
In the hour of trial, 324
Keep thyself pure, 281
My soul, be on thy, 321
O Jesus, I have promised, 343
Our Father who art, 627
Sweet hour of prayer, 296

TEN COMMANDMENTS
Scripture Reading, 655

THANKSGIVING
Scripture Readings, 658, 674, 675, 676, 678, 706, 707, 709, 710
For the beauty, 58
My God, I thank Thee, 267
Now may He, who from, 506
Now thank we all, 31
O praise ye the Lord, 596
Ye servants of God, 100

TRAVELERS
(See PILGRIMAGE)
Scripture Reading, 677

TRIALS
Scripture Readings, 694, 696, 714

TRINITY
Scripture Reading, 701
All creatures, 51, 52
All glory be to God, 38
All praise to Thee, 496
Awake, my soul, 485
Christ is made, 219
Come, Holy Spirit, 214
Come, O Creator, 211
Come, Thou Almighty, 4

TOPICAL INDEX

Cry out with joy, 618
Eternal Father, 37
Father, we praise, 480
Glory be to God, 632
Glory be to the Father, 640, 641, 642
Holy, holy, holy, 5
Holy God, we praise, 1
Jehovah, let me now, 8
Jesus, with Thy church, 379
Jerusalem the golden, 416
Joy dawned again, 181
Lift up your heads, 120
Lord Jesus Christ, 91
My God, accept my, 399
Now praise we Christ, 598
O Christ, our hope, 288
O gladsome light, 489
O love that casts out, 287
O perfect love, 412
Of the Father's love, 92
Praise God from whom, 638
Praise, O praise, 518
Rejoice, ye pure, 277
Sing, my tongue, 404
The God of Abraham, 11
Thou, whose almighty, 429

TRUST

Scripture Readings, 663, 665, 666, 669, 671, 673, 682, 690

All the way my Savior, 573
As pants the hart, 285
As the hart, 284
Be not dismayed, 574
Be still, my soul, 73
Come, come, ye saints, 312
Father, whate'er, 336
God is my light, 85
God moves, 80
God of our life, 603
Great God, we sing, 508
How lovely are Thy, 393
If thou but suffer, 314
I love Thy kingdom, 380
I waited for the Lord, 302
Jesus, keep me near, 560
Lord, all my heart, 608
Lord of the worlds, 392
My hope is built, 558
O God of love, O King, 454
O Lord of life, 418
Peace, perfect peace, 271
Take Thou my hand, 318
Teach me the measure, 315
Thy way, not mine, 341
What God hath done, 77
When we walk, 577

TRUTH

Scripture Readings, 670, 701

Before Jehovah's aweful, 48
Eternal One, 313
God the omnipotent, 86
I love Thy kingdom, 380
Lead us, O Father, 317
O wonderful, wonderful, 587
O Word of God, 219
Send out Thy light, 631
Teach me Thy truth, 438
The heavens declare, 220

UNITY

(See CHURCH: Unity of)

VICTORY

(See also Conflict and Victory, 321-332)
Scripture Readings, 659, 669, 673, 703, 706, 717

A safe stronghold, 597
Alleluia! the strife, 183
Am I a soldier, 348
Awake, my soul, 110
Christ has for sin, 562
Christ is arisen, 612
Encamped along, 589
For all the saints, 395
Forty days and forty, 144
God is working, 605
Hail the day, 185
Heart and mind, 362
I will sing, 554
If ye then with Christ, 564
Jerusalem the golden, 416
Lead on, O King, 443
Look, ye saints, 186
Low in the grave, 567
O where are kings, 378
Onward, Christian, 591
Peace, perfect peace, 271
Ride on, ride on, 156
Rise, glorious, 188
Sing, my tongue, 404
Stand up, stand up, 592
The day of resurrection, 174
The head that once, 189
The Savior died, 268
Thine is the glory, 180
This is the day, 499
Wake the song, 199
We have heard a joyful, 594
We welcome glad Easter, 474

VISION

Be Thou my vision, 300
God of our life, 603
Not always, 153
O holy city, 450

WAITING FOR GOD

Scripture Readings, 665, 682, 685

WALKING WITH GOD

Scripture Readings, 663, 677, 715

Come, we that love, 529
Forth in Thy name, 430, 432
I love the Lord, 617
In heavenly love, 252
O for a closer walk, 305
O happy day, 398
O Master, let me walk, 440
So let our lips, 327
The Lord's my Shepherd, 67
To Thy temple I repair, 390
Walk in the light, 282
When we walk, 577

WARNING

Scripture Readings, 655, 662

A charge to keep, 350, 351
Come with thy sins, 548
O wherefore do, 202
The Lord is King, 204
This body in the grave, 417

WATCHFULNESS

Scripture Reading, 694

A charge to keep, 350, 351
Am I a soldier, 348
Awake, my soul, 485
It may be at morn, 570
My soul, be on thy, 321
Rejoice, all ye, 194
The bridegroom soon, 195
Wake, awake, for night, 118

WATCH-NIGHT HYMNS

(See also Old and New Year, 508-511)
God is working, 605

WEDDING HYMNS

(See MARRIAGE HYMNS)

WHIT SUNDAY

(See HOLY SPIRIT)

WINTER

Great is Thy, 534
'Tis winter now, 512

WISDOM

Scripture Reading, 659

WITNESSING

(See also Evangelism and Missions, 419-429)

Scripture Readings, 670, 691, 697, 712, 716
Faith of our fathers, 262
Heart with loving, 386
I love to tell, 593
Jesus, from whom all, 372
Lord, speak to me, 389
O Master of the loving, 145
Savior, Thy dying, 355
Spread, still spread, 224
Take my life, 358

WORD OF GOD

(See BIBLE)
Scripture Readings, 655, 681, 686, 697, 713, 714

WORLD FRIENDSHIP AND PEACE

(See also PEACE—AMONG MEN)
Hope of the world, 295

WORSHIP AND PRAISE

Scripture Readings, 658, 664, 665, 671, 674, 675, 688, 689, 692, 708, 717, 718, 719

YOUTH, HYMNS FOR

All creatures, 51, 52
All hail the power, 95
Away in a manger, 472
Be Thou my vision, 300
Come, Thou Almighty, 4
Day is dying, 493
Dear Lord and Father, 274
Fairest Lord Jesus, 97
Faith of our fathers, 262
Hark! the herald, 135
Heralds of Christ, 420
Holy, holy, holy, 5
How firm a foundation, 260
In the cross of Christ, 169
Jesus shall reign, 203
Joyful, joyful, 13
Joy to the world, 122
Just as I am, 354
O little town, 133
O young and fearless, 459
Rejoice, ye pure, 277
The church's one, 375
This is my Father's, 49
When morning gilds, 107

ZEAL

A charge to keep, 350, 351
Awake, my soul, 332
Christ, of all my, 286
Jesus merciful, 339
My soul, be on thy, 321
O God, Thou faithful, 352
Rise up, O men of God, 441
Strive aright, 328

Index of First Lines

A charge to keep I have............ 350
A charge to keep I have............ 351
A gladsome hymn of praise......... 464
A mighty fortress is our God....... 325
A safe stronghold our God is still... 597
A wonderful Savior is Jesus........ 546
Abide, O dearest Jesus............ 308
Abide with me 495
Above the trembling elements..... 290
According to Thy gracious Word... 400
Across the sky the shades......... 511
Ah, holy Jesus 158
Alas! and did my Savior bleed..... 170
All creatures of our God and King.. 51
All creatures of our God and King.. 52
All glory be to God on high........ 38
All glory, laud, and honor......... 154
All hail the power of Jesus' name... 95
All hail the power of Jesus' name... 601
All my heart this night rejoices.... 124
All my hope on God is founded.... 291
All people that on earth do dwell... 2
All people that on earth do dwell... 3
All praise to Him who reigns above. 32
All praise to our redeeming Lord... 383
All praise to Thee, my God........ 496
All the way my Savior leads me.... 573
All things are Thine.............. 365
All things come of Thee........... 636
Alleluia! the strife is o'er......... 183
Almighty Father, hear our prayer. 629
Almighty Maker of my frame..... 369
Am I a soldier of the cross........ 348
Amazing grace! how sweet........ 242
Amens 648-653
Angels from the realms of glory.. 128
Angels holy, high and lowly....... 30
Angels we have heard on high..... 127
Another year is dawning.......... 510
Approach, my soul, the mercy seat.. 239
Arise, my soul, arise.............. 244
Art thou weary, art thou languid... 230
As lives the flower within the seed.. 568
As pants the hart................. 285
As the hart with eager yearning... 284
As with gladness men of old....... 142
At even, ere the sun was set....... 494
At the name of Jesus.............. 94
Awake, my soul, and with the sun.. 485
Awake, my soul, awake my tongue.. 69

Awake, my soul, in joyful lays..... 110
Awake, my soul, stretch every nerve 332
Away in a manger................ 472

Be known to us in breaking bread.. 402
Be not dismayed whate'er betide... 574
Be present at our table, Lord...... 639
Be still, my soul.................. 73
Be Thou my vision............... 300
Before Jehovah's awful throne.. 48
Behold the glories of the Lamb.... 109
Beneath the cross of Jesus........ 171
Bless, O my soul, the living God.... 72
Bless Thou the gifts.............. 634
Blessed assurance 544
Blessed Jesus, at Thy word...... 391
Blessed Savior, we adore Thee..... 545
Blest are the pure in heart........ 279
Blest be the tie that binds........ 385
Bread of heaven! on Thee we feed. 401
Bread of the world............... 607
Bread of the world in mercy...... 407
Break forth, O beauteous
  heavenly light 609
Break Thou the bread of life...... 222
Breathe on me, Breath of God..... 216
Brightest and best............... 143
Built on the Rock................ 615
By Christ redeemed.............. 409

Cast thy burden upon the Lord..... 643
Children of the heavenly Father... 335
Christ for the world we sing....... 424
Christ for the world we sing....... 425
Christ has for sin atonement made. 562
Christ is arisen 612
Christ is coming! let creation...... 193
Christ is made the sure foundation. 373
Christ is our cornerstone......... 374
Christ is the world's true light..... 198
Christ lay awhile in death's
  strong bands 611
Christ of all my hopes............ 286
Christ, the life of all the living..... 168
Christ the Lord is risen again..... 177
Christ the Lord is risen today..... 179
Christ, we do all adore Thee....... 644
Christ who left His home in glory.. 566
Christ, whose glory fills the skies... 478
Christians, awake 123

INDEX OF FIRST LINES

Come, come, ye saints	312
Come down, O Love divine	210
Come, every soul by sin oppressed	553
Come, gracious Spirit	215
Come, Holy Spirit, come	214
Come, let us all unite	528
Come, let us join	105
Come, let us join our friends	394
Come, let us join with one accord	501
Come, let us tune our loftiest song	93
Come, my soul, thou must be	477
Come, my Way, my Truth, my Life	445
Come, O come, Thou quickening Spirit	212
Come, O Creator Spirit, come	211
Come, O my soul, in sacred lays	53
Come, O Thou Traveler unknown	322
Come, risen Lord, and deign	403
Come, Thou Almighty King	4
Come, Thou Fount	310
Come, Thou long-expected Jesus	115
Come to the Savior now	225
Come unto Me, ye weary	226
Come, we that love the Lord	529
Come with thy sins	548
Come, ye disconsolate	333
Come, ye faithful, raise the strain	178
Come, ye thankful people, come	519
Comfort, comfort ye My people	121
Create in me a clean heart	628
Cross of Jesus, cross of sorrow	166
Crown Him with many crowns	191
Cry out with joy	618
Day is dying in the west	493
Dayspring of eternity	484
Dear Father, whom we cannot see	453
Dear Lord and Father of mankind	274
Dear Lord, who sought at dawn	309
Deck thyself with joy	406
Depth of mercy	233
Draw Thou my soul, O Christ	307
Each little flower that opens	465
Ein' feste Burg ist unser Gott	597
Encamped along the hills	589
Ere the blue heavens	19
Eternal Father, when to Thee	37
Eternal One, Thou living God	313
Eternal Source of joys divine	275
Extol the love of Christ	410
Fairest Lord Jesus	97
Faith is a living power	249
Faith of our fathers	262
Far, far away	243
Father eternal, ruler of creation	447
Father, I stretch my hands to Thee	256
Father, we praise Thee	480
Father, we thank Thee for the night	475
Father, whate'er of earthly bliss	336
Father, whose will is life and good	422
Fierce raged the tempest	148
For all the saints	395
For God so loved us	471
For the beauty of the earth	58
For Thy mercy and Thy grace	509
Forget them not, O Christ	427
Forth in Thy name	430
Forth in Thy name	432
Forty days and forty nights	144
From all that dwell below	36
From every stormy wind	331
From heaven above to earth	134
From the eastern mountains	140
Give to our God immortal praise	34
Give to the winds thy fears	340
Glorious things of thee are spoken	376
Glory be to God on high	632
Glory be to the Father	640
Glory be to the Father	641
Glory be to the Father	642
Glory to God on high	101
Go, labor on	431
Go to dark Gethsemane	160
God be in my head	645
God, be merciful to me	238
God be with you till we meet	503
God be with you till we meet	504
God Himself is with us	7
God is love, His mercy brightens	71
God is my light	85
God is my strong salvation	342
God is the refuge of His saints	326
God is working His purpose out	605
God moves in a mysterious way	80
God my Father, loving me	476
God of grace and God of glory	434
God of our fathers	448
God of our life	603
God of our strength	533
God of the earth, the sky, the sea	54
God of the fertile fields	360
God, the Lord, a King remaineth	602
God the Lord omnipotent	55
God the omnipotent	86
God who madest earth and heaven	60
God, whose giving	363
Grace to you and peace	646

INDEX OF FIRST LINES

Gracious Savior, who didst honor	460
Gracious Spirit, Holy Ghost	270
Gracious Spirit! Love divine	206
Grant us, Lord, the grace of giving	635
Great God, how infinite art Thou	46
Great God, indulge my humble claim	35
Great God, Thou Giver of all	637
Great God, we sing that mighty	508
Great is Thy faithfulness	534
Guide me, O Thou great Jehovah	311
Hail the day that sees Him rise	185
Hail to the brightness	423
Hail to the Lord's anointed	113
Happy the home when God	461
Hark! ten thousand harps	201
Hark, the glad sound	112
Hark! the herald angels sing	135
Hast thou not known	81
Have faith in God, my heart	255
He is coming, the Man of sorrows	569
He leadeth me, O blessed thought	543
He wants not friends	397
He who would follow Christ	344
He who would valiant be	323
Hear Thou our prayer	630
Heart and mind, possessions, Lord	362
Heart with loving heart united	386
Heaven and earth, the sea and air	59
Help me to be holy	580
Heralds of Christ	420
Here, O Lord, Thy servants gather	377
Here, O my Lord, I see Thee	405
High in the heavens, Eternal God	39
Holy God, we praise Thy name	1
Holy, holy, holy is the Lord	536
Holy, holy, holy, Lord God Almighty	5
Holy, holy, holy, Lord God of hosts	622
Holy Lord, holy Lord	24
Holy Spirit, truth divine	207
Hope of the world	295
Hosanna, loud hosanna	155
How beauteous were the marks	103
How bright appears the morning star	141
How firm a foundation	260
How firm a foundation	261
How great Thou art	535
How lovely are Thy dwellings fair	393
How shall I follow Him	349
How sweet the name of Jesus	102
I am the Lord, O hear	329
I am Thine, O Lord	581
I bind my heart this tide	353
I hear Thy welcome voice	549
I heard a sound of voices	366
I heard the voice of Jesus	231
I heard the voice of Jesus	232
I know not why God's wondrous	586
I know that my Redeemer liveth	565
I lay my sins on Jesus	248
I look to Thee in every need	334
I love the Lord	617
I love Thy Kingdom, Lord	380
I love to tell the story	593
I love to think that Jesus saw	467
I need Thee every hour	578
I owe the Lord a morning song	479
I sing the mighty power of God	50
I sing with exultation	40
I sought the Lord	228
I stand amazed in the presence	540
I to the hills will lift mine eyes	258
I waited for the Lord my God	302
I will ever sing Thy praises	33
I will sing of my Redeemer	554
I will sing the wondrous story	551
If thou but suffer God to guide	314
If ye then with Christ be risen	564
I'll praise my Maker	25
I'm pressing on the upward way	582
Immortal, invisible, God	43
Immortal love, forever full	150
In Christ there is no East or West	387
In heavenly love abiding	252
In loving kindness Jesus came	547
In the cross of Christ I glory	169
In the hour of trial	324
In the land of strangers	588
In Thee is gladness	90
It came upon the midnight clear	126
It may be at morn	570
I've found a friend	542
Jehovah, let me now adore Thee	8
Jerusalem! my happy home	370
Jerusalem the golden	416
Jesus calls us	229
Jesus came, the heavens adoring	197
Jesus Christ, my sure defense	182
Jesus, friend, so kind	414
Jesus, from whom all blessings flow	372
Jesus, joy of man's desiring	599
Jesus, keep me near the cross	560
Jesus, lover of my soul	236
Jesus, lover of my soul	237
Jesus merciful	339
Jesus, priceless treasure	600
Jesus shall reign where'er the sun	203

INDEX OF FIRST LINES

Jesus, stand among us. 624
Jesus, still lead on 319
Jesus, the very thought of Thee. . . . 108
Jesus, Thou divine companion. 433
Jesus, Thou joy of loving hearts. . . 98
Jesus, Thou mighty Lord. 96
Jesus, Thy boundless love to me. . . . 266
Jesus, where'er Thy people meet . . . 381
Jesus, with Thy church abide. 379
Joy dawned again on Easter day. . . 181
Joy to the world. 122
Joyful, joyful, we adore Thee. 13
Judge eternal, thronged 446
Judge me, God of my salvation. 571
Just as I am, Thine own to be. 354
Just as I am, without one plea 235

Keep thyself pure. 281
Kindly spring again is here. 514

Lamp of our feet 223
Lead, kindly Light. 316
Lead on, O King eternal 443
Lead us, O Father, in the paths. . . . 317
Let all mortal flesh keep silence. . . . 117
Let all the world. 22
Let all together praise our God. 136
Let the whole creation cry 62
Let the words of my mouth. 633
Let there be light. 455
Let us with a gladsome mind 70
Lift up your heads, ye mighty gates 120
Lift your glad voices. 175
Light of light, enlighten me. 486
Lo! He comes 192
Lo, how a rose e'er blooming. 131
Lo, what a pleasing sight 382
Look, ye saints 186
Long ago when Jesus. 469
Lord, all my heart is fixed on Thee. . 608
Lord, as to Thy dear cross we flee. . . 451
Lord, bless and pity us. 419
Lord Christ, when first Thou cam'st 247
Lord, dismiss us with Thy blessing. 502
Lord, from the depths to Thee 241
Lord God of morning. 481
Lord, I am fondly, earnestly. 585
Lord, I want to be a Christian 293
Lord, it belongs not to my care. 371
Lord Jesus Christ, be present now. . 91
Lord Jesus, I long. 583
Lord Jesus, think on me 246
Lord of all being, throned afar. 57
Lord of light, whose name. 436
Lord of our life, and God. 456

Lord of our life. 346
Lord of the home. 462
Lord of the worlds above. 392
Lord, should rising whirlwinds 525
Lord, speak to me. 389
Lord, Thou dost love the cheerful giver 361
Lord, Thou hast searched and seen . 79
Lord, Thou hast searched me. 619
Lord, Thou shalt early hear 482
Lord, Thy mercy now entreating. . . 240
Lord, Thy Word abideth. 221
Lord, what a change within us. 299
Lord, who can be with Thee compared 26
Love consecrates the humblest act. . 411
Love divine, all loves excelling. 75
Love divine, all loves excelling. 76
Love of the Father. 604
Low in the grave He lay. 567

Majestic sweetness sits enthroned. . 187
Man of Sorrows, what a name. 561
Marvelous grace of our loving Lord. 541
Master, speak! Thy servant heareth 347
May the grace of Christ our Savior. 647
May the Holy Spirit's sword. 209
More love to Thee, O Christ. 539
Must Jesus bear the cross alone. . . . 345
My dear Redeemer and my Lord . . . 147
My faith looks up to Thee. 251
My God, accept my heart. 399
My God, how endless is Thy love . . . 18
My God, I thank Thee 267
My hope is built on nothing less. . . . 558
My Jesus, I love Thee. 265
My Shepherd will supply my need. . 63
My song is love unknown. 172
My soul, awake and render. 17
My soul, be on thy guard. 321

Nearer, my God, to Thee. 289
Nearer, still nearer 579
New every morning is Thy love. . . . 483
Not always on the mount. 153
Now is eternal life. 367
Now may He who from the dead . . . 506
Now on land and sea descending. . . 492
Now praise we Christ 598
Now thank we all our God. 31
Now the day is over. 490
Now to the King of heaven. 623

O bless the Lord, my soul. 245
O brother man, fold to thy heart. . . 435

INDEX OF FIRST LINES

O Christ, our hope	288
O come, all ye children	470
O come, all ye faithful	132
O come, let us worship	626
O come, loud anthems let us sing	14
O come, O come, Emmanuel	111
O could I speak	99
O day of God, draw nigh	88
O day of sacred rest	497
O for a closer walk with God	305
O for a faith that will not shrink	259
O for a heart to praise	283
O for a thousand tongues	104
O gladsome light, O grace	489
O God of Bethel	83
O God of earth and altar	457
O God of love, O King of peace	454
O God of mercy! hearken now	298
O God, our help in ages past	84
O God, the Rock of Ages	42
O God, Thou faithful God	352
O God, we praise Thee	28
O grant us light	444
O happy day, that fixed my choice	398
O happy home where Thou art	463
O have you not heard	556
O holy city, seen of John	450
O holy Savior, friend unseen	263
O Holy Spirit, enter in	208
O how happy are they	272
O how shall I receive Thee	119
O Jesus Christ, our Lord most dear	415
O Jesus Christ, to Thee may hymns	616
O Jesus, I have promised	343
O Jesus, Thou art standing	227
O Lamb of God all holy	173
O Life in whom is life indeed	584
O little town of Bethlehem	133
O Lord my God	535
O Lord of heaven and earth	523
O Lord of life, where'er they be	418
O Lord of love, Thou Light divine	625
O Lord, our Lord, in all the earth	47
O Lord, within my soul	590
O love divine	306
O love of God, how strong	64
O love that casts out fear	287
O love that wilt not let me go	269
O Master, let we walk with Thee	440
O Master of the loving heart	145
O Master workman of the race	458
O my soul, bless thou Jehovah	531
O perfect love	412
O power of love	106
O praise ye the Lord	596
O sacred Head, now wounded	159
O Savior, rend the heavens wide	116
O sons and daughters, let us sing	610
O Spirit of Life	205
O Spirit of the living God	421
O Splendor of God's glory	44
O Splendor of God's glory	45
O that I had a thousand voices	10
O Thou, in whose presence	273
O Thou, who through this holy week	157
O where are kings and empires now	378
O wherefore do the nations rage	202
O wonderful, wonderful Word	587
O Word of God incarnate	219
O worship the King	15
O young and fearless Prophet	459
O Zion, haste	428
Of the Father's love begotten	92
On Jordan's stormy banks	294
Once in royal David's city	466
Onward, Christian soldiers	591
Open now Thy gates of beauty	6
Our Father God, Thy name we praise	384
Our Father who art in heaven	627
Out of the depths I cry to Thee	234
Peace in our time, O Lord	449
Peace, perfect peace	271
Pour down Thy Spirit	452
Pour out Thy Spirit from on high	388
Praise God from whom	606
Praise God from whom	638
Praise Him! praise Him!	530
Praise, my soul, the King of heaven	16
Praise, O praise our God and King	518
Praise our Father for this Sunday	498
Praise the Lord, His glories show	61
Praise the Lord, ye heavens	27
Praise thou the Lord, O my soul	20
Praise to God, immortal praise	524
Praise to the Lord, the Almighty	9
Praise waits for Thee in Zion	82
Prayer is the soul's sincere desire	297
Prince of Peace, control my will	276
Purer in heart, O God	280
Rejoice, all ye believers	194
Rejoice, the Lord is King	184
Rejoice, ye pure in heart	277
Ride on, ride on in majesty	156
Rise, glorious Conqueror	188
Rise up, O men of God	441
Rock of ages! cleft for me	254

INDEX OF FIRST LINES

Savior, again to Thy dear name	505
Savior, like a shepherd lead us	572
Savior, Thy dying love	355
Seek ye first the kingdom	200
Send out Thy light and Thy truth	631
Shepherd of souls, refresh and bless	320
Shepherd of tender youth	413
Silent night, holy night	130
Sing, my tongue	404
Sing praise to God	21
Sing to the Lord of harvest	520
Sing we the song	368
Sing we triumphant hymns	190
Sinners Jesus will receive	550
So let our lips and lives express	327
Soldiers of Christ, arise	330
Sometimes a light surprises	253
Son of God, eternal Savior	359
Songs of praise the angels sang	29
Spirit of God	217
Spirit of holiness, descend	213
Spread, still spread, thou mighty Word	224
Stand up, stand up for Jesus	592
Strive aright when God doth call	328
Strong Son of God	442
Summer suns are glowing	516
Sun of my soul, Thou Savior dear	491
Sweet hour of prayer	296
Take my life	358
Take Thou my hand, O Father	318
Take up thy cross, the Savior said	357
Teach me, my God and King	301
Teach me, O Lord	356
Teach me the measure of my days	315
Teach me Thy truth, O mighty One	438
That day of wrath	87
That man hath perfect blessedness	278
The bridegroom soon will call us	195
The church's one foundation	375
The day of resurrection	174
The day Thou gavest, Lord	488
The duteous day now closeth	487
The first noel the angel did say	137
The glory of the spring	513
The God of Abraham praise	11
The God of harvest praise	522
The Head that once was crowned	189
The heavens declare Thy glory	220
The King of love my Shepherd is	65
The King shall come	196
The Lord is in His holy temple	620
The Lord is in His holy temple	621
The Lord is King	204
The Lord is King, O praise His name	89
The Lord is risen indeed	176
The Lord is risen indeed	613
The Lord my Shepherd is	66
The Lord's my Shepherd	67
The love of God	538
The sands of time are sinking	292
The Savior died, but rose again	268
The spacious firmament on high	56
The work is Thine, O Christ	426
The year is swiftly waning	517
There is a green hill far away	473
There were ninety and nine	552
There's a wideness in God's mercy	78
Thine arm, O Lord, in days of old	152
Thine is the glory	180
This body in the grave we lay	417
This is my Father's world	49
This is the day of light	500
This is the day the Lord hath made	499
This joyful Eastertide	614
Thou art the Way	149
Thou didst leave Thy throne	563
Thou, Lord of life	437
Thou to whom the sick and dying	151
Thou true vine, that heals	304
Thou, whose almighty word	429
Throned upon the awful tree	162
Through all the changing scenes	41
Thy life was given for me	557
Thy way and all thy sorrows	338
Thy way, not mine, O Lord	341
Thy Word, O Lord, like gentle dews	218
'Tis midnight, and on Olive's brow	161
'Tis the promise of God	537
'Tis winter now	512
To God be the glory	532
To God the only wise	507
To Thy temple I repair	390
To us a child of hope is born	125
'Twas on that night	408
Under His wings	575
Unto the hills around	257
Veiled in darkness Judah lay	114
Wake, awake, for night is flying	118
Wake the song of jubilee	199
Walk in the light	282
We come unto our fathers' God	396
We give Thee but Thine own	364
We have heard a joyful sound	594
We plow the fields, and scatter	521

We praise Thee, O God	527	When I survey	165
We praise Thee, O God, our Redeemer	12	When in the hour of utmost need	264
We thank Thee, Lord	526	When morning gilds the skies	107
We walk by faith	250	When morning gilds the skies	595
We welcome glad Easter	474	When peace, like a river	576
We would extol Thee	23	When we walk with the Lord	577
We would see Jesus	303	Where cross the crowded ways	439
Were you there	164	While shepherds watched	138
What a friend we have in Jesus	337	Wise men seeking Jesus	468
What child is this	129	With songs and honors	515
What God hath done is done aright	77	Wonderful Savior, Redeemer	559
What mercy and divine compassion	68	Worship the Lord	139
What wondrous love is this	163	Would you be free	555
When all Thy mercies, O my God	74	Ye fair green hills of Galilee	146
When I survey	167	Ye servants of God	100

Index of German First Lines

Allein Gott in der Höh sei Ehr	38	Nun danket alle Gott	31
Die Sach ist dein	426	O Gott Vater, wir loben dich	384
Ein feste Burg ist unser Gott	597	So lange Jesus bleibt der Herr	89
Gott ist die Liebe	471	So nimm denn meine Hände	318
Grosser Gott, wir loben dich!	1	Stille Nacht, heilige Nacht!	130
Ich weiss einen Strom	556	Was Gott tut, das ist wohlgetan	77
Jesu, geh voran	319	Wer nur den lieben Gott lässt walten	314
Lobe den Herren, den mächtigen König	9		